CAROLINGIAN CATALONIA

Drawing on a range of evidence related to royal authority, political events, and literate culture, this study traces how kings and emperors involved themselves in the affairs of the Spanish March, and examines how actively people in Catalonia participated in politics centred on the royal court. Rather than setting the political development of the region in terms of Catalonia's future independence as a medieval principality, Cullen J. Chandler addresses it as part of the Carolingian 'experiment'. In doing so, he incorporates an analysis of political events alongside an examination of such cultural issues as the spread of the Rule of Benedict, the Adoptionist controversy, and the educational programme of the Carolingian reforms. This new history of the region offers a robust and absorbing analysis of the nature of the Carolingian legacy in the March, while also revising traditional interpretations of ethnic motivations for political acts and earlier attempts to pinpoint the constitutional birth of Catalonia.

CULLEN J. CHANDLER is Associate Professor and Chair of the Department of History at Lycoming College in Williamsport, Pennsylvania. He has, with Steven Stofferahn, co-edited a *Festschrift* in honour of John J. Contreni, and his first article, 'Between Court and Counts', won the *Early Medieval Europe*-Blackwell Essay Prize.

Cambridge Studies in Medieval Life and Thought
Fourth series

General Editor
ROSAMOND MCKITTERICK
Emeritus Professor of Medieval History, University of Cambridge, and Fellow of Sidney Sussex College

Advisory Editors
CHRISTOPHER BRIGGS
Lecturer in Medieval British Social and Economic History, University of Cambridge
CHRISTINE CARPENTER
Emeritus Professor of Medieval English History, University of Cambridge
ADAM J. KOSTO
Professor of History, Columbia University
ALICE RIO
Professor of Medieval History, King's College London
MAGNUS RYAN
University Lecturer in History, University of Cambridge, and Fellow of Peterhouse

The series *Cambridge Studies in Medieval Life and Thought* was inaugurated by G. G. Coulton in 1921; Professor Rosamond McKitterick now acts as General Editor of the Fourth Series, with Dr Christopher Briggs, Professor Christine Carpenter, Professor Adam J. Kosto, Professor Alice Rio and Dr Magnus Ryan as Advisory Editors. The series brings together outstanding work by medieval scholars over a wide range of human endeavour extending from political economy to the history of ideas.

This is book 111 in the series, and a full list of titles in the series can be found at:
www.cambridge.org/medievallifeandthought

CAROLINGIAN CATALONIA

Politics, Culture, and Identity in an Imperial Province, 778–987

CULLEN J. CHANDLER

Lycoming College

CAMBRIDGE
UNIVERSITY PRESS

CAMBRIDGE
UNIVERSITY PRESS

University Printing House, Cambridge CB2 8BS, United Kingdom

One Liberty Plaza, 20th Floor, New York, NY 10006, USA

477 Williamstown Road, Port Melbourne, VIC 3207, Australia

314–321, 3rd Floor, Plot 3, Splendor Forum, Jasola District Centre, New Delhi - 110025, India

79 Anson Road, #06-04/06, Singapore 079906

Cambridge University Press is part of the University of Cambridge.

It furthers the University's mission by disseminating knowledge in the pursuit of
education, learning and research at the highest international levels of excellence.

www.cambridge.org
Information on this title: www.cambridge.org/9781108465199
DOI : 10.1017/9781108565745

© Cullen J. Chandler 2019

First published 2019
First paperback edition 2020

A catalogue record for this publication is available from the British Library

ISBN 978-1-108-47464-1 Hardback
ISBN 978-1-108-46519-9 Paperback

For Amy and Cate

CONTENTS

ACKNOWLEDGEMENTS

It took much longer for this book to appear than I had thought it would. I therefore owe thanks to everyone who encouraged me to continue making progress after long periods of turning my attention to other matters. First, my colleagues at Lycoming College fostered an environment that allowed me to devote myself to undergraduate teaching and to serving an institution that does good work for our students and their world. When the time came that I made this book my top professional priority, those same colleagues were very supportive. Students likewise proved to be a source of inspiration, repeatedly assuring me that they looked forward to reading the book when it appeared. I will forgive them if they do not. And, to friends and colleagues in the field who came to recognize me as the one working on the Spanish March and asked from time to time when the book would be finished: I am sorry that it took so long, but quite happy with how it turned out.

Certain individuals deserve special mention in these pages. For too long I failed to avail myself of the good nature of other historians and Carolingianists and approached the work of a scholar as that of a hermit. John Contreni knew this project throughout that time. He read the complete work in its early stages and pointed out many potential improvements, then read successive versions. Tom Noble subjected a draft of the full manuscript to friendly but critical scrutiny, and Marty Claussen lent his expertise and keen reader's eye. The work exists in its current form, completely different from the doctoral dissertation from which it allegedly derives, thanks to them. Paul Dutton and Paul Kershaw read individual chapters and offered their critiques, as did Jeffrey Bowman and Celia Chazelle, although so long ago that they may no longer recall how helpful they were. My colleagues from Purdue, the *comitatus*, were good friends, especially in the early days, and have remained so: Amy Bosworth, Demetrius Glover, Steven

Stofferahn, and Jim Williams all shared their thoughts about my work and formed a great support network. Marta VanLandingham and Jim Farr offered crucial advice even before this project had got off the ground. Rosamond McKitterick and anonymous readers for Cambridge University Press helped to push me to consider various avenues of study that early drafts had left under-explored. I owe a significant debt of gratitude to Liz Friend-Smith of Cambridge University Press, whose patience and, on one key occasion, necessary sternness, guided this ship into port. This book is therefore the product of not only my labour, but of all of theirs as well. And yet, as it is my name attached to the title, responsibility for any shortcomings that remain in this book lies at my feet, not theirs.

A historian works neither totally alone nor self-sufficiently. The dissertation in which I first tested some of the ideas present in this book was funded by the Purdue Research Foundation in the form of a two-year grant. Victor Farías twice arranged for me to have access to residence in Barcelona and to the facilities at the Universitat Pompeu Fabra, especially in the Jaume Vicens i Vives Institute of History. I cannot say enough in gratitude to Alberto Torra and the immeasurably helpful staff of the Archivo de la Corona de Aragón, as well as Ana Gudayol and the very kind people at the Biblioteca de Catalunya. Most of the time I worked much closer to home, where I came to rely on Alison Gregory and Sue Beidler at Snowden Library and the interlibrary loan staff, who never failed to locate and acquire obscure volumes on my behalf. My work and travel were supported more than once by Lycoming College Professional Development Grants, and by Spain's Ministry for Education, Culture and Sports grants from the Program for Cultural Cooperation (now known as Hispanex), which allowed me to study in Barcelona. Nearer the end of the process Julie Polcrack, Abbie Bendick, and Joanna Wagner provided invaluable editorial assistance, and Kayla Everett helped with the maps.

Finally and most of all, thanks go to family. I promised not to have to apologize to them for my obsessive pursuit of this project, for absence and neglect. Of all the various victories one must achieve to write a book, the most significant one for me is having lived up to that promise. Patty and Jim Chandler brought me up to be the person who wrote this book and always offered moral support in my quest to learn about 'Frank'. My brothers Andy and Jimmy came through with the occasional yet necessary heckling. Everyone who knows my wife and daughter knows that Amy and Cate are beyond wonderful. Even though I tried not to let my work interfere in their lives, they had to live with 'Daddy at Work' signs in the house during nice summer days and to put up with my time away one winter when I went to study in Barcelona. They deserve the most and highest thanks I can give, and I can only hope that they can be proud of this book dedicated to them.

ABBREVIATIONS

AB	*Annales Bertiniani*
ARF	*Annales Regni Francorum*
CC 1	R. d'Abadal i de Vinyals. *Catalunya Carolíngia 1: El domini carolingi a Catalunya.* Barcelona 1986.
CC 2	R. d'Abadal i de Vinyals, ed. *Catalunya Carolíngia 2: Els diplomes carolingis a Catalunya.* 2 vols. Barcelona, 1926–52.
CC 3	R. d'Abadal i de Vinyals, ed. *Catalunya Carolíngia 3: Els comtats de Pallars i Ribagorça.* 2 vols. Barcelona, 1955.
CC 4	R. Ordeig i Mata, ed. *Catalunya Carolíngia 4: Els comtats de Osona i Manresa.* Barcelona 1999.
CC 5	S. Sobrequés Vidal, S. Riera i Viader, M. Rovira i Sola and R. Ordeig i Mata, ed. *Catalunya Carolíngia 5: Els Comtats de Girona, Besalú, Empúries i Peralada.* Barcelona 2003.
CC 6	P. Ponsich, and R. Ordeig i Mata, ed. *Catalunya Carolíngia 6: Els comtats de Rosselló, Conflent, Vallespir i Fenollet.* Barcelona 2006.
CCSL	*Corpus Christianorum Series Latina*
CMM	*Chronicon Moissiacense Maius*
EME	*Early Medieval Europe*
HGL	*Histoire Générale de Languedoc*
MGH	*Monumenta Germaniae Historica*
Capit.	*Capitularia*
Conc.	*Concilia*
Epp.	*Epistolae*
LL nat. Germ.	*Leges nationum Germanicarum*
Poetae	*Poetae latini carolini aevi*

SS	*Scriptores* (in Folio)
SS rer. Germ.	*Scriptores rerum Germanicarum in usum scholarum separatim editi*
PL	J.-P. Migne, ed. Patrologiae Cursus Completus, Series Latina. Paris, 1841–55.

MAPS

Map 1   Charlemagne's empire in 814

GIRONA Principal counties
RAZES Other areas
☦ Monasteries
● Episcopal sees
○ Other towns

CARCASSONNE   NARBONNE

Carcassonne ●   Narbonne ●

RAZES

ROUSSILLON

VALL
D'ARAN

San Miquel
de Cuixà   Elna ●

RIBAGORCA

PALLARS   ANDORRA   CAPCIR   CONFLENT

PALLARS JUSSÀ   SOBIRÀ

CERDANYA   PERALADA

Sant Pere
de Camprodon ☦   BESALÚ   EMPÚRIES

La Séu
d'Urgell

Roda
d'Isàvena

R. Fluvia   Castelló
d'Empúries

Santa Maria
de Ripoll   Sant Joan
de Ripoll   Besalú

URGELL   *BERGA*

Casserreso   R. Ter

R. Segre   Roda de Ter   Girona

OSONA   GIRONA

Cardona   Vic

R. Llobregat

Manresa ○   Sant Benet
de Bages

○ Lleida   BARCELONA

Sant Cugat ☦
del Vallès

Barcelona ●

M e d i t e r r a n e a n   S e a

● Tarragona

```
0      20     40     60     80    100 km
0    10   20   30   40   50   60 miles
```

Map 2   The Carolingian Spanish March

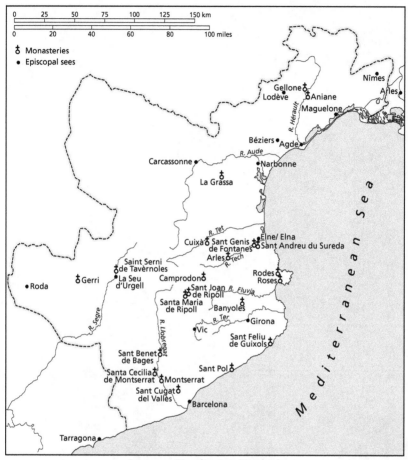

Map 3   Carolingian 'Gothia'

INTRODUCTION

A pedestrian strolling along Carrer Trafalgar, window shopping in Barcelona's Barri Gòtic, may, if alert, catch a glimpse of a street sign indicating the Carrer Lluís el Piadós – Louis the Pious Street. The street sign informs the reader that Louis was king of Aquitaine and conqueror of Barcelona in 804 (the date is now known to be 801). His street is very short, only a couple of blocks, in a city where more important avenues recall Catalonia's heroes of the high and late Middle Ages – when Catalonia was the centre of the Crown of Aragon's wealth and power in the western Mediterranean – or revolutionaries of the nineteenth century. Students of medieval history know Louis as the Frankish emperor whose reign has sometimes in the past been depicted as the beginning of the decline of the Carolingian dynasty, but the short street serves to remind *barcelonins* and visitors of the importance of Frankish rule south of the Pyrenees. How are the histories of Louis the Pious and Barcelona entwined, and why? What happened under Carolingian rule after Louis's conquest that positioned Barcelona to become the centre of a principality that would come to such prominence later in the Middle Ages? The connections between the Carolingians and Catalonia, known to the Franks as *marca hispanica*, or the Spanish March, form the basis of the study that follows.

On Easter Sunday in 801, Louis, as king of Aquitaine, entered Barcelona in triumph. His campaign and capture of the city marked the most important step towards Frankish control of territory south of the Pyrenees, erasing his father's failure to take Zaragoza in 778.[1] The generation that witnessed these campaigns was the first to experience Frankish overlordship in the region now called Catalonia, a region whose

---

[1] Astronomer, *Vita Hludowici imperatoris*, MGH SS, 2 (Hanover, 1829), 604–48. c. 13; Ermoldus Nigellus, *In honorem Hludowici*, MGH Poetae, 2 (Berlin: 1884), 1–91, bk. 1.

I

ruling counts continued to observe loyalty to the kings until the end of the Carolingian dynasty nearly two centuries later. By then, conditions had changed so greatly that the Frankish rule was arguably theoretical and sometimes not observed at all. The final cleavage between counts and kings is often traced to the events of 985–8, including the sack of Barcelona by the Muslim general al-Mansur, the replacement of the last Carolingian king by Hugh Capet, and that king's inability or unwillingness to provide military support and secure the homage of Borrell, count of Barcelona.[2] By the end of the tenth century, the power of the West Frankish kings had virtually vanished from the Spanish March. Kings made no journeys there, nor did they often reinforce their authority via old practices such as directly appointing counts and issuing diplomas. Counts and bishops in the March, for their part, travelled to Francia less frequently. This set of circumstances stands in marked contrast to the generation of Louis the Pious, conqueror and king, and clearly marks the end of what we can call 'Carolingian' Catalonia.[3] Some therefore argue, not without reason, that 'Carolingian' hardly describes any part of the tenth century.[4] Despite such opinions, one of the arguments of this book is that the Carolingian conquest of the region was of fundamental importance for its later history.

The primary concern of this study is the question of how the Spanish March became integrated into the Carolingian empire, judging primarily from the evidence related to royal authority, political events with regional and wider significance, and literary culture. In order to ask this question, 'integration' must be defined. This study traces how kings and emperors involved themselves in the affairs of the March, and gauges the degree to which people in Catalonia participated in politics centred on the royal

---

[2] The two modern historians who have written the most on these issues are Michel Zimmermann and Paul Freedman. See M. Zimmermann, 'Western Francia: the Southern Principalities', in *The New Cambridge Medieval History*, vol. 3, c.900–c.1024 ed. T. Reuter (Cambridge, 1999), 420–55; M. Zimmermann, 'De pays catalans à la Catalogne: genese d'une représentation', in *Histoire et archéologie des terres catalanes au Moyen Age*, ed. P. Sénac (Perpignan, 1995), 71–85; M. Zimmermann, 'Entre royaume franc et califat, soudain la Catalogne', in *La France de l'an mil*, ed. R. Delort (Paris, 1990), 75–100; M. Zimmermann, 'La prise de Barcelone par Al-Mansûr et la naissance de l'historiographie catalane', *Annales de Bretagne et des pays de l'Ouest* 87 (1980), 191–218; P. Freedman, 'Symbolic Implications of the Events of 985–988', in *Symposium internacional sobre els orígens de Catalunya* vol. 1 (Barcelona, 1991), 117–29; P. Freedman, 'Cowardice, Heroism and the Legendary Origins of Catalonia', *Past and Present* 121 (1988), 3–28. See also A. Benet i Clarà, *El procés d'independència de Catalunya* (Sallent, 1988).

[3] For the reign of Louis, see R. d'Abadal i de Vinyals, *La Catalogne sous l'Empire de Louis le Pieux*, Études Roussillonnaises: 4 (1954–5): 239–72; 5 (1956): 31–50, 147–77; 6 (1957): 267–95. Reprinted, in Catalan, in Abadal, CC 1, 217–303.

[4] See, for example, F. Udina i Martorell, 'Llegat, sediment i consciència visigòtica a la Catalunya dels segles VIII–XI', in X. Barral i Altet et al., eds, *Catalunya i França meridional a l'entorn de l'any Mil* (Barcelona, 1991), 368–73 at 371–3.

court and in court-sponsored reform initiatives. Charlemagne, Louis the Pious, and their successors granted properties and privileges to churches, monasteries, and lay people in Catalonia. These acts established and strengthened ties between the monarchy and the March, and continued to be sought after well into the tenth century. Integration into Carolingian structures can also be traced in terms of culture, as developments in doctrine, monastic observance, and educational reform bear the imprint of the movement known as the Carolingian renaissance. A great deal of modern scholarship treats the developments of the later part of the period, tracing how the tenth-century March, if not devoid of direct Carolingian political involvement, certainly became increasingly detached from the monarchy and started to become a principality in its own right. By looking to the ninth century, when the royal presence in the March was stronger, this study can make a fair attempt to shed more light on Carolingian political culture, in a sense by looking from the outside in. When the tenth century is understood in the light of the ninth rather than the eleventh century, new conclusions become apparent.[5] Catalonia is a good test case for such an investigation because of its geography and previous history.

GEOGRAPHICAL AND HISTORICAL BACKGROUND

Catalonia was a Carolingian creation. Although the region boasts a history from the Roman era to the Visigothic kingdom to a relatively brief Muslim occupation, the crucible of the later medieval principality was the Spanish March that separated Frankish Gaul from Muslim al-Andalus. Had not Carolingian authority been imposed, Barcelona and other places probably would have continued under Muslim rule, as did cities farther south like Tortosa and Tarragona. Although part of the Romano-Visigothic province of Tarraconensis, the territorial extent of Spanish March did not correspond to the province's entirety, but rather clung to the Pyrenees and the Mediterranean coast north of the Ebro. From this nucleus, settlement under Christian rule expanded into loosely controlled areas, beginning in the late ninth century. Even though the dynasty of Wifred 'the Hairy' (r. 870–98), count of Barcelona, Osona, Cerdanya, and Urgell, governed most of the region and guided it down its own path in the wake of fading royal power, the fact remains that that same royal power carved out the very

---

[5] This tactic is aligned with the similar approach of C. West, *Reframing the Feudal Revolution: Political and Social Transformation between the Marne and Moselle, c. 800–c. 1100* (Cambridge, 2013).

counties in which Wifred and his heirs made themselves rulers. The existence of the new polity was a function of Carolingian imperialism, so a study of the March also becomes a study of the practices of empire.[6]

Catalonia offers an interesting and significant vantage point from which to examine the meaning of empire in the Carolingian age. Unlike Brittany, Catalonia was completely integrated into Frankish political networks. Like Saxony, the Spanish March required some thirty years to stabilize under Carolingian control, but the military opposition was Muslim rather than pagan. Further, the armies that fell to Frankish forces did not represent the people who came under their rule; Catalonia, as part of the former Visigothic kingdom, was heir to the rich Christian heritage of Isidore of Seville and others. Unlike the Lombard kingdom, which was an established polity absorbed wholesale into Frankish expansion, and saw some degree of migration of northerners, that is, Franks, Alemanni, Bavarians, and Burgundians, the Spanish March was not a cohesive principality until after the period of Carolingian control; neither did it see the widespread settlement of Franks from over the mountains. To understand the Spanish March as a part of the empire is to understand the meaning of the Carolingian conquest of Catalonia not just for the region, but the wider empire. Further, it is important to ask what the lasting effects of the conquest were. How did political and social institutions resulting from the conquest of the Spanish March affect the region's development as Frankish authority waned? What can the conquest and incorporation of the March tell us about Carolingian power structures and political relationships in general? Answers to these questions will help fill out our understanding of regional practices and polities in Carolingian Europe and their relation to the wider empire.

Today, the land area of what was the Carolingian Spanish March lies in Catalonia, one of the autonomous regions of modern Spain, much larger than the March of the early Middle Ages. That area corresponds to what is now called Catalunya Vella, Old Catalonia, the parts nearest the Pyrenees and along the Mediterranean coast from the Carolingian-era counties of Empúries and Peralada south to Barcelona, the city itself lying near the Christian–Muslim frontier for much of the period.[7] Whether the

---

[6] Some discussion in this volume, especially regarding Charlemagne, agrees with the broad argument in J. R. Davis, *Charlemagne's Practice of Empire* (Cambridge, 2015).

[7] For reference, see the *Atles dels comtats de la Catalunya carolíngia* series: J. Bolòs and V. Hurtado, *Atles del comtat de Besalú (785–988)* (Barcelona, 1998); *Atles dels comtats d'Empúries i Peralada (780–991)* (Barcelona, 1999); *Atles del comtat de Girona (785–993)* (Barcelona, 2000); *Atles del comtat de Manresa* (Barcelona, 2001); *Atles del comtat d'Osona* (Barcelona, 2001); *Atles del comtat d'Urgell* (Barcelona, 2006); J. Bolòs, V. Hurtado, and R. Català, *Atles dels comtats de Rosselló, Conflent, Vallespir i Fenollet* (Barcelona, 2009); J. Bolòs and V. Hurtado, *Atles dels comtats de Pallars i Ribagorça* (Barcelona, 2012). See also V. Hurtado, J. Mestre, and T. Miserachs, *Atles d'història de Catalunya* (Barcelona, 1992).

Carolingians based their administration on old Visigothic counties is unclear, but they set up the counties of Roussillon north of the Pyrenees, Empúries and Peralada just south of the mountains, Girona and Barcelona along the coast, and Cerdanya, Urgell, and Pallars and Ribagorça in the uplands to the west. Towards the end of the ninth century and the early years of the tenth, new districts arose: the counties of Osona and Manresa and *pagi* of Vallespir and Berguedà as a result of expanding Christian settlement, Besalú from the partition of rule amongst members of the comital family. Ecclesiastically, most traditional sees maintained their status, from Elna north of the Pyrenees to Girona, Barcelona, and Urgell beyond them, although Empúries and Egara lost episcopal status, and the see of Vic was re-established in the late ninth century to govern the churches of Osona and Manresa. All were subject to the archbishop of Narbonne until the late eleventh century, when the old Visigothic metropolitanate at Tarragona rejoined Christendom.[8]

Catalonia's flair for legalism, often noted by students of its medieval history, could be related to its convoluted topography.[9] Its plains are neither numerous nor very large, so farms and estates had to follow the contours of the lush hills and rugged mountains that dominate the land-scape. Property disputes could easily arise in places whose boundaries were surveyed only with difficulty.[10] Most of the population in the Carolingian period was concentrated in and around the valleys, rivers, and streams that cut through the high terrain. The headwaters of the major rivers, the Tet, Ter, and Segre, almost meet at the upper ridge of the Pyrenees in Cerdanya. From there, the Segre flows south-west to la

---

[8] R. d'Abadal i de Vinyals, *Historia dels catalans*, vol. 2: *Alta Edat Mitjana* (Barcelona, 1963); Benet i Clarà, *El procés*; H. J. Chaytor, *A History of Aragón and Catalonia* (London, 1933).

[9] See, for example, J. M. Salrach, *Justícia i poder a Catalunya abans de l'any mil* (Vic, 2013); J. A. Bowman, *Shifting Landmarks: Property, Proof, and Dispute in Catalonia around the Year 1000* (Ithaca, 2004); M. A. Kelleher, 'Boundaries of Law: Code and Custom in Early Medieval Catalonia', *Comitatus* 30 (1999), 1–10; J. M. Salrach, 'Prácticas judiciales, transformación social y acción política en Cataluña (siglos IX–XIII)', *Hispania* 47 (1997), 1009–48; P. H. Freedman, *Church, Law, and Society in Catalonia, 900–1500*, Variorum Collected Studies Series (Aldershot, 1995); R. Collins, *Law, Culture, and Regionalism in Early Medieval Spain* (Aldershot, 1992); A. Kosto, *Making Agreements in Medieval Catalonia: Power, Order, and the Written Word, 1000–1200* (Cambridge, 2001); P. H. Freedman, *The Origins of Peasant Servitude in Medieval Catalonia* (Cambridge, 1991).

[10] For exemplary studies handling evidence for disputes and their resolutions in the early Middle Ages, see W. Davies and P. Fouracre, eds, *The Settlement of Disputes in Early Medieval Europe* (Cambridge, 1986) and W. Brown, *Unjust Seizure: Conflict, Interest, and Authority in Early Medieval Society* (Ithaca, 2001); L. F. Bruyning, 'Lawcourt Proceedings in the Lombard Kingdom before and after the Frankish Conquest', *Journal of Medieval History* 11 (1985): 193–214. On Catalonia in particular, see Bowman, *Shifting Landmarks*; Kosto, *Making Agreements*; J. M. Salrach, 'Conquesta de l'epsai agrari i conflictes per la terra a la Catalunya carolíngia i comtal', in X. Barral i Altet et al., eds, *Catalunya i França meridional a l'entorn de l'any Mil* (Barcelona, 1991), 203–11.

Seu d'Urgell and turns southward. Along its course it picks up the waters of the Noguera Pallaresa and the Noguera Ribagorçana before emptying into the Ebro well beyond the *limes* of the Carolingian empire. The Tet and the Ter both flow eastward towards the Mediterranean, and provided fertile areas for many monasteries, including Santa Maria and Sant Joan de Ripoll (the latter now also known as Sant Joan de les Abadesses) (Ter), Eixalada-Cuixà (Tet), and cities such as Vic and Girona (Ter). The plain of Vic, watered by the Ter, was the primary target for migrations down from the mountains in the 870s and 880s. Knowledge about settlement in the valleys of Barcelona's rivers, the Llobregat and Besós, is scanty; the Llobregat did mark the area where the Carolingian empire began to meet al-Andalus, but did little to protect the city from Muslim attacks. The line of the frontier doubtless appears more solid in modern atlases than in the everyday life of the ninth and tenth centuries.[11] As for the Mediterranean coast, Barcelona was no major trade centre, as it would be later in the Middle Ages, and little naval activity is reported, save the occasional Muslim seaborne raid on Carolingian territory. During the ninth century, the Franks seldom mounted offensives via the sea; this mirrors the trend of their operations in the North Sea and English Channel.[12]

Society in the March, as in high-elevation areas elsewhere in early medieval Europe, throve in the river valleys that cut through the mountains, and took advantage of such plains as there were that stretched out just south of the slopes. The Roman Via Augusta connected the March to southern Gaul, and from there travellers could journey up the Rhône to Burgundy and continue overland to Paris, much as the ninth-century monks Usuard and Odilard did on their return to St-Germain-des-Prés from Spain.[13] Local inhabitants blazed their own trails, building and maintaining new roads after the Frankish conquest, especially as ties to Francia weakened and local economic activity took off, in no small part fuelled by trade with Muslim Spain.[14] Carolingian Catalonia embodied tradition and innovation in its administration, infrastructure, and more.

---

[11] See J. M. H. Smith, '*Fines imperii*: the Marches', in R. McKitterick, ed., *The New Cambridge Medieval History*, vol. 2 (Cambridge, 1995), 169–89 at 179.

[12] B. S. Bachrach, 'Pirenne and Charlemagne', in A. C. Murray, ed., *After Rome's Fall: Narrators and Sources of Early Medieval History. Essays Presented to Walter Goffart* (Toronto, 1998), 224–5. John Haywood, *Dark Age Naval Power: a Reassessment of Frankish and Anglo-Saxon Seafaring Activity* (London and New York, 1991), 95–109, 113–15.

[13] P. M. Duval, 'Les plus anciennes routes de France: les voies gallo-romaines', in G. Michaud, ed., *Les routes de France. Depuis les origines jusqu'à nos jours* (Paris, 1959), 9–24; J. Hubert, 'Les routes du Moyen Age', ibid., 25–56; L. Harmand, *L'Occident romain: Gaule, Espagne, Bretagne, Afrique du Nord (31 av. J. C. à 235 ap. J. C.)* Bibliothéque Historique (Paris, 1960).

[14] A. M. Mundó, *De quan hispans, gots, jueus, àrabs i francs circulaven per Catalunya*. Seminari de Paleografia, Diplomàtica i Codocologia Monografies (Bellaterra, 2001).

Introduction

Such is the geography, physical and political, of the March, the subject of this examination. The region has a rich historiography, but often remains in non-Catalan historians' blind spots, even for specialists of the period.[15] In the early stages of this study, it became apparent that there exist, in general, two branches of Anglophone scholarship on the early Middle Ages. Work on the Carolingian period in general often neglects the Spanish March, and historians who study early medieval Spain tend to ignore the Carolingian March in order to focus on the Visigothic kingdom, the kingdom of Asturias, or al-Andalus. Even recently, Carolingian history has often been the history of kings, aristocrats or the court scholars.[16] While those characters are by no means absent from this study, and indeed are often key players, the focus is on events and conditions in the Spanish March, not the larger constellation of concerns occupying minds at the imperial centre. Put differently, many know the story of Bernard of Septimania, but they know little about the place he governed as count of Barcelona and *marchio*.

What follows is a corrective. This project is about neither kingship nor what it meant to be an aristocrat. Rather, it is about how the empire held together, from the perspective of a conquered province. Rosamond McKitterick observed that the Spanish March was not integrated under Charlemagne, and in her more recent study, Jennifer Davis follows that interpretation.[17] In what follows, we shall see that perhaps the process of integration was gradual, but it did begin under Charlemagne. Kings implemented strategies of rulership; aristocrats worked with or against kings according to strategies of their own. Everyone had loyalties to ruler, lord, family, followers, dependents, and religion. What was the role of learned culture or of perceived community or ethnic identity in shaping these sometimes conflicting loyalties? It is my aim to determine how the

---

[15] C. J. Chandler, 'Carolingian Catalonia: the Spanish March and the Franks, c.750–c.1050', *History Compass* 11 (2013): 739–50.

[16] For example, on kings: R. McKitterick, *Charlemagne: the Formation of a European Identity* (Cambridge, 2008); R. Collins, *Charlemagne* (Toronto and Buffalo, 1998), 234; E. Boshof, *Ludwig der Fromme* (Darmstadt, 1996); J. L. Nelson, *Charles the Bald* (London, 1992); E. J. Goldberg, *Struggle for Empire: Kingship and Conflict under Louis the German, 817–876* (Ithaca, 2006); S. MacLean, *Kingship and Politics in the Late Ninth Century: Charles the Fat and the End of the Carolingian Empire* (Cambridge, 2003); aristocrats: the essays collected in S. Airlie, *Power and its Problems in Carolingian Europe* (Farnham, 2012); R. Le Jan, *Famille et pouvoir dans le monde franc (VIIe–Xe siècle): essai d'anthropologie sociale* (Paris, 1995); the essays in Le Jan, ed. *La royauté et les élites dans l'Europe carolingienne (début IXe siècle aux environs de 920)* (Villeneuve d'Ascq, 1998); and scholars: C. Chazelle, *The Crucified God in the Carolingian Era: Theology and Art of Christ's Passion* (Cambridge, 2001); D. A. Bullough, *Alcuin: Achievement and Reputation* (Leiden, 2004).

[17] McKitterick, *Charlemagne*, 133–4, 136; Davis, *Charlemagne's Practice*, 242–3 and 415.

various strategies employed played themselves out in the fashioning of a multi-ethnic empire.

Other, relatively simple, issues that have arisen in the historiography of 'Carolingian Catalonia' have conspired to keep it buried deeper underground than it deserves. First, there is a divide between Catalan-language scholarship (and to a lesser degree, that in other European languages), and an English-speaking audience all too under-informed on the Carolingian and 'comital' periods in the region. Historians in Catalonia and France have been the primary champions of the study of the region's early medieval history. But for early medievalists, especially Carolingianists in North America, the United Kingdom and beyond who are interested in continental developments, and for their colleagues interested in the later medieval Crown of Aragon, this study helps to illuminate a pivotal period in a region that was key both to the Carolingian empire and to the high and late-medieval Mediterranean world. The rapidly growing body of English-language scholarship on Catalonia and the Crown of Aragon points to the region's significance, yet the earlier period has for too long escaped the attention of numerous historians.[18] Within the last decade or so, however, a small handful of scholars have turned their attention to Carolingian connections south of the Pyrenees and to the politics and society of the Spanish March in particular, yet there remains no full-scale treatment of the early period of true and meaningful connections to the larger Carolingian enterprise.[19]

[18] The starting point is T. N. Bisson, *The Medieval Crown of Aragón: a Short History* (Oxford, 1986). For somewhat more recent work, C. Stalls, *Possessing the Land: Aragon's Expansion into Islam's Ebro Frontier under Alfonso the Battler 1104–1134*, The Medieval Mediterranean: Peoples, Economies, and Cultures, 400–1453 (Leiden, 1995); S. P. Bensch, *Barcelona and Its Rulers, 1096–1291* (Cambridge, 1995); Kosto, *Making Agreements*; M. VanLandingham, *Transforming the State: King, Court, and Political Culture in the Realms of Aragon (1213–1387)*, The Medieval Mediterranean: Peoples, Economies, and Cultures, 400–1453 (Leiden, 2002); Bowman, *Shifting Landmarks*; B. A. Catlos, *The Victors and the Vanquished: Christians and Muslims of Catalonia and Aragon, 1050–1300* (Cambridge, 2004).

[19] For connections to Spain, see F. Riess, 'From Aachen to Al-Andalus: the Journey of Deacon Bodo (823–76)', *EME* 13 (2005): 131–57; C. J. Chandler, 'Between Court and Counts: Carolingian Catalonia and the *aprisio* grant, 778–897', *EME* 11 (2002): 19–44; 'Heresy and Empire: the Role of the Adoptionist Controversy in Charlemagne's Conquest of the Spanish March', *International History Review* 24 (2002): 505–27; 'Land and Social Networks in the Carolingian Spanish March', *Studies in Medieval and Renaissance History*, third series, 6 (2009): 1–33; 'Barcelona, BC 569, Dhuoda's *Liber manualis*, and Lay Culture in the Carolingian Spanish March', *EME* 18 (2010): 265–91; and 'A New View of a Catalonian *Gesta contra Iudaeos*: Ripoll 106 and the Jews of the Spanish March', in C. J. Chandler and S. A. Stofferahn, eds, *Discovery and Distinction in the Early Middle Ages: Studies in Honor of John J. Contreni* (Kalamazoo, MI, 2013). See especially the work of J. Jarrett: 'Power over Past and Future: Abbess Emma and the Nunnery of Sant Joan de les Abadesses', *EME* 12 (2003): 229–58; 'Settling the Kings' Lands: *Aprisio* in Catalonia in Perspective', *EME* 18 (2010): 320–42; 'Caliph, King, or Grandfather: Strategies of Legitimization on the Spanish March in the Reign of Lothar III', *The Mediaeval Journal* 1 (2011): 1–22; 'Archbishop Ató of Osona: False Metropolitans on the *Marca Hispanica*', *Archiv für*

The most prominent of the twentieth-century non-Catalan works that treat Catalonia at all are very broad in chronological and geographical scope, and consider developments in the history of the region, often along with that of Aquitaine, over centuries. Such studies highlighted Catalonia's connection to Aquitaine and the Frankish kingdom, casting the region as one of many where political machinations and developing societal trends had played themselves out. Lordship in Catalonia has long been a central topic; older scholarship charts the changes from royal to papal protection of monasteries and the development of lordship from early medieval office-holding. These early works provide useful guides, but now show their age.[20]

The medieval history of Spain posed problems for historians in the twentieth century, many for political reasons. The regime of Francisco Franco (1939–75) was characterized by fierce centralization in Spain, and much historical scholarship produced in his time and since has tended to privilege the history of Castile as 'Spanish' history, largely marginalizing the distinct histories of other regions.[21] Reflecting their need for regional identity, Catalan historians, especially Ramon d'Abadal i de Vinyals in the Franco era and many others since the dictator's death, have produced a vibrant literature on the history of Catalonia, relishing the uniqueness of their land. The Carolingian period figures prominently in this effort to write a history as the era of Catalonia's 'national formation'.[22] Since the 1970s, other European scholars have taken a keen interest in the region's Carolingian history. In the late 1980s and 1990s, conferences and volumes published to coincide with millenary anniversaries enlisted Catalan and French scholars to commemorate Hugh Capet, Gerbert of Aurillac, the kingdom of France at the millennium and the

Diplomatik 56 (2010): 1–42; and 'Centurions, Alcalas, and *Christiani Perversi*: Organisation of Society in the Pre-Catalan "Terra de Ningú"', in A. Deyermond and M. J. Ryan, eds, *Early Medieval Spain: a Symposium* (London, 2010), 97–128. J. Jarrett, *Rulers and Ruled in Frontier Catalonia, 880–1010: Pathways of Power* (London, 2010) is an admirable study of the local social and political structures on the frontier, but it is not a study of the region's Carolingian history.

[20] L. Auzias, *L'Aquitaine carolingienne* (Toulouse, 1937); O. Engels, *Schutzgedanke und Landherrschaft im östlichen Pyrenäenraum (9.–13. Jahrhundert)* (Münster in Westfalen, 1970); A. Lewis, *The Development of Southern French and Catalan Society, 718–1050* (Austin, 1965); and even J. M. Salrach, *El procés de feudalització (segles III–XII)*, ed. P. Vilar, 2nd ed., Història de Catalunya 2 (Barcelona, 1987). See also M. Rouche, *L'Aquitaine des Wisigoths aux Arabes, 418–781*. Editions de l'Ecole des hautes études en sciences sociales (Editions Touzot: Paris, 1979).

[21] P. Linehan, *History and the Historians of Spain* (Oxford, 1993).

[22] Term taken from the title of Salrach, *El procés*; see also R. d'Abadal i de Vinyals, *Historia dels catalans* 2; Zimmermann, 'De pays catalans à la Catalogne', and the collection of his earlier work in *En els orígens de Catalunya: emancipació política i afirmació cultural*, trans. from French into Catalan by A. Bentué (Barcelona, 1989); and of course the essays in *Symposium internacional sobre els orígens de Catalunya (segles VIII–XI)*, 2 vols (Barcelona, 1991).

'origins of Catalonia'.[23] Most recently, the massive and magisterial *thèse* of Michel Zimmermann has synthesized and advanced his own previous work on literacy and culture in the region from the Carolingian period to the dynastic union with Aragon in the twelfth century.[24] Despite the significance of this body of scholarship, Carolingian Catalonia has largely escaped English-language historiography. Until the last decade or so, when Anglophone scholars have addressed conditions or developments in the region in major works, it has often been within other studies as a frontier, the viewpoint from the centre out, or as major figures happened to be involved with the March, rather than treating Catalonia in its own right; some comparative studies on social and economic history have featured the region.[25]

European initiatives have indeed examined the Spanish March on its own terms, emphasizing local developments. The major, comprehensive works of the Franco era were primarily political history and drew on the wider imperial context to explain the region's budding independence, its detachment from the Carolingian empire. Cultural developments garnered some attention, giving the local context primacy of place. This common commitment to Catalonia's history was coloured by nationalism even as it cautioned against reading a Catalan national identity back into the ninth and tenth centuries.[26] Early studies of the Spanish March as part of the Carolingian empire emphasized the gradual independence of the counts as royal power weakened.[27] Later efforts built on these foundations and concentrated on the society and culture of the March, deliberately eschewing overtly nationalist approaches. These studies shed light on marriage patterns, agricultural exploitation, lordship and learned culture, but the relationship of the March to the empire is all but omitted in

---

[23] X. Barral i Altet et al., eds, *Catalunya i França meridional a l'entorn de l'any mil / La Catalogne et la France méridionale autour de l'an mil*, Colloque international DNRS, Hugues Capet 987–1987, La France a l'an mil (Barcelona, 1991); I. Ollich i Castanyer, ed., *Actes del Congrés Internacional Gerbert d'Orlhac i el seu temps: Catalunya i Europa a la fi del Ir mil.leni* (Vic, 1999); R. Delort, ed., *La France a l'an mil* (Paris, 1990); and the *Symposium internacional*.

[24] M. Zimmermann, *Écrire et lire en Catalogne (IX–XII siècle)* (Madrid, 2003).

[25] See the works cited in note 13 above, as well as C. Wickham, 'European Forests in the Early Middle Ages: Landscape and Land Clearance', in *Land and Power: Studies in Italian and European Social History, 900–1200* (London, 1994), 155–99 and 'Problems of Comparing Rural Societies in Western Europe', in ibid., 201–27, and his more recent *Framing the Early Middle Ages: Europe and the Mediterranean, 400–800* (Oxford, 2007).

[26] See R d'Abadal i de Vinyals, *Dels visigots als catalans*, ed. J. Sobrequés i Callicó. 2nd ed., vol. 2 (Barcelona, 1974), 158–9.

[27] The fundamental works are Abadal, *Els primers comtes catalans,* Biografies Catalanes (Barcelona, 1958); his collected essays in *Dels visigots als catalans*; Abadal, CC 1; Abadal, *Els temps i el regiment del comte Guifré el Pilós*, ed. J. Sobrequés i Callicó (Sabadell, 1989); and Salrach, *El procés.*

favour of legacies of the pre-Carolingian past.[28] For example, the survival of Visigothic law, which became the basis for the medieval *Usatges* of Barcelona when they were redacted in the late tenth century, is often cited as evidence of the Carolingians' meagre influence on Catalonia.[29] In fact, however, it was standard Carolingian practice to allow the continued use of local legal traditions, as was the case in Burgundy, Bavaria, and Italy. Legal culture when understood in an imperial context then serves to underscore how much Catalonia had in common with other Carolingian provinces rather than to stress its remoteness from the Carolingian world. It sheds light on what should be seen as an element in Carolingian notions of empire, including the court's emphasis on the several subject peoples it ruled.[30]

As historians attempt to deepen our understanding of the Carolingian world, regional studies have loomed large in contemporary English-language scholarship on the period. In the last generation, several major works have been dedicated to such investigations.[31] Whether on the edge of the empire near potential enemies or well within the heartland, these regional studies reveal much about Carolingian society. They address such issues as how the Carolingian rulers and their aristocratic partners governed areas, whether old or newly acquired by expansion, and how

---

[28] For representative studies, see the following: on marriage patterns: M. Aurell, 'Pouvoir et parenté des comtes de la Marche Hispanique (801–911)', in R. Le Jan, ed., *La royauté et les élites dans l'Europe carolingienne (début IXe siècle aux environs de 920)* (Villeneuve d'Asq, 1998), 467–81; agriculture: G. Feliu, 'Societat i economia', in *Symposium internacional*, 1, 81–116; and Salrach, 'La Catalunya de Gerbert entre dues èpoques: estructura del territori i dinàmica político-econòmica', in I. Ollich i Castanyer, ed., *Actes del Congrés Internacional Gerbert d'Orlhac i el seu temps: Catalunya i Europa a la fi del Ir Mil.leni* (Vic, 1999), 45–67; lordship: Salrach, 'Societat i poder als comtats pirinencs als segles IX i X', in *Mil.lenari de Catalunya i la Cerdanya* (Barcelona, 1989), 23–36; learned culture: J. Alturo, 'La cultura latina medieval a Catalunya. Estat de la qüestion', in *Symposium internacional*, 1, 21–48.

[29] R. Collins, *Visigothic Spain, 409–711* (Oxford, 2004), 223–39, esp. 226.

[30] For other discussion on notions of empire, see M. de Jong, 'The Empire that Was Always Decaying: the Carolingians (800–888)', *Medieval Worlds: Comparative & Interdisciplinary Studies* 1 (2015): 6–25.

[31] W. Davies, *Small Worlds: the Village Community in Early Medieval Brittany* (Berkeley and Los Angeles, 1988) and C. Wickham, *The Mountains and the City: the Tuscan Apennines in the Early Middle Ages* (Oxford, 1988) have led the way, followed by J. M. H. Smith, *Province and Empire: Brittany and the Carolingians* (Cambridge, 1992). See, in addition to the works cited below, R. Collins, 'Pippin I and the Kingdom of Aquitaine', in P. Godman and R. Collins, eds, *Charlemagne's Heir: New Perspectives on the Reign of Louis the Pious (814–840)* (Oxford, 1990), 363–89; T. F. X. Noble, 'Louis the Pious and the Frontiers of the Frankish Realm', in ibid., 333–47. There has been a similar trend also for Continental scholars, exemplified by M. Rouche, *L'Aquitaine*; C. Lauranson-Rosaz, *L'Auvergne et ses marges (Velay, Gévaudan) du VIIIe au XIe siècle: Le fin du monde antique?* (Le-Puy-en-Velay, 1987) and G. Albertoni, *L'Italia carolingia* (Rome, 1997). For surrounding areas, see C. R. Bowlus, *Franks, Moravians, and Magyars: the Struggle for the Middle Danube, 788–907* (Philadelphia, 1995), F. Curta, *The Making of the Slavs: History and Archaeology of the Lower Danube* (Cambridge, 2001) and N. Everett, *Literacy in Lombard Italy, c.568–774* (Cambridge, 2003).

their subjects responded. The Spanish March is noticeably absent from the roster of these regional studies. For Bavaria, such studies have found that existing local customs continued to influence dispute settlements under the Carolingians, and have also illuminated how tensions between local traditions of loyalty and Carolingian dominion made territorial rule precarious.[32] We have been able to see a study of the small but important area of the Middle Rhine Valley draw large conclusions about how 'state' and 'society' collapsed into one another in the early medieval world, challenging long-held assumptions of Carolingian government based on a constitutional view of power rather than a social one.[33] These studies and others show that, in order to enforce their authority, kings had to insinuate themselves into local networks of power.[34] Before any of these studies were published, the case of Brittany had already shown that, even while emerging as a separate and independent principality in the late ninth and tenth centuries, the region was nonetheless a Carolingian creation, its very autonomy originating in its rulers' participation in Carolingian politics.[35] The common thread running through all these works is the nature of a region's participation in the Carolingian world. While this project takes up the same thread, it raises further questions about the role of identity in forming the empire.

This study carries the banner of regional studies into Catalonia, focusing on the period that can properly be called Carolingian. In doing so, it undertakes something rather more comprehensive than the excellent studies mentioned above. They largely examine charter evidence and feature other kinds of textual sources in supporting roles. This project certainly avails itself of royal and local charters when they are available, but also takes in a wide variety of source material as it investigates a series of fairly wide-ranging issues. It modifies the received understanding of the Spanish March in the light of the questions more recent regional studies have investigated and attempts to facilitate productive comparisons between regions, without being designed as a comparative study per se. Influential works, informed by anthropological approaches and based on the idea that power in agrarian societies was rooted in control of land and exercised through reciprocity, have been devoted to local studies

---

[32] W. Brown, *Unjust Seizure: Conflict, Interest, and Authority in Early Medieval Society* (Ithaca, 2001); K. L. R. Pearson, *Conflicting Loyalties in Early Medieval Bavaria: a View of Socio-Political Interaction, c.680–900* (Aldershot, 1999).

[33] M. Innes, *State and Society in the Early Middle Ages: the Middle Rhine Valley, 400–1100* (Cambridge, 2000); this study has had a significant impact on how I see the Carolingian world.

[34] See especially H. Hummer, *Politics and Power in Early Medieval Europe: Alsace and the Frankish Realm, 600–1000* (Cambridge, 2005), which emphasizes the roles monasteries played in both local and royal power.

[35] Smith's *Province and Empire* has been very influential indeed for the present study.

of charter evidence. The results speak to the role of central authority and the means by which control of property was converted into political power across Europe.[36] The present study takes up similar issues, notably the activities of kings in granting land to parties in the March and enforcing the rights and privileges contained in the grants. Amongst other aspects of early medieval society addressed here are the role of monasteries in networks of learned culture in the exchange of texts and ideas from place to place in the Carolingian realms and beyond their borders.[37]

Very recent efforts in Carolingian history complement the findings of this study. To highlight just two such works, by Jennifer Davis and Charles West, will suffice for present purposes. Davis puts forth a refreshing interpretation of Charlemagne's rule: that the king dealt effectively using the limited tools at his disposal, choosing carefully and strategically which political battles really needed to be fought. The empire Charlemagne built was always a work in progress, not any kind of system driven by ideology.[38] We can see developments that support just such an interpretation in the formative age of the Carolingian Spanish March. Meanwhile, West argues for a degree of continuity in sociopolitical structures from the Carolingians all the way to the early twelfth century. There were changes in how power was organized, but those changes were rooted in the outcomes of the Carolingian reforms. Power had become quite localized and identified as property; rights had become jurisdiction.[39] As we shall see below, the structures of power that the Carolingians helped to establish in the Spanish March would remain in place while also undergoing change in the degree to which the Carolingian dynasty 'owned' power. Yet even by the late tenth century, Carolingian institutions still preserved the legitimacy that allowed kings to wield power in the March.

---

[36] H. Fichtenau, *Das Urkundenwesen in Österreich vom 8. bis zum frühen 13. Jahrhundert* (Vienna, Cologne, Graz, 1971), 56–72. Davies and Fouracre, eds, *The Settlement of Disputes in Early Medieval Europe*; W. Davies and P. Fouracre, eds, *Property and Power in the Early Middle Ages* (Cambridge, 1995).

[37] On monasteries' roles see R. McKitterick, ed., *The Uses of Literacy in Early Medieval Europe* (Cambridge, 1990); M. de Jong, 'Carolingian Monasticism: the Power of Prayer', in R. McKitterick, ed., *The New Cambridge Medieval History*, vol. 2, c.700–c.900 (Cambridge, 1995), 622–53; B. H. Rosenwein, *To Be the Neighbor of Saint Peter: the Social Meaning of Cluny's Property, 909–1049* (Ithaca, 1989). For the cultural roles of monasteries, see R. E. Sullivan, 'The Context of Cultural Activity in the Carolingian Age', in R. E. Sullivan, ed., *'The Gentle Voices of Teachers': Aspects of Learning in the Carolingian Age* (Columbus, 1995), 51–105; J. J. Contreni, 'The Carolingian Renaissance: Education and Literary Culture', in McKitterick, ed., *The New Cambridge Medieval History*, vol. 2, c.700–c.900, 709–757; Pierre Riché, *Ecoles et enseignement dans la Haut Moyen Age: fin du Ve siècle–milieu de XIe siècle* (Paris, 1989).

[38] Davis, *Charlemagne's Practice*.   [39] West, *Reframing the Feudal Revolution*.

In the past two decades, some shorter studies have addressed early medieval Spain, but the Spanish March has escaped their reach.[40] As an exception to this trend, a piece by Roger Collins, published over twenty-five years ago, served to emphasize the need for further study of the region.[41] It is time to pursue the promise the March offers. More recent research has been looking into earlier and earlier periods of Catalonia's history, stretching back into the tenth century, but the true meaning of Carolingian rule remains unassessed.[42] These newer works, like most regional studies of Carolingian societies, emphasize law and the settlement of disputes. Adam Kosto's meticulous investigation of *convenientia* focuses on judicial and administrative practice in the development of the Catalonian feudal regime after the year 1000. Jeffrey Bowman, although sympathetic to the Carolingian era, studies the development of law, legal methods and mentalities in Catalonia in the decades around 1000 and joins the debate on the Feudal Revolution. Both revise earlier positions about the process by which 'public' power was 'privatized', as well as the supposedly violent atmosphere in which this transformation took place. Such themes, without doubt, are important avenues into understanding the mentalities of medieval people, and the realities of power in their lives. But what escapes the view of most such efforts, in Carolingian history as well as Catalonian, is the crucial idea of the Carolingian empire itself. Sometimes termed an 'experiment', the empire was made up of component regions including Bavaria, Alemannia, Italy, Burgundy, Aquitaine, and Saxony. The understanding of regions has become key to understanding the empire. Likewise, students of later developments should recognize the value of Catalonia's early medieval history for both the early medieval period and for the region's later developments.

Along with these lines of inquiry, this study must engage with the notion of 'frontier' on some level. Notions of frontier are important for understanding the political relationship between the marcher region of Catalonia and the Carolingian cultural centres of northern Europe. The historiography on frontiers in the Middle Ages, especially in the USA, has its roots in Frederick Jackson Turner's famous frontier thesis, which defines the frontier as the boundary between civilization and savage wilderness, a place where individual freedom reigns and the

---

[40] See for example C. C. de Hartmann, 'The Textual Transmission of the Mozarabic Chronicle of 754', *EME* 8 (1999): 13–29; J. A. Bowman, 'Councils, Memory and Mills: the Early Development of the Peace of God in Catalonia', *EME* 8 (1999): 99–130. See also J. L. Nelson, 'The Franks, the Martyrology of Usuard, and the Martyrs of Cordoba', *Studies in Church History* 30 (1993): 67–80.

[41] R. Collins, 'Charles the Bald and Wifred the Hairy', in M. T. Gibson and J. L. Nelson, eds, *Charles the Bald, Court and Kingdom* (Aldershot, 1990), 169–88.

[42] Kosto, *Making Agreements*, Bowman, *Shifting Landmarks*, and Kelleher, 'Boundaries of Law'.

power of the central government is weak.[43] Later work on the 'frontier', in American history has criticized the Turner thesis.[44] Medievalists have studied the concept of frontiers well, and have worked with the European definition of the term, as denoting a political and military boundary.[45] Central governments can either attempt to tighten their grip on frontier areas at the risk of losing their authority, or appease their residents while maintaining only a weak sort of authority.[46] Historians have seen frontiers in the Carolingian world as dynamic and expanding, composed of rings of subjected peoples,[47] or have pointed to the varied and continually developing concept of the frontier in late antiquity and the early Middle Ages, a concept that, far from constituting a barrier, allowed for controlled interaction between groups of people.[48] Those who have studied Catalonia adopt a multivalent use of the concept of the frontier. On the one hand, they fully accept that the *marca hispanica* was, to the Frankish rulers, a wide band of territory encompassing several counties.[49] On the other, these modern scholars tend to see a frontier line that shifted over time.[50] Important developments transpired in the frontier area that would define the history of Catalonia as a region.

Peter Sahlins, a historian of the early modern period, has approached the notion of frontier in Catalonia in yet another way. He understands that what happened at the farthest reaches of the early modern kingdoms of France and Spain helped determine the shape of the developing states. Cerdanya, a part of Catalonia in the Pyrenees, saw the delineation of the border between the two countries in the seventeenth century, and has been divided between them since then; people at the border defined

[43] F. J. Turner, *The Frontier in American History* (New York, 1920).

[44] P. N. Limerick, *The Legacy of Conquest: the Unbroken Past of the American West* (New York and London, 1987); P. N. Limerick, C. A. Milner II, and C. E. Rankin, eds, *Trails: Toward a New Western History* (Lawrence, KS, 1991).

[45] R. I. Burns, 'The Significance of the Frontier in the Middle Ages', in R. Bartlett and A. MacKay, eds, *Medieval Frontier Societies* (Oxford, 1989), 307–30; A. R. Lewis, 'Cataluña como frontera militar (870–1050)', *Anuario de Estudios Medievales* 5 (1968), 15–29. See also the essays collected in D. Power and N. Standen, eds, *Frontiers in Question: Eurasian Borderlands, 700–1700* (New York, 1999).

[46] See the treatment of frontier governance in A. Stieldorf, *Marken und Markgrafen. Studien zur Grenzsicherung durch die fränkisch-deutschen Herrscher.* Monumenta Germaniae Historica Schriften, 64 (Hanover, 2012).

[47] Noble, 'Louis the Pious and the Frontiers of the Frankish Realm'; Smith, '*Fines imperii*'.

[48] See the essays gathered in *The Transformation of Frontiers: From Late Antiquity to the Carolingians*, eds W. Pohl, I. Wood, and H. Reimitz, The Transformation of the Roman World, 10 (Leiden, 2001), esp. H.-W. Goetz, 'Concepts of Realm and Frontiers from Late Antiquity to the Early Middle Ages: Some Preliminary Remarks', at 73–82; G. Ripoll López, 'On the Supposed Frontier between the *Regnum Visigothorum* and Byzantine *Hispania*', at 95–115; and H. Wolfram, 'The Creation of the Carolingian Frontier-System c. 800', at 233–45.

[49] Abadal, *Dels visigots als catalans*, 173–9.

[50] Lewis, 'Cataluña como frontera militar (870–1050)'.

themselves as French or Spanish just as the monarchies underwent the processes of nation-building.[51] Building upon Sahlins's insights, this project approaches Catalonia indeed on its own terms, but also from the perspective of its importance for the Carolingian empire. How did the governors of the Spanish March and local events there reflect or even shape the political culture of the empire as a whole? Studying the formation of a new polity at the frontier reveals as much about the centre as it does about the periphery, and indeed induces hesitation about the use of such loaded terms as these.

Cautious about the use of the 'frontier' as a conceptual tool, this study also questions the common understanding of the Carolingian 'periphery'.[52] To ask how the Spanish March was integrated is to a degree asking how the March functioned as a component part of the larger empire. That necessitates approaching the region in itself not merely as a periphery. It was not a periphery to the people who lived there, for it was the centre of their lives. At the same time, it was connected to the wider empire, and figures such as Count Bera of Barcelona, Bernard of Septimania and Dhuoda, and others were interested in the kingdom as a whole as well as in the Pyrenean region. The same principle holds true for intellectual culture. The Carolingian 'renaissance' was a court programme, and the relationship between the ideals of this initiative and local realities is an important theme in Carolingian history. To look at the impact of any centralizing impetus on the Spanish March is not to marginalize the region, but to begin to sense to what degree this particular locality, like any other in the empire, participated in royal initiatives. The region's status as a recently conquered province made it special, and since it was one of the few areas bordering on territory not subject to the Franks, people there operated under special circumstances at one level. That fact cannot be denied, but this project is a regional study more than strictly a frontier study.

With the fall of communist regimes in Eastern Europe and the advancing unification of western Europe in the last decade of the twentieth century, concerns about ethnic traditions and history stretching back to the Middle Ages and even the *Völkerwanderungszeit* became front-page news.[53] Medievalists, led by Walter Pohl and others centred in Vienna, understandably sought the origins of ethnic groups, ultimately coming to

---

[51] P. Sahlins, *Boundaries: the Making of France and Spain in the Pyrenees* (Los Angeles, 1989).

[52] Smith, *Province and Empire*, 2–3. See also Hummer's perspective, *Politics and Power*, 8.

[53] P. J. Geary, *The Myth of Nations: the Medieval Origins of Europe* (Princeton, 2002) is a good example of how the work of medieval historians can be of immediate and practical benefit to the larger public, with these issues given primary importance.

question the very notion of ethnicity itself.[54] Ethnicity as it is now understood was and is fluid, defined as much against an out-group as by articulation of an in-group.[55] This kind of identity is of some importance for the present study, which seeks to tell the history of a region, peopled by members of at least one recognized *gens* and conquered by another. Whether such identities carried significance or posed hurdles to the construction of the Carolingian empire in the Spanish March, whether they played a part in the weakening of royal power and whether they mattered much in the politics and culture of the March are threads running throughout the chapters that follow.

Ultimately, even though the Carolingians seem to have paid more attention to ethnic identity than previous dynasties amongst the barbarian kingdoms,[56] such labels or the perceived ethnic differences behind them simply did not matter for the politics in the empire. The sources yield no evidence that any individual concerned with the Spanish March acted politically because of a perceived Gothicness or Frankishness. Contemporaries recognized differences in law codes and languages, and knew that the kingdom included Franks, Goths, Bavarians, Lombards, and others. Ultimately, this study concludes that, despite their recognition of such facts, political actors between the eighth and tenth centuries did not care about them the way twentieth- or twenty-first-century people might because the labels were *ethnic* – that is, each denoting a 'people' with its own history that could be read or talked about – but not *racial* – meaning indicative of a difference that would cause discrimination or persecution. Where the sources for the March actually reveal unfavourable treatment, it is because of religion. Take, for example, Charlemagne's court and the scholars he attracted to it: Anglo-Saxon,

---

[54] The literature is vast and growing. The early works that inspired this study include W. Pohl, 'Conceptions of Ethnicity in Early Medieval Studies', *Archaeologia Polona* 29 (1991): 39–49, reprinted in L. K. Little and B. H. Rosenwein, eds, *Debating the Middle Ages: Issues and Readings* (Oxford, 1998), 15–24. See also T. Anderson Jr., 'Roman Military Colonies in Gaul, Salian Ethnogenesis and the Forgotten Meaning of *Pactus Legis Salicae* 59.5', *EME* 4 (1995): 129–44 and P. Amory, 'The Meaning and Purpose of Ethnic Terminology in the Burgundian Laws', *EME* 2 (1993): 1–28.

[55] See the studies in H.-W. Goetz, J. Jarnut, and W. Pohl, eds, *Regna and Gentes: the Relationship between Late Antique and Early Medieval Peoples and Kingdoms in the Transformation of the Roman World*. Transformation of the Roman World 13 (Leiden, 2003), esp. A. Christys, 'The Transformation of Hispania after 711', at 219–41; H.-W. Goetz, '*Gens*, Kings and Kingdoms: the Franks', at 307–44; M. Schmauder, 'The Relationship between Frankish *Gens* and *Regnum*: a Proposal Based on the Archaeological Evidence', at 271–306; I. Velázquez, '*Pro patriae gentisque Gothorum statu* (4th Council of Toledo, Canon 75, a. 633)', at 161–217; and P. Wormald, 'The *Leges Barbarorum*: Law and Ethnicity in the Post-Roman West', at 21–53.

[56] W. Pohl, 'Telling the Difference: Signs of Ethnic Identity', in W. Pohl with H. Reimitz, eds, *Strategies of Distinction: the Construction of Ethnic Communities, 300–800*, The Transformation of the Roman World, 2 (Leiden, 1998), 17–69 at 45.

Irish, Lombard, and Visigothic/hispanus. The labels indicate points of origin for individuals, not 'who they were' as an identity.[57] Carolingian rulers tended to emphasize these labels more than contemporaries in the locales concerned, to the effect of trumpeting the imperial nature of their rule over different subject peoples.

SOURCES AND METHODS

The study of the early Middle Ages is often hampered by the paucity of surviving sources. Catalonia, however, is unusually rich in documentary materials, for over 5,000 charters survive from the tenth century, and a healthy 350 or so from the ninth. This body of evidence includes charters of local origin, preserved in numerous originals and even more medieval cartularies, as well as over 100 diplomas from the Frankish royal court. Since the 1920s, these documents have fallen under the purview of the Catalunya carolíngia enterprise, begun by Ramon d'Abadal i de Vinyals and continued to the present day.[58] Key to this study is the royal diplomas' illustration of the degree to which the Frankish monarchy involved itself in the region's affairs. In addition, individuals and teams have made available the material from the cartularies of several regional monasteries and cathedrals. These efforts have made thousands of documents available, enabling more researchers to turn their attention to the region. The documents have long been used to trace the development of monastic houses as nodes of wealth and culture, while more recent studies of the individual vendors, purchasers, donors, and the monasteries and churches that acquired property also reveal social power relationships. As important as charters are for understanding the early Middle Ages, it is paramount to read them critically. Decades of charter study have emphasized that such texts are records of orally and ritually public acts, not necessarily constitutive acts in and of themselves. Over time charters became dominant evidence in disputes, yet we also see that human memories could reconstitute lost archives. More recent work treats charters as their own narratives with their own agendas, not merely as

---

[57] These ideas arise not only from the sources that follow, but also from consideration of the scholarship in the preceding notes, along with critiques found in A. Gillett, ed., *On Barbarian Identity: Critical Approaches to Ethnicity in the Early Middle Ages* (Turnhout, 2002), esp. Gillett, 'Introduction: Ethnicity, History, and Methodology', in ibid., 1–18 and W. Goffart, 'Does the Distant Past Impinge on the Invasion Age Germans?', in ibid., 21–38.

[58] This team of Catalan scholars has produced critical editions of the documents pertaining to the royal Carolingian declarations (vol. 2, 1926–52) and charters of the counties of Pallars and Ribagorça (vol. 3, 1955), Osona and Manresa (vol. 4, 1999), Girona, Besalú, Empúries and Peralada (vol. 5, 2003), and Roussillon, Conflent, Vallespir, and Fenollet (vol. 6, 2006), while volumes on Barcelona and on Urgell and Cerdanya are promised.

records of things done.[59] Most important for present purposes are the royal diplomas issued to recipients in the Spanish March and Septimania, as their study can yield a view of the relationship between the region and the Carolingian dynasty.

Even more than the richness of charter evidence, this investigation draws on a wider array of sources for insight into the integration of Catalonia into Carolingian politics and culture. There are no narrative sources from the Carolingian Spanish March, so it must rely on sources from the 'centre' about the 'frontier'; this yields an interesting and significant opportunity to examine interaction in both directions. Certain annals and chronicles exhibit a familiarity with, and interest in affairs in Spain and the southern reaches of Frankish dominion, while the royalist Frankish sources highlight events in the March as they affected royal and imperial politics and policies. Because of their bias in favour of the royal court, however – a bias in terms of political slant as well as amount of material – the annals cannot paint a complete picture of the Spanish March.[60] Thus, capitularies, royal diplomas, and indeed charters corroborate and supplement narratives. Church councils, too, demonstrate the degree of Catalonian integration into Frankish institutions. Insofar as the edicts of the councils touch on Christian doctrine and learning, they serve as evidence for intellectual culture. For this study, though, ninth- and tenth-century manuscripts have yielded far more. Monastic manuscripts preserved at the Archive of the Crown of Aragon have generated a considerable wealth of information on the culture of the March. Latin literacy and manuscripts have long been of interest to scholars of the area, and the power of the written word for various aspects of culture is now well recognized.[61] For present purposes, emphasis is

---

[59] The work on charters and the regional studies just cited are also examples of key literature on this aspect of charter studies. Most recently, G. Koziol, *The Politics of Memory and Identity in Carolingian Royal Diplomas: the West Frankish Kingdom (840–987)* (Turnhout, 2012) makes important observations regarding royal documents. Essays collected in W. C. Brown, M. Costanbeys, M. Innes, and A. J. Kosto, eds, *Documentary Culture and the Laity in the Early Middle Ages* (Cambridge, 2013) are also important for our understanding of charter production, use, and preservation. See also R. McKitterick, *History and Memory in the Carolingian World* (Cambridge, 2004), chapter 7 on cartularies, which those who investigate charters must consider. H. Fichtenau, '"Politische" Datierungen des frühen Mittelalters', in *Intitulatio*, II: Lateinische Herrscher- und Furstentitel im neunten und zehnten Jahrhundert (Vienna, 1973), 453–522; E. Screen, 'The Importance of the Emperor: Lothar I and the Frankish Civil War, 840–843', *EME* 12 (2003), 25–51.

[60] Narrative sources have come under the scrutiny especially of R. McKitterick, in *History and Memory*, and more recently of H. Reimitz, in *History, Frankish Identity and the Framing of Western Ethnicity, 550–850* (Cambridge, 2015).

[61] M. C. Diaz y Diaz, *Index scriptorum Latinorum medii aevi Hispanorum* (Salamanca, 1959); Z. García Villada, *Bibliotheca Patrum Latinorum Hispaniensis*, Vol. 2 (Vienna, 1915); R. Beer, 'Die Handschriften des Klosters Santa Maria de Ripoll', *Sitzungsberichte der philosophisch-historischen*

placed on the educational setting of monastic schools as an indicator of what kinds of things the elite, at least, thought worthy of teaching.[62] The investigation thus can reveal points of influence from the Carolingian court initiatives as well as the legacy of the learning of the Visigothic era.

Of course, all these sources have provided grist for scholars' mills for generations. This study aims to build on and modify earlier findings by asking new and different questions. Rather than attempting to determine when and how Catalonia became independent from Frankish rule, I ask how the region and its people functioned as parts of the Carolingian empire, in times when the monarchy was strong as well as when it was weak. Instead of seeking the ways indigenous counts made their territories into states, I highlight the long tradition of counts wielding power in Catalonia without strict oversight from kings, yet largely adhering to their agendas. In the end, one cannot but conclude that Catalonia, although distant from royal courts, was indeed connected to the Carolingian world, that it became an important part of that world, that in turn that world became important to Catalonia and that the relationship can sometimes be seen more clearly through the lens of troubled times. These results of the study take on a wider significance because they demonstrate that traditional sources can be used to question traditional paradigms.

THE PRESENT STUDY

In what follows, the first three chapters explore Carolingian involvement in Catalonia, from the Frankish conquest of Septimania in the mid-eighth century to the death of Charles the Bald and succession of his son Louis the Stammerer, bringing us up to the year 878. As political history, these chapters revisit the paths beaten by earlier studies, especially those of Ramon d'Abadal, Archibald Lewis, and Josep María Salrach. What I present reinterprets the events in question and people behind them from a different vantage point, looking at them as they related to the Carolingian world as well as the local context, an approach informed by more recent ideas of early medieval politics, culture, and identities in general. Chapter 1 examines the region from its pre-Carolingian history up to Charlemagne's invasion of Spain in 778, with one eye on the

---

Klasse der Kaiserlichen Akademie der Wissenschaften 155, 158 (1908): 1–112, 1–117, with plates; Zimmermann, *Écrire et lire*.

[62] See the studies collected in J. J. Contreni, *Carolingian Learning, Masters and Manuscripts*, Variorum Collected Studies Series (Aldershot, 1992) and R. McKitterick, *The Frankish Kings and Culture in the Early Middle Ages* (Aldershot, 1990).

meaning of Gothic and Frankish identity in the eighth century. The formation of the Spanish March is the focus of Chapter 2, which constitutes an investigation of regional and royal power up to the death of Louis the Pious in 840. The imposition of Benedictine monasticism and doctrinal dispute over Spanish Adoptionism serve as case studies in Carolingian cultural centralization. The third chapter turns to the Spanish March as a functioning part of the empire and the western Frankish kingdom in the period 840–98. Royal authority in distant Septimania and Catalonia are the central issues. Carolingian rulers continued to grant land and immunities, sent armies to solidify the frontier and quell revolts, and changed their strategy in appointing counts to office in the March. Again, notions of identity form a thread running through these chapters.

The last three chapters of the book address the period long held to have witnessed the decline of Carolingian authority in the Spanish March and the rise of a regional dynasty. Chapter 4 investigates the relationships between that dynasty and the kings from the installation of Wifred the Hairy to several counties in the 870s, through the rule of his sons. During this period of the late ninth century and early tenth, the Carolingian family lost its monopoly on the throne of the West Frankish kingdom, as members of the family later known as the Capetians alternated with Carolingians. The fluctuations in dynastic fortune were significant for royal relations with the leaders of the Spanish March. Chapter 5 treats developments in learning and culture during the same period, assessing the degree to which Catalonia participated in the Carolingian renaissance; at issue are the political ramifications of intellectual dependence on the Frankish texts and programmes as opposed to the region's Visigothic heritage. Here again our view takes in the tenth century, thanks to the survival of manuscript evidence, the most important example of which dates from the late ninth century and the first decades after 900. Looking into the tenth century allows us to discern how integrated the Spanish March had become culturally by the time centrifugal forces politically pulled the empire apart. The final chapter analyses the exercise of power and authority in the Spanish March after 947, and considers the end of Carolingian royal presence in the region. Along these lines, it suggests a modification of existing interpretations of Catalonia's nascent independence. Counts, chief amongst them Borrell II of Barcelona, took over many of the duties of kings in this period, but royal presence was not simply replaced by comital 'sovereignty'. The counts looked to Muslim neighbours as nominal overlords, while churches turned to the papacy; the Frankish monarchy remained a viable, if symbolic, source of legitimacy. How locals identified themselves, and how the royal court identified them, as members of *gentes* and as wielders of power, reveals much about the nature of the Carolingian legacy. Catalonia's uniqueness must be balanced with a view of generally waning royal authority. The region is only unique in its later 'statehood' and conjunction with the kingdom of Aragon in the high Middle Ages, while other former Carolingian territories were eventually reabsorbed by the French crown. The theme of power and authority at the end of the Carolingian age holds great significance for our understanding of the Spanish March and the wider Carolingian world.

* * *

I use the toponyms 'Spanish March', 'the March' and much less frequently 'Catalonia', interchangeably. This will strike some as anachronistic, since there was no concept of or word for 'Catalonia', in the period under investigation.[63] Frankish sources are the only ones to designate the entire region with one name, and these use such locutions as 'Septimania' or 'Gothia', albeit to refer to a wider area than Old Catalonia. Some contemporary sources employ *marca hispanica*, less frequently *limes hispanicus*, to indicate the narrower area with which this study concerns itself. Some sources even use the term *Hispania*, denoting the Iberian Peninsula beyond the Pyrenees, and making it hard to distinguish Catalonia from al-Andalus or Asturias. Because of these inconsistencies, I use 'Catalonia' or 'Spanish March' to designate the area reaching from the county of Roussillon, south to the county of Barcelona, and westward as far Pallars and Ribagorça. I do this so that 'Septimania' and 'Gothia' can be used to refer to the whole region up to the Rhône. To adhere strictly to contemporary toponymy, as do other works of Carolingian history, which refer to 'Frankish Gaul', 'Francia', or 'Neustria', would make consistency and clarity difficult to achieve. I thus occasionally use 'Catalonia' for clarity, and beg readers' pardon for the anachronism. Furthermore, I use the adjectival form 'Catalonian', rather than 'Marcher', to refer to social and cultural developments. I do this in preference to the modern linguistic and ethnic term 'Catalan'. My usage of 'Catalonia' and 'Catalonian', then, both gives a sense of unity to all the counties conventionally subsumed under the label 'Spanish March', in the light of these realities – especially since the count of Barcelona often held other counties as well – and avoids overly wordy circumlocutions to express a more or less simple geographic

---

[63] Abadal, *Dels visigots als catalans*, 158–72; M. Aurell, 'Pouvoir et parenté', 467, especially fn 462, critiquing the use of 'Catalonia' based on the nationalism of Abadal in the 1950s and Salrach in the 1970s. But see also R. Collins, *Early Medieval Spain: Unity in Diversity, 400–1000*, 2nd ed. (New York, 1995), 256, in defence of the convenience of the modern place name.

concept. This is to some degree a concern of style, to avoid overuse of 'the (Spanish) March'. Yet I also wish to paint a picture of some cultural unity for the region in the ninth and tenth centuries; much like today, it embraced broadly similar cultural, social, and political features, even while local norms and conditions could vary.

Chapter 1

GOTHIC CATALONIA AND SEPTIMANIA TO 778

In 759, the inhabitants of the city of Narbonne handed their city over to Pippin, king of the Franks, apparently on the condition that they retain the use of their own law code.[1] This code was the Visigothic law, and Narbonne, although under Muslim control as a result of earlier fighting in the eighth century, had been one of the last outposts of the Visigothic kingdom north of the Pyrenees. The surrounding area, known as Septimania or 'Gallia Narbonensis' to the Visigothic regime that was centred on Toledo in the seventh century, even had its own Visigothic kings in the 720s after the rest of the Gothic realm fell to Arab and Berber invaders. Coincidentally, it was also the sole area of Gaul to remain under Visigothic rule after the Franks had expelled the Goths from their former base in Aquitaine very early in the sixth century. To some degree, this Gallic province of the Visigothic kingdom of Toledo had always been somewhat removed from the centre of royal power. So, too, were the farthest reaches of the ecclesiastical province of Tarraconensis, south of the Pyrenees. Bishops of cities like Barcelona and Girona sometimes found it difficult to attend important church councils held in Toledo. From time to time, nobles who sought to cast off royal control or otherwise alter the high politics of the kingdom used these regions as bases of power; they were also the pathways for occasional Frankish interference in Visigothic affairs. By the early ninth century, these regions had formed new provinces of the Carolingian Frankish kingdom but,

---

[1] *Annales d'Aniane* in *Histoire Générale de Languedoc*, eds C. Devic and J. Vaisette, Vol. 2 (Toulouse: Privat, 1875), col. 7. This text has benefitted from the recent edition by J. M. J. G. Kats, 'Chronicon Moissiacense Maius: a Carolingian World Chronicle from Creation to the First Years of Louis the Pious', prepared and revised by D. Claszen, 2 vols. (MPhil thesis, Leiden, 2012) available online at https://openaccess.leidenuniv.nl/handle/1887/20005. On this source, see below. This reference is found in Kats's edition of the text, vol. 2, 118. The edition is henceforth cited as *CMM*, while the introduction is cited by the editors' names and specifies vol. 1 of the work. For historical background, see F. Riess, *Narbonne and Its Territory in Late Antiquity: From the Visigoths to the Arabs* (Farnham, 2013).

thanks to their previous history, they presented special opportunities and challenges to their rulers.

This chapter presents a brief, historical survey of the Visigothic areas of Catalonia and Septimania that Pippin and Charlemagne had added to their expanding kingdom, from their functioning as part of the Visigothic kingdom of Toledo near the beginning of the eighth century up to the early phases of Carolingian dominion before the century's end. In doing so, its aim is not to tell the full story of these provinces during the periods of Visigothic rule and Muslim occupation, but rather to establish the main features of institutional and cultural survivals that the Carolingians inherited when they conquered the areas. For example, the case of the Muslim garrison that Pippin had to encourage the residents of Narbonne to betray was matched by other, similar ones throughout Catalonia and Septimania.[2] Certainly Charlemagne and Louis the Pious encountered Muslim warriors defending positions in Catalonia in the period 778–815. The strongholds that housed these garrisons were largely surviving Visigothic fortifications, which in many cases had been continuously used since Roman times.[3] Cities, counties, and fortresses all provided Muslim and later Frankish conquerors of the north-eastern corner of the Visigothic kingdom with the means to govern and defend the region without having to build them from nothing. The inhabitants of Septimania and the eastern Pyrenees may or may not have embraced royal authority, but their section of the kingdom did follow a different path in its history by joining the Frankish realm. Even then, though, an interesting and dynamic relationship between central power and regional autonomy was present in the Carolingian world as well.

This chapter progresses chronologically, beginning with its overview of Visigothic Catalonia. It first addresses the issues of Catalonia's supposed separateness as well as notions of identity found (at least in their subtexts) in the classic treatments of the region by scholars such as Ramon d'Abadal i de Vinyals.[4] Building on more recent studies of identity, the argument here is that there was no strong or distinct sense of identity amongst those

---

[2] *CMM* 118; J. M. Wallace-Hadrill, ed., *The Fourth Book of the Chronicle of Fredegar with Its Continuations* (London, 1960), 93–5; A. R. Lewis, *The Development of Southern French and Catalan Society, 718–1050* (Austin, 1965), 9.

[3] Although see J. Albert Adell i Gisbert and J. Josep Menchon i Bes, 'Les fortificacions de la Frontera Meridional dels comtats catalans, o les fortificacions de la Marca Superior d'al-Àndalus', *Lambard: Estudis d'Art Medieval* 17 (2004–5): 65–84 for the identification of some fortified sites in the area around Tarragona as dating to the period of Muslim occupation. For a broader picture, A. Christys, 'Christian-Muslim Frontiers in Early Medieval Spain', *Bulletin of International Medieval Research* 5 (1999): 1–19, esp. 5–7 with literature cited.

[4] Especially the first volume of his studies collected in *Dels visigots als catalans*. R. Abadal i de Vinyals, ed. J. Sobrequés i Callicó, 2nd ed., 2 vols (Barcelona, 1974). Note that the same subtext is absent from the long-view account in J. M. Salrach, *El procés de feudalització (segles III–XII)*, Història de

in the north-east of the Visigothic kingdom of Toledo. In the early eighth century, the kingdom of Toledo fell in the wake of a Muslim invasion from Africa. As we will see below, the Muslim conquest of Spain occasioned mixed results for Catalonia. Without doubt there was some violence and displacement of those who governed and lived in the region, but overall the conquest did not leave a heavy imprint on local society and culture. In part this was because the conquerors preferred treaties to sieges, and in part it was because of the limited span of time during which they occupied the Tarraconensis and Gallia Narbonensis areas before the Franks arrived on the scene. Next, this chapter turns its attention to the early phases of Frankish involvement in Catalonia, from Pippin's takeover of Narbonne to the eve of Charlemagne's invasion of Spain in 778. Identity again becomes a theme of the investigation, as the conquering Franks had to deal effectively with local people and incorporate Goths into prevailing Frankish-style sociopolitical networks. It will be seen that any supposed ethnic differences between Goths and Franks formed no obstacles to political cooperation in the time of Charles Martel and Pippin. Finally, Charlemagne's invasion through the Pyrenees takes the stage. This chapter sketches out the events surrounding the Frankish king's intervention, its execution, and its ultimate failure. Along the way, I offer some reappraisals of traditional thinking about and explanation of the first, abortive attempt to establish Frankish royal authority south of the Pyrenees.

CATALONIA AND SEPTIMANIA IN THE LATE VISIGOTHIC PERIOD

Underneath a veneer of centralized government and unification, Visigothic rule in Spain was characterized by a degree of tension between the monarchy seated in Toledo and the power of regional authorities.[5] The secular administration of the Visigothic kingdom of Toledo was carried out on the local level by counts. These officials, holdovers from the Roman administrative apparatus, had fiscal and military responsibilities and were based in towns.[6] Towns thus appear to have been key to the governance of the kingdom. For the eastern Pyrenean region, we have evidence that the province of Gallia, or Narbonensis, was governed by

Catalunya 2 (Barcelona, 1987), 53–90, although he pays special attention to Catalonia in his brief discussion of church organization, 110–12.

[5] This is of course the overarching theme of R. Collins, *Early Medieval Spain: Unity in Diversity, 400–1000*, 2nd ed. (New York, 1995) and Collins, *Visigothic Spain, 409–711* (Oxford, 2004). See, amongst other works, J. Orlandis, 'Le royaume wisigothique et son unité religieuse', in *L'Europe Héritière de l'Espagne wisigothique*, eds J. Fontaine and C. Pellistrandi (Madrid, 1992), 9–16.

[6] See P. S. Barnwell, *Kings, Courtiers and Imperium: the Barbarian West, 565–725* (London, 1997), Part II; Collins, *Early Medieval Spain*, 162.

counts, and that a mint operated at Narbonne until the early eighth century.[7] To keep law and order, the counts could turn to Visigothic law, which has long been subjected to study. The language of the code itself, the origins of its content, successive kings' contributions to it, and its interplay with contemporary society are all important themes that modern historians have addressed.[8] While this is not the place to delve into a deep examination of the history of law in the Gothic kingdom of Spain, it does merit some attention here in the form of a few brief remarks. Visigothic law stems from the Code of King Euric (466–84) and the Breviary of Alaric (King Alaric II, son of Euric, r. 484–507), written when the seat of royal authority was still at Toulouse. Euric's Code was influential beyond his own kingdom, providing some material for the later Bavarian law code. Meanwhile, the Breviary, an abridgement of Roman law and jurisprudential texts, was perhaps the most important transmitter of the Theodosian Code in early medieval Europe.[9] For now it is sufficient to note that several kings during the sixth and seventh centuries added to the legal corpus inherited from Toulouse, and that all these laws were superseded in 654 by the publication of the *Liber Iudicum*, which kings in the later seventh century updated, and which became the font for legal practice throughout the early Middle Ages in Spain. Many modern studies have addressed law as arguably a defining feature of Gothic identity.[10] More than a few point to the very long period during which the law was put to use in Catalonia and Septimania as evidence for the region's distinct character in the early Middle Ages, indeed down to the twelfth century.[11]

---

[7] Ardo, *Vita Benedicti Anianensis*, in G Waitz, ed., *MGH SS*, 15, (Hanover, 1887), 201. Lewis, *The Development of Society*, 7. For mints, *HGL*, 7, 324; F. Mateu y Llopis, 'De la Hispania Tarraconense visigoda a la Marca Hispánica carolina', *Analecta Sacra Tarraconensia* 19 (1947): 21. See now P. Grierson and M. Blackburn, *Medieval European Coinage: With a Catalogue of the Coins in the Fitzwilliam Museum, Cambridge* vol. 1 The Early Middle Ages (5th–10th centuries) (Cambridge, 1986), 39–54, esp. 43–4, 48–9, and 52–3.

[8] See, in the first instance, P. D. King, *Law and Society in the Visigothic Kingdom* (Cambridge, 1972).

[9] Ibid., 232 and I. Wood, 'The Code in Merovingian Gaul', in J. Harries and I. Wood, eds, *The Theodosian Code* (London, 1993), 161–77.

[10] Aside from traditional Catalan work as cited above, the idea is implicit in R. Collins, 'Visigothic Law and Regional Custom in Disputes in Early Medieval Spain', in W. Davies and P. Fouracre, eds, *The Settlement of Disputes in Early Medieval Europe* (Cambridge, 1986), 85–104; see also the insights of P. Wormald, 'Lex Scripta and Verbum Regis: Legislation and Germanic kingship from Euric to Cnut', in P. Sawyer and I. Wood, eds, *Early Medieval Kingship* (Leeds, 1977), 105–38; Wormald, 'The Leges Barbarorum: Law and Ethnicity in the Post-Roman West', in H.-W. Goetz, J. Jarnut, and W. Pohl, eds, Regna *and* Gentes: *the Relationship between Late Antique and Early Medieval Peoples and Kingdoms in the Transformation of the Roman World*, The Transformation of the Roman World 13 (Leiden, 2003), 21–55; and T. Faulkner, *Law and Authority in the Early Middle Ages: the Frankish Leges in the Carolingian Period* (Cambridge, 2016), 1–23.

[11] See W. Kienast, 'La pervivencia del derecho godo en el sur de Francia y Cataluña', *Boletín de la Real Academia de Buenas Letras de Barcelona* 35 (1973–4): 265–95; M. Zimmermann, 'L'Usage du

Despite the potentially unifying force of the law code, the politics of the Visigothic kingdom of Toledo featured regional deviation from the aims of its recognized central authority.[12] The kingdom is also associated with a vibrant intellectual culture that featured such figures as Fructuosus of Braga, Braulio of Zaragoza, Julian of Toledo, and perhaps most famous of all, Isidore of Seville. These men of the church, bishops all, and others like them studied Christian letters, wrote treatises, and influenced, or attempted to influence, kings and aristocrats. Their legacy reached throughout western Europe in the early Middle Ages, and indeed Carolingian court-sponsored scholars built upon solid foundations in reading and using their works.[13] Julian, for one, paid substantial attention to the 'Gauls' within the Visigothic kingdom of his time, chastising them for their disloyalty.[14] Earlier in the seventh century, the bishop of Barcelona, Quiricus, had been translated to the see of Toledo in a move highlighting the pre-eminence of the *urbs regia*.[15] On the one hand, then, these examples show that Catalonia and Septimania were indeed fully part of the Toledan kingdom and that their inhabitants were expected, at least by those in Toledo, to behave as loyal subjects. Archaeological finds support the notion of sustained links between Hispania and Septimania, and of the Gallic region's integration into the kingdom.[16] Yet on the other hand, it is clear that certain people, based in these rather distant areas, sought to escape from the reach of centralizing authority and break with the ideal of rule by consensus in order to follow their own aims.

In the twentieth century, historians detected the scent of animosity between the people of the two parts of the Visigothic kingdom of

---

droit wisigothique en Catalogne du IXe au XIIe siècle', *Mélanges de la Casa de Velázquez* 9 (1973): 233–81, as well as J. M. Salrach, 'Práctica judiciales, transformación social y acción política en Cataluña (siglos IX–XIII)', *Hispania* 47 (1997): 1009–48; M. A. Kelleher, 'Boundaries of Law: Code and Custom in Early Medieval Catalonia', *Comitatus* 30 (1999): 1–10. Most recently, J. A. Bowman, *Shifting Landmarks: Property, Proof, and Dispute in Catalonia around the Year 1000* (Ithaca, 2004) and Salrach, *Justícia i poder a Catalunya abans de l'any mil* (Vic, 2013).

[12] Collins, *Visigothic Spain*; R. L. Stocking, *Bishops, Councils, and Consensus in the Visigothic Kingdom, 589–633* (Ann Arbor, 2000); Abadal, *Dels visigots als catalans*, 57–94; E. A. Thompson, *The Goths in Spain* (Oxford, 1969).

[13] See the essays collected in J. Fontaine and C. Pellistrandi, *L'Europe héritière de l'Espagne wisigothique* (Madrid, 1992).

[14] Julian, *Historia Wambae, Iudicium in tyrannorum perfidia promulgatum*, and *Insultatio uilis storici in tyrannidem Galliae*, in *Sancti Iuliani Toletanae sedis episcopi opera*, J. N. Hillgarth, ed., CCSL 115; R. Collins, 'Julian of Toledo and the Education of Kings in Late Seventh-Century Spain', in *Law, Culture and Regionalism in Early Medieval Spain* [originally published as Julian of Toledo and the Royal Succession in Late Seventh-Century Spain] (Hampshire, 1992), 1–22.

[15] Collins, *Visigothic Spain*, 100.

[16] G. Ripoll López, 'Las relaciones entre la Península Ibérica y la Septimania entre los siglos V y VIII, según los hallazgos arqueológicos', in *L'europe héritière de l'Espagne wisigothique*, eds J. Fontaine and C. Pellistrandi (Madrid, 1992), 285–301.

Toledo, Hispania on one hand and the much smaller Gallia, or Septimania, on the other.[17] Septimania, the only Gothic province north of the Pyrenees, was the vestige of the fifth-century kingdom's occupation of Aquitaine, lost to Clovis in 507. More recent views dismiss the notion of deeply held enmity between people of the different regions of the kingdom; holders of such views are careful to withstand the influence of later historical events on their understanding of the general contours of society. Rather than resulting in enduring hostility, distance from the royal seat in Toledo and proximity to the growing power of the Franks contributed to repeated attempts by secular and ecclesiastical lords in Septimania to resist central authority.[18] The actions in the seventh century of the usurping King Sisenand and the rebel Duke Paul lend credence to such a view. In addition, these events inspired the composition of texts that shed some light on the degree to which people during the seventh century may have seen different regional identities within the Gothic kingdom of Toledo.

The usurper Sisenand was the face of a plot against the reigning King Suinthila (r. 621–31), whom different sources describe in contradictory ways. For some, Suinthila was a successful king who defeated enemies and ruled morally. Later, his name was denounced at the Fourth Council of Toledo in 633.[19] Apparently, it was the aristocracy of his realm that saw to Suinthila's undoing. Upon Sisenand's request and bribe, the Frankish King Dagobert invaded Spain with an army from Burgundy, in what amounted to the first Frankish invasion since 588.[20] Because the king of the Franks was involved in this intrigue, Frankish historians recorded it. Recent studies interested in the political uses of history have framed the efforts of these early medieval historians, including 'Fredegar' and his continuators, in terms of their subtext concerning the cohesion of Frankish politics or the creation of a Frankish identity in the period the texts were composed rather than for the events they record per se.[21] Here is evidence of the political class of Franks exercising their might beyond their own kingdoms. It was also the last Frankish invasion of Spain until Charlemagne's own. Dagobert arrived with military support for the forces looking to remove Suinthila in 631. His army joined up with

---

[17] See Thompson, *The Goths in Spain*, 227–8 and Abadal, *Dels visigots als catalans*, 57–94.

[18] Collins, *Early Medieval Spain*, 250–1.

[19] J. Vives, ed., *Concilios Visigóticos e Hispano-Romanos* (Barcelona, 1963), 221; see also the letters of Braulio of Zaragoza in *PL* 80: 650; Thompson, *The Goths in Spain*, 168–9.

[20] *The Fourth Book of the Chronicle of Fredegar with Its Continuations*, ed. Wallace-Hadrill, 61–2; Thompson, *The Goths in Spain*, 171–2.

[21] The reference of first resort is R. McKitterick, *History and Memory in the Carolingian World* (Cambridge, 2004), esp. Ch. 5, 'Politics and History'. See more recently H. Reimitz, *History, Frankish Identity and the Framing of Western Ethnicity, 550–850* (Cambridge, 2015).

Sisenand's at Zaragoza just as Suinthila abdicated.[22] The former king, along with his family, faced banishment rather than execution. Sisenand, as new king, was present for the opening of the Fourth Council of Toledo, which, ironically, recognized him as legitimate while also denouncing coups such as his own and propounding the principle of elective kingship.[23] Despite these decrees, rebellion was the rule, rather than the exception in royal politics for roughly a decade.

Julian of Toledo's *Historia Wambae regis* provides an account of the later King Wamba's war to suppress a revolt that happened in Gallia during the years 672–3.[24] Julian's perspective from Toledo is certainly biased in favour of Wamba as the legitimate king, but he articulates a difference between the inhabitants of 'Gaul', or Septimania, and those of Spain. Paul, a count apparently in good standing at the new royal court of Wamba, led the revolt against his king after being sent to crush a rebellion, and also looked to Franks for support as he declared himself king.[25] According to Julian, Wamba was legitimately elected, installed, and anointed by Bishop Quiricus of Toledo, who had been translated from Barcelona. All of these procedures followed the rules established at earlier councils of Toledo.[26] But the new king already had to confront a conspiracy in Gallia, led by Ilderic, count of Nîmes, Bishop Gumild of Maguelonne, and Abbot Ranimir, who seem to have wanted to hand over their territory to the Franks.[27] Basque raids broke out too, into the upper Ebro valley. Wamba personally led forces to respond to the Basque raids, while sending Paul to deal with Ilderic, Gumild, and Ranimir. Paul had previously been involved with Wamba's succession, and may have harboured ambitions for the crown himself, having probably been in the inner circles of highest politics since at least 653. When Paul arrived in Gallia, he found that the bishop of Nîmes had been replaced by Ranimir. Paul himself decided not to attack the rebels, but instead threw his lot in with theirs, and indeed gained leadership of the

---

[22] *The Fourth Book of the Chronicle of Fredegar with Its Continuations*, 61–2; Collins, *Visigothic Spain*, 78.

[23] Vives, ed., *Concilios Visigóticos e Hispano-Romanos*, 217–19; Thompson, *The Goths in Spain*, 172, 174.

[24] The *Historia* and its related texts – a letter from Paul to Wamba, Julian's *Insultatio* and *Iudicium* – are edited in Julian, *Sancti Iuliani Toletanae sedis episcopi opera*, ed. J. N. Hillgarth, vol. 1 CCSL 115 (Turnhout, 1976) and translated by J. Martínez Pizarro, ed., *The Story of Wamba: Julian of Toledo's Historia Wambae Regis* (Washington, DC, 2005).

[25] Thompson, *The Goths in Spain*, 221.

[26] Toledo VIII and X: Vives, ed., *Concilios Visigóticos e Hispano-Romanos*, 260–96 and 308–24; Collins, *Visigothic Spain*, 92–5.

[27] Julian, *Historia Wambae*, 8; Ian Wood, *The Merovingian Kingdoms, 450–751* (London, 1994), 88–101 for a similar phenomenon occurring repeatedly amongst the Franks, who governed borderlands and transferred loyalty to improve their situations.

movement, with the support of the duke of Tarraconensis, Ranosind.[28] So Paul's challenge to Wamba was serious but not inevitably fatal. It seems that Paul envisaged a split of the kingdom, with himself as 'King of the East' and Wamba as 'King of the South'.[29] Wamba, who appears to have disregarded the offer if it was made, moved to confront Paul's forces at the close of his campaign against the Basque raiders, marching down the Ebro and then up to Narbonne. Barcelona and Girona capitulated with little resistance, and Paul was forced to flee Narbonne for Nîmes, where his ally Ranimir was ruling as bishop and could be counted on to offer hospitality.[30] There he surrendered after failing to hold his position in a fortified amphitheatre.[31] Roger Collins notes that the high walls typical of amphitheatre construction actually made sense for those seeking handy fortified locations, especially in cities with diminished populations relative to their high point during the empire's golden age.[32] Wamba took Paul to Toledo for ritual humiliation and imposed a sentence of exile upon him.[33] The political culture of the Visigothic kingdom seems to have avoided extremes whenever possible, so Paul and his party were not executed, and indeed many of his supporters were not even punished with permanent removal from the political sphere and confiscation of wealth.[34]

Sisenand's coup surely indicates that aristocratic opinion of the king in certain circles was quite low, and not that people in any one region of the Gothic kingdom felt the need to break away politically from the court in Toledo. The facts that he based his military activity in the Ebro valley and called on Frankish military support are attributable to simple strategic thinking. Sisenand saw that his position was not strong enough to remove Suinthila without a fight and that that fight would require aid from outside the kingdom. Further, in order both to mount his own forces and to join with Dagobert's, Sisenand needed to be geographically removed from Toledo and nearer to Dagobert's point of entry into Spain. Paul's rebellion, forty years later, likewise shows no proclivity towards autonomy or independence on the part of the inhabitants of the Tarraconensis-Narbonensis region vis-à-vis the central authority of Toledo. The rebellion clearly emanated from personal or factional rivalry between Paul and Wamba, but it does at least show that those aristocrats

---

[28] There is a brief treatment of this affair in Stocking, *Bishops, Councils, and Consensus*, 184–6.
[29] Julian, *Epistola Pauli*.   [30] Julian, *Historia Wambae*, 11–17.
[31] Julian, *Historia Wambae*, 18; Pizarro, *The Story of Wamba*, xvi–xvii.
[32] Collins, *Visigothic Spain*, 220–1.
[33] Julian, *Iudicium in tyrannorum perfidia promulgatum*, in *Historia Wambae*, 6–7.
[34] Pizarro, *The Story of Wamba*, 95.

who dared to challenge the authority of a new king did so by consistently using those areas as a power base.

Another interesting aspect of Paul's rebellion is the nature of the source material it generated. In addition to the narrative *Historia Wambae regis*, Julian of Toledo also authored a pair of shorter, accompanying texts, the *Insultatio vilis storici in tyrannidem Galliae* and the *Iudicium in tyrannorum perfidiam promulgatum*. Of these, the *Insultatio* merits some consideration for what it can reveal about attitudes and identities within the Gothic kingdom. In it, Julian lashes out against the land that supported the rebels, addressing his highly rhetorical invective towards Gallia herself.[35] Gallia, or Gaul, is 'the nurse of scandal, the igniter of evil, the mother of blasphemers, stepmother of treachery, stepdaughter of deceit, timber of brothels, den of betrayal, fountain of perfidy, murderess of souls'.[36] The bishop, supporter of the rightful King Wamba, denounces Gaul for seeking a second king as he would an adulterous wife who sought another man.[37] The rebels were cowards, fighting by means of the women's weapons of tricks and poison, rather than with fortitude and strength.[38] By contrast, the 'Spaniards' who came to subdue the revolt were virtuous and manly warriors who used their swords to defeat a treacherous enemy.[39] Gaul was reduced to deserving servitude, but the righteous King Wamba, who had always been a friend, ally, and protector, bestowed freedom. The 'Spaniards' had been kind to Gaul, but Gaul repaid them with deceit in return for peace, destruction for its own defence, and invited foreigners to overthrow the Spaniards when they rode with arms to defend Gaul's freedom.[40] All this is clearly rhetoric, an invective that inverts the formula of panegyric. It does not indicate any sense of identity, but rather in a gendered way attributes all manner of vices to the region where the rebels made their base. The closest Julian comes to marking out the people of Gallia as separate from those of Hispania is when he contrasts the virtue of the *Spani* to Gallic perfidy. This, too, is rhetorical flourish rather than evidence of identity, but it does apply to people the labels deriving from geography, and this in itself may indicate a process of defining communities.[41] Julian clearly took the side of the 'Spaniards' and highlighted the alterity of the people and places

---

[35] Pizarro, *The Story of Wamba*, 89–95, 98–109, 153–63.
[36] Julian, *Insultatio*, in *Historia Wambae*, 2; trans. Pizarro, 224.   [37] Julian, *Insultatio*, 3.
[38] Julian, *Insultatio*, 5.
[39] Julian, *Insultatio*, 7. 'Spaniard' is Pizarro's translation of Julian's 'Spanus'. See ibid. 227, with note 153 that contrasts Julian's use of the term 'exercitus Hispaniae' in the *Historia* proper (chapter 13).
[40] Julian, *Insultatio*, 8.
[41] My use of this concept derives from the essays collected in R. Corradini, M. Diesenberger, and H. Reimitz, eds, *The Construction of Communities in the Early Middle Ages: Texts, Resources and Artefacts*, The Transformation of the Roman World 12 (Leiden, 2003), esp. W. Pohl,

beyond the Pyrenees. The distant province of Gallia proved challenging to rule from the centralizing perspective of the royal court and associated church leaders. What is more, Julian allowed his strident anti-Judaism to come to the surface, castigating Gallia for not only perfidy and murder, but also for associating too closely with Jews.[42]

The presence of a prominent Jewish community was indeed one aspect of society that set Gallia apart from the Spanish areas of the Gothic kingdom.[43] This community was prominent enough to influence royal policy, as some kings would court Septimanian Jews while others would act against them to gain popularity with other groups elsewhere in the kingdom. Kings could restore a depleted fisc by divesting the magnates, or even Jews, of their funds.[44] The Sixth Council of Toledo (638), for instance, reinforced earlier pronouncements that, it declared, had successfully brought the Jews to heel, and called upon future kings to ensure that such a state endured. The bishops especially warned against kings allowing any Jewish resurgence out of want of financial resources.[45] Isidore disapproved of Sisebut's forced conversion of Jews.[46] Further, Toledo XII spelled more bad news for the Jews of the kingdom, apparently as a result of the influence of Julian of Toledo.[47] The council restricted Jews' rights to marry, the reading of certain books deemed contrary to Christian faith, and their religious practice, amongst other limitations on their lifestyle.[48] Yet because there was broad opposition to anti-Jewish policies, and these policies proved difficult to enforce when they were enacted, it seems the Jewish population was quite significant in the north-east, in contrast to the rest of the kingdom.[49]

Long ago, E. A. Thompson pointed out that the bishops of Septimania attended seventh-century councils less regularly than their peers in other parts of the kingdom. Bishops or their deputies often had good reason for missing a council, perhaps because of plague, distance, weather, or infirmity, while sometimes the death of a bishop or vacancy in the see could explain a lack of representation.[50] The evidence of most of the

---

'The Construction of Communities and the Persistence of Paradox: an Introduction', 1–16 and D. Harrison, 'Structures and Resources of Power in Early Medieval Europe', 17–38.

[42] Julian, *Insultatio*, 2.

[43] For this point see discussions throughout older scholarship, e.g., Thompson, *The Goths in Spain*; Lewis, *The Development of Society*, 12.

[44] Abadal, *Dels visigots als catalans*, 66–7.

[45] Vives, ed., *Concilios Visigóticos e Hispano-Romanos*, 580.   [46] Collins, *Visigothic Spain*, 76.

[47] Vives, ed., *Concilios Visigóticos e Hispano-Romanos*, 395–7; Abadal, *Dels visigots als catalans*, 82–3; Collins, *Visigothic Spain*, 236.

[48] Vives, ed., *Concilios Visigóticos e Hispano-Romanos*, 580.

[49] See especially B. S. Bachrach, 'A Reassessment of Visigothic Jewish Policy', *American Historical Review* 78 (1973): 11–34.

[50] Thompson, *The Goths in Spain*, 285–6.

Toledan councils, on the contrary, shows that most bishops in the kingdom, or their legates, did participate. And sometimes, even when relatively few of the realm's bishops were in attendance, these included
representatives from Catalonia and Gallia. For example, at Toledo V in
636, twenty bishops were present. Although none traversed the Pyrenees
from the Narbonne province, one, the bishop of Barcelona, came from
Catalonia.[51] The council was primarily concerned with stabilizing high
politics, pronouncing statements on matters relating to the high aristocracy, and electing the king. The descendants of kings and royal council-
lors were to enjoy the inheritance of property left to them in wills, and
only members of the highest echelon of the aristocracy were to participate
in elections.[52] Forty-one bishops or episcopal representatives attended
Toledo VII, amongst them the archbishop of Tarragona and the bishop of
Empúries. This was another council aimed at strengthening the monarchy, as its first canon dealt harshly with traitors; there was a separate act
specifically concerning the clergy of Gallia.[53] Toledo VIII was better
attended, featuring bishops from modern Catalonia (Ausona, Girona,
Urgell, Empúries, Tortosa, Lleida, and Egara), and from Gallia (Agde,
Carcassonne); the bishop of Egara did not attend but instead sent
a representative.[54] This council may have been deemed important
enough for distant bishops to attend because it dealt with serious political
issues of kingship, as King Chindasuinth established the principle of
hereditary kingship. The record of the council even shows that it took
place under the auspices of Chindasuinth's son Reccesuinth, in the
fifth year of his reign as co-ruler.[55] Explaining the absence of the trans-
Pyrenean bishops is thus more difficult. Gallia, which seems to have been
considered something of a 'problem area', was nonetheless firmly part of
the kingdom; it had been the location of ritual practices that had earlier
been banned by Toledo IV.[56] Toledo XII in 681 legitimized the reign of
Ervig, who had supplanted Wamba in 680. Julian of Toledo anointed the
new king, in the presence of thirty-one bishops and four vicars, and the
council recognized the right of the metropolitan of Toledo to consecrate
all bishops in the kingdom. The council also enacted twenty-eight laws
against the Jews and revised the Visigothic law code, the *Forum Iudicum*.[57]
Of the bishops in attendance, representatives came neither from

[51] Vives, ed., *Concilios Visigóticos e Hispano-Romanos*, 230.
[52] Vives, ed., *Concilios Visigóticos e Hispano-Romanos*, 227–9.
[53] Vives, ed., *Concilios Visigóticos e Hispano-Romanos*, 253–9; Abadal, *Dels visigots als catalans*, 75–7.
[54] Vives, ed., *Concilios Visigóticos e Hispano-Romanos*, 287–8.
[55] Abadal, *Dels visigots als catalans*, 77–9. The full *acta* are in Vives, ed., *Concilios Visigóticos e Hispano-Romanos*, 260–93.
[56] Stocking, *Bishops, Councils, and Consensus*, 80, 159–60.
[57] Vives, ed., *Concilios Visigóticos e Hispano-Romanos*, 380–410.

Tarraconensis, including Catalonia and the Ebro valley and western Pyrenean dioceses, nor from Gallia.[58] Abadal suggested that they disagreed with the raising of Ervig after his coup against Wamba, who had replaced nearly the entire episcopate of two formerly rebellious provinces with men who were fiercely loyal to him. Those bishops seem to have enacted a boycott of the installation of his successor.[59] The next kingdom-wide council, Toledo XIII, is taken to epitomize the search for political equilibrium.[60] That might explain the attendance by most of the episcopate, with forty-four bishops and twenty-six vicars participating. The archbishops of Narbonne and Tarragona sent representatives, as did the bishops of Lodève, Elna, Carcassonne, Agde, and Uzès from Gallia, as well as those of Barcelona, Zaragoza, Egara, Urgell, Empúries, Girona, and Osona from Tarraconensis. The bishops of Béziers and Maguelonne from Gaul, amongst others from different regions, attended personally.[61] Over the course of the seventh century, then, church councils articulated an ideal of unity, which clearly included the north-east of the kingdom and the province beyond the Pyrenees, even though bishops' intermittent participation in those councils underlines the difficulties inherent in making that ideal a reality.

After this brief survey of the evidence for the major events in the history of Catalonia and Septimania within the Gothic kingdom of Toledo, it is important to consider whether the regions really had a notion of separateness from the larger part of the realm, or if they were simply the locations where these important events took place. In the case of the rebel count Paul, there was no home-grown separatist movement. Instead, what is traceable in the surviving evidence was simply a group of nobles working against the king in order to overthrow him and take the reins of the monarchy themselves. They based themselves in the north-east because it was a strategic location or perhaps because they had property or family connections in the area, enabling them to build up armies there.[62] Alternatively, the writings of Julian of Toledo may raise the possibility of regional tensions within the kingdom, if his *Insultatio* is not to be dismissed as purely rhetorical. To do so, however, is to fall into a trap. In short, there were no separatists detectable in the evidence amongst the inhabitants of Catalonia and Septimania. It is highly possible that the ruling aristocrats in the area sometimes strove for

---

[58] The subscription list is found in Vives, ed., *Concilios Visigóticos e Hispano-Romanos*, 401–3.

[59] Abadal, *Dels visigots als catalans*, 82–3.

[60] Vives, ed., *Concilios Visigóticos e Hispano-Romanos*, 411–40.

[61] Vives, ed., *Concilios Visigóticos e Hispano-Romanos*, 431–4 for the subscriptions. Abadal, *Dels visigots als catalans*, 83–5.

[62] On property or family ties, Lewis, *The Development of Society*, 4.

autonomy from the monarchy or to unseat a reigning king out of simple ambition, without the motivating factor of a regional identity, and chose the most favourable location to stage their coups. After all, Paul arrived on the scene in the first place in order to quell the rebellion of Ilderic and his company. Indeed, some recent work has pointed to aspirations for autonomy on the part of regional aristocrats as the reasons for the failure of Hispania (including Gallia) to coalesce into a nation.[63] This interpretation is potentially teleological, whereas a closer reading of the evidence shows merely the consistent work by kings and councils to establish and maintain political stability for the Visigothic kingdom of Toledo.

THE MUSLIM CONQUEST

In the early eighth century, most of the Visigothic kingdom's military forces were concentrated in the north-eastern provinces of Tarraconensis and Gallia, as those were the regions considered most at risk of possible attack, from either the Franks or the dukes of Aquitaine. Roger Collins further links the presence of large numbers of troops to the fact that, during the seventh century, challenges to the Toledan kings originated in the north-east, as we have seen.[64] By the dawn of the eighth century, then, the degree to which the central monarchy exerted influence in the extreme north-east of the kingdom is questionable. In this sense, the political developments of the seventh century, when kings had to fight hard to maintain unity under the monarchy, resulted in a pattern in the deployment of military resources that would have grave consequences in the face of the Muslim invasion in the early eighth century.

In order to understand the invasion and conquest of Spain as it relates to the history of Catalonia, the textual sources must be reconsidered. For present purposes, the most important of the texts are the *Chronicle of 754* and the *Chronicon Moissiacense Maius (CMM)*, which itself seems to contain information derived from the former.[65] There are several medieval Arabic historical, geographical, or ethnographical texts that cover the conquest, but all of them date from much later than the events they represent, some by centuries. Moreover, the first half of the eighth century in al-Andalus is arguably the most sparsely documented period in Islamic historiography.

---

[63] I. Velázquez, '*Pro patriae gentisque gothorum statu* (4th Council of Toledo, Canon 75, a. 633)', in H.-W. Goetz and J. Jarnut, eds, *Regna and Gentes: the Relationship between Late Antique and Early Medieval Peoples and Kingdoms in the Transformation of the Roman World* (Leiden, 2003), 161–217.

[64] Collins, *Visigothic Spain*, 141.

[65] For a general treatment of the source material pertaining to the Muslim conquest in general, see; R. Collins, *The Arab Conquest of Spain, 710–797* (Oxford and Malden, MA, 1994), 23–36. P. Chalmeta, *Invasión e islamización: La sumisión de Hispania y la formación de al-Andalus* (Jaén, 2003), 31–68 includes an extensive discussion.

While this study does call upon those sources in an effort to glean as much as can safely be used, it relies more on texts that do not suffer the same weaknesses. Closer in chronological and geographical proximity are the aforementioned *Chronicle of 754*, composed in Spain in the middle of the eighth century, and the *CMM*, which builds on the foundation of several earlier texts but is also clearly well informed on events in Septimania in the eighth century. In recent decades archaeological excavations have produced helpful findings, so the treatment here will draw on some of that work to a degree as well.

For its part, even though its author was likely not exactly contemporary with the events of the Muslim invasion and early conquest and in any case composed the work in decades afterwards, the *Chronicle of 754* is considered an 'eyewitness account' and 'intrinsically credible' in modern scholarship.[66] The first part of the *Chronicle* is in fact a universal chronicle that charts its years by the *anno mundi* system and also according to the reigns of Byzantine emperors, beginning with Heraclius.[67] It also employs the Spanish 'era', which is an independent dating system similar to but 38 years ahead of that of Anno Domini, which became prominent later in the West.[68] In the twentieth year of Heraclius's reign and the era 669, the Chronicle starts to date by the 'years of the Arabs', in this case the fourteenth year after the *hijrah* or flight from Mecca to Medina, when Umar succeeded Abu Bakr as caliph. As this instance shows, the chronology is not always precisely that which is known to modern historians, who would date the twentieth year of Heraclius to AD 630, which would be the eighth year from the *hijrah*, but Umar succeeded in 634. After that point, the era is the predominant dating mechanism, while Visigothic kings are mentioned alongside Byzantine emperors and the 'year of the Arabs' is also given. By the early eighth century, the chronology remains tricky to figure, but the account of the events is trustworthy. The *Chronicle of 754* is the best source on the Muslim conquest of Spain. The main drawback of the text for the interests of this study is that it pays no special attention to the north-east of the peninsula or Gallia.

For areas further north we must turn to the *CMM*. This text has recently had the benefit of a new edition, which sorts out the complex manuscript history and corrects the errors of earlier, partial critical

---

[66] C. Cardelle de Hartmann, 'The Textual Transmission of the Mozarabic Chronicle of 754', *EME* 8 (1999): 13–29 calls it an 'eyewitness', while Collins, *The Arab Conquest of Spain*, 36, views it as 'intrinsically credible both in terms of historical methodology and common sense'.

[67] *Chronica Muzarabica*, in J. Gil, ed., *Corpus Scriptorum Muzarabicorum*, 2 vols. (Madrid, 1973) (henceforth *Chron. 754*), vol. 1, 16.

[68] See the study in J. E. López Perreira, *Estudio crítico sobre la Crónica Mozárabe de 754* (Zaragoza, 1980), and an edition of the text: J. E. López Perreira, *Crónica muzárabe de 754* (Zaragoza, 1980).

editions.[69] Such editions, such as those in the *Monumenta Germaniae Historica* and the *Histoire General de Languedoc*, identified three separate but related texts: the *Chronicle of Moissac*, the *Annals of Aniane*, and the *Chronicle of Uzés*.[70] These three texts, each existing in an individual manuscript, can be shown to have shared material that derives from a common ancestor, a now-lost 'southern' source.[71] As the manuscripts that preserve these texts post-date the Carolingian period and contain interpolated material, they invite questions as to how trustworthy they are for relating the history of the eighth century.[72]

The *CMM* exists because of three stages in its history. First, the original composer used Bede and other late antique and early medieval sources for the early part of its own universal history.[73] A compiler in the early ninth century brought the story forward, building on more recent texts, and finally an eleventh-century copyist preserved the text in the format that exists today. The eleventh-century manuscript is considered a faithful copy of its exemplar, in large part because it also includes marginal notations.[74] For the history of the eighth century, the compiler copied the earlier universal chronicle in its entirety, and for the eighth century began to rely on Frankish material such as the *Lorsch Annals*, as well as the lost 'southern' source that provided material on Spain, Septimania, and Aquitaine. Its manuscript is missing folios that would cover the decades between 741 and 770, but manuscript evidence allows us to follow the text of the *Annals of Aniane* for this period as the other witness to the lost 'southern' source.[75] The information recorded for the period after 770 contains clues that the compiler was based in Septimania, where he had access to that now-lost source, even though he was intently interested in Charlemagne and the rise of the Carolingian empire.[76] Therefore, the *CMM* is a useful source for the early Frankish involvement in Septimania that followed a generation or so after the Muslim conquest. What started

[69] Kats and Claszen, ed. *CMM.*, as in note 1.
[70] *MGH* SS 1 (Hannover, 1826), 280–313; *HGL* 2, col. 1–12; *HGL* 2, col. 23–9.
[71] Kats and Claszen, ed., *CMM*, vol. 1, 13 and 24.
[72] The manuscripts are Paris, BNF lat. 4886, which contains the *Chronicle of Moissac*, BN lat. 5941, dated to the twelfth century for the *Annals of Aniane* and also contains a copy of the *Gesta comitum Barcinonesium*, and BNF lat. 4974, dated to the fourteenth century, for the *Chronicle of Uzés*.
[73] Kats and Claszen, ed., *CMM*, vol. 1, 27–30 give the full contents of the manuscript.
[74] Kats and Claszen, ed., *CMM*, vol. 1, 31.
[75] Kats and Claszen, ed., *CMM*, vol. 1, 13–14 and 119; R. Kramer, 'Great Expectations: Imperial Ideologies and Ecclesiastical Reforms from Charlemagne to Louis the Pious (813–822)' (PhD diss., Freie Universität Berlin, 2014), 338–53. I thank Dr Kramer for giving me a copy of his dissertation.
[76] P. Geary, 'Un fragment récemment découvert du *Chronicon Moissiacense*', *Bibliothèque de l'École des Chartes* 136 (1978): 69–73. See also P. Buc, 'Ritual and Interpretation: the Early Medieval Case', *EME* 9 (2000): 183–210, which expresses hope that the lost common ancestor of both the Moissac and Aniane texts could be reconstructed.

as a universal chronicle became more and more a Carolingian history, the Aniane branch incorporating material even from the *Annales Regni Francorum* and Einhard's *Vita Karoli*. For these reasons, we shall return to the *CMM* below.[77] For now, because the surviving manuscript is considered a faithful copy of its early medieval exemplar, it is useful for a discussion of the Muslim occupation of parts of Catalonia.

Blaming the decadence of Witiza's reign for these events, the *CMM* briefly accounts for Roderic's installation as king and his failure on the battlefield against Tariq at Guadalete following the invasion of 711. In doing so, it provides basically the same interpretation as do sources from Spain. Within two years, these annals report, the invading Muslims subdued almost the entire peninsula.[78] Such a rapid subjugation is explained in part by the treaties Visigothic nobles made with their conquerors, allowing local aristocrats to maintain their power under Muslim overlords. In this way, the conquest of Spain took place, to a significant degree, by negotiation.[79] The prime example of this method of consolidating rule over new territory in Iberia is known as the treaty 'of Tudmir' or 'of Orihuela'. Tudmir, or Theodemir, was a secular magnate with authority in Murcia who came to an agreement with the Arab leader Abd al-Aziz in 713, by which Theodemir retained his position and the people of a series of cities under his rule were to suffer no molestation.[80] While spared from death, imprisonment, and religious persecution, Theodemir and his followers were subject to the payment of an annual tax in coin and kind, the *jizyah*.

Although Theodemir was a leader in south-eastern Spain, the example may hold for other regions. Evidence of resistance to the Muslim advance in the north-east is scarce, so it may be fair to base conclusions on the patterns established in the early Islamic conquests, both in the Near East and earlier in Spain.[81] It may be, however, that the Muslim conquest of parts of the region was violent, as some studies have hinted at pockets of

---

[77] Reimitz, *History, Frankish Identity and the Framing of Western Ethnicity*, chs. 8, 9, and 10 in particular shed light on how these and related texts contributed to the formation of Frankish identity in the period.

[78] *CMM*, 111.

[79] Chalmeta, *Invasión e islamización*, 206–13; Lewis, *The Development of Society*, 6; Collins, *Early Medieval Spain*, 159–60 and 203.

[80] The famous treaty, found in F. J. Simonet, *Historia de los Mozárabes de España* (Madrid, 1903), is translated by O. R. Constable in *Medieval Iberia: Readings from Christian, Muslim, and Jewish Sources*, ed. O. R. Constable (Philadelphia, 1997), 37–8.

[81] On the evidence, P. Chalmeta, 'El sugar de una formación: Al-Andalus', in *El Islam y Cataluña* (Barcelona, 1999), 39–49, at 47. For the likelihood of treaties, M. Sánchez Martínez, 'Catalunya i al-Àndalus (segles viii–x)', in *Catalunya a l'època carolíngia: art i cultura abans del romànic (segles IX i X)* (Barcelona, 1999, 29–35), with English trans. 431–5; Pere Balañà i Abadia, *L'Islam a Catalunya (segles VIII–XII)* (Barcelona: Dalmau, 1997), 14.

resistance in certain areas.[82] In either case, it is likely that Muslims entered the region via the Roman road from Zaragoza.[83] Areas farther inland seem to have been spared the most significant effects of conquest, as some evidence indicates the survival of native church and monastic traditions.[84] In the end, it is clear that people in some locales resisted the Muslim advance, while others in different places submitted relatively peacefully. A review of the narrative of events bears this out.

To begin with, it is possible that Roderic's succession to the throne was unpopular and thus challenged.[85] The base of this challenge was in the north-east part of the kingdom, the provinces of Tarraconensis and Gallia, where earlier challenges to royal authority had also been based. The leader of the uprising seems to have been a man named Achila, perhaps a son of the former king Witiza, and Roderic was never able to confront him, thanks to the Arab invasion.[86] Achila set up his rule, apparently supported by the relatively large and politically important Jewish population of the region; the Jews opposed Roderic because of his anti-Jewish policies, which were popular elsewhere in the kingdom. The presence of Jewish collaborators led to some instances of local Jews allying with the invading Muslims, probably because of generations of royal and ecclesiastical anti-Jewish policy, perhaps recently reversed by Witiza but reinstated under his successor.[87] Seville, Córdoba, and Toledo even received Jewish garrisons. Achila certainly had other followers, many of whom numbered amongst Roderic's own troops, fighting in 711 against first Basques and later Muslims. These supporters seem to have deserted Roderic in his encounter with Tariq, thus allowing their own lord, Achila, to assert his kingship while also paving the way for the collapse of his kingdom by giving ground to the invaders.[88] Numismatics show Achila's kingdom survived Muslim conquest for at least three years, for coins struck in Achila's name originated from mints in Narbonne, Girona, Tarragona, and Zaragoza. There is evidence of a campaign to Zaragoza in spring 713 led by the Arab governor of western Africa,

---

[82] For example A. Pladevall, 'L'organització de l'Església a Catalunya carolíngia', *Catalunya a l'època carolíngia: art i cultura abans del romànic (segles IX i X)* (Barcelona, 1999), 53–8, with English trans. 444–8. Discussion of the resistance follows below.

[83] Balañà, *L'Islam a Catalunya*, 12–13.

[84] See for the example of Urgell, R. d'Abadal i de Vinyals, 'El paso de Septimania del dominio godo al franco a través de la invasión sarracena (720–768)', *Cuadernos de Historia de España* 19 (1953): 9–15. Reprinted in Abadal, CC 1, 1–37.

[85] Chalmeta, *Invasión e islamización*, 134–43.

[86] Abadal, CC 1, 9; Collins, *The Arab Conquest of Spain*, 32–3.

[87] Bachrach, 'Visigothic Jewish Policy', 33, with note 85.

[88] *Chron. 754*, 31–2; Bachrach, 'Visigothic Jewish Policy', 32–3 and sources literature cited therein.

Musa, after which Achila disappears from the record.[89] Using Roman roads, it would have taken at least to the end of 713 to complete the conquest of the north-east.[90] Barcelona and Girona, along with Lleida and Tarragona, fell by the end of that year.[91] Unfortunately, it remains unclear whether these cities capitulated or went down fighting.[92]

The new king in the north-east was Ardo, who reigned until about 720, and for whom no physical evidence, such as coins or official documents, exists.[93] He appears only in a regnal list, given a reign of seven years.[94] By the time he succeeded Achila, the Tarraconensis had fallen into Muslim hands, leaving Ardo in possession of Gallia. Resist though he might, Ardo and his remnant kingdom eventually fell. Chronology is difficult to follow clearly in the main sources, the *Chronicle of 754* and the *CMM*. In the period 716–21, Muslim forces first consolidated the area from Barcelona to the Pyrenees and then crossed into Gaul.[95] According to earlier studies, the *wali* al-Hurr took Barcelona.[96] The Christians mounted a counter-attack and regained territory, prompting the caliph in Damascus to send a new commander, al-Samh, to Spain. Al-Samh continued the campaign, taking Narbonne itself in 719 or 720.[97] He later pushed onward to besiege Toulouse. Eudo, duke of Aquitaine, came to the city's rescue in the summer of 721, and al-Samh fell in battle.[98] Eudo's victory inspired resistance in Septimania, so the next emir Ambasa needed to bring the province back to heel with expeditions to Carcassonne and Nîmes.[99] The Gothic count of Carcassonne stayed in place according to an agreement similar to the Treaty of Tudmir, and Nîmes capitulated along similar lines ('pace conquisivit'), giving basically all of Septimania to Ambasa by 725.[100] The *CMM* reports another campaign in 725, this time

---

[89] Abadal, CC 1, 5–6.   [90] Balañà, *L'Islam a Catalunya*, 15–16.

[91] Sanchez Martínez, 'Catalunya i al-Àndalus', 29.

[92] One view is that the nobles of the region disliked Achila's penchant for negotiation and could have elected someone else in his place, in order to resist the Muslims. Abadal, CC 1, 9; Collins (*The Arab Conquest of Spain*, 45) agrees that the next king put up some resistance.

[93] Thompson, *The Goths in Spain*, 249–51. See also C. Miles, *The Coinage of the Visigoths of Spain: Leovigild to Achila II* (New York, 1952), 40–3, 444–7; Mateu y Llopis, 'De la Hispania Tarraconense visigoda a la Marca Hispánica carolina', 1–122 at 121.

[94] Ibn al-Athir, Catalan trans. in J. M. Millàs i Vallicrosa, *Textos dels historiadors àrabs referents a la Catalunya carolíngia* (Barcelona, 1987), no. 25; Collins, *Visigothic Spain*, 139–40.

[95] *Chron. 754*, 36.   [96] Abadal, CC 1, 10.

[97] *CMM*, 112; P. Sénac, 'Las incursions musulmanes más allá de los Pirineos (siglos VIII–XI)', in *El Islam y Cataluña* (Barcelona, 1999), 51–5, on the basis of several Arabic sources; Balañà, *L'Islam a Catalunya*, 16.

[98] Abadal, CC 1, 12, following the *Liber Pontificalis* for some details.

[99] *Chron. 754*, 37–38; *CMM*, 112; Balañà, *L'Islam a Catalunya*, 16; Sanchez Martínez, 'Catalunya i al-Àndalus', 29; and Sénac, 'Las incursions musulmanes', 51–2.

[100] Ibn al-Athir in Vallicrosa, *Textos dels historiadors àrabs*, 38–40. See also *CMM*, 112.

to Autun, where the Muslims sacked the city and took treasure.[101] The campaign extended to Sens, where Ambasa was killed during a siege that lasted into early 726.[102] The conquest of the Visigothic lands was then complete, as raiding activity extended into Aquitaine and the Frankish kingdom.

Ambasa's death started a brief period of peace for Septimania and the eastern Pyrenees. Then in 730, a rebellion broke out there, led by a Berber commander named Munussa. The example of the bishop of Urgell, Nambad, who held office during the eighth century and met an unfortunate end, could serve as evidence of a sometimes violent Muslim consolidation in the far north-east of the Visigothic kingdom.[103] Apparently, Munussa burned the bishop to punish Christians for fomenting unrest in Cerdanya.[104] To solidify the territory further, Munussa married Duke Eudo's daughter, cementing an alliance between Muslim and Christian, which would enable each regional lord to resist his more powerful neighbour.[105] Munussa rebelled against the emir in Córdoba, Abd al-Rahman, while Eudo could defy the overtures of the Frankish mayor of the palace, Charles Martel. Abd al-Rahman, however, struck out and besieged Munussa in Llívia, the principal town of Cerdanya.[106] Munussa tried to escape but was captured and committed suicide. Abd al-Rahman, in recognition of his success and service, received an honourable salutation from the caliph in Damascus, to whom he sent Eudo's daughter as a prize.[107] The new *wali* in Septimania, Yusuf ibn Abd al-Rahman al-Fihri (734–41), worked on his own accord, but not in opposition to the emir in Córdoba, to renew raiding and attacks in Gaul.[108] The narrative of the *Chronicle of 754* signals that these actions during his reign resulted in Charles Martel's intervention, as it flows freely from these developments to the confrontation against the Franks without stopping to mark the new era or regnal year.[109]

---

[101] *CMM*, 114; See Tessier, *Recueil des actes de Charles le Chauve*, no. 23 for a precept of Charles the Bald confirming rights granted by Louis the Pious to the bishop of Autun because of the losses incurred.

[102] Ibn al-Athir in Vallicrosa, *Textos dels historiadors àrabs*, nos. 38–9; Abadal, CC 1, 15.

[103] A. Pladevall, 'L'organització de l'Església a Catalunya carolíngia', 53–8, with English trans. 444–8.

[104] *Chron. 754*, 42.

[105] *Chron. 754*, 42; Balañà, *L'Islam a Catalunya*, 25; Sanchez Martínez, 'Catalunya i al-Àndalus', 29; and Sénac, 'Las incursions musulmanes', 52–3.

[106] *Chron. 754*, 41.

[107] Balañà and Sanchez Martínez, as above; Abadal, CC 1, 15–17 attributes Bishop Nambad to the see of Urgell. Abadal also sees Munussa's revolt as a precursor to the civil unrest that marked a large part of the history of medieval al-Andalus.

[108] Vallicrosa, *Textos dels historiadors àrabs*, no. 43. See also Abadal, CC 1, 19–22.

[109] *Chron. 754*, 42–3.

A few factors can help explain the supposed tendency of *walis* in the north of al-Andalus to defy their superiors. For instance, most Muslims who settled into the mountainous areas of Spain were Berbers; their Arab superiors tended to settle in river valleys and less rugged terrain.[110] While one explanation of this settlement pattern is that the Arab leadership took over the best land, it is now rather seen as the migration of these two Muslim groups to the land in Spain that most resembled that of their homelands.[111] The Berbers who made up the bulk of the invasion force could indeed have felt resentment at being allocated more marginal land, even though such land was generally similar in climate and topography to their homeland in North Africa.[112] The mid-eighth century also saw the Abbasid revolution, which resulted from, at least in part, the frustration of non-Arab Muslims who wanted more participation in the political culture of the Islamic world. Berbers in Spain, where the Umayyad dynasty remained in power, possibly wanted an equal footing or some measure of autonomy from their co-religionists commensurate with their contribution to the conquest of Spain. Full-scale Berber revolts in North Africa and Spain in this period are also attributable to these developments.

The Muslim invasion of Spain marked the end of the Visigothic kingdom, and the raids and campaigns in the former Tarraconensis and Gallia provinces could have wreaked havoc on the local populations in certain areas like Urgell, to be sure. Yet the long-term impact of the Muslim conquest on the daily life and institutions of the area for future generations must be said to have been minimal. Evidence is almost non-existent for ecclesiastical or secular administrative activity in the north-east during the eighth century. From what scant clues do survive, however, it seems that, as elsewhere in places Arabs conquered in the seventh and eighth centuries, Islamic rule did not change much in local administration, whether civil or ecclesiastical, other than the imposition of the *jizyah*.[113] Of course, the Tarraconensis and Gallia regions received Muslim governors and garrisons, and the higher authorities tended to appoint the governors for the north-east in groups. Meanwhile, their garrisons did not often mix with locals in centres of population. For example, Cardona and Casserres de Berguedà were fortified places, distant from the major towns, that the Franks occupied and refortified in

---

[110] P. Guichard, *Al-Andalus: estructura antropológica de una sociedad islámica en Occidente* (Barcelona, 1976) on these settlement issues.

[111] Collins, *The Arab Conquest of Spain*, 49–50.

[112] Chalmeta, *Invasión e islamización*, 281, following *Chron. 754*, 41, and 298–305 for the revolt of 739.

[113] Pladevall, 'L'organització de l'Església a Catalunya carolíngia', 54–7; Balañà, *L'Islam a Catalunya*, 16–17. The greater part of Chalmeta, *Invasión e islamización*, i.e., 242–305, is an account of administration, progressing by named governors of al-Andalus.

798. The siting of many garrisons away from urban centres perhaps accounts for the glaring lack of Arabic documentation for Gallia and Tarraconensis.[114] Alternatively, there could be little documentation because the relatively small number of centres that would have produced it fell victim to the brunt of the destructive force of the conquest, while other areas were hardly affected at all. What we must remember is that narrative sources that relay accounts of campaigns and raids tell only part of the story. Violence might dominate the narrative, but that may be because peaceful takeovers rarely offer sufficient drama.

One way the initial social dislocation can be traced is in the fates of monasteries. Older studies concluded that monasteries in the eastern and central Pyrenees suffered a profound decline in the wake of the Muslim conquest in comparison to their heyday in the seventh century. While monasteries continued to exist in some places throughout the eighth century and are documented in charters from the reigns of Pippin and Charlemagne, others seem to have been deserted.[115] It is likely that even abbeys that survived lost at least parts of their landed endowments. Earlier studies sought evidence of abandoned monasteries in surviving place names, but that is no certain proof, since place names could simply reflect that a plot of land had been monastic property, not necessarily the site of the monastic house itself.[116] Antoni Pladevall argues that monasteries experienced more intensely than dioceses and parishes the impact of the religious collapse that came with the Muslim conquest. This is a reasonable conclusion given the pattern of some garrisons being established outside cities, if the monasteries' lands were confiscated while diocesan and parochial organization was mostly untouched, but evidence is scarce. The Urgell area seems to have been the most fertile ground early on for both continuing and new monastic development, probably because it was the least affected by the Muslim conquest and the farthest geographically from the devastation of continuous raids and campaigns. Even the gruesome end that befell Bishop Nambad is not attributable to unrest in the Urgell area, as his horrific story took place in Cerdanya to the east, closer to the main routes of campaigns crossing the Pyrenees.[117] It is easy to imagine a couple of generations of demographic fluctuation because of refugees leaving their homes in a few areas that were on the

---

[114] Balañà, *L'Islam a Catalunya*, 17–18, which points out the reliance on archaeology and toponymy studies in the absence of textual evidence. See also Mateu y Llopis, 'De la Hispania Tarraconense visigoda a la Marca Hispánica carolina', *Analecta Sacra Tarraconensia* 19 (1947): 1–122; and Joaquín Vallvé, *La division territorial de la España musulmana* (Madrid, 1986).

[115] See for example *HGL* 2, cols. 45–7, 50–2, 52–4.

[116] Abadal, *Dels visigots als catalans*, 371–3; L. Nicolau d'Olwer, 'Le cadre historique et social', in *La Catalogne à l'epoque romane* (Paris, 1932), 18–19.

[117] Pladevall, 'L'organització de l'Església a Catalunya carolíngia', 57–8.

routes that raiding armies followed, despite the overall peaceful nature of accords that the conquerors and conquered reached. There would have been enough fighting during the 710s and 720s to throw life into confusion for some time; documentation would have been scarce during that period, and indeed for some time after stability had returned.

Because documentary evidence is so sparse and narrative sources focus on the great deeds of leaders, precious little information survives for demographics and the possible conversion of local people to Islam. Overall, it is clear that Christianity survived and remained quite strong amongst the general population despite the sporadic violence of the era. Elsewhere in al-Andalus, Christians were able to rebuild churches, and monastic communities were able to survive into the ninth century, when groups of particularly zealous monks sought martyrdom.[118] Even in the wide areas that remained under Muslim control well into the Middle Ages, the Christian religion and its culture were under no great threat in the eighth century. Modern studies have detected 'remarkable continuity' in the types of texts produced.[119] And indeed, in the absence of an official drive to convert Christians to Islam, there remained large numbers of Christians in Spain to the end of even the tenth century. Those who did convert had personal, social and economic, or even political reasons for doing so.[120]

The landmark study of Richard Bulliet has framed discussion about the issue of conversion to Islam in Spain for decades.[121] Bulliet's quantitative methods yield plausible estimates for the proportion of the population that converted to Islam over time. According to these figures, about 40 per cent of the Christian population of Spain had converted to Islam by the end of the eighth century, increasing only to half by the middle of the tenth century.[122] Yet other estimates are possible. Mayte Penelas urges caution when consulting Bulliet's figures, as he imported his methodology from his study of Iran, discounting the different social, religious, and cultural contexts of Spain and also the differences in source survival.[123] Meanwhile, Mikel de Epalza argues that most Christians in

---

[118] A. Linage Conde, 'El monacato mózarabe hacia la benedictinización', in *Cristianità d'occidente e cristianità d'oriente (secolo VI–XI)* Settimane di Studio della Fondazione Centro Italiano de Studi sull'Alto Medioevo LI (Spoleto, 2004), 337–461, at 382–3 and 415–20.

[119] Christys, 'Christian-Muslim Frontiers', 16–17.

[120] Chalmeta, 'El sugar de una formación: Al-Andalus', 48. Linage Conde, 'El monacato mózarabe', 337–44 states that the conversion to Islam in Spain was quick, but the only time frame given is 'by the eleventh century', so it is difficult to see what that means.

[121] R. Bulliet, *Conversion to Islam in the Medieval Period* (Cambridge, MA, 1979).

[122] Bulliet, *Conversion to Islam*, 116, cited by Balañà, *L'Islam a Catalunya*, 20–1 and Christys, 'Christian-Muslim Frontiers', 14–15.

[123] M. Penelas, 'Some Remarks on Conversion to Islam in al-Andalus', *Al-Qantara* 23 (2002): 193–200.

the conquered areas of Spain had converted by the end of the eighth century.[124] Choosing a more conservative approach, Thomas Glick postulates that only 16 per cent of Christians converted in the century that followed the 'installation' of Islam in Spain.[125] Given this range of numbers for the whole of Muslim Spain, it may seem that assessing the degree of 'Islamicization' in the poorly documented Catalonia is impossible to do with certainty, yet tentative conclusions are possible.

As the discussion above indicates, documentary and material evidence from the north-eastern provinces of Tarraconensis and Gallia strongly suggests a light Muslim footprint.[126] Kenneth Wolf argues that Christians in Spain first wrote about Islam in the late eighth to early ninth centuries, rather than in prior periods, because Islam was not a threat before then. Cultural segregation, favourable terms of surrender and rule, and Christians' protected status as *dhimmi* all made Islamic rule palatable. It was only when cultural barriers broke down about a century later and more Christians converted to Islam that some Christian leaders started to speak out and write about Islam, and by then they knew enough about the religion to repudiate it.[127] With that in mind, it matters less what proportion of the population had converted by the end of the eighth century and more what the political context was at a given time. In the north-east, there probably was less cultural integration between conquerors and subjects, and the military occupation most assuredly was much shorter there than elsewhere in the former Visigothic kingdom, lasting only decades rather than centuries. Thus the political context does not point to any sort of thorough conversion to Islam in the future Catalonia. Keeping with Bulliet's reckoning as the middle way between conservative and generous estimates, it would have taken until 814–20 for even 40 per cent of Christians in Catalonia and Septimania to convert to Islam.[128] The region, of course, had already been conquered by the Franks by that time. It is indeed difficult to see how the Muslim conquest made any significant social, cultural, or religious impact on daily life in the forty years until Pippin conquered Narbonne, or the seventy to eighty or

---

[124] M. de Epalza, 'Mozarabs: an Emblematic Christian Minority in Islamic al-Andalus', in S. Khadra Jayyusi, ed., *The Legacy of Muslim Spain* (Leiden, 1992), 149–70. Epalza's estimate would seem to confirm Linage Conde's remark ('El monacato mozárabe', 337–44) that the conversion to Islam in Spain was quick.

[125] T. F. Glick, *From Muslim Fortress to Christian Castle: Social and Cultural Change in Medieval Spain* (Manchester, 1995), 52.

[126] For artistic products, see J. D. Dodds, 'Islam, Christianity, and the Problem of Religious Art', in *The Art of Medieval Spain, AD 500–1200* (New York, 1993), 27–37.

[127] K. Baxter Wolf, 'The Earliest Spanish Christian Views of Islam', *Church History* 55 (1986): 281–93.

[128] See Balañà, *L'Islam a Catalunya*, 18–24, which also stresses that any estimate is only counting from an original Christian population, paganism still existed in the interior and mountain regions.

so years until Charlemagne and Louis the Pious gained control of areas south of the Pyrenees. Except perhaps for a few aristocrats who converted to Islam for social and political reasons, people in Septimania and the future Spanish March would largely still have been Christian.[129]

In terms of the identities attributed to people in these areas by those who compiled documents, the Muslim conquest of the early eighth century perhaps left a perceptible imprint on how they used terms grounded in geography. As this study will bear out, the destruction of the Gothic kingdom of Toledo cemented a bifurcation of terminology applied to those living in or originating in its former territories in the Iberian peninsula. As if taking a cue from Julian of Toledo, the Franks called those from south of the Pyrenees *hispani*, but unlike Julian, they used *Gothi* for those in Gallia, as in the case of the Goths of Narbonne with whom Pippin negotiated for control of the city.[130] The Frankish use of these terms, as documented by court-sponsored annalists and the royal chancery, may have changed slightly over time, as Frankish authority extended over the mountains, and any relation to the cultural inheritance of the Gothic kingdom is almost impossible to trace through them. The perspective of our sources changed from a Gothic to a Frankish point of view during the eighth century because of Frankish involvement in Catalonia and Septimania during the latter half of the century.[131] Not only did this change in circumstance mean a difference in the nature of surviving sources, but it also charted a new course for the history of the regions, tying them to the Franks under the Carolingian dynasty for the next two centuries.

FRANKISH INVOLVEMENT IN SEPTIMANIA

The southern material found in the *Chronicon Moissiacense Maius* describes Muslim forays north of the Pyrenees in the 720s. As we saw above, Narbonne and other cities in Septimania and Aquitaine were captured or ravaged. When Carcassonne and Nîmes fell, hostages were sent to the

---

[129] See also Glick, *From Muslim Fortress to Christian Castle*, 60 as well as Balañà, *L'Islam a Catalunya*, 18–20.

[130] *CMM*, 118 states '*quo facto: ipsi Goti Sarracenos . . . occidunt*'. We will encounter a document from around 801, the year that Louis the Pious took Barcelona, which mentions Goths (CC 2, 415–16). I suggest that those Goths were men who travelled from Septimania, perhaps as part of the army, and intended to settle in the Barcelona region, or even resettle if they or their families had previously fled north.

[131] For the peninsular perspective, which seems likewise to have maintained the notion of Hispania as a geographical concept, see A. Christys, 'The Transformation of Hispania after 711', in H.-W. Goetz and J. Jarnut, eds, *Regna and Gentes: the Relationship between Late Antique and Early Medieval Peoples and Kingdoms in the Transformation of the Roman World* (Leiden, 2003), 219–41.

Muslim base at Barcelona.[132] Eudo, 'prince of Aquitaine', fought off the Muslims for a time.[133] The raiding parties even reached Autun in the middle of the decade, sacking the city and returning with booty to Spain.[134] Despite these raids, the Frankish ruling elite were not very worried about Muslims until early 730s, when the Emir Abd al-Rahman invaded Aquitaine via the western Pyrenees and defeated Eudo. This defeat drove Eudo to seek help from Charles Martel as Muslim forces advanced northward towards Poitiers.[135] It is important to remember that throughout this period, Muslim military activity in Aquitaine and nearby regions was limited to raiding. No source records entire populations put to the sword, and certainly no territory fell under the rule of the emir or his subordinates. Yet the movements of armies and their leaders could and did have important ramifications.

After emerging victorious from the battle with a Muslim raiding party near Poitiers in 733, Charles Martel showed little sustained interest in taking the initiative in Aquitaine, although he was evidently quite concerned about developments there. The following year, Charles was campaigning in Frisia, but hastened to face Muslim forces in Septimania and Provence. The Franks dispatched Muslim forces at Avignon, crossed the Rhône, besieged their Muslim enemies at Narbonne, defeated reinforcements from Spain, and set fire to the amphitheatre and city gates of Nîmes.[136] Thus Charles defeated the Saracens, but returned to Francia without occupying territory.[137] In the end, the best evidence indicates that Muslim operations extended to Burgundy, that they despoiled and depopulated parts of Septimania,[138] and that the mayor of the palace was alarmed enough to take sweeping measures against them, calling on troops from Burgundy and other Frankish-related areas. The Continuations of the *Chronicle of Fredegar*, which the *CMM* seems to depend on for part of its information, relates that Charles Martel attacked the cities of Nîmes, Agde, and Béziers before returning to Francia. Further, the continuator describes a second campaign to the

---

[132] *CMM*, 112; Collins, *Early Medieval Spain*, 163.
[133] *CMM*, 112. See also M. Rouche, *L'Aquitaine des Wisigoths aux Arabes, 418–781: naissance d'une région* (Paris, 1979), 111–20.
[134] *CMM*, 114.
[135] *CMM*, 114. See the older view of L. Halphen, *Charlemagne and the Carolingian Empire*, trans. G. de Nie (New York, 1977), 14, who paints Martel as the saviour of Christendom. See now P. Fouracre, *The Age of Charles Martel* (London, 2000), 84–8.
[136] *CMM*, 115; J. M. Wallace-Hadrill, *The Frankish Church* (Oxford, 1983), 93–5. See also Abadal's fuller discussion in Abadal, CC 1, 19–22.
[137] *CMM*, 115.
[138] It is worth emphasizing that modern investigations reveal almost no truly depopulated areas, but some settled areas suffered from diminished population and disorganization.

south, again to help defend Provence from the Arabs.[139] The *CMM* is silent on most of this. Abadal argued that it is likely that locals loyal to their leader Maurontus, the duke or *patricius* of Provence, resisted Charles Martel's advance in the area of Avignon, and that Charles punished the cities of Septimania for their apparent loyalty to the Muslims.[140] The *Annals of Aniane*, problematic though they are, add an account of Charles Martel's siege of Narbonne in 738, noting that he failed to take the city. This report may be misinformed or simply have its chronology off by a few years.[141] The discussion above, however, shows the evidence as disinclined to reveal the Muslim conquest as making a significant impression on the society of Septimania, so Abadal's characterization of the Frankish campaign as punitive needs to be reconsidered. It is more reasonable on the basis of the evidence to conclude that the Christians of Septimania were conquered people who wanted peace. They were in no position to halt or hinder the Muslim ventures deeper into Gaul. Any devastation Frankish armies visited on the cities of Septimania had to have the objective of weakening the Muslim powers that controlled them, not punishing the Christians who inhabited them. One can understand frustration on the part of Charles or the annalists favourable to his family, for the damage the Muslim raids inflicted was known far and wide. For example, in a letter to the king of Mercia, the missionary Boniface warns that his royal duty was to reform his people, lest they face the wrath of God as the people of Spain, Provence, and Burgundy had done.[142] By his death in 741, Charles Martel exercised no real control over Aquitaine, although he had established a foothold in Septimania and Provence.[143] In the 750s, after a lull the previous decade, Frankish activity intensified in the south. By the end of the decade, Pippin, son of Charles Martel, father of Charlemagne, and first Carolingian king of the Franks, firmly controlled Septimania.

Frankish dominion over the old Gothic region relied on the personal relationships Pippin forged with leading nobles there. It was important for Pippin, as a Christian ruler and conqueror, to court the goodwill of the ecclesiastical hierarchy of the region, bestowing grants upon the church of Narbonne, as can be seen in an 844 precept of

---

[139] *The Fourth Book of the Chronicle of Fredegar with Its Continuations*, ed. Wallace-Hadrill, 96.

[140] Abadal, CC 1, 23–6 paints the picture of Charles Martel punishing the Goths for loyalty to Muslims.

[141] *Annals d'Aniane*, as in note 1, col. 6 suggest that Charles had besieged the city and abandoned the operation because of the arrival of a Muslim force. See also Lewis, *The Development of Society*, 23; Fouracre, *The Age of Charles Martel*, 88–9.

[142] *MGH* Epp. 3, 340–5, at 343.

[143] Lewis, *The Development of Society*, 21–4; Bachrach, *Early Carolingian Warfare: Prelude to Empire* (Philadelphia, 2001), 33–4. See also Fouracre, *The Age of Charles Martel*, 88–9.

Charles the Bald, which mentions Pippin's no-longer-extant grant.[144] Walled cities were very difficult to take, as Charles Martel had found during his siege of Narbonne. Yet Pippin was apparently more able or more determined to take the city than his father had been, relying on relationships with locals rather than siege engines. The most important connection was the one Pippin made with Ansemundus, a man usually identified as a Goth.[145] He appears with no title in the sources but seems to have been pre-eminent amongst the regional political class of Septimania, and allied with Pippin. Negotiations between Ansemundus and Pippin turned over to the Frankish king the cities of Nîmes, Agde, Bèziers, and Maguelonne in 752. From that day, the *CMM* composer says, the Franks were set on Narbonne. Ansemundus was assassinated in Narbonne in 754 by a group led by his own supporter Ermeniard. Pippin, in a move demonstrating his authority, then appointed the Frankish nobleman Radulf as count of Nîmes to fill the void.[146] This chain of events marks the beginning of the end of autonomous rule for Septimania, for the Frankish king now appointed the rulers of cities. Another chronicle, linked to the *CMM* as having been written from a common source, the *Chronique d'Uzès*, notes the significance of the event, relating that the city had now been given over to Frankish rule, ending the rule of the Goths.[147] But the murder of Ansemundus also shows that the leading figures of Septimania were not all of one mind.[148] Ermeniard may have opposed Frankish influence in the area in favour of local autonomy, or he may have been merely ambitious, seeking to supplant Ansemundus. In any event, Pippin was able to establish himself in Septimania with relatively little fighting, in contrast to his prolonged struggles in Aquitaine and Gascony.

The chroniclers state that after Ansemundus and his associates had delivered their cities to Pippin, the Franks turned their attention to Narbonne, the crown jewel of Septimania. Further, the annals mention that Waifar, *princeps Aquitaniae*, invaded the Narbonne area, making the overall situation in the region more troublesome for

---

[144] Tessier, no. 49, mentions the equal split of toll revenues between the church and the count of the city. See Abadal, CC 1, 32–3.

[145] *CMM*, 118 names him 'Ansemundus gotus'.

[146] Later Ansemundus's widow was killed in Nîmes. J. M. Salrach, *El procés de formació nacional de Catalunya (segles VIII–IX)*, 2 vols. (Barcelona, 1978), vol. 1, 5–6; Lewis, *The Development of Society*, 24–6. See also Rouche, *L'Aquitaine*, 121.

[147] Ancienne chronique d'Uzès, in C. Devic and J. Vaisette, eds, *Histoire Générale de Languedoc*, 2 (Toulouse, 1875), cols. 23–9; col. 25.

[148] Abadal, CC 1, 30–1.

Pippin.[149] Abadal pursued this issue, noting the difficulty that would have faced Pippin had he tried to besiege Narbonne and simultaneously chase Waifar. Pippin, he argued, won over Goths of the other cities for an attack on Narbonne, while simultaneously Waifar had his eyes on the same prize. According to this line of reasoning, Pippin was preparing for a multi-front fight for the city, pitting his own troops, with allied Goths, against both the Muslim garrison and Waifar's forces.[150] On this point Abadal's reasoning is sound. Ultimately, Pippin succeeded in both driving away Waifar and coaxing submission out of the defenders of Narbonne. According to the different accounts based on the lost 'southern' source, different details are available. Synthesizing all three surviving texts, it seems that the king allowed them to keep their traditional Gothic law, their leader, Count Milo, and the lucrative tolls to the church of Narbonne.[151] Roussillon, further south and resting at the feet of the Pyrenees, was next to come under Pippin's control, even though this probably resulted from the work of his allies as much as that of his own men. Solidifying control of Septimania provided Pippin with a stable front so that he could confidently launch a campaign into Aquitaine. That campaign was long and arduous, but by 768 he had established control over most of Gaul, creating a division between Frankish territory and Hispania at the Pyrenees.[152] He also had managed to work local Gothic nobles into the prevailing Frankish political networks. His strategy of building personal networks and preserving local legal traditions allowed for the incorporation of Septimania into the Frankish kingdom.

Labels that modern readers may take as markers of identity difference, such as Frank or Goth, were no impediments to the extension of Frankish control or even to direct relationships between Gothic nobles and the Frankish king. The sources do make a point that Ansemundus was a Goth, suggesting that the annalist was cognizant of some kind of difference. The writer may have pointed out the distinction to show Pippin in alliance with a local; that he came to authority in the area not by force but by the willingness of the local people. In the final reckoning, the fact that Ansemundus was a Goth clearly was no obstacle to his

---

[149] *CMM*, 118.   [150] Abadal, CC 1, 29–30.

[151] *Chron. Moissac*, 294; *Annales d'Aniane*, cols. 6–7; *Chron. d'Uzès*, col. 26. Lewis, *The Development of Society, 718–1050*, 26; Abadal, CC 1, 31–2.

[152] For a more detailed summary of the events and dates of the 'Frankish Reconquista' see O. Engels, *Schutzgedanke und Landherrschaft im östlichen Pyrenäenraum (9.–13. Jahrhundert)* (Münster in Westfalen, 1970), 7–8. The re-establishment of the ancient boundary between Gaul and Spain by removing control over Septimania from a regime centred south of the Pyrenees features in Bachrach, *Early Carolingian Warfare*, especially at 44–6, 48–9.

cooperation with Pippin, and Franks like Radulf could be sent into Gothic areas and be expected to function in them in terms of governance; outsiders could begin social manoeuvring and networking within channels of power. Michel Zimmermann suggests that the conquest of Septimania was to serve as a model for Catalonia in terms of economy and religion.[153] This, however, was not the only case the Carolingians rulers had from which to learn the lesson. The extension of Carolingian power often featured locals functioning as entry points for kings to exert power in the locality, for the dynasty's experience in other areas, such as Alemannia and Bavaria, was quite similar.[154]

THE MARCH ACROSS THE PYRENEES

Nine years of relative peace elapsed in Aquitaine and Septimania after Pippin's completion of the conquest in 768.[155] A decade later, Pippin's son Charlemagne invaded Spain in an unsuccessful attempt to take control of a handful of cities south of the Pyrenees. His failure and the ambush of his rearguard in the Pyrenean pass of Roncesvalles as the army returned to Francia provided the inspiration for the later medieval *Song of Roland*. While Pippin seemed content with his kingdom's borders in the Pyrenean region, a new opportunity presented itself to his successor with the arrival in Charlemagne's court of envoys from al-Andalus in 777. The motivation for the Muslim embassy has been explained by the distance of local governors from their superiors and their proximity to the Franks, the temptations of geography guiding their ambition to a tipping point concerning revolting against central authority. This would fit into a pattern established by the Berber leader Munussa in his revolt based in Cerdanya 731.[156] As was noted above, the whole affair did not end well for Munussa, but that is not to say that others would not think to take advantage of the geographical situation after him. As for Charlemagne, the opportunity for expansion of his authority to Christian communities he could liberate, the promise of plunder, and the fulfilment of his role as war-leading king of the Franks provided ample motivation for a new campaign.

---

[153] M. Zimmermann, 'Origines et formation d'un etat Catalan (801–1137)', in J. N. Farreras and P. Wolff, eds, *Histoire de la Catalogne* (Barcelona, 1982), 237.

[154] For Alemannia, see H. Hummer, *Politics and Power in Early Medieval Europe: Alsace and the Frankish Realm, 600–1000* (Cambridge, 2005) and for Bavaria, W. Brown, *Unjust Seizure: Conflict, Interest, and Authority in Early Medieval Society* (Ithaca, 2001). See now also J. R. Davis, *Charlemagne's Practice of Empire* (Cambridge, 2015), 239–92 on Charlemagne and his men learning from experimentation in Bavaria and Italy.

[155] Lewis, *The Development of Society*, 28–9.   [156] For this argument, Salrach, *El procés*, vol. 1, 7.

When Frankish power began to reach into the affairs of Hispania following the conquest of Aquitaine and Septimania, rebels in the northern reaches of Muslim-controlled territory could call on the Franks for help against the central power, which by the 770s was the emirate based in Córdoba.[157] In any case, the beginnings of heavy Carolingian involvement in the area that became the Spanish March can be traced to that meeting of Muslim messengers and the Frankish king at Paderborn. Charlemagne held an assembly there in 777, the major importance of which was that the baptism of many Saxons took place there; but in addition to Saxon converts, Charlemagne received the envoys from Muslim rebel leaders proposing Frankish military intervention into the affairs of the Ebro valley.[158] The *wali* of Zaragoza submitted to Charlemagne himself and the cities over which the 'king of the Saracens' had placed him.[159] Abbasid moves to exert caliphal authority in Spain, in addition to Yemeni and Berber uprisings, made for an uncertain political environment, and perhaps an opportunity for ambitious local governors.[160] Suleiman ibn al-Arabi, governor of Barcelona and Girona, was fighting against the emir's forces and made the appeal to the Frankish king, who had proven himself against the Saxons and Lombards.[161] Suleiman and his son Yusuf offered Charlemagne a sort of protectorate over cities and a promise of collaboration.

Charlemagne was concerned with affairs on multiple fronts in 777, when the envoys came to Paderborn.[162] There is no sign that Charlemagne was interested in Spain before that moment. His father and grandfather had restored the Frankish kingdom to the historical boundaries of Gaul, and the risk was great and unknown.[163] But, since Italy was settled and the Saxon affairs seemed to be developing in his favour, Charlemagne was open to the idea. He accepted the rebels'

---

[157] Collins, *Early Medieval Spain*, 251.

[158] *ARF, MGH SS rer. Germ.*, 48–9, 51. The Reviser states that the emissaries surrendered their cities to Charlemagne. For further treatment and re-evaluation of this source, see R. Collins, 'The "Reviser" Revisited: Another Look at the Alternative Version of the *Annales Regni Francorum*', in A. C. Murray, ed., *After Rome's Fall: Narrators and Sources of Early Medieval History: Essays Presented to Walter Goffart* (Toronto, 2000), 191–213. See now R. McKitterick, *Charlemagne* (Cambridge, 2008), 27–31 and Reimitz, *History, Frankish Identity and the Framing of Western Ethnicity*, chs. 11, 12, and 13 on the *ARF* as contributing to the construction of Frankish identity.

[159] *ARF MGH SS rer. Germ.*, 48–51.

[160] J. J. Saunders, *A History of Medieval Islam* (London, 1965; reprinted 1996), 95–8, 115.

[161] Abadal, CC 1, 41–2.

[162] As the annals make clear, the king was preoccupied first and foremost with the Saxons, as they hold the first place in the year's entry; the fact that he was at Paderborn for the assembly is also telling. See the entries for the years 776 and 777 in *ARF MGH SS rer. Germ.*, 42–51. See Abadal, CC 1, 39–41, which points out that Arabic chroniclers downplay the significance of the meeting.

[163] Abadal, CC 1, 43.

invitation to invade Spain and in 778 crossed the Pyrenees. The king himself, with a force made up of Burgundians, Austrasians, and Bavarians, made his way to Zaragoza via Pamplona, while a second army consisting of men from Septimania, Provence, and Lombardy was to meet him after first coming through the eastern passes, probably by the Roman Via Augusta to Barcelona.[164] Historians note that troops were called in from all over the kingdom and its various parts. Eastern territories of the Frankish realm provided troops to participate in the eastern entrance of Pyrenees, while soldiers from the western territories entered Spain at the western end of the mountains.[165] This enabled Charlemagne to arrange his forces for a pincer movement like the one he had used during the Lombard campaign.[166] No contemporary or near contemporary gives an account of what the army did in the mountains. The Astronomer early in his *Vita Hludovici* alludes to Pompey's and to Hannibal's crossings of the Pyrenees, but relays no specific information about the difficulties the Franks faced and how they managed the passages.[167] Charlemagne's detachment crossed through Navarre, while the other passed through Septimania towards Barcelona, probably to meet up with Suleiman's rebelling army, to make its way then to Lleida, Huesca, and finally Zaragoza.[168] But no source gives an explanation as to why Charlemagne's prospective allies failed to join forces with him. One reason could have been that they came simply gave up in the face of looming, overwhelming opposition or else placation from the Emir Abd al-Rahman. Alternatively, they enticed the Frankish king with lofty promises, planning to deliver on those promises as little as possible and therefore maximize gain for themselves. Most Latin annals agree on the events of the campaign, which by all accounts, ended badly with the Basque ambush at Roncevalles. Despite his ultimate failure, Charlemagne appears to have realized something of a victory in conquering Pamplona without a fight, taking hostages from the governor of the city.[169] At Zaragoza, however, he was less successful. Again, two later sources based on the lost 'southern' source give alternate details. The *Annales*

[164] *ARF*, 50–3; Engels, *Schutzgedanke und Landherrschaft*, 8. See also R.-H. Bautier, 'La campagne de Charlemagne en Espagne (778): la réalité historique', in *Roncevaux dans l'histoire, la légende et le myth: Actes du colloque organisé à l'occasion du 12e centenaire de Roncevaux, Saint-Jean-Pied-de-Port, 1978*, vol. nouv. série, 135 (Bayonne, 1979), 1–47.

[165] See, on raising troops, G. Halsall, *Warfare and Society in the Barbarian West, 450–900* (London, 2003), 71–110.

[166] *ARF*, 35–6.

[167] Astronomer, *Vita Hludowici imperatoris*, in MGH SS 2 (Hanover, 1829), 604–8.

[168] Abadal, CC 1, 48–50, offers a reconstruction of the routes taken by the divisions of the Frankish armies. This view, from the early twentieth century, has largely remained the accepted account of events.

[169] *CMM*, 121; *ARF*, 51.

d'Aniane report that the Franks killed thousands of Muslims in battle, before having to withdraw in order to deal with a Saxon force that had crossed the Rhine.[170] Meanwhile, the *Chronicle of Moissac* states merely that the Saxons rebelled while Charles was away in Spain, apparently causing the king to return home.[171] The royal annals here differ from the southern sources; according to the court source, Charles only learned of the Saxon activity when he arrived at Autun on the way back from Spain, so he sent a force against them.[172] If he heard about Saxon revolt on the way back from Spain, this concern could not have been the reason for his withdrawal, as is at least implied in the southern sources because of the order in which they relate the stories. We should instead attribute the Frankish withdrawal to the difficulties the campaign encountered.[173] Charlemagne never returned to the southern theatre again, depending on subordinates and his son, Louis, to control and expand Carolingian holdings in the area.

The primary explanation for Charlemagne's refusal to intervene personally in campaigns into Hispania has long been the emotional and psychological impact of the catastrophe at Roncesvalles. After leaving Zaragoza frustrated, the king turned his attention towards Pamplona, a city he had probably passed before on his campaign route. There, as noted, he took hostages, but he seems not to have made much progress beyond the city before a small Arab strike freed the prisoners.[174] This setback effectively erased Charlemagne's one small victory from the campaign, but the situation deteriorated from there. The few sources to mention the loss in the Pyrenees are the Revised *Annales Regni Francorum*, Einhard's *Vita Karoli*, and the Astronomer's life of Louis.[175] As to where the Basque attack happened, nineteenth- and twentieth-century scholars took some time to settle the question, ultimately coming down in favour of Roncesvalles. Abadal supported the idea that the location was along the route of the old Roman road from Bordeaux to Astorga, the most logical route Charlemagne would have taken. Abadal adds that the fighting would have been on the crests, not in the valleys, because that is the topography the Roman roads followed.[176] This information adds weight to the account in the *Annales Regni Francorum* that the Basques had the upper hand because of terrain. Besides providing

---

[170] *Annales d'Aniane*, cols. 8–9.   [171] *Chron. Moissac*, 296.   [172] *ARF*, 52–3.
[173] I agree with Abadal, CC 1, 51–2 that the story in the *Annales d'Aniane* version is merely an excuse made up after the fact.
[174] Vallicrosa, *Textos dels historiadors àrabs*, no. 72; Abadal, CC 1, 52–3.
[175] *ARF*, 51; Einhard, *Vita Karoli, MGH SS rer. Germ.* 25, 12–13; Astronomer, c. 2.
[176] Abadal, CC 1, 65, and literature cited therein.

the initial kernel of legend for the story in the *Song of Roland*, the disaster at Roncesvalles contributed to Charlemagne's decision never to campaign personally in Spain again because of the substantial risk involved.[177] Instead, he left military affairs to his very young son, Louis, and the counts of Toulouse during Louis's long minority. Chorso filled this office for several years, succeeded by Charlemagne's trusted cousin William.

Because identity and ethnicity have long been key themes in Catalan scholarship of the early medieval period, because they have emerged to take a prominent place more generally in studies in the late twentieth and early twenty-first centuries, and indeed because those concepts have been motivating factors for this study, a brief discussion of the identity of the attackers at Roncesvalles is germane to the investigation of the Carolingian conquest of Catalonia. The attackers were Basques, or in Basque territory, which excludes Navarre, then under nominal Frankish rule. Abadal, in his discussion of the battle, took some pains to draw a distinction between 'Basques' from Hispania and French 'Gascons'.[178] This is a problematic distinction to make for the eighth century, and seems to arise from Abadal's twentieth-century Catalan nationalist outlook rather than any sense of early medieval identity. In fact, there is no distinction to be made even between modern 'Basques' and 'Gascons', as the only difference between them is the modern nation-state boundary between Spain and France; there are two 'Basque countries' for one modern ethnic group that straddles the Pyrenees.[179] Further, Abadal's somewhat extended discussion of the matter seems to go against the grain of his parallel thinking, published elsewhere, that the designation 'Marca hispanica' to indicate the region that Charlemagne's and later Louis's forces conquered was a geographical term, not one with an official political or constitutional meaning.[180] Likewise, it is best to understand that, when sources denote Gascony as the region between the Garonne and the Pyrenees, it is merely a geographical designation,

---

[177] While the Spanish campaign is not directly addressed in the work, B. S. Bachrach, *Charlemagne's Early Campaigns (768–777)* (Leiden, 2013) suggests that Charlemagne rarely undertook any military operation without a very high level of confidence in its success.

[178] Abadal, CC 1, 54–5.

[179] For a general account of Basque history, see R. Collins, *The Basques* (Oxford and New York, 1986). Interested readers can also turn to his other works, including R. Collins, 'The Basques in Aquitaine and Navarre: Problems of Frontier Government', in J. Gillingham and J. C. Holt, eds, *War and Government in the Middle Ages: Essays in Honor of J. O. Prestwich* (Cambridge, 1984), 3–17; R. Collins, 'Spain: the Northern Kingdoms and the Basques, 711–910', in R. McKitterick, ed., *The New Cambridge Medieval History*, vol. 2, c.700–c.900 (Cambridge, 1995), 272–89.

[180] Abadal, *Dels visigots als catalans*, 173–9.

not an ethnic one, distinct from the territory of the 'Basques' farther south.

The aftermath of Charlemagne's failed expedition to Zaragoza in 778 seems to have been disastrous for monasteries in the eastern Pyrenees, many of which were abandoned. Military activity in the area caused teams of hispani monks to migrate to Septimania, north of the Pyrenees.[181] After the Muslim invasion in the early eighth century, there was no corresponding major emigration of hispani into Christian territory. Yet after 778, as far as can be known, many people left the Ebro valley for Frankish-controlled territories: monks to practise their spiritual observance, lay people to avoid second-class 'protected' status as *dhimmi*, everyone to take advantage of free and available land in Septimania.[182] Charlemagne had well-documented economic and military reasons for accepting immigrants, who could bring the agricultural land in areas of Septimania back into viability while also providing soldiers to defend the region against potential future raids and campaigns from the south.[183]

In the light of his failure to conquer Zaragoza and other cities in Spain, Charlemagne's strategic rationale for invading has proved puzzling. Few seem to question his reasons for waging his other, successful wars, but the failure in Spain seems, for some reason, more fascinating. The *Annales Regni Francorum* give no insight, and Einhard simply gives an account of all of the wars as being worthy of memory. Yet it is possible that Charlemagne had designs for a protectorate consisting of territory south of the Pyrenees to serve as a buffer against Muslim attacks if necessary.[184] Abadal dismissively points to the reality, as the next decade or so would prove, that there were no prospects of an imminent Muslim invasion of southern Gaul.[185] But it is far from certain that Charlemagne would have seen such an attack as unlikely, given the chain of events in the eighth century. He could have operated very well under the idea that safe was better than sorry, or his Muslim guests or court advisors could have eventually convinced him that a buffer was necessary, if only in order to further their own ends.[186] In the end, it is plausible to conclude that

---

[181] Abadal, *Dels visigots als catalans*, 375–6.

[182] These themes will be addressed in the next chapter.

[183] Chandler, 'Between Court and Counts.' Abadal, CC 1, 75–6.

[184] See a manner of justification in *Codex Carolinus MGH Epp. Merovingici et Karoli aevi 1* (Berlin, 1892), no. 61.

[185] Abadal, CC 1, 65–7.

[186] This is essentially the argument in T. F. X. Noble, 'Louis the Pious and the Frontiers of the Frankish Realm', in P. Godman and R. Collins, eds, *Charlemagne's Heir: New Perspectives on the Reign of Louis the Pious (814–840)* (Oxford, 1990), 333–47. The Franks in several places campaigned beyond their borders to create something like demilitarized zones.

Charlemagne wanted a military buffer, whether hindsight proved he needed it immediately or not, and perhaps a zone for Christian missionizing, such as those that existed at that time near other frontiers of the kingdom. Charlemagne was not aiming to effect the wholesale destruction of the Muslim population or the liberation of Christian inhabitants throughout all of Spain.

CONCLUSIONS

As is clear from the discussion here, the Gothic areas of Septimania and Catalonia shared a somewhat peculiar history. On the one hand, they had been part of the Visigothic kingdom of Toledo for over a century, but on the other they were sometimes seen as problematic provinces. They were repeatedly the origin points of trouble in the kingdom of Toledo, particularly when they served as staging areas for rebellions against the crown. And yet, with the fall of the Toledan regime, the north-eastern region represented the lone continuation of royal self-rule, at least for a time. During the early eighth century, both Catalonia and Septimania fell to the Arab conquest, but only after negotiations and intermittent yet fierce fighting. Moreover, the geographical links to Aquitaine and the Frankish kingdom precipitated frequent eruptions of localized warfare in Septimania, which presented an opportunity to the Franks after about 730.

The growing power of the Franks under the Carolingians brought some degree of stability in the last half of the century, so that Charlemagne felt secure enough in his southern Gallic territories to venture a campaign south of the Pyrenees. Stability such as this was the result of incorporation into Frankish structures of governance, that is to say, by the forging of personal links between the king and the regional and local power brokers. Pippin had accomplished this by working through the Goth Ansemundus, later establishing the Frank Radulf as count in Nîmes, and by showing favour to the church of Narbonne, the region's chief city. As king of the Franks, Pippin had also ensured the incorporation of the Septimanian Goths into his kingdom by allowing them to keep their own legal customs. All of Pippin's manoeuvres show that separate identities, namely, those of Frank and Goth, were distinguished; annalists, biographers, chroniclers, and perhaps political leaders perceived them and used specific terms to represent them. It is important that the writers who applied identifying labels in surviving Latin texts did so from the Frankish court's point of view, probably in order to portray the kings' actions in a positive light. These were different uses of such labels from those

Julian of Toledo had employed in his highly charged rhetoric generations earlier. Yet in the eighth century, identity difference was no obstacle to political cooperation.

Charlemagne followed up on Pippin's successful annexation by launching his campaign to Spain in 778, which failed. The Franks remained undeterred, however, and over the next couple of decades successfully created the Spanish March in Catalonia, using essentially the same combination of military activity and sociopolitical integration of the area's Christian leaders. It is the task of the next chapter to reconstruct how that happened.

Chapter 2

CREATING THE SPANISH MARCH, 778–840

In January 820 the Emperor Louis the Pious held an assembly in Aachen to deal with various matters of state, including the actions of the Slavic leader Liudewit against the Franks' eastern borders. One of the other topics for deliberation at the assembly concerned the frontier area at the opposite end of the empire. Bera, count of Barcelona and a noble of Gothic heritage, whose family apparently was based in Septimania, a region also known in Carolingian sources as 'Gothia', was accused of treason. In the trial by combat that ensued, Bera was defeated, and thus found guilty. The capital sentence that could have befallen him, however, was commuted to exile by the emperor, and Bera spent his time of banishment in Rouen.[1] According to the Astronomer's biography of Louis, Bera's accuser was Sanila, also a Goth, so they were entitled to settle their case by combat 'according to their own law'.[2] The *Annales Regni Francorum* inform us that the combat took place on horseback, but imply, rather than declare, that mounted duel deviated from Frankish practice.[3] Although we cannot ascertain the degree of similarity or difference between Gothic and Frankish ordeal by combat from this episode, it stood as an important enough marker of distinction to the Astronomer for him to record it in his narrative as something that distinguished one people from another, although it may reveal more about the Astronomer's reading in classical texts than about true differences in lifestyle in the early

---

[1] *ARF 741–829 qui dicuntur Annales Laurissenses maiores et Einhardi,* in G. Kurze, ed., *MGH SS rer. Germ.,* I (Hanover, 1895), 152.

[2] Astronomer, *Vita Hludowici imperatoris,* c. 34 in *MGH SS,* 2 (Hanover, 1829), 625. There is a recent translation in T. F. X. Noble, *Charlemagne and Louis the Pious: Lives by Einhard, Notker, Ermoldus, Thegan, and the Astronomer* (University Park, PA, 2009), 219–302.

[3] *ARF,* 152 and Astronomer, c. 33 *MGH SS* 2, 625, with E. Nigellus, *In honorem Hludowici, MGH Poetae latini aevi Carolini,* 2. ed. E. Dümmler (Berlin, 1884), 1–91. Ermoldus's poem has also been translated by Noble, *Charlemagne and Louis the Pious,* 119–86, with the passage on Bera at 168–9.

ninth century.[4] This account also tells us that, if an accusation of treason levied by one Goth against another were to be valid, then loyalty to the Frankish Carolingian ruler was expected of Goths by Goths. Carolingian rule of 'Gothia' was to be upheld and not resisted or subverted. This chapter examines the processes by which the Spanish March was integrated into the political networks of the Carolingian empire.[5] Charlemagne and Louis the Pious faced many challenges in ruling the Spanish March, including distance, the fact that they had precious few previous relationships with individual figures in local and regional society, and religious differences. The concept of ethnic identity, however, was not amongst the various obstacles in their path. Indeed, the Carolingian sources place more emphasis on ethnic labels than is warranted by the events they describe. This discrepancy can be attributed to the discourse on empire, in that by highlighting the diversity of peoples they ruled, Charlemagne and Louis the Pious (and those who wrote for them) exalted their own authority.

This chapter will progress more or less chronologically, picking up where the previous chapter left off, after Charlemagne's campaign to Zaragoza in 778. By means of military conquest, royal grants to local individuals and monastic communities, and the imposition of court-sponsored religious programmes, the integration of the Spanish March into Carolingian political institutions tapped into and altered social and power networks on the local level. Some aspects of the integration call into question surviving elements of Visigothic culture and identity. After 800, the Carolingian rulers carried the title of emperor, but continued to employ the same means of rule as before: the assignment of aristocrats to govern the Spanish March and the use of personnel and royal interventions to ensure loyalty on the part of locals to the emperors and to provide limitations of comital authority. The case of Bera shows that loyalty was expected on both sides; his removal began a period of rule in the Spanish March by powerful magnates from the Frankish heartlands. Any tensions between the locals and the Franks brought about by conflicts rooted in ethnicity could have spelled trouble for the new March, but none can be proven. As it turned out, Bernard of Septimania, the first of the series of great Frankish magnates holding office in the Spanish March, was the first to make significant trouble for Carolingian kings. Bernard's rise to

---

[4] W. Pohl, 'Telling the Difference: Signs of Ethnic Identity', in W. Pohl with H. Reimitz, eds, *Strategies of Distinction: the Construction of Ethnic Communities, 300–800*, The Transformation of the Roman World 2 (Leiden, 1998), 17–69 at 27–34.

[5] R. McKitterick, *Charlemagne: the Formation of a European Identity* (Cambridge, 2008), 133–4, 136; J. R. Davis, *Charlemagne's Practice of Empire* (Cambridge, 2015), 242–3 and 415.

prominence at court in many ways was the direct result of his activity in the March, and became in turn a source of trouble for Louis the Pious. In Bera's case, he was dealt with before much potential damage could be done, but Bernard's behaviour was part of a series of tumultuous events that culminated in the emperor's temporary downfall. These and other developments of the ninth century show that before the end of Louis's reign, the Spanish March had become firmly incorporated into political and religious practices that had direct links to the Carolingian dynasty.[6] Incorporation like this was a process, not an event, begun by Charlemagne. Evidence shows that by 814–15, the March was part of a centralized governance structure, and by 840 was contested as a prize for aristocrats to claim. No *marchio* or count, however powerful and ambitious, sought to throw off Carolingian authority over the region. Meanwhile, by incorporating an area historically separate and distinct from the Frankish kingdoms, the Carolingian dynasty was able to emphasize its claims to broader, imperial authority.

CAMPAIGNS AND CONQUESTS, 778–800

The narrative sources relating to the conquest of the Spanish March after Charlemagne's campaign into Spain are not numerous. We have seen the *Chronicon Moissiacense Maius* (*CMM*) and the *Annales Regni Francorum* already in Chapter 1. The royal annals become a more important source for this study in the late eighth century and into the ninth, as the particular, southern perspective of the chronicle of Moissac gives way. For what they reveal that is not found in the more official line in the royal annals, this chapter will occasionally employ other annalistic texts that were friendly to the Carolingian dynasty but written rather independently of direct royal influence. Because of the significant role Louis the Pious as king of Aquitaine played in the campaigns that settled the limits of Frankish rule, it is also important to draw on information from the Astronomer, the anonymous author of a text known as *Vita Hludovici imperatoris*.[7] This person was evidently well connected at Louis's court in Aquitaine before 814 and continued to stay close to the emperor throughout his reign. It is even conceivable that the Astronomer, so called

---

[6] For a similar idea see J. L. Nelson, *The Frankish World, 750–900* (London: Hambledon, 1996), xiii–xxxi.

[7] Deeper study of the Astronomer and his work can be found in Noble, *Charlemagne and Louis the Pious*, 219–26; Ernst Tremp's introduction to the text in *MGH SS rer. Germ.* 64 (Hanover, 1995), 53–152; Tremp, *Die Überlieferung der Vita Hludowici imperatoris des Astronomus MGH* Studien und Texte 1 (Hanover, 1991); W. Tenberken, *Die Vita Hludowici Pii auctore Astronomo* (Rottweil, 1982).

because of an interest in celestial occurrences seen occasionally in the text, was an aristocrat of some standing from Septimania.[8] As far as his reliability as a witness to the events he records is concerned, for the early years and the Aquitainian phase of Louis's career he draws upon the work of Einhard and the now lost account of Adhemar, who may be identified as the count of that name in the Astronomer's text. The anonymous biographer also draws from, without mindlessly copying, the *Annales Regni Francorum* for the first decade of Louis's reign as emperor, and there is a degree of overlap with the account found in the lay author Nithard; both authors seem to have worked from common source material. In general terms, scholars have found the Astronomer to be a dependable and important source.

Louis the Pious was born during the campaign of 778; three years later he was named king of Aquitaine. By reorganizing the region as a subkingdom under his son (as he also did in Italy under Louis's brother Pippin), Charlemagne did not merely give a nod towards the fact that Aquitaine had until recently been ruled by its own duke, but indeed made for more efficient management of his vast kingdom's resources as well as a foothold for further involvement in Spain.[9] Indeed, there is no indication that Charlemagne or his court saw this new 'kingdom' of Aquitaine as an unchanging entity, as the *Divisio regnorum* of 806 would have split Louis's territories between his brothers in the event of his death.[10] Charlemagne's reorganization of Aquitaine and policy towards these regions has been attributed to the failure of the Zaragoza campaign. Although the Franks took a somewhat less aggressive posture thereafter, Spain presented attractive possibilities for further intervention.[11] The first opportunity was in 785, when 'the men of Girona delivered the city . . . to king Charles' even though Charlemagne was in Saxony that year, and indeed never personally campaigned south of the Pyrenees after 778.[12]

---

[8] He was almost assuredly from the western parts of the kingdom. See Noble, *Charlemagne and Louis the Pious*, 220 and literature cited there.

[9] The argument that the move placated Aquitanian particularism stems from the harsh fighting earlier in the eighth century. See L. Auzias, *L'Aquitaine carolingienne* (Toulouse, 1937), 1–63. Lewis, *The Development of Southern French and Catalan Society, 718–1050* (Austin, 1965), 51, discusses the region's particularism as a possible motivation behind the creation of the kingdom. But see R. Collins, *Charlemagne* (Toronto and Buffalo, 1998), 70 and 73.

[10] *Divisio regnorum* of 806 *MGH* Cap. 1, no. 45, 127–8. Although Aquitaine and Gascony were separated from Septimania and Burgundy with Provence, these terms were retained as geographical labels. J. L. Nelson, 'Frankish Identity in Charlemagne's Empire', in I. H. Garipzanov, P. J. Geary, and Przemyslaw Urbanczyk, eds, *Franks, Northmen, and Slavs: Identities and State Formation in Early Medieval Europe* (Turnhout, 2008), 71–83, at 72–3.

[11] Lewis, *The Development of Society*, 29.

[12] J. M. J. G. Kats, *Chronicon Moissiacense Maius: a Carolingian World Chronicle from Creation to the First Years of Louis the Pious*, prepared and revised by D. Claszen, 2 vols. (MPhil thesis, Leiden, 2012), henceforth *CMM*, 125; Collins, *Charlemagne*, 70.

Nevertheless, the successful annexation of Girona resulted in the creation of the first county in the Spanish frontier area, with the aristocrat Rostagnus as its count.[13]

In the 790s, the Franks regained the initiative. Expansion into Hispania took the form of numerous campaigns, carried out in Louis's name for several years by high-ranking counts. The Astronomer's and various annalists' accounts of Louis's reign in Aquitaine reveal just how great the effort was. To begin with, Charlemagne had appointed trusted men as court advisors and counts and bishops throughout the new kingdom of Aquitaine, including Chorso, named count of Toulouse.[14] These men had to deal with both Basques and Muslims. Chorso himself was captured by Basques, humiliated, and released; Louis and his men decided to avenge him by trying the Basque leader at an assembly.[15] Hostages were exchanged, but no trial held until 790, when Charlemagne held an assembly at Worms. There, the Basque leader, whom the Astronomer names Adelericus, could not purge himself through oath and thus was exiled.[16] Chorso, meanwhile, was removed from office on account of his disgraceful carelessness. As a result, Charlemagne's cousin William was appointed count of Toulouse, and took charge of most military matters associated with the Spanish March.[17]

Just as Charlemagne had received envoys from Muslim leaders in 777, Louis repeatedly dealt with such messengers. A Muslim leader in northern Spain named Abu Thawr, who accompanied Suleiman to meet Charlemagne in Paderborn, sent delegates to Toulouse to seek peace with Louis as king of Aquitaine in 790, as the Astronomer records.[18] Louis

[13] Rostagnus may have already been count in the city, perhaps leading in its submission to the Franks. See See J. M. Salrach, *El procés*, 1, 17–19; R. d'Abadal i de Vinyals, *Dels visigots als catalans*, J. Sobrequés i Callicó, ed, 2nd ed. (Barcelona, 1974), 155, 202. The main source is Astronomer, c.13 *MGH SS* 2, 612.

[14] *Vita Hludowici*, Astronomer, c. 3 *MGH SS* 2, 608.

[15] *Vita Hludowici*, Astronomer, c. 5 *MGH SS* 2, 609. See Noble, *Charlemagne and Louis the Pious*, 231–2, with footnote 25: The name of the estate where the assembly was held was Mourgoudou, in Latin Mors-Gothorum, 'Death for the Goths'. This place name may recall the fighting of the early and middle eighth century.

[16] See the brief discussion of this name in Noble, *Charlemagne and Louis the Pious*, 231, with footnote 23. See also the identification as the son of Lupus, duke of Gascony, in Lewis, *The Development of Society*, 38, with notes 7 and 8. Adelericus might seem more a Frankish than Basque name, but a Frankish name need not indicate Frankish ethnicity. See J. Jarnut, 'Nomen et gens: Political and Linguistic Aspects of Personal Names between the Third and the Eighth Century', in W. Pohl with H. Reimitz, eds, *Strategies of Distinction: the Construction of Ethnic Communities, 300–800* (Leiden, 1998), 113–16 with Pohl, 'Telling the Difference: Signs of Ethnic Identity', in ibid., 25 and G. Ripoll López, 'The Arrival of the Visigoths in Hispania: Population Problems and the Process of Acculturation', in ibid., 153–87 at 165–6.

[17] The Worms assembly is recorded in *ARF* for 790. For details about the exile of Adelericus, removal of Chorso and appointment of William, see Astronomer c. 5 *MGH SS* 2, 609.

[18] See Astronomer, *Vita Hludowici*, cc. 5 and 8 *MGH SS* 2, 609 and 611.

agreed. Even Alcuin mentioned Spanish affairs in a letter which shows that he seems to believe the Franks to possess a considerable strip of land in Spain, even though their control over the Basque area was slight, and their authority recognized in the central Pyrenees only freshly established.[19] Parts of this region, namely Urgell and Cerdanya, were incorporated into the new kingdom of Aquitaine and placed in the hands of the young Louis and his advisors, while Pallars and Ribagorça may have been considered marches of Toulouse and governed more directly by William, or else the count served as a conduit for royal power and religious reform.[20] In 793, the year Louis turned fifteen, William led Frankish forces against the Saracens, who had ventured forth from Hispania into parts of Gothia and terrorized the Christians there.[21] The Muslim raid may have been prompted by Charlemagne's attention to other matters, namely in Saxony and his canal project designed to link the Rhine and Danube.[22] Some Frankish sources report that the Saracens believed Charlemagne to be fighting the Avars, and took the opportunity to attack across the Pyrenees.[23] Other combat followed, often instigated by the Franks after Louis reached his majority.

Louis undertook further campaigns to extend Carolingian power in the March throughout the rest of his reign in Aquitaine. The Astronomer reports a rather significant campaign in the late 790s that burned the city of Lleida and ravaged the countryside around Huesca, but no permanent conquest resulted.[24] Louis later set his sights on cities farther south. Because of this campaign, he was able to inflict damage on the Muslim troops raised to stop him and return to Aquitaine with booty plundered from along the route, including the cities of Tarragona and Tortosa.[25] These and other minor campaigns did not result in further conquest so much as

[19] Alcuin, Ep. 7, *MGH Epp.* 2, 32. See Abadal, CC 1, 74.

[20] Astronomer, *Vita Hludowici,* cc. 3–4 *MGH SS* 2, 608–9. See also Louis's portion of the Frankish kingdom as spelled out in the *Divisio regnum MGH LL nat. Germ.* 1, 140–1. Abadal, CC 3, 89–91 demonstrates that the counts of Toulouse, rather than the Frankish kings, were the rulers of the Pyrenean areas of Pallars and Ribagorça, issuing diplomas as the kings did elsewhere. See now A. Miro, 'Les comtes de Toulouse en Pallars et Ribagorce au IXe siècle: princes souverains ou agents du prince?' *Territorio, Sociedad, y Poder* 6 (2011): 23–52.

[21] *Annales Laureshamenses,* in G. H. Pertz, ed., *MGH SS,* 1 (Hanover, 1826), 33. See also for the leadership of William *Annales Alamannici,* in G. H. Pertz, ed., *MGH SS,* 1 (Hanover, 1826), 47; CMM, 131.

[22] See ARF, 93, for the year 793; M. McCormick, *Origins of the European Economy* (Cambridge, 2001), 399; H. H. Hoffmann, 'Fossa Carolina. Versuch einer Zusammenschau', in W. Braunfels, ed., *Karl der Grosse, Lebenswerk und Nachleben* (Düsseldorf, 1965), vol. 1, 437–53 at 444–50; W. D. Pecher, *Der Karlsgraben – wer grub ihn wirklich?* (Treuchtlingen, 1993) and W. E. Keller, *Der Karlsgraben-Fossa Carolina* (Treuchtlingen, 1993). See also Collins, *Charlemagne,* 127–8.

[23] ARF, 95; CMM, 131.   [24] Astronomer, *Vita Hludowici,* c. 8 *MGH SS* 2, 611.

[25] Astronomer, *Vita Hludowici,* c. 14 *MGH SS* 2, 613–14.

shows of Frankish strength.[26] In 798, Louis ordered frontier defences refortified along the Ter and extending westward from where the river bends, including at Vic, Cardona, and Casserres, amongst other *oppida deserta*, an effort he entrusted to a Count Borrell.[27] Not much evidence survives about Borrell, but he was presumably count of Urgell, which had come under Carolingian control by about 790; at the least, its bishop could be compelled to attend a synod that Charlemagne convened in Regensburg in 792.[28] The most important military positioning of the period revolved around the city of Barcelona. The city first enters the picture in 778, and by 797 the Franks had formally acquired it by negotiation, but its Muslim governor Zatun seems never actually to have surrendered it.[29] The fortifications of 798 would have aided in severing Barcelona from Muslim territory, as well as offering protection to the areas that had come under Frankish control in the decade or so prior. When all is taken into account, the Carolingian kings had to engage in intermittent fighting from 778 to beyond 800 to expel Muslim forces and consolidate control of the Christian population in the Spanish March. This was roughly the same length of time as they needed to accomplish the conquest of pagan Saxony.

FORMING A FRONTIER, 801–820

Charlemagne's imperial coronation in 800 seems to have had no effect on the governance and military activity in the Spanish March, most of which was continued under the direction of his now adult son Louis as king of Aquitaine. Louis needed a campaign that concluded after his father's imperial coronation to affirm Carolingian control of Barcelona, which was to become the principal seat of power in the March. After a meeting at Toulouse to develop strategy, the king of Aquitaine set off for Barcelona in 800. He divided his army

[26] *ARF*, s.a. 809, *MGH SS rer. Germ.*, 6, 127. See especially the many *ARF* and other entries for the 790s and early 800s.

[27] Astronomer, *Vita Hludowici*, c. 8 *MGH SS* 2, 611. The classic treatment is Abadal, *Dels visigots als catalans*, vol. 1, 309–11. See I. Ollich i Castanyer, 'Vic: la cuitat a l'època carolíngia', in J. Camps, ed., *Catalunya a l'època carolíngia: art i cultura abans del romànic (segles IX i X)* (Barcelona, 1999), 89–94, trans. as 'Vic: the Town in the Carolingian Age', ibid., 464–6; also her 'Roda: l'Esquerda. La ciutat carolíngia', ibid. pp. 84–8, trans. as 'Roda: l'Esquerda. The Carolingian Town', ibid., 461–3.

[28] M.-M. Costa, 'Les genealogies comtals catalanes', in *Symposium internacional*, 447–62; on the synod, see *ARF* s.a. 792, *MGH SS rer. Germ.*, 6, 91.

[29] Collins, *Charlemagne*, 74, emphasizes Louis's role in enforcing the treaty. *ARF*, s.a. 797, *MGH SS rer. Germ.* 6, 100–1 highlight the presence of the Muslim governor Zatun in Aachen. Astronomer, *Vita Hludowici*, c. 10 *MGH SS* 2, 611 states that Zatun met Louis on the king's earlier campaign into Spain but did not hand over Barcelona.

into three parts: the first he held in reserve under his own command north of the Pyrenees in Roussillon, the second went to besiege Barcelona under Count Rostagnus of Girona and apparently Bera of Roussillon in command of the 'Gothi', while the third under William and Ademar of Narbonne set off westward to head off any Muslim relief forces coming by the old Roman road from Zaragoza.[30] Despite hopeful expectations that Barcelona would surrender like Narbonne and Girona, it seems that Louis set off with ample preparations for a long siege.[31] William and Ademar's force did indeed block Muslim relief forces; these Muslims withdrew, freeing William and Ademar to join Rostagnus at Barcelona, where resistance was tough. The siege of Barcelona lasted into winter, proving a longer operation than the Franks were accustomed to, but causing the city to suffer and become demoralized; the Astronomer reports that some residents jumped from city walls in desperation. Louis appeared with his reserve troops in early 801, and six weeks later Barcelona capitulated, allowing the king a triumphal entrance on Easter Sunday 801.[32] Ermoldus Nigellus offers an account of the conquest of Barcelona that takes up the first book of his poem *In honorem Hludowici*.[33] In it, the poet, who was not an eyewitness to the campaign but rather cast the events as an epic tale, portrays an act of strength by Louis, his throwing of a spear into the city, as the key to victory. It lodged in a stone wall, aweing the inhabitants.[34] Ermoldus marks Easter Sunday as the celebration of Louis's victory and triumphal entrance into the city, and elaborates on the religious purification that took place by order of the king, before he left it in the charge of guardians and returned to Aquitaine.[35]

While the conquest of Barcelona marks the furthest Carolingian expansion south of the Pyrenees, it may not have been the final objective. The apparent goal was to set the frontier at the Ebro, whose marshes and topography provided a better natural defence than the Llobregat near Barcelona. Louis the Pious directed several campaigns against Tortosa before his accession as emperor, none of which succeeded. Using Arabic sources and the Astronomer's accounts of the campaigns, modern

---

[30] Astronomer, *Vita Hludowici*, c. 13 MGH SS 2, 612. See also Lewis, *The Development of Society*, 41.

[31] Salrach, *El procés*, vol. 1, 14–24; Abadal, CC 1, 183–216. ARF s.a. 801, MGH SS rer. Germ. 6, 116 mention a two-year siege, which is surely an error.

[32] Astronomer, *Vita Hludowici*, c. 13 MGH SS 2, 612–613; CMM, 142, which places the campaign in 803.

[33] See also M. McCormick, *Eternal Victory: Triumphal Rulership in Late Antiquity, Byzantium and the Early Medieval West* (Cambridge, 1990), 374–5.

[34] Ermoldus, *In honorem Hludowici*, ll. 515–20, MGH SS 2, 476.

[35] Ibid., ll. 525–34, MGH SS 2, 477.

historians have been able to chart three expeditions.[36] The first, in 805, destroyed the fortifications of Tarragona and burned much of the area as the Franks moved south along the coastal route.[37] Borrell of Urgell and Cerdanya commanded the second branch of the Frankish army.[38] In the second attempt on Tortosa, in 809, the Franks were thwarted, according to the Astronomer because the shrewd Muslims noticed horse dung floating in the Ebro that was the result of the Franks having camped upriver. Although the Franks defeated Muslim forces and returned home with loot, they did not capture the city.[39] Finally, in 810, Louis found mixed success, as he was able at least to besiege Tortosa.[40] The Arab historian al-Maqqari simply reports that the Franks were defeated and returned home, and the *Annales Regni Francorum* confirm that they were unable to take the city.[41] A treaty agreed between the two sides in 810 set the limits of Frankish dominion south of the Pyrenees just beyond Barcelona, thus ending the enterprise of establishing the frontier at the Ebro.[42]

Events in the fledgling kingdom of Aragon to the west, where *walis* tended to rebel against emirs in Córdoba, also pressed the Franks to forego further conquest in Spain. The Franks established there, in Zaragoza, a Count Aureolus, but at his death the *wali* Amrus established himself and sent to Charlemagne for aid against the emir.[43] The emir proposed a separate peace agreement in 810, by which the Franks agreed to give up their designs on Tortosa and Zaragoza, which they did not directly control, while the Muslims accepted Frankish control of Barcelona and had the freedom to deal with Amrus.[44] Also in 810, Muslim pirates raided the Balearics and Corsica, causing Charlemagne to legislate for the provision of naval protection for his coasts.[45] The Astronomer reports not only campaigns against Tortosa, but also against the inland cities of Pamplona and Huesca.[46] Carolingian attempts

---

[36] Astronomer, *Vita Hludowici*, c. 14 MGH SS 2, 613–14. P. Wolff, 'Aquitaine et ses marges', in Braunfels, ed., *Karl der Große*, vol. 1, *Persönlichkeit und Geschichte* (Düsseldorf, 1965); Salrach, *El procés*, vol. 1, 32–7.

[37] Astronomer, *Vita Hludowici*, c. 14, MGH SS 2, 613. He reports that Borrell's men crossed the Cinca and the Ebro above Tortosa by swimming.

[38] Astronomer, *Vita Hludowici*, c. 14 MGH SS 2, 613–14.

[39] Astronomer, *Vita Hludowici*, c. 15 MGH SS 2, 614–15.

[40] See especially Salrach, *El procés*, vol. 1, 37. Note however, that the Astronomer, *Vita Hludowici*, c. 16 MGH SS 2, 615.

[41] Al-Maqqari, in J. M. Millàs i Vallicrosa, *Textos dels historiadors àrabs referents a la Catalunya carolíngia* (Barcelona, 1987), nos. 98–9; *ARF*, s.a. 809, MGH SS rer. Germ. 6, 127.

[42] *ARF*, s.a. 810, MGH SS rer. Germ. 6, 130.   [43] *ARF*, s.a. 810, MGH SS rer. Germ. 6, 130.

[44] Salrach, *El procés*, vol. 1, 37–8.

[45] *ARF*, s.a. 810, MGH SS rer. Germ. 6, 130; Wolff, 'Aquitaine et ses marges', 282.

[46] Astronomer, *Vita Hludowici*, cc. 16–18 MGH SS 2, 615–16.

at expansion into Spain ended with the 812 siege of Huesca, intended to retake a position from which Muslims had ousted them the previous year.[47] The siege failed, and with it the Carolingian intervention into the central Pyrenees that began in 778. The Astronomer blamed the impudent youth of the Frankish troops.

Fighting erupted between the Franks and the Basques in 815 and 816, according to the *Chronicon Moissiacense Maius*. There seems to have even been a rift amongst the Basques, whom the authors paint as rebels, as a new leader had emerged and been killed by 817.[48] The narrative, clearly dependent on another source for this information, does not provide any clue as to why a new leader would rise and fall so quickly. Perhaps his strategies vis-à-vis his Frankish and Muslim neighbours played a role. In the middle of the decade, a Muslim attack on Barcelona was repulsed in large part by the success of Bera and local fighters, both Gothi and hispani, many of whom had claimed direct relationships with and protection from the kings.[49] The *Annales Regni Francorum* report that in 816, after a brief peace between the Franks and the Muslims, war again resumed because Louis the Pious deemed the peace useless, perhaps because it failed to provide him an advantage against the Basques. The following year, envoys arrived at the emperor's court to seek peace again.[50] The two sides agreed a truce for 817–20.[51] After these developments, the Carolingian dominion across the Pyrenees settled in the region now known as Catalunya Vella, or Old Catalonia.[52] While the boundary near the coast was just south of Barcelona, further inland it barely came down from the mountains.

After the campaigning and eventual peace of the 810s, Frankish control of some Pyrenean areas proved ephemeral. Events in the real world tend to be much messier than the plans of kings, so the incorporation of a conquered area must be understood as a gradual process rather than a solitary accomplishment. In the 820s local leaders in western lands, such as those of Aragon and Pamplona, asserted their autonomous rule of their localities. The expulsion of Asnar Galindo from Aragon and his settlement in Carolingian Urgell was a symptom of this movement. Asnar, favoured by the Franks in the early years of the ninth century, seems to

---

[47] Astronomer, *Vita Hludowici*, c. 17 MGH SS 2, 615.   [48] CMM, 148.

[49] For the characterization of the soldiers involved as 'local hispano-gothic forces', Salrach, *El procés*, vol. 1, 43–4. On their direct relationship with the monarchs, see below in the chapter section 'Networks of Loyalty'.

[50] ARF, s.a. 816, MGH SS rer. Germ 6, 143.

[51] ARF, s.a. 817, MGH SS rer. Germ 6, 145. The Astronomer, *Vita Hludowici*, c. 25 MGH SS 2, 620 refers to a three-year truce, but includes its mention amongst events and actions from prior years.

[52] Salrach, *El procés*, vol. 1, 37–9.

have held the honour of count in Aragon before being expelled by his son-in-law around 820. Because Borrell, the count who had fortified a line of defence in Urgell and Cerdanya, had died in that year, Louis appointed Asnar as successor.[53] Perhaps similar grumblings sounded in the eastern Pyrenees, but there the Frankish royal presence was stronger. From 812 to 816, Charlemagne and Louis were able to intervene with authority, and always looked for ways to link themselves to locals in the eastern counties. There, especially along the frontier, it has been argued that some nobles seem to have pushed for a split with the Carolingian monarchy, following their neighbours to the west, while others wanted peace with Muslims at any cost, including subordination to the Franks.[54] Taking this argument further, some even posit an ethnic motivation for throwing off Carolingian authority.[55] This recent work argues that locals in the Spanish March had been 'Islamicized' to a degree and supposedly tended to align more with Muslim overlords or the nearby Banu Qasi than with the Franks. If these factions had applied pressure on Bera to keep peace with Muslims and to flex his own authority after the expiry of the truce in 820, his actions along those lines could have prompted the accusation of treason. Yet no solid evidence in texts of the time can be cited to uphold this view, so the question of the relationship between identity and political loyalty is not so easily dealt with.

ETHNIC IDENTITY AND THE SPANISH MARCH

It has long been held that the Carolingian conquest of Septimania was accomplished with the cooperation of notable individuals with family roots in the area, usually referred to as Goths, and their role is supposed to be even more important for the frontier south of the Pyrenees. That seems to have been the case, at least for Girona's capitulation in 785, which came about because the 'men of the city' capitulated to the king even while he was on campaign in Saxony.[56] But regionally based supporters of the Carolingians were important in other ways as well, for in the conquest of territory beyond the mountain frontier, Gothic counts and soldiers from Septimania played key roles. In the fundamental modern Catalan works on the period, the Gothic ethnicity of these individuals

---

[53] CC 2, 325–6. This is not a document so much as Abadal's argument for the existence of a document from the 820s; documentation on Asnar Galindo is very thin indeed. See further discussion in Abadal, *Els primers comtes catalans*, Biografies Catalanes (Barcelona, 1958), 222–30.

[54] Salrach, *El procés*, 1, 45–6.

[55] This is the line of reasoning in Ollich, 'Vic', 91, and 'Roda', 86, admittedly for events later in the decade.

[56] CMM, 125.

is more often asserted than demonstrated, yet their contributions are borne out by examination of sources.[57] Count Borrell, presumably a Goth because of his family's base in Septimania, carried out Louis's orders to fortify Vic, Cardona, and Casseres west of Girona in the late 790s.[58] And the noble Bera, whose mother was a Goth, became Barcelona's first Carolingian count in 801, although he did not command any of the main branches of the army that conquered the city.[59]

In addition to Goths and Franks, some evidence highlights the importance of Jews in the establishment of the Spanish March. Earlier, in consolidating his control of Septimania, Pippin recognized the elevated standing of the Jewish population there and favoured them with legal freedoms they did not always enjoy under Visigothic kings; Charlemagne followed Pippin's example along these lines.[60] The plain of Vic, fortified in the late 790s, was already at least partially populated at the time the Franks arrived.[61] The only investigation so far into the role of Jews in the Frankish conquest of the March, by Bernard Bachrach, found that all holders of allods in this part of the Visigothic kingdom were obliged to render military service under the command of the counts and that Jews numbered amongst these allod holders.[62] Bachrach maintains that, because the campaign for Barcelona included levies from Aquitaine, Burgundy, Gascony, Provençe, and 'Gothia' (Septimania),[63] which was home to many Jews, then Jews may have formed part of the army that took Barcelona.[64] Interesting as this idea seems, there is no direct evidence to support it, though the circumstantial argument is tempting. No Jew ever attained the rank of count in the 'Gothic' or marcher areas.[65] Those posts were the preserve of the Christian aristocrats who participated directly in the conquest or came from families of note in the Frankish realms. Aristocratic families with members involved in the

[57] See, for example, Rostagnus as 'probably a Goth' according to Salrach, *El procés*, 1, 27.

[58] Astronomer, *Vita Hludowici*, c. 8 *MGH SS* 2, 611. These areas are now central in terms of Catalan geography, but in the 790s were the frontier.

[59] Astronomer, *Vita Hludowici*, c. 13 *MGH SS* 2, 613.

[60] B. S. Bachrach, 'On the Role of the Jews in the Establishment of the Spanish March (768–814)', in J. M. Sola-Solé, ed., *Hispanica Judaica: Studies in the History, Language and Literature of the Jews in the Hispanic World* (Barcelona, 1980), 11–19.

[61] The Astronomer's account attributes 'repopulation' to Louis's initiative, c. 8 *MGH SS* 2, 611, but the details he gives are of fortifications to existing settlements.

[62] Bachrach, 'On the Role of the Jews', 14–19.

[63] *CMM*, 142. For Septimanian Jews, see in Chapter 1.

[64] Bachrach, 'On the Role of the Jews', 18–19.

[65] The arguments of A. J. Zuckerman, *A Jewish Princedom in Feudal France, 768–900* (New York, 1972) notwithstanding, there is no evidence that Jews wielded considerable political power in the south-western territories of the Carolingian Empire. See the reviews by B. S. Bachrach, *American Historical Review* 78 (1973): 1440–1; and P. Wormald, 'Review of *A Jewish Princedom in Feudal France, 768–900*', *English Historical Review* 89 (1974): 415–16.

conquest established themselves in powerful positions early on and drew on their ties to the Carolingians to obtain and retain power in the March.

In this light, attributing Bera's treason and exile to pressure from locals to align more closely with nearby Muslim powers is tempting but problematic. If the count was attempting to maintain peace on the frontier, that in itself would not constitute treason, even if he relied on his own authority rather than consulting with Louis first.[66] Alternatively, Bera's removal in 820 took place in the context of the revolts of his neighbours in the western Pyrenees. It was the consequence of a possible move of the count acting on his own to establish a base of power independent from the king.[67] Neither of these factors, however, constitutes an ethnic motivation for treason. Furthermore, there is reason to believe his treason was not even real, but rather a trumped-up charge propagated by his enemies. The *Annales Regni Francorum* report that locals brought charges against him, without using language that implies passing judgement; thus it is difficult to assess the official court position. Indeed, Bera lost his duel, but Louis the Pious apparently did not consider him a dangerous criminal and so commuted the capital sentence to exile to Rouen.[68] It seems that after the tragedy of his nephew Bernard of Italy, Louis was wary of capital punishment, or any harsh punishment; his penance at Attigny in 822 at any rate was aimed at expiating the sin of Bernard's death following his blinding.[69] Sanila, who made the formal accusation against Bera, was a Goth like Bera (who was really only half-Goth, being born to a Frankish father), but also a friend and subordinate of Gaucelm, Bera's half-brother and rival.[70] Gaucelm was also a son of William of Gellone, by his second, Frankish wife, and held extensive interests in Septimania and the March.[71] The two lines of descent from the Carolingian monarchs'

---

[66] A. Stieldorf, *Marken und Markgrafen: Studien zur Grenzsicherung durch die fränkisch-deutschen Herrscher, MGH* Schriften 64 (Hanover, 2012), ch. II, esp. 54–68.

[67] See Lewis, *The Development of Society*, 42–4, who views Bera's alleged treason as following this pattern. See also Aurell, 'Pouvoir et parenté des comtes de la Marche Hispanique (801–911)', in R. Le Jan, ed., *La royauté et les élites dans l'Europe carolingienne (début IXe siècle aux environs de 920)* (Villeneuve d'Ascq, 1988), 470–1.

[68] *ARF*, s.a. 820, *SS rer. Germ.* 6, 152. The duel was fought on horseback, as noted previously. Salrach states that this indicates the use of 'light weapons', Salrach, *El procés*, vol. 1, 46.

[69] Amongst other works on Louis, his methods of rule, and the role public penance played, see E. Boshof, *Ludwig der Fromme* (Darmstadt, 1996), 148–51 and 192–203; M. de Jong, *The Penitential State: Authority and Atonement in the Age of Louis the Pious, 814–840* (Cambridge, 2009); and C. Booker, *Past Convictions: the Penance of Louis the Pious and the Decline of the Carolingians* (Philadelphia, 2009).

[70] One identification of both Sanila and Bera as Goths comes from Ermoldus Nigellus, *In honorem Hludowici MGH SS* 2, 501.

[71] Aurell, 'Pouvoir et parenté', 469–70. Salrach proposed that Sanila and his followers brought charges against Bera defending their own interests in the wake of the loss of Pamplona and Aragon. Lewis, *The Development of Society*, 45, following R. d' Abadal i de Vinyals, 'La Catalogne sous

staunchest supporter in Aquitaine, Septimania, and the Spanish March found a great deal of power in the frontier concentrated in their hands, but their fates had nothing to do with any supposed notion of ethnic identity.

For one thing, Bera seems to have been one of the emperor's men. As has been noted, following the pattern of his neighbours in the western Pyrenees, areas that were only loosely connected with the old Visigothic kingdom before the Muslim conquest, any powerful marcher count in the 810s could have declared himself king of his territory and tried to back up his claim by fighting the Franks. Since Bera did not do this – in part because the eastern Pyrenees were more strongly connected to Frankish dominion via roads, and in part because Bera himself came from Septimania, a region that did not really exhibit independence-minded, 'pro-Visigothic' political proclivities under decades of Carolingian rule – any notion that Visigothic identity was the root of political activity in the Spanish March seems to be more an assumption on the part of nine-teenth- and twentieth-century scholars. To arrive at an understanding of Bera's case, and the role of identity in the Spanish March, we should reconsider the motives of those who accused Bera of treason and brought about his downfall. It seems that Bera acquired more territories over time, having already been 'sub-count' of Razès and Conflent from about 790, ruling in association with his father, William. He became count of Barcelona, and then in the early 810s acquired Besalú and Girona when their count died.[72] Traditional Catalan historiography holds that Bera wanted to make peace with the Muslims nearby, and that he headed a pro-Visigothic faction in the Spanish March, against Gaucelm's pro-Frankish, pro-war faction.[73] But it also seems that Gaucelm, who governed Roussillon and Empúries,[74] was losing out in terms of power and prestige in Septimania and the Spanish March, despite his exceptionally high birth and whatever other merits he possessed. Furthermore, the Astronomer's account that named Sanila as Bera's accuser emphasizes that Sanila was a Goth.[75] One Goth accusing another Goth of treason against the Frankish emperor, with whom the accused served and for whom he governed the city they took, cannot indicate politicized

l'Empire de Louis le Pieux', *Études Roussillonnaises* 4–6 (1955–7): 147–52 and Abadal, *Els primers comtes*, 222–30 views the removal of Bera as part of a family rivalry between the descendants of William of Gellone (Gaucelm and Bernard of Septimania) and those of Bello of Carcassonne. This interpretation is preferable to the notion of latent Catalan nationalism, but does not hold up in the light of Aurell's findings that Bera was also William's son and not Bello's.

[72] J. M. Salrach, *El procés de feudalització* (Barcelona, 1987), 141–2. [73] For example, ibid., 142–3.
[74] Ibid., 141. Salrach calls Gaucelm count of 'Empúries-Roselló', 142.
[75] Astronomer, *Vita Hludowici*, c. 33 *MGH SS*, 2, 625. Sanila has been called a friend and subordinate of Gauclem's in Salrach, *El procés de feudalització*, 143.

ethnicity. It seems, then, that instead of ethnic tension, that is, a Frankish Gaucelm in conflict with a Gothic Bera, this case is more about aristocratic rivalries that had Bera his job and honour.

Fundamentally, this case shows that identity or ethnic labels did not matter in the politics of empire in Septimania and the Spanish March. No evidence in narrative sources can confirm that any individual acted a certain way politically because of a perceived Gothicness or Frankishness.[76] To judge from the law codes, people understood that there were Franks, Goths, Bavarians, Lombards, and other groups within the kingdom; however, although such labels may have been ethnic, that is, each denoting a 'people' with its own history that contemporaries could read or discuss, they were not so in the modern sense of a difference that would put individuals at an advantage or disadvantage. Some fairly recent and influential work on ethnic identities notes that the Carolingian monarchs and their associates paid more attention to ethnic identity than other early-medieval ruling groups.[77] Einhard, for one, knew what it meant to dress like a Frank, the same way the Astronomer knew what it meant to dress like a Basque.[78] The ethnic labels seem to indicate places of origin rather than identities. Despite the suggestions of Catalan scholars, who seem to want to detect a regional flair for separatism in the Carolingian period, the evidence has to be interpreted as meaning that ethnic labels did not matter in terms of politics. Court-affiliated writers like Einhard and the Astronomer, as well as anonymous annalists, bestowed more significance on the labels than events warranted. In doing so, they elevated the imperial status of Charlemagne and Louis by highlighting the many different peoples over whom they ruled.

NETWORKS OF LOYALTY

In the aftermath of conquest, the Carolingian rulers needed to integrate their new territories into the existing institutions of the kingdom.[79] Aside

---

[76] Close reading of narratives is precisely the methodological approach advocated in the major enterprise on early medieval ethnicity: P. Heather, 'Disappearing and Reappearing Tribes', in Pohl and Reimitz, eds, *Strategies of Distinction*, 95–111.

[77] W. Pohl, 'Telling the Difference: Signs of Ethnic Identity', in Pohl and Reimitz, eds, *Strategies of Distinction*, 17–69 at 45.

[78] Einhard, *Vita Karoli, MGH SS rer. Germ.* 25 (Hanover and Leipzig, 1911), ch. 23; Astronomer, *Vita Hludovici*, c. 4 MCH SS 2, 609. Note that Pohl, in his discussion cited above, mistakenly cites Thegan rather than the Astronomer.

[79] Davis, *Charlemagne's Practice*, Part II, provides a stimulating discussion of conquered regions. See esp. pp. 172–3 for an overview of her argument on centralization and regional diversity, which aligns very well with my argument, and ch. 4, pp. 175–238. C. West, *Reframing the Feudal Revolution: Political and Social Transformation between the Marne and the Moselle, c.800–c.1100* (Cambridge, 2013), 19–48, gives an overview of Carolingian governing institutions.

from the straightforward management of personnel, kings employed institutional means, both political and cultural. Following established patterns, they did so in a variety of ways. Two methods arose from the kingdom's laws, and two others stemmed from the active religious reform the royal court sponsored. Evidence concerning Visigothic law, the *aprisio* land grants, monastic observance of the Rule of Benedict, and the doctrinal controversy over Spanish Adoptionism allows a fuller understanding of how the Carolingians were able to make the Spanish March a well-functioning, albeit distant, province of their growing empire.

First, the precedent Pippin had set by preserving Visigothic law for his new subjects in Septimania extended south of the Pyrenees. This agreement can be seen to relate to concepts of the personality and territoriality of law, but recent studies rightly question these notions.[80] It is very likely that, rather than 'Goths' maintaining Gothic law because it was part of their self-identity as a group from time immemorial, the situation was reversed. The use of Visigothic law instead became part of the definition of being a Goth during the Carolingian period. A *gens* did not have a *lex*, but the *lex* made the *gens*. Presumably, the inhabitants of Girona handed their city over to the Franks with a similar agreement, although the evidence for the transfer of power to Charlemagne does not explicitly mention law. After the unsettling chain of events earlier in the eighth century, the benefits of Carolingian rule would have been clear to the locals of the newly forming Spanish March. Carolingian diplomacy attempted to neutralize the ever-present Muslim threat from emirs, and Carolingian rule meant continuity with regards to law and order, order that was based on Visigothic law. Arguably the agreement to maintain the law was pivotal in the success of the campaigns. Roger Collins has noted that the practice of following written law in Septimania and the Spanish March probably resulted in a tradition of fairly robust local governance.[81] Previous studies have demonstrated the survival of Visigothic law throughout the Carolingian period and beyond in the language of local charters, repeated citations of the code itself in documents, the use of panels of judges, the importance of boundary markers, and the practice of writing *exuacuationes*, or promises by those who have previously claimed property to

---

[80] See P. Amory, 'The Meaning and Purpose of Ethnic Terminology in the Burgundian Laws', *EME* 2 (1993): 1–28. Now, and even more especially, T. Faulkner, *Law and Authority in the Early Middle Ages: the Frankish* Leges *in the Carolingian Period* (Cambridge, 2016), esp. 9–22 and 46–83. His discussion is very useful, and we will return to it.

[81] R. Collins, 'Charles the Bald and Wifred the Hairy', in M. Gibson and J. Nelson, eds, *Charles the Bald: Court and Kingdom*, 2nd ed. (Aldershot, 1990), 183.

leave it.[82] In short, despite the military upheavals of the late eighth and early ninth centuries, the region was blessed with stability in terms of preserving local law and order, which continued to be based upon Visigothic law, while the Carolingian monarchy upheld the code in order to complete the conquest and annexation of the territory and its people.

Without taking some measure to ensure political order and social stability, Charlemagne would have had to deal with great uncertainty in his 'Gothic' territories, both on the frontier itself and in Septimania. Because these areas were so distant from the Frankish heartlands, the king could not involve himself personally in their affairs as easily as he could in other places, such as Saxony, whither he made repeated visits.[83] Throughout the Carolingian realms, counts were the primary wielders of power on the local level, their power limited by institutions such as *missi dominici*, royal immunities, or private lordship, as well as the need for local acceptance and consent.[84] Obviously Charlemagne had to delegate power to counts throughout the empire, but equally clearly he required safeguards to ensure that justice was done and royal authority observed. Diffusing power amongst hundreds of counts, interspersing bishops amongst them, and sending *missi* to visit various areas were all means at the king's command.[85] In extreme cases, counts were removed from office, as in the case of Bera of Barcelona, whose story began this chapter.[86] *Marchiones* in border areas acted not only as powerful political figures in their regions, but also served as intermediaries between the king and the other counts of the marches, who reported directly to the *marchiones*.[87] The limitation of comital power was even more important

---

[82] Zimmermann, 'L'Usage du droit wisigothique', *Mélanges de la Casa de Velázquez* 9 (1973): 233–81; W. Kienast, 'La pervivencia del derecho godo en el sur de Francia y Cataluña', *Boletín de la Real Academia de Buenas Letras de Barcelona* 35 (1973), 265–95; J. M. Salrach, 'Práctica judiciales, transformación social y acción política en Cataluña (siglos IX–XIII)', *Hispania* 47 (1997), 1009–48; M. A. Kelleher, 'Boundaries of Law: Code and Custom in Early Medieval Catalonia', *Comitatus* 30 (1999), 1–10; and R. Collins, 'Visigothic Law and Regional Custom in Disputes in Early Medieval Spain', in W. Davies and P. Fouracre, eds, *The Settlement of Disputes in Early Medieval Europe* (Cambridge, 1986), 85–104, with Appendix of Latin texts, 252–7 and Collins, '*Sicut lex Gothorum continent*: Law and Charters in Ninth- and Tenth-Century León and Catalonia', *English Historical Review* 100 (1985): 489–512.

[83] On Charlemagne's travels, see McKitterick, *Charlemagne*, 178–86.

[84] M. Innes, 'Charlemagne's Government', in J. Story, ed., *Charlemagne: Empire and Society* (Manchester, 2005), 71–89; Lewis, *The Development of Society*, 54. For immunities, see B. H. Rosenwein, *Negotiating Space: Power, Restraint, and Privileges of Immunity in Early Medieval Europe* (Ithaca, 1999).

[85] K. F. Werner, as in note 87, was an early and influential voice on Carolingian administration. See now Davis, *Charlemagne's Practice of Empire*, esp. 78–9, 99–107 on these issues.

[86] See also Davis, *Charlemagne's Practice of Empire*, 107–18 on dismissing counts from office.

[87] K. F. Werner, 'Missus-Marchio-Comes: entre l'administration centrale et l'administration locale de l'empire carolingien', in W. Paravicini and K. F. Werner, eds, *Histoire comparée de*

in the Spanish March with its potentially fluid cross-border political loyalties, given the relatively unstable political situation in the Pyrenees in the late eighth century.

To address these challenges, Charlemagne needed to establish direct ties between himself and local figures. Beginning in the late eighth century, documentation arises for a particular kind of land grant in Septimania and the Spanish March, in many instances made to refugees – known as hispani, fleeing Muslim Spain – in recognition of their efforts at clearing and working new land. This practice, known as *aprisio*, featured deserted fiscal land, and royal grants enumerated settlers' rights and immunities.[88] The phenomenon was not a Frankish invention, but rather Charlemagne's co-option of a local and regional practice of homesteading. Supposedly deserted land was automatically claimed for the royal fisc, and the apparently novel bestowal of rights and protection to these settlers reflects the knack the king had for improvising solutions to the various problems of governance.[89] One recent argument, by Jonathan Jarrett, highlights the importance of the *aprisio* for local society and land usage. There is significant value in that perspective; however, it tends to minimize the importance of the royal impetus to protect the *aprisio* settlers and therefore does not sufficiently consider the context of Charlemagne's reign.[90] Jarrett does raise important questions about the nature of the surviving evidence and to what degree it unquestionably demonstrates connections between the notion of *aprisio*, the hispani refugees, and immunities. Yet in seeking to emphasize local conditions and practices, often drawing upon evidence from a much later period in order to do so, he downplays the fact that the evidence for the first *aprisiones* is in fact from the royal perspective of the late eighth and ninth

---

l'administration (IVe–XVIIIe siècle), Beihefte der Francia, vol. 9 (Munich, 1980), 191–239; Lewis, *The Development of Society*, 50–68 and 114–35.

[88] Much of what follows was argued in Chandler, 'Between Court and Counts: Carolingian Catalonia and the *aprisio* Grant, 778–897', *EME* 11 (2002): 19–44, here revised with consideration of newer scholarship. See also E. Müller-Mertens, *Karl der Grosse, Ludwig der Fromme und die Freien: wer waren die liberi homines der karolingischen Kapitularien (742/743–832)? Ein Beitrag zur Sozialgeschichte und Sozialpolitik des Frankenreiches* (Berlin, 1963), 62 ff.

[89] See J. L. Nelson, 'Charlemagne and Empire', in J. R. Davis and M. McCormick, eds, *The Long Morning of Medieval Europe: New Directions in Early Medieval Studies* (Aldershot, 2008), 223–34 and J. R. Davis, 'A Pattern for Power: Charlemagne's Delegation of Judicial Responsibilities', in ibid., 235–46. Davis, *Charlemagne's Practice* argues for Charlemagne's adaptiveness throughout; see 104–5 for explicit discussion of the *aprisio*, where she follows Jarrett's argument, which is discussed later in this paragraph.

[90] J. Jarrett, 'Settling the King's Lands: *aprisio* in Catalonia in Perspective', *EME* 18 (2010): 320–42 offers a useful overview of the term, its meaning, and its use, while affirming my central argument concerning Charlemagne's approach to the settlers. Jarrett's argument touches on the ninth century but is more useful for settlement practices in the tenth century.

centuries.[91] Indeed, Jarrett concedes that Charlemagne could very well have come to the protection of the hispani in part to see to his own interests as ruler, which for present purposes is the most important point.[92] Other recent work supports the idea that royal documents issued for holders of *aprisiones* were re-affirmations of these relationships that represented the entry of royal authority into the localities of Septimania and the Spanish March.[93]

Ramon d'Abadal, the editor of Carolingian royal diplomas issued to recipients in Septimania and the Spanish March, presumed that the earliest grant of fiscal land as *aprisio* was made around 780, in the aftermath of Charlemagne's failed invasion of Spain. Adabal reconstructed this putative grant to a group of hispani on the basis of language used in later royal documents, their allusions to conditions that prevailed around 780, and their citation of the principle taken from Visigothic law that fiscal land became the full and indisputable property of grantees after thirty years.[94] The language of later documents states that the recipients were indeed fleeing from the Saracens and voluntarily placing themselves under the protection of the Frankish king to settle in Septimania and the Spanish March.[95] The origin of these hispani is uncertain, but it could have been the region of Tudmīr in south-eastern Spain, named after the Visigothic noble Theodemir who had maintained power in the area after making a treaty with the conquerors in the early eighth century; there is perhaps more support in the evidence for the northern areas nearer the Pyrenees,

---

[91] See the earlier work of A. Barbero, 'La integración social de los "hispani" del Pirineo oriental al reino carolingio', in P. Gallais and Y.-J. Riou, eds, *Mélanges offerts à René Crozet* (Poitiers, 1966), 67–75.

[92] Jarrett, 'Settling the King's Lands, 322–3. See also Davis, *Charlemagne's Practice*, Part II on 'Center and Region', which emphasizes Charlemagne's ability to seize on circumstances and turn them to the benefit of royal authority. See esp. pp. 218–19 for the argument of granting land technically from the fisc, which in conquered and border areas did not diminish royal land-holdings.

[93] See G. Koziol, *The Politics of Memory and Identity in Carolingian Royal Diplomas: the West Frankish Kingdom (840–987)* (Turnhout, 2012), 60–1 for an argument similar to mine.

[94] Abadal's reconstructive methodology is laid out in CC 2, 399–411; it is based on the references to earlier documents of Charlemagne made in documents of Louis the Pious and Charles the Bald. For further observations on the thirty-year law, see A. Udina i Abelló, 'L'aprisió i el problem del repoblament', in *Symposium internacional*, 159–70, at 163. (Udina uses and cites Abadal's reconstruction of the 780 document, as I did in 'Between Court and Counts', but only explains it as a reconstruction in the footnote.) The Visigothic law itself is *Lex Visigothorum* 10.2.4, *MGH LL nat. Germ.* 1, ed. K. Zeumer (Hanover, 1902), 392–3.

[95] In this case, the language of the so-called *Constitutio de Hispanis* of Louis the Pious in 815, *MGH Capit.* 1, 261, edited by Abadal in CC 2, 417: 'de partibus Hispaniae ad nos confugerunt, et in Septimania atque in ea portione Hispaniae quae a nostris marchionibus in solitudinem redacta fuit sese ad habitandum contulerunt, et a Sarracenorum potestate se subtrahentes nostro dominio libera et prompta voluntate se subdiderunt ...' See also Dupont, 'L'aprision et le régime aprisionaire dans le Midi de la France', *Le Moyen Age* 71 (1965, 1966): 177–213, 375–99, at 183–98.

like Zaragoza.[96] Whatever their origins, the new settlers obtained the right to pass on the land they settled in inheritance, or to alienate it to other hispani, just as if it were their own property. According to the dominant recent interpretation that land termed waste or desert in the sources was merely neglected rather than truly depopulated, these settlers represent the imposition of political, social, and economic organization in these areas as much as the clearing of land.[97] To reflect their new political status, the hispani were to perform the required military service to the king in whichever county they settled, just as other free men were to do, by participating in patrols and keeping watch.[98] One reason Carolingian monarchs bestowed *aprisio* grants, even if in recognition of clearances and settlements already made, was to integrate productive farmers and potential soldiers, most of whom were hispani immigrants from al-Andalus, into Carolingian political structures.[99] Indeed, the largest *aprisio* holders owed military service to the monarchs for their land.[100]

Beyond this the evidence suggests that *aprisio* grants constituted another weapon in the Carolingian arsenal of royal power that monarchs could wield to maintain their authority in a newly conquered and unstable province of a far-flung empire.[101] Early Carolingian legislation stipulated that the *aprisio* settlers were to bring land back into cultivation from waste, and in return were to hold the land completely and without obligation to local authority. In particular, they were free from payment of the *cens*.[102] Holders of *aprisiones* additionally were explicitly granted retention of their customary, presumably Visigothic laws, when executing transactions of *aprisiones* amongst themselves, and exemption from

---

[96] Chandler, 'Between Court and Counts', 25 follows the speculation of R. Collins, *The Arab Conquest of Spain, 710–797* (Oxford, 1994), 174. Jarrett, 'Settling the King's Lands', 323, cites a letter of Einhard on behalf of Charlemagne sent to recipients in Spain as evidence for a northern area of origin for the refugees. This letter, however, may date to closer to 830, written on behalf of Louis the Pious: *Charlemagne's Courtier: the Complete Einhard*, ed. and trans. P. E. Dutton (Peterborough, ON, 1998), no. 39, p. 148.

[97] Udina i Abelló, 'L'aprisió', 159–60. See also C. Wickham, 'European Forests in the Early Middle Ages: Landscape and Land Clearance', in *Land and Power: Studies in Italian and European Social History, 400–1200* (London, 1994), 155–200 at 156–8, with emphasis on such land constituting part of the royal fisc and having been granted out to settlers by kings.

[98] CC 2, 417–18. '... sicut caeteri liberi homines cum comite suo in exercitum pergant ... in marcha nostra juxta rationabilem ejusdem comitis ordinationem atque admonitionem explorationes et exculbias, quod usitato vocabulo wactas dicunt, facere non neglegant.'

[99] CC 2, 313–14 names forty-two hispani.

[100] A. Dupont, 'L'aprision', and also A. Dupont, 'Considerations sur la colonisation et la vie rurale dans la Rousillon et la Marche d'Espagne', *Annales du Midi* 57 (1955): 223–45. Lewis, *The Development of Society*, 70–4 emphasizes the military and political aspects. Udina i Abelló, 'L'aprisió, 165–6 is a reminder that nobles as well as smallholders were *aprisio* proprietors.

[101] See literature cited in Chandler, 'Between Court and Counts'.

[102] CC 2, 413, based on the language used in the so-called *Constitutio pro Hispanis* of 815, ibid., 418.

comital jurisdiction in legal disputes.[103] These rights and privileges, defended by the emperor Charlemagne himself in favour of a group of land-holders more than thirty years after his military intervention in Spain, provide insight into a complex tenurial and political situation in Septimania and the Spanish March. In 812, a group of forty-two land-holders journeyed from the Spanish March all the way to Aachen. They went before Charlemagne to lodge a group complaint against their local counts; the document their pleas generated is the oldest royal judgement concerning the hispani as a group. The hispani claimed that 'they had sustained many oppressions' at the hands of their counts, who are named in the document, and subordinate officials.[104] They complained that the counts unlawfully charged the *cens*, to which they were exempt. Not only that, the locals, termed *pagenses* and presumably not immigrants, had violated the rights of the hispani in the extreme, depriving them of land over which they exercised full property rights, while the hispani were subjected to other demands through pressure from *saiones* and other legal authorities. Charlemagne ordered these wrongs to be reversed, and commanded both his *missus*, Archibishop John of Arles in Provençe, and his son Louis, then king of Aquitaine, to oversee the rehabilitation of the hispani.[105]

Past scholarship raised doubts as to the efficacy of Carolingian royal government.[106] There is no proof, for example, that the case of the hispani in 812 was in fact resolved to their (and Charlemagne's) satisfaction. The most forceful pronouncements of capitularies and royal judgements may not have been enforceable in the least beyond the royal court itself, as evidence for the actual execution of legislation is hard to come by.[107] Other recent work, however, points to the very fact of the Carolingian empire's existence, namely Charlemagne's successful military campaigns and the rulers' ability to hold disparate regions together in one political system, as the only evidence we should need to understand the effectiveness of royal and imperial governance.[108] For present

---

[103] Ibid., with the same qualification.

[104] The document, edited as CC 2, 313-14, survives in a twelfth-century copy from Narbonne, now Paris, BNF lat. 11015, f. 8 available online at http://gallica.bnf.fr/ark:/12148/btv1b520009994 / r=manuscrits+latins+11015.langFR.

[105] Ibid.

[106] For two examples, see F. L. Ganshof, *The Carolingians and the Frankish Monarchy* (Ithaca, 1971) and Collins, *Charlemagne*, 171–4.

[107] H. Nehlsen, 'Zur Aktualität und Effektivität germanischer Rechtsaufzeichnungen', in P. Classen, ed., *Recht und Schrift im Mittelalter* (Sigmaringen, 1977), 449–502. See now for a different perspective C. Pössel, 'Authors and Recipients of Carolingian Capitularies', in R. Corradini et al, eds, *Texts and Identities in the Early Middle Ages* (Vienna, 2006), 253–74.

[108] B. S. Bachrach, *Charlemagne's Early Campaigns (768–777)* (Leiden, 2013), introduction. See also West, *Reframing the Feudal Revolution*, ch. 1 and Faulkner, *Law and Authority*, chs. 3 and 4 for how

purposes, the fundamental point is that, if governmental power was too minimal, from the perspective of loyal subjects, it would not have been worth receiving an immunity from the king and then going all the way from Septimania and the March to Aachen to get the king to hear complaints and uphold the rights of the immunity. Not much evidence survives of royal pronouncements actually being followed, but there is the question of how much such evidence should be expected and why anyone should record instances of law being followed rather than broken.[109] There is, after all, the Basel Roll, which documents the efforts of royal emissaries carrying out Charlemagne's orders to survey churches in the Holy Land for the purposes of distributing alms to them.[110] Without the survival of a single manuscript fragment, the only textual reference to the emperor's grand plans would have been a reference in Einhard's *Vita Karoli*, and scholars would no doubt have been highly sceptical of the veracity of Einhard's remarks.[111] The evidence of the hispani of 812 making good on their right to royal protection indicates both an earlier grant of such protection to them and the effectiveness of Carolingian royal government.

Study of royal documents concerned with *aprisiones* also reveals how the legal practices of those who followed Visigothic law were integrated into Frankish governance. Jarrett questions the importance of the 'thirty-year rule' to the *aprisio* as a method of clearance and the kings' role in establishing pathways for their power to enter Septimania and the March.[112] Yet it is important to note that the 'thirty-year rule' does not indicate that the holders of *aprisio* lands had no rights to them until after thirty years had passed, but rather that the land in question became fully their property after that time rather than a revocable grant.[113] In its description of the settlement of the matter by assigning it to a *missus* and Louis as sub-king, the 812 diploma further reveals the structure of authority in the March,[114] indicating that although empire-wide the patchwork of *regna* provided the advantages of regionalized governance, Charlemagne maintained ultimate authority.[115] Upon his succession,

---

royal authority and written law was effective, even as local understanding and implementation varied.

[109] On these points, I agree with Innes, 'Charlemagne's Government', 79–85.

[110] M. McCormick, *Charlemagne's Survey of the Holy Land: Wealth, Personnel, and Buildings of a Mediterranean Church between Antiquity and the Middle Ages* (Washington, DC, 2011).

[111] Einhard, *Vita Karoli, MGH SS rer. Germ.* 25, 31–2.

[112] Jarrett, 'Settling the Kings' Lands', 325–7.

[113] Note the argument in Jarrett, 'Settling the Kings' Lands', which implies that I had previously argued otherwise in 'Between Court and Counts'.

[114] Werner, 'Missus-Marchio-Comes', 197; CC 2, 314.

[115] See the notion of frontiers in T. F. X. Noble, 'Louis the Pious and the Frontiers of the Frankish Realm', 333–47. More recent studies of Carolingian frontiers can be found in W. Pohl, I. Wood,

Louis followed the model, confirming and clarifying the rights of the *aprisio* settlers. A capitulary dated to 815 limited the recourse to self-adjudication using Visigothic law by specifying offences as 'major cases' to be decided at the counts' courts, including theft, robbery, and the severing of limbs.[116] Even though Louis restrained the rights of the settlers to a degree by this act, he maintained the direct ties between them and the royal court. Grants of immunity to lay land-holders re-affirmed royal authority.

Jarrett's argument seeks to de-emphasize the role of kings in the clearance and settlement of land by *aprisio*, observing that it makes little sense to find 'clues to the status of tenth-century settlers' in the royal legislation of the ninth century.[117] That assertion is no doubt correct, as is the argument that local individuals carried out the hard work of bringing abandoned or underdeveloped land into cultivation without having first been prompted by the kings to do so. But at the same time, the reverse of Jarrett's proposition is also true: it makes precious little sense to study the evidence for local settlement patterns in the tenth century in order to understand royal policies of the ninth. Charlemagne and Louis the Pious did indeed intervene in the affairs of locals, to legislate the rights of hispani who made *aprisio* clearances.[118] Jarrett also rightly notes that the word 'hispani' does not appear in Louis's first document; however, the phrase 'de partibus Hispaniae ad nos confugerunt' does. If the definition of hispani is, as Jarrett allows, people who came from Hispania, then it remains clear that Louis was concerned with hispani. Given the danger of using evidence from one period as valid for another, it may be too optimistic to conflate royal evidence from 816, 862, and local charters from the early tenth century to dissociate the hispani from being identified as *aprisio* holders, as if conditions had not changed in over a century

---

and H. Reimitz, eds, *The Transformation of Frontiers: From Late Antiquity to the Carolingians*, The Transformation of the Roman World 10 (Leiden, 2001); see especially for general remarks about forming frontiers around the period in question H. Wolfram, 'The Creation of the Carolingian Frontier System c. 800', in ibid., 233–46. For more detail on marches and their counts in the Carolingian period, Stieldorf, *Marken und Markgrafen*, 36–107, 188–229, and 350–423.

[116] CC 2, 418: 'Ipsi vero pro majoribus causis, sicut sunt homicidia, raptus, incendia, depraedationes, membrorum amputationes, furta, latrocinia, alienarum rerum invasiones, et undecunque a vicino suo aut criminaliter aut civiliter fuerit accusatus et ad placitum venire jussus, ad comitis sui mallum omnimodis venire non recusent. Ceteras vero minores causas more suo, sicut hactenus fecisse noscuntur, inter se mutuo definire non prohibeantur'. This paragraph broadened the category of 'major cases', which originally had included only murder, rape, and arson.

[117] Jarrett, 'Settling the Kings' Lands', 334.

[118] CC 2, 312–14 is Charlemagne's response to the complaint by the hispani, and CC 2, 417–19 and 420–1 are constitutions by Louis.

nor from royal perspective to local.[119] Even allowing for a degree of continuity in royal purpose and documentary procedures, the shift in evidence to the local point of view means that the texts are about different situations.[120] Jarrett further cites a royal diploma that mentions hispani without the word *aprisio* or its derivatives appearing. Yet that document mentions the land of the hispani as an exception to the grant, along with land possessed by Bishop Frodoin of Barcelona, and specifies that the hispani took their land from waste – *de heremo traxerunt* – in an echo of the language of *aprisio*; the appearance of the words hispani and *de heremo traxerunt*, moreover, are separated by a lacuna, as indicated in the edition.[121] It is entirely conceivable that the term *aprisio* did in fact appear in the original document, which strengthens the connection between the hispani and *aprisiones*. Another example of hispani turning up in a royal document without *aprisiones* is Louis's second constitution, dated to 816.[122] Jarrett is correct that the word *aprisio* does not appear.[123] But Louis also explicitly refers to the precise conditions of migrating refugees settling in Frankish-controlled territory and their receiving precepts from Charlemagne and Louis as their legal right to hold the land, as well as other circumstances that in earlier documents accompany the concept of *aprisio*. Nor does the text mention any other form of land acquisition, whether by inheritance or purchase, but according to Jarrett's own argument the absence of those terms does not render impossible the ability of hispani to own land by those means. It seems clear that primarily, cleared land, which is the meaning of *aprisio,* is central to the royal legislation concerning these hispani. The connection between refugee migration and increased clearance and settlement of wasteland in Septimania and the Spanish March at the time of Charlemagne and Louis the Pious is indeed supported by a reasonable amount of evidence.

The political situation surrounding frontier areas, those areas where the physical presence of the king was non-existent and that of potential enemies strong, is an important context for understanding the *aprisio* as a tool of the monarchy in the early ninth century.[124] In this context, the right of *aprisio* holders to appeal directly to the king for justice reinforced their special relationship to the rulers, and the grant consolidated the structures of Carolingian politics. For *aprisio* holders, the royal court

---

[119] Jarrett, 'Settling the Kings' Lands', 324–5, especially note 16, which cites evidence from 862, 816, and 927.

[120] This point is important in terms of methodology in general, but especially as regards the debate over *aprisiones*, as Jarrett in his article uses a similar argument against reading forward and backward in time from Charlemagne to Charles the Bald and back.

[121] CC 2, 355–8.   [122] CC 2, 420–1.   [123] 'Settling the Kings' Lands', 325 with n. 16.

[124] J. M. H. Smith, *Province and Empire: Brittany and the Carolingians* (Cambridge, 1992), 2–3.

served as a resource for justice in local controversies and thus facilitated the binding of the marcher areas more closely to the monarchy.[125] Distance, however, posed problems for *aprisio* holders, counts, and kings alike. The settlers had to deal with the realities of local power,[126] while the rulers and their subordinates faced the difficult situation of insinuating themselves into the political networks of a newly conquered area. Constant military activity, predicated on the proximity of Muslims, enhanced the power of the local warrior class, especially the counts. The counts of militarily charged frontier areas like the Spanish March possessed more extensive political and judicial authority than their counterparts elsewhere in the Carolingian world.[127] Their remoteness from the king allowed counts in the Spanish March freedom to exercise their authority independently, while their proximity to prospects for tribute and plunder as well as potential Muslim aggression encouraged them to strengthen their own control of the region.[128] These conditions made all the more urgent the king's task of establishing links between himself and local laymen of the military class. About twenty years after he must have made the first *aprisio* grant to hispani fleeing from Muslim rule, existing evidence suggests that Charlemagne granted similar rights to Goths and hispani living in Barcelona and the fortress Terrassa. In fact, Charles the Bald issued a capitulary for the hispani of Barcelona and Terrassa, almost surely the descendants of the immigrants of previous generations, that explicitly mentions the precedents of Charlemagne and Louis the Pious.[129] Such an act suggests that the earlier Charles, now emperor, recognized the usefulness of the guarantee of rights, in some ways

---

[125] A similar situation prevailed for monasteries in Alsace. See H. Hummer, *Politics and Power in Early Medieval Europe: Alsace and the Frankish Realm, 600–1000* (Cambridge, 2005), 62–4.

[126] See local disputes involving *aprisio* holders and local bishops, e.g., J. M. Marquès, ed., *Cartoral, dit de Carlemany, del bisbe de Girona (s. IX–XIV)* 1 (Barcelona, 1993), nos. 8 and 9. J. L. Nelson, *The Frankish World, 750–900* (London, 1996), xxv–xxvi; H.-W. Goetz, 'Social and Military Institutions', in R. McKitterick, ed., *The New Cambridge Medieval History*, vol. 2, c.700–c.900 (Cambridge, 1995); J. M. Salrach, 'Conquesta de l'espai agrari i conflictes per la terra a la Catalunya carolíngia i comtal', in X. Barral i Altet, et al., eds, *Catalunya i França meridional a l'entorn de l'any Mil* (Barcelona, 1991), 206–9 addresses the *aprisio* in this context. See also Nelson, 'Dispute Settlement in Carolingian West Francia', in W. Davies and P. Fouracre, eds, *The Settlement of Disputes in Early Medieval Europe* (Cambridge, 1986), 48 for an example from north of the Pyrenees.

[127] Werner, 'Missus-Marchio-Comes', 195 on the role of the *marchiones* vis-à-vis the king and local counts, 212–18 on the roles and powers of *marchiones*.

[128] Ibid; T. Reuter, 'Plunder and Tribute in the Carolingian Empire', *Transactions of the Royal Historical Society 5th series* 35 (1985): 75–94.

[129] CC 2, 415–16, based on documents of Louis the Pious and Charles the Bald at 417–19 and 422–5 (also edited by Boretius, *MGH Capit.* I, 261–263 and Tessier, no. 46); see again Abadal's criteria for reconstructing the document, 399–411. Lewis, *The Development of Society*, 73.

resembling immunity, in preventing his marcher counts from ensuring their own authority.

Royal recognition of *aprisiones* as grants of fiscal land was one way that the monarchs established and strengthened ties to individuals in Septimania and the Spanish March. The *aprisio* does not appear in documentation from Carolingian territory before the Frankish conquest of Catalonia. Further, of all the realms governed by the Franks, it appears only in Catalonia, serving the needs of the local population of immigrants and the desire of kings to increase settlement.[130] The special circumstances of its locality, moreover, allowed the Carolingian rulers to ensure the presence of their own authority in the March through their protection of *aprisio* immunities.[131] We can see in the *aprisio* grant the role of local elements within broader Carolingian structures of power. Moreover, it is clear that the two main groups in the society of the Spanish March were the Goths, who ran the region prior to the Carolingian conquest, and the hispani, immigrants from elsewhere in Spain. What seems to have been most important for their identity, as far as the Frankish court was concerned, was place of origin. The counts of the region made up a third important component of the regional society, and all three confronted each other regarding the possession of land. When land had been granted by kings to hispani as *aprisiones*, the tenure and rights of the immigrants were upheld, and amongst these rights was recourse to their traditional law.[132] By trumpeting the variety of peoples under their rule and the number of laws at their disposal, Carolingian rulers could subtly lay claim to universal, imperial authority. This process of incorporating the Spanish March began under Charlemagne and continued under Louis the Pious.

THE POLITICS OF CULTURE

By the time of the first royal *aprisio* grants, immunities were a normal cog in Carolingian political machinery.[133] Holders of royally sanctioned *aprisiones* possessed not only land, but also immunity: they stood outside the jurisdiction of the counts. Not only did grants of *aprisiones* chronologically and geographically coincide with grants of immunity to

---

[130] A. Dupont, 'Considerations sur la colonisation', 223–45; A. Dupont, 'L'aprision', 177–213, 375–99. See more recently C. Duhamel-Amado and A. Catafau, 'Fidéles et aprisionnaires en réseaux dans la Gothie des IXe et Xe siècles', in *La royauté et les élites dans l'Europe carolingienne (début IXe siècle aux environs de 920)*, ed. R. Le Jan (Villeneuve d'Ascq, 1998), 437–65 and Udina i Abelló, 'L'aprisio', 159–70, with appendix.

[131] Chandler, 'Between Court and Counts', 19–44.   [132] CC 2, 312–14.

[133] Rosenwein, *Negotiating Space*, 97.

monasteries, but they also contained immunities from jurisdiction similar to those contained in the diplomas issued to monasteries. *Aprisio* holders and royal monasteries fulfilled similar functions, both in repopulating the region and as recipients of a privileged judicial status that bound them to the king. The expansion of monastic enterprises in Catalonia, including settling in new lands and establishing new houses, developed almost in tandem with *aprisiones* and the concomitant expansion of land under cultivation. In the Pyrenean region as in the rest of the empire, monastic immunities provided another means to this end. Carolingian rulers placed monasteries in the March under royal protection just as they did *aprisiones*, as the wealth of immunity charters demonstrates. Charlemagne himself made perhaps only one grant of immunity to a monastery in Catalonia, that of Santa Maria of Arles in modern Roussillon.[134] It is more certain that in 820, Louis the Pious bestowed immunity on Arles. Much of the monastery's land was formerly deserted, indicated by the phrase *ab heremo*.[135] The act of 820 is representative of the other immunities, in that it concedes to the monastery three elements: royal protection, termed *tuitio* or *mundeburdium*, a no-entry clause prohibiting interference from any *iudex publicus* or other official, and the right to elect succeeding abbots.[136]

Monasteries in the Spanish March had to be protected for a few different but related reasons. First, the discussion in Chapter 1 pointed to a possible decline in the number and vitality of monastic houses in the region and in neighbouring Septimania during the eighth century. Of course, the principal 'evidence' for that conclusion is a stunning lack of documentation, rather than positive accounts of monasteries having been abandoned. Further, Carolingian kings used monasteries as points of contact in the social fabric of the localities of the empire.[137] No less important was the concept of spiritual patronage, that by helping monasteries and churches as institutions, one procured benefit for one's soul.[138] There is also the related notion that the

---

[134] CC 2, 22–3, which give not a document but speculation on the existence of one based on later textual sources. This is Arles-sur-Tech (dep. Pyrénées-Orientales), not to be confused with Arles in dep. Bouches-du-Rhône.

[135] Ibid., 24–6.   [136] Rosenwein, *Negotiating Space*, 42–52.

[137] This idea will be explored below, but see the recent studies that have influenced the approach taken, especially Innes, *State and Society in the Early Middle Ages: the Middle Rhine* Valley, *400–1100* (Cambridge, 2000), as well as Hummer, *Politics and Power*. See the earlier work by Davies, *Small Worlds: the Village Community in Early Medieval Brittany* (Berkeley and Los Angeles, 1988).

[138] See B. H. Rosenwein, *To Be the Neighbor of Saint Peter: the Social Meaning of Cluny's Property, 909–1049* (Ithaca, 1989). There is application of the idea to the study of social and political networks on the local level in Innes, *State and Society*, 13–50; C. Wickham, *The Mountains and the City: the Tuscan Apennines in the Early Middle Ages* (Oxford, 1988).

monarchs were charged with fostering the development of the Christian religion in their realms, which led Charlemagne to promote educational, clerical, and social reform initiatives.[139] The drive for correctness that characterized the Carolingian *renovatio* extended to monastic observance, favouring the Rule of St. Benedict.[140] In examples from the Spanish March, the receipt of royal grants shows the connections being forged between the rulers and their partners. Benedict's Rule did not address this fundamental aspect of Carolingian monasticism, namely, that monasteries would function in concert with royal initiatives to work with wealthy and powerful men in localities throughout the empire and to establish footholds in new regions.[141] Yet, as elsewhere in the empire, emperors could intervene in the affairs of monasteries as a way to further their control of sociopolitical situations.[142]

In the Spanish March, however, many existing monasteries followed the traditional Visigothic Rule of St Fructuosus.[143] The first attested Catalonian monastery, Santa Maria of Arles, appears in documents from around the year 780 as having been founded by a refugee named Castellanus; in 820 Louis granted the abbey royal privileges and protection because it followed Benedictine observance.[144] Other monasteries also received royal grants on the condition that the Rule of Benedict governed their communities. Charlemagne favoured the monastery of Gerrí in the western counties of Pallars and Ribagorça, and the Visigothic-era foundations of St-Andreu de Tresponts and Tavèrnoles in Urgell itself.[145] After the military and cultural storms associated with the Spanish March had died down, Louis still enforced the adoption of Benedict's Rule in

---

[139] M. de Jong, 'Carolingian Monasticism: the Power of Prayer', in R. McKitterick, ed., *The New Cambridge Medieval History*, vol. 2, c.700–c.900 (Cambridge, 1995), 622–53; W. Ullmann, *The Carolingian Renaissance and the Idea of Kingship* (London, 1969); A. Angenendt, *Taufe und Politik in Frühen Mittelalter* (1973), 143–68.

[140] J. Semmler, 'Benedictus II: Una Regula – Una Consuetudo', in W. Lourdaux and D. Verhelst, eds, *Benedictine Culture 750–1050* (Leuven, 1983). See also P. Riché, *Ecoles et enseignement dans la Haut Moyen Age, Fin du Ve siècle – milieu du Xie siècle* (Paris, 1989), 87.

[141] A. Diem, 'The Carolingians and the *Regula Benedicti*', in R. Meens, et al, eds, *Religious Franks: Religion and Power in the Frankish Kingdoms: Studies in Honour of Mayke de Jong* (Manchester, 2016), 243–61.

[142] J. Semmler, 'Benediktinische Reform und kaiserliches Privileg. Die Kloster im Umkreis Benedikts von Aniane', in G. Arnaldi, et al, eds, *Società, istituzioni, spiritualità. Studi in onore di Cinzio Violante*, 2 vols. (Spoleto, 1994), vol. 2, 787–823.

[143] J. M. Salrach, *El procés*, vol. 1, 71. See also a royal diploma in CC 2, 46–7, that mentions the monks living *sub normam religionis*, which does not necessarily mean the Rule of Benedict, but closes by insisting upon Benedictine observance.

[144] CC 2, 66; Lewis, *The Development of Society*, 48.

[145] CC 2, 260–2; CC 3, 20–35; Lewis, *The Development of Society*, 48–9.

the Spanish March when he granted land and privileges to several monasteries in the years around 820.[146] Thereafter, Benedictine practice gradually spread to monasteries throughout the Spanish March.[147] Like the integration of the March into political networks, the process of monastic reform was gradual.

Likewise, the Carolingians' conquest of the Spanish March is best understood within the context of their complementary concern with orthodox religion.[148] Charlemagne and others treated the region as if it were clearly part of his kingdom. That meant the 'Gothic' inhabitants were expected to accept the court-sponsored programme of cultural reform. If religious practice deviated, reform was encouraged; this was the case with Benedictine observance in monastic communities, but also with doctrine and teaching in the work of secular clergy. Without instituting religious reform, Charlemagne and the Franks could incorporate Catalonia into their civilization neither politically nor culturally. Just as reform initiatives were designed to bring about correct belief and practice in the Frankish heartland, missionary activity went hand in hand with the establishment of Carolingian authority over newly conquered territories.[149] Similarly, preaching and writing against a new perceived threat to orthodoxy, Spanish Adoptionism, were necessary to integrate the Spanish March with the rest of realm. When seen in this context, the rebuttal of late eighth-century Adoptionism emerges not only as an important theological dispute, but also as a political issue. It was a means to establish cultural hegemony in this conquered area in an effort to stabilize it as a new part of the Carolingian kingdom during the ongoing process of incorporation under Charlemagne and Louis the Pious.[150]

[146] These are discussed below.
[147] C. J. Bishko, 'The Pactual Tradition in Hispanic Monasticism', reprinted in *Spanish and Portuguese Monastic History, 600–1300* (Aldershot, 1984), 1–16; A. M. Mundó, 'Monastic Movements in the East Pyrenees', in N. Hunt, ed., *Cluniac Monasticism in the Central Middle Ages* (Hamden, CT, 1971), 98–122; M. Zimmermann, *Écrire et lire en Catalogne (IX–XII siècle)* (Madrid, 2003), 550–68; 761–3.
[148] For a consideration of three major doctrinal controversies in this period, see H. Nagel, *Karl der Große und die theologischen Herausforderungen seiner Zeit: Zur Wechselwirkung zwischen Theologie und Politik im Zeitalter des großen Frankenherrschers* (Frankfurt am Main, 1998).
[149] See R. E. Sullivan, 'The Carolingian Missionary and the Pagan', *Speculum* 28 (1953): 705–40, and J. Palmer, 'Defining Paganism in the Carolingian World', *EME* 15 (2007): 402–25. Particularly on the case of Saxony, A. Angenendt, *Kaiserherrschaft und Königstaufe: Kaiser, Könige und Päpste als geistliche Patrone in der abendländischen Missionsgeschichte* (Berlin, 1984), C. Carrol, 'The Bishoprics of Saxony in the First Century after Christianization', *EME* 8 (1999): 219–45.
[150] C. J. Chandler, 'Heresy and Empire: the Role of the Adoptionist Controversy in Charlemagne's Conquest of the Spanish March', *International History Review* 24 (2002): 505–27. See also U. Vones-Liebenstein, 'Katalonien zwischen Maurenherrschaft und Frankenreich. Probleme um die Ablösung westgotich-mozarabischer Kirchenstrukturen', in R. Berndt, ed., *Das*

The controversy and debate surrounding Spanish Adoptionist doctrine was developed by Elipandus, the elderly archbishop of Toledo and primate of the church in Spain under Muslim rule, and defended by Felix, bishop of Urgell, which came into Carolingian hands by about 790.[151] In broad terms, these prelates claimed that whereas Christ, in his divine nature, is the true Son of God, in his human nature he was the adoptive Son of God.[152] The root of the problem for Alcuin, the most active scholar on the Carolingian side of the debate, hinged on the use of the word *adoptiuus*, rather than *assumptus* to describe the human form, the man Jesus.[153] In other words, for Elipandus and Felix, the key issue was the self-emptying or self-abasement of the Word to take human form, but for the Carolingians it was the reverse, the assumption of a sinless human nature up into the divine Trinity. In short, the Carolingian side interpreted the Adoptionist position as constituting a denial of the unity of Christ's two natures in one person. While modern understandings have accepted that the Carolingian side of the debate cannot be said to represent their opponents accurately, accusations of Nestorianism rang out in the ninth century. As the work of Susan Keefe has shown in her study of Frankish commentaries on the Creed, the Carolingians were very concerned about belief in the Trinity. The survival of hundreds of texts in manuscripts attests to a considerable preoccupation.[154] Several of these texts concern the Adoptionist controversy directly,[155] tempting the observation that the controversy, which took place early in the reform movement under

---

Frankfurter Konzil von 794: Kristallisationspunkt karolingischer Kultur, vol. 1: *Politik und Kirche* (Mainz, 1997), 453–505 for a broader perspective than that taken in this chapter, but not one at odds with the larger study as a whole.

[151] The best treatment of the controversy is Cavadini, *The Last Christology of the West* (Philadelphia, 1993); see also C. Chazelle, *The Crucified God in the Carolingian Era: Theology and Art of Christ's Passion* (Cambridge, 2001), 52–99. For earlier work see the introduction to G. Blumenshine, ed., *Liber Alcuini contra haeresim Felicis: Edition with an Introduction* (Vatican City, 1980); W. Heil, 'Der Adoptianismus, Alkuin, und Spanien', in B. Bischoff, ed. *Karl der Große*, vol. 2 *Das geistige Leben* (Düsseldorf, 1965); E. Amann, *L'Epoque Carolingienne*, eds A. Fliche and V. Martin, *Histoire de l'Eglise* vol. 6 (Paris, 1947).

[152] Cavadini, *Last Christology*, 80–3 and Appendix 81, 107–27, explains the teachings of Felix.

[153] Alcuin, *Contra Felicem Urgellitanum libri VII*, in *PL*, 101, ed. J.-P. Migne (Paris, 1844), 172, 213; *idem* in Blumenshine, ed., *Liber Alcuini*, 31, 32. Ganz, 'Theology and the Organization of Thought', in R. McKitterick, ed., *The New Cambridge Medieval History, vol. 2, c.700–c.900* (Cambridge, 1995), 762–63. See Nagel, *Karl der Große und die theologischen Herausforderungen seiner Zeit*, 94.

[154] See S. Keefe, *A Catalogue of Works Pertaining to the Explanation of the Creed in Carolingian Manuscripts* (Turnhout, 2012).

[155] Keefe, *A Catalogue*, nos. 50, 95, 165, 167, 307, 315, 316, 317.

Charlemagne, was important for shaping the Carolingian fixation on the Trinity.[156]

It must be made clear that, rather than setting out to destroy the indigenous Visigothic church, Charlemagne and his scholars wanted simply to rid the Frankish kingdom of what they perceived as the danger of heresy that had infiltrated a newly conquered territory, and to correct its perpetrators beyond their borders.[157] The danger of Spanish Adoptionism, as the Carolingian court saw it, was that it attracted followers, and that would pose problems for integrating the new region 'into the Carolingian fold'.[158] The threat of heresy was sufficiently strong to muster resources against it almost on a par with those employed in more renowned Carolingian efforts to combat Byzantine iconodulism.[159] Both issues shared attention at the great Council of Frankfurt in 794.[160] In any case, Charlemagne saw himself and his court as the final voice on orthodox belief, within the bounds of his kingdom and beyond. His scholars exerted themselves to organize missions to the pagans and to compose a refutation to the perceived Byzantine error; the activity directed towards the

[156] C. J. Chandler, 'Agobard and Adoptionism: a Controversy Continues', in proceedings of Colloque international: Lyon dans l'Europe carolingienne – Autour d'Agobard (816–2016) (Lyon, forthcoming) will address this theme.

[157] See the interesting argument of B. Effros, '*De Partibus Saxoniae* and the Regulation of Mortuary Custom: a Carolingian Campaign of Christianization or the Suppression of Saxon Identity?' *Revue Belge de Philologie et d'Histoire* 75 (1997): 267–86, which somewhat parallels the point made here. Another parallel argument is made by Y. Hen, *The Royal Patronage of Liturgy in Frankish Gaul to the Death of Charles the Bald (877)* (London, 2001).

[158] R. Kramer, 'Adopt, Adapt and Improve: Dealing with the Adoptionist Controversy at the Court of Charlemagne', in R. Meens et al., eds, *Religious Franks: Religion and Power in the Frankish Kingdoms: Studies in Honour of Mayke de Jong* (Manchester, 2016), 32–50. The nice turn of phrase is found at 33. See also M. Innes, '"Immune from Heresy": Defining the Boundaries of Carolingian Christianity', in P. Fouracre and D. Ganz, eds, *Frankland: the Franks and the World of the Early Middle Ages. Studies in Honour of Dame Jinty Nelson* (Manchester, 2008), 101–25.

[159] T. F. X. Noble, *Images, Iconoclasm, and the Carolingians* (Philadelphia, 2009) is an excellent study of the history of the controversy over images, which situates the eighth-century dispute in its historical context and wider development from the seventh to ninth centuries. Cavadini, *The Last Christology of the West*, as noted, is very valuable for understanding the intricacies and fine points of the competing doctrines of the so-called Adoptionist controversy, but there is no work on the subject comparable to Noble's in terms of placing the controversy in its wider context.

[160] *MGH* Conc. 2, 1, 110–71. See also some of the essays generated by a commemorative conference: J. Marenbon, 'Alcuin, the Council of Frankfort and the Beginnings of Medieval Philosophy', in *Das frankfurter Konzil von 794: Kristallisationspunkt karolingischer Kultur*, ed. R. Berndt, vol. 2: *Kultur und Theologie* (Mainz, 1997), 603–15; J. L. Nelson, 'The Siting of the Council at Frankfort: Some Reflections on Family and Politics', in ibid., vol. 1, 149–65; T. Hainthaler, 'Von Toledo nach Frankfurt: dogmengeschichtliche Untersuchungen zur adoptianistischen Kontroverse', in ibid., vol. 2, 809–60; J. C. Cavadini, 'Elipandus and His Critics at the Council of Frankfort', in ibid., vol. 2, 787–807.

Gothic provinces was in the same vein.[161] Two of these scholars, Alcuin and Paulinus of Aquileia, as well as a series of church councils, condemned Spanish Adoptionism throughout the 790s.[162]

Older studies of the Carolingian cultural reform too often interpreted such efforts as little more than intellectual posturing. They criticize Carolingian opposition to the doctrines of others as arising from misunderstanding or overzealous promotion of their own intellectual and political positions.[163] However, for the Carolingian period, it is impossible to separate political motives from religious ones. Alcuin and Paulinus, and later Benedict of Aniane and Agobard of Lyon, tried, by so vigorously combating the Spanish Adoptionist doctrine, to ensure correct belief as they saw it throughout the Frankish kingdom. That is certainly true, but proper understanding of their work evades us when isolated from the political concerns of the age. The Adoptionist controversy represents an attempt to buttress orthodox Christianity in a recently acquired territory as that territory and its people became part of the Carolingian kingdom.

Certain elements of the controversy point to differences in culture and tradition between the Spanish Adoptionists and the Carolingians.[164] To be precise, Spanish Adoptionism began with the reaction of Elipandus, in his capacity as archbishop of Toledo, to an odd doctrine preached by a certain Migetius, a priest from the Muslim-held southern province of Baetica who taught that each divine person of the Trinity made a historical appearance on earth in human form.[165] Some modern scholars have argued that Adoptionism was influenced by Islam. That is, by making Christ the adopted Son of God, Christianity would be more

---

[161] See R. E. Sullivan, 'Carolingian Missionary Theories', *The Catholic Historical Review* 42 (1956), 273–95; J. Deér, 'Karl der Große und der Untergang des Awarenreiches', in H. Beumann, ed., *Karl der Große 1 Persönlichkeit und Geschichte*, ed., vol. 1 (Düsseldorf, 1965), 719–91; Noble, *Images, Iconoclasm, and the Carolingians*, chs. 3–4; A. Bonnery, 'A propos de Concile de Francfort (794). L'action de moines de Septimanie dans la lutte contre l'Adoptianisme', in *Das frankfurter Konzil*, vol. 2, 767–86.

[162] In addition to the works cited above, see G. Fedalto, 'Il significato politico de Paolino, Patriarca de Aquileia, e la sua posizione nella controversia Adozionista', in *Das frankfurter Konzil*, vol. 1, 103–23.

[163] T. F. X. Noble, 'The Papacy in the Eighth and Ninth Centuries', in R. McKitterick, ed., *The New Cambridge Medieval History*, vol. 2, c.700–c.900 (Cambridge, 1995), 563–86 at 578–69 for a synopsis of this traditional view. See also J. Herrin, *The Formation of Christendom* (Princeton, 1987), 434–45. Amongst older works see H. Fichtenau, *The Carolingian Empire*, Peter Munz trans. (Oxford, 1957), 69–70.

[164] See W. Heil, *Alkuinstudien 1: Zur Chronologie und Bedeutung des Adoptianismusstreites* (Düsseldorf, 1970), 66–72 for chronology of the controversy.

[165] A. von Harnack, *History of Dogma*, vol. 5, trans. J. Millar, 3rd German ed. (New York, 1958), 281; J. F. Rivera Recio, *El Adopcionismo en España siglo VIII: Historia y Doctrina* (Toledo, 1980), 31–2.

acceptable to the Muslim rulers of al-Andalus.[166] Others have seen the formulation as a way for Christians in Asturias to break with the Visigothic past.[167] The Carolingian denunciation of Spanish Adoptionism as Nestorianism coloured the traditional view of Adoptionism so that only in the last generation or so has it been understood as an independent development. These older views have been revised in favour of one situating Spanish Adoptionism in a more strictly Western heritage that, due to its location in Spain, was rather isolated from the fifth-century Eastern councils, especially that of Chalcedon, and emphasizing the conditions facing the church in eighth-century Spain.[168] Since Alcuin and others drew upon the Eastern councils for their authoritative statements against earlier, somewhat similar teachings, it stands to reason that the debaters spoke at cross-purposes, both in face-to-face confrontations and in their writing. Thus, the very core of the dispute illustrates the need for cultural integration that would bring Charlemagne's new subjects in line with the religious teachings being propounded across the rest of the Frankish realms.

How the so-called Adoptionist doctrine reached Urgell in the Pyrenees from Toledo in Muslim territory remains uncertain, but it is likely that Elipandus and Felix communicated with one another as members of a still-unified Visigothic church that existed despite Muslim control over most of the peninsula. Elipandus may have been searching for support against anti-Adoptionists in the fledgling Christian kingdoms in the north, and Felix perhaps sought to build the prestige of his own see by closer association with Toledo.[169] By 789 the unity of Elipandus and Felix's church was in jeopardy.[170] On one hand, kings and prelates in Asturias seem to have drawn on Carolingian influence as a way to develop their own independence from the defunct Visigothic

---

[166] J. McWilliam, 'The Context of Spanish Adoptionism: a Review', in M. Gervers and R. Jibran Bikhazi, eds, *Conversion and Continuity: Indigenous Christian Communities in Islamic* Lands, *Eighth to Eighteenth Centuries*, Papers in Mediaeval Studies 9 (Toronto, 1990), 75–88.

[167] A. Frez, 'El adopcionismo i la evoluciones religiosas i politicas en el reino astur', *Hispania: Revista Española de Historia* 58 (1998): 971–93; Frez, 'El adopcionismo: disidencia religiosa en la Península Ibérica (fines del siglo VIII–principios del siglo IX)', *Clio i Crimen: Revisto del Centro de Historia de Crimen de Durango* 1 (2004): 115–34.

[168] See Cavadini, *Last Christology*, 5–7. Also see K. Schäferdiek, 'Der adoptianische Streit im Rahmen der spanischen Kirchengeschichte', *Zeitschrift für Kirchengeschichte* 80–1 (1969–1970): 291–311, 1–16 and A. Cabaniss, 'The Heresiarch Felix', *The Catholic Historical Review* 39 (1953): 129–41 at 130.

[169] Cavadini, *Last Christology*, 71–2; R. d'Abadal i de Vinyals, *La batalla del adopcionismo en la desintegración de la iglesia visigoda* (Barcelona, 1949), reprinted with augmentation in Abadal, CC 1, at 76–7, states that the two 'were lifelong friends'.

[170] The classic overall study is Abadal, *La batalla*, 93–181.

kingdom.[171] On the other, once Carolingian forces occupied the region around Urgell, Felix's teachings attracted the attention of a king and court bent on religious reform. The Carolingian kings used church personnel and resources as an integral part of their rule; attempts to reform religious practice aimed at the salvation of souls, but also the stability of society and royal rule.[172] Religious observance could serve the king as a primary unifying factor in his vast dominions, since it was not Carolingian policy to eradicate all aspects of existing culture in conquered areas. The parallel practice most applicable to the Goths of Septimania and the Spanish March is the continued use of Visigothic law. In a kingdom with many personal laws, the law of God was universal. The *Admonitio generalis* and other documents served as calls for orthodoxy and proper comportment.[173] It was precisely the universality and unity Carolingians strove for that Spanish Adoptionism stood to thwart.

Deeply rooted local culture survived, in its ever-developing form, even in those regions that Pippin III had added to the kingdom in the 750s.[174] People in the Frankish kingdom, whether established there or newly arrived immigrants (the hispani), shared the Visigothic liturgy from which Elipandus drew the language of Adoptionism.[175] Despite these indications that deeply ingrained elements of religious culture could have occasioned the actual teaching of and adherence to Adoptionist doctrine in Septimania and the Spanish March, Donald Bullough asserted that Adoptionism probably never was an important social issue for the Carolingian regime.[176] In a letter to Archbishop Arn of Salzburg of 796, however, Alcuin boasted that 20,000 heretics, men and women from all strata of society, had been converted in Septimania and the Spanish March.[177] Although some historians who studied the controversy

---

[171] J. Escalona, 'Family Memories: Inventing Alfonso I of Asturias', in I. Alfonso, H. Kennedy, and J. Escalona, eds, *Building Legitimacy: Political Discoures and Forms of Legitimacy in Medieval Societies* (Leiden, 2004), 223–62, at 226–32.

[172] J. L. Nelson, 'Kingship and Empire in the Carolingian World', in R. McKitterick, ed., *Carolingian Culture: Emulation and Innovation* (Cambridge, 1994), 52–87 at 50–1, 64.

[173] J. J. Contreni, 'The Carolingian Renaissance: Education and Literary Culture', in R. McKitterick, ed., *The New Cambridge Medieval History*, vol. 2, c.700–c.900 (Cambridge, 1995), 709–57, at esp. 709–25. E. Magnou-Nortier, 'L'*Admonitio generalis*. Étude critique', in Josep Perarnau, ed., *Jornades internacionals d'estudi sobre el bisbe Feliu d'Urgell* (Barcelona, 2000), 195–242 puts forth an interesting, if not altogether convincing, reassessment of the *Admonitio generalis*.

[174] Riché, *Ecoles et enseignement dans la Haut Moyen Age*, 87.

[175] R. E. Reynolds, 'The Visigothic Liturgy in the Realm of Charlemagne', in *Das frankfurter Konzil*, vol. 2, 919–45; Ganz, 'Theology and the Organization of Thought', 762.

[176] Bullough, 'Alcuin and the Kingdom of Heaven', 48, 50, 58–59. See also 43, where he notes that Alcuin's letter to 'the monks of Gothia' concerns baptism explicitly.

[177] Alcuin, *Ep.* 208, *MGH Epp.* 4, 345–6.

supposed that most followers of Felix in Carolingian realms were monks and secular clergy, Alcuin mentions the *populus*, including lay men and women.[178] The number 20,000 is, of course, a symbolic exaggeration, but Alcuin's use of it, along with vocabulary indicating common lay people's involvement, nonetheless reveals an official perception of Adoptionism as a major problem on the ground and not only as a theological argument amongst intellectual elites. In any case, Charlemagne, along with his bishops and other advisers, was acutely worried about anything that challenged the orthodox interpretation of the Trinity. Spanish Adoptionism posed just such a threat and had to be dealt with very seriously, and individuals in Septimania and the Spanish March had to be taught correct belief so that the kingdom would be free of error.

The conquest of the Spanish March provides context for the Adoptionist controversy. The Carolingians needed to reinforce their military overlordship and political patronage with cultural harmony. Their armies struggled against Saracens while their preachers fought the Felicians.[179] Early medieval ecclesiastics and rulers drew no distinction between internal and external missionizing, which is to say that missionaries and teachers preaching the true religion were needed within the kingdom's bounds as well as outside the kingdom amongst pagans.[180] It may have been Alcuin who coordinated a preaching mission in the Spanish March, Septimania, and southern parts of Aquitaine conducted by Benedict of Aniane, Bishop Leidrad of Lyon, and Archbishop Nibridius of Narbonne.[181] Leidrad and Nibridius were respected churchmen whose sees were quite near to the area concerned, and thus made for logical selection for the missionizing duty. In an earlier study, I suggested that, in the light of John Cavadini's argument that the Carolingians and Adoptionists were at odds because of the way their different cultural

---

[178] See Ganz, 'Theology and the Organization of Thought', 763–4; Blumenshine, 'Alcuin's *Liber Contra Haeresim Felicis* and the Frankish Kingdom', 222–33 at 228, who posits the wide acceptance of Adoptionism in Southern Gaul and assumes most Adoptionists to be monks, although he presents no evidence.

[179] See the study, much more detailed than space here permits, of C. Baraut, 'La intervenció carolíngia antifeliciana al bisbat d'Urgell i les seves conseqüències religioses i culturals (segles viii–ix)', in *Jornades internacionals d'estudi sobre el bisbe Feliu d'Urgell*, ed. Josep Perarnau (Barcelona, 2000), 155–93.

[180] S. Vanderputten, 'Faith and Politics in Early Medieval Society: Charlemagne and the Frustrating Failure of an Ecclesiological Project', *Revue d'histoire ecclésiastique* 96 (2001): 311–32, at 99. See also H. Mayr-Harting, 'The West: the Age of Conversion (700–1050)', in J. McManners, ed., *The Oxford Illustrated History of Christianity* (Oxford, 1990), 92–121; S. Airlie, 'True Teachers and Pious Kings: Salzburg, Louis the German, and Christian Order', in R. Gameson and H. Leyser, eds, *Belief and Culture in the Middle Ages: Studies Presented to Henry Mayr-Harting* (Oxford, 2001), 89–105 at 191.

[181] Bonnery, 'A propos de concile de francfort', 767–86.

traditions shaped their Christologies, Benedict's Visigothic heritage was significant for his role in preaching against Adoptionism.[182] The baptism liturgy has long served as an indication of the religious language that the Old Spanish rite and Adoptionist teachings shared, and I previously high-lighted its place in the controversy.[183] Those conclusions should be tempered. For one thing, Roger Reynolds has shown that the liturgy promulgated throughout the Frankish kingdom, in particular the rituals related to baptism and marriage, was permeated with Old Spanish influences.[184] For another, Yitzhak Hen has pointed out that there is no real evidence for Charlemagne's court-sponsored reforms having sought to eliminate the varied regional liturgical practices within his realm.[185] Indeed, they clearly embraced texts and practices from beyond the Frankish and Roman traditions strictly defined. The reformers indeed used texts from Visigothic Spain alongside those from papal Rome and allowed for people in different parts of the empire to continue their traditional practices. In short, for the Carolingian reform effort, unity of purpose did not require uniformity in practice.[186]

Seventy years ago, the idea of embracing Adoptionist teaching was interpreted as an anti-Carolingian, anti-papal move by those in Spain and the Spanish March to preserve their independence.[187] But this idea cannot be sustained. First, the doctrine was articulated outside the context of Carolingian expansion and within the context of a controversy in Spain; Charlemagne intervened later. Kings and two bishops in Asturias took stances against the doctrine as part of their reform of royal authority; they were copying the Carolingian position in order to act regally and to distance themselves from the Visigothic kingdom's legacy. Rather than oppose the Carolingians' foreign interference, these Asturians embraced the Frankish understanding of orthodoxy. Of course the same can be said of bishops and counts in Septimania and the Spanish March.

---

[182] Chandler, 'Heresy and Empire', 525–6, building on Cavadini, *Last Christology*, 24–44, 71–102, see also 104.

[183] Chandler, 'Heresy and Empire', 516–17, citing R. E. Reynolds, 'The Organisation, Law, and Liturgy of the Western Church, 700–900', in R. McKitterick, ed. *The New Cambridge Medieval History*, vol. 2, c.700–c.900 (Cambridge, 1995), 587–621 at 619–620; Ganz, 'Theology and the Organization of Thought', 762. See also Bullough, 'Alcuin and the Kingdom of Heaven', 43, where he notes that Alcuin's letter to 'the monks of Gothia' concerns baptism explicitly.

[184] R. E. Reynolds, 'The Visigothic Liturgy in the Realm of Charlemagne', in *Das frankfurter Konzil*, vol. 2, 919–45, at 925–6 for baptism, and 927 for marriage.

[185] Hen, *The Royal Patronage of Liturgy*, 69–89.

[186] Ibid. For more on this line of argument, Davis, *Charlemagne's Practice*, esp. Part II and McKitterick, *Charlemagne*, ch. 4. Even Theodulf articulated the idea that unity meant in the faith, not in the details of celebrating the service, which were free to vary from place to place. See the *Opus Caroli regis*, ed. A. Freeman in *MGH Conc.* 2, Supp. 1, 135–6.

[187] See, for example, A. Cabaniss, 'The Heresiarch Felix', *The Catholic Historical Review* 39 (1953): 129–41, as well as Catalan-language works cited above.

Furthermore, modern historians do a disservice to honest belief on the part of medieval people when they offer political motives always and everywhere to explain religious positions. What we can say is that the archbishop of Toledo articulated Adoptionism, and that many of the clergy in Spain seem not to have objected. Likewise, Felix as bishop of Urgell was in a position to preach Adoptionism in the Carolingian-held Pyrenees, and others there followed him. The period when the controversy flared up was one of considerable change – even upheaval – in the northern parts of the Iberian peninsula especially, and some people in Asturias and the Spanish March may have followed the tradition of allegiance to Toledo while others saw Rome and the Franks as the true path.

By Charlemagne's imperial coronation in late 800, the Adoptionist controversy was, from the court's perspective, definitively settled. The 'preaching infantry' led by Benedict of Aniane still had work to do, but the Spanish March had become part of the Carolingian empire. Its bishops answered to the court, its counts received their offices from the king, and monasteries and even individual lay people sought and received grants of land and privileges from the ruler. Felix ended his life an exile in Lyon in 818, closing the active controversy over his Adoptionist teachings. Succeeding bishops of Urgell received grants of land by royal precept.[188]

THE ERA OF BERNARD OF SEPTIMANIA, 820–840

Perhaps to avoid intrigues rooted in family rivalries similar to those surrounding Bera's fall from power, Louis the Pious installed Rampo, a Frankish magnate with no such stake in the March, as Bera's successor. Rampo took his new office with a record of loyal service to both Charlemagne and Louis. The practice of appointing a Frank to office in the conquered territory only after the departure of a figure with more local clout mirrors Carolingian policy in Italy after the conquest in 774, where many Lombard counts retained their offices, with Franks succeeding.[189] Despite having responsibility for the key strategic area of the Spanish March, Rampo appears only in documents from the inland *pagus* Besalú. Since Besalú was under the authority of the count of Girona in the early ninth century, it is generally taken that Rampo held that post.

---

[188] CC 2, 276–8 for introduction, 279–85 for documents, including reconstructions of lost charters by Charlemagne and Louis, referred to by later confirmations.

[189] The fundamental treatment for the migration of northerners into Italy under the Carolingians is E. Hlawitschka, *Franken, Alemannen, Bayern und Burgunder in Oberitalien, 774–962: Zum Verständnis de fränkischen Königsherrschaft in Italien* (Freiburg im Breisgau, 1960).

Rampo comes is documented in a grant of Louis the Pious to Banyoles, as the intercessor on behalf of the monastery, located in the *pagus* of Besalú, later its own county separate from Girona.[190] His title in another document, *marchio*, indicates that he may have governed Barcelona, since that title seems in some respects to have been reserved for those whose authority included the extreme border of the empire.[191] As no other count of Barcelona is known to immediately follow Bera, and Rampo was *marchio* in the nearby area, it has long been accepted that he ruled the counties of both Girona and Barcelona.[192]

Concerning the events in and pertaining to the Spanish March, the surviving sources reveal a fair amount of activity. An assembly in 821 discussed organizing raids beyond the *limites* of the Spanish March, but the implementation probably took a year to finalize.[193] The next year *comites* of the March undertook a raid across the river Segre, which may have served to mark the boundary. Although the annalist did not name leaders of the operation, narrative sources show that they were the counts Rampo, Gaucelm of Empúries and Roussillon, and Asnar of Urgell and Cerdanya, likely accompanied by Berengar of Toulouse, whose Pyrenean counties of Pallars-Ribagorça were near the theatre of action, and possibly Oliba of Carcassonne.[194] As *marchio*, it would seem that Rampo served as commander of the expedition over the other counts except Berengar; none save perhaps Oliba was a Goth.

At Rampo's death in 825, claimants struggled over the succession to his *honores* in the March, with conflict pitting the followers of Bera's family against the camp surrounding his supposed rival Gaucelm. In the end, Barcelona and Girona, with its *pagus* Besalú, devolved to Bernard of Septimania, Gaucelm's younger brother. Previous historians have attributed this development as the primary factor triggering a revolt in 826–7, led by the mysterious figure Aizo and Willelmundus, son of Bera and nephew of the new *marchio* Bernard.[195] The uprising was successful largely because of help recruited from al-Andalus, making it an

---

[190] CC 2, 46.
[191] CC 2, 7, features a monastery built *per licentiam Ramponi marchioni*. This document, however, is a precept of Charles the Bald confirming the rights of the monastery, dated to 844, so the original language used to describe Rampo is not entirely recoverable; it does, however, show that someone within a generation or so thought Rampo should be entitled *marchio*.
[192] Salrach, *El procés*, 1, 47. See also the discussion in Abadal, *Dels visigots als catalans*, 89–90.
[193] *ARF SS rer. Germ.* 6,154.
[194] Astronomer, *Vita Hludowici*, c. 35 MGH SS 2, 626–27; *ARF SS rer. Germ.*, 158–9. But see Miro, 'Les comtes de Toulouse', for refining the relationship between the Pyrenean counties and the magnates based in Toulouse.
[195] Salrach, *El procés*, 1, 48–9; Abadal, *Dels visigots als catalans*, 1, 311–15.

intriguing case study for the role of identity in ninth-century politics and diplomacy.

The actions Louis ordered against the revolt were the first order of business for the annalist of 827, and the Astronomer discusses them as well.[196] To quell this revolt, Louis commanded Bernard of Septimania to take the field against Aizo and his reinforcements from al-Andalus. The emperor committed further Frankish forces, sending the chancellor Helisachar and counts Hildebrand and Donatus, and then reinforcing these troops by ordering his son Pippin, king of Aquitaine, into action.[197] The leaders of Pippin's army, counts Hugh of Tours and Matfrid of Orléans, delayed their advance, some say intentionally, giving the rebels and their friends ample time to lay waste to much of the countryside, endangering the cities of Girona and Barcelona, and costing them royal favour and their offices.[198] A re-interpretation of the events, based on a common-sense appreciation of ninth-century military logistics, questions the idea of delay, referring to the amount of time needed to muster forces and march to Barcelona. Thus Louis may have decided beforehand to dismiss Hugh and Matfrid.[199] Bernard, in any event, did the most he could with the military resources at his disposal and managed ultimately to fend off Aizo and Willelmundus. The Muslim forces that came to Aizo's aid, however, succeeded in helping him to occupy a good deal of territory. The Franks lost the plain of Vic, parts of Berguedà and Urgell, and the buffer region south and west of Barcelona that was later known as Osona, and regained them only near the end of the century.[200] Bernard acquitted himself well, despite the late help from Aquitaine, and within the next year found himself promoted to the imperial court serving as chamberlain to Louis.

It is important that Aizo, not Willelmundus, appears in the sources as the leader of the rebellion. If the affair were a result of family rivalries between the two branches of descent from William of Gellone, Willelmundus should have had sufficient cause and support to take up arms against Bernard, as Bernard held *honores* previously invested in

---

[196] *ARF, MGH SS rer. Germ.* 6, 172–3; Astronomer, *Vita Hludowici,* cc. 40–1, *MGH SS* 2, 629–31.

[197] Astronomer, *Vita Hludowici,* cc. 40–1 *MGH SS* 2, 629–31; *ARF, MGH SS rer. Germ.* 6,172–3.

[198] Thegan, *Vita Hludowici imperatoris,* in *MGH SS,* 2 (Hanover, 1829), 597; Nithard, *Historiarum Libri IIII,* in *MGH SS,* 2 (Hanover, 1829), 651–2; *Annales Xantenses et Annales Vedastini,* in *MGH SS rer. Germ.,* 12, ed. B. von Simson (Hanover, 1909), 7. Lewis, *The Development of Society,* 47 and n. 52 ties this behaviour to the attempt to create a kingdom for Charles the Bald.

[199] R. Collins, 'Pippin I and the Kingdom of Aquitaine', in P. Godman and R. Collins, eds, *Charlemagne's Heir: New Perspectives on the Reign of Louis the Pious (814–840)* (Oxford, 1990), 363–89.

[200] *ARF,* s.a. 820, 826, *MGH SS rer. Germ.* 6, 152, 170–1. See also Abadal, 'Louis le Pieux', 147–77; Abadal, *Dels visigots als catalans,* 309–21; R. Collins, 'Pippin I and the Kingdom of Aquitaine', 373–80.

Willelmundus's father. But as Aizo was the prime mover, his motives merit a full understanding. Salrach, consulting Arabic sources along with Frankish accounts, rehabilitated an older thesis that Aizo should be identified as the Muslim *wali* 'Aysun, who with his brother controlled the areas of Girona and Barcelona before the Frankish conquest.[201] According to this view, 'Aysun revolted against Abd ar-Rahman I in the late eighth century, later reconciled with the emir, and participated in the siege of Zaragoza after Charlemagne's failed expedition. At the fall of Girona to the Franks in 785, 'Aysun would have been captured and taken to the Carolingian court, finally escaping just before the revolt in 826, when he would have been an old man. Willelmundus then joined in, looking to damage Bernard's reputation and power base, and perhaps planning to double-cross 'Aysun and take the marcher counties for himself. At any rate, 'Aysun's involvement and his putative connections to Córdoba are taken to explain the involvement of troops from farther south. Salrach elaborates a double scenario, seeing on one hand the personal ambitions of local nobles, Franks and Goths alike, looking to improve their power relative to rivals both Muslim and Christian, and on the other hand native Goths and perhaps Muslims, wanting peace at the frontier and unwilling to accept the culturally homogenizing policy of the royal court.[202]

The case of this rebellion is enlightening for the question of identity in the Spanish March and must be reconsidered. On Aizo's identity, the sources do not reveal much. A recent argument holds that Aizo was an 'Islamicized Goth' who led the revolt out of a sense that the Franks had wronged the Goths of the March by getting rid of Bera and replacing him with Frankish counts.[203] An interpretation that stays close to the sources, however, will conclude that Aizo was not a pro-Visigoth, anti-Frank freedom fighter. If he had been in residence at the royal court, or at one of the royal palaces, before starting or joining the uprising in the Spanish March, that is an indication that he was something of a high-level hostage.[204] All this could mean that Aizo was indeed not the *wali* himself but the son of the old *wali* of Barcelona, Sulayman al-Arabi, an

---

[201] Salrach, *El procés*, 1, 80–3, 85–7, citing F. Codero y Zaidín, 'El Godo o moro Aizón', in *idem, Estudios críticos de historia árabe española* vii (Madrid, 1917). Abadal suggested that Aizo was a Gothic noble: *Dels visigots als catalans*, 1, 311–15. Aurell, 'Pouvoir et parenté', 470–1 follows Salrach.

[202] Salrach, *El procés*, vol. 1, 90.

[203] I. Ollich i Castanyer, 'Vic: la ciutat a l'època carolíngia', in J. Camps, ed., *Catalunya a l'època carolíngia: art i cultura abans del romànic (segles IX i X)* (Barcelona, 1999), 89–94, trans. as 'Vic: the Town in the Carolingian Age', ibid., 464–6; also her 'Roda: l'Esquerda. La ciutat carolíngia', ibid., 84–8, trans. as 'Roda: l'Esquerda. The Carolingian Town', ibid., 461–3.

[204] A. J. Kosto, 'Hostages in the Carolingian World (714–840)', *EME* 11 (2002): 123–47.

identification that would militate against Aizo's being a staunch Visigoth. Even if he were the *wali*'s son, he could not have been younger than Louis the Pious, because Arabic sources have him leading soldiers against the Franks in 778. Figuring him a young adult of twenty or twenty-five years old when he commanded troops, he would be in his sixties or near seventy by the time of the revolt in 826. Another problem with the pro-Visigoth argument is that it favours the so-called policy change from appointing Visigoths to appointing Franks to office in the March as a trigger for the revolt, but there was a delay of over five years between Bera's removal and Aizo's rebellion. Even given the time necessary to send messages to the right people, escape from the palace, and travel from Francia to the March, it should not have taken five years to launch the operation.

Aizo's identity has thus been subject to much speculation. He could have been the son of the leader of a Muslim garrison in a key location in the Spanish March, handed over to the Franks as the garrison left as a safeguard against a future attack. Alternatively he could have been the son of an important leader in Barcelona, sent to Louis in 801 as security against treachery from within the city, in case the Muslims should try to take it back. This would still allow him to be a son of an important individual in the region, a hostage of some rank and former prominence in the Spanish March escaped from a palace in Francia to head home for a rebellion. The Frankish sources do not label Aizo as a Muslim or 'Saracen', a point in favour of the idea that Aizo was not Muslim. In fact, the only 'ethnic' attribution for Aizo is in the later Frankish *Annals of Fulda*, wherein he is called 'Aizo Gothus', which of course has led to the long-standing attribution of Gothic ethnicity.[205] The only proposed alternative identification, calling Aizo a Muslim, is in a literary tale from the Arabic perspective, dating to the eleventh century.[206] The safest conclusion is that Aizo was a 'Goth' in the eyes of maybe a single annalist, who from an East Frankish perspective could well have had no knowledge or memory of his actual origins. Whatever such ethnic labels meant, they meant more as symbols of power to the Carolingian court than to those governed and governing in the Spanish March. As to how Aizo built a power base, he must have had connections in the region around Vic. Perhaps some of the old Muslim garrison at Barcelona, or alternatively his 'Gothic' family, established themselves there after they lost the city, or perhaps his family was based in Vic or somewhere nearby. In any

---

[205] *Annales Fuldenses*, in G. H. Pertz, ed., *MGH SS*, I (Hanover, 1826), 359. English translation by T. Reuter, *Annals of Fulda* (Manchester, 1993).
[206] See the modern Spanish translation in F. de La Granja in 'A marca superior en la obra de Al-Udri', *Estudios de la Edad Media de la Corona de Aragón*, VIII (1967): 457–61.

case, this appears not to have been a pro-Visigoth insurrection, but a more straightforward power grab, making use of old relationships to carve out a lordship where he could.

Meanwhile, the relationships between emperor and locals, established by *aprisio* grants and other royal acts, seem to have held firm. Individuals in Barcelona and Terrassa would have been on the front lines, fighting off the rebels, suffering the most from their attacks, and remaining loyal to the Carolingians, despite the role in the revolt played by Bera's son Willelmundus. This seems counter-intuitive if the revolt were fuelled by pro-Visigoth sentiment, because the presumably Visigothic son of the ousted Visigothic count of their area was one of the rebels. Perhaps the hispani who were under royal protection would be even more anti-Muslim than the local Goths? Those who fled the Muslims, as well as their descendants alive during the 820s, would perhaps be more likely to stay loyal to the kings. Individual Goths, as well as hispani, also received grants from kings, and it would seem that the indigenous families remained loyal to the kings as well. Both groups also would have had a full generation of living under Bera and yet felt no residual loyalty to him or his son. Presumably they would have done a lot of the fighting, and that under the command of Bernard of Septimania, the second Frankish count of Barcelona and *marchio*, and were far from averse to serving Franks against Goths. The evidence simply cannot support the notion that Aizo's revolt was a pro-Visigoth, anti-Frank affair. Indeed, perhaps that is why the event is known as Aizo's revolt rather than Willelmundus's. Willelmundus would have been the more likely candidate to capitalize on any Gothic feeling, yet he played second fiddle.

As to why the revolt succeeded in setting up an area outside Carolingian control, the best answer is that it was only loosely under their control in the first place. The surviving evidence, from both texts and archaeology, shows that a line of fortifications was set up through the middle of what became Osona, along the river Ter.[207] No royal documents from before the revolt pertain to the area. This is not an indication that nobody lived there, just that the kings were not insinuating themselves into local sociopolitical networks, at least as far as is visible in the surviving sources.[208] All of this indicates that the kings did not consider the territory to be theirs yet. Thus Aizo took an area that the Carolingians did not really strongly hold. This was his best chance, because his actions

---

[207] See the works by Ollich cited above for the archaeology.

[208] Abadal, *Dels visigots als catalans*, 1, 312 argues that the area was only sparsely populated, guarded by a few scattered castles, and hard to reach from most places.

in more firmly held areas near Barcelona did not succeed in conquest, and in fact the narrative sources portray him as an invader. That also helps to explain why he and apparently at least one successor were able to maintain their independence from both the Carolingians and Umayyads; they were on the frontier itself.

Besides altering the power relations amongst the Frankish nobility, and indeed the imperial court, with Bernard's elevation and the dismissal from their *honores* of Hugh and Matfrid, the end of Aizo's revolt set the bounds of the Carolingian empire in the Spanish March until nearly the end of the ninth century. No major campaigns moved the frontier to benefit either Franks or Muslims, and the border stability allowed the counties of the March to function in the politics involving kings and the nobility just as any other Carolingian counties. It has been argued that if there ever had been any Islamic influence in marcher politics, the revolt ended it. The same holds true for any supposed 'Visigothism' that may have factored into political behaviour such as Bera's alleged treason.[209] These ideologies have been understood as disappearing after 827 to be replaced by family rivalries between the lines of Bera and Bernard. All this is an old interpretation based on modern nationalist presuppositions, however, and a clear understanding of the period on its own terms necessitates a challenge to the older view.[210] Following the pattern of neighbours in the western Pyrenees who were only very loosely connected with the old Visigothic kingdom before the Muslim conquest, any powerful marcher count could have declared himself king of his territory and tried to back up his claim by fighting the Franks. Since this did not happen, in part because the eastern Pyrenees were more strongly connected to Frankish dominion via roads,[211] and in part because Willelmundus's family came from Septimania, a region that did not exhibit 'pro-Visigothic' tendencies under Carolingian rule, any notion that Visigothic identity was the root of political activity in the March seems to be more of an assumption on the part of modern scholars.

Bernard of Septimania, at any rate, was a Frank on both sides of his family. His stock rose sharply in the years after Aizo's revolt thanks to his

---

[209] Salrach, *El procés*, vol. 1, 90. See also Aurell, 'Pouvoir et parenté', 470–1; Engels, *Schutzgedanke und Landherrschaft*, 3.

[210] Aurell, 'Pouvoir et parenté', 469–71.

[211] P. M. Duval, 'Les plus anciennes routes de France: les voies gallo–romaines', in *Les routes de France. Depuis les origines jusqu'a nous jours*, ed. G. Michaud (Paris, 1959), 9–24; J. Hubert, 'Les routes du Moyen Age', in ibid., 25–56; L. Harmand, *L'Occident romain: Gaule, Espagne, Bretagne, Afrique du Nord (31 Av. J. C. à 235 Ap. J. C.)* (Paris, 1960), 395–431.

success in combating the rebels and their allies. Upon the death in 828 of the Septimanian magnate Leibulf, Bernard received the counties of Narbonne, Bèziers, Agde, Maguelonne, Nîmes, and perhaps Uzès. By 830 he had amassed so much power in the region that Nithard dubbed him 'dux Septimaniae'.[212] The territory Bernard and his brother Gaucelm held as *honores* now included every county from the Rhône to the Pyrenees, and from there to the very bounds of the empire just south of Barcelona.[213] He became chamberlain, a promotion that led to significant problems for the emperor Louis, the empress Judith, and their son Charles. For whatever reasons, whether dynastic rivalries, individual vendettas, jealousy, or something else entirely, Bernard was accused of all manner of misdeeds, precipitating a crisis that resulted in rebellion against Louis, part of arguably the greatest crisis faced by a Carolingian monarch.[214]

Bernard did not give up *honores* in the Spanish March and Septimania to become *camerarius*. When he went to court, taking his four-year-old son William with him but leaving his wife Dhuoda in Uzès, his brother Gaucelm ran affairs in his stead.[215] The evidence for Gaucelm's activity is a now-lost charter for the monastery of Amer in Girona, one of Bernard's counties.[216] The charter allegedly demonstrated that Gaucelm was exercising jurisdiction in Girona, thus implying his involvement elsewhere. Matthew Innes has challenged the idea that counties were strictly defined jurisdictional units, at least in the Middle Rhine Valley, so perhaps Gaucelm's act in place of his absentee brother is evidence of similar conditions in the Spanish March.[217] Along this line of reasoning, since Gaucelm was count, outranking any other officials and even Bernard's wife Dhuoda, who no doubt ran the household affairs,[218] it would be his place as a count *in* Girona to grant charters, despite not being the count *of* Girona.

---

[212] Nithard, *Vita Hludowici*, 652.

[213] Salrach, *El procés*, vol. 1, 93–4, where he claims that the union of Narbonne and Barcelona, with their respective satellite counties, as a single geopolitical unit, remained to 878 and contributed directly to weakening the Empire.

[214] The severity of the crisis has long been recognized, but there has recently been a shower of attention rained upon it. Using sources also cited below, de Jong, *The Penitential State*, 41–4 gives a general overview of developments; likewise, Booker, *Past Convictions*, 151–4 emphasizes, amongst other misdeeds, charges of sorcery.

[215] Abadal, *Dels visigots als catalans*, 182.

[216] Salrach, *El procés*, vol. 1, 97, posits this conclusion based on the note of the charter in CC 2, 10–13. Gaucelm is believed to have had comital authority in Roussillon since Bera's removal in 820: Abadal, *Dels visigots als catalans*, 155.

[217] Innes, *State and Society*, 94–140.

[218] Dhuoda, *Liber manualis*, 10.4 in Marcelle Thiébaux, ed. and trans. (New York, 1998), 226–7.

Once at court, Bernard found himself in waters particularly hard to navigate. Paschasius Radbertus's account of his alleged adultery with the empress Judith is well known.[219] As Nithard reports, when Bernard fled court in 830 to his southern lands, he left behind his partisans, including his brother Eribert, who was captured, blinded, and sent to Italy as an exile. Gaucelm, Bernard's other brother who wielded power in the Spanish March, went into exile to family lands in Burgundy with his old friends, including, it seems, the same Sanila who accused Bera in 820. Bernard may or may not have gone to Burgundy to firm up support; maybe he held the Septimanian area of Razès-Conflent by force, having been dispossessed for a time, but all sources state he went to live in Septimania.[220] The fates of Bernard's relatives later weighed heavily on Dhuoda as she wrote her manual of moral instruction for their son William.[221] When, in late 831, Pippin of Aquitaine rebelled against Louis the Pious, Bernard changed sides and cast his fortunes with the rebels. Louis's campaign against his son Pippin commenced early the next year; his supporter, Berengar of Toulouse, moved against Bernard.[222] Berengar seized Roussillon by February of 832, to judge from a local document recording a dispute settlement, as part of his manoeuvres to take control of Bernard's *honores*.[223] In the end, the emperor put down the revolt of his son. Amongst the Frankish nobility, Berengar profited most from the conflict, having been given the counties of Toulouse with Pallars and Ribagorça, Uzès, Nîmes, Maguelonne, Agde, Bèziers, Narbonne, Razès, Conflent, Roussillon, Vallespir, Peralada, Empúries, Besalú, Girona, and Barcelona.[224] Bernard of Septimania, as defender of the emperor's interests in the Spanish March, had become second in the empire in 829, but by 833 he was ousted from power, not to regain it even upon the emperor's restoration. Berengar of

---

[219] Paschasius Radbertus, *Epitaphium Arsenii*, ed. Ernst Dümmler, *Abhandlungen der königlichen Akademie der Wissenschaften zu Berlin, Philologische und historische Klasse* 2 (1900): 1–98; D. Ganz, 'The *Epitaphium Arsenii* and Opposition to Louis the Pious', in P. Godman and R. Collins, eds, *Charlemagne's Heir: New Perspectives on the Reign of Louis the Pious (814–840)* (Oxford, 1990), 527–50; E. Ward, 'Caesar's Wife: the Career of the Empress Judith, 819–829', in ibid., 205–27 and A. Koch, *Kaiserin Judith: Eine politische Biographie* (Husum, 2005). For more, G. Bührer-Thierry, 'La reine adultère', *Cahiers de civilisation medieval, Xe–XIIe siecles* 35 (1992), 299–312 and E. Ward, 'Agobard of Lyons and Paschasius Radbertus as Critics of the Empress Judith', *Studies in Church History* 27 (1990), 15–25.

[220] Astronomer, *Vita Hludowici*, c. 44 MGH SS 2, 632–33; Nithard, *Historiae*, MGH SS 2, 652.

[221] Dhuoda, 3.4 in Thiébaux, ed., 92–3; Glenn W. Olsen, 'One Heart and One Soul (Acts 4:32 and 34) in Dhuoda's "Manual"', *Church History* 61 (1992): 23–33 at 26.

[222] Salrach, *El procés*, vol. 1, 100–1.

[223] Pierre de Marca, *Marca hispanica sive limes hispanicus*, 2 vols. (Paris, 1688), app. 5.

[224] See the discussion in Salrach, *El procés*, vol. 1, 101.

Toulouse was then the most powerful magnate in the realm and governor of the Spanish March.

Royal diplomas reveal the emperors' relations with locals in the March during this turbulent time.[225] Confirmations of previous grants as well as new arrangements were very important for both the king and the recipient of the grant. As noted above, *aprisio* holders and monasteries obtained security in their possessions when succeeding kings reiterated the terms of earlier agreements. Kings used confirmations as opportunities to express their power, or to 'perform' their roles as kings. Louis the Pious confirmed and modified his father's arrangements. Louis's son, Lothar, followed suit during the time he had seized power after the rebellion of 833. A series of royal diplomas from the middle 830s, each concerning an ecclesiastical beneficiary, is of particular interest for tracing royal power in the Spanish March. The first in the series is Lothar's confirmation of his father's grant for Sant-Genís, dated to 834 and surviving in two fragments in a cartulary, which stands as a standard reiteration of the rights and privileges Louis the Pious had granted in 819; the fragmentary nature of the text's survival makes more detail impossible to retrieve.[226] Documents like this were common when new kings succeeded, but this one is evidence of Lothar acting as emperor in his own right; the dating clause names the first year of his reign in Francia and thirteenth in Italy. At about the same time, the new emperor seems to have confirmed the possessions of the monastery of Oveix and granted the house immunity.[227] Lothar issued another precept around the same time, to the bishop of Elna in Septimania, affirming the church's possessions brought into cultivation *ex heremo* as well as a half interest in the local market. The text of this diploma is intriguing, because it gives the bishop jurisdiction over land that the bishop's men organized along the lines of *aprisio*, although that term does not appear in the document.[228] These documents show Lothar performing rulership, acting the part of emperor at just the moment when he needed to shore up support. Louis the Pious acted in much the same way once he had regained power. Late in 834, he

---

[225] This paragraph builds on the interesting recent work of Koziol, *The Politics of Memory*, esp. 40–8, 60–1.

[226] CC 2, 208–9.

[227] CC 2, 471–2. Like other items Abadal included in his edition, this entry is not a document but rather an argument in favour of the existence of such a text based on a later reference dated to 1010, which itself is a conflict resolution that has Count Sunyer evacuating the villa of Somponiu in favour of the monastery of Sant Vincenç of Oveix. The abbot had a document to prove that the monastery was the rightful owner of the villa, and Abadal surmised that this document, referred to in 1010 as '*ab antiquis temporibus, de domno Leutario imperatore*' must have been a confirmation of goods by Lothar in 834, about the same time as the diplomas concerning the church of Elna and monastery of Sant Genís les Fonts were issued.

[228] CC 2, 101–3.

placed the cathedral church of Girona, with its possessions given by Charlemagne and others, *sub nostra tuicione*.[229] In March 835, he responded to the petition of Bishop Sisebut of Urgell to confirm Charlemagne's and Louis's own earlier grants of jurisdiction over parishes and that no count may interfere or hold in benefice the parish of Llívia.[230] A grant for the monastery of Tavèrnoles made at the same time reinforces the idea that networks of royal association with religious foundations served to bind March to monarchy.[231] The restored emperor Louis issued his own grant to the episcopal church of Elna in 836, but rather than enumerate the estates concerned, he more generally placed the church and its properties under royal protection.[232] Clearly Louis had to perform his restoration, to reaffirm his power after regaining the throne while also cementing his relationship with the bishops and abbots in Septimania and the Spanish March.

When Lothar fell from power and fled to Italy, he was able to meet some supporters, including exiles from Septimania and the Spanish March, such as Archbishop Bartholomew of Narbonne and Bishop Salomon of Elna.[233] Twentieth-century scholars sometimes linked support of Lothar in the Spanish March to the existence of a political 'party' grouped around the ideology of imperial unity, opposed to other 'parties': the 'legitimists', committed to the idea that the emperor's will was law and who thus threw their lots in with the young Charles the Bald, and the 'regionalists,' who backed Pippin of Aquitaine out of their desire for regional autonomy.[234] While it is difficult to disprove such ideological stands on the parts of aristocrats in the ninth century, general patterns of political activity in the period point to different factors. It seems much easier to believe that certain counts, bishops, and others were partisans of particular royal-family members linked by social or patronage networks.[235]

After Louis was restored as emperor, for example, his ally Berengar began to build a network of supporters in the Spanish March, calling on men not previously attached to his rival

---

[229] *Cartoral*, ed. Marques, no. 2, re-edited in CC 2, 120.   [230] CC 2, 282–5.

[231] CC 2, 246; CC 2, 282.   [232] CC 2, 104–6.   [233] Salrach, *El procés*, I, 103.

[234] Here the traditional Catalan historiography has unfortunately built on the ideas of, e.g., W. Mohr, 'Die kirchliche Einheitspartei und die Durchführung der Reichsordnung von 817', *Zetschrift für Kirchengeschichte* 72 (1961): 1–45.

[235] For the early medieval aristocracy, R. Le Jan, *Famille et pouvoir dans le monde franc (VIIe–Xe siècle): essai d'anthropologie sociale* (Paris, 1995). The work of Stuart Airlie has also been influential for this study. See especially Airlie, 'The Palace of Memory: the Carolingian Court as Political Centre', in S. Rees Jones, R. Marks, A. J. Minnis, eds, *Courts and Regions in Medieval Europe* (York, 2000), 1–20; Airlie, 'Semper Fidelis? Loyauté envers les Carolingiens comme constituant de l'identité aristocratique', in Régine Le Jan, ed., *La royauté et les élites dans l'Europe carolingienne* (Villeneuve d'Ascq, 1998), 129–43.

Bernard. Thus a certain Sunifred, probably the son of a Count Bello of Carcassonne, appears as count of Urgell and Cerdanya, along with his brother Sunyer, and Alaric, son of Bera of Barcelona, in Roussillon and Empúries; all three men were members of regionally based families.[236] Sunifred had an older brother, Count Oliba of Carcassonne, who had inherited their father's office. An original manuscript shows that in 829, Louis the Pious had granted to his *fidelis* Sunifred the villa of Fontcuberta in Septimania.[237] Clearly this generation came from a high enough lineage to merit the office.[238] In addition, Berengar kept direct control of the counties of Barcelona, Girona, and Narbonne, along with other maritime counties in Septimania. Salrach argued that these counts of Septimanian origin were 'legitimists', aligned with Berengar and by extension Louis the Pious because it was the ruler's will that Berengar lead the governance of the March; the argument implies that their loyalty saw them rewarded with marcher *honores*. Again, while their political ideologies, if any, are impossible to prove or disprove, the available evidence allows us only to state that these men owed their installation as counts to their support of Berengar and the fact that they were not associated with Bernard. It is likely that their *honores* were indeed rewards for loyalty, but assigning them adherence to a 'legitimist' political party is unwise. It seems clear that Louis needed to find locally based individuals to serve as channels for royal authority to reach into the inland reaches of the Spanish March. We can safely interpret this turn of events as Berengar's staking a claim to power in the March, conceived as a project that would require the aid of local notables to counterbalance the influence of Bernard's own followers who remained in the area.

If Berengar perceived that he would have difficulty reasserting his authority in the March, he was not mistaken. Galindo, count of Urgell and Cerdanya, had asserted his own power by occupying

---

[236] M.-M. Costa, 'Les genealogies comtals catalanes', in *Symposium internacional*, vol. 1, 447–62, building on the earlier work of Abadal, *Els primers comtes*, P. Ponsich, 'El problema de l'ascendència de Guifré el Pelós', *Revista de Catalunya* 23 (1988): 35–44. See also M. Aurell, 'Jalons pour une enquête sure les strategies matrimoniales des comtes catalans (IXe–XIe s.)', in *Symposium internacional*, 1, 281–364, which intently studies the very late ninth and tenth centuries, but includes helpful tables for the earlier period as well.

[237] CC 2, 323–4.

[238] Salrach, *El procés*, 1, 104–5. Abadal, *Els primers comtes*, 20–2. See K. F. Werner, 'Important Noble Families in the Kingdom of Charlemagne: a Prosopographical Study of the Relationship between King and Nobility in the Early Middle Ages', in T. Reuter, ed. and trans., *The Medieval Nobility: Studies on the Ruling Classes of France and Germany from the Sixth through the Twelfth Century* (New York, 1979), 137–202 for the argument that royal choices of whom to appoint were limited by the status of aristocratic families.

Pallars-Ribagorça, and Bernard was active in his old *honores*, angry at the deaths of friends and family in recent conflicts.[239] Galindo, the duly installed and recognized count of Urgell and descendant of the earlier count of that region, Asnar Galindo, took advantage of the chaos of the 833 revolt to expand his power westward, in the direction of Pallars and Ribagorça, Berengar's first territories in the Spanish March. In the 820s Asnar Galindo may have received the single largest grant of fiscal land in the Spanish March, for the purpose of repopulating areas in Urgell and Cerdanya. Although no royal diploma survives to provide details, a charter from a later generation refers to imperial recognition of fiscal land as Asnar's *aprisio*.[240] His son, whom Salrach identifies as 'probably a "unitarist"', meaning he favoured maintaining the empire's integrity by supporting Lothar, appears in the evidence merely to have been an opportunist. Probably as a punishment for his actions, Louis and Berengar formally stripped Galindo of his *honores*, but he refused to leave. After a hard struggle, the *fidelis* Sunifred was able to oust Galindo and claim his appointment.[241] This conflict disrupted life in the Urgell area, as exemplified by its bishop asking Louis the Pious to fix his rights, which had been usurped in the parishes. Louis's diploma, dated to 835, reveals details about Galindo's machinations or the general lapse of episcopal authority that arose in the confusion of the times. In particular it specifies that no count or public officer may usurp the tithes or other duties due to the bishop from nine parishes, including Pallars and Ribagorça. A tenth location, Llívia, is expressly designated as outside the benefice of any count.[242] The places named in the diploma show the areas where Galindo tried to exercise authority. These were places whence Berengar, Sunifred, and Bishop Sisebut had to remove him. Berengar also encountered hostility from Bishop Wimar of Girona, a former supporter of Lothar. A grant of immunity from Louis in 834 pacified Wimar, affirming the bishopric's possession of a series of villas and *villares* in the counties of Girona and Empúries, some with castles, and a one-third part of the tolls in associated properties and *pagi*.[243]

---

[239] Bernard's friends and family were Sanila, Gaucelm, Eribert, and Gerberga, who was drowned by Lothar and his supporters as a witch – see Astronomer, *Vita Hludowici*, c. 52 MGH SS 2, 638–9; *Annales de Saint-Bertin*, eds F. Grat, J. Vielliard, and S. Clémencet (Paris, 1964), 14.

[240] The discussion in CC 2, 325 provides orientation. Abadal there dates the putative diploma to 820–30.

[241] See also Salrach, *El procés*, vol. 1, 102–4; R. d'Abadal i de Vinyals, 'Un diplôme pour le comte Oliba', *Annales du Midi* 61 (1949): 346–52.

[242] Louis helped the bishop: CC 2, 282–5.   [243] CC 2, 122–3; Salrach, *El procés*, vol. 1, 105–6.

The situation thus had begun to favour Berengar and Sunifred by the mid-830s. Berengar was master of much of the southern extremities of the empire and his authority was solidifying, but Bernard of Septimania was still a powerful challenger. Louis the Pious called both men to an assembly at Crémieux near Lyon in 835 to settle things between them. Berengar died on his way to the council, so Bernard regained Toulouse and the counties of Septimania and the Spanish March, save those allotted to Sunifred, Sunyer, Alaric, and Oliba.[244]

As the Astronomer relates in his *Life* of Louis the Pious, Bernard's second rule in Septimania and the Spanish March began with *missi* working in the area to correct conditions that required improvement according to the complaints of the 'Gothi'.[245] According to Salrach, this time around, Bernard's rule was 'despotic'.[246] At an assembly at Quierzy-sur-Oise in 838, a group of marcher nobles appealed to the emperor against the abuses to which Bernard subjected them.[247] Traditional Catalan historiography holds that Visigothic identity could have factored into their complaints, as most of them were indigenous Goths, while Bernard represented Frankish dominion. Yet the nobles appealed to the emperor, a Frank himself. Certainly Bernard had to reaffirm his power because of absence. He was at Louis the Pious's court and involved in the civil wars of 830s, followed by his deposition 832–5, during which time viscounts, subordinates, and other counts operated entirely without his involvement, as did a Viscount Wifred.[248] It is therefore likely that any harshness he exhibited could be traced to the need to reassert his personal authority after a string of defeats, by turning out individuals whose loyalty he questioned. Any argument that locals resented Bernard's second rule in Septimania and the Spanish March is based on speculation rather than evidence. It is better to conclude that the Spanish March had become politically integrated into Carolingian sociopolitical networks to the same degree that other regions had. That need not mean absolute cultural uniformity, but it did mean that *honores* in the March were distributed like those elsewhere, that monasteries and individuals below the rank of the high aristocracy had some direct ties to the king, and that those who governed the areas on his behalf were expected by locals to do so

---

[244] Salrach, *El procés*, vol. 1, 106.   [245] Astronomer, *Vita Hludowici*, c. 57 MGH SS 2, 642.

[246] 'Despotic' rule of Bernard: Salrach, *El procés*, vol. 1, 110.

[247] For this council, see Astronomer, *Vita Hludowici*, c. 59 MGH SS 2, 643–4 and MGH Conc. 2, 768–82.

[248] Salrach, *El procés*, vol. 1, 110–12 and literature discussed therein. This Wifred is not to be identified with Sunifred's son and later count of Cerdanya, Urgell, and Barcelona, known now as Wifred the Hairy.

loyally and in adherence to royal promulgations, regardless of their places and families of origin.

CONCLUSIONS

The political manoeuvring centred on the Spanish March drew in kings, great magnates like Bernard and Berengar, and more local figures like Sunifred. Tracing the developments that placed marcher counties in the hands of various nobles shows the thoroughness of the Carolingians' success at politically integrating Catalonia into their empire by 840, or indeed even by 820. Cultural differences still existed between Goths and Franks, but the gulf between them was narrowing as the ninth century wore on, as the texts and even the script of Carolingian reform found their way into Catalonia.[249] Political integration is evidenced by the ways that *honores* in the March were carefully distributed by rulers who strove to maintain a balance of power across different families. Unlike great nobles closer to royal authority, the leaders of the March had many opportunities to flout royal authority and increase their own power. The results of Aizo's revolt are revealing. Aizo rose against Carolingian rule and carved out a space of his own, but rather than indicate that the whole Spanish March had failed to be integrated, it in fact shows the opposite. The rest of the March was indeed strongly integrated, because no other political actor in the area could disregard the monarchy. Charlemagne and Louis the Pious strove to place loyal men in high positions and bolstered royal authority by directly linking themselves to intermediate levels of marcher society by means of immunities and the enigmatic *aprisio* land settlements. Supposed ethnic identity was not a factor. In the second half of the ninth century, the Spanish March was so thoroughly integrated into the West Frankish kingdom that its governors, in part through the power they gained by holding the March, became major players on the stage of high politics.

[249] See Chapter 5 in this volume.

Chapter 3

MARCH AND MONARCHY, 840–878

Amongst the difficulties facing Charles the Bald as he assumed rule in the western Frankish kingdom after 840 was establishing his authority throughout his realm. Pippin II of Aquitaine and his supporters made trouble for Charles, and the *fideles* the new king put in place to govern encountered various problems. Amid the turmoil of the late 840s William, son of Bernard of Septimania, assembled a force and took the city of Barcelona, apparently killing the king's appointed steward in the process. This event and the royal response in the Spanish March both mark the importance of the region as a part of the Carolingian realms worth fighting for. It was significant strategically as a frontier, for a disruption there could create military problems for the kingdom; it was perhaps symbolically important to William as a portion of what he may have assumed to be his patrimony; and it was significant as a potential *honor* and power base for aristocrats concerned with internal competition within the Frankish realms. Barcelona was more important than a mere local or regional centre. The March also figured in the high politics of the period. The episode of William's seizure of power and his subsequent fall are also typical of the longer-term challenges Charles the Bald faced in appointing individuals to *honores* in the Spanish March. William, his father Bernard, and their successors Odalric, Humfrid, and Bernard of Gothia were all Franks sent to govern the March; they all acted against Charles the Bald, and even his son Louis the Stammerer. Locally appointed counts, especially Sunifred and his descendants, never did so.

This chapter examines evidence that indicates that the Spanish March was an integrated province of the West Frankish kingdom and the wider Carolingian world. It will proceed more or less chronologically, first examining the decade after the death of Louis the Pious, which featured controversy and conflict that reveal a great deal about how the March functioned in the political universe of loyalty and identity in the Carolingian world. Those years saw the careers of Bernard of

Septimania, his son William, and the locally based Sunifred, who served Charles the Bald as a conduit for royal influence into the region. After 850, Charles eschewed the model of appointing figures based in Hispania or Gothia. Instead he turned to great magnates to serve as *marchiones* in order to secure the March in the hands of men he could trust and to win powerful allies in the struggle against his kin, especially Pippin II of Aquitaine. During the same period, relations between the king and others in the March, including churches and monasteries, show the extent to which local individuals and institutions remained connected to the monarchy. By 870, Charles no longer faced fierce competition from his relatives, and the last years of his reign saw the return to the pattern of appointing lesser nobles with local power bases to *honores* in the March, as the king needed ties of patronage to greater numbers of figures in the region. These included Wifred 'the Hairy', who much later gained legendary status as founder of Catalonia while in his own time maintaining loyalty to the Carolingian dynasty. By the 870s, despite the behaviour of the Frankish magnates who held the offices of the March, royal influence still mattered.

CONFLICT IN THE MARCH, 840–850

Just as with other historical narratives sources we have encountered, it is worth discussing the principal source for the later ninth-century West Frankish kingdom, namely, the *Annales Bertiniani*, or *Annals of St-Bertin*. We have seen how chroniclers and annalists were not mere reporters of fact, but that they chose their information carefully to suit other agendas. Perhaps they sought to raise the prestige of their monasteries, perhaps they were instruments or associates of the royal court seeking to communicate ideas about royal authority or promote a common sense of identity amongst the political class.[1] The *Annales Bertiniani* (*AB*) are no different. The narrative begins in 830, picking up at the point the *Annales Regni Francorum* (*ARF*) end in 829, originally as a continuation of the older royal annals.[2] They were composed by different authors up to the death of Archbishop Hincmar of Rheims, their final author, in 882. For the early years, there is no known, single author, and the enterprise may have been a group effort attached to the royal court. After about 835, the effort was taken over by Prudentius, a hispanus who resided at court and

---

[1] These are the chief lessons learned from studies such as R. McKitterick, *History and Memory in the Carolingian World* (Cambridge, 2004) and H. Reimitz, *History, Frankish Identity and the Framing of Western Ethnicity, 550–850* (Cambridge, 2015), esp. Part III on the Carolingian period.

[2] See J. L. Nelson, trans. *The Annals of St-Bertin*, Ninth-Century Histories 1 (Manchester, 1991), 'Introduction', 1–19.

later was appointed bishop of Troyes. He gave more information in his yearly entries than the previous authors and wrote a more independent account once he became bishop. For the years up to around 860, perhaps because of the origins of their author, the *AB* contain information pertinent to Spain and the Spanish March. Prudentius died in 861, after which year Hincmar took up authorship of the annals. Already a long-serving bishop, Hincmar was involved in the high affairs of the empire, more so than Prudentius had been, and as such his annals are sometimes coy when dancing around a sensitive issue, sometimes fiery in criticism of political actors including Charles the Bald. In total, the *AB* do not present an official, royal perspective on history, but they are a well-informed source for the events of the West Frankish kingdom. They do not continue the tradition of history-writing before them, stretching back to the eighth century, of defining the identity of the Franks.[3] For that reason, discussion of identity in this chapter turns to other sources.

Given the back-and-forth struggles of Berengar of Toulouse and Bernard of Septimania in the 830s addressed in the previous chapter, it is not surprising to find that the Spanish March and Septimania were divided, just like the rest of the West Frankish kingdom, between fol-lowers of Charles the Bald and Pippin II of Aquitaine. Nithard, layman, grandson of Charlemagne, and courtier of Charles the Bald, reports that men based in Aquitaine raised Pippin II to kingship, but performed homage to Charles upon Emperor Louis's orders.[4] Later events prove that to have been either an ineffectual performance or a fabrication on Nithard's part. During the early period of Charles's reign, the March took on a strategic importance it had not held for a generation, only in this context the strategy concerned internal politics rather than expanding the kingdom's borders. Especially in these years, Charles needed to involve himself in the March to counter the support his nephew Pippin II found there. Meanwhile, Bernard of Septimania apparently thought his position strong enough to take a middle ground between Charles the Bald on the one hand and Lothar and Pippin II on the other. Again according to Nithard's testimony, Bernard swore primary loyalty to Pippin, and Charles was vexed by Bernard's continued misleading words and deeds.[5] Others in the March, especially the recently appointed and regionally based counts Sunifred, Sunyer, and Alaric, seem to have supported

---

[3] Reimitz, *History, Frankish Identity and the Framing of Western Ethnicity*, 430–3.

[4] Nithard, *Histoire des fils de Louis le Pieux*, ed. and trans. P. Lauer (Paris, 1964), 1.8.

[5] Nithard, *Histoire*, 2.5: Nithard does not specify the *seductiones quas patri fecerat et actenus illi faciebat* ('the tricks this man had played first on his father and now on him'). Translation in B. W. Scholz with B. Rogers, *Carolingian Chronicles: Royal Frankish Annals, Nithard's Histories* (Ann Arbor, 1972), 145–6.

Charles.[6] This may be attributed, at least in part, to their status. As lesser aristocrats beneath the level of Bernard, who had connections owing to kin networks and inherited possessions also in Burgundy as well as Septimania and the March,[7] they felt a more acute need for royal patronage and saw Charles as the best source of it. Bernard himself, trying to hedge his bets in the conflict between Pippin II and Charles, refused to aid Charles until forced to do so, and even then did not provide the help he had promised.[8] Bernard's most damning misstep was at the field of Fontenoy, where, torn between loyalty to Pippin and to Charles, he withheld his troops from battle until Charles's victory was certain, then agreed to hand over to Charles his young son William as a hostage to guarantee loyalty in the future.[9] Charles remained suspicious of Bernard, supporting Sunifred in 843 with grants of property to counter the Frankish *marchio*'s power in the March. Sunifred gained several *villas* both north of the Pyrenees, in Roussillon and the Conflent, and south of the mountains in Urgell and Cerdanya in return for his loyalty.[10]

The next year saw a series of events that in retrospect would prove very important for the future of the Spanish March, although at the time they were just further developments in Charles the Bald's attempts to strengthen his rule. Bernard, once more trying to move between sworn allegiances to both Charles and Pippin II, faced a difficult situation. Charles besieged Pippin's forces at Toulouse, and, although the sources do not mention who commanded them, they do reveal that Bernard was captured and executed in Aquitaine.[11] Charles bestowed Bernard's *honores* and authority in the Spanish March and Septimania to a man of proven fidelity, Sunifred, newly named *marchio*.[12] In a later generation, Sunifred's sons succeeded to the counties of the Spanish March and developed their autonomy, but such an outcome cannot, of course, be attributed to the intentions of either Charles or Sunifred in 844. The significance of this Aquitainian campaign to a king showing himself as authoritative in the region explains a flurry of activity during May and June of 844 that saw Charles issue several privileges to churches,

---

[6] Salrach, *El procés*, 1, 115.

[7] See, for example, J. L. Nelson, *Charles the Bald* (New York, 1992), 103.

[8] Nithard, *Histoire*, 2.5.

[9] Astronomer, *Vita Hludowici imperatoris,* in *MGH SS*, 2 (Hanover, 1829), 657, 662; Nithard, *Histoire*, 82–4; Nelson, *Charles the Bald*, 120. On hostages, see A. J. Kosto, 'Hostages in the Carolingian World (714–840)', *EME* 2 (2002): 123–47.

[10] CC 2, 332–4.

[11] *AB*, 45; Ann. Lorsch, 34; L. Malbos, 'La capture de Bernard de Septimanie', *Le Moyen Age* 76 (1970): 7–13; Nelson, *Charles the Bald*, 139–40.

[12] CC 2, 335–7 mentions Sunifred as *marchio* in mid-May of 844. Salrach, *El procés*, 1, 119; Nelson, *Charles the Bald*, 140–1.

monasteries, and individuals in the Spanish March. He had to perform kingship in order to win support, and that meant acting like a king by recognizing the rights and properties his petitioners possessed, in holding court during the siege.[13]

Charles the Bald's diplomas from the spring of 844 are illuminating. On 11 May, the king granted a series of lands to abbot Donnulus of St Peter of Albanyà in Besalú. He also placed the monastery under royal protection and immunity, specifying also that the Rule of St Benedict be observed. This was no new foundation, as the document mentions that Donnulus had built the monastery *'per licentiam Ramponi marchionis'*, Bernard of Septimania's predecessor in that *honor*.[14] A few days later, Charles confirmed to the monastery of Amer in Girona another grant of immunity and protection, and the right to abbatial election, renewing the tie between the king and the house established by his father and the preceding abbot.[15] Abbot Adulfus of Sant Martin of Les Escaules in Besalú sought and received a royal grant of his house's properties, along with immunity; the lands included those that the monks had developed *tam ex aprisione quam ex heremo*, showing the continued recognition of the *aprisio* grant in the royal repertoire, as well as further organization of settlements in the ninth century.[16] As the spring progressed, so did the siege of Toulouse.[17] Charles issued grants into June, as more petitioners came to seek him out. The king confirmed to Agila, abbot of Santa Grata in Pallars, the grant of immunity and properties that Louis the Pious had made at the petition of Count Matfrid of Orléans, whom the emperor later deposed.[18] Reversing his predecessor's allegiance to Lothar,[19] Bishop Gondemar of Girona received confirmation of his see's properties and rights from Charles, who augmented them as well.[20] On 25 June, Charles confirmed a similar grant of his father's to the monastery of Santa Maria of Arles (modern Arles-sur-Tech, dep. Pyrénées-Orientales, not to be confused with Arles, dep. Bouches-du-Rhône).[21] Abadal, the early leader of the drive to edit and publish charters and royal diplomas

---

[13] G. Koziol, *The Politics of Memory and Identity in Carolingian Royal Diplomas: the West Frankish Kingdom (840–987)* (Turnhout, 2012), 69–71.

[14] CC 2, 6–8.

[15] CC 2, 11–13. Louis's document does not survive, but Charles's is preserved in its original form in Paris, BNF, Nouv. acq. lat. 2579, f. 1.

[16] CC 2, 154–6. Other grants from this spring near Toulouse concerned the *aprisiones* of lay individuals. See CC 2, 335–7, 338–40, and 422–25; also Chandler, 'Between Court and Counts', and Koziol, *The Politics of Memory*, 71–2 with note 23.

[17] Also dated to this period, CC 2, 270–272, for Sant Andreu of Sureda.

[18] CC 2, 263–265, with the earlier grant at 259–62.

[19] CC 2, 117 (Abadal's editorial commentary) and 120–4 for a diploma issued by Lothar preserved in a tenth-century copy.

[20] CC 2, 125–30.   [21] CC 2, 27–9.

concerning 'Carolingian Catalonia', reconstructed other documents that he argued Charles had drawn up for other monasteries. Amongst them was Banyoles in Besalú, which received a grant of immunity and protection, along with various *cellae* in the vicinity.[22] A final document, a capitulary issued in June 844, regulated the obligations of the priests in Septimania towards their superior bishops to protect them from abuses of episcopal authority; it is usually presumed that the dioceses south of the Pyrenees were intended to abide by these pronouncements as well.[23] In all, this series of a dozen diplomas and the capitulary show Charles acting as king, connecting and reconnecting with royal *fideles* in Septimania and the Spanish March, tying individuals on the ground to royal authority.

These abbots may also have desired stability in their own areas before seeking privileges from the king, or indeed felt the need to confirm their rights in the wake of recent disturbances, not all of which related directly to the civil wars amongst Carolingian family members. Before being named *marchio*, Sunifred had demonstrated his competence in leading the military defence of the March. In 841–2, Emir Abd ar-Rahman II ordered a raid on Narbonne. The Muslim leaders, Abd al-Wahid and Musa ibn Musa of the Banu Qasi, governor of Tudela, took an inland route through areas that had already been affected by Aizo's revolt in the 820s.[24] Perhaps the emir sought to capitalize on the upheaval in the early 840s in the Carolingian empire, or perhaps the timing of the attack on the Frankish march was coincidental. Most Frankish sources do not mention this raid, suggesting that it went badly for them, or that the Frankish chronicles were preoccupied with the internal clashes. The regions of Bages, Lluçanes, and Osona were particularly hard hit before Sunifred was able to mobilize in reaction. It would appear that Sunifred's success against this Muslim invasion of 841–2 helped him gain higher office.[25]

Charles the Bald kept the group of counties from the Rhône to the Pyrenees intact after the fall of Bernard of Septimania, perhaps also as a

---

[22] CC 2, 48–54, where Abadal has compared the text of two other 844 diplomas with that of a later confirmation on the rights of Banyoles, issued by Charles himself in 866, to suggest the text of a grant to Banyoles in 844. See also CC 2, 179–82 for Saint Climent in Roussillon, to which only one document pertains.

[23] *MGH Cap.* 2, no. 255 (pp. 256–8); CC 2, 426–9, with Abadal's note on the dioceses of Girona, Barcelona, and Urgell.

[24] Modern historians have not agreed on the leadership. See É. Levi-Provençal, 'España musulmana hasta la caída del califato de Córdoba (711–1031)', in *Historia de España dirigida por R. Menéndez Pidal* vol. 4 (Madrid, 1950), 142 against Abadal, *Els primers comtes catalans*, Biographies Catalanes (Barcelona, 1958), 174. Salrach, *El procés*, vol. 2, 14–17 wisely returns to the Muslim sources. See in particular those translated in J. M. Millàs i Vallicrosa, *Textos dels historiadors àrabs referents a la Catalunya carolíngia* (Barcelona, 1987), nos. 104 and 105.

[25] Salrach, *El procés*, vol. 2, 14–17; Abadal, *Els primers comtes*, 174.

counter to the kingdom of Aquitaine, where he faced difficulties.[26] The only evidence indicating that Sunifred succeeded to all of Bernard's *honores* in Septimania and the March is the fact that he is called *marchio* in a royal document from 844.[27] Counts of Barcelona received this title because they were directly responsible for the frontier, and for much of the ninth century the same men also held Narbonne. The diploma that refers to Sunifred as *marchio* concerns landed property in Béziers, north of the Pyrenees, so the fact that it refers to Sunifred also suggests that he was the highest ranking official in that area as well. In the period 844–8 only Sunifred is titled *marchio* throughout the area, so previous historians have concluded that he did indeed acquire the Septimanian and marcher counties Bernard previously had possessed.[28] Sunifred apparently maintained peaceful relations with his Muslim neighbours after the 842 raid. The *AB* report a peace mission from Abd ar-Rahman II to Charles the Bald in 847, and there is no record of hostilities along Sunifred's border.[29] His rule as *marchio* was relatively short, only about four years to judge from documents relating the names of new counts in Agde, Barcelona, and Girona for 848 and 849.[30] Therefore Sunifred probably died in 848 – the same year that counts Bera II, the grandson of Bera who was the first count of Barcelona, in Razès and Conflent, and Sunyer I of Empúries and Roussillon dropped from the historical record.[31] Perhaps all of these men fell in the revolt of William, eldest son of Bernard of Septimania.[32] These disappearances indicate that Charles the Bald's hold on the Spanish March had weakened from its strongest point in the spring of 844.

Beyond the turbulent political events of the Spanish March, William is known as the addressee of his mother Dhuoda's *Liber manualis*. Indeed, Dhuoda warned her son in her little book about deviating from orthodox teaching on the Trinity while living in Septimania and the Spanish March.[33] The Adoptionist formulation, which had arisen in Spain but spread to the Gothic areas of the Carolingian domains, including Dhuoda's home in Uzés, was held by Carolingian thinkers to call into question the nature of Christ, thereby undermining the co-eternality and consubstantiality of the

[26] See Salrach, *El procés*, vol. 2, 17–18 on the 'bloc' of counties.   [27] CC 2, 335–7.
[28] As Salrach reasons, consolidating earlier arguments, *El procés*, 2, 17–19.   [29] *AB*, 53.
[30] Count Apollonarius of Agde in 848: *HGL*, 2, 277–279. Count Aleran of Barcelona in 849: *Les premières annales de Fontanelle (Chronicon Fontanellense)*, in *Mélanges de la Société de l'Histoire de Normandie*, ed. J. Laporte (Rouen, 1951), 80–3. Count Wifred of Girona in 850: *Marca Hispanica*, 783–4.
[31] M.-M. Costa, 'Les genealogies comtals catalanes', in *Symposium internacional*, 447–62.
[32] This is suggested in Salrach, *El procés*, vol. 2, 27–8.
[33] See C. J. Chandler, 'Barcelona BC 569 and a Carolingian Programme on the Virtues', *EME* 13 (2010): 265–91.

three persons of the Trinity.[34] For her part, Dhuoda instructed William to 'read the volumes of the orthodox Fathers, and you will find what the Trinity is'.[35] She further declares concern for those who may swerve from their faith in the Trinity.[36] For all the effort and ink spent fifty years previously, Adoptionism was still a sufficiently alarming issue, for others in the empire raised concerns about the potentially lingering heresy.[37] The learned monk Haimo of Auxerre, writing against false doctrines as late as the middle of the ninth century, recalled Charlemagne's fight against Adoptionism.[38] And indeed, even later in the ninth century Hincmar of Rheims owned a codex full of texts related to the controversy.[39] The impact that the controversy had on Carolingian thought and action was pronounced and prolonged, on a par with that of the controversy over images, which has attracted more attention in modern times.[40] Thus the Carolingian conquest of the Spanish March had a long-term impact throughout the empire.

No evidence exists for how well William heeded his mother's Trinitarian exhortations, but the young man certainly played a significant role in the politics of the Spanish March. During the time of Sunifred's rule in Septimania and the Spanish March in the 840s, Pippin II, through a settlement with Charles the Bald, had been able to re-establish his authority in Aquitaine. Yet matters were still not settled between the two kings. Pippin managed to mint coins, issue charters, and recruit followers from amongst the southern nobility.[41] William, like his father Bernard, was amongst these followers, despite having been sent to Charles as a hostage in 841 after

---

[34] Alcuin, the chief Carolingian anti-Adoptionist writer, was concerned about this controversy even as he penned his work dedicated to the Trinity. See J. C. Cavadini, 'The Sources and Theology of Alcuin's *De fide sanctae et individuae trinitatis*', *Traditio* 46 (1991): 123–46.

[35] Dhuoda, *Liber manualis*, 2.1, in *Dhuoda, Handbook for Her Warrior Son: Liber Manualis*, ed. and trans. M. Thiébaux (New York, 1998), 72–3 with fn 1. See also E. Amann, *L'Epoque Carolingienne, Histoire de l'Eglise depuis les origines jusqu'à nos jours* vol. 6, ed. Augustin Fliche and Victor Martin (Paris, 1941), 149–150.

[36] *Liber manualis* 8.13, ed. Thiébaux, 200–201 with fn 11.

[37] C. Chazelle, *The Crucified God in the Carolingian Era: Theology and Art of Christ's Passion* (Cambridge, 2001), 120, 127–8.

[38] J. J. Contreni, '"By Lions, Bishops are Meant; By Wolves, Priests": History, Exegesis, and the Carolingian Church in Haimo of Auxerre's *Commentary on Ezechiel*', *Francia: Forschungen zur westeuropäischen Geschichte* 29 (2003): 1–28.

[39] This is now ms Reims, BM 385. See S. Keefe, *A Catalogue of Works Pertaining to the Explanation of the Creed in Carolingian Manuscripts* (Turnhout, 2012), 332.

[40] Amann, *L'epoque carolingienne*, 129–152; Chazelle, *The Crucified God*. See now T. F. X. Noble, *Images, Iconoclasm, and the Carolingians* (Philadelphia, 2009).

[41] S. Coupland, 'The Coinages of Pippin I and II of Aquitaine', *Revue numismatique* 6 (1989): 194–222.

the battle at Fontenoy.[42] William pledged homage to his king and in return received the Burgundian lands of his uncle Theodoric. It was not long, however, before the relationship soured. William was already working against Charles in 844 just before his father fell, teaming up with Pippin in an ambush of Charles's army as it headed south to assist in the siege of Toulouse.[43] This ambush proved devastating to the upper ranks of the West Frankish aristocracy, forcing Charles to redistribute many *honores*, ecclesiastical as well as secular.[44] During the siege, Charles performed his royal role and supported his followers in the Spanish March and Septimania, but the ambush of his men altered both his standing and affairs in the March.

In the wake of the siege of Toulouse in 844, it seems that William received from Pippin II his father's responsibility for that county, probably with its Pyrenean appendages, Pallars and Ribagorça.[45] Pippin was in a position to appoint counts in Aquitaine, even ruling without the royal title his father had possessed, according to an agreement he had reached with Charles in 845.[46] William also gained the county of Bordeaux and duchy of Gascony in 845, giving him a solid power base in southern and south-western Aquitaine.[47] But just as the rival kings jostled for position in Aquitaine, it seems that William faced competition for the *honor* of Toulouse, if he had been appointed to it at all. Another noble from Aquitaine, Fredol, may also have expected to command the area. Charter evidence shows Fredol acting as the chief authority in Toulouse, recognizing the *aprisiones* of settlers in Pallars and Ribagorça by 849 at the latest.[48] Perhaps he was appointed to Toulouse after William's succession to Gascony, as a useful actor on behalf of Charles, who needed a counter to Pippin's man William.

---

[42] Leonce Auzias, *L'Aquitaine carolingienne* (Toulouse, 1937), 209, 259–60; Kosto, 'Hostages in the Carolingian World'.

[43] *AB*, 46–47 lists those killed.

[44] Nelson, *Charles the Bald*, 141–2 emphasizes ecclesiastical involvement in military affairs.

[45] Salrach, *El procés*, vol. 2, 25–6; Leonce Auzias, *L'Aquitaine*, 260, based on a fragment of the *Chronicle* of Ademar of Chabannes.

[46] Nelson, *Charles the Bald*, 143–4; Auzias, *L'Aquitaine*, 216–32.

[47] Auzias, *L'Aquitaine*, 161, 257–60. Abadal, in CC 3, 110 stated that a Count Fredol was governing Toulouse by 845, but Salrach could not identify the source. Salrach agrees with Abadal that William received Gascony and Bordeaux from Pippin II in 845, thus explaining Fredol's role in Toulouse.

[48] CC 3, no. 40 and 41. See Auzias, *L'Aquitaine*, 260, arguing that William held Toulouse until 848; Abadal, *El primers comtes*, 175–6, suggests that Fredol was on the scene as early as 845; Salrach, *El procés*, vol. 2, 26 offers no conclusive finding but affirms William acting as count in Bordeaux; Nelson, *Charles the Bald*, 156 suggests that Fredol was 'presumably Pippin's appointee'.

In 848, because of Pippin II's failure against a raiding band of Northmen, William was captured in Bordeaux, and a good many Aquitainians deserted to Charles the Bald. The defection threatened both the Northmen and Pippin, leading them to come to an agreement freeing William so that he could raise the March in rebellion against their common enemy, Charles, who was too successful for both sides' liking.[49] All evidence indicates that William took the opportunity of his release from captivity to attack the Spanish March, overthrowing and perhaps even killing the counts Sunifred, Sunyer, and Alaric in 848, all of whom disappear from the historical record around that time.[50] Perhaps he was motivated in part by a desire to reclaim the *honores* of his father. It is just as likely, however, that William's actions stemmed from his partisanship to Pippin II, and that he undertook his Barcelona campaign in order to damage Charles the Bald. In so doing, he might very well have derived satisfaction from harming the king who had executed his father four years earlier, claiming his father's *honores*, and maintaining his father's loyalty to Pippin. The question of William's motivation will never be fully understood. Whether he acted out of desire for what he considered his patrimony, revenge for his father, or even to uphold Pippin's claims for royal authority cannot be established. Bernard and William are unfairly characterized as rebels, however, if they merely upheld their loyalty to Pippin, even at Charles's expense. Indeed, William was Charles's hostage to ensure his father's oath sworn in 841, but he could have understood his father's execution as ending his relationship with Charles. Whereas Bernard eventually became trapped while playing both sides, William's behaviour paints him as Pippin II's partisan from early on.

At the high point of William's campaign, Charles was forced to appoint new counts in the March at an assembly held in October 849 in Narbonne: Aleran to Barcelona as well as to Empúries and Roussillon, Wifred to Girona and Besalú, and Salomo to Urgell, Cerdanya, and Conflent.[51] Their first order of business was to expel William; the task fell especially to Aleran, who was given a second-in-command, Isembard, son of the powerful Burgundian magnate Warin.[52] We know Aleran only through the

---

[49] *AB*, 56–7; Salrach, *El procés*, vol. 2, 26; Nelson, *Charles the Bald*, 150–1 and 160 on William.

[50] See *AB*, 56 and also for Charles's actions in 849, 58. Compare the events related for 850, *AB*, 58–9, with the account of the *Chron. Font.* (as in note 26), 83 and *Frag. Chron. Font. MGH SS* 2, 302–3.

[51] *AB*, 68: 'Marcam quoque Hispanicam pro libitu disponit'. Aleran is mentioned as *custos* of the city of Barcelona and the *limitis Hispanici* in the *Frag. Chron. Font., MGH SS* 2, 302. Salrach, *El procés*, vol. 2, 28 specifies the assignments.

[52] Nithard, *Histoire*, 4.4 mentions Warin having responsibility for Charles's interest in Aquitaine. See also *AB*, 68, with note 7 and Abadal, *Els primers comtes*, 176.

accounts of the *AB* and the *Chronicon Fontanellense*; no other text mentions him, but he was probably a count from Troyes.[53] Aleran may have been the son of William, count of Blois, and thus nephew of Charles the Bald's father-in-law, which perhaps placed him in the king's inner circle.[54] Isembard possibly came to the March at the head of an army of Burgundian troops.[55] Charles brought notable personnel and resources from across his kingdom to bear on the situation in the Spanish March.

William's activity, for its part, was one strand of a web of alliances incorporating him, Northmen, Basques, and Pippin II of Aquitaine all arrayed against Charles the Bald, thus tying the events surrounding William and the Spanish March more closely to the kingdom-wide conflicts than is usually appreciated. His activity created a second theatre for Charles, to the benefit of Pippin II. It seems that William called on the emir of Córdoba for help against royal Frankish troops, bringing another group of outsiders into the web.[56] That is the ultimate irony, for William's father Bernard had gained so much for his role in putting down a revolt aided by Muslim arms. Around 850, the Muslim general Ibn Mugīth led an expedition that had laid waste to some areas and besieged Girona. Aleran and Wifred held their commands firm against the Muslim incursion, but William captured Aleran and Isembard by means of trickery. The king's men were not held for long. Royal reinforcements soon defeated the rebel, and when William sought refuge in Barcelona, Isembard and Aleran defeated him. William was captured, and then executed.[57] Thus ended the revolt.

CHARLES THE BALD AND MARCHIONES, 850–865

The rest of Charles the Bald's reign after William's uprising saw the Spanish March under the control of powerful *marchiones* from prominent families of the Frankish aristocracy. It was in this period that the term *marchio* itself began to designate a rank of nobility rather than simply a frontier responsibility.[58] Traditional interpretations view the

---

[53] See brief discussions of Aleran and his family in C. West, *Reframing the Feudal Revolution: Political and Social Transformation between the Marne and Moselle, c.800–c.1100* (Cambridge, 2013), 53 and R. Le Jan, *Famille et pouvoir dans la monde franc (VIIe-Xe siècle): essai d'anthropologie sociale* (Paris, 1995), 213 and 256.

[54] William's brother was Odo of Orléans, the king's father-in-law. See Nelson, *Charles the Bald*, 81.

[55] *Frag. Chron. Font., MGH SS* 2, 302; *AB*, 69. Salrach, *El procés*, 2, 28–9 and 33.

[56] *Chron. Font.*, 83–5; Auzias, *L'Aquitaine*, 260.

[57] *AB*, 58–9 for the events of 850. See also *Frag. Chron. Font. MGH SS* 2, 302–3 for events in 849 and 850.

[58] A. Stieldorf, *Marken und Markgrafen: Studien zur Grenzsicherung durch die fränkisch-deutchen Herrscher* (Hanover, 2012), 188–349.

developments after Sunifred's death and those of Bera II and Sunyer as the 'return' of the governance of most of the Carolingian Spanish March to 'Frankish' hands until the 870s. At the time of William's fall, Sunifred's heirs probably were all minors, for there is no record of their political or legal activities; thus Charles resorted again to installing Franks in the March and Septimania.[59] The period of Frankish *marchiones* coincides with a dearth of narrative information on the Spanish March in comparison to other regions in the kingdom. Royal diplomas proliferated under Charles the Bald, including several pertaining to local interests in the March after 844. Unlike the earlier period when Louis the Pious was king of Aquitaine and events in the March were chronicled by the court-centred Astronomer and *ARF,* the best-informed surviving narrative sources are the *AB,* which pay brief and occasional attention to the southern territories. The attention given the March in the *AB* may be a function of authorial interest for, as we have seen, the record of these years at least was written by the hispanus Prudentius of Troyes. After his death in 861, the annals provide nothing on the March until they mention the accession of Wifred the Hairy in the 870s.[60] The thirty-year period of Prudentius's authorship and the career of Bernard of Septimania spanned the time when the Spanish March was not a marginal frontier zone, but a key element in the conflicts amongst the highest Frankish nobility. Powerful magnates with familial bases elsewhere in the kingdom controlled the region as they vied for supremacy with each other and stood up to the royal family. Narrative sources record the bold acts of the magnates but largely neglect the affairs of the March itself.

A Muslim incursion during 850–1 may have been conducted in retaliation for William's execution. Prudentius, in his annal entry for 852, reports that the attack on Barcelona found aid amongst the Jews of the city, but gives no details beyond the fact that Muslims killed Christians, laid waste to the city, and returned without reprisal.[61] That they did not occupy the city when, by Prudentius's account, they could have done, supports the idea of the raid as punishment rather than a campaign of conquest. Aleran, supporter of Charles the Bald and victor over the rebel William, fell in the sack leading the resistance. Abd ar-Rahman sent a peace mission to Charles soon after the sack of Barcelona, so the fight must have been

[59] R. Collins, 'Charles the Bald and Wifred the Hairy', in Margaret T. Gibson and Janet L. Nelson, eds, *Charles the Bald, Court and Kingdom* (Aldershot, 1990), 173.

[60] See *Annales de Saint-Bertin,* eds F. Grat, J. Vielliard, and S. Clémencet (Paris, 1964), v–xvi (hereafter cited as AB); Nelson, *The Annals of St-Bertin,* 6–13, esp. 7–9 on Prudentius. Salrach, *El procés,* vol. 2, 23–4 also notes the nature of the sources.

[61] *AB,* 64. Note the similar implication of Jews in the fall of Bordeaux in 848.

tremendous.[62] Also, in Gascony, it seems Charles and Musa ibn Musa of the Banu Qasi agreed to address Gascon threats jointly, and Pippin II, captured by his former supporter Sancho, was handed over to Charles, who incarcerated him in the monastery of St-Médard, Soissons in September 852.[63] Given all the travails of the previous four years, Charles himself was in a good position by the end of 852. By finally overcoming Pippin II, Charles brought under effective control Aquitaine, Septimania, and the Spanish March, and he established new people in charge of the March area counties.

Unfortunately, very little information exists about these new counts. Wifred of Girona and Besalú is perhaps known through only one document, a record of dispute settlement between the bishop of Girona and a layman named Leo dating to 851. His name may not even appear in the document, for different editors have read the same name in different ways, as either 'Uuifred' or 'Unifred'.[64] Unifred is the same name as Humfrid, who is known to be count of Barcelona and *marchio* later in the 850s; some have seen in this support for reading the name in the 851 document as his. Yet Humfrid only became count and *marchio* in 858, after the tenures of Aleran and his immediate successor, Odalric. Since there is such a gap in time between Humfrid's putative appearance in the 851 dispute record and his known appointment to marcher *honores*, it does seem safe to read the charter as giving the name of a Count Wifred. We have more, yet also questionable, evidence regarding Salomo of Urgell, Cerdanya and Conflent, who appears as a villain in the mostly legendary *Gesta comitum Barcinonensium*.[65] This twelfth-century account of the deeds of the counts was written to lend prestige to the house of Barcelona during the generation after their holdings had been merged with the kingdom of Aragon by marriage, and so is not a viable source for events of the ninth century. Established interpretation takes Salomo and Wifred as Goths from the regional minor nobility, probably related to or allied to Sunifred's family.[66]

Evidence from contemporary sources indicates that the disbursal of *honores* was one of Charles the Bald's chief tools to use in managing affairs in the Spanish March. The new *marchio* installed in 852 upon Aleran's death

---

[62] *AB*, 65. Salrach, *El procés*, vol. 2, 32–3.

[63] *AB*, 64–5, but they do not mention Musa; see Nelson, *Charles the Bald*, 162.

[64] Salrach, *El procés*, vol. 2, 33. Wifred appears in MH ap. 21 cols. 783–4. J. M. Marquès, ed., *Cartoral, dit de Carlemany, del bisbe de Girona (s. IX-XIV)* I (Barcelona, 1993), no. 8, revises the name 'Uuifredi venerabilis comitis' to 'Unifredi'.

[65] L. Barrau-Dihigo, ed., *El 'Gesta Comitum Barcinonensium'* (Barcelona, 1925), now in a newer edition by S. M. Cingolani, *Les Gesta Comitum Barchinonensium (versió primitiva), la Brevis Historia i altres textos de Ripoll* (Valencia, 2012).

[66] Abadal, *Els primers comtes*, 29–40. For the sources on Salomo see CC 6, nos. 56 and 60.

was Odalric, who came to the March from a powerful, East Frankish family. A document of a *placitum* held in the territory of Narbonne reveals some of his early activity as *marchio*. The document records a dispute between the monastery of Caunes and the layman Odilo.[67] The monastery's *mandatarius* was apparently able to produce, in the presence of Odalric and other assembled local notables, an imperial grant awarding the property to Caunes. This was a testimony Odilo was unable to refute and he therefore evacuated the property. Another document, dated to 854, shows Odalric, given the title *marchio*, petitioning Charles the Bald for a grant of property to the king's *fideles*, the 'Goths' Sumnold and Riculf.[68] Odalric aided Charles the Bald during the king's problems with Louis the German and Louis the Younger, who invaded on behalf of a group of Aquitainians in 854, and then in the agreement between Charles and Pippin II to instal Pippin's son as king of Aquitaine.[69] Muslim attacks, not noted in Frankish sources but mentioned in later Arabic accounts, targeted Barcelona in 856, wreaking much havoc and destruction.[70] The Carolingian fortress at Terrassa probably fell to Muslim hands for a time because of the raiding.[71] Odalric's suspected incompetence in defending the March probably played a role in his removal the following year, but other factors, namely questionable loyalty to Charles the Bald, were important as well. Odalric found himself dismissed from marcher office in late 857 after a series of defections throughout the kingdom that came to a head in 858; amongst the rebels was Odalric's brother, Abbot Adalard of St-Bertin. His brother's involvement suggests that Odalric himself was either in league with the rebels or simply appeared guilty by association.[72] These nobles rebelled against Charles' strong hand, extracting tribute from locals in order to sway a pair of leaders of the Northmen into agreements of loyalty.

Humfrid, Odalric's successor as *marchio*, was an East Frank himself, probably already with the title of count in Rhaetia or Alemannia, who fell out with Louis the German and transferred his loyalty to Charles the Bald.[73] By 858 Charles had given him the Spanish March and also *honores*

---

[67] *HGL* 2, no. 77.   [68] *HGL* 2, no. 144.

[69] *AB*, 77; *Annales Alamannici*, in G. H. Pertz, ed., *MGH SS*, 1. (Hanover, 1826), 44; Nelson, *Charles the Bald*, 169–73. See also M. Chaume, 'Onfroi, marquis de Gothie: ses origines et ses attaches familiales', *Annales du Midi* 52 (1940): 113–36.

[70] As reported in the Arabic histories of Ibn Idari, Ibn al-Athir, Ibn Khaldun, and al-Maqqari, translated in Millàs, *Textos dels historiadors àrabs*, nos. 111, 112, 113, and 114.

[71] See Ibn Idari and Ibn al-Athir as in note 70. See also Salrach, *El procés*, vol. 2, 51–2.

[72] *AB*, 72–9, for the years 856–8, discuss the machinations of nobles against Charles the Bald's interest; *AF*, 49–50 provide more details, including some intended to disparage Charles. Salrach, *El procés*, vol. 2, 52–4; Nelson, *Charles the Bald*, 186–8.

[73] An imperial aristocrat, Humfrid may have been the son of Count Hunruoch of Ternois and Engeltruda, thus Odalric's half-brother. See Chaume, 'Onfroi, marquis de Gothie', 128; Salrach,

in Burgundy. We know from the account of Aimoin, master of the school of St-Germain and chronicler of the translation of relics from Córdoba, that the monks Usuard and Odilard journeyed between Paris and Córdoba via Burgundy, visiting Humfrid, to whom Aimoin accords the title 'marchio Gothiae', in Beaune.[74] The monks negotiated a treaty with the Muslim leader of Zaragoza, and carried letters from Humfrid to important figures in Hispania and took the responses back with them on the return trip home.[75] The treaty allowed the new *marchio* to avoid entanglements in the March and thus free himself to deal in the wider politics of the kingdom. In the revolt of 858, when Odalric defected to Louis the German, Humfrid stayed loyal to Charles, leading forces from Septimania northward to assist Charles against the invasion of Louis the German.[76] After helping to defeat the eastern king in 859, Humfrid was able to turn to his southern *honores* and assume the leadership of Charles's supporters in March.[77]

In doing so Humfrid, whom a royal diploma calls 'dearest count' (*carissimi nobis comitis*) of Barcelona and *marchio*, is known to have interceded on behalf of individuals in Septimania and the Spanish March for royal favours. A man named Gomesindus, a *fidelis* of Charles the Bald, benefitted from his connection to Humfrid by receiving properties in the Narbonne *pagus* by royal grant in 859.[78] That same year, Charles bestowed two other properties in Narbonne, particularly at Humfrid's intercession, on Isembard, who in the previous decade had played a role in defeating William at Barcelona, but who more recently had deserted Charles in favour of Louis's invasion.[79] A third *fidelis*, Aureolus, received lands in his father Alaric's county Empúries.[80] Previous studies have connected these bestowals to the networks of noble families in the area.

El *procés*, vol. 2, 54–5, highlights this putative relationship but admits that it cannot be demonstrated.

[74] Aimoin, *De Translatione ss. martyrum Georgii monachi, Aurelii et Nathaliae*, in *PL*, 115, 940B. J. L. Nelson, 'The Franks, the Martyrology of Usuard, and the Martyrs of Cordoba', *Studies in Church History* 30 (1993): 67–80 at 74. See also A. Christys, 'St-Germain-des-Près, St Vincent, and the Martyrs of Cordoba', *EME* 7 (1998): 199–216, on the problems inherent in Aimoin's text. Christys's arguments about confusion of the date of Usuard's travels are compelling, but *AB*, 79 corroborates Usuard and Odilo's return to Francia in 858.

[75] Aimoin, *Trans. Georgii, Aurelii et Nathaliae*, 942C–94. Stieldorf, *Marken und Markgrafen*, 221–30: *Marchiones* in the ninth century made diplomatic treaties on their own initiative. See the evidentiary basis for this in the admittedly later text, Hincmar of Rheims, *De ordine palatii*, *MGH Fontes iuris Germanici antique* 3 (Hanover, 1980), c. 30.

[76] Koziol, *The Politics of Memory*, 132 with note 47; Collins, 'Charles the Bald and Wifred the Hairy', 174; J. Dhondt, *Études sur la naissance des principautés territoriales en France (IXe-Xe siècles)* (Bruges, 1948), 176.

[77] Salrach, *El procés*, vol. 2, 54–5, who again uses the term 'legitimists' for Charles's allies.

[78] *HGL* 2, no. 152.   [79] *HGL* 2, no. 151. See Koziol, *The Politics of Memory*, 136 and 185.

[80] *HGL* 2, no. 153, also *CC* 2, 352–4, a grant of royal land at the request of Humfrid.

Salrach argued that these documents and others like them show existing warm relations between Frankish *marchiones* and locally powerful families.[81] A better explanation is that high nobles like Humfrid depended on personal relationships with local people in order to govern effectively. Besides, the recipients of the diplomas are referred to as the *fideles* of Charles the Bald, not of Humfrid himself, although their relationship with Humfrid would have been crucial in linking them favourably with the king. This kind of activity does not preclude amiability, but neither does it require it; it is simply patronage. The diplomas featuring Humfrid show his power in both Septimania and the Spanish March, but they also show Charles the Bald as the area's chief patron. Ties between the March and the monarchy were strong.

In 859, some Aquitainians, identified as 'regionalists' by earlier generations of studies, incited Charles the Younger, son of Charles the Bald, to rebel against his father; an accusation of treachery levelled against Humfrid in 862 may indicate that he had joined the rebellion.[82] Charles the Bald disposed of Humfrid and gave a series of *honores* to Sunyer, probably the son of the earlier Sunyer who had been count of Empúries and Roussillon along with Alaric.[83] Humfrid held on to Narbonne and moved against Toulouse in 863 in coordination with other notables in the region.[84] He took the city by the treachery of its residents, their Count Raymond having fallen in battle. Charles the Bald apparently did not fight the rebels but first secured peace with Muslims to their south, and sent *missi* to receive the loyalty of several cities and castles in the south.[85] By the end of 863, the king's troops occupied the Burgundian estates, Pippin II was in custody, and Charles the Younger's revolt had lost momentum. Charles the Bald dispossessed his son, and Humfrid decided to flee to Italy.[86]

A TROUBLESOME MARCH, 865–878

Humfrid's successor as *marchio*, Bernard of Gothia, was the last Frankish aristocrat appointed to the post, having taken up the position in 865.[87] Salrach proposed that Bernard's rule paved the way for Catalonia's progress towards independence.[88] It is true that the years 865–78 saw the

---

[81] See commentary in Salrach, *El procés*, vol. 2, 55–8.
[82] *AB*, 90–1; Auzias, *L'Aquitaine*, 305–13, Salrach, *El procés*, vol. 2, 59.
[83] *CC* 2, 355–58, on which more below. For familial relationships, see Costa, 'Les genealogies comtals catalanes', 449–50, 452–4.
[84] *HGL*, 2, 331–6; Salrach, *El procés*, vol. 2, 61.
[85] *AB*, 103–4 and 105; Salomo, count of Urgell and Cerdanya, was the envoy to Córdoba for neutrality: Aimoin, *Translatio Beati Vincentii*, PL 126: 1018A.
[86] *AB*, 104 and 112–13.   [87] *AB*, 117.   [88] Salrach, *El procés*, vol. 2, 67.

revolts and crises of Charles the Bald's last years, the rocky start to the reign of Louis the Stammerer, and the appointment of local counts to positions of power in the March. It is also true, however, that the distancing of the March from the monarchy had less to do with Bernard's activity as *marchio*, and more to do with kingdom-wide developments and completely separate Carolingian dynastic tragedies that together resulted in a diminished royal presence in the March. In the context of the middle and late ninth century, we must also remember the rivalry amongst royal brothers and nephews, and that nobles in the various regions of the empire backed one king or another to suit their own interests. They could renege on their promises to Charles the Bald and throw their support behind Louis the German, for example. Such behaviour was impossible under earlier emperors, who had no royal brothers with whom to contend, and only became an option when the adult sons of Louis the Pious could serve as rallying points. Again it was the Frankish magnate, Bernard in this case, not those with roots in the Spanish March, who rebelled.

The first order of business for the king following Charles the Younger's revolt and Humfrid's deposition was to redistribute vacant counties taken from the rebels. Charles the Bald took advantage of the passing of a generation to allot various *honores* to his followers. The years 862–5 saw a change in the allocation of *honores* in the March and Septimania, a departure from the previous royal practice of consolidation of power in the hands of only a few counts.[89] Prevailing interpretations held that finally, after a series of rebellious *marchiones*, the king realized that such a 'supercount' constituted a threat to royal authority. More recently, Simon MacLean has argued that large magnate-ships, at least in Charles 'the Fat' III's reign, stood in for the royal sons' sub-kingdoms of earlier generations.[90] It may be, however, that the quest for constitutional history prevented generations of historians from seeing family of origin for the new counts as the main reason Charles changed his tactic in making appointments. Historians have long been engaged in a hunt for constitutional origins but have had this answer right under their noses for a very long time. Even Pertz mentioned it as such in his apparatus published 1826.[91] Beginning with Bernard Septimania, the maritime

---

[89] Salrach, *El procés*, vol. 2, 68–9 for orientation. Abadal, *Els primers comtes*, 3–6 for revision of earlier interpretations, especially that of Calmette, that Catalonia was 'invented' in the redistribution of *honores* in 865. See J. Calmette, 'Les origines de la première maison comtale de Barcelone', *Mélanges d'archeologie et d'histoire* 20 (1900): 299–306, amongst his other works that touch on the issue.

[90] S. MacLean, *Kingship and Politics in the Late Ninth Century: Charles the Fat and the End of the Carolingian Empire* (Cambridge, 2003), 75–80.

[91] *MGH SS* 1, 467.

provinces were bestowed upon 'Franks', while 'Goths' received inland *honores*. After Humfrid, though, some coastal counties south of the Pyrenees went to men of local families: Empúries and Peralada to the brothers Sunyer II and Dela, Girona and its *pagus* Besalú to Otger. Salomo continued to hold Urgell and Cerdanya inland.[92] The central Pyrenean counties Pallars and Ribagorça went to Bernard of Toulouse as appendages to his county.[93] Carcassonne was in the hands of Oliba II, nephew of Sunifred, the *marchio* of local origin who had governed in the 830s and 840s.[94] Charles offered property near Barcelona to Sunyer, giving some fiscal lands to him and others to Bishop Frodoin.[95] The *honor* of Barcelona itself, however, was given to Bernard 'of Gothia', who also held the Septimanian counties of Narbonne, Agde, Béziers, Nîmes, Maguelonne, Roussillon, and Razès.[96] Thus the practice of having the lion's share of Septimania and the March in one man's hands was not completely undone, but contemporaries may have made more of a distinction between lands north and south of the Pyrenees. This was not anything like the constitutional formation of Catalonia. Instead, 865 saw the king distributing the counties so that more men from local families could hold *honores*. This gave Charles more points of connection and patronage. It also gave the governance of the March better custodians, because individuals who would govern their counties while residing in them rather than elsewhere could focus on local affairs. Such men would also be less likely to forsake the March in favour of participation in the wider political activities of the realm. Again, this can be attributed to their somewhat lesser status, especially when compared to Humfrid. These were neither ethnic nor constitutional concerns, but rather a king changing established patterns of patronage to ensure more direct links between himself and the secular leaders of the Spanish March.

Three great magnates in control of territory in the southern reaches of the West Frankish kingdom, all named Bernard, played major roles in the politics of the later 860s and 870s. Bernard of Toulouse, son of Humfrid's victim Raymond, Bernard 'Plantapilosa', son of Bernard of Septimania, and Bernard of Gothia governed in Aquitaine, Septimania, and the Spanish March under a new sub-king, Charles the Bald's son Louis.[97] Charles organized this sub-kingdom carefully, mindful of these counts'

---

[92] Abadal, *Els primers comtes*, 8–9.
[93] *HGL*, no. 164 shows Bernard with the title *comes et marchio Tolosensis*; Auzias, *L'Aquitaine*, 322 and 340.
[94] Salrach, *El procés*, vol. 2, 69.
[95] CC 2, 355–8 for Sunyer's property, 430–3 for Frodoin's rights.
[96] *AB*, 117, (for year 865) have Charles sending Bernard to Gothia, with 'part of the March' entrusted to him. See Abadal, *Els primers comtes*, 8–9; Auzias, *L'Aquitaine*, 342.
[97] Auzias, *L'Aquitaine*, 339–42.

potential influence; royal *fideles* exercised most of the important administrative duties.[98] These new appointments in the early 860s established a balance of power, but did not leave any of the great magnates with enough power and dignity to satisfy them. Each Bernard could have complained about the *honores* not assigned him. Traditional Catalan historiography holds that all three men became bitter and began to struggle for more.[99] Situations like this helped foster competition amongst the great aristocrats, who, in the absence of opportunities for external conquest, sought to enhance their own positions by striving against each other and against Charles himself.[100] In order to ensure the effective administration of Aquitaine and provide an avenue to *Königsnähe* for the magnates, Charles installed his son Louis ('the Stammerer') as king of Aquitaine in place of the deceased Charles the Younger, who had died in 866 as a result of a head injury suffered in 864.[101] This move continued the Carolingian practice, initiated by Charlemagne, of providing a royal son as king for the large and populous region of Aquitaine, together with the adjacent areas of Septimania and the Spanish March. Charles must have imagined that the court of his son would serve as a centre of gravity for ambitious nobles.

Balancing that kind of ambition with other priorities of royal administration proved challenging. As count of Roussillon and Barcelona, Bernard of Gothia came into conflict with Bishop Frodoin of Barcelona, appointed by Charles the Bald, who granted to his bishop fiscal lands and rights usually reserved for counts. In a document no longer extant but knowable from a later confirmation by Louis the Stammerer after he had succeeded his father, Charles granted the bishop immunity, lands, and one-third of the toll to which Bernard as *marchio* would otherwise have been entitled.[102] Charles perhaps attempted to make up for the perceived slight by reassigning a county in Bernard's favour. By

---

[98] R. McKitterick, *The Frankish Kingdoms under the Carolingians* (London, 1983), 77–105; K. F. Werner, '*Missus-Marchio-Comes*. Entre l'administration central et l'administration locale de l'Empire', in W. Paravicini and K. F. Werner, eds, *Histoire comparée de l'administration (IVe-XVIIIe siècle) Beihefte de Francia* 9 (Munich, 1980), 190–239.

[99] Abadal, *Els primers comtes*, 8–9; Salrach, *El procés*, vol. 2, 68–74.

[100] This suggestion follows the line of argument in T. Reuter, 'The End of Carolingian Military Expansion', in P. Godman and R. Collins, eds, *Charlemagne's Heir: New Perspectives on the Reign of Louis the Pious (814–840)* (Oxford, 1990), 391–405.

[101] *AB*, 112 and 134; 138 for Louis assuming the kingship of Aquitaine. Hincmar as annalist of course does not note the role of *Königsnähe* in arranging the subkingdoms, but this statement follows the reasoning of MacLean, *Kingship and Politics*, 48 and 64–75. See also Nelson, *Charles the Bald*, 210–12 for the case of Aquitaine in the 860s.

[102] Salrach, *El procés*, vol. 2, 74–5. CC 2, 66–7 for Abadal's editorial discussion of the missing document, 69–71 for Louis's confirmation, which spells out that Bernard accepted the condition of the toll *per preceptum genitoris nostri*.

870, counts Salomo and Otger had died, so Charles assigned the *honores* of Urgell, Cerdanya, and Conflent to the sons of the Sunifred who had presumably been killed in William's insurrection of 848. Wifred received Urgell and Cerdanya, and Miro Conflent, likely at an assembly at Attigny in 870.[103] Neither succeeded to Otger's Girona and Besalú, and as evidence is lacking, it is assumed that these regions went to Bernard of Gothia on the premise that they were usually tied to Barcelona.[104] That was not so under Otger, or his predecessor, also named Wifred. Girona and Besalú, rather than somehow constitutionally linked with Barcelona as earlier interpretations would hold, shared a coastline with that county. Thus it fits with another pattern of Frankish appointments in the region, that of great magnates holding the maritime counties, perhaps in part because of their ability to mount and control naval defences. Regardless of the reason why he received these *honores*, by these means Bernard of Gothia was able to expand his power.

If Charles did grant Girona to Bernard, it was not enough to satisfy the count's ambition to out-manoeuvre his peers. Bernard, along with three other great magnates, refused to attend an assembly at Quierzy-sur-Oise in the summer of 877, famous for its capitulary, which was formerly interpreted as legitimating hereditary succession to *honores* and thus weakening kingship in favour of territorial aristocracy.[105] Others view the capitulary as the king asserting his rights while preparing for the possibility of his own death on campaign.[106] The capitulary indeed shows Charles as a strict manager of his kingdom and his son Louis.[107] While on the campaign, Charles stayed at Pavia and Tortona with Pope John VIII. Having received word that Karlmann, son of Louis the German, was planning to attack, Charles waited for *primores regni sui*, Abbot Hugh, Boso, Count Bernard ('Plantapilosa') of Auvergne, and Bernard, '*markio*' of Gothia, all of whom Charles had ordered to join him in Italy.[108] The magnates, however, 'had conspired and formed a plot against him together with the other leading men of the realm, with a few exceptions, and also the bishops'.[109] So they did not come, raising their arms against the king instead. Simon MacLean

---

[103] Abadal, *Els primers comtes*, 42–5 argues this rather convincingly from circumstantial evidence.

[104] Salrach, *El procés*, vol. 2, 78.

[105] *AB*, 212–13. See also *MGH Cap*. 2, 355–61. For the older interpretation that the assembled nobles protected their hereditary rights to *honores*, see for example A. R. Lewis, *The Development of Southern French and Catalan Society, 718–1050* (Austin 1965), 111.

[106] S. Airlie, 'The Aristocracy', in R. McKitterick, ed. *The New Cambridge Medieval History*, vol. 2, c.700–c.900 (Cambridge, 1995), 431–50, at 448–50; R. McKitterick, *The Frankish Kingdoms under the Carolingians* (New York, 1983), 182–4; Dhondt, *Études sur la naissance des principautés territoriales*, 204–17 and 231–58.

[107] I must agree here with Nelson, *Charles the Bald*, 248–50.   [108] *AB*, 215–16.

[109] *AB*, 216; the translation is Nelson's, 201–2.

has argued, concerning the downfall of Charles the Fat a decade later, that great magnates desired *Königsnähe* and rebelled in order to claim the attention and direct patronage of kings as a way to reinforce their own power locally.[110] It is hard to see the same logic apply in this case. If this group in the 870s were angered by some of the actions of Charles the Bald, now emperor, turning his attention to other realms and other aristocrats, they were so deeply committed to their uprising that his death and a change of direction under Louis the Stammerer did nothing to stop them. The new king, as former sub-king in Aquitaine, demanded a strong royal presence in the south, a stand apparently unacceptable to the rebels, even though it would seem to fit any desire on their part for *Königsnähe*. It is also important that both Bernard of Gothia and Boso had been appointed to the Aquitainian court of Louis the Stammerer, while Bernard of Toulouse was left out of the sub-king's inner circle. If any one of them had reason to feel slighted by being closed off from the king, it would have been this latter Bernard, yet he was not numbered amongst the rebels.[111] If anything is clear from this episode, it is that putative ethnicity had nothing to do with rising or falling political fortunes in the late-ninth-century West Frankish kingdom.

As fate would have it, Charles the Bald died on the way home from Italy.[112] The new regime as drawn up at Quierzy apparently removed Bernard of Gothia and Boso from the inner circle at the new royal court under Louis the Stammerer.[113] Upon his succession, Louis attempted to ensure loyalties by making grants, but apparently some of the *primores* of the kingdom, abbots as well as counts, were 'outraged by his granting out *honores* without their consent'.[114] He made his way to Compiègne only to find the great magnates, alongside his stepmother Richildis, ravaging everywhere they went; negotiations by messenger between Louis and the leading men of the realm ensued.[115] The magnates were divided amongst themselves into factions, one led by Abbot Hugh and the other by Abbot Gauzlin. In other words, those whose patronage was threatened positioned themselves against those who stood to gain.[116]

---

[110] MacLean, *Kingship and Politics*, 81–122.

[111] *AB*, 177–8 for the year 872 show some concessions given to Bernard of Toulouse, though not a place at Louis the Stammerer's court or higher power in the kingdom of Aquitaine.

[112] *AB*, 216–17.

[113] *MGH Cap.* 2, 358–9 in c. 12 names some individuals tasked with executing Charles the Bald's will should he die, and those individuals are not named; ch. 31 expressly concerns the *honores* of Bernard and Boso. Nelson, *Charles the Bald*, 248–51.

[114] *AB*, 218, with English, trans. Nelson, 203. Nelson, 203, n. 19 gives the details of the grants.

[115] *AB*, 218.

[116] *AB*, trans. Nelson, 203 with fn. 19 and O. G. Oexle, 'Bischof Ebroin von Poitiers und seine Verwandten', *Frühmittelalterlichen Studien* 3 (1969): 138–210 identify the factions.

Eventually, all agreed to peace, and Louis held his coronation at Compiègne, with Archbishop Hincmar of Reims presiding. There, bishops, lay abbots, and magnates all commended themselves and promised loyalty.[117]

Negotiations amongst all parties mediated by Archbishop Hincmar of Rheims ended with only Bernard of Gothia still in revolt, competing with Bernard Plantapilosa for supremacy in the south. The Council of Troyes in 878 stripped Bernard of Gothia of his *honores*, reassigning them to loyal counts in the Spanish March and Septimania.[118] These loyal counts included Wifred and his brother Miro, sons of Sunifred. In September 878, the demands of some of the magnates forced a response from Louis. Hugh, son of Lothar II, and Imino, brother of Bernard of Gothia, were excommunicated along with their accomplices.[119] Meanwhile, *honores* were redistributed. Bernard of Gothia lost out as punishment for his brother's actions; Bernard Plantapilosa and men of lesser status with bases in the Spanish March gained.[120] After Christmas, Louis the Stammerer moved towards Autun against the rebellious *marchio* Bernard of Gothia. But the king fell ill, so he sent his son Louis to Autun in his stead. Abbot Hugh, Boso, and Bernard Plantapilosa all accompanied the younger Louis on this expedition.[121] It is clear that 'the Spanish March' as a region with a supposed personality was not in revolt, but rather that the Frankish magnate appointed to its governance, a man with no family ties to the region, acted in response to what he perceived to be an affront to his honour, even seeking an alternative power base in the light of his dismissal and the reapportioning of the *honores* of the March.

The particular dynastic problems of the late 870s and 880s, when male members of the Carolingian family died at young ages, no doubt caused consternation amongst the great magnates of the Frankish kingdoms. Bernard of Gothia, of course, was removed from power and, although he caused trouble for kings as he tried to re-establish himself, never regained high status. Boso, as is known, claimed kingship for himself; Hincmar stresses that he was induced into doing so by his wife.[122] After a few years, his territories were reintegrated into direct Carolingian rule. For his part, Bernard Plantapilosa became one of 'Charles the Fat's key supporters west of the Rhine', active in Boso's old power bases in

---

[117] *AB*, 219.   [118] Abadal, *Els primers comtes*, 53–72; Salrach, *El procés*, vol. 2, 82–6, 104–5.

[119] *AB*, 222 relate that Imino had caused trouble, even ravaging lands like Northmen.

[120] *AB*, 229–230.

[121] *AB*, 234. On Hincmar's own importance, see M. McCarthy, 'Hincmar's influence during Louis the Stammerer's reign', in R. Stone and C. West, ed., *Hincmar of Rheims: Life and Work* (Manchester, 2015), 110–29.

[122] *AB*, 239.

Provence and Burgundy.[123] Again, the question arises as to how much access he had to a king based in Alemannia as compared to one based in Aquitaine. Bernard died in 886, and his sons succeeded to family lands in Burgundy, but not the *honores* elsewhere. In the case of 877–8, the magnates involved did not seek another Carolingian king but rebelled against the one best placed to offer patronage. Their uprising can best be understood in terms of forcing negotiations. They had been left out of considerations at Quierzy because their *honores* were not in question, so they needed to voice their concerns about the new regime. Perhaps in the end, these aristocrats were indeed concerned with access to the king, as a key element in defining their own status. They knew that they would uphold Louis the Stammerer's kingship. These 'rebels' were not actually rebels. In order to signal that they wanted to negotiate, they laid waste to a few fields here and there. This was at much less cost to themselves than to the peasants who eked livings from those fields. In any case they were interested in their status, their access to the court, and their roles in the court as well as their *honores* and everything related to their places in the kingdom, so they used the 'rebellion' as a way to bring about negotiations. A later chapter will take up the examination of those lesser nobles who were not amongst the rebels. Nowhere in the rebellions of the 870s is there regional separatism to be found on the part of counts, viscounts, and *fideles* of the Spanish March whose families were based there.

MONARCHY, MARCH, AND IDENTITY UNDER CHARLES THE BALD

There is no evidence that the nobles' supposed ethnic identities as Goths or Franks was a factor in the appointments of individuals to *honores* in the Spanish March. It is a preoccupation of the nationalistic line of thinking amongst Catalan historians. In the aftermath of William's uprising in the late 840s, there were positions to be filled. As we saw above, the information about the men who took office in this period is scant. The early preoccupation with the 'ethnicity' of Salomo, the new count of Urgell and Cerdanya, seems to have been a settled question by the late twentieth century, when it became accepted that he came from a family that also produced counts for Carcassonne, Roussillon, and Empúries.[124] Aleran, appointed to Barcelona, and his successors, all are identified as coming from Frankish families. As they all also held the maritime counties, the allocation of inland counties to men of local, 'Gothic' origin and lesser

---

[123] MacLean, *Kingship and Politics*, 69–70. See also M. Innes, *State and Society in the Early Middle Ages: the Middle Rhine Valley, 400–1100* (Cambridge, 2000), 222–4.

[124] Costa, 'Les genealogies comtals catalanes', 450.

status could have been intended to establish a balance of power in the March.[125] Salrach, who espouses this idea, also admits it is a fragile thesis because of the sparse documentary support. An alternative view is that Charles the Bald appointed Franks from the upper echelon of imperial society to the maritime region because they possessed the resources necessary to maintain naval defences. The absence in the record of references to Muslim raids along the coasts of Gothia in the 850s may lend support to this idea or even indicate that no defences were necessary. The *AB* record river raids into the Spanish March, Septimania, or Aquitaine for the years 842 and 844, but mention no such raids for the 850s. It could be that raids never took place, or perhaps defences were more up to the task of defending against them. Yet the 'balance of power' thesis is unsatisfactory, and the 'maritime resources' view only partially satisfying. It is better to see instead that the major magnates were awarded the Spanish March territories in order to secure their loyalty during Charles the Bald's struggles against his relatives. He wanted major players on his side, and the March *honores* were amongst the tools he had at his disposal.

Clearly there was no 'ethnic' tension in Gothia, the Spanish March, or elsewhere at the root of turmoil in the 850s. Sumnold and Riculf, *fideles* of Charles the Bald, are the only individuals identified by ethnic labels in the source material. They are not known to have had any role in the rebellion; the attribution of 'Gothic' identity merely marked them as members of the politically active class in Roussillon and enhanced the aura of Carolingian imperialism. In the end, Charles the Bald was able to recruit support away from his brother Pippin II of Aquitaine for a period of years, using the landed wealth of 'Gothia', now an integrated province of the empire, as a lure.

As noted, earlier scholarship framed the revolt of 859–63 in terms of those supporting Aquitanian regional autonomy, emblematized by Pippin II, against those who remained loyal to the 'legitimate' ruler, Charles the Bald. Some have even proposed that national separatism provided the rationale for the revolt.[126] Yet the leaders of the insurrection have been shown to be Franks appointed by the king to direct the affairs of the March and Aquitaine. The major figure of local, 'Gothic' lineage in the affair was Salomo, who proved his loyalty to Charles the Bald by securing peace with the caliph in Córdoba. As events would play out in the following decade, Frankish magnates continued to cause more

[125] Salrach, *El procés*, 2, 39–40.
[126] Dhondt, *Études sur la naissance des principautés territoriales*, 210, in which Dhondt identified Humfrid as a sort of Goth patriot. Collins, 'Charles the Bald and Wifred the Hairy', 178–9, argues otherwise. Obviously the account here accepts the identification of Humfrid as a Frank.

problems for Charles than the loyal nobles of local descent. This evidence leads to the conclusion that ethnicity or ethnic labels were not the driving force behind political action. Men of lesser status needed their connections to the king, while great magnates had some reason to be upset and supported the rebellion of the royal son – it is important to note that they were not trying to overthrow the monarchy or the dynasty, just to replace the king with a member of his own family. Probably their objective was not even really to overthrow Charles the Bald, but rather to bring their grievances to his attention. The chief source for the period, the *Annales Bertiniani*, concentrates on royal concerns and so does not provide insight as to the complaints of these nobles against Charles. Nevertheless, given what we do know, ethnicity cannot be said to have played a role.

Despite the machinations of the most highly placed aristocrats in the West Frankish kingdom, during the reign of Charles the Bald there was remarkable consistency in the relationships cultivated between the kings and more regionally based actors, whether individual laymen, bishops, or monasteries. Indeed, a series of royal documents illustrates that the king valued his connections to his friends on the ground in the Spanish March, thus anchoring the March to the monarchy. It was likely the existence of these ties that resulted in Bernard of Gothia carrying out his rebellion in Burgundy rather than the March in the first place, as the king's *fideles* built a firm footing for his authority in the region they called home.

As the monk Aimoin's account of his *frater* Usuard's journey from Saint-Germain-des-Prés to Córdoba and back indicates, Humfrid was often absent from the March while he held the title, both before and after the rebellion of 858. That left subordinates known as viscounts to govern the area. One such man, Sunifred of Barcelona, is recorded in Aimoin's text, while another viscount, Richelm of Roussillon, figures in a dispute charter from that area.[127] Other Frankish *marchiones* in the middle of the ninth century also had subordinates to assist in the mundane governance of their regions. Viscounts are known throughout the area from Roussillon to Urgell.[128] Unlike the usurper Galindo or Raymond of Toulouse, the magnates of the 860s and 870s were too busy pursuing their objectives elsewhere to be concerned with matters in the March, even when they did control Toulouse with its marcher territories in Pallars and Ribagorça. In contrast to the findings in other regions of the Carolingian realms, royal patronage of monasteries does not seem to have

---

[127] Aimoin, *De Translatione ss. martyrum Georgii monachi, Aurelii et Nathaliae,* in *PL* 115. For Richelm, *HGL* vol. 2, no. 150.
[128] A. de Fluvià, *Els primitius comtats i vescomtes de Catalunya* (Barcelona, 1989), 125–232.

been prominent in the Spanish March, although kings did sometimes issue diplomas to houses in the region.[129] Therefore, *marchiones* relied on lay individuals and families with firmer connections to local sociopolitical networks, and indeed Charles the Bald saw value in emphasizing his own relationship to such men, naming them as *fideles* and *missi*.[130]

There were, moreover, individuals who received royal grants from Charles. In 847 the king granted recognition of proprietorship of lands in the Narbonne *pagus* to his *fideles* Adefonsus and his kin Gomesindus and Durannus. Abadal, editor of the royal diplomas issued to recipients in the Spanish March, usually did not include documents concerning land outside of the modern areas of Catalan culture but made an exception in this case because he believed the *fideles* in this instance to have been Catalans from Roussillon. The diploma recognizes at least part of the properties as having been *aprisiones* in an earlier generation and upholds the family's rights. Yet Abadal's interpretation is perhaps more noteworthy in that it exhibits the latent nationalism bound up with the early study of 'Carolingian Catalonia', for nowhere in the text are Adefonsus and his kin referred to by any supposed ethnic label.[131] Kings simply wanted to extend and confirm patronage to individuals as a means to tap into local networks of association and thereby ensure loyalty.

Two years later, when Charles was present in Narbonne, he recognized the full proprietorship of Teudefred over the villa of Fontejoncosa and its associated villae, which Teudefred's father John had acquired by *aprisio* in the time of Charlemagne. Teudefred himself had sought and received confirmation of the properties from Charles near Toulouse in 844, as John had likewise done before Louis the Pious in 815; the 849 diploma represents an augmentation of the possessions concerned.[132] Here is evidence of a sustained relationship between the Carolingian royal family and a locally based family in Septimania over generations; Charlemagne, Louis, and Charles supported and enhanced the claims of their *fideles* for about fifty years, extending patronage networks that provided pathways for royal power to penetrate to the March. In these diplomas from the 840s, Charles is recognized as the legitimate source of that royal power, and the locals of his 'Gothic' provinces bound themselves to him.[133]

---

[129] See for example the prominence of monasteries as the centres of political networks in Alsace as described by H. Hummer, *Politics and Power in Early Medieval Europe: Alsace and the Frankish Realm, 600–1000* (Cambridge, 2005).

[130] Lewis, *The Development of Society*, 114–15 with references (although his citation in fn. 8 to CC 2, 325–6 is erroneous).

[131] CC 2, 340–2.   [132] CC 2, 343–5, with the preceding grants 307–11, 320–1, 338–9.

[133] See a similar argument regarding Charles's Toulouse diplomas in Koziol, *The Politics of Memory*, 71.

Another faithful supporter of Charles the Bald's, a man named Teutmundus, is known from only one extant document. Charles bestowed upon Teutmundus seven manses of royal property in Roussillon in 853.[134] He repeated a gift of royal property in the same county the next year, to the benefit of his *fideles* Sumnold and Riculf, whom the text identifies as Goths.[135] As a later chapter will discuss, the term 'Goth' by the end of the ninth century may have become less an ethnic label than a designation of owning certain property,[136] so it may be that Sumnold and Riculf were either soldiers or claimants to such properties; certainly they were not considered immigrants from al-Andalus, to whom the label *hispani* would have applied. Regardless of Sumnold and Riculf's lineage, it is clear that the foremost issue in earning royal patronage was loyal service, not any identification that modern observers would call ethnicity.

The same pattern persisted throughout the 850s and 860s. Humfrid, as *marchio*, interceded on behalf of men based both north and south of the Pyrenees, successfully procuring grants of royal property for individuals named Aureolus and Gomesindus.[137] While Humfrid may have been the key figure for causing the grant to take place, owing to his position as *marchio* placing him as a liaison between the local men and the king, Charles the Bald was careful to name each man *fidelis noster*. There would be no confusion as to where Aureolus and Gomesindus should place their ultimate loyalty, if Charles could help it. They were his faithful men and received grants from his own property. Likewise, having dismissed Humfrid for his role in the rebellion, the king seems to have referred to Sunyer as *fidelis* in a grant of royal property in the *pagus* of Barcelona. The surviving documentation, an eighteenth-century copy, is in poor condition, but editorial reconstruction has had reason to feature Sunyer as the recipient. The dating clause of the diploma is intact, making it clear that the grant was issued on 19 August 862, and the letters 'Su' follow the phrase *fideli nostri* in spelling out the beneficiary of the decree. Abadal reasoned that Sunyer was here receiving the land that Humfrid had held in benefice from the king. The grant expressly excludes possessions of Bishop Frodoin of Barcelona and the lands that certain *servi* had brought into cultivation from waste.[138] In studies of the period, Sunyer is referred

---

[134] CC 2, 345.　　[135] CC 2, 347 (also cited above as evidence of Odalric's role as *marchio*).

[136] J. Lalinde Abadía, 'Godos, hispanos y hostolenses en la órbita del rey de los francos', in *Symposium internacional*, vol. 2, 35–74.

[137] CC 2, 352, a diploma which exists as a parchment original and cited above with *HGL* 2, no. 153 as evidence of Humfrid bearing the title *marchio*, bestows to Aureolus properties in the counties of Empúries and Peralada; *HGL* 2, no. 152 grants to Gomesindus lands *in pago Narbonense*.

[138] CC 2, 355–7 for Abadal's justification of editorial choices, 357–8 for the text of the document.

to amongst the 'Goths' who served Carolingian kings in the Spanish March, but in this admittedly fragmentary evidence, no such ethnic label appears.

By the end of the 860s, labels emphasizing differences amongst the parts of the West Frankish kingdom, though not its people, perhaps begin to proliferate. A royal diploma dated to 869, surviving in a seventeenth-century copy, uses the term *Septimaniae regnum* to locate the royal properties granted to the *fideles* Dodo and Otger in the *pagus* of Roussillon.[139] These men, like the others discussed here, are not identified by an ethnic label. A later chapter will take up the issue of later Carolingian kings' perception of Septimania as a 'sub-kingdom' within their realm, or at least their use of such terminology in royal documents. For present purposes, the document confirms that ethnic terminology as applied to individual laymen was very limited in the time of Charles the Bald, who placed more emphasis on the status of such men as *fideles* who could support royal authority in Septimania and the Spanish March. As seen above, these links proved useful in this period, when the *marchiones* themselves could not be trusted to remain loyal to Charles in the face of competition from royal relatives.

In addition to that from laymen, Charles the Bald counted on support from monasteries and episcopal churches in the Spanish March, and so he extended patronage to them. No fewer than nine royal diplomas to such recipients were issued during his reign, most of which survive in later copies. One that does survive in the original is a diploma of confirmation Charles issued for the monastery of Amer in Girona. Acts of confirmation were of course a vital function for new kings to perform, and indeed Charles did just that for the same house in 844.[140] The later confirmation, made at the instigation of the abbot Theodosius, solidifies the royal immunity and guarantee of the monks' right to elect their abbot that had originally been established by Louis the Pious.[141] In 860, Charles also extended the immunity to new properties in Girona.[142] The context for the diploma is of course the monastery's acquisition of these properties, including a church that had only recently been built, but also the political and military strife facing Charles throughout his kingdom at the time. Theodosius needed a royal document to support his immunity for the new properties, and Charles needed to act as a king, that is to say as a benefactor of his followers and as the fount of authority. In 869 Charles

---

[139] CC 2, 359–60.
[140] Articulated most recently by Koziol, *The Politics of Memory*, esp. in chapters 2 and 3; CC 2, 11–13.
[141] Louis's diploma no longer exists, even in copies, but both of Charles's documents refer to it. See CC 2, 10.
[142] CC 2, 14–16.

again issued a second diploma for a monastery to which he had made an earlier grant in 844, this time for Arles in Roussillon.[143] The text of the document gives a considerable list of properties concerned in the immunity, but does not explicitly confirm and expand the earlier grant.[144] Rather, it takes the form of a completely new act, largely because a Viking attack had damaged the monastery and its archive.[145] Abbot Hilperic understood Charles to be the only legitimate authority to guarantee the monastery's rights; indeed, as the house had been placed under royal protection, it was Charles's duty to do so. Charles could perform the role of king for his distant subjects no better than in making this grant. Another confirmation made in 869, for the monastery of Sureda, concerns the community's possessions, immunity, and right to elect the abbot. The text refers explicitly to Louis the Pious but does not appear, as others do, to re-use the language of Louis's document.[146] These acts of confirmation show the monasteries of the Spanish March to have been crucial nodes in the network of association connecting the March to the Carolingian kings. Louis's acts represented the first stages of integrating the March into the empire, while Charles's show that the integration of the frontier province had been firmly established. Abbots asked the king for confirmation of their houses' rights; if they had not imagined themselves as part of the community of which the king was head, they would have had no reason to seek him out.

In 860, Charles confirmed the jurisdiction of the church of Urgell over the parishes in the western reaches of the Spanish March, including Cerdanya, Berga, Pallars, and Ribagorça.[147] The king also confirmed the Urgell church as in possession of various properties and rights, *sicut aliae ecclesiae Septimaniae*, Urgell's in particular pertaining to the *pagus* of Andorra, the phrase 'just as other churches in Septimania' implying that the March south of the Pyrenees was seen as part of Septimania. The importance of personal relationships is highlighted in this act, which was possible partly because of Bishop Wisadus's participation at the Council of Tusey, which placed him in much closer contact with Charles than was possible in his home diocese. In a grant dated to early 866, to the monastery of Banyoles in Besalú, a *pagus* usually associated with the county of Girona, Charles again referred to his father's earlier act when renewing royal recognition of the monastery's lands; he further granted immunity to Banyoles.[148] The Besalú area received more attention the

---

[143] CC 2, 30–2.   [144] For the 844 document, see above and CC 2, 27–9.
[145] The text makes no mention of the attack; evidence comes from a letter Abbot Hilperic sent to Charles the Bald. See Abadal's introduction to the text, CC 2, 30.
[146] CC 2, 273–5. See Koziol, *The Politics of Memory*, 98–9 for re-use of language.
[147] CC 2, 286–8.   [148] CC 2, 55–7.

next day when, upon the intercession of Otger, count of Girona, Charles granted immunity to a new *cella* and placed it under royal protection. The diploma names the *villare* Revidazer as one of the properties of the new monastery, noting the place as having been put to the plough 'by certain Goths and Gascons' at an unspecified time.[149] Finally, two documents from 871 helped to establish other new monasteries. For the small house at Aguges in Besalú, only one Carolingian royal diploma exists: Charles the Bald's recognition of Abbot Ricimir's foundation and confirming its possessions. The text clearly exempts the *aprisiones* made by hispani in the area but does not refer to any individuals as either Goths or hispani.[150] The other document concerns the founding of Sant Andreu de Eixalada, which later moved to become Sant Miquel de Cuixà after a devastating flood. That flood destroyed the original diploma, but copies were made which allow the text to survive. Protasius, the founding abbot, along with six other priests and a following of free men, left the parish of Urgell with the permission of Bishop Wisadus to establish a community living under the Rule of Benedict.[151] Clearly, these were men of local origin, but the text does not identify them as Goti or hispani.

The entire series of documents issued in the 860s shows a tendency by either Charles or those who drew up his documents, or both, to make distinctions based on geographical conceptions. As in earlier generations, Septimania was the collection of counties on the coast from the Rhône to the Pyrenees, now explicitly indicated to extend over the mountains into Urgell. Meanwhile hispani were those whose families had originated in areas under Muslim control. Urgell was within the ecclesiastical province of Narbonne, a city that was also the political centre of Septimania, so identifying Urgell as part of Septimania follows the logic of church organization. As was the case with the laymen discussed above, the abbots, monks, bishops, and priests named in these documents are not identified by 'ethnic' labels. These points taken together suggest that the Carolingian court in the time of Charles the Bald thought more along the lines of personal ties of loyalty and patronage rather than ethnicity.

THE CHURCH IN THE MARCH

Ecclesiastical politics in the March provide some further insight about how the region fit into the wider Carolingian world. A telling episode

---

[149] CC 2, 219–1: 'quoddam villare nomine Revdazer in eodem pago a quibusdam Gotis et Guasconibus exartatum'.

[150] CC 2, 176–7.

[151] CC 2, 85–90. See also J. A. Bowman, *Shifting Landmarks: Property, Proof, and Dispute in Catalonia around the Year 1000* (Ithaca, 2004), 155–6 for the reconstruction of the archive after the flood.

revolves around the cult of Saint Eulalia of Barcelona. According to tradition, Eulalia was a young girl from Roman Barcelona who found martyrdom in the persecutions of Diocletian's reign. There seems to have been a local cult in and around the city from at least the sixth century, and perhaps since the fourth. If the text from late medieval manuscripts of the *Translatio beatae Eulaliae* can be trusted as relaying a story from the ninth century, the relics of the late antique martyr-saint of Barcelona were moved from a church outside the city walls to the cathedral within the city in the 870s thanks to Bishop Frodoin. According to this text, Frodoin rediscovered Eulalia's remains and translated them to the cathedral, accompanied by appropriate public fanfare, in 877.[152] To commemorate this act, he set up an inscription.[153]

Compilers of martyrologies – from Bede in the eighth century to the Anonymous of Lyon, followed by Florus and Ado, and finally Usuard – were all familiar with Eulalia's story, even if they confused some of the details, like the date of her martyrdom, with those pertaining to Eulalia of Mérida. Usuard in particular deserves brief attention, because he is known to have travelled to Spain, and the text that records his journey mentions Eulalia as a martyr venerated in the towns Usuard visited along the way to Córdoba.[154] An entry for Eulalia appears in Usuard's martyrology, under the correct, locally observed date of 12 February.[155] Usuard travelled to Barcelona, but it remains unknown whether his entry for Eulalia of Barcelona was based on knowledge of the Barcelona tradition or on the text known in Gaul. That he has the date correct might indicate that he knew the Barcelona tradition, but there are texts from ninth-century Gaul that also have the correct feast date of 12 February. Furthermore, Usuard gives no information about Eulalia's martyrdom, while his entry for Eulalia of Mérida, for 10 December, has more details about her tortures, which are the same as those the Barcelona saint is said to have suffered in the Barcelona text. It seems that Usuard followed his textual sources and corrected the date for Eulalia of Barcelona according to what he learned on his travels, but made no further changes to his work.

At about the same time that Usuard was finishing his martyrology, a new bishop took office in Barcelona. Just a few years later, this bishop, Frodoin, had found Eulalia's relics and translated them to the

[152] See also Abadal, *Els primers comtes*, 68–70.
[153] See the transcription in A. Elías de Molins, *Catálogo del Museo Provincial de Antigüedades de Barcelona* (Barcelona, 1888), 169.
[154] See J. Dubois, ed., *Le Martyrologe d'Usuard: texte et commentaire* (Brussels, 1965), introduction: 'La vie d'Usuard', 133.
[155] Dubois, ed., *Le Martyrologe d'Usuard*, 179.

cathedral.[156] The text commemorating the translation survives in three manuscripts of the cathedral archive in Barcelona, all of which date to the fourteenth or early fifteenth century.[157] According to the text, the provincial archbishop, Sigebod of Narbonne, came to Barcelona in order to find Eulalia's remains and take them back with him, to instal her relics in a new church he was building and dedicating to her name. After gruesome tortures at the hands of Roman persecutors, Eulalia had been buried at a location now unknown.[158] After centuries of rest in that place, her faithful felt forced to move her remains in 713 because of the Muslim invasion of Spain. In the 870s Sigebod attempted to find them in a church outside the city walls, ostensibly to translate them to his church in Narbonne. The enterprise took much longer than the archbishop had anticipated, so he left before the searchers could find the saint.[159] There have been few studies of the *inventio* and *translatio* of Eulalia of Barcelona, but there is a consensus that the text's portrayal of trouble locating her tomb served as an indication that she wanted to stay in Barcelona – the city of her birth, short life, and martyrdom – despite the fact that as important a person as the archbishop made the trip intending to translate her to his own, more prestigious church. One scholar even argues that his failure enhanced the holiness of the relics; that is, Eulalia herself appeared more exalted thanks to the presence of the archbishop.[160]

After Sigebod's departure, 'the man of God, Bishop Frodoin' led all the people in a three-day fast, and then personally took up the task of finding her. His men finally located Eulalia's resting place, where they noticed a sweet odour emanating from her tomb.[161] Frodoin's success in finding the relics after his archbishop's departure is more significant to issues of prestige, for both the martyr and the bishop, than the earlier failure to do so. The church where Frodoin and his crew found Eulalia was outside the city walls, her remains still positioned as they had been in the eighth century, so they had to carry them to the gate, draped in a white stole and accompanied by candles. Her marble tomb became too heavy to carry, so

---

[156] Edited in Á. Fàbrega Grau, *Santa Eulalia, de Barcelona: revisió de un problema histórico* (Rome, 1958), 151–5, as well as by S. Puig y Puig, Episcopologio de la Sede Barcinonense (Barcelona, 1929), 357–9, but without critical apparatus.

[157] Fàbrega Grau, *Santa Eulalia*, 151, reviews the manuscripts.

[158] According to tradition, as part of these tortures, Eulalia was rolled in a barrel down the little street now called Baixada de Santa Eulalia, or 'Saint Eulalia's descent'.

[159] Fàbrega Grau, *Santa Eulalia*, 151–2.

[160] J.-F. Cabestany Fort, 'El culte de Santa Eulàlia a la catedral de Barcelona (s. ix–x)', *Lambard* 9 (1997): 159–65, at 162. See also Puig y Puig, *Episcopologio*, 357–9 (the edition of the text) and Abadal, *Els primers comtes*, 68.

[161] Fàbrega Grau, *Santa Eulalia*, 152–3. The translation is mine.

Frodoin ordered his men to genuflect and pray earnestly to God, who enabled them to complete the task.[162] After a week-long celebration with candles, fasts, vigils, prayers, and so forth, Frodoin began to build a crypt.[163] When it came time to lower Eulalia's remains into the new crypt, they again became too heavy to move. Following a miracle involving the theft and restoration of one of the saint's fingers, Frodoin and his men were finally able to lay her body at rest.[164]

This episode certainly possesses significance beyond the translation itself, to the issue of what Frodoin stood to gain, and why he would move Eulalia's body. The text points to Sigebod's designs on the relics as the initial impetus, which makes Frodoin appear far more humble, and thus more worthy, than his superior. Note that Frodoin only became determined to find Eulalia after the enterprise had already begun at the archbishop's initiative. It is widely accepted, especially in Catalan historiography, that Frodoin was probably a Frank, entrusted with a 'complex and difficult mission' to contribute to the administration of the county and bishopric of Barcelona and the neighbouring county of Girona, and maybe even the bishopric of Girona until the appointment of Teuter to the office of bishop there.[165] The argument that Frodoin was a Frank beset by trouble in a Gothic land assumes that he had to confront the last vestiges of Visigothic liturgy and thought, which had posed challenges for Carolingian administrators and religious scholars nearly a century earlier in the controversy over Spanish Adoptionism, in that its language tended to make Adoptionist teaching readily palatable for local audiences.[166] Moreover, the argument hinges on the claim that '[a] certain resistance' to the Frankish church was fomented by newly arrived clergy and laity from Muslim-held territories who were faithful to the authority of the archbishop of Toledo.[167] There is no evidence whatsoever concerning Frodoin's origin or identity, nor is there textual evidence that he attempted to enact liturgical change. Yitzhak Hen argues that the

---

[162] Fàbrega Grau, *Santa Eulalia*, 153.   [163] Fàbrega Grau, *Santa Eulalia*, 153–4.

[164] Fàbrega Grau, *Santa Eulalia*, 154.

[165] Cabestany Fort, 'El culte de Santa Eulàlia', 159. The tradition goes back at least to Abadal, *Els primers comtes*, 6–7 and 177–8. See also A. M. Mundó, 'Les changements liturgiques en Septimnie et en Catalogne pendant le période préromaine', *Les cahiers de Saint-Michel de Cuxa* 2 (1972): 29–42 at 38 and G. Feliu i Montfort, 'Els inicis del domini territorial de la Seu de Barcelona', *Cuadernos de historia económica de Cataluña* 14 (1976) 45–61 at 46. See for information on Frodoin and the royal diploma CC 2, 65–7.

[166] Cabestany Fort, 'El culte de Santa Eulàlia', 159–60 and Chandler, 'Heresy and Empire: the Role of the Adoptionist Controversy in Charlemagne's Conquest of the Spanish March', *International History Review* 24 (2002): 505–27. 505–27. Cabestany Fort cites no sources for these two important aspects of interpretation, that Frodoin was a Frank charged with these tasks, and the existence of resistance to the Roman liturgy being imposed by Frankish authority.

[167] Cabestany Fort, 'El culte de Santa Eulàlia', 159–60.

Carolingians were not as staunchly opposed to regional variations in liturgy as was commonly held for a long time and emphasizes that 'Visigothic' elements were incorporated into royally approved liturgy during the reign of Charles the Bald.[168] Further, in outperforming his own superior, Frodoin would seem to have upheld local customs more than submission to the norms of the Frankish kingdom. It seems more likely that Frodoin engaged in what would today be termed 'community building'. As the new bishop, he needed to affirm his role amongst his flock in Barcelona, or even to establish himself amongst his peers in the March.[169] In any case, trying to find explanations for behaviour in terms of ethnicity is unhelpful for understanding the more general power structures linking the Spanish March to the Frankish monarchy.

Frodoin's precarious political situation was clear at the 874 Council of Attigny, where he presented wrongs done to him and exposed the impediments to his administrative and organizational work, as well as problems with pastoral care in the bishopric of Barcelona.[170] A priest named Tyrsus from Córdoba usurped Frodoin's rights by setting up a small church in the city. Tyrsus's presence may support the idea of the existence in Barcelona of a community of immigrants from al-Andalus, even though there is no indication in the text of a body of followers he brought with him. Through the 'insolence' of a priest (probably Tyrsus), a 'faction of Baio' had claimed the castle of Terrassa, which by rights ought to have been under Frodoin's jurisdiction. Other men, named Madascius and Ricosind and identified as Goths, usurped property rights in the locality. The council of course supported Frodoin's rights and authority.[171] It also appears that during 877, Charles the Bald sent ten pounds of silver to Frodoin to help defray the costs of repairs or improvements to the church building.[172] The following year, Louis the Stammerer honoured the bishop by confirming to the see immunity, lands, and a third part of the toll of Barcelona, raising the prestige of Frodoin himself and also of the see of Barcelona; the diploma mentions that Eulalia rested in the church of the Holy Cross, an indication that she

---

[168] Y. Hen, *The Royal Patronage of Liturgy in Frankish Gaul to the Death of Charles the Bald* (London, 2001), esp. 138–46.

[169] F. Lifshitz, *The Norman Conquest of Pious Neustria* (Toronto, 1995), 18–99 on the notion of celebrating local cults as acts of resistance to external political pressure.

[170] Feliu i Montfort, 'Els inicis', 46–50 has a good discussion of these and related issues.

[171] *MGH Conc.* 4, 597–600. See also *MGH Cap.* 2, no. 303 and CC 2, 430–3. Tyrsus is indeed the primary concern of the Attigny *acta*. The entire document is devoted to Frodoin's problems, and the other offenders are named. See also Cabestany Fort, 'El culte de Santa Eulàlia', 159–160.

[172] Abadal, *Els primers comtes*, 55, 59, 63. See CC 2, 434–5 for what may be a letter directly from Charles the Bald to his loyal supporters in Barcelona, dated to 877. The document survives as an original in the ACB; see Abadal's discussion, with references to earlier scholarship, on the controversy as to whether the parchment contains an autograph note by the emperor himself.

had already been translated.[173] Ricosind's property was revoked by both Louis and the Council of Troyes in 878.[174] The councils and the kings' interventions show Barcelona as a fully functioning part of the West Frankish kingdom. It is clear that Frodoin sought benefits from earthly and heavenly patrons alike.

It is reasonable to conclude that Frodoin moved Eulalia to the cathedral in order to create a bond between the saint and himself. By forging and strengthening the physical and spatial connection between bishop and patron saint, the bishop could legitimize his own position as spiritual leader of the city and the diocese. Eulalia was a fairly famous saint who could very well have been familiar to Frodoin because of the existence of her cult in Gaul and beyond, as evidenced by the independent textual tradition, or through other channels, such as the martyrologies produced in Lyon. As bishop in Barcelona, Frodoin could harness the saint's popularity for his benefit, while reciprocating by giving her a worthier resting place.

Bishops were men of power in the Catalonian counties.[175] Besides acting as powerful men locally just as counts, bishops in the Spanish March connected themselves to the wider empire by participation in councils. Although evidence for their participation is sparse for the first half of the ninth century, as subscription lists for the councils are unavailable, marcher bishops participated at synods in the second half of the century, especially when synodal business concerned them directly. Unfortunately, we have no evidence for the participation of bishops from the Pyrenean region in the councils held elsewhere in the empire for most of the ninth century. One document, issued during Charles the Bald's siege of Toulouse in 844, directs priests' behaviour towards bishops, governs the intake of their daily bread, and spells out other pastoral and administrative responsibilities. The decree notably and explicitly draws on councils of the Visigothic kingdom.[176] Between the final council of the Adoptionist Controversy (799) and the accession of King Odo in Francia (888), marcher bishops were present at three synods: Tusey in 860, Attigny in 874, and Troyes in 878. As a later chapter will show, bishops from the Spanish March thereafter took part in the

---

[173] CC 2, 68–71.

[174] For an overall account of the important Council of Troyes, W. Hartmann, *Die Synoden der Karolingerzeit im Frankenreich und in Italien* (Paderborn, 1989), 336–40; see also the royal diploma of Louis, CC 2, 68–72.

[175] The general work on bishops during the Carolingian period is now S. Patzold, *Episcopus. Wissen über Bischöfe im Frankenreich des späten 8. bis frühen 10. Jahrhunderts* (Ostfildern, 2008).

[176] CC 2, 426–9; also *MGH Cap.* 2, no 255, cited above. It mentions councils of Toledo IV and Braga III concerning the measures of grain, wine, and such things that bishops might legitimately accept.

provincial synods of Arnustus, the active archbishop of Narbonne from about 890 to 920, and sporadic meetings throughout the rest of the tenth century.

Felix of Urgell participated famously in the Council of Aachen, admitting his error for the final time in the presence of Charlemagne and the churchmen of the kingdom. The only other clergy from the Spanish March known to have been in attendance were also from the Urgell diocese.[177] At that time Girona and Elna were the only other established Carolingian bishoprics in the area, for Barcelona was not yet in Frankish hands, and Vic did not have a bishop until seventy years later when its area was reorganized. The lack of a surviving subscription list for the great council means that the participation of other marcher prelates remains unknown.

Three bishops from the Spanish March attended the synod of Tusey (860), which brought together bishops from the kingdoms of Charles the Bald, Lothar II, and Charles of Provence, under their archbishop, Fredold of Narbonne. Bishops Audesindus of Elna (852–85), Ataulf of Barcelona (known only by his subscription to the synod), and Wisadus of Urgell (857–72) all subscribed to the *acta* of the synod dedicated to the issues of predestination and church robbers.[178] More important for the church in the March were the proceedings of the council of Attigny (874).[179] The entire convocation concerned conflict in the diocese of Barcelona.[180] Its bishop, Frodoin (c.862–74), complained that Tyrsus, the migrant priest from Córdoba, celebrated Mass in the diocese without episcopal permission, and also that he baptized and administered Communion. The council excommunicated Tyrsus. It also took measures against a certain Baio, who illegally celebrated festivals in Terrassa, outside the city of Barcelona and the location of the defunct Visigothic-era bishopric of Egara. The final act of the council treated a dispute over possession of land by two Goths, Madascius and Ricosindus, who had obtained it by means of dubious documents. The church of St Stephen claimed ownership of the property Madascius held, while the cathedral of Santa Eulalia, the see of Barcelona, contested Ricosindus. The matter was to be taken up by royal *missi*. In 874, the affairs of the Spanish March were important

---

[177] *Concilium Aquisganense, MGH* Conc. 2, ed. A. Werminghoff (Hanover, 1906). These were the priests Emanus, Ildesind, Exsuoperius, Gundefredus, Sidonius, and Ermegildus, the deacon Wittildus, Wittiricus, and other clerics.

[178] Council of Tusey (860), in W. Hartmann, ed., *MGH* Conc. 4, (Hanover, 1998), 12–42. See also Hartmann, *Die Synoden*, 265–6, 270–2. P. R. McKeon, 'The Carolingian Councils of Savonnières (859) and Tusey (860) and their Background', *Revue Bénédictine* 84 (1974): 74–110.

[179] Council of Attigny (874), in W. Hartmann, ed., *MGH* Conc. 4, (Hanover, 1998), 597–600, and Hartmann, *Die Synoden*, 333.

[180] For the disputed lands, see CC 2, 349, 351, and 430–3 (the capitulary emanating from the council).

enough to be considered at a kingdom-wide church council. The March was clearly an integrated part of the kingdom.

In September 878, and in connection to a church council held at Troyes, Louis the Stammerer granted a document to Barcelona's Bishop Frodoin, in which the disputed land was restored to the see and Ricosindus's claims dismissed.[181] By issuing a diploma like this upon his succession, Louis moved to confirm the act of the Council of Attigny, which had already resolved the issue of the property rights of the Barcelona church. Furthermore, Louis bestowed on Frodoin the rights to tolls held by the *marchio* Bernard of Gothia, who was deposed at about the same time.[182] Even Pope John VIII (872–82) paid careful attention to the controversies surrounding the see of Barcelona. The pope, in Troyes to perform Louis's coronation, issued declarations of excommunication against those who rebelled against the new king.[183] Amongst all the other important business he carried out in conjunction with the Council of Troyes, John also issued a judgement concerning the bishops, priests, and even counts and secular officials in 'Gothia' and 'Hispania'.[184] There can be presumed to have been a question arising from the deeds of Tyrsus, Ricosindus, and Madascius as to whether they had committed sacrilege, or what the punishment for such an offence should have been. Archbishop Sigebod of Narbonne approached the pope with a book of Gothic law, wherein there was no provision for sacrilege. Pope John, in order to rectify this oversight, consulted the law of Justinian, but rejected it in favour of Charlemagne's law and pronounced the penalty for sacrilege at 600 solidi of pure silver, and for the guilty to be excommunicated until the fine were paid.[185] This law was to be written into the law books used in 'Gothia' and 'Hispania'. Clearly, rather than seeming to be distant and foreign, the governance of the Spanish March was of great concern to pope and king alike. The controversies of Barcelona having been dealt with, Louis turned his attention while still at Troyes to other affairs of the Spanish March. Thus he issued diplomas confirming the properties and immunities of the monasteries of Arles and Banyoles, as his

---

[181] CC 2, 68–71.

[182] *AB*, 229–30. See also Abadal's analysis of the document and argument against the previous interpretation of Calmette that the Bernard mentioned in the text was Bernard 'Plantapilosa' of Auvergne, CC 2, 69.

[183] *AB*, 223–7.

[184] The pope's letter, omitted from *MGH Epp.* VII, can be found in CC 2, 436–7.

[185] Justinian's *Novellae* could have been available in the Latin *Epitome Juliani*, and the *Codex* was possibly also available, as the earliest extant manuscript is Italian. See C. M. Radding and A. Ciaralli, *The* Corpus Iuris Civilis *in the Middle Ages: Manuscripts and Transmission from the Sixth Century to the Juristic Revival* (Leiden, 2007). Ibid., 54 highlights two other of John VIII's citations of Justinianic law, but relegates this instance to a footnote without attempting to identify the citation.

father had done.[186] Curiously, his document for Arles does not mention Charles the Bald or any other previous king, while the text of the Banyoles grant does refer to Charles. The grant to Arles does, however, use much of the language of his father's diploma, even as it adds a considerable list of properties to those over which the monastery had rights. A final grant from 878, in favour of Bishop Teotarius and the church of Girona, was also drawn up at Troyes, according to Abadal.[187] Similar diplomas from later Carolingian kings do exist, one of them an original, so it would seem odd for Louis not to have followed both his predecessors and successors in favouring the see of Girona upon his succession. Louis as king did a great deal over the course of one month to ensure that the ties between the king and his clerical supporters in the Spanish March bound them firmly to one another.[188]

The evidence that exists indicates that connections between the Spanish March and the Carolingian monarchs were maintained throughout the later ninth century. While few bishops from the March attended the synods and councils north of the Pyrenees, they and their monastic counterparts continued to seek royal protection and guarantees of their rights to property and immunity. As in previous generations, the kings did not take it upon themselves to issue diplomas for recipients in the March, but responded favourably when approached by supporters. In doing so, Charles the Bald and Louis the Stammerer acted as kings should. When matters became very serious, with threats to the property and prerogatives of the bishop of Barcelona, they acted effectively. Church councils, assembled nobles, and the pope himself watched and supported the kings in their moves to uphold previous royal pronouncements. All the while, 'ethnic' labels rarely appeared in documentation. Only in the case of Frodoin of Barcelona's problems are they used, and only to identify those on the wrong side of justice. That is not to say that 'Goths' were always villains, as documents discussed above concerning lay people show. The sparing use of the terms, however, does raise their profile when they do appear. 'Goth' in the late ninth century probably indicated a connection to certain properties or military responsibilities linked to such land.[189] At the very least, it was a term that denoted some sense of belonging to a community. It was not an 'ethnic' marker in the modern sense, nor did it contribute to a psychological distance between the monarchs and the March.

---

[186] CC 2, 33–6 for Arles-sur-Tech, 58–61 for Banyoles.   [187] CC 2, 131–4.

[188] See M. J. McCarthy, 'Power and Kingship under Louis II the Stammerer, 877–879', PhD diss. (University of Cambridge, 2012), which unfortunately I have been unable to consult.

[189] J. Lalinde Abadia, 'Godos, hispanos y hostolenses en la órbita del rey de los Francos', in *Symposium internacional*, vol. 1, 35–74.

CONCLUSIONS

The Spanish March was an integral part of the empire, and later of the West Frankish kingdom, throughout the period 840–78. It was only after the Council of Troyes that the region started to become marginal from the point of view of the great Frankish nobles, and then only because none possessed it. Likewise, as a later chapter will show for the counts of the March, the kingdom also began to become marginal, increasingly so during the tenth century. Yet, as we shall also see, personal relationships with monasteries and lay families on both sides of the Pyrenees continued to flourish, and a series of episodes involving regional bishops demonstrates a continued link to the Frankish ecclesiastical realm down to 899. The churches maintained ties with the Frankish church and with the papacy as well. It is clear from the ninth-century evidence that the later development of a principality centred on Barcelona can be traced to the Carolingian conquest of the region. The more powerful Frankish *marchiones* of the ninth century served Charles the Bald's purposes by providing counters to his royal rivals, first Pippin II of Aquitaine, then Charles's son Charles the Younger. High-ranking Franks exhibited a tendency to desert the king, while lesser nobles with local power bases proved loyal to the king who granted them their *honores*.

Jinty Nelson once suggested that the label 'Frank' during the eighth and ninth centuries became less an ethnic label and more a status denominator, and more recently has argued that ethnic identity was 'an operational tactic' used to negotiate rights.[190] These concepts would apply to all nobles, especially as intermarriage and cultural practices blurred the lines between ethnic groups at court and throughout the empire, and evidence indicates that people cared more about such status markers than ethnic identifiers. In terms of the language used in accounts of the politics of the Spanish March, the marker 'Goth' was in fact imbued with importance by those associated with the court and the high affairs of the kingdom. As late as the 870s, the magnate Bernard was known to Hincmar as 'Gothiae markionis', an appellation that connected him not to a people, but to a locale.[191] There remained, to a degree and from the royal court's perspective, a sense of geographical distance and regional variation in customs. At the same time, Catalan nationalist historians amongst others perhaps too hastily sought to ascribe a nationality to

---

[190] J. L. Nelson, *The Frankish World 750–900* (London, 1996), xvii–xix. See now her 'Frankish Identity in Charlemagne's Empire', in I. H. Garipzanov, P. J. Geary, and P. Urbanczyk, eds, *Franks, Northmen, and Slavs: Identities and State Formation in Early Medieval Europe* (Turnhout, 2008), 71–83.

[191] *AB*, 229.

historical figures, since in the ninth century people did not conceive of themselves in the same terms.[192] Using the terminology of what modern societies call 'ethnicity' or 'nationality' served to enhance the imperial stature of the Franks and of Charles the Bald; and this was done much more frequently by annalists than by those who drew up documents on behalf of the king himself. By no means did ethnicity present an obstacle to political unity for the Carolingian empire. For most of the ninth century, the Spanish March functioned as a source of power for magnates, just as *honores* functioned elsewhere in the empire. Politically, then, the frontier had been incorporated into Frankish power structures.

---

[192] P. J. Geary, *The Myth of Nations: the Medieval Origins of Europe* (Princeton, 2002).

Chapter 4

COUNTS, CHURCH, AND KINGS, 877–947

Amongst the results of the Council of Troyes of 878 was that Wifred, often known now as 'the Hairy', count of Urgell and Cerdanya, received the *honores* of Barcelona and Girona, while his brother Miro was granted Roussillon. Throughout the twentieth century, historians took these assignments as the foundation of Catalonia in the hands of its own ruling dynasty,[1] although it is doubtful that anyone at the time foresaw that. Indeed, Wifred and Miro proved to be the last counts in the March appointed by a king of the Franks. According to later legend, Wifred was a knight, son of Wifred of Arrià. The elder Wifred was so extraordinary in virtue, arms, and council that the king of the Franks named him count of Barcelona. This legend of Wifred the Hairy, recounting his rise to power in the March and struggles against Saracen foes, derives from the first two chapters of the *Gesta comitum Barcinonensium*, written between 1162 and 1184.[2] In fact, Wifred's family had no such illustrious beginnings.[3] Rather, it seems that they sought to capitalize on the events of 876–8, moving against Bernard of Gothia. Miro, for his part, found himself castigated by Pope John VIII for occupying fortifications in Roussillon by force of arms, although the king, Louis the Stammerer, legitimated his authority.[4] Traditional historiography, not altogether wrongly, attributed this family's rise to power to their continuing loyalty to the Carolingian

---

[1] For example, R. d'Abadal i de Vinyals, *Els primers comtes catalans*, (Barcelona, 1958), 65–6.

[2] See Barrau-Dihigo, ed., *El 'Gesta Comitum Barcinonensium'* (Barcelona, 1925), now in a newer edition by S. M. Cingolani, *Les Gesta Comitum Barchinonensium (versió primitiva), la Brevis Historia i altres textos de Ripoll* (Valencia, 2012); Collins, 'Charles the Bald and Wifred the Hairy', 169; Abadal, *Els primers comtes*, 26, 209–16; Salrach, *El procés*, 2, 88–94 for a study of the *Gesta* and legend.

[3] See now, for the origins of Wifred's family and the development of family and marriage patterns in the period this chapter concerns, S. Cingolani, 'The Family of Wilfred I, the Hairy: Marriage and the Consolidation of Power, 800–1000', *Imago Temporis: Medium Aevum* 4 (2010): 119–40.

[4] *MGH Epp. Karolini aevi* 5, no. 119. See also Salrach, *El procés*, vol. 2, 103 and Abadal, *Els primers comtes*, 59–60.

kings. For example, Josep Maria Salrach identified Wifred and his family leading others in a loyal, 'legitimist' party.[5] Yet it is fair to ask whether their acts reflect loyalty to the 'legitimacy' of the royal will or opportunism. The great families of the nobility changed sides when it suited them, as had been the case in earlier generations. Wifred and Miro, though not great magnates, likewise took advantage of the weakening rebel momentum to strengthen their own position, knowing that by opposing Bernard of Gothia and his allies, they stood to gain much.

Wifred and his contemporaries thus acted as participants in the politics of the West Frankish kingdom no less than their predecessors. Indeed, even though the counts of the next generation succeeded to their positions without royal intervention, formal connections between the March and the monarchy persisted. Contrary to traditional interpretations, the late ninth and early tenth centuries were not a period when the leaders of the Spanish March began to chart a course intentionally separate from that of the kingdom. Like their ninth-century predecessors, the counts acted on their own initiative regarding diplomatic and military affairs vis-à-vis their Muslim neighbours, but they also sought and received royal affirmation for their authority. Moreover, the bishops of the March continued to function within the ecclesiastical province of Narbonne, despite the flaring up of individual ambition. Whereas earlier Carolingian kings relied upon personal bonds with locals to ensure the presence of royal authority in the March, during the later Carolingian period locals in the March needed to forge and renew bonds with kings in order to enhance their own positions in the local context.

This chapter continues to address the issues affecting royal and local power in the Spanish March chronologically. In particular, it will consider first the era of Wifred the Hairy in a rather local context, then the role of contemporary kings from Louis the Stammerer to the first non-Carolingian king, Odo. A good portion of the royal diplomas from Odo's reign in fact concern ecclesiastical affairs of the same period, which merit separate discussion. The years around 900 mark something of a milestone, for both royal and local comital successions caused what might have become a crisis. The events of that generation are considered first from the perspective of the local counts, then of the king's role in the time of Charles the Simple. At every stage, evidence demonstrates that kings wanted to intervene in the business of the Spanish March, and that locals needed them to do so to legitimize their claims to rights and properties

---

[5] Salrach, *El procés*, vol. 2, 103 following Abadal, *Els primers comtes*, 59–60. R. Collins, *Early Medieval Spain: Unity in Diversity, 400–1000*, 2nd ed. (New York, 1995), 254–6 mentions the continued loyalty of the local counts, though he eschews the older labels.

and also their connections to channels of power. Finally, the ecclesiastical politics of the early tenth century show that, far from acting on any presumed desire to separate from the Frankish kingdom and the church province of Narbonne, bishops and monastic communities in the Spanish March, in particular those south of the Pyrenees, participated in a fully integrated fashion in the functioning of those institutions. In short, despite the installation of what proved centuries later to be a regional dynasty, the political culture of the Spanish March in the late Carolingian period continued its dependence on the Frankish monarchy.

WIFRED THE HAIRY AND REGIONAL AUTHORITY, 877–898

For tracing developments on the local level in the Spanish March, away from the deeds of kings and the annalists who recorded them, historians have for a long time turned to the hundreds of surviving charters produced in the area. While these documents, usually but not always concerning the ownership and transferral of land, can shed light on how society functioned and how counts behaved, those who study them need to be aware of the conditions affecting their production and survival.[6] On the one hand, there is no royal propaganda permeating the pages of local charters as is the case with the royal annals. But on the other hand, landed wealth translated into power, and charters could be made to tell the stories that the powerful wanted to tell.[7] Also, almost all of the charters that survive to the present day do so because they were preserved in episcopal and monastic archives. Even charters that document transactions between lay people are preserved in most cases because the property in question eventually came into the hands of church institutions. Even though there are many originals preserved for our region, there are many, many charters that exist today because they were copied into cartularies for preservation in such local archives. For these reasons, the problems of interpretation are complex. Untold numbers of documents no longer exist because the property never devolved to a church or monastery. Other documents may no longer exist that could complete the picture of transactions, disputes, and relationships. Copies may contain errors or interpolations, scribes can create forgeries to reflect reality as they knew it,

---

[6] These observations draw on insights from a wide-ranging body of study and debate, but see M. Innes, 'Archives, Documents and Landowners in Carolingian Francia', in W. C. Brown et al., eds, *Documentary Culture and the Laity in the Early Middle Ages* (Cambridge, 2013), 152–88 and H. Hummer, 'The Production and Preservation of Documents in Francia: the Evidence of Cartularies', in ibid., 189–230 for helpful discussion and synthesis.

[7] The essays in W. Davies and P. Fouracre, ed. *The Settlement of Disputes in Early Medieval Europe* (Cambridge, 1986) and *Property and Power in the Early Middle Ages* (Cambridge, 1995) have been especially influential in the last few decades concerning the study of charters.

and the practices and assumptions about record-keeping in the early medieval period do not always align with our own. Moreover, to approach charters as if their writers had no ulterior motives despite the form and process of composing the texts is to make a mistake.[8] These sources present just as many challenges as any others, but it remains possible that reasonable conclusions can be drawn. For present purposes the issues of scribal practices, literacy, autograph signatures, and witness lists are not as important as they would be for seeking answers to other questions. Genuine charters kept in order to preserve claims to property can reveal the concerns, intentions, and behaviours of the counts in the Spanish March. These sources are, after all, the traces that we have to study, and we must allow that, despite opportunities for manipulation and misrepresentation, they can provide good information.[9]

Wifred, when appointed count of Barcelona, seems to have left authority in some areas to his brothers. Conflent went to Miro in 870, when they were both given *honores* in the March; Radulf received Besalú in 878 at Wifred's accession to Barcelona.[10] These events have been interpreted as pointing to shifting notions of office. At the beginning of the ninth century, counts were agents of the king, but at the century's end, they were regional dynasts. Wifred could have seen the precedent of his father Sunifred as count of the same places as giving him a right to them, and thus he had a duty to delegate jurisdictional powers to his brothers. But offices could not pass to their heirs as a patrimony; those *honores* returned to Wifred or his heirs at the king's behest. It has been argued that a new, hereditary–familial conception of countship led the wives of counts to begin to be styled 'countesses'.[11] It is important, though, to note the fact that Wifred did not succeed to office until more than thirty years after his father had died. To what extent would he have seen his own holding of these counties as birthright? Wifred and

---

[8] On these and other concerns, see in addition to the works cited just above, P. Geary, *Phantoms of Remembrance: Remembering and Forgetting in the Tenth and Eleventh Centuries* (Princeton, 1985), 85–114.

[9] H. Mordek, 'Karolingische Kapitularien', in Mordek (ed.), *Überlieferung und Geltung der Normativer Texte des frühen und hohen Mittelalters* (Sigmaringen, 1986), 25–50 esp. at 30. I thank J. Jarrett for this reference.

[10] Abadal, *Dels visigots als catalans*, ed. J. Sobrequés i Callicó, 2nd ed., 2 vols (Barcelona, 1974), vol. 1, 319 admits that there is no surviving source that shows bestowal of these *honores*, but evidence from later on corroborates that these people held authority in the areas concerned. See his discussion in Abadal, *Els primers comtes*, 65–6.

[11] The best known of these women was Winidilda, Wifred's wife. See CC 4, no. 4; *Archivo Condal*, no. 6. See R. Le Jan, *Famille et pouvoir dans le monde franc (VIIe–Xe siècle)* (Paris, 1995), 344–65. Earlier works noted this development: A. R. Lewis, *The Development of Southern French and Catalan Society, 718–1050* (Austin, 1965), 123; Salrach, *El procés*, vol. 2, 105–6. See now J. A. Bowman, 'Countesses in Court: Elite Women, Creativity, and Power in Northern Iberia, 900–1200', *Journal of Medieval Iberian Studies* 6 (2014): 54–70.

Miro first gained their *honores* by appointment from Charles the Bald, in keeping with the king's policy of installing local nobles alongside great Frankish magnates in the March; throughout the ninth century counts from local families administered these same counties. When Wifred became count of Barcelona and *marchio* in 878, he was the first man in that position since the 840s to have had family roots in the Spanish March. Thus it is difficult to attribute dynastically strategic planning to Wifred concerning the delegation of some authority to his kin. Based on his experiences as count of Urgell and Cerdanya since 870, he had some activities under way, such as encouraging the settlement of the valleys of Osona and fighting against neighbouring Muslims. He may have relinquished some authority elsewhere in order to devote himself to these endeavours.

More or less 'natural' migrations down from the mountains had begun by the 870s as people left to find opportunities in new, deserted – or at least unorganized – lands. Useful lands in the eastern territories were relatively crowded, making it difficult to start new cultivation. Thus, the settlers almost by default headed for the area lost since Aizo's revolt in 827.[12] This grass-roots development was well under way before Wifred took action to foster it. He cast himself as defender, propagandist, and consolidator of the migration movement, and as such saw to the repair and re-garrisoning of the sites originally fortified by Borell in 798.[13] At first settlers maintained peaceful relations with the Muslims nearby. As Christian settlement increased, tensions mounted, and Wifred came to see the recently fortified Muslim base at Lleida as a threat and attacked it in 883–4. Unfortunately for the *marchio*, striking first did not translate into victory, and the March could not be completely safe. Throughout this period, Wifred also established a new county, Osona, created or took up sponsorship of new parishes and monasteries – Santa Maria de Ripoll and Sant Joan de Ripoll – and restored the old bishopric of Ausona, now located at Vic, all of which helped to organize settlement in the area.[14]

---

[12] Abadal, 'La plana de Vic', in *Dels visigots als catalans*, vol. 1 309–21 is the fundamental study of the phenomenon.

[13] Abadal, 'La plana de Vic', in *Dels visigots als catalans*, vol. 1 321; Ollich, 'Vic: la ciutat a l'època carolingia', in J. Camps, ed., *Catalunya a l'època carolíngia: art i cultura abans del romànic (segles IX i X)* (Barcelona, 1999), 89–94.

[14] Ripoll: the archives of Ripoll were destroyed in the 1835 fire, so the original documents of foundation are lost, leaving Ordeig, *Les Dotalies de les Esglesies de Catalunya*, nos. 11, 14 and *Marca Hispanica*, ap. 123; Sant Joan: CC 4, no. 4 and *Archivo Condal*, no. 3; Vic: Abadal, *Dels visigots als catalans*, vol. 1, 317–19; CC 2, 293–9 and *Archivo Condal*, no. 7, both of which are later documents that confirm the earlier establishment of the diocese.

Wifred projected an image of himself as a patron of religion and culture as well as a leader of his people.[15]

Later documents show Wifred the Hairy acting as a powerful count, handing out privileges to settlers as the kings did in earlier generations. Before he was named count of Barcelona, he issued a charter of exemptions to the inhabitants of Vall de Lord at the southern reaches of the county of Urgell.[16] We do not know the precise terms of this charter, as it does not survive but is known from later documentation. Perhaps we can gain some insight from another, likely similar, act. As the area of settlement under his rule expanded, Wifred granted a charter of settlement to the castle of Cardona on or very near the edge of Christian territory at the confluence of Osona's *pagus* Manresa, Urgell, and the Berguedà, Wifred's extension of Cerdanya. With this charter, dated to the 880s, the count granted Cardona's settlers security in person and goods, double compensation for stolen goods, partial exemption from tolls and other tribute, and full immunity to criminals within the settlement.[17] The final feature of the grant, immunity to criminals, illustrates Wifred's sponsorship of the enterprise and need to attract further settlers to the area. This grant fills the same needs for Wifred as did Charlemagne's privileges granted to hispani immigrants settling the *aprisiones* a century earlier, except that whereas Charlemagne dealt with refugees, Wifred resolved to pardon indigenous criminals in order to open up land. And, lest we forget the martial nature of Wifred's 'colonization' initiative, the document concerns the jurisdiction of the castle at Cardona.[18] We should also note that in some respects Wifred recognized a fait accompli; the criminals and their neighbours already had settled into the area and the castle stood to protect them. Like many earlier, royal documents, this comital charter indicates that those in power both sponsored and legitimated re-population efforts. What is

---

[15] Salrach, *El procés*, vol. 2, 107–8, 136–7; P. Bonnassie, *La Catalogne du milieu du Xe siecle à la fin du XIe siècle: croissance et mutations d'une société* (Toulouse, 1975), 99–106; Abadal, *Els primers comtes*, 73–114. On these monastic foundations, Abadal, ibid., 130–47. See also P. Balañà i Abadia, *L'Islam a Catalunya* (Barcelona, 1997), 32–3. E. J. Goldberg, 'More Devoted to the Equipment of Battle than the Splendor of Banquets: Frontier Kingship, Martial Ritual, and Early Knighthood at the Court of Louis the German', *Viator* 30 (1999): 41–78 shows how Louis the German cultivated a similar warrior ethic in his rule of frontier Germany, but without a reputation for cultivating letters. More recently, on Louis the German and cultural developments, H. Hummer, *Politics and Power in Early Medieval Europe: Alsace and the Frankish Realm, 600–1000* Cambridge, 2005), 130–54.

[16] J. M. Font Rius, ed., *Cartas de poblacion y franquicia de Cataluña* 1 (Madrid–Barcelona, 1969), no. 3; Abadal, *Els primers comtes*, 82.

[17] Font Rius, ed., *Cartas*, no. 4. Wifred's document is not extant, but known from a 986 charter of his grandson, Borrell II, that refers to it. See also ibid., no. 9.

[18] For the term 'colonization' see A. Dupont, 'Considerations sur la colonisation et la vie rurale dans la Rousillon et la Marche d'Espagne', *Annales du Midi* 57 (1955): 223–45. See also Lewis, *The Development of Society*, 130–5 on the function of castles.

most important to understand for comital power in the period is that the initiative here was Wifred's, not the king's.

After the rapid successions of Charles the Bald's son Louis (d. 879) and grandsons Louis (d. 882) and Carloman (d. 884), the West Frankish kingdom devolved to Charles the Fat, son of Louis the German. This Charles briefly ruled a unified empire, but frequently encountered problems, especially with the Northmen.[19] With his deposition in 887 and death in 888 the Carolingian empire effectively ended. The dynasty would continue to rule in the east until 911 and in the west until 987, but any ideal of unity ended with the successions of Arnulf, the illegitimately born king of Germany, and Berengar of Friuli as king in Italy, Radulf in Burgundy, Louis the Blind in Provence, and Odo in the western kingdom.[20] The idea of Carolingian kingship was, however, still powerful. Berengar was the son of Eberhard of Friuli and the Carolingian Gisela; Louis was the grandson of Louis II of Italy through his mother, Ermengard, who had married Boso. In the Spanish March, Wifred the Hairy neither proclaimed loyalty to Odo, nor acted in open insubordination. Contrary to the old interpretation,[21] the election of Odo did not so much sever the bonds between kings and the counts of the Spanish March as it capped off trends of the late 870s and 880s that challenged the traditional relationships between centre and peripheries throughout the empire. It was not Odo's election per se, but the circumstances that warranted it, that caused a potential crisis for the relationship between March and monarchy. Local problems in northern Francia, especially dealing with Northmen, prevented both Charles the Fat and Odo from intervening more frequently in the Spanish March. Dynastic problems, which resulted in the reunification of the empire in Charles's hands and then to the rise of local *principes*, made *Königsnähe* difficult for the Marcher counts to obtain.[22] Distance from the royal court without the intermediary of a junior Carolingian sub-king in Aquitaine made the forming of political relationships all the more difficult; whatever bonds with earlier

---

[19] See now, for a reinterpretation of his reign, S. MacLean, *Kingship and Politics in the Late Ninth Century: Charles the Fat and the End of the Carolingian Empire* (Cambridge, 2003).

[20] AF, 405–6; Regino, *Chronicon*, in G. H. Pertz, ed., *MGH SS* 1 (Hanover, 1826), 598–9. See P. Riché, *The Carolingians: a Family Who Forged Europe*, trans. M. I. Allen (Philadelphia, 1993), 207–38. These new rulers were sons of powerful magnates; Boso had pronounced himself king in Provence in 880.

[21] For which see Salrach, *El procés*, vol. 2, 112, Lewis, *The Development of Society*, 92, 103, 111, 113; Abadal, *Els primers comtes*, 153–4.

[22] Regino, abbot of Prüm, remarked along these lines in his chronicle, *Reginonis Prumiensis Chronicon*, ed. F. Kurze, *MGH SS* rer. Germ. 50 (Hanover, 1890), 129.

kings that counts in the March had been able to claim no longer existed by 888.[23] Odo's ability to deal effectively with local issues in Francia resulted in his election, but the counts of the Spanish March did not share the concerns of the new king and those who elected him. Tenuous ties to the royal court and Wifred's personal role in reorganizing Osona, the area lost to Christian authorities since 827, enhanced the stature of the *marchio* in the March. Yet the counties of the March remained part of the western kingdom.

The monastic houses of Sant Joan and Santa Maria de Ripoll have always loomed large in the historiography of the organization of settlement in Osona. Sant Joan, now widely known as Sant Joan de les Abadesses because it was a convent for nuns, seems to have benefitted greatly from the largess of Wifred and his wife Winidilda in 885. According to surviving documents, some of which are problematic, the count and countess endowed the house well in order to secure its future and its place in leading the organization of the community, giving the comital family a strong presence in the locality. The first document gave the monastery wide-ranging properties in the area under settlement in the Ripoll valley, including the castle of Mogrony, but also in Conflent and elsewhere, but it is heavily interpolated and so is best disregarded as evidence for present purposes.[24] In a second charter, dated to the first year of the reign of Charles the Fat, Wifred carries the titles of count and *marchio*, while Winidilda is countess. Yet this charter survives only in a copy from the eleventh century, which suffers from errors in transcription. It is therefore not highly reliable evidence for the intentions of Wifred and Winidilda, nor for their titles. We are on surer footing with other charters. The couple returned to Sant Joan in June of 887, when Bishop Gotmar of Vic consecrated the church there.[25] The momentum that Wifred and Winidilda gave to the building of communities in the Ripoll valley seems to have continued, as Sant Joan became a more effective hub of activity and as unrelated individuals came together to build and endow their own churches. Gotmar was called to the castle of Tona in Osona by such a band of settlers in early 888 to consecrate a church dedicated to St Andrew.[26] Later that year, Odo's succession to the

---

[23] See the more widely ranging discussion in MacLean, *Kingship and Politics*, 64–80.

[24] CC 4, no. 4. See J. Jarrett, 'Power over Past and Future: Abbess Emma and the Nunnery of Sant Joan de les Abadesses', *EME* 12 (2003): 233–57 for the history of Sant Joan, 237–41 for discussion of the document.

[25] CC 4, no. 8. Udina, the editor of Sant Joan's charters for *Archivo condal*, believed the endowment and consecration documents to be forgeries. R. Ordeig i Mata, 'La consagracio i la dotacio d'esglesies a Catalunya en els segles IX–XI', in *Symposium internacional*, vol. 2, 85–102 confirms the consecration on 24 June 887. Ordeig i Mata also edited CC 4.

[26] CC 4, no. 9.

West Frankish throne seems to have been recognized in a charter drawn up to record the consecration of the church at Santa Maria de Ripoll. The text as it now exists, the original having been lost, probably in a fire in 1835, features Gotmar and the count and countess Wifred and Winidilda coming together for the solemn occasion in 'anno primo imperii Odonis regis'.[27] The existence of two early modern copies of the document means that it cannot be taken as clear evidence for the titles of local or royal authority, but its modern editors have confidence that their version reflects accurately the text of the Ripoll original. In 889, Wifred and Winidilda bought properties near the Llobregat from a group of lay people, perhaps augmenting their holdings in the area for further re-distribution, but also perhaps to cement ties to the local community by becoming landowners in the area.[28] And a document from 890 firmly shows that Odo's succession was recognized without controversy by Wifred and the elite of his territories, as Gotmar was called by the count and countess to consecrate a church in honour of St Peter in the Ripoll valley.[29] This series of charters shows Wifred acting as count, often without reference to the title *marchio*, in consort with Winidilda. Together the pair appear as guardians and sponsors of churches and communities in Osona, projecting strength and authority in the areas where settlement needed to be organized.

Wifred needed to burnish his image as the personification of power in the area with his activity in battle against the Saracens who menaced the new settlements – likely because the settlements encroached on Muslim territory. The Banu Qasi continued to strengthen their presence to the south and west of Wifred's territories, so he took action for strategic reasons as well as for prestige. Throughout the 890s, Wifred acted as patron to the re-population initiative, taking the offensive as the decade progressed, and finally falling on the field at Odera, now Valldora, in 898.[30] Upon his death, his sons assumed a joint countship without waiting for royal appointment. This turn of events marks for many modern historians, politicians, and Catalan citizens the de facto autonomy of the Spanish March, although in many respects evidence points to a surviving local perception of the March being a part of the Frankish kingdom.

---

[27] CC 4, no. 10.

[28] *Archivo condal*, no. 6. For the idea that such transactions had social as well as economic significance, see C. J. Chandler, 'Land and Social Networks in the Carolingian Spanish March', *Studies in Medieval and Renaissance History*, third series, 6 (2009): 1–33.

[29] CC 4, no. 16.

[30] See Abadal, *Els primers comtes*, 191–8, L. Auzias, *L'Aquitaine carolingienne* (Toulouse, 1937), 264–6 and É. Levi-Provencal, *Histoire de l'Espagne musulmane*, vol. 1 (Leiden, 1950 and 1957), 314 for the death of Wifred in battle against the Banu Qasi.

Even though performing the role of leader and providing patronage to local churches was crucial, the foundation of comital power in the Spanish March during the later ninth century was royal patronage. Counts in the March made their authority known by granting charters, to be sure, but their positions were granted and revoked by kings, especially Charles the Bald. When, in the 870s, Charles came to appoint figures of local or regional stature rather than great magnates, these men needed royal patronage even more than their predecessors because they were lesser aristocrats. Odalric, Humfrid, and the like possessed patrimonies removed from the March, so when they lost their *honores*, they were able to maintain themselves or even transfer loyalty to another Carolingian king. The local men, however, had no such options, which helps to explain their consistent loyalty. The succession of the next generation around the turn of the tenth century may not have depended so heavily on royal patronage, but the earlier generations – Sunifred, his sons Wifred and Miro, and their cousins Sunyer and Dela, discussed in Chapter 3 – certainly did. Even so, though Wifred's sons succeeded without royal appointment they maintained the comital title. Moreover, church administration and monasticism remained quite dependent on royal patronage.

As in earlier chapters, royal diplomas again provide evidence for the relationship between kings and counts in the Spanish March. Just as with charters, royal diplomas are not always precise indicators of where a king was or who exactly put ink to parchment in the way that historians used to treat them in order to reconstruct royal itineraries and court personnel.[31] These texts were written with political agendas underlying them, and the agenda was often to create an understanding of history and of royal authority, even to give a sense of the ruler's presence through the parchment, composition, and seal.[32] Through the documents, we can therefore glimpse the creation and maintenance of bonds of patronage and clientship, as kings sought to ensure that their authority would be recognized in the Spanish March, while political actors in the region depended on links to the monarchy for legitimation and legal standing.

During his stay in Troyes, site of his coronation and of a church council at which Pope John VIII presided, Louis the Stammerer issued royal

---

[31] G. Koziol, *The Politics of Memory and Identity in Carolingian Royal Diplomas: the West Frankish Kingdom (840–987)* (Turnhout, 2012). Although devoted to a king in a different period, the conclusions of R. McKitterick, *Charlemagne: the Formation of a European Identity* (Cambridge, 2008), 137–213 are instructive.

[32] Koziol, *The Politics of Memory*, 32–9; I. Garipzanov, *Symbolic Language of Authority in the Carolingian World (c.751–877)* (Leiden, 2008), 18–21 and 30–2.

diplomas for recipients in the Spanish March.[33] Amongst them was Bishop Frodoin of Barcelona, who gained royal confirmation of his church's possessions following on the controversy treated at Attigny in 874.[34] Of course, Louis also dealt with other matters. For one, he issued royal immunity and protection to Abbot Castellanus and the monastery of Santa Maria of Arles in the Vallespir *pagus* of Rousillon, in imitation of an earlier grant his father had made in 869, but apparently without explicitly confirming the earlier act. Indeed, Louis's diploma expanded considerably the holdings of the monastery included in the immunity beyond Charles's grant, listing the properties that had already been covered as well as numerous additions.[35] Also at Troyes, Louis confirmed and augmented a grant by Charles to the monastery of Banyoles in Besalú.[36] Abadal, in editing the royal diplomas issued to recipients in the Spanish March, also deduced another document drawn up at Troyes to the benefit of the episcopal church of Girona, although no trace or copy of it survived into the modern era.[37] Later confirmations by his successors point to a diploma Louis issued to Bishop Theotarius, so Abadal's conclusions are convincing. The new king, no longer answerable to his father, acted as required and saw to the needs of his faithful supporters in the March. For their part, the abbots and bishops of institutions long associated with the Carolingians likewise depended on their continued cultivation of relationships with the kings in order to solidify their positions as leaders in the local society.

The short reign of Louis the Stammerer meant that his son and successor Carloman rather quickly came to rule the southern part of the West Frankish kingdom, which included the Spanish March. In August 881, Carloman issued no fewer than three diplomas for churches in the March. The king's first diploma in this series, surviving today in a later copy, granted to the monastery of Santa Cecilia d'Elins, in Urgell, immunity and the right to elect the abbot. The diploma is the only document issued by a Carolingian king for this house, which seems to have been newly founded, as the king recognizes the rights of Abbot

---

[33] For the pope's role in the council, see the bull published in CC 2, 436 discussed in Chapter 3 of this volume.

[34] See Chapter 3 and CC 2, 68–71.

[35] CC 2, 33–6. In fact, Charles had issued two earlier diplomas to Santa Maria of Arles, one in 844 and the other 869. The 844 document refers to his own father Louis's grant, while the 869 text does not. The difference does not seem attributable to the practices of copyists who preserved the text in later centuries.

[36] CC 2, 58–61; the document does not survive in a medieval copy but rather the nineteenth-century transcription of J. Villanueva, *Viage literario a las iglesias de España*, vol. 14 (Madrid, 1802–52), 249.

[37] CC 2, 131–4.

Edifredus and his subject monks to wasteland (*heremum*) that they had brought into cultivation.[38] In a diploma that exists in its original parchment form, Carloman acted upon the request by Bishop Theotarius of Girona for confirmation of the possession of several villas in the *pagi* of Girona and Empúries. The document refers to an act by *pater noster Lhudovicus*, showing Carloman to be following a time-honoured tradition of protecting the property of the bishops of Girona; it also supports the idea that Louis had indeed issued a diploma for Girona that no longer survives.[39] The final act of the month was a grant to Santa Maria of Arles that seems mostly to have been a copy of the diploma of Louis the Stammerer, save for the substitution of the abbot's name to reflect the succession of Sunifred to that position.[40] Carloman acceded to rule of the whole western kingdom when his brother Louis died in 882, but no diplomas relating to the Spanish March survive from after the period of activity in the summer of 881.

Upon Carloman's death while hunting in 884, his cousin Charles the Fat added the western kingdom to his conglomeration of eastern and Italian *regna*, reuniting the Carolingian empire. As the king of the Franks and *imperator augustus*, Charles is known to have issued only one diploma for the Spanish March, namely a confirmation of the immunity and holdings of Bishop Theotarius of Girona.[41] In the text, Charles refers to earlier grants to the Girona church by his imperial forebears, Charlemagne and Louis the Pious, but does not mention his predecessors who ruled in the time of the divided kingdoms after 840. This rhetorical device emphasized Charles's imperial dignity, in that he names only those illustrious ancestors who bore the imperial title themselves and ruled the empire in its entirety. Bishop Theotarius is also noteworthy as a petitioner of all the Carolingian kings of this period; it seems that he was keen to obtain royal confirmation of his see's holdings and was perhaps able to secure it quite quickly. Certainly the surviving evidence shows that the bishop's contemporaries also could and did find royal patronage; perhaps Theotarius was more anxious to do so than they were, or perhaps the Girona archive was more fortunate in preserving a record of his activities. Either way, links between the Carolingian monarchy and the Spanish March continued to function as they long had. Royal grants provided opportunities for kings to perform their necessary roles as patrons, while the bishops and abbots of the March still saw royal writ as key guarantor of their worldly positions.

---

[38] CC 2, 250–2.   [39] CC 2, 135–7.

[40] CC 2, 37–9. Perhaps because it was almost a verbatim copy of his father's grant of 878, Carloman's diploma does not explicitly identify itself as a confirmation.

[41] CC 2, 138.

The non-Carolingian king Odo issued as many diplomas as did any of Charles the Bald's successors. In part this is due to the latters' short reigns, and in part it is attributable to an ecclesiastical controversy vexing the Spanish March during Odo's own ten-year hold on the West Frankish throne. There may have been hesitation on the part of authority figures in the Spanish March in terms of recognizing Odo's succession, but before very long his affirmation was sought by beneficiaries in the March. An original manuscript placing the new monastery of Fontclara under royal protection and immunity dates itself to the second year of Odo's reign and the year 888 of the Incarnation, a seeming contradiction given Odo's accession upon the deposition of his predecessor Charles the Fat in 887.[42] Yet the document may be dated to Odo's coronation, which happened later. Around the same time, June of 888, another diploma also carrying the same dating formula survives thanks to nineteenth-century efforts to transcribe important documents. It affirms the possession of lands held by three brothers in Besalú – lands that had been brought into cultivation from waste by their grandfather.[43] Trace evidence survives of a diploma dated to 890 for the monastery of Amer, the first royal diploma for that house in thirty years.[44] Another original parchment preserves an act from the following year in which Odo granted to the layman Petronius a villa in the *pagus* of Girona.[45] A document of the early tenth century refers to an act of Odo's, again benefitting a lay recipient.[46] In all these diplomas, Odo appears acting out the role that his Carolingian predecessor had played in affirming rights to properties. It was the place of the king to grant privileges and confirm the possessions and rights of his faithful followers. For the early years of Odo's reign, however, it seems that most of those followers in the Spanish March were non-elite lay individuals rather than institutions of the church and secular aristocracy. That is likely the case because the counts and bishops of the March had other concerns.

ECCLESIASTICAL AFFAIRS, 878–900

The Council of Troyes (878), called by Pope John VIII, as noted in the previous chapter, saw the installation of Wifred 'the Hairy' as count of

---

[42] CC 2, 113–15. For more on Odo's struggles during his first years claiming kingship, and the dating of these diplomas in the context of others issued at the same time, see Koziol, *The Politics of Memory*, 81–5.

[43] CC 2, 363–4. [44] CC 2, 17, with discussion 9.

[45] CC 2, 365–6. The grant was made at the intercession of Bishop Servus Dei, a central figure in the ecclesiastical controversy discussed just below.

[46] CC 2, 367.

Barcelona and his brother Miro to office in Roussillon.[47] The congregation included both Frankish and Italian bishops, with Theotarius of Girona, Frodoin of Barcelona, Audesindus of Elna, and Nantigisus of Urgell numbered amongst them.[48] A truly great council, Troyes addressed business from throughout the kingdom, especially that of the Spanish March, whose counts and bishops clearly were no outsiders.

Salrach called the archbishops of Narbonne of the ninth and tenth centuries 'pro-Frankish' because they supported the kings' appointments of prelates to sees in the March. He attributed this behaviour to the increased independence of action on the part of counts – in order for the archbishop to maintain power in the area, he had to install such men in ecclesiastical offices as counterweights to comital pressure. Thus the archbishops of Narbonne served as champions of what Salrach termed the 'royal policy of assimilation', acting as guardians of royal interest and in liturgy as opponents of what he called Visigothism, which is an unhelpful, nebulous term.[49] Yet a strand of scholarship on Carolingian reforms, especially amongst more recent work, seeks to revise the interpretation of Charlemagne and his successors as ceaselessly striving for strict religious uniformity.[50] The next chapter will address liturgy and reform, leaving aside for present purposes the question of personnel.

An apparent controversy in the ecclesiastical politics of the late ninth-century Spanish March arose, attributable to the machinations of a local noble in Cerdanya named Sclua.[51] First, Sclua gave up secular pursuits in the 880s and had himself named bishop of Urgell in 885, while the incumbent Ingobert was ill but still living; Ingobert recovered, but Sclua refused to step down. Wifred the Hairy, as count of Urgell, apparently did not oppose this usurpation of the see.[52] Catalan historians of the twentieth century postulated that Sclua harboured ambitions to recreate the ancient metropolitanate of Tarraconensis, but to centre it on Urgell rather than Tarragona, which was in Muslim hands.[53] According

---

[47] See H. Mordek and G. Schmitz, *Papst Johannes VIII. und das Konzil von Troyes (878) in Geschichtsschreibeung und geistiges Leben im Mittelalter, Festschrft für H. Löwe* (Cologne and Vienna, 1978), 179–225.

[48] W. Hartmann, *Die Synoden der Karolingerzeit im Frankenreich und in Italien*, Konziliengeschichte Reihe A (Paderborn, 1989), 338, note 15.

[49] Salrach, *El procés*, vol. 2, 115–16.

[50] See in particular Y. Hen, *The Royal Patronage of Liturgy in Frankish Gaul to the Death of Charles the Bald (877)* (London, 2001), 69–89 and R. E. Reynolds, 'The Visigothic Liturgy in the Realm of Charlemagne', in *Das frankfurter Konzil*, vol. 2, 919–45, but also the earlier work of McKitterick, *The Frankish Church and the Carolingian Reforms: 789–895* (London, 1977), esp. 128–30.

[51] Abadal, *Els primers comtes*, 154–66.   [52] Salrach, *El próces*, vol. 2, 115–16.

[53] Salrach repeated the narrative as found in Abadal's work, despite the examination of R.-H. Bautier, 'La prétendue dissidence de l'épiscopat catalan et le faux concile de « Portus » de 887–890', *Bulletin philologique et historique (jusqu'à 1610) du Comité des Travaux Historiques et*

to this interpretation, Sclua's actions as would-be archbishop amounted to an early case of Catalan separatism. Abadal, for his part, seems to have fallen into the trap of modern nationalist sentiment in following the trail of evidence in the later – and fictional – *Vita sancti Theodardi* for a break-away archbishop and new metropolitanate for Catalonia.[54] A closer look at the documents concerned, however, reveals just how much the politics, ecclesiastical as well as secular, of the Spanish March depended on the Frankish kings in the late ninth century.

Sclua's upheaval particularly affected the bishopric of Girona. Theodardus, the archbishop of Narbonne who had acted as Wifred's ally in the establishment of the diocese of Ausona and the installation of its bishop, Gotmar, at Vic, appointed another, aptly named man, Servus Dei, to the vacant bishopric of Girona in 887 – a move supposedly reflecting the 'uniformizing' royal policy. Sclua apparently supported a different candidate, named Ermemir. It is not clear whether Ermemir contested Servus Dei directly in Girona or was named bishop of Empúries, an old Visigothic see which was no longer canonical but was within territory Sunyer II, not Wifred the Hairy, controlled.[55] Sunyer II by implication favoured the formation of the province headed by Urgell so that Ermemir would serve as bishop of Girona; he would then have had allies in two of Wifred's territories, or at least in one of Wifred's counties in addition to a bishop of his own. Wifred, who for his part as count of Urgell sat by as Sclua usurped that episcopal seat, could not stand for a similar development in Girona, and so now found himself opposing Sclua and Ermemir as uncanonical appointments. Abadal supposed that a diploma from Odo granted property and rights to collect revenue through tithes and tolls to Bishop Gotmar, at the request of Ermemir, who is identified as bishop.[56] If this were true, Sclua, and by extension Sunyer II, took advantage of Wifred's hesitation to recognize Odo as legitimate king by hastening to build a relationship with him. As Robert-Henri Bautier showed, though, this diploma is problematic, in that it survives thanks to a convoluted pattern of copying and revision, and cannot

---

Scientifiques 1961 (Paris 1963): 477–98. See also J. A. Jarrett, 'Archbishop Ató of Osona: False Metropolitans on the Marca Hispanica', *Archiv für Diplomatik* 56 (2010): 1–42, at 9–12.

[54] As is the general argument in Bautier, 'La prétendue dissidence', although without accusations of nationalist bias in Abadal's work.

[55] Abadal, *Els primers comtes*, 156–7; Salrach, *El procés*, vol. 2, 116. The more focused study of Bautier, 'La prétendue dissidence', is of course useful. J. M. Morera Sabater, 'Un conato de secesión eclesiástica en la Marca Hispánica en el siglo IX' *Anales del Instituto de Estudios Gerundenses* 15 (1962): 293–315 offers a dissenting view.

[56] CC 2, 296–8.

be trusted.[57] Abadal further held that Odo enacted a revision of the diploma, dated to 890, which wrote out the usurping bishop in favour of Archbishop Theodardus in the clause referring to the intercessor on Gotmar's behalf, and bestowed upon Gotmar royal rights with the consent of local counts.[58] This demonstrated to Abadal's satisfaction that Wifred and Theodardus realized they had been out-manoeuvred, and sought out Odo as the controversy unfolded, in order to influence the king in their favour. Yet the textual basis for this claim is as dubious as that for Ermemir's receipt of a diploma.[59]

Wifred and others did indeed initially reserve recognition of Odo, and their change of tune is evident in a brief comparison of documents. A charter from the spring of 888, in which Wifred and his siblings gave properties to the monastery of La Grasse, does not recognize Odo as king, as it features the dating clause 'madii, anno quod obiit Karolus imperator, [Christo] regnante rege expectante'.[60] In January of 889, though, a charter that still exists as an original in the archive of Vic records a sale by a lay couple to Bishop Gotmar. Its dating clause recognizes Odo's reign as being in its third year.[61] As the land being sold was in Wifred's county of Osona and the document drawn up in the presence of his man, Gotmar, it is clear that recognition of Odo as king was common enough to be reflected in everyday documents. By 890 Theodardus also offered recognition to Odo and even received precepts for himself and his supporters.[62] As indication that Servus Dei had won the day, a royal document of 891 names him as bishop of Girona while granting his church immunity and placing it under royal protection.[63] Servus Dei likely was in the presence of the king that summer, when he is attested at a synod at Meung-sur-Loire.[64]

Abadal argued that during the height of controversy Servus Dei had been expelled and ultimately given refuge at Banyoles by Wifred and his brother Radulf. Salrach proposed another interpretation – that Servus Dei had not been expelled, but that there was a seizure of territory, and Ermemir acted as bishop in parts Sunyer II held by force.[65] Yet the case is

---

[57] See the discussion in CC 2, 293–6. The text is heavily interpolated. See Bautier, 'La prétendue dissidence', 478.

[58] CC 2, 298–9. [59] Bautier, 'La prétendue dissidence', 478. [60] CC 6, no. 144.

[61] CC 4, no. 12.

[62] See also I. Schröder, *Die westfränkischen Synoden von 888 bis 987 und ihre Überlieferung*, Monumenta Germaniae Historica Hilfsmittel 3 (Munich, 1980), 106–9 and 122–38.

[63] CC 2, 141–3.

[64] J. D. Mansi, ed., *Sacrorum conciliorum nova et amplissima collection* (Florence, 1767; Paris, 1902), 18 A, col. 119D–120E.

[65] Salrach, *El procés*, vol. 2, 115–19; Abadal, *Els primers comtes*, 154–166; Morera, 'Un conato de secesión eclesiástica', 293–315.

so riddled with problematic evidence that an ultimate determination is unlikely. Despite the difficulties with sources, we can see that the controversy arose and found resolution. A series of documents from 892 and 893 shows Servus Dei claiming properties for his see in Empúries, where the contest had been most heated. In one charter, an individual named Wadamir made official recognition that the see of Girona owned one-sixth of a vineyard he had purchased, rendering its sale invalid.[66] Another man, Revellus, appears in three charters as having recognized his unjust possession of different properties, including houses, fields, and a mill, all in the *term* of Bàscara.[67] He evacuated all three properties in favour of Servus Dei and the church of Girona. A fourth document also featuring Revellus has him admitting to cutting down seventeen fig trees from the bishop's garden in Bàscara.[68] Servus Dei and Theodardus had carried the day, thanks to their cooperation with Odo, who in turned gained recognition as the legitimate king throughout the Spanish March. It was once believed that Ermemir ultimately was removed and eventually excommunicated at a synod in Port, but Bautier has shown that the documentary evidence for the council was forged.[69] In 897 Servus Dei requested and received a papal grant confirming the properties and rights of the Girona church, even the islands of Mallorca and Minorca, as well as confirming his rival Ermemir's expulsion and excommunication.[70] By 899, the king, now the Carolingian Charles the Simple, confirmed Servus Dei's office, reiterating the rights and privileges of his church.[71]

Another apparent element of Sclua's plot was to create a diocese in the western part of the Spanish March. Adulf, bishop of this newly formed diocese of Pallars, continued to hold office separate from the diocese of Urgell until his death.[72] Count Ramon of Pallars and Ribagorça seems to have supported the idea of an independent bishop for his territory but was otherwise not directly involved in the confusing affairs to his east.[73] For his part, Sclua was deposed and may have contented himself with serving as Sunyer II's personal bishop.[74] After the whirlwind of controversy in ecclesiastical politics in the

---

[66] J. M. Marquès, ed., *Cartoral, dit de Carlemany, del bisbe de Girona (s. IX–XIV)* vol. 1 (Barcelona, 1993), no. 16.

[67] Marquès, ed., *Cartoral, dit de Carlemany*, nos. 14, 15, 17.

[68] Marquès, ed., *Cartoral, dit de Carlemany*, no. 18.

[69] Bautier, 'La prétendue dissidence', 495–497; Hartmann, *Die Synoden*, 381–2; I. Schröder, *Die westfränkischen Synoden von 888 bis 987 und ihre Überlieferung*, no. 15; and Mansi, *Sacrorum Conciliorum Nova Amplissima Collectio*, 18 A, col. 179B–182B.

[70] Marquès, ed., *Cartoral, dit de Carlemany*, no. 20.

[71] Marquès, ed., *Cartoral, dit de Carlemany*, no. 21; CC 2, 144.

[72] Abadal, *Dels visigots als catalans*, 2, 65–8.   [73] Abadal, *Els primers comtes*, 157–69.

[74] Jarrett, 'Ató of Osona', 11, with literature cited therein.

Spanish March, the authoritative position of the archbishop of Narbonne stood affirmed. Theodardus struggled and succeeded at keeping the power of his see felt in the March, relying on the king for support. His successor as archbishop, Arnustus, even sought and received formal papal sanction for intervening in episcopal elections concerning Narbonne's suffragan dioceses.[75]

What both Salrach and Abadal failed to emphasize properly is that this episode shows Frankish kingship to have been important in the Spanish March. Wifred, Theodardus, and Servus Dei gained the upper hand when local documents recognized Odo as king. The charters from 892 and 893 that document Servus Dei as claiming property were all dated by the regnal years of Odo, following on the bishop's receipt of a grant from the king at the council at Meung-sur-Loire. Clearly the seeds of this controversy were power struggles sown within the Spanish March and Septimania, indeed seeming to emanate from within the diocese of Urgell. If national or Gothic separatism were really the motivations behind Sclua's and Sunyer II's machinations,[76] they failed at stirring their neighbours to join them. Again, it seems rather to have been the opposite; that Wifred and Theodardus, who had at first withheld recognition from Odo, changed course and emerged in a superior position. Having royal backing enhanced the legitimacy of their position in the context of the more local rivalries. Furthermore, one of the bishops often believed to have supported Sclua in his nomination of Ermemir to the see of Girona was Frodoin of Barcelona, who is unanimously considered a Frank himself and a royal appointee, even though there really is no evidence for it. The motivation on the parts of all these actors had more to do with ambitions for status in the Spanish March than any notion of Gothic identity surging against Frankish overlordship. In the end, the March and Septimania are seen to have been fully integrated provinces, secular and ecclesiastical, of the Frankish empire.

Salrach's 'pro-Frankish', 'pro-assimilation' interpretation needs to be revised. What we see here is not a culture war between Frankish and Visigothic sympathies, but more basic questions of ecclesiastical administration. Furthermore, it is better to understand the issue as one of following the continuing court and ecclesiastical reform programme, the region and its people already having been incorporated into the empire. After all, it is very difficult to argue from surviving

---

[75] Abadal, *Els primers comtes*, 167–8.

[76] As not only the traditional works by Abadal and Salrach imply, but as also found in the more recent work of A. Pladevall, 'L'organització de l'Església', in *Catalunya a l'època carolíngia: Art i cultura abans del romànic (segles IX i X)* (1999), 53–8, with English translation, 444–8.

sources that any region or people was truly 'assimilated' into the Carolingian empire in a cultural sense, whatever that would mean,[77] as opposed to having been 'integrated' into its sociopolitical networks. While political networks and bonds of patronage could bind the kings and magnates to supporters and monastic houses in the March and the court could sponsor campaigns against perceived heresy, regional differences continued to exist and to flourish, and religious practices varied even within the 'centre' of the *regnum Francorum*.[78] As has been noted, different laws survived in various parts of the empire.[79] Doctrinal controversies were not limited to conquered areas of non-Frankish cultural heritage, namely the predestination and *filioque* controversies of the mid-ninth century.[80] Church councils convened throughout the Carolingian realms to address both major controversies and shortcomings within the church, wherever they happened to arise. For example, councils debated the attempted divorce of Lothar II, the conflict between Hincmar of Laon and his superior, Hincmar of Rheims, and church policies.[81] In this sense, the Spanish March was no different from any other province of the empire. Indeed, the cultural history of the Carolingian Spanish March merits a much fuller discussion in the next chapter. The ecclesiastical controversy of the late eighth century, for its part, shows that the counts and bishops of the Spanish March needed the kings to legitimate their positions, just as in previous generations the kings used local figures to enhance royal authority in the March.

---

[77] Astronomer, *Vita Hludovici imperatoris*, in *MGH SS*, 2 (Hanover, 1829), 604–48, c. 4 reports that even Louis the Pious, in his youth, was said to dress according to the Basque custom in his kingdom of Aquitaine, an example of a Carolingian king 'assimilating' to the customs of his subjects, rather than vice versa.

[78] See R. McKitterick, 'Unity and Diversity in the Carolingian Church', in R. Swanson, ed. *Unity and Diversity in the Church* (Oxford, 1996), 59–82. For an allied argument for the Spanish March, see M. Zimmermann, 'Conscience gothique et affirmation nationale dans la genèse de la Catalogne (IXe–XIe-siècles)', in J. Fontaine and C. Pellistrandi, eds, *L'Europe héritière de l'Espagne wisigothique* (Madrid, 1992), 51–68 at 58–9, although Zimmermann pushes the argument too far elsewhere and excessively downplays the degree to which the Spanish March was integrated into Carolingian political structures.

[79] P. Amory, 'The Meaning and Purpose of Ethnic Terminology in the Burgundian Laws', *EME* 2 (1993): 1–28; L. F. Bruyning, 'Lawcourt Proceedings in the Lombard Kingdom Before and After the Frankish Conquest', *Journal of Medieval History* 11 (1985): 193–214.

[80] Prudentius and Hincmar as annalists mention *filioque* and predestination in AB, 76–7, 93, and 141–2. See Hartmann, *Die Synoden*, 261–6 and 303. *MGH Conc.* 3, 294–7 on the Council of Quierzy that discussed predestination, *MGH Conc.* 4, 246–311 on the 868 Council of Worms that addressed the *filioque* controversy.

[81] See Hartmann, *Die Synoden*, 274–85 on Lothar II, 321–8 on Hincmar of Laon, and 245–60, 328–30 on general reform in this period.

THE HEIRS OF WIFRED, 898–947

By the late 890s, Wifred the Hairy found himself in firm control of most of the Spanish March; he had even augmented the territory under his direct rule while leaving some regions to his brothers.[82] Nearby lands to the south gradually fell away from the effective control of the emirs in Córdoba, al-Mundir (886–888) and 'Abdallah ibn Muhammad (888–912). The northern frontier of Islamic territory became the province of local strongmen, and it may be that the resettlement and reorganization of Osona Wifred sponsored gave these new powers reason to feel uneasy about the growing Christian power.[83] Indeed, the count conducted two major campaigns against the Banu Qasi, one to stop the fortification of Lleida in 885 or so against Ismail ibn Musa, and the other in 898 against Lubb ibn Musa.[84] It is significant that both were offensive actions taken by the Christian count, and the major fighting took place in Banu Qasi territory in and around Lleida. Two generations after losing territory in Aizo's uprising, the leading count of the Spanish March sought to restrict Muslim activity on the other side of the frontier and to expand Christian influence. Both campaigns, however, went badly for Wifred, and in the latter he lost his life.

At that time, Odo was king in West Francia. Wifred the Hairy and his brothers ruled all of the counties of the Spanish March except for Empúries and Roussillon, where their cousin Sunyer II was count, and Pallars and Ribagorça, ruled by Ramon II. All three lineages came from families based in Septimania and the Pyrenean regions, not Francia or Burgundy. Wifred had given Besalú over to his brother Radulf, unintentionally initiating the territory's separation from the county of Girona, and their brother Miro already died in 896. At Wifred's death, it seems his sons simply took their places as counts in the Spanish March, without waiting for or seeking royal approval. Much has been made of this turn of events, as it has been seen as pointing the way to an independent Catalonia.[85] Wifred the Hairy was, admittedly, the last count and *marchio*

---

[82] Miro had already been appointed count for Cerdanya by Charles the Bald, and Radulf joined their rank as count of Besalú. See Salrach, *El próces*, vol. 2, 105–6.

[83] M. Sánchez Martínez, 'Catalunya i al-Àndalus (segles viii–x)', in *Catalunya a l'època carolíngia* (Barcelona, 1999), 29–35 (English translation at 431–5) at 433. For Wifred's initiatives, see Abadal, *Dels visigots als catalans*, vol. 1, 309–21 and *Els primers comtes*, 73–114.

[84] Arabic sources edited and translated into Catalan in Millàs, nos. 128–9 and D. Bramon, ed., *De quan erem o no musulmans: textos del 713 al 1000. Continuació de l'obra de J. M. Millàs i Vallicrosa* (Vic 2000), no. 316 with notes. See also P. Balañà, *L'Islam a Catalunya (segles VIII–XII)* (Barcelona, 1997), 33 with notes 125 and 126.

[85] It has been addressed by Salrach, *El procés*, vol. 2, 141–57; Abadal, *Els primers comtes*, 219–315; Abadal, *L'abat Oliba, bisbe de Vic, i la seva època* (Barcelona, 1948), 33–4 (reprinted in *Dels visigots als catalans*, vol. 2, 141–278); Abadal, *Historia dels catalans* vol. 2, 706; Abadal, 'Un gran comte de

appointed by the Frankish kings, and a century after his rule his successors acted independently in many ways. Social forces may have played a role in the shift from royal appointment to hereditary succession, as the age-old argument holds that great magnates began to treat their *honores* as personal property by the end of the ninth century.[86] Yet a different factor surely played an important part. The ruling king of the West Franks, Odo, was formerly count of Paris and wielder of substantial power during the reign of Charles III 'the Fat'.[87] Powerful as Odo was, he was not a descendant of Charlemagne and thus, arguably in the context of the time and in the eyes of the counts in the Spanish March, not a legitimate king. Of course, there were no true legitimate heirs to the Frankish throne at the death of Charles III in 888, at least none of age, so the northern Frankish nobility had to come to some decision.[88] The aristocrats in the Pyrenean reaches of the kingdom, however, seem to have felt no need to recognize Odo's authority immediately upon their accessions a decade later. One good reason they had was that there was the mounting conflict between the ageing Odo and the resurgent Carolingian Charles the Simple. So in 898, when the sons of Wifred the Hairy took their places as counts, they were not exactly certain which northerner would sit as king. Such a mindset can be seen in the dating clauses of charters, an issue to which we shall return, but can also explain why Wifred the Hairy's sons saw no need to receive royal permission to succeed their father. Within a few months, though, there was a new king – Charles the Simple, son of Louis the Stammerer, the king who had appointed Wifred the Hairy as count of Barcelona. With the return to Carolingian rule and apparent stabilization of the monarchy, the new count of Barcelona did seek and receive royal blessing for his de facto power.

Previous studies have noted that there was no sense of true or natural unity to the territories Wifred the Hairy had governed, that he came to hold them by a sort of accidental conglomeration.[89] This is borne out by the succession of his sons, each of whom came to power in a different county. Presumably the oldest, a son also named Wifred, inherited Barcelona and Girona, perhaps the most prestigious *honores*, as well as Osona, the area reorganized under his father's reign. Barcelona and Osona, moreover, marked most of the limits of the Spanish March.

Barcelona preterit: Guifré-Borrell (897–911)', *Cuadernos de Arqueología e Historia de la Ciudad de Barcelona* 5 (1964): 102–11 (reprinted in *Dels visigots als catalans*, vol. 1, 323–62).

[86] J. Dhondt, *Etudes sur la naissance des principautés territoriales en France, IXe au Xe siècle* (Bruges, 1948); Lewis, *The Development of Society*, 121–4.

[87] See the discussion in MacLean, *Kingship and Politics*, 48–80 for a balanced treatment of the relationship between Charles and Odo.

[88] MacLean, *Kingship and Politics*, 75–80, 102–9.

[89] The classic is Abadal, *Els primers comtes*, at 249. See also his *Dels visigots als catalans*, vol. 1, 338–9.

Another son, Sunifred, took over in Urgell, another territory occupied since the days of Charlemagne, which also afforded a frontier. Miro succeeded in Cerdanya, with its surrounding *pagi*, and the youngest son Sunyer was still a minor entrusted to the tutelage of his brother Wifred.[90] A fifth son, Radulf, was already an inmate at the monastery of Santa Maria de Ripoll. Indeed, it seems that Wifred possessed some sort of prestige over all of his brothers, as the titles of *marchio* and even *princeps* given him in documents indicate.[91]

Wifred had a second name, Borrell, which eventually became how he was known to his descendants.[92] Modern historians thus call him Wifred-Borrell. His pre-eminence over his brothers, and perhaps the other counts of the Spanish March, stemmed not from the titles given to him in documents, but from the wealth he controlled. By governing Barcelona, Girona, and Osona, Wifred-Borrell had at his disposal more territory to bestow upon followers than any of his peers. Recognizing the succession of Charles the Simple helped him in that regard. The king granted him legitimate rule of his territories, as well as rights to all fiscal and deserted lands within them, and the right to take profit from the minting of coins in his lands.[93] This is admittedly a problematic document, as the original diploma is no longer extant. The rights granted to Wifred-Borrell have been adduced by recourse to later documents, which refer to properties and rights given to him by royal precept. Properties and rights are not, of course, the same as a royal appointment to his *honores*. Indeed, this is a case of mutual recognition of both men's successions to dynastic positions. Charles gained the loyalty of a count who otherwise could have deserted him, while Wifred-Borrell secured legitimacy for his rule from the rightful king.[94] In a document from April 898, Girona features a figure recorded as *Gauzfredus comes* residing *in Gerundam ciuitatem*. Abadal, figuring Gauzfredus was perhaps a variant spelling of *Guifredus*, identified him as Wifred-Borrell.[95] This identification never won universal acceptance, and the most recent editors of the charter posit that another individual took up the comital prerogative of holding a court to judge

---

[90] Abadal, *Els primers comtes*, 249–50. See also Salrach, *El procés,* vol. 2, 141–50.

[91] *HGL* 5, no. 35 for *comes*, Sant Cugat, no. 2 for *comes et marchio*. *España sagrada*, vol. 43, ap. 15 for *princeps maximus marchio*.

[92] For example, Sant Cugat, no. 3, which names Wifred as 'Wifredo, comite hac marchio, que vocant Borrellus'. Abadal, *Dels visigots als catalans*, vol. 1, 323–62 is a reprint with some revisions of the author's earlier treatment of Wifred-Borrell's career. That article, like much of Abadal's work, is still useful in many ways and has to serve as the starting point for what follows. See 323–4 for discussion of Wifred-Borrell's name.

[93] CC 2, 375–7.   [94] Admittedly, Abadal argued this some time ago: *Els primers comtes,* 259–60.

[95] Abadal, *Dels visigots als catalans*, vol. 1, 325–6. Abadal should have realized that most documentary attestations of the name in the period used the spelling Wifredus over Guifredus, favoured in later generations.

disputes.[96] If this identification is accurate – and it seems to be, based on the detailed study in the edition – 'count' Gauzfredus would presumably have constituted a rival to Wifred-Borrell, perhaps adding urgency to the trip to Tours-sur-Marne in 899 to recognize King Charles and win royal affirmation of his authority in the Spanish March.

Whatever the status of Gauzfredus, we know nothing of him beside his appearance in the judgement document of 898 and its related charter of evacuation, no longer extant.[97] Wifred-Borrell, on the other hand, was already behaving as a man of status by the end of 898. A charter records the sale of property in Osona by a man named Daniel and his wife to Wifred-Borrell and his wife Garsenda; the document was lost in the Ripoll fire of 1835, as the properties in question were bequeathed to the monastery in the count's will, but survives in later copies.[98] The act recorded in the charter upholds the pattern seen for property transactions elsewhere in the Spanish March in the late ninth and early tenth centuries, whereby people of lesser status would sell properties to gain the patronage of wealthier individuals.[99] Wifred-Borrell was active in supporting other monasteries in his territories as well. He is recorded as donating property to the abbot and community of Sant Cugat in 904, when the bishop of Barcelona also ceded jurisdiction over nearby churches to the monastery.[100] The next year, Wifred-Borrell was present, alongside his brother Miro and Bishop Nantigisus of Urgell, at the consecration and endowment of a new church in the area where the counties of Osona and Cerdanya met.[101] The uncertainty of boundaries likely played a role in calling both counts out for the event. At any rate, Wifred-Borrell appears to have been quite active in the ecclesiastical affairs of the areas where his father had encouraged and sponsored settlement and organization.

The ecclesiastical politics of the age have long been recognized as a driving force behind the production of documentation. Such is the case for a document dated to 907, recounting the synods of Barcelona and St-Thibéry (diocese of Agde).[102] Wifred-Borrell was present in the church, which carries in the document the name of the Holy Cross but not of St Eulalia.[103] At stake in the deliberations was freedom from *cens* payments for the church of Vic and the convent of Sant Joan, won by both houses.

---

[96] CC 5, no. 91, with editorial introduction.   [97] CC 5, no. 92.
[98] Abadal, *Dels visigots als catalans*, vol. 1, 326.   [99] Chandler, 'Land and Social Networks', 1–33.
[100] Sant Cugat, nos. 2 and 4. There are two versions of this record in the cartulary, one dated 904 and the other 910. The latter is a brief copy of the former that makes some clarifications. See Abadal, *Dels visigots als catalans*, vol. 1, 328–9.
[101] Abadal, *Dels visigots als catalans*, vol. 1, 329–30.
[102] Abadal, *Dels visigots als catalans*, vol. 1, 330. See also Schröder, *Die Synoden*, 172–3 and 174–81.
[103] HGL 5, col. 114–19. St Eulalia was translated to the cathedral church in 878 and later was recognized as its nominal co-patron – see Chapter 3.

The *marchio*, as reason would dictate, attended the synod held in his chief city, especially as it concerned two important establishments in his territory. Late in 908 Wifred-Borrell was present at the installation of the new bishop of Girona, Wigo, a royal appointee, along with the important prelates Arnustus of Narbonne, Teudericus of Barcelona, and Nantigisus of Urgell. The nature of this document provides insight into protocol and recording practices in the Spanish March of the early tenth century. Bishop Nantigisus is listed as amongst those present at Wigo's inauguration, but he did not sign the document. Idalguer of Vic signed in his stead, an indication that the document was drawn up after the fact. Therefore the assembly at which the count and clergy were present was the constitutive act, and the parchment record simply an aid to memory.[104] It is also important to note that Urgell was not amongst the territories Wifred-Borrell governed, but that Vic, the seat of Osona, was. It seems that in the time between Wigo's actual installation and the composition of the document, Nantigisus had returned to Urgell, and the count had to call on a nearby prelate to help validate the document.

Also in 908, Trasovadus, the judge active with Wifred-Borrell earlier that same year, sold to the count and countess substantial properties in the county of Barcelona for the price of 2,000 solidi.[105] Trasovadus himself came to own the property by purchasing it from Sunyer II of Empúries, who had inherited it from his father. Sunyer I, in his time, had received the land from Charles the Bald, who had granted fiscal wealth in 862 to both the count and to Bishop Frodoin of Barcelona in a move against the rebellious *marchio* Humfrid. In any case, Trasovadus must have been a man of considerable status in the Spanish March, for although not a count himself, he interacted with counts of different – and sometimes competing – families, and the value of the property was quite considerable.

Finally, four documents reveal the last of Wifred-Borrell's acts, although he was young enough not to anticipate that they would be his last. In 910, a woman and her four sons sold property to Wifred-Borrell and his wife Garsenda.[106] The next year, the *princeps et marchio* passed away. A document still extant records the distribution of alms in his memory to the episcopal churches of his domains, and a later charter shows that the activity continued five years later.[107] Meanwhile, a funerary stone at the church of Sant Pau de Camp bears his name.[108] The small

---

[104] Villanueva, *Viage literario* vol. 13, ap. 9. See the discussion in Abadal, *Dels visigots als catalans*, vol. 1, 333. The document is dated by the Incarnation.
[105] Sant Cugat, no. 3; Abadal, *Dels visigots als catalans*, vol. 1, 331–2.
[106] Udina, *Archivo Condal* no. 30. Abadal, *Dels visigots als catalans*, vol. 1, 334.
[107] Udina, *Archivo Condal* no. 33, plus CC 2, 166–74. Abadal, *Dels visigots als catalans*, vol. 1, 335–7.
[108] Abadal, *Dels visigots als catalans*, vol. 1, 334.

Romanesque church, now well within the bounds of Barcelona, was in the tenth century a small monastery beyond the city walls, as its name (Saint Paul of the Field) indicates. Wifred-Borrell is the only member of his family buried in Barcelona. Other members of the family who shared his names are buried at other locations, Wifred the Hairy at Ripoll and Borrell II at Castellciutat. Rather than establish a dynastic necropolis, these counts were buried where they died. Such dispersed practices hint at the decentralized nature of their power in the Spanish March of the period, and serves as one more reminder not to read too much national pride back into the intentions of the early medieval counts.

THE REIGNS OF WIFRED-BORRELL'S BROTHERS, 897–947

It is unfortunate that the deeds of most of Wifred-Borrell's brothers are poorly documented. Sunifred, the next oldest, seems not to have shared his brother's interest in recognizing Charles the Simple and receiving confirmation in return. Instead he succeeded to rule in Urgell without royal permission.[109] Perhaps Wifred-Borrell's status was enough for the entire family; the case of Wifred the Hairy appointing his own brother Radulf to comital rank in Besalú may have suggested a precedent. At any rate, the new count of Urgell is only scarcely attested to in the surviving record, and what does exist gives little clue as to how he governed his territory.[110] In 948 at Sunifred's death, his nephew Borrell succeeded to govern Urgell.[111] The next brother, often known as Miro the Younger, became count of Cerdanya and later Besalú in this second generation. He succeeded Wifred the Hairy in Cerdanya in 898, while his uncle Radulf maintained authority in Besalú. Radulf died in 913, allowing Miro to take office there.[112] In 904 Miro is documented exercising his jurisdiction by presiding over a judgement involving property in Cerdanya claimed by his sister, Abbess Emma of Sant Joan, on behalf of her community.[113] Two laymen recognized the abbey's claims, based on the written testimony of one of the nuns, to land called *aprisiones*. Miro presided at another dispute settlement in 913, alongside his younger brother Sunyer who had succeeded to comital rank for Barcelona, Girona, and Osona. This case was again decided in favour of Emma and Sant Joan.[114] Together, these cases show the authority possessed by Wifred the Hairy's

---

[109] Abadal, *Els primers comtes*, 245, 250, 267.
[110] It is most telling that Sunifred merits only seven mentions in all of Abadal, *Els primers comtes*. See, in addition to instances cited in the previous note, pp. 81, 118, and 147. The only documents Abadal refers to are Villanueva, *Viage literario* vol. 10, app. 13 and 15.
[111] Abadal, *Els primers comtes*, 292.   [112] Abadal, *Els primers comtes*, 292–3.
[113] *Archivo Condal*, no. 16   [114] *Archivo Condal*, no. 38. See also CC 4, 119.

sons, their fraternal cooperation, and also potential confusion over to which jurisdiction Sant Joan and its properties pertained.[115]

The youngest of Wifred the Hairy's sons, Sunyer, succeeded Wifred-Borrell in Barcelona, Girona, and Osona.[116] Sunyer was one of the executors of Wifred-Borrell's will, and gifts to the churches of Ripoll, Girona, and Barcelona in his own right were for the purposes of benefitting his brother's soul.[117] Abadal concluded that Sunyer was to inherit Besalú upon the death of Radulf (Wifred the Hairy's brother, Sunyer's uncle), thereby assigning the youngest of his sons the smallest of his territories. Wifred-Borrell, however, predeceased Radulf, paving the way for Sunyer to inherit Barcelona, Girona, and Osona. Thus a deal was struck by which Miro took over Besalú as compensation for his younger brother succeeding to more substantial and more prestigious counties.[118] That, apparently, is the explanation behind Sunyer and Miro ceding property in the valley of Ripoll, county of Osona, to Emma and Sant Joan in 913 – two years after the death of Wifred-Borrell and one year after the death of their uncle Radulf. A document represents Miro's *mandatarius* Oliba forsaking comital rights to these properties in favour of their sister's community, but Miro must have come to have those rights only by acquiring the land from Sunyer.[119]

Arabic sources record that Sunyer achieved some military successes against the Muslims.[120] After 900, the Banu Qasi were eclipsed by the Banu Sabrit. Muhammad al-Tawil of this family controlled a few cities in the northern frontier area and led his own campaign against the Christians of the Spanish March. The sources show al-Tawil raiding in Pallars,[121] and perhaps Urgell[122] in 909 and 910. Ibn Idari records a raid into the territory of Barcelona and Terrassa in 912, which Sunyer rode out to meet in nearby canyons. The Muslims won the victory, but the contest between them was not over.[123] In 913 al-Tawil was bound for the Christian Spanish March again, to rebuild fortifications at Tortosa, not

---

[115] On Emma's strategies as abbess and the early history of Sant Joan, see J. Jarrett, 'Power over Past and Future', 229–58.

[116] Surprisingly, despite his importance and appearance in no fewer than forty-three charters from Osona and Manresa (four times as many as his older brother), there exists no substantial study of Sunyer beyond P. Bofarull y Mascaró, *Los condes de Barcelona vindicados, y cronología y genealogía de los reyes de España considerados como soberanos independientes de su marca* (Barcelona 1836, repr. 1990), vol. I, 64–138.

[117] *Archivo Condal*, no. 33 for the Ripoll area.

[118] Abadal, *Dels visigots als catalans*, vol. 1, 342–4.

[119] Udina, *Archivo Condal*, ap. 2–A. See also CC4, no. 120.

[120] For a brief overview of further interactions, see Sánchez Martínez, 'Catalunya i al-Àndalus (segles viii–x)', 29–35 (English at 431–5) at 433. See also Abadal, *Els primers comtes*, 313–14.

[121] Ibn Idari, in Bramon, *De quan erem o no musulmans*, no. 335.

[122] Al-Udri, in Bramon, *De quan erem o no musulmans*, no. 336 and Ibn Idari in no. 338.

[123] Bramon, *De quan erem o no musulmans*, no. 339.

too far from Barcelona, but was defeated and killed.[124] After al-Tawil's death, the key Muslim city of Lleida was in the hands of the Tudjibides family of Zaragoza, loyal to the caliph. The frontier found peace for about twenty years.

These years mark a transition, away from the power of the Banu Qasi and towards a re-invigorated central, caliphal authority. 'Abd al-Rahman III took over in Córdoba and began to strengthen his control of local potentates in al-Andalus. By 928 he had asserted his authority in the northern frontier, diminishing the locals' abilities to deal independently with neighbouring Christian leaders from the Spanish March or the kingdom of León.[125] Reflecting the new state of affairs, the Arabic narrative sources begin to rather favour direct diplomatic relations between the counts of the Spanish March and the caliph in Córdoba over frontier raids and campaigns, save for naval expeditions.[126] A change in practice like this may be the result of a change in the sources that record the history of the period, but given the amount of energy the caliphs used to exert more control over their own domains, a genuine change in diplomatic practice towards the Spanish March is not out of the question. Nor is it a complete switch away from military raids. The use of an improved navy for punitive raids against the Christians is a signal of caliphal control over the external affairs of al-Andalus and of Abd al-Rahman III's success in taking the initiative away from the frontier commanders.

Sunyer, as count of Barcelona and Girona, was vulnerable to seaborne attacks and held the responsibility for meeting them. The caliph in 933 ordered a sea campaign, but it was turned back by a storm near the Balearic Island of Mallorca.[127] Another campaign, setting out from Almería in 935, reached the coast as far as Empúries, attacking the counties of Girona and Barcelona. The forces at Barcelona came to meet the aggressors in the open on land, but the Muslims won victory near the city at the mouth of the Llobregat.[128] In 936 Count Sunyer of Barcelona went on the offensive, encouraged by the insurgence of frontier leader Muhammad ibn Hasim al-Tugibi. Sunyer did not succeed, as his force was countered by the caliph's men besieging Zaragoza.[129]

---

[124] Al-Udri, in Bramon, *De quan erem o no musulmans*, no. 340, Ibn Hayyan in no. 341, and Ibn Idari in nos. 342–3.

[125] Sánchez Martínez, 'Catalunya i al-Àndalus (segles viii–x)', 29–35 (English at 431–5) at 433.

[126] Sánchez Martínez, 'Catalunya i al-Àndalus (segles viii–x)', 29–35 (English at 431–5) at 433 does not explicitly state that the caliph preferred sea attacks in order to weaken the positions of frontier leaders, but that conclusion is reasonable.

[127] Ibn Hayyan, in Bramon, *De quan erem o no musulmans*, no. 374.

[128] Ibn Hayyan, in Bramon, *De quan erem o no musulmans*, no. 382.

[129] Ibn Hayyan, in Bramon, *De quan erem o no musulmans*, no. 386.

Under the weight of a decade's pressure, Sunyer had to agree to peace with the caliph in 940. Parties to the treaty included Hugh of Provence and Riquilda of Narbonne (Sunyer's sister and wife of the viscount), who gained security from attacks against them from Fraxinetum, the Balearic Islands, and other bases. Sunyer and his older brother Sunifred of Urgell agreed 'to break up any alliances against the caliph' who in return would 'suspend all hostilities against the region' i.e., the Spanish March. It seems that two fleets crept up the coastline while negotiations developed, dispersing only when they learned that peace had been agreed. Obviously, the implication is that that they would have attacked if the Christians refused to agree. Bishop Gotmar of Girona travelled back to Córdoba with the caliph's ambassador, bringing as a gift a book apparently detailing aspects of Frankish history.[130] Sunyer renewed the peace the next year by sending a new embassy.[131] Before the end of his reign, though, Sunyer would gain the upper hand in the contest for frontier territory.[132] Sunyer's reign was long and eventful, more than a mere transitional period between those of his brother and son.

COUNTS OF OTHER FAMILIES

Beyond the direct lineage of Wifred the Hairy, the leading nobles elsewhere in the Spanish March were active in Frankish politics, especially those based in coastal Empúries and in Roussillon. The count of these lands, Sunyer II (d. 915), alone of his peers of the March, was present at Orléans to recognize the election of king Odo in 888. His cousin Wifred was apparently less enthusiastic about the succession. Sunyer II also played an important part in the controversy over the bishopric of Girona between Servus Dei and Ermemir, conflicting with the archbishop of Narbonne. At the opening of the tenth century, only Sunyer II amongst the counts of the March had received his office from a king.[133] One document produced in Sunyer II's territories even seems to hesitate in recognizing Odo's successor, the Carolingian Charles the Simple. It is a charter recording the sale of somewhat valuable properties by a priest named Romanus and his sister Chilio to Riculf, the bishop of Elna. The scribe, also a priest, dated the document to Odo's thirteenth year – 'anno XIII regnante Oddone rege' – which is a bit alarming, given that Odo reigned only ten years from early 888 to his death in January 898.[134]

---

[130] Ibn Hayyan, in Bramon, *De quan erem o no musulmans*, no. 399, al-Masudi in no. 400, and al-Udri in no. 401.
[131] Ibn Hayyan, in Bramon, *De quan erem o no musulmans*, no. 404.
[132] Al-Masudi, in Bramon, *De quan erem o no musulmans*, no. 411 and al-Maqqari in no. 412.
[133] Salrach, *El próces*, vol. 2, 173–5.   [134] CC 6, no. 162.

Extending the length of the king's reign is either a slip of the pen, perhaps giving the Roman numeral *x* in place of *v*, or else an indication of reluctance to recognize the new king. Supposing that scribes were aware that Sunyer II's comital peer Wifred-Borrell had sought to reciprocate legitimation with Charles, this dating clause could have been a political statement.

Unlike Wifred-Borrell, Sunyer II of Empúries did not do much to curry royal favour. It has long been held that Wifred-Borrell travelled to Tours-sur-Marne to recognize Charles the Simple and receive recognition in return; Sunyer II made no such journey.[135] Quite to the contrary, Charles supported his own faithful men with gifts of considerable properties in Sunyer II's area of authority. One *fidelis*, named Stephen, received properties in the *pagus* of Narbonne, Roussillon, and Besalú, at least in part through the intervention of Archbishop Arnustus of Narbonne and the king's mother Adelaide.[136] This Stephen held the rank of viscount of Narbonne. His wife, Anna, is named in the document. Her grandfather, Bera, was the first count of Barcelona under Carolingian rule.[137] While Charles made the grant of new properties, as well as confirming possessions already Stephen's and Anna's by purchase at the behest of other parties, a slight hint of animosity between the king and Count Sunyer II is evident in the dating clause at the end of the diploma. According to the notary, Heriveus, the grant was made in the seventh year of Charles's reign, with modern editors assigning it to 899 at Tours-sur-Marne. It is held that Stephen accompanied Wifred-Borrell to meet the king.[138] In that case, the summer of 899 would represent not the second year of Charles's reign after the death of Odo, but rather the seventh year as recognized by partisans aligned against Odo, the king who after all initially supported Sunyer in the ecclesiastical controversy of the bishopric of Girona.[139] Another *fidelis*, Theodosius, received lands in the same counties the previous year, given as the sixth in the reign of 'the most serene king Charles'.[140] Theodosius was not from a local family, as Stephen seems to have been at least by marriage, but rather the client of the king's former tutor, Duke Robert.[141] His grant includes what

---

[135] CC 2, 375–7, as noted earlier.   [136] CC 2, 371–4.

[137] See the editorial discussion in CC 2, 371–2, based on documentation in *HGL* 2, app. 136, 139, 169, and 190; *HGL* 5, col. 1504; and MH, ap. 62.

[138] Abadal, *Dels visigots als catalans*, vol. 1, 346–54.

[139] In many cases, documents from the Spanish March date Charles's reign by Odo's death, as is the case in Villanueva, *Viage* 10, 83–5 and *Archivo Condal*, no. 10. Schröder, *Die Synoden*, 152 discusses the challenges in working out dates for these years.

[140] CC 2, 368–70.

[141] See the editorial introduction to the document as well as Abadal, *Dels visigots als catalans*, vol. 1, 349–50.

amounts to lordship, in that men who live on the properties in question are to offer service to Theodosius, the hispani just as much as the rest. The document also contains for the first time an important geographical designation of the broader region within which the hispani and others lived, *regno nostro Gothiae uel Septimaniae*. These diplomas show Charles working to safeguard his authority in the eastern Spanish March against Sunyer by supporting loyal men with generous grants and by re-affirming his status as king over what appears to be gaining recognition as a distinct section of the king's realm.[142]

Meanwhile, Sunyer II remained in office despite whatever friction may have existed between him and Charles. As the reigning count of Empúries, he had responsibilities to tend to, amongst them leading a naval expedition of fifteen ships in 889–90 to the Muslim maritime base of Pechina, where he met with some success.[143] After that, by all indications there was peace between Sunyer and the Muslims of the coast, the only non-Christians he was able to attack. Meanwhile, the controversy over the episcopal seat of Girona in the 880s cast a long shadow. An ecclesiastical council at Jonqueres in 909 seems to have at least conditionally eased the conditions placed on Sunyer II for his role, provided he made good on promises to Archbishop Arnustus.[144] Sunyer II was after all appointed by a Carolingian king, but his sons, like those of his early contemporary Wifred the Hairy, succeeded by heredity. Counts still maintained some degree of connection to the Frankish monarchy even though they did not depend on kings for their offices.

At the other end of the Spanish March, in the counties of Pallars and Ribagorça, another dynasty was taking shape.[145] Comital power in these western areas arose in the upheavals of the early 870s, when competition for the *honores* of Toulouse allowed local power brokers to assert themselves.[146] The first independent count, Ramon, involved himself in the politics of the Basque areas of the Spanish March that had long before established a greater degree of independence from Carolingian overlordship; the count himself came from a Basque family.[147] Ramon then supported the creation of a new diocese, separate from Urgell – the would-be bishopric of Pallars – and succeeded for a time.[148] Two

---

[142] This concept deserves more scrutiny, which it shall receive below.

[143] Ibn Hayyan, in Bramon, *De quan erem o no musulmans*, no. 309; Sánchez Martínez, 'Catalunya i al-Àndalus (segles viii–x)', 29–35 (English at 431–5) at 434.

[144] *HGL* 5, col. 126–7; discussion in Schröder, *Die Synoden*, 186–9 and Abadal, *Els primers comtes*, 259.

[145] The fundamental account is still that of Abadal, CC 3, part 1, 116–27.

[146] CC 3, part 1, 112–16.   [147] See the genealogy provided CC 3, part 1, 127.

[148] Salrach, *El próces*, vol. 2, 173–5.

consecutive bishops, Adulf and Ató, Ramon's son, governed for decades.[149] The Muslim leaders of the frontier were quite strong, so castles proliferated in Pallars and Ribagorça, though issues of social and economic organization may have been as important as military considerations.[150] In addition, Ramon allied with the Banu Qasi and agreed to buy Zaragoza from them, only to have the agreement fall apart because of the intervention of the emir's army.[151] Lubb ibn Musa led a campaign against Pallars in late 904, attacking fortifications and taking many prisoners.[152] This was one of a series of raids throughout the first decade of the tenth century, resulting in the acquisition of sufficient booty to fund the improvement of defences at nearby Osca.[153]

Ramon governed both Pallars and Ribagorça as count from roughly 872 until his death in around 920, but, as was the case with Wifred the Hairy's sons, his heirs succeeded in different areas and ruled independently. Isarn and Lupus came to rule in Pallars, while Bernard and Miro governed Ribagorça.[154] Nothing much is known about the activities of these counts or of the society they governed in the tenth century, owing to the relatively patchy documentary record.[155] Fewer than 300 documents dating to the period exist for Pallars and Ribagorça, compared to several hundred or even more than a thousand each for the more easterly regions. Muhammad ibn Lubb of the Banu Qasi, related by marriage to the ruling family of Pallars and Ribagorça, was struggling to maintain his position in this area as well. The two families did not, however, always get along. One particular confrontation, or ambush, in 929 led to Muhammad's death and the end of the Banu Qasi's power.[156] Unlike the eastern counties, where counts became princes by the early eleventh century, authority in Pallars and Ribagorça continued to be partitioned in successive generations until neighbouring rulers asserted their own power, absorbing the lands into their own realms.

---

[149] CC 3, part 1, 170–7. An ecclesiastical document attests to Adulf's participation at a synod near Narbonne in 911: CC 3, no. 117.

[150] See the building of castles as a social and economic development in Italy: C. Wickham, *Framing the Early Middle Ages: Europe and the Mediterranean, 400–800* (Oxford, 2005), 464 and his *The Mountains and the City*.

[151] Ibn Hayyan, in Bramon, *De quan erem o no musulmans*, no. 294.

[152] Ibn Idari, in Bramon, *De quan erem o no musulmans*, no. 328; Sánchez Martínez, 'Catalunya i al-Àndalus (segles viii–x)', 29–35 (English at 431–5) at 433.

[153] P. Balaña, *L'Islam a Catalunya (segles VIII–XII)* (Barcelona, 1997), 33.

[154] Abadal, CC 3, part 1, 128.

[155] See, for example, A. Benet i Clarà, 'Castells i línies de reconquesta', in *Symposium internacional*, vol. 1, 365–391 at 388. Abadal has furnished the basis of understanding for this period in CC 3, part 1, 128–64 focusing on the counts, and 165–93 for bishops; the social structures are illuminated at 71*–80* and 193–202.

[156] Al-Udri, in Bramon, *De quan erem o no musulmans*, no. 370; Balaña, *L'Islam a Catalunya*, 36.

REPRESENTATIONS OF AND RELATIONS WITH KINGS

When Charles the Simple took the crown in 898, secular and ecclesiastical magnates from the Spanish March came to recognize him, travelling to meet with him and allowing dating by his reign in local charters. Abadal attributed this to a 'traditional legitimist position in the family of our counts'.[157] His observation merits two remarks. First is his characterization of the counts of the Spanish March as legitimists. Dating clauses in documents do, as he demonstrates, favour members of the Carolingian family, emphasizing their legitimate claims to rule by noting their royal descent; descendants of Odo and Robert are not so recognized in Catalonian documentation. But the use of the label 'legitimist' recalls other such vocabulary that twentieth-century Catalan scholarship of the period – legitimist, unitarist, regionalist – applied to Wifred-Borrell's predecessors and that simply has no grounding in the political thought of the early Middle Ages. Second, Abadal's repeated use of the term 'our counts' betrays his explicit warning against nationalism. He strongly cautions against the nationalism the term Catalonia causes to project back to the ninth and tenth centuries. The formulation 'pre-Catalunya' is therefore intended as an alternative to avoid placing a sense of nationalism in the ninth and tenth centuries, and yet it remains a teleological term referring to the 'natural' boundaries of the future territory.[158] It will do to recognize the tendency by those in the Spanish March to accept Carolingians' successions rather warmly and Robertians' only belatedly, but modern historians should not ignore the political circumstances prevailing at the time of each succession, and the effect those may have had on the relationships between kings and the counts and notaries of the March.

For his part, Charles the Simple granted most of his diplomas for the Spanish March in the first years of his rule. He issued seven in 898 and 899, while five date to his last year as king; another three documents, now lost, are known from other sources that mention them.[159] Amongst the early diplomas were those to his *fideles* Theodosius and Stephen to shore up his position against Count Sunyer II of Empúries. He also supported the bishop of Elna, in Sunyer II's other county of Roussillon, by granting to Riculf properties, fiscal rights, and immunity 'in omni regno nostro

---

[157] Adabal, *Dels visigots als catalans*, vol. 1, 348.

[158] See Abadal, *Els primers comtes*, 3–12; and use of 'pre-Catalunya' in the title of his article, 'La institucio comtal carolingia en la pre-Catalunya del segle IX', reprinted in *Dels visigots als catalans*, vol. 1, 181–226, where he discusses the term 'pre-Catalunya'.

[159] Another, CC 2, 375–7, as noted above in the context of Count Wifred-Borrell's power and authority, is adduced on the basis of later evidence and cannot be dated with certainty.

Goticae siue Hispaniae'.[160] The king re-affirmed the status of Servus Dei as bishop of Girona by confirming possessions and immunity,[161] and even placed the convent of Sant Joan, led by Abbess Emma, under royal protection.[162] A further act to protect church property favoured Archbishop Arnustus of Narbonne, likely in order to settle confusion arising in the unsettled times of the *marchio* Bernard of Gothia.[163] One other diploma, procured by the intercession of Arnustus, benefitted lay supporters with royal legitimation of possessions on both sides of the Pyrenees.[164] After a hiatus of about sixteen years, royal intervention in the Spanish March was sought again. In 916 Charles renewed the grant of immunity to the abbey of Banyoles made by his predecessors.[165] This marks what many regard as the more passive phase of Carolingian kingship in regards to the Spanish March. Yet clearly the king was active. Even if diplomas were granted only in response to petitions, it must be observed that most grants to recipients in the March had always been made in such fashion, from the earliest surviving grant of Charlemagne to the series of diplomas by his namesake a century later. The churches and monasteries of the March sought out royal diplomas in order to legitimize their rights and possessions, and Charles seized the opportunity to pronounce his authority and role as protector of the church.[166]

King Charles did intervene in at least one other substantial way in the affairs of the Spanish March – appointing a bishop. From the document on the installation of Wigo as bishop of Girona in 908, it is noteworthy that not only was Wigo appointed from the 'aula regia' but also took his place amongst the bishops 'of Gothia'.[167] The language used here recalls that of ten years earlier, in noting *nostro regno Gothiae*.[168] It had been quite some time since a king of the Franks had appointed a bishop to the Spanish March. For example, in Elna, Count Miro was able to appoint his brother Riculf, following the careers of two of Sunyer II's sons.[169] Later, in 922 the king moved to affirm the immunity and possessions of the church of Girona for Bishop Wigo, the king's man.[170] Charles acted nearly simultaneously at Wigo's request on behalf of the monastery of Amer, and also in favour of a family headed by an archdeacon and *fidelis* of

---

[160] CC 2, 107–8; CC 2, 109–11.   [161] CC 2, 144–7.

[162] CC 2, 215–17, a document which survives in original.

[163] The document survives in only one copy, from the twelfth century. CC 2, 438–40.

[164] CC 2, 371–4, cited above in a different context.   [165] CC 2, 62–4.

[166] Koziol, *The Politics of Memory*, 494–8 discusses the diplomas in similar context.

[167] Villanueva, *Viage literario* vol. 13, ap. 9: 'a aula regia prolatum et eius iussone atque sanctorum Episcoporum Gothiae electum'.

[168] CC 2, 368–70.   [169] Abadal, *Els primers comtes*, 261–2.

[170] CC 2, 148–51. The document refers to previous grants by the kings Charles the Bald and Louis the Stammerer, but not to the reigning king's own grant from 899.

the bishop's to protect their property, whether acquired by gift, *aprisio*, or purchase, throughout 'Gozie uel Hispanie'.[171] Wigo may have been at court with Charles, for in a charter dated only a few days later and in a different place, the king confirmed the properties in the county of Girona to another of the bishop's *fideles*, again whether by gift, *aprisio*, or purchase, throughout Gothia and Hispania.[172] It is interesting to note that, given the attention modern historians have paid to the counts' emphasis on Carolingian legitimacy, Charles the Simple's confirmations refer explicitly to the grants made by his father and grandfather but never mention any royal acts of Odo. This is especially noteworthy for the bishopric of Girona, which possesses diplomas issued by the non-Carolingian king. Charles wished to stress his legitimacy, and even diminish Odo's, at least as avidly as parties in the March wished to recognize him.

After Odo's reign, royal documents reveal a difference in the perceived relationship between the monarchy and the March. Charles the Simple styled himself *rex Gothorum* in addition to *rex Franchorum* in grants issued shortly after his coronation, marking the first time a Carolingian king used such a title. His charters also call the territories either side of the Pyrenees the *regnum Goticae sive Hispaniae*.[173] His predecessors used the term 'Septimania' in royal documents dating from Charlemagne's first *aprisio* grant. Ninth-century kings named Septimania as the region concerned when the lands in question lay north of the Pyrenees, as Charles the Bald did in 844.[174] The toponymy used around the turn of the tenth century signals what in some respects was the age-old royal approach to Septimania and the Spanish March, parallel to Charles the Simple's adoption of a second title as 'king of the Franks and of the Goths'. Abadal saw the new title as an attempt to recover royal authority in the region after Odo's usurpation, which regional counts in the March recognized only slowly, if at all. Charles sent a message that he was their king as well as the king of his Frankish subjects.[175] While this interpretation has merit, the fact that the ethnic element to the geographical designation 'Gothia' gained currency at about the same time must

---

[171] CC 2, 18–19 for Amer; CC 2, 378–80 for the family; both dated to 922. The latter document exists in the twelfth-century capitulary copy of the Girona church archive, which may account for the unusual orthography.

[172] CC 2, 381–2. Again, the document uses odd spellings – *Gozie uel Yspanie* – and again survives in the Girona archive in cartularies. Unlike the previous diploma, there are two copies, in different cartularies.

[173] CC 2, 109–10, 369–170; Abadal, *Dels visigots als catalans*, vol. 1, 167–8.

[174] CC 2, 339, regarding the villas of Fonts and Fontjoncosa, both in the county of Narbonne. CC 2, 360 names land in Roussillon as being in Septimania.

[175] Abadal, *Dels visigots als catalans*, vol. 1, 167.

not be overlooked. Taken together, the title and toponymy employed by the royal court emphasized the royal claim to authority over distant lands and peoples, stressing the friendship between Charles as a Frank and the local 'Goths', and trying to paint Odo as not only a king of questionable legitimacy but also as a king largely disinterested in the affairs of faraway subjects.[176] Locally in the March, labels like Frank and Goth seem to have lacked any value as identity markers and thus were not used. This could be because no large Frankish population ever settled there, or alternatively because ethnic differences were not considered important in the first place. Really, only documents emanating from the royal court continued to distinguish ethnicities. The very Goths whom the royal court emphasized as a separate people in order to claim royal authority continued to see themselves as members of a Frankish kingdom.

CHURCHES AND COUNCILS AFTER WIFRED THE HAIRY

In addition to the behaviour of the counts of the Spanish March, the activities of the region's bishops and abbots in the tenth century merit attention.[177] At the same time that comital ambivalence held sway in Catalonia's secular political culture, a similar trend obtained in the ecclesiastical hierarchy. The leaders of church houses often had great incentive to maintain direct ties to the Frankish kings, as they placed great value on the legal legitimacy of royal grants for their lands and rights. Yet further links connected the churches of the March to the institutions of the Frankish kingdom, most importantly involving the administration of ecclesiastical affairs. While the bishops of the Spanish March only occasionally attended the great church councils of the ninth century, they participated actively in the provincial synods of Narbonne. In doing so they maintained the position the dioceses of the March had had with Frankish structures since the days of Charlemagne and Louis the Pious.

As seen above in relation to the controversy surrounding Sclua, the churches of the Spanish March of the tenth century were still part of the ecclesiastical province of Narbonne. The active Archbishop Arnustus called as many as seven provincial synods from 897 to his death in 912–13, and bishops from south of the Pyrenees participated regularly. The earliest provincial synod of Narbonensis on record for

---

[176] Koziol, *The Politics of Memory*, 497–8, makes a similar argument simply on the basis of legitimate, Carolingian, 'public' order as seen against the power-grabbing of the Robertians; he does not discuss royal titles and their inclusion of toponymy.

[177] The church certainly has not been ignored: M. Riu, 'L'Església catalana al segle X', in *Symposium internacional*, vol. 1, 161–90.

this period was reputedly held at Port in 897, but likely never took place.[178] Nantigisus of Urgell and Riculf of Elna accompanied Servus Dei of Girona to a synod at Narbonne concerned with episcopal authority over the churches in the possession of Abbess Emma and Sant Joan, scattered as they were across jurisdictional boundaries and the responsibilities for the parishes having become entangled.[179] No bishop of Barcelona is recorded as having attended the synod, because the see was vacant for several years after Frodoin's death in 890. In 902 Arnustus and his colleague Rostagnus of Arles convoked a council for the provinces of Narbonne and Arles, held at Attilian. The council's business dealt with jurisdictional matters in Béziers, but the same three bishops from the March attended.[180] The bishops of the province finally met south of the Pyrenees in 906 in Barcelona, where Wifred-Borrell was present. All the canonical bishops of the Spanish March were there, unsurprisingly, representing the sees of Barcelona, Girona, Vic, Urgell, and Elna; accompanying them were several of their colleagues from outside the March, as well as Abbess Emma and other regional abbots and clerics.[181] The business concerned Sant Joan's possessions, as had been the case in the earlier synod at Narbonne, but also the tribute due to the archbishop from the still poorly organized diocese of Vic. A follow-up council the next year at St-Thibéry saw to Idalguer of Vic's concern, much to his relief. This synod was also well attended by the bishops of the March and others in the province.[182] At Jonqueres in 909 the bishops convened to absolve Count Sunyer II of Empúries of his excommunication; interestingly, only Nantigisus of Urgell represented the bishops south of the Pyrenees.[183] By 911, Wigo had succeeded Servus Dei as bishop in Girona, and there was a new diocese in the Pyrenees, that of Pallars, to be addressed. The bishops of 'Gothia' gathered at Fontcouverte and recognized Adulf as bishop of Pallars after twenty-three years of his see's existence apart from Urgell. The

---

[178] *HGL* 3, pp. 56–7. The council record was denounced as a forgery in Bautier, 'La prétendue dissidence', 477–98, citing in turn É. Griffe, *Histoire religieuse des anciens pays de l'Aude. Tome I: des origines chrétiennes à la fin de l'époque carolingienne* (Paris, 1933): 252–63. See also Schröder, *Die Synoden*, 146–53, who found no solid evidence confirming that the synod took place.

[179] *HGL* 5, col. 114–16 and Schröder, *Die Synoden*, 150–3; see also O. Engels, 'Der Weltklerus und das Pfarrnetz', in *Symposium internacional*, 477–90 on the network of parishes, even though his study pertains to the diocese of Urgell.

[180] *HGL* 5, col. 109–11; Schröder, *Die Synoden*, 160–3.

[181] *HGL* 5, col. 114–16; Schröder, *Die Synoden*, 172–3 and 175–7 for bibliography.

[182] *HGL* 5, col. 116–19; Schröder, *Die Synoden*, 174–81.

[183] *HGL* 5, col. 126–7; Schröder, *Die Synoden*, 186–9.

synod allowed Adulf to retain his position, but the diocese of Pallars was to die with him.[184] Only a year later, Arnustus himself met a terrible fate, for along the road to another provincial synod in the Spanish March, his party was attacked. The marauders blinded the archbishop and cut out his tongue; he later died from these injuries, despite the aid of the bishops of Béziers and Urgell, who found him on the road. The murder has been a mystery for more than a thousand years, with the best hypothesis laying blame at the feet of Sunyer II of Empúries, on the grounds that he had not kept his promises and would have been excommunicated again at the synod Arnustus was set to convene.[185] All told, the synodal activity of the very early tenth century shows the churches of the Spanish March still fully integrated into the ecclesiastical framework of the Frankish kingdom. While Sclua and a few others in the 890s may have had designs on ignoring the authority of the archbishop of Narbonne, the activity of the March's bishops in the period after the controversy shows the majority to have held no such notions. The administration of the church established in the time of Charlemagne held firm a century later.

After Arnustus's archiepiscopate, synodal activity dropped off considerably for the rest of the tenth century. Documentation survives from only four additional synods from 913 to 947 in the Narbonne province. The earliest of the four seems to have involved exclusively clergy from the Carcassonne region.[186] In 937, what may loosely be termed a synod of the province met without any representatives from south of the Pyrenees. The only participants from areas traditionally aligned with the leading families of the Spanish March were Wadaldus, bishop of Elna, and Abbot Sunyer II of La Grassa.[187] The gathering featured clerical and lay individuals of some status, but dealt with founding the monastery of St-Pons-de-Thomières, a rather local affair for Aquitainians. Another meeting of the clergy and laity of Narbonensis again numbered amongst its participants Wadaldus and Sunyer, and perhaps the bishop of Urgell, again to attend to the business of St-Pons.[188] Bishop Wadaldus died in early

---

[184] CC 3, no. 117: 'conventus sinodalis sanctorum episcoporum Gocie'; Schröder, *Die Synoden*, 197–202.

[185] Abadal, *Els primers comtes*, 262–3.   [186] HGL 5, col. 155–6; Schröder, *Die Synoden*, 226–8.

[187] HGL 5, col. 176–9; Schröder, *Die Synoden*, 235–40. The next generation of counts would consciously pursue building strong relationships with comital families and monastic houses in Aquitaine: M. Aurell, 'Jalons pour une enquête sure les strategies matrimonials des Comtes Catalanes (ix^e–xi^e s.)', in *Symposium internacional*, 281–364, esp. 290–2.

[188] HGL 5, col. 185–7; Schröder, *Die Synoden*, 241–5.

947, and a synod affirmed Riculf II as his successor, but no one from south of the Pyrenees attended.[189] For whatever reasons, synodal activity diminished greatly without Arnustus's leadership, and the local focus characterizing church business attracted only the clergy of the March who were based nearby, north of the Pyrenees.

CONCLUSIONS

The evidence for the late ninth and early tenth centuries shows no signs of a fledgling Catalonia stretching its wings and attempting to fly a course separate from the West Frankish kingdom. If anything, the relationships between kings, counts, and bishops show that the old networks of political ties were still valued, especially by those in the Spanish March. Even when they did not succeed to office because of royal appointment, the counts of the March recognized kingship as the root of their authority when they travelled to show loyalty, as Wifred-Borrell did in 899. Bishops and abbots repeatedly sought royal diplomas as confirmation of their rights and the extension of rights to new properties. Even scribes made political statements by naming kings in the dating clauses of charters. Simply put, the Carolingian kings were important to people in the Spanish March.

Beyond articulating political positions with the words they wrote, scribes indicated their allegiance to the Carolingian kings in another way. The very script they used to compose their documents was a Carolingian importation. Indeed, the minuscule so prevalent in the Frankish heartland was used to write books of liturgy, learning, and law in the Spanish March. The texts those books contained stand to reveal a good deal of information about the cultural connections that bound the Spanish March to the Carolingians' royally sponsored reform movement. Indeed, the next chapter will explore the realms of books and learning in the March during the late ninth and early tenth centuries, highlighting the under-appreciated degree to which masters and pupils participated in the programme known as the Carolingian renaissance.

---

[189] *HGL* 3, 135; Schröder, *Die Synoden*, 251–4.

Chapter 5

LEARNED CULTURE IN CAROLINGIAN CATALONIA

The Archive of the Crown of Aragon (Archivo de la Corona de Aragón in Spanish, Arxiu de la Corona d'Aragó in Catalan, or ACA) in Barcelona houses many medieval manuscripts. One of them in particular, today with the shelf mark Ripoll 40, provides evidence for the legacy of connections between the Spanish March and the Carolingian monarchy. Produced in the early eleventh century, Ripoll 40 is a copy of an earlier collection of mostly Carolingian royal documents, including the compilation of capitularies made by Ansegisus, abbot of Fontanelle (d. 834), around 827.[1] The Barcelona manuscript was originally kept at the monastery of Santa Maria de Ripoll. Ripoll 40 stands as an example of two different periods of textual linkages between the Spanish March and the Carolingian rulers: the first dating to the period of the exemplar or exemplars of these Carolingian texts from which Ripoll 40 in turn was made, and the second to the early eleventh century, when the dynasty no longer ruled but locals in the March deemed its legacy important enough to maintain.[2] As the purpose of this book has been to explain the relationship between March and monarchy, the notion of legacy embodied in Ripoll 40 is significant, for it gives us a glimpse of how important the period of Carolingian rule over the region was for its history. Ripoll 40 is full of texts, including not just the collection by Ansegisus but also two

---

[1] The manuscript was apparently unknown or inaccessible to Boretius, the editor of Ansegisus's collection for the Monumenta Germaniae Historica, although it became known to the enterprise by 1996. *MGH Leges* 1, 256–325 and *Cap.* 1, 382–450; the 1996 edition, by G. Schmitz, in *MGH Cap.* NS 1 (Hanover, 1996). See García Villada, *Bibliotheca Patrum Latinorum Hispaniensis*, 559–60; G. Schmitz, 'The Capitulary Legislation of Louis the Pious', in P. Godman and R. Collins, *Charlemagne's Heir: New Perspectives on the Reign of Louis the Pious* (Oxford, 1990), 425–36; M. Zimmermann, *Écrire et lire en Catalogne (IX–XII siècle)* (Madrid, 2003), 763–7.

[2] See, for different kinds of texts but the same pattern, R. Kramer, 'Great Expectations: Imperial Ideologies and Ecclesiastical Reforms from Charlemagne to Louis the Pious (813–822)', PhD diss., (Freie Universität Berlin, 2014), 344; A. Remensyder, *Remembering Kings Past: Monastic Foundation Legends in Medieval Southern France* (Ithaca, 2005).

epistolary treatises by Hincmar of Rheims and the legalistic compilation of Benedictus Levita, which would speak to the rights of churches and clergy.[3] The Spanish March must have been truly integrated into the Carolingian empire for the royal documents to have been considered so important locally in the generation after the end of the dynasty.

This chapter takes on the issue of integration by highlighting the Frankish kings' programme of cultural reform, the Carolingian renaissance. As the example of Ripoll 40 shows, manuscript evidence is crucial to examine for traces of influence from north of the Pyrenees. Ansegisus's assembly of capitularies and the other texts were desired in the Spanish March of this later period, but so were other texts, especially during the earlier period of Carolingian rule. The Carolingians' drive to have people in all parts of the empire using authoritative texts in correct ways is well known, and it stands to reason that the rulers as well as the locals would have wanted at least certain key texts in the possession of churches and schools in the Spanish March. In addition to manuscripts from the March showing evidence of participation in the Carolingian reforms, locals made use of a variety of texts in creative ways to suit their own needs, especially in educating students in the liberal arts and solving practical problems related to increasingly well-organized Christian settlement in parts of the region. When taken together, the evidence for texts emanating from Frankish areas as well as from Gothia and Hispania indicates that elements of Carolingian reform and intellectual culture took root in the Spanish March, cementing the notion that, rather than a semi-foreign or backwater area, the March was a full-fledged part of the empire. Centres of learning in the Spanish March were concerned with the same issues and read and copied some of the same texts as their counterparts elsewhere in the empire, for all participated in the Carolingian renaissance.

THE CAROLINGIAN RENAISSANCE

First it should be helpful to define briefly the elements of culture that usually find themselves included under the label 'Carolingian renaissance'.[4] 'Carolingian' learned culture, as this chapter uses the

---

[3] Hincmar's writings in *PL* 125:1035C–1070C and 126:94D–99A. For Benedictus Levita, see now T. Faulkner, *Law and Authority in the Early Middle Ages: the Frankish Leges in the Carolingian Period* (Cambridge, 2016), 155–92. Other capitularies, the *acta* of church councils, and two hymns with neumes also appear in the manuscript.

[4] See J. J. Contreni, 'The Carolingian Renaissance: Education and Literary Culture', in R. McKitterick, ed., *The New Cambridge Medieval History*, vol. 2, c.700–900 (Cambridge, 1995), 709–57; G. Brown, 'Introduction: the Carolingian Renaissance', in R. McKitterick, ed., *Carolingian Culture: Emulation and Innovation* (Cambridge, 1994), 1–51; R. E. Sullivan, 'The Context of Cultural Activity in the Carolingian Age', in *The Gentle Voices of Teachers: Aspects of*

term, was Christian and based on the Latin language. It built on the foundations of a long tradition stretching back through the period of Merovingian rule, including its late Roman, Anglo-Saxon, Irish, and indeed even Visigothic influences.[5] Reform for the Carolingians meant literally to 're-form' their present according to ideals from this past.[6] The key texts for understanding the Carolingian renaissance as a reform movement are the *Admonitio generalis* and the *Epistola de litteris colendis*, both of which are taken to have been produced in the 780s.[7] These documents spelling out the parameters and goals of the effort to renew Christian society emanated from Charlemagne's court, for the king had the primary responsibility as ruler of the faithful. Those goals were for everyone in Frankish society to become more fully Christian: to learn the teachings of the faith and to live by its morals.[8] Kings of course had to rely on others to carry out the reforms, and that task fell to the clergy. That in turn necessitated addressing the organization and function of the church itself, largely through a series of councils. Canon law provided the foundation for reforming the church so that clergy could lead. A third text thus occupied a position of particular significance: the *Dionysio-Hadriana*, a compilation of the pronouncements of earlier church councils made by the monk Dionysius Exiguus in the sixth century and supplemented in the eighth by Pope Hadrian I, who presented a copy to Charlemagne. So fundamental was this collection that the *Admonitio generalis* is largely based on its contents. Taken together, these texts lay out Charlemagne's platform on education: that monasteries and bishoprics establish schools for grammar and other liberal arts in order to produce a better clergy.

Learning in the Carolingian Age (Columbus, 1996), 51–105; H. Liebeschutz, 'Wesen und Grenzen des karolingischen Rationalismus', *Archiv für Kulturgeschichte* 33 (1950): 17–44.

[5] For much more on the developments in culture across Europe, P. Riché, *Education and Culture in the Barbarian West: Sixth through Eighth Centuries*, trans. J. J. Contreni (Columbia, SC, 1976), esp. 177–246, 266–74, 279–85, 290–3, 324–36, 421–46 on Frankish Gaul.

[6] M. A. Claussen, *The Reform of the Frankish Church: Chrodegang of Metz and the Regula canonicorum in the Eighth Century* (Cambridge, 2004), 1–19. J. Barrow, 'Ideas and Applications of Reform', in T. F. X. Noble and J. M. H. Smith, eds, *The Cambridge History of Christianity*, vol. 3: *Early Medieval Christianities c.600–c.1100* (Cambridge, 2008), 345–62.

[7] *Admonitio generalis*, c. 70, spells out the aims: *MGH Fontes iuris germanici antique in usum scholarum* 16, ed. H. Mordek, K. Zechiel-Eckes, and M. Glatthaar (Hanover, 2012), 222–4; the *Epistola de litteris colendis, MGH Cap.* 1, 79, addressed to Abbot Baugulf of Fulda but intended to be copied and circulated throughout the kingdom, directs abbots and bishops to educate the next generations of clergy. Their significance is highlighted in Contreni, 'The Carolingian Renaissance'.

[8] Contreni, 'The Carolingian Renaissance'; Brown, 'Introduction: the Carolingian Renaissance'; McKitterick, *The Frankish Church and the Carolingian Reforms* (London, 1977); J. M. Wallace-Hadrill, *Early Germanic Kingship in England and on the Continent* (Oxford, 1971), 100–8; W. Ullman, *The Carolingian Renaissance and the Idea of Kingship* (London, 1969).

While royal patronage fuelled the 'Carolingian renaissance', its execution was a largely clerical undertaking, geared at reforming clergy and society through a Christian-based education. Almost every known author of the ninth century was a man in holy orders. This does not mean, however, that lay aristocrats were largely illiterate, as popular culture has long held. In fact, much excellent historical scholarship, especially since the 1980s, has put that myth to rest.[9] Sons of kings were educated at monasteries, and rulers for generations sponsored the development of religious culture and church reform.[10] Charlemagne himself is credited with expanding the ambition and scope of the reform and educational movement, breathing new vigour into a slow and gradual development. As is clear from abundant evidence, the court-sponsored reform movement met with some success. Although many monasteries and cathedrals lacked the resources to support schools, no one can deny the literary output of the age. The poetic, historiographic, theological, and moralizing works of the ninth century were built on a foundation of successful schools.[11] Legislation by Charlemagne's successors Louis the Pious and Charles the Bald upheld the aims of their predecessor's *Admonitio generalis*. For example, Louis the Pious mandated that only monks should be educated in monastic schools;[12] presumably other pupils would find cathedral or parish schools, or else be educated in a monastery's 'external school'.[13] Theodulf, the hispanus or Goth bishop of Orléans, encouraged the clergy in his diocese to establish

---

[9] The essays collected in P. Wormald and J. L. Nelson, eds, *Lay Intellectuals in the Carolingian World* (Cambridge, 2007) are now the starting point for study of the phenomenon. See also R. McKitterick, *The Carolingians and the Written Word* (Cambridge, 1989) and R. McKitterick, ed., *The Uses of Literacy in Early Medieval Europe* (Cambridge, 1990).

[10] Einhard famously recorded that Charlemagne saw to the education of his children, and that the king himself was both a student and a proponent of the liberal arts: *Vita Karoli*, cc. 19 and 25. Claussen, *The Reform of the Frankish Church* delves into an earlier Carolingian reform movement. R. E. Sullivan, 'The Carolingian Age: Reflections on Its Place in the History of the Middle Ages', *Speculum* 64 (1989): 267–306; Sullivan, 'The Context of Cultural Activity 51–105.

[11] On poetry, P. Godman, *Poets and Emperors: Frankish Politics and Carolingian Poetry* (Oxford, 1987); for history-writing, R. McKitterick, *History and Memory in the Carolingian World* (Cambridge, 2004); on religious history, see E. Amann, *L'Epoque Carolingienne, Histoire de l'Eglise*, vol. 6. ed. A. Fliche and V. Martin (Paris, 1947), but then A. Angenendt, *Das Frühmittelalter: die abendländische Christenheit von 400 bis 900* (Stuttgart, 1990). Of course for schools, P. Riché, *Ecoles et enseignement dans la Haut Moyen Age, Fin du Ve siècle- Milieu de Xie siècle* (Paris, 1989). See, on more practical and mundane matters, B. Bischoff, 'Libraries and Schools in the Carolingian Revival of Learning', in *Manuscripts and Libraries in the Age of Charlemagne*, trans. M. Gorman (Cambridge, 1994), 93–114.

[12] *Capitulare monasticum*, c. 45 in *MGH Cap.* 1, 346.

[13] See M. M. Hildebrandt, *The External School in Carolingian Society* (Leiden, 1992) for a general picture of how the 'external school' of a monastery may have functioned to teach those not vowed to cenobitic life.

schools not only for future clergy, but for lay children as well.[14] In later generations, major monasteries continued to be the principal centres of learning. Houses such as Fulda, Lorsch, and St-Gall had large libraries in the ninth century, and Fulda in particular had a renowned school.[15] Cathedrals in some locations flourished as well. In Laon, Lyons, and Würzburg, for example, schools and libraries prospered, often thanks to the collegial exchange of books with other houses.[16] These books included scripture, patristics, and even classics. Much the same culture was present in the Spanish March as well.

The liberal arts provided the foundation of learning. These divided into the trivium, or arts of letters, and the quadrivium, or arts dealing with numbers. Without training in grammar and rhetoric, no student could hope to comprehend the Bible, the church fathers, or frankly much else. Poetry was learned because the Bible is partially metrical, especially the Psalms.[17] Rising above the arts of the quadrivium arguably stood computus, famously concerned with fixing the date of Easter. Study ranged from counting on the fingers, to knowing the divisions of time, to describing the celestial bodies and their movements, and to calculating a wide variety of phenomena using various algorithms.[18] Even pagan classical authors produced works that could be of use for learning how to understand God's creation. Once the study of the fundamental liberal arts was complete, Carolingian scholars could consider the deeper issues of the Christian religion. The most authoritative texts for such study were of course the Bible, then the writings of late antique church fathers, especially Augustine of Hippo. For more mundane pursuits, classical texts were mined as needed. Originality of thought was frowned upon, but Carolingian authors found ways to innovate while seeming to rely on their authorities, by means of selecting extracts and organizing their texts to suit their purposes.[19]

---

[14] *Capitula ad presbyteros*, c. 20 in *PL* 105, 196D.

[15] On Lorsch and libraries, see B. Bischoff, *Die Abtei Lorsch in Spiegel ihrer Handschriften*, 2nd edn. (Lorsch, 1989), McKitterick, *The Carolingians and the Written Word*, 165–210, and A. Häse, *Mittelalterliche Bücherverzeichnisse aus Kloster Lorsch. Einleitung, Edition und Kommentar* (Wiesbaden, 2002).

[16] J. J. Contreni, *The Cathedral School of Laon: Its Manuscripts and Masters* (Munich, 1978) is an excellent case study. R. McKitterick, *The Frankish Kingdoms under the Carolingians* (London, 1983), 201–10, provides an overview of this context of learned culture.

[17] C. W. Jones's editorial introduction to Bede, *Opera Didascalica CCSL* 123 A (Turnhout, 1975), xi, lays out this point.

[18] J. J. Contreni, 'Counting, Calendars, and Cosmology: Numeracy in the Early Middle Ages', in J. J. Contreni and S. Casciani, eds, *Word, Image, Number: Communication in the Middle Ages* (Rome, 2002), 43–83.

[19] The articles collected in J. J. Contreni, *Carolingian Learning, Masters and Manuscripts* (Variorum, 1992) form a starting point for exploring this idea.

The key to this enterprise, of course, was the acquisition of appropriate books, which had to be orthodox and authoritative. Those working to reform church and society had to be able to base their thoughts and deeds on the authority and wisdom of their forebears.[20] The copying of old books and the composition of new works, great and small, happened predominantly in monasteries connected to royal or aristocratic families.[21] When the Carolingian dynasty ruled as kings, their 'renaissance' was not only court-sponsored, but largely monastery-based. Of course, not every library possessed all of the sources necessary, nor did every source include material that may be useful to a writer's purpose. When their source material was lacking, reformers had to cobble together material in order to create the past that they needed. Even earlier in the eighth century, Bishop Chrodegang of Metz embodied what this movement was to become, in that he was concerned not only with reforming the habits of the clergy, but of the whole society, reaching back to the models of the past and modifying them for present purposes when necessary.[22] The treatises and commentaries written in the later eighth and ninth centuries show a propensity to do the same. Indeed, examples of this method appear in surviving manuscripts from the Spanish March. By the middle of the eighth century the main centres of learning in the Carolingian world, especially as measured by book production, were located north of the Loire and in Germany. A long-standing view holds that two generations of nearly constant warfare in Aquitaine, Provence, and Burgundy almost guaranteed the decline of literary activity in these regions.[23] Septimania and Catalonia were not immune to the destruction, as noted earlier in Chapter 1.

Invasions, civil wars, and the break-up of empire into constituent *regna* governed by different members of the Carolingian family during the second half of the ninth century would all suggest the continuation of a

---

[20] D. Bullough, 'Roman Books and Carolingian *Renovatio*', in *Carolingian Renewal: Sources and Heritage* (Manchester, 1991), 1–37; F. Brunhölzl, 'Die Bildungsauftrag der Hofschule', in B. Bischoff, ed., *Karl der Grosse: Lebenswerk und Nachleben 2: Das geistige Leben* (Dusseldorf, 1965), 28–41; M. Innes and R. McKitterick, 'The Writing of History', in *Carolingian Culture*, 193–220; M. Garrison, 'The Franks as the New Israel? Education for an Identity from Pippin to Charlemagne', in Y. Hen and M. Innes, ed., *The Uses of the Past in the Early Middle Ages* (Cambridge, 2000), 114–61.

[21] For example, B. Bischoff, 'Benedictine Monasteries and the Survival of Classical Literature', in *Manuscripts and Libraries in the Age of Charlemagne*, trans. Michael Gorman (Cambridge, 1994), 134–60.

[22] Claussen, *Reform of the Frankish Church*, 5.

[23] L. Auzias, *L'Aquitaine carolingienne* (Toulouse, 1937), 72–6, while not mentioning schools directly, strongly implies a steep decline in religious and cultural activity, as well as sociopolitical and economic, in the wake of devastation. See also, for example, Abadal, 'L'Entrada des sarraïns a la peninsula i l'enfonsada del regne de Toledo. La reacció dels francs i llur occupació de Septimània', in Abadal, CC 1, 1–37.

poor environment for schools and learning in Gothia and the Spanish March. Despite the uncertain conditions surrounding the monarchy in the face of first the civil war amongst the sons of Louis the Pious and later the dynastic crisis of the late ninth century, and then the occasional loss of the throne from 888 through the tenth century, however, teachers taught and pupils learned throughout the Frankish kingdoms. During the time of heated rivalry between the sons and grandsons of Louis the Pious from roughly 840 to 876, learned culture in fact continued to thrive. Literature, teaching and moralizing, hagiography, exegesis, and expositions of doctrine, often linked to disputes, all continued to be the subjects of new works based on the study of scripture or other authoritative texts. After that period, whereas the patronage of the kings was at some degree of remove, the regional nobles tended to stand as the immediate benefactors of monasteries, which were still the main centres of literate culture. This was precisely the case in the Spanish March, where Wifred the Hairy and his descendants controlled and founded major religious houses. As for the nature of the culture these establishments fostered, evidence from the early-to-middle decades of the ninth-century activity is quite sparse, all but forcing the conclusion that the impetus for cultural production, primarily the copying of texts, had to have been the region's integration into the Carolingian empire and reform movement.

Emphasizing Carolingian cultural influence is not to deny the legacy the Visigothic kingdom left to the Spanish March. The work of Isidore of Seville, especially, laid the groundwork for a good deal of intellectual activity in the Spanish March during the late ninth and tenth centuries, for which evidence is more abundant than it is for earlier periods.[24] Isidorian texts were widely disseminated throughout the Carolingian realms, and so formed a basis for European cultural more generally defined.[25] Textual studies have revealed the subtly hidden traces of Visigothic liturgy in the official practices promoted by the Carolingian reforms.[26] The influence of Iberian learned culture on Europe north of the Pyrenees was also embodied in the contributions of individuals who emigrated from Spain into the Frankish kingdoms, such as Theodulf of Orléans, Agobard of Lyons, Claudius of Turin, and Prudentius of Troyes.

---

[24] Zimmermann, *Écrire et lire*, 632–48; Zimmermann, 'Conscience gothique et affirmation nationale dans la genèse de la Catalogne (IXe–XIe-siècles)', in J. Fontaine and C. Pellistrandi, eds, *L'Europe héritière de l'Espagne wisigothique* (Madrid, 1992), 55–6.

[25] J. Fontaine, 'La figure d'Isidore de Séville à l'époque carolingienne', in J. Fontaine and C. Pellistrandi, eds, *L'Europe héritière de l'Espagne wisigothique* (Madrid, 1992), 195–212. See also his 'Mozarabie hispanique et monde carolingien: les échanges culturels entre la France et l'Espagne du VIIe au Xe siècle', *Anuario de Estudios Medievales* 13 (1983): 17–46.

[26] R. E. Reynolds, 'The Visigothic Liturgy in the Realm of Charlemagne', in *Das frankfurter Konzil*, vol. 2, 919–945, at 925–6 for baptism, and 927 for marriage.

Ever since the time of Charlemagne, notable hispani had left Spain for the royal court and episcopal offices in Francia, so the intelligentsia who could have illuminated the Spanish March were not there to do so, supposing their families had been based there and not elsewhere in Spain.[27] As has been pointed out, the Ebro served as more of a frontier than the Pyrenees, so these immigrants were almost naturally drawn northward.[28] They embody the reciprocal impact that the conquest of the March had on the culture of the empire, but this study will maintain its focus on developments within the March itself. Nevertheless, by virtue of having been connected to the cultural currents of the Visigothic kingdom, the Spanish March could both build on what might be termed its cultural patrimony and bolster it by participating in the Carolingian movement.

A long-standing interpretation of the Latin culture of the Spanish March has maintained that from the time the Adoptionist controversy settled down early in the ninth century, the Spanish March lay dormant from the standpoint of cultural creativity.[29] Even when studies admit that the educational and intellectual infrastructure in the Spanish March could not have been truly annihilated by decades of warfare – after all, Felix of Urgell was possible in the eighth century, as were those lay persons who signed their own names to documents during the ninth – they fall back on the region's inheritance of literate forms of culture from the Visigothic period as explanation.[30] Indeed, twentieth-century Catalan historiography is riddled with the notion of a strong Visigothic identity opposing Frankish intrusion, culturally as well as politically.[31] In a relatively recent, sweepingly magisterial study of the literate culture of Catalonia from the ninth through twelfth centuries, Michel Zimmermann has even called

---

[27] P. Riché, 'Les réfugiés wisigoths dans le monde carolingien', in J. Fontaine and C. Pellistrandi, eds, *L'Europe héritière de l'Espagne wisigothique* (Madrid, 1992), 177–83. For Theodulf in particular, A. Freeman, 'Theodulf of Orléans: a Visigoth at Charlemagne's Court', ibid., 185–94. On Claudius, J. Vezin, 'Le commentaire sur la Genèse de Claude de Turin, un cas singulier de transmission des textes wisigothiques dans la Gaule carolingienne', ibid., 223–30. Also J. Vezin, 'Manuscrits presentant des traces de l'activité en Gaule de Theodulfe d'Orléans, Claude de Turin, Agobard de Lyon et Prudence de Troyes', in *Coloquio sobre Circulación de codices y escritos entre Europa y la Peninsula en los siglos VIII–XIII* (Compostela, 1988), 57–71.

[28] R. Guerreiro, 'La rayonnement de l'hagiographie hispanique en Gaule pendant le haut Moyen Âge: circulation et diffusion des *Passions* hispaniques', J. Fontaine and C. Pellistrandi, eds, *L'Europe héritière de l'Espagne wisigothique* (Madrid, 1992), 137–57.

[29] Abadal, *La batalla del Adopcionismo en la desintegración de la Iglesia visigoda* (Barcelona, 1949); J. Alturo, 'Manuscrits i documents llatins d'origen català del segle IX', in *Symposium internacional*, 273–80 at 280.

[30] J. Alturo and A. H. Ballina, 'El sistema educativo en la Cataluña altomedieval'. *Memoria ecclesiae* 12 (1998): 31–61.

[31] See, for readily apparent examples in the most fundamental scholarship, Salrach, *El procés*, vol. 1, 71 and 2, 74–5.

the region 'a conservatory of Visigothic culture' that claimed a Gothic heritage as a way of preserving a regional identity within the Frankish kingdom, in spite of the Carolingian drive towards uniformity.[32] Thus there appears to be a consensus of received wisdom that the Visigothic heritage was more important for the literate culture of the Spanish March than any Carolingian influence in the region. More recent scholarship stresses that Charlemagne and his successors, however, strove more to set general standards than to enforce uniformity.[33] It is clear that for the Spanish March, as for any region, existing cultural and intellectual traditions and institutions would be of fundamental importance for developments during the period of Carolingian rule. Yet it also stands to reason that, if Carolingian rule had any discernible impact on the literate culture of the Spanish March, traces could be found in surviving manuscripts. Unfortunately, the sack of Barcelona during a Muslim raiding campaign in 985 appears to have destroyed almost all evidence for cultural activity in the city before that date.[34] Only the evidence from other centres can provide any knowledge of what learned culture was like in the Carolingian Spanish March.

Throughout the ninth century, centres for education and culture survived and even grew.[35] Documentary evidence shows that several houses were founded, often at comital initiative in the later ninth century, while many others received royal immunities and protection as early as the late eighth. Throughout the eighth and ninth centuries, smaller houses may have lost their independence, but continued to function as subordinates of larger, more powerful foundations.[36] During and after the conquest of the Spanish March, the Carolingians worked to establish their religious institutions in Catalonia, including the Rule of Benedict and opposition to Spanish Adoptionism. Those sent to reform the March brought important texts, including monastic regulations, such as the *De*

---

[32] M. Zimmermann, *Écrire et lire*, 620–74, with an explicit statement of these views in English at 1352. See also his earlier work, 'Conscience gothique et affirmation nationale dans la genèse de la Catalogne (IXe–XIe-siècles)', cited earlier in note 24.

[33] J. R. Davis, *Charlemagne's Practice of Empire* (Cambridge, 2015), esp. Part II and Y. Hen, *The Royal Patronage of Liturgy in Frankish Gaul to the Death of Charles the Bald (877)* (London, 2001).

[34] That does not make investigation impossible. See J. Alturo, 'Un Seduli amb glosses de Remi d'Auxerre copiat a començos de segle X (a Barcelona?)', *Analecta Sacra Tarraconensia* 695 (1996): 5–28. More generally, G. Feliu i Montfort, *La presa de Barcelona per Almansor: història i mitificació; discurs de recepció* (Barcelona, 2007) and M. Zimmermann, 'La prise de Barcelone par Al-Mansûr et la naissance de l'historiographie catalane', *Annales de Bretagne et des pays de l'Ouest* 87 (1980): 191–218.

[35] Abadal, *Dels visigots als catalans*, ed. J. Sobrequés i Callicó, 2nd ed., 2 vols (Barcelona, 1974), vol. 1 363–494.

[36] As was the case with Sant Pere d'Albanyà, a small monastery that became dependent on Santa Maria d'Arles in Vallespir. See CC 2, 6–8 and 30–32. Sant Julià del Mont, which ended up dependent on Banyoles: CC 2, 219–221 and 258–261. See also Salrach, *El procés*, vol. 1, 58–61.

institutione canonicorum, De institutione sanctimonialium, and *Capitulare monasticum.*[37] Some of the monasteries, at least, built schools, and the manuscripts that survive from them provide the best evidence of the intellectual culture of the region. Before the end of the ninth century, Wifred, count of Barcelona, and his wife Winidilda bolstered Catalonian monasticism with their patronage of the monastery of Santa Maria de Ripoll, which became a major centre of learning.[38] Even into the tenth century, even as Carolingian royal power found it more difficult to manage the affairs of the Spanish March directly, a sort of cultural allegiance remained.[39] While not denying the importance of regional traditions, it is the purpose of this chapter to highlight the Carolingian impact on the learned culture of the Spanish March and even to feature some locally produced texts which show that the concerns of locals fit in quite well with the Carolingian educational programme and even applied texts to local situations.

Pathways of Carolingian influence on the regional literate culture are easy to see. First, we have only to point to a handful of examples of individuals who travelled between Francia and the Spanish March to cement the idea that people and their ideas could flow over the Pyrenees. The adoption of a school grammar text written by the 'northern' monk Usuard for use at the most important monastery in the March shows clear ties to a house with royal connections. The earliest texts in circulation in the March, furthermore, and indeed the very script used to copy them, indicate a familiarity with patristic learning and other typically 'Carolingian' practices. By the late ninth century and early tenth, the Spanish March had functioning schools and libraries which housed texts directly connected to the Carolingian reforms, including the *Dionysio-Hadriana.* Especially at the monastery of Santa Maria de Ripoll, manuscripts survive that feature authors such as Bede and Alcuin, whose importance to Carolingian initiatives is unassailable. Finally, local production is important to highlight, and the Ripoll library provides crucial evidence for how locals used the intellectual resources at their disposal.

---

[37] Salrach, *El procés,* vol. 1, 70–1. For the texts, see *MGH Conc.* 2, 312–421; 422–56 and *MGH Cap.* 1, 343–9.

[38] Ripoll's significance has been acknowledged, even by those who do not study Catalonia primarily. See R. W. Southern, *The Making of the Middle Ages* (New Haven, 1953), 119–121, but also Abadal, *Dels visigots als catalans,* vol. 1, 485–94. The books of Santa Maria's library are featured in this chapter.

[39] The notion has long been recognized in classic Catalan scholarship, such as Abadal, *Els primers comtes catalans* (Barcelona, 1958), 271–326 and Abadal, *Dels visigots als catalans,* vol. 1 139–72. A. Kosto, *Making Agreements in Medieval Catalonia: Power, Order, and the Written Word, 1000–1200* (Cambridge, 2001), 4–9 admits as much as he establishes post-Carolingian Catalonia as a viable subject of study.

Two texts can serve as examples, first and in greater detail below that of Gisemundus, who names himself in his work. A second, found under the heading *Contra Iudaeos*, highlights the currents common in religious thought in both the Frankish core areas and the Spanish March. Admittedly, the survival of evidence means that we really have only glimpses at the late ninth and early tenth centuries, but nonetheless such evidence reveals that Carolingian cultural and intellectual reforms had taken root in the Spanish March by the rise of the generation after Wifred the Hairy. In other words, the March evinces cultural integration into the Carolingian empire by the very time that the royal dynasty's political grasp on the region is supposed to have slipped.

TIES ACROSS THE PYRENEES

The history of the production of the well-known martyrology by the monk Usuard of St-Germain-des-Prés in Paris can serve as a gateway to the study of intellectual culture in the Spanish March.[40] Usuard's work, fundamental to the martyrology tradition of the church down to modern times, was one of the first in the Frankish tradition to include information about martyrs from Ireland, including Columban, and from Spain.[41] Especially significant for the course of cultural interchange between Francia and the Spanish March was the trip Usuard made in 857 with his *frater* Odilard to collect relics and stories related to the martyrs of Córdoba. Charles the Bald was deeply involved in Usuard and Odilard's mission from the beginning. In fact, the king ordered it. We know from the account of Aimoin, master of the school of St-Germain and chronicler of the translation of relics from Córdoba, that the monks journeyed between Paris and Córdoba via Burgundy, visiting the villa of the noble Humfrid, whom Charles had recently invested with lands in both Burgundy and the Spanish March.[42] The pair also negotiated a treaty with the Muslim leader of Zaragoza, and carried letters from Humfrid to important figures in Hispania and took the responses back with them on

---

[40] Usuard's work is edited in J. Dubois, ed., *Le martyrologe d'Usuard: Texte et commentaire* (Brussels, 1965). See also Guerreiro, 'La rayonnement de l'hagiographie hispanique en Gaule pendant le haut Moyen Âge.'

[41] See J. L. Nelson, 'The Franks, the Martyrology of Usuard, and the Martyrs of Cordoba', *Studies in Church History* 30 (1993): 67–80 at 69. More generally, J. M. McCullogh, 'Historical Martyrologies in the Benedictine Cultural Tradition', in W. Lourdaux and D. Verhelst, eds, *Benedictine Culture 750–1050* (Leuven, 1983), 114–31; F. Lifshitz, *The Name of the Saint: the Martyrology of Jerome and Access to the Sacred in Francia, 627–827* (Notre Dame, IN, 2006), esp. 129.

[42] Aimoin, *De Translatione ss. martyrum Georgii monachi, Aurelii et Nathaliae*, in PL, 115, ed. J.-P. Migne (1852). Nelson, 'Usuard', 74. See also A. Christys, 'St-Germain-des-Près, St Vincent, and the Martyrs of Cordoba', *EME* 7 (1998): 199–216, on potential problems inherent in Aimoin's text.

the return trip home.[43] Both on the way to Córdoba and on the way back home, the monks passed through and stayed in the Spanish March. It is important to note that the monks were travelling south to bring knowledge of the south and its saints to the north. In a very real sense, this exchange is emblematic of reciprocity in the relationship between people in Francia and their counterparts in Catalonia.

Thus it is clear that Usuard's journey was not intended solely to retrieve relics for transport back to St-Germain. Yet that goal was the central issue; without it, the king could have found other ambassadors to send instead of Usuard and Odilard. Devotion to martyr cults was an age-old tradition for the Franks, through which they both showed and received God's favour. The tradition can be seen as far back as the sixth century, when Gregory of Tours compiled stories of past martyrs, and the genre of *passiones* was strong into the seventh century.[44] From 838–55, Florus of Lyon, Hrabanus Maurus in Mainz, Wandalbert at Prüm, and Ado of Lyon all compiled calendars of festivals. The location of all these centres in Lothar's kingdom cannot be explained by mere coincidence; the Middle Kingdom embraced the Frankish heartland, the centre of Frankish identity. As the geographical core of the New Israel, Lothar's realm fostered a sense of centrality in the Christian world, of which the martyr-saints were living members.[45] Charles the Bald, not wanting to be outdone by his elder brother, then commissioned Usuard's martyrology. Apart from their devotional value, martyrologies also had a political dimension; whoever controlled relics and cults held spiritual and cultural authority.[46] Such elements of power were not as intangible for Charles as may appear to modern eyes, and he needed them. Because of the mid-century geopolitical situation of the Spanish March, acquiring relics and information on martyrs from Spain took on added significance.

During that period of Charles's reign in the West Frankish kingdom, the Spanish March took on a strategic importance it had not held for a generation. By 850, it had become clear to Charles that, since his kingdom could not expand at the expense of Lothar to the east, the Spanish

---

[43] A. Stieldorf, *Marken und Markgrafen: Studien zur Grenzsicherung durch die fränkisch-deutschen Herrscher* (Hanover, 2012), 221–30: *Marchiones* in the ninth century made diplomatic treaties on their own initiative. See the evidentiary basis for this in the admittedly later text, Hincmar of Rheims, *De ordine palatii*, MGH Fontes iuris Germanici antique 3 (Hanover, 1980), c. 30.

[44] Nelson, 'Usuard', 67; H. Reimitz, 'Social Networks and Identities in Frankish Historiography: New Aspects of the Textual History of Gregory of Tours' *Historiae*', in R. Corradini and M. Diesenberger and H. Reimitz, eds, *The Construction of Communities in the Early Middle Ages* (Leiden, 2003), 229–68; W. Goffart, *The Narrators of Barbarian History* (Princeton, 1988), 112–234 for Gregory, 127–53 for the *Miracula* in particular.

[45] Nelson, 'Usuard', 68; J. M. McCullough, 'Historical Martyrologies', 114–31.

[46] Nelson, 'Usuard', 67–9.

March offered opportunities to gain both physical and spiritual manifestations of power. The mid-century martyrdom movement in Córdoba presented Charles with a chance to express his devotion to Christian martyr-saints, and perhaps to forge a stronger sense of solidarity with his subjects in the southern reaches of his kingdom.[47] An enhanced royal presence in the March stood to help Charles in his internecine struggles while simultaneously providing him with a theatre for external action.[48]

Besides Usuard's journey, evidence points to other travels and points of contact between people from both sides of the Pyrenees. There is the case of the apostate deacon Bodo, who during the reign of Louis the Pious converted to Judaism and took the name Eleazar, moved to Spain, and began to preach against Christianity there.[49] Throughout the ninth century, bishops, monks, and counts, notably Bernard of Septimania, obviously moved from Gaul into Septimania and the Spanish March. Meanwhile, from almost the beginning of Carolingian involvement in Spain, individuals and groups are known to have migrated to points north of the Pyrenees, as attested in the examples of *hispani* who went to Aachen to argue for their *aprisio* property rights and other notable *hispani* intellectuals who took up positions at court or in episcopal offices throughout the kingdom in the ninth century.[50]

Eulogius of Córdoba, another of the people Usuard met in his travels, proved to be a valuable source of information about the Córdoban martyrs of the 850s, to Usuard and modern scholars alike. At the earliest we know of him, Eulogius (d. 859) had embarked on an ecclesiastical career as priest in Córdoba; he later won election as bishop of Toledo but found martyrdom before he could take office. His writings, the *Memoriale sanctorum* and the *Apologetica martyrum*, written during the 850s, defend and glorify the martyr movement.[51] Usuard set himself to writing his martyrology just after returning from Spain, before news arrived of

---

[47] On the martyr movement, see J. A. Coope, *The Martyrs of Córdoba: Community and Family Conflict in an Age of Mass Conversion* (Lincoln, NE, 1995) and K. B. Wolf, *Christian Martyrs in Muslim Spain* (Cambridge, 1988). For my purposes here, Nelson, 'Usuard', 75–8. See also the discussion in Chapter 3.

[48] For another perspective on this aspect of Charles the Bald's reign, see G. Koziol, *The Politics of Memory and Identity in Carolingian Royal Diplomas: the West Frankish Kingdom (840–987)* (Turnhout, 2012), 69–74 and Chapter 3 in this volume.

[49] *AB*, 41–2, 65. Also see F. Riess, 'From Aachen to al-Andalus: the Journey of Deacon Bodo (823–76)', *EME* 13 (2005): 131–57.

[50] See A. Barbero, 'La integración social de los "hispani" del Pirineo oriental al reino carolingio', in P. Gallais and Yves-Jean Riou, eds, *Mélanges offerts à René Crozet* (Poitiers, 1966), 67–75; Riché, 'Les réfugiés wisigoths dans le monde carolingien', 179–81 on Theodulf, Leidrad, Claudius, Smaragdus, and Prudentius.

[51] The works of Eulogius are in J. Gil, ed., *Corpus Scriptorum Muzarabicorum*, 2 vols (Madrid, 1973), vol. 2, 363–503.

Eulogius' own holy death, and revised it throughout the 860s.[52] Around 848 Eulogius started a journey from Córdoba with the goal of reaching Francia to check on his *fratres* who had some time earlier set off for Mainz. The political difficulties in and near the Carolingian Spanish March at the time, however, forced him to turn back before he crossed the Pyrenees. Roger Wright has suggested that if Eulogius or, perhaps more accurately, his *fratres*, had arrived at Strasbourg at the time of the oaths sworn amongst Charles the Bald, Louis the German, and their followers in 842, they would have been able to understand the Romance version of the oaths.[53] These interesting findings are important, for they hint that, regardless of the success or failure of Eulogius' journey, ninth-century travellers between Hispania and Francia, including Usuard and Odilard and Eulogius's *fratres*, undertook their expeditions with little risk of linguistic confusion, even in terms of everyday speech. Communication between the Frankish royal court and northern monasteries on the one hand, and the magnates and monks of the March on the other, may well have been easier than that between western and eastern Franks.[54]

All these examples point to the ample opportunity for cultural influence to cross the Pyrenees. Just as the learned culture of Francia accepted the contributions of individuals like Theodulf of Orléans and others from Spain, as well as the texts of figures like Isidore of Seville, the Frankish realms were able to return the favour by bringing the Spanish March under the umbrella of the Carolingian reforms. The decentralized nature of those reforms makes it difficult to trace the nature of Carolingian influence on the texts copied and used in the Spanish March, but gradual changes in script and other practices, as well as the presence of key reform texts make it clear that the Carolingian renaissance did reach the March and that its impact should not be discounted.

SCRIPTS AND TEXTS

The copying and dissemination of correct and authoritative texts was the keystone of the Carolingian reforms and intellectual activity, and the surviving manuscripts thus provide crucial evidence for related developments in the Spanish March. Overall, the state of survival for the evidence

---

[52] Nelson, 'Usuard', 78.

[53] R. Wright, 'Early Medieval Pan-Romance Comprehension', in J. J. Contreni and S. Casciani, eds, *Word, Image, Number: Communication in the Middle Ages* (Rome, 2002), 25–42.

[54] See, for example, Lupus, Ep. 70 in *Servati Lupi Epistolae*, ed. P. K. Marshall (Leipzig, 1984), 73–4; J. J. Contreni, 'The Carolingian Renaissance', 731. M. Banniard, 'Language and Communication in Carolingian Europe', in R. McKitterick, ed., *The New Cambridge Medieval History*, vol. 2, c.700–c.900 (Cambridge, 1995), 695–706; M. Banniard, *Viva Voce: communication orale et communication écrite en occident latin (IVe–IXe siècle)* (Paris, 1992).

is not as strong as could be hoped, rendering it quite difficult to draw conclusions about the use of various texts in ecclesiastical centres in different places in the March and at different specific times. One particular artefact stands as stunning testimony to the production and collection of sometimes grand codices. It is a beautiful, artistic silver book cover from the Carolingian period that today contains no actual parchment folios.[55] The ornate cover could be the only remaining portion of an evangelary, an early example of the *textum argentum* type that proliferated especially in the tenth century. Although this surviving element of ninth-century learned culture offers nothing to study of literary activity in the Spanish March, it does provide valuable evidence of the production or acquisition of high-quality books in the area during the Carolingian period. Even though there were few literary creations, books were valued. This becomes even clearer in written records of books owned and given away by ecclesiastical centres and individuals. In 807 the priest Spanellus, founder of the monastery of Gerri, endowed it with books.[56] Bishop Sisebut of Urgell compiled a basic description of ten books in his cathedral's holdings in 839.[57] The important monastery of Eixalada-Cuixà, north of the Pyrenees, listed twelve books in its catalogue of 854, and in 878 at the death of its second founder, Protasius, there were thirty.[58] Riculf, bishop of Elna, left his collection of books to his church upon his death in 915.[59] The jewel in the crown of scholarly activity in Carolingian Catalonia was the monastery of Santa Maria de Ripoll, founded at about the time of the second Cuixà catalogue.[60] By the close of the period of Carolingian influence in the area during the 980s, Ripoll had sixty-five books in its possession. By the time of the compilation of its catalogue in 1047, after the death of its great Abbot Oliba, it had 245.[61] In the early days, the Ripoll library was not extravagant compared

---

[55] MS Barcelona, Biblioteca de Catalunya (BC) 3724. I thank Ana Gudayol of the Biblioteca de Catalunya for first drawing my attention to this item and its characteristics. See an image in A. M. Mundó, 'La cultura escrita dels segles IX al XII a Catalunya', in *Obres completes* (Barcelona, 1998), 547.

[56] CC 3, no. 1. See also A. M. Mundó, 'La cultura i els llibres [a Catalunya, ss. VIII a XII]', in *Obres Completes*, Vol. 1 (Barcelona: Edicions 62, 1998), 465.

[57] Mundó, 'La cultura i els llibres', 465.

[58] Abadal, *Dels visigots als catalans*, 377–484 is a study of the birth and growth of Eixalada-Cuixà, founded as Eixalada and then reformed as Cuixà after a disastrous flood in 878, through a thorough study of its charters; see for the books Mundó, 'La cultura i els llibres', 466.

[59] CC 6, no. 189; A. M. Udina i Abelló, *La successió testada a la Catalunya altomedieval* (Barcelona, 1984), ap. 5 with references.

[60] See above, Chapter 4 (pp. 158–59), on the early history of the monastery and its sister house, Sant Joan.

[61] These lists are synthesized in Mundó, 'La cultura i els llibres', 465–66; the Ripoll catalog of 1047 is studied in Zimmermann, *Écrire et lire*, 559–78, where he does not treat the manuscripts discussed in this chapter except when he attributes mss 74 and 106 to the eleventh century (!).

to other famous monastic libraries, such as St-Gall, which held approximately 264 books in the ninth century,[62] or Corbie, which housed about 250 including fragments;[63] the great monastery of Lorsch possessed over 450.[64] Throughout medieval Europe, a single manuscript codex could contain any number of discrete texts, so the monastic library at Ripoll was indeed extensive.[65] In the decades around 900, Ripoll stood at the forefront of the Spanish March.

Bishops and cathedral schools, especially in Girona and later in Vic, too supported education and culture. Girona, along with Felix's Urgell, was a functioning bishopric that Charlemagne incorporated into the Frankish kingdom's ecclesiastical structure, subjecting trans-Pyrenean churches to the authority of the archbishop of Narbonne. The Girona cathedral scriptorium produced a copy of Augustine's *Liber de dono perseuerentiae* in the 870s.[66] The old episcopal see of the Visigothic era, Ausona, was reconstituted by Wifred at the city of Vic and became an important centre as the tenth century dawned.[67] A few generations later, the thriving culture of churches in this region, linked to developments in both Francia and al-Andalus, must have been something noteworthy to draw the monk Gerbert away from his cloister in Aurillac to study the mathematical and scientific arts in 'Hispania citerior'.[68]

It is in the production of books that perhaps the most telling sign of Catalonia's cultural incorporation into the Frankish cultural orbit is revealed: the gradual replacement of Visigothic script by the Carolingian standard minuscule. From what evidence that remains, it appears that early ninth-century manuscripts from the area were written largely in traditional Visigothic script, but some Carolingian influences were creeping into scribal practice. Script changed in stages during the successive generations, becoming a mixed Visigothic-Carolingian script by the end of the first third of the ninth century. There are many examples of mixed script in codices and documents. But before the end of the century, Carolingian minuscule was written as a matter of course in the Barcelona comital scriptorium and at major cathedral and monastic

---

[62] McKitterick, *The Carolingians and the Written Word*, 169–96.

[63] D. Ganz, *Corbie and the Carolingian Renaissance* (Sigmaringen, 1990), 124–58.

[64] B. Bischoff, *Lorsch im Spiegel seiner Handschriften* (Munich, 1974), 15.

[65] Southern, *The Making of the Middle Ages*, 121 notes Ripoll as a large library in its heyday.

[66] J. Alturo, 'Un manuscrito del *Liber de dono perseuerantiae* de san Agustín copiado en Gerona an torno al decenio 870–880', *Revue des Études Augustiniennes* 43 (1997): 105–10. The manuscript in question is ACA Frag. Ms. 157.

[67] P. H. Freedman, *The Diocese of Vic: Tradition and Regeneration in Medieval Catalonia* (New Brunswick, 1983); Abadal, 'La reconquesta d'una regió interior de Catalunya: la Plana de Vic (717-886)', in *Dels visigots als catalans*, vol. 1, 309–22.

[68] Richer of Saint-Rémi, *Histories*, ed. and trans. J. Lake (Cambridge, MA, 2011), vol. 2, 62–3.

centres.[69] By the 880s the standard, with few exceptions, was a Carolingian library script with only a few Visigothic survivals, which had died out by the end of the decade.[70]

The progressive dominance of Carolingian script practically leaps off the parchment in existing manuscripts. Viewed as a series, the ninth-century fragments and tenth-century codices reveal these developments. A modern composite of four fragments, now in the Biblioteca de Catalunya, serves as an excellent example.[71] Early samples are unmistakable in their Visigothic features, including open 'a', an eye on 't', a straight descender on 'g', and distinctive ligatures of 'e' with 't', 'c', and 'x'. A commentary on Matthew in this collection shows these traits, and also some instances of 'e' leaning right.[72] The most recent surviving folios in the series have lost most of these distinctive elements, such as the 't' form and 'g' descender, and employ both open and closed forms of 'a'. The chronological change is clearly visible when all of the folios are viewed together. The ascender on 'd' changes as well, from a pronounced slant, to alternating slanted and vertical forms, to a decidedly vertical line. Other ninth-century fragments show the same development, from the early Visigothic-script fragments, to the closed 'a' and eyeless 't' of an Augustinian fragment copied in the 870s.[73] An Isidorian fragment exhibits several palaeographical features that other early manuscripts in Visigothic script do not share, including a rare abbreviation for '-orum' and a vowel-t ligature where a small 't' is written over the last minim of the vowel.[74] The bar through the descender of the 'p' in 'per' abbreviations begins with a short downward mark before crossing the descender, causing the loop of the 'p' to look as if it rests atop a '4'. These features suggest a mid-ninth-century date for the manuscript. A later law book, dated to around 880, exhibits a mixture of Visigothic and Carolingian scripts.[75] A liturgical text of just before 890, with mixed script indicative of rural production, is contained in the oldest codex with musical notation in Catalonia.[76] Another Isidore manuscript, of the very late ninth

[69] Mundó, 'La cultura i els llibres', 463–4
[70] Alturo, 'Manuscrits', 275. See also A. Millares Carlo, *Tratado de paleografía española*, 3 vols, 3rd ed. (Madrid, 1983). More recently, see for example A. Castro Correa, 'Visigothic vs. Carolingian script. Context (I)', *Littera Visigothica* (March 2014), http://litteravisigothica.com/visigothic-vs-carolingian-script-context1 (ISSN 2386-6330).
[71] This is BC 2451; the fragments are numbered 1–5, omitting the number 3.   [72] BC 2451, 4.
[73] These manuscript fragments are Barcelona, ACA fragments nos. 22, 33, 154, 157, 395, and 396.
[74] Barcelona, ACB Codex 131.   [75] Alturo, 'Manuscrits', 277; Vic, col. particular.
[76] Alturo, 'Manuscrits', 277; MS Tarragona, Arx. Hist. Arxdioc., frag. 22, 1. Musical notation, in the form of 'Catalano-Narbonese neumes' can be found in Barcelona, BC parchment, 9135 2-VIII-2, an original of a charter of consecration of a church in Osona, dated 888 and published in CC 4, no. 9. See S. Zapke, 'Notation Systems in the Iberian Peninsula: From Spanish Notations to Aquitanian Notation (9th–12th Centuries)', in S. Zapke, ed., *Hispania Vetus: Musical-Liturgical*

century, displays Carolingian script but with Visigothic traits, including uncial 'G'.[77] The script of many codices from Santa Maria de Ripoll is virtually identical with that of manuscripts from Frankish centres. Ripoll's earliest codices feature the script that had become prominent in the Spanish March by the time they were produced.

Jesús Alturo compiled a solid survey of ninth-century manuscripts that serves as a starting point for investigating the contents of books produced in the Spanish March during the ninth century.[78] According to his findings, the only manuscript of certain ninth-century Catalonian origin is a *Liber iudicum*, the surviving version of Visigothic law current in the Spanish March; the manuscript contains a reference to events in Girona in 827 as well as corrections by two distinct but contemporary hands.[79] Very probably from Catalonia, but now housed in collections in other countries, are copies of Isidore's *Differentiae*, a *Liber commicus* and a *Liber iudicum*, all Visigothic-era texts.[80] Of course, most regionally used, Carolingian-era manuscripts can be found today in modern Catalan depositories. These include another *Liber iudicum*, which exhibits a mixture of Visigothic and Carolingian scripts, datable to around 880.[81] From 890, a manuscript containing Isidore's *Sententiae* and *Commentarium in Genesim* displays Carolingian script but with Visigothic traits.[82] The surviving manuscripts show both a preoccupation with late antique and Isidorian texts and the gradual assimilation of Carolingian scribal methods.

Monasteries and cathedrals, the cultural centres of the March, naturally collected religious and moral texts. A few manuscript fragments of this nature survive from the ninth century. One manuscript fragment, now in a very bad state of conservation, once formed part of an orational of Hispanic origin written in Visigothic script.[83] As it stands today, it contains the Completuria, the Benediction of the Vespers of the feast of St Vincent, and the incipits of the first antiphon and of the first prayer of the Matins of the same feast. Perhaps a product of the Barcelona cathedral, the fragment seems to have served as the cover of another manuscript.[84]

Manuscripts from Visigothic Origins to the Franco-Roman Transition (9th–12th Centuries) (Bilbao, 2007), 189–243 at 215.

[77] Montserrat, Bibl. Monest. 1104-I. See also Alturo, 'Manuscrits', 277.

[78] For a more complete discussion of what follows in this paragraph, see Alturo, 'Manuscrits', 275–8.

[79] The manuscript identified is Paris, BNF, lat. 4667.

[80] These are mss. Paris, BNF lat. 609, BNF lat. 2269, and R* Kopenhagen, Univ. Bibli. 1927 (AM 795, 4). See A. M. Mundó, 'El commicus palimpsest Paris B.N. Lat. 2.269. Amb notes sobre la litúrgia i manuscrits visigòtics a Septimania i Catalunya', in *Liturgica I. I.A. Schuster in memoriam* (Montserrat, 1956), 151–276.

[81] Vic, col. particular, as mentioned above.

[82] MS Montserrat, Bibl. Monest. 1104-I, also noted above.

[83] ACB Codex 187-B (*olim* Fragmenta Codicum 10, B 14).

[84] The 'Liber primus Panfilii' of ACB Codex 178-1 (*olim* Fragmenta codicum 1).

Other religious texts dating from the ninth century also survive in fragments: parts of Psalms 145 and 146;[85] the last part of the book of the
prophet Micah and an incipit and two lines of a prologue for the book of
Nahum;[86] and a later copy of a florilegium of texts from Proverbs,
Ecclesiasticus, the Book of Wisdom, and Ecclesiastes.[87] More Psalms
appear in yet another codex.[88] Such texts constituted the foundation of
the religious life for monastic and cathedral centres, and even lay libraries
as well, in the Carolingian world. While not proof of direct Carolingian
intervention in the intellectual affairs of the Spanish March, the aims of
study these manuscripts represent do align with the aims and scope of
Carolingian reforms.

Along with Scripture and liturgical books, early medieval churches and
their schools depended on patristics and canon law. Augustine's
Soliloquiae were copied in a manuscript used at, if not made at, the
monastery of Santa Maria de Ripoll, while patristic study is further
exemplified in an earlier fragment of Jerome's commentary on
Matthew.[89] Scholars in the Spanish March could have studied church
history through an early ninth-century copy of Eusebius, given to Ripoll
at the beginning of the tenth century.[90] The catalogue of the Biblioteca
de Catalunya in Barcelona identifies another late antique text rather
unceremoniously as a canon-law connection, namely Dionysius
Exiguus' *Collectio canonum*, surviving in a manuscript produced in
Francia but taken to Catalonia during the second half of the ninth
century.[91] It is, however, none other than the *Dionysio-Hadriana*, the
key canon-law text of the Carolingian renaissance, and so serves as
evidence that the Spanish March was part of the reform movement.
The manuscript that contains it, BC 945, shows evidence of having
been completed in two locations. It survives today complete with a
wooden cover and latch, its script a fine Carolingian minuscule. Early
studies of the manuscript revealed that the copying effort had begun in
what might be termed the Carolingian heartland, but that the work was
finished in the Spanish March.[92] The first hand, responsible for all but a
few lines, has been identified as a scribe from northern Francia of the
ninth century; the second, contributing only some passages at f. 46 r, is a

---

[85] ACA frag. ms. 395.   [86] BC 2541, 1.
[87] The florilegium survives in BC 569, a fourteenth-century manuscript that preserves early medieval texts that may have survived in Barcelona for centuries. See Chandler, 'Barcelona, BC 569',
265–91.
[88] ACB Codex 137.
[89] ACA, Ripoll 106 contains the Augustinian text, BC 2541, 4 that of Jerome.
[90] ACA, Frag. cod. 22; Mundó, 'La cultura i els llibres', 470, 472.   [91] BC 945.
[92] A. Mundó, 'La cultura escrita dels segles IX–XII a Catalunya', in *Obres completes* (Barcelona, 1998),
572.

Ripoll hand of the early-to-middle tenth century.[93] Palaeography suggests, then, not only that the *Dionysio-Hadriana* was in demand in at least some quarters of the Spanish March in the later ninth century, but also that locals in the March had connections to their counterparts farther north, to whom they could turn for copies of important texts. The text may well have circulated south of the Pyrenees as well. There was at least one other copy of the *Dionysio-Hadriana* in the Spanish March, identified in the Ripoll library by J. Villanueva.[94] He dated this manuscript to the twelfth century, but Zimmermann attributes its existence to Carolingian influence.[95] Given the poor general state of the survival of evidence, it is impossible to draw conclusions about the use of this text in ecclesiastical centres either in earlier decades of the century or in other places in the March. Nonetheless, the transmission of this important reform text and its preservation at Ripoll is a clear indication of the Carolingian renaissance having taken root in Catalonia. Other fragments also contain the remnants of texts that would have been useful in ecclesiastical settings. For example, Hispanic liturgical texts copied in the ninth century in Barcelona are accompanied by a near-contemporary copy of Isidore's *De ecclesiasticis officiis*.[96] These are the kinds of texts, and in the case of the *Dionysio-Hadriana* precisely the key text, one would expect to find in an area more normally associated nowadays with the Carolingian reform movement.

One final manuscript preserving a late antique text, one of the oldest copies of Sedulius' *Carmen paschale*, survives in the Barcelona cathedral chapter archive and carries glosses by Remigius of Auxerre.[97] This manuscript, dated to the early tenth century, may have been produced in the decade or so after the great teacher died in 908, judging from the script. According to Alturo, furthermore, it is likely that the manuscript originated from the Barcelona cathedral scriptorium.[98] For the this text to circulate south of the Pyrenees so close to its author's passing, along with the *Dionysio-Hadriana*, suggests key conclusions about the literate culture of the Carolingian Spanish March. They are clear evidence of a fairly strong network of scholars and reformers traversing the mountains, made

---

[93] A. Mundó and Anna Gudayol, 'Manuscrits altmedievals amb caplletres i altres il.lustracions', in *Catalunya romànica*, vol. 26 (Barcelona, 1997), 447–51 at 448.

[94] J. Villanueva, *Viage literario a las iglesias de Espana* (Madrid, 1802–52), vol. 8, 55.

[95] Zimmermann, *Écrire et lire*, 767.

[96] ACB Codex 187-B for the liturgical texts, ACB Codex 131 for Isidore.

[97] Alturo and Ballina, 'El sistema educativo en la Cataluña altomedieval'; Alturo, ' Un Seduli amb glosses de Remi d'Auxerre copiat a començos de segle X (a Barcelona?)', *Analecta sacra Tarraconensia* 69 (1996): 5–28 on ACB 178.

[98] Alturo, 'Un Seduli amb glosses de Remi d'Auxerre', 10–13.

up of individuals and communities in the March who desired, sought, and copied mainstream Carolingian texts.

For the ninth century, it is difficult to discern the nature of schools in the Spanish March from the point of view of their texts, as little evidence survives. Perhaps some ninth-century texts that survive only in tenth-century copies stocked libraries at one time but are now lost. In this early period, it seems that cathedrals were more prominent centres for education than were monasteries. Alturo argues that in rural areas, parishes had their own schools, even if it was only the local priest training his successor in basic literacy.[99] Although it seems reasonable to conclude that schools at monasteries and cathedrals existed in the ninth century, the only evidence for a functioning major school in that period is found in early manuscripts from Girona that later made their way to a monastic library. The flyleaves of one surviving manuscript were once part of a law codex, suggesting the study of Visigothic law at the Girona cathedral school for the training of judges.[100] Santa Maria maintained the largest monastic school in the region during the tenth century, and it seems clear that cathedrals not only at Girona, but also at Barcelona and Vic ran schools as well. Although the Ripoll evidence does not necessarily speak for the rest of the March, it is clear that different communities in monasteries and cathedrals in the area kept in communication with one another and with centres in Francia and al-Andalus, allowing the conclusion that other and smaller centres participated in cultural activity of the same kind, if not degree, as Ripoll.

Visigothic law was practised throughout the period, as witnessed by several manuscripts whose remnants are widely scattered in modern Catalan and European libraries and archives. One ninth-century fragment, surviving only as the flyleaves of another codex, is probably the sole survivor of three 'vetustissima' codices mentioned in the 1047 Ripoll catalogue.[101] Because Ripoll was not founded until late in the ninth century, the law fragment must have been produced elsewhere. On palaeographical grounds, the cathedrals of Girona and Urgell are candidates for its production. Scholarly opinion is split, with the majority favouring Girona, which also was the origin of another ninth-century

---

[99] See the general picture painted by Alturo and Ballina, 'El sistema educativo en la Cataluña altomedieval', at 42–9.

[100] Barcelona, ACA, Ripoll 46, discussed above. See Zimmermann, *Écrire et lire*, 922–40 for Visigothic law in use, although most of his evidence comes from the eleventh century.

[101] The flyleaves in question are those of Ripoll 46.

Visigothic law book.[102] It is interesting to note the copying and preservation of these manuscripts in religious houses. Such a history suggests that churches and monasteries were the centres of legal education, and hints that church centres knew and used law. That is not to say that the church had a monopoly. One manuscript now housed in the archive of Vic was probably copied by a lay judge in Osona, the territory of Vic's jurisdiction.[103] For general purposes, including dispute settlement in the Spanish March, Visigothic law prevailed. The use of that law code, which Pippin III granted to the Goths of Narbonne in 759 and Charlemagne to the hispani settlers after 778, obviously stands as an element of traditional Visigothic culture, despite one claim that the hispani were left to their own unique, not Visigothic, law.[104] For our entire period and beyond, this element of Visigothic identity survived Frankish dominion. Indeed, the very survival of the traditional law text forms a lynchpin in the argument that survivals of Visigothic culture were more important than any Carolingian intervention.[105] Yet the fact that several of these copies of law survive only as flyleaves also attests to their physical marginality. Legal practices continued to develop, as did the instructional and studious needs of the communities that needed books.[106] Furthermore, Carolingian rule did not eliminate local laws and legal practices elsewhere in the empire, so the persistence of Visigothic law is not a special case and should not be seen as outweighing the Carolingian contribution to learned culture in the Spanish March.

Before one could become learned, it was necessary to gain basic literacy. Indeed, correct Latin and the liberal arts were the root of education in the Carolingian period, while education in turn was the root of the reform movement. Schooling in the early Middle Ages began with the trivium, the foundation of which was grammar. It should come as no surprise, then, that grammatical texts are found in the schoolbooks of the Spanish March. The oldest surviving text for the study of education in the region is one such teaching text composed by Usuard, the traveller from Francia. The information gathered in the martyrology was the

---

[102] A. M. Mundó, 'Els manuscrits del "Liber iudiciorum" de les comarques gironines', in J. Portella i Comas, ed., *La formació i expansió del feudalisme català: Actes de col.loqui organizat pel Col.legi Universiari de Girona (8-11 de gener de 1985)* (Girona, 1985), 77–86 at 80–1, recounting earlier arguments. F. Mateu i Llopis and M. C. Díaz y Díaz argued for Girona. Mundó supported Urgell, but most recently, Alturo, 'Manuscrits', 276–77, concludes that the law book was likely produced in Girona. The other manuscript is Paris, BNF lat. 4667.

[103] Alturo, 'Manuscrits', 277.

[104] Barbero, 'La integración social de los "hispani" del Pirineo oriental al reino carolingio', 75; see also the discussion above in Chapters 1 and 2.

[105] Zimmermann, 'Conscience gothique et affirmation nationale', 57–8.

[106] Faulkner, *Law and Authority in the Early Middle Ages*, ch. 4 is a good example of studying the local uses of law codes.

Frankish monk's primary accomplishment, and proved its worth through the centuries, but the grammar holds more significance for present purposes. Grammar during the Carolingian period was built on the works of the late Latin authors Donatus and Priscian; Anglo-Saxon and Irish experience with learning Latin as a foreign language spurred the writing of commentaries on those authoritative texts, and in turn the commentaries proved their utility for teachers and students throughout the Frankish kingdoms in the ninth century.[107] Itself largely based on commentaries on Priscian and Donatus, Usuard's work dates from before his journey to Córdoba.[108] Despite Usuard's composition of the grammar in and for the monastery of St-Germain-des-Prés, the only three extant copies now exist in two manuscripts housed in the ACA in Barcelona, originally part of the library at the monastery of Santa Maria de Ripoll.[109] The survival of three apparently successive versions of the same, northern text at a single, southern house demonstrates again the exchange of manuscripts between Catalonia ánd Francia in the second half of the ninth century, and probably indicates that such interaction had been established earlier, either before Usuard's trip to Córdoba or as a consequence of it. Usuard may well have met like-minded fellows and made contacts in Hispania and maintained them after his return to Paris. If his grammar found its way to the Spanish March before Ripoll's foundation, it proved worthy of space in that monastery's library soon afterwards.

The example of Usuard's grammar is clear evidence of the influence of the Carolingian education programme on schools in the Spanish March. In addition to the possession of contemporary texts and the transmission of older ones, evidence survives of local use and modification of the tools at hand, whether originally at Ripoll or elsewhere in the Spanish March. The three copies (designated 'a', 'b', and 'c' based on date of creation) appear in what are now two manuscript codices, which very probably indicates that the grammar was once present in three different volumes in the Ripoll library.[110] Further, there is the use of a Gothic name, Sunnia,

---

[107] C. Jeudy, 'Donat et commentateurs de Donat à l'abbaye de Ripoll au Xe siècle (ms. Barcelona, Archivo de la Corona de Aragón, Ripoll 46)', in G. Cambrier, C. Derous, and J. Préaux, eds, *Lettres latine du Moyen Age et de la Renaissance* (Brussels, 1978); Vivien Law, 'The Study of Grammar', in R. McKitterick, ed., *Carolingian Culture: Emulation and Innovation* (Cambridge, 1994), 88–110; L. Holtz, *Donat et la tradition de l'enseignement grammatical: étude sur l'Ars Donati et sa diffusion (IVe–IXe siècle) et édition critique* (Paris, 1981).

[108] For other evidence of the study of the two late antique grammarians at Ripoll, see P. Edward Dutton and A. Luhtala. 'Eriugena in Priscianum', *Mediaeval Studies* 56 (1994): 153–63, although their evidence is the eleventh-century manuscript Ripoll 59.

[109] The grammar has been discussed and edited by J. M. Casas Homs, 'Una gramàtica inèdita d'Usuard', *Analecta Montserratensia* 10 (1964): 77–129.

[110] The manuscripts are Ripoll 46 and 74. See Z. García Villada, *Bibliotheca Patrum Latinorum Hispaniensis* (Vienna, 1915), 563–7 and 580–4.

in the first declension chart found in the 'c' version rather than in the oldest, 'a' version in one of the manuscripts. A much-later schoolmaster or some other user also inserted a note in the 'c' version of Usuard, hinting to readers that if they are uncertain whether an ablative noun ends with 'a' or 'o', to check the genitive plural.[111] These modifications indicate that Usuard's text found audiences for generations and served in some small way to connect students in the Spanish March with the culture of learning nearer the Frankish heartlands, even as they stand as evidence of regional variation on a more universal theme. Usuard's personal connection to the Spanish March did not make possible the teaching and learning of Latin grammar in local schools, but it did represent a link to Francia and indeed made possible the survival of his text to the present day.

Usuard's grammar appears in its two Ripoll manuscripts along with Bede's *De arte metrica*; a third copy of Bede's text survives today in a different codex.[112] Bede's work, dated to just after 700 along with his *De schematibus et tropis*, was copied and used in many parts of the Carolingian world for instruction in grammar and rhetoric.[113] The appearance of Bede's text in Ripoll is thus further evidence of the Carolingian influence in Catalonian culture.[114] Such activities in the teaching of the trivium, the basis for future study in the liberal arts, provide evidence also of a lively literary culture in the Spanish March, which would lead in time to what is now recognized as the 'poetic school of Ripoll'.[115]

Ripoll 74 also contains a formulary, which is fairly well known thanks to the work of Michel Zimmermann.[116] The formulary has been dated to

---

[111] Barcelona, ACA Ripoll 74, f. 5v.

[112] Manuscripts Ripoll 46, 74, and 106. See R. Beer, 'Die Handschriften des Klosters Santa Maria de Ripoll I', *Sitzungsberichte der Philosophisch-Hostorischen Kalsse der Kaiserlichen Akademie der Wissenchaften* 155 (1908): 1–112, with plates, at 59, 67, 92–5 for grammar texts in these codices; also García Villada, *Bibliotheca*, 563–7, 580–4, and 597–9. In the introduction to the *CCSL* edition of Bede, *Opera Didascalica*, ed. C. W. Jones, *CCSL* 123 A (Turnhout, 1975), Ripoll 46 is mentioned as carrying the text, but mss. 74 and 106 are not. Neither does Laistner mention these mss. in his hand-list: M. L. W. Laistner, *A Hand-List of Bede Manuscripts* (Ithaca, 1943), 134, where he lists Ripoll 46.

[113] Bede, *Opera Didascalica*, 74. For a later date, see C. Vircillo Franklin, 'The Date of Composition of Bede's *De schematibus et tropis* and *De arte metrica*', *Revue bénédictine* 110 (2000): 199–203. See also G. Björkvall and A. Haug, 'Verslehre und Ververtonung im lateinischen Mittelalter', in U. Schaefer, ed., *Artes im Mittelalter* (Berlin, 1999), 309–23; A. Holder, '(Un)dating Bede's *De arte metrica*', in J. Hawkes and S. Mills, eds, *Northumbria's Golden Age* (Stroud, 1999), 390–5; N. Wright, 'The Metrical Art(s) of Bede', in K. O'Brien O'Keeffe and A. Orchard, *Latin Learning and English Lore*, vol. 1 rd (Toronto, 2005), 150–70.

[114] Zimmermann, *Écrire et lire*, 753–6.

[115] L. N. d'Olwer, 'L'Escola poètica de Ripoll en els segles X–XIII', *Anuari d'Institut d'Estudis Catalans* 6 (1920), 3–84.

[116] Ripoll 74, ff. 145v-156v. See M. Zimmermann, 'Un formulaire du Xème siècle conservé à Ripoll', *Faventia* 4 (1982): 25–86; Zimmermann, *Écrire et lire*, 251–63. See also J. Alturo, 'La

around 980 and consists of thirty-eight mostly partial models for documents of various purposes, including letters, sales, donations, exchanges, even for the consecration of a church or the report of an election of an abbot. Many elements of the formulae recall the Visigothic law, such as the act of writing itself being mandated by the law and mentioning the Visigothic era in the dating clause. Others show direct influences from old Frankish practices, including the dating clause given according to the reign of the Frankish king. The several folios in Ripoll 74 are the sole surviving witness to the formulary, which had escaped the attention of early editors. Yet they stand as one more testimony to the vibrancy of literate culture in the Spanish March.

While the Ripoll school seems to have first flourished in the tenth century, it was obviously built on the foundations of the ninth. Poetic composition, as seen in tenth-century manuscripts from Ripoll,[117] was possible in part thanks to the development of schools under Carolingian influence, which itself is traceable in the presence of Bede's work and its accompanying verses by Alcuin.[118] It is perhaps dangerous to attempt to attribute this cultural development to any influence the Frankish conquest of Catalonia may have had. However, as Bede only finished the work at around the same time that the kingdom of Toledo fell, it stands to reason that scholars and students in the Visigothic kingdom never had much of a chance to read his works.[119] It is in this case safe to claim that Bede's work appears in the Spanish March because of the importation of Carolingian culture, just as the Carolingians themselves were influenced by Northumbrian developments. The connection is strengthened by the presence of Alcuin's verses accompanying Bede's treatise on metre. Certainly the work of a leading scholar associated with the court of Charlemagne did not find its way to the Spanish March outside the context of Frankish control of the region. Overall, Carolingian learned culture was pan-European in some sense. The scholars Charlemagne gathered around himself hailed from England, Ireland, Italy, and Spain. The textual sources for the religious and educational enterprise termed the Carolingian renaissance likewise originated from throughout the Latin West. For the rest of the ninth century, and into the tenth, individuals from all corners flocked to the Frankish realms. The presence

---

Glossa VI del ms 74 de Ripoll: un epítom isidorià incorporat al Liber glossarum', *Faventia* 18 (1996): 67–91.

[117] N. d'Olwer, 'L'Escola poètica de Ripoll en els segles X–XIII.'

[118] Alcuin's poem is edited in *MGH Poetae* 1, 347–8.

[119] Bede's influence on Spaniards of a much later era has been traced in H. Heidenreich, 'Beda Venerabilis in Spain', *MLN* 70 (1985): 120–37.

of texts by Bede and Alcuin can thus serve as evidence for Catalonia having entered the same network.[120]

The March's manuscripts also document interest in numeric and scientific studies. Students in Catalonian schools practised arithmetic and chant; astronomy was always important, but became a focal point during the tenth century as contact with the world of Arabic science increased.[121] The so-called mechanical arts also had a place in instruction as well. Geometry and surveying held a special place in the Spanish March as settlement expanded into areas described as waste. The most original intellectual contributions of Catalonians came in these fields. Such practical texts, large and small, serve as our windows into the 'scientific' education of Carolingian Catalonia.[122]

Training in computus was perhaps the most important of the numerical arts of the quadrivium. Calculating the date of Easter and marking the timing of significant events in world history required complex skills. Several of the Ripoll manuscripts contain computistical efforts, in tables from both the ninth and tenth centuries. Bede's treatises on reckoning time appear in later codices, as his works apparently gained readers as the Anno Domini dating system replaced the Visigothic 'era'.[123] The 'era', in this sense, was a reckoning of years, taking 38 BC as its base year and thus thirty-eight years ahead of the Anno Domini reckoning; it had been used in the Visigothic kingdom and endured into the Christian culture under Muslim rule.[124] A computistical table and rules for the calculation of the calendar even nestles between the 'a' and 'b' versions of Usuard's grammar.[125] This brief interlude of mathematical work in a codex otherwise dedicated to the trivium may be explained by frugality. Parchment was so expensive that schoolmasters and their pupils wrote on whatever surfaces presented themselves. It also illustrates, however, that these same

---

[120] Evidence exists, just barely, of another ninth-century copy of a Bedan text in the flyleaves of a Catalonian manuscript: J. Alturo, 'Los folios de guarda del manuscrit Paris, Bibl. Nat. Lat. 6113: un *Commentarium in Lucam* de Beda del siglo IX', *Historia. Instituciones. Documentos* 19 (1992): 1–6.

[121] For orientation, see Riché, *Ecoles et enseignement*, 267–84; Contreni, 'The Carolingian Renaissance', 725–47.

[122] Zimmermann, *Écrire et lire*, 949–82 provides much more discussion than is possible here.

[123] D. P. McCarthy, 'The Emergence of *Anno Domini*', in *Time and Eternity: the Medieval Discourse*, eds G. Jaritz and G. Moreno-Riaño (Turnhout, 2003), 31–54; G. Declercq, *Anno Domini: the Origins of the Christian Era* (Turnhout, 2000), 149–95; Faith Wallis's introduction to Bede, *The Reckoning of Time*, trans. F. Wallis (Liverpool, 1999), xv–ci, but esp. xxxiv–lxiii for 'A Brief History of the Christian Calendar before Bede'; D. M. Deliyannis, 'Year-Dates in the Early Middle Ages', in C. Humphrey and W. M. Ormrod, eds, *Time in the Medieval World* (Rochester, NY, 2001), 5–22.

[124] Traditionally, Christians under Muslim rule in Spain have been called 'mozarabs'. R. Hitchcock, *Mozarabs in Medieval and Early Modern Spain: Identities and Influences* (Aldershot, 2008) argues against such an identity in the early Middle Ages.

[125] Ripoll 74; García Villada, *Bibliotheca Patrum Latinorum Hispaniensis*, 580–4.

masters and pupils understood the *artes liberales* as a coherent enterprise. There may have been a time for letters and a separate time for numbers, but both helped the student along the path to understanding God.[126]

One of the oldest manuscripts from the Ripoll collection dates to the ninth century and contains Boethius's *De arithmetica*.[127] The manuscript, Ripoll 168, which some had dated to the eleventh century at least in part on the basis of Arabic marginalia, was well suited to quadrivial study at Ripoll, and is now recognized as a creation of the ninth century.[128] It may well have originated in a Frankish centre outside the Spanish March, given its date and palaeographical characteristics. Its current binding restores the folios to the correct order after mistakes made in the nine-teenth century. The script employed to copy the text was Carolingian minuscule, but there is evidence of early, local use in the marginalia in Visigothic script on folios 5v, 6r, and 57v. The ink and script, moreover, do not match the types employed to create manuscripts that certainly were produced in the March. Regionally produced manuscripts feature a trademark brownish ink with orange-red rubrics, while Ripoll 168 was written in a darker, black ink and exhibits no rubrics in different colours. Such physical evidence may indicate that the manuscript had been imported from north of the Pyrenees. Then, at some point during the tenth century, it found its way into the hands of someone who apparently knew both Latin and Arabic, as demonstrated by the presence of Arabic notations in margins on folios 42r (in the last chapter of Boethius, bk. 1), 62r–v (bk. 2.25), and 91r (2.54, which the manuscript combines with 2.53). These notations clearly indicate that the manuscript of Frankish origin played a role in the intellectual exchange between people in the Spanish March and al-Andalus known to have taken place in the tenth century.

Other manuscripts show interest in computus and also the influence of the Carolingian renaissance in the form of Bede. For example, Ripoll 59, a manuscript dating to the very end of the Carolingian period in Catalonia, contains a calendar and, on its last folios, the thirteenth and twenty-third chapters of Bede's *De tempore ratione*, to explain how to use

---

[126] For recent treatments on this idea, see J. J. Contreni, 'Counting, Calendars, and Cosmology: Numeracy in the Early Middle Ages', in J. J. Contreni and S. Casciani, eds, *Word, Image, Number: Communication in the Middle Ages* (Rome, 2002), 43–83, at 48–9, and W. M. Stevens, 'Fields and Streams: Language Practice of Arithmetic and Geometry in Early Medieval Schools', in ibid., 113–204.

[127] See the modern editions: Boethius, *Institution arithmétique* ed. and French trans., J.-Y. Guillaumin (Paris, 1995), and H. Oosthout and J. Schilling, *Anicii Manlii Severini Boethii De arithmetica CCSL* 94 A (Turnhout, 1999).

[128] Guillaumin's editorial introduction makes this clear, Boethius, *Institution arithmétique*, lxvi.

tables of letters and numbers.[129] The chapters from Bede may have been added to the codex after it was initially produced.[130] Alternatively, the calendar itself arguably derives from Bede's work, so the two elements may both be original to the composition of the manuscript.[131] Two columns of narrow line ruling contain chapter 45 of Bede's *De tempore ratione*, along with part of a commentary of chapter 42.[132] Meanwhile, computus also appears within a very special manuscript, Ripoll 106, considered in more detail below. The evidence of these manuscripts illustrates that the principal cultural centres of the Spanish March were well harmonized with learned culture elsewhere in the Carolingian world by the tenth century, and would compare favourably with many other centres in other regions.

Other manuscripts, as noted above, provide evidence on the learning provided in schools. Chief amongst them was the school at Ripoll. Barcelona, ACA, Monacals, Ripoll 106, arguably the most interesting and most important manuscript of the period from the Spanish March, unlocks many secrets about the climate of Carolingian Catalonia's most important centre of learned culture. One of the oldest manuscripts in the collection, most of it was created in the late ninth century.[133] Despite the fact that, for over a century, the codex has been recognized as one of the richest manuscripts of the period, it deserves to be more widely known than it is.[134] This manuscript contains much that would have been useful for a Carolingian monastic school. The first eight folios are twelfth-century additions, and folio 26 is another later and smaller insertion from when the codex was bound into its current format. Between these later additions, on folios 9–25, are a medicinal recipe and Bede's *De arte metrica*, followed immediately by a short computus discussion. The manuscript also includes texts related to religious study, including patristics and texts with musical notations, which strongly suggest a Carolingian influence.[135] A table of constellations precedes a compilation of geographical surveying texts, while the last third of the codex is made up of smaller, near-contemporary texts, including a short introduction to

[129] García Villada, *Bibliotheca Patrum Latinorum Hispaniensis*, 575–6.
[130] A. Cordoliani, 'Los manuscritos de cómputo eclesiástico en las bibliotecas de Barcelona', *Analecta sacra Tarraconensia* 23 (1950): 104–7.
[131] M. C. Diaz y Diaz, *Index scriptorum Latinorum medii Aevi Hispanorum* (Salamanca, 1959), 146.
[132] Cordoliani, 'Los manuscritos de cómputo', 107–10.
[133] L. Toneatto, 'Manoscrito dell'Ars gromatica Gisemundi', in *Codices artis mensoriae i manoscriti degli antichi opusculi latini d'agrimensura (V–XIX sec.)*, vol. 3 (Spoleto, 1995), 997–1012 at 999; Beer, 'Handschriften', 239.
[134] Beer, 'Handschriften', 59–67. Also Zimmermann, *Écrire et lire*, 958, where he dates its compilation to c. 900.
[135] Zimmermann, *Écrire et lire*, 564 notes a 'liturgie romano-franque', on the basis of clues in Ripoll 106 and 74; no sacramentary survives. See also ibid., 626–32.

numbers and some poetic and religious works. The last few folios contain an inventory note and hymn. Ripoll 106 contains other short computistical works and tables as well. Amongst the tables is a chart of the zodiac constellations and their path through the solar calendar. Astronomical interests extended through the tenth century, spurred on by intellectual contacts with Muslim scholars elsewhere in Spain. The variety of texts included in its covers, the fact that some of these texts have long escaped serious scrutiny, and the fact that many of the studies that have been done tend to isolate texts present opportunities to learn about the educational culture of the late Carolingian Spanish March.

The moral and religious texts in Ripoll 106 demand attention. It also preserves one of the two oldest copies of Sedulius' *Carmen paschale* in Spain, along with the same author's Hymn I. The other survives in the Barcelona chapter archive, with its glosses by Remigius of Auxerre.[136] Ripoll 106 as a whole reflects the interests of Carolingian masters like Remigius. For example, in addition to the liberal arts, Ripoll's students, whether oblates or laymen, received moral instruction through Augustine's *Soliloquiae* and the *Disticha Catonis*, with which Remigius himself was familiar. It is clear that the Ripoll copy is a very early and quite independent manuscript in the tradition of the *Disticha Catonis*.[137] Other late antique moral and spiritual texts in this rich codex guided monks and their students in the contemplation of God and of man's creation. A fragment of the confession of the fifth-century African bishop Leporius found its way into the codex alongside Bede, computus, and other scientific tracts. Other religious texts, such as the *Epigrammatum liber* of Prosper of Aquitaine, a fragment of a commentary on Kings, and excerpts from Gregory of Nyssa's *De opificio hominis* translated by Dionysius Exiguus, were originally part of another book, but later users bound them into the current codex.[138] The presence of these late antique texts in a ninth-century Ripoll manuscript suggests that the monks of Carolingian Catalonia worked within a tradition of study throughout the ninth and tenth centuries, a tradition held in common with their counterparts elsewhere in the Frankish kingdoms.

Clearly, education and culture in the Spanish March followed the pattern of the Carolingian renaissance by using the script and even some crucial texts imported from north of the Pyrenees. That is not to

---

[136] ACB 178, discussed above.

[137] T. González Rolán, 'La tradición de los Dicta Catonis y el Ripollensis 106', *Habis* 5 (1974): 93–106.

[138] Prosper: L. Toneatto, 'Manoscrito dell'Ars gramatica Gisemundi', in *Codices artis mensoriae i manoscriti degli antichi opusculi latini d'agrimensura (V–XIX sec.)*, vol. 3 (Spoleto, 1995), 997–1012 at 1001; Cordoliani, 'Los manuscritos de cómputo', 107. Gregory: *PL* 67: 370B–377C.

say that learning in the Spanish March had become 'Frankish', whatever that might mean, for the cultural basis of the Carolingian reforms was largely not 'Frankish' itself, but rather biblical and patristic. Major studies of these issues often prioritize the region's later political autonomy and read backwards into the past a streak of independence-mindedness on the part of people in the March.[139] Emphasizing that monasteries and chapters of canons in the March possessed texts from elsewhere in Spain, and holding that as an indication of cultural autonomy, tends to elide the fact that many Carolingian reform initiatives themselves were informed and influenced by Visigothic-era texts and shared the same textual inspiration and sources.[140] An adjustment in emphasis is in order, to a position that views the Carolingians not as bent on uniformity but as tolerant of local custom to a degree, and that views the continued use of 'Visigothic' rather than 'Frankish' texts as drawing as necessary on local sources for authorities – as regional variation on the wider theme of reform rather than stubborn clinging to a cultural patrimony.

LOCAL PRODUCTIONS

The Ars Gisemundi

Putting aside the common educational tradition and networks of association between the Spanish March and the rest of the Frankish kingdoms under Carolingian rule, a few texts contained in Ripoll 106 are especially interesting for what they reveal about the creation of works in the Spanish March. These include the *Ars gromatica* of Gisemundus. His compilation appears in the first section of the codex as now bound, a section that dates to the late ninth century and perhaps constituted its own book at that time.[141] Gisemundus' gromatical texts do not seem like academic exercises, but may well be related to sociopolitical-economic developments in

---

[139] Zimmermann, *Écrire et lire*, 768–71. See also 559–78, where he states that no manuscript earlier than the eleventh century exists from the Ripoll library. Studies of some manuscripts, however, contradict that statement, including that of Zimmermann himself as in note 135. As this chapter shows, there are clear survivals from before 1000 in the archive in Barcelona.

[140] Examples come from liturgy: Reynolds, 'The Visigothic Liturgy in the Realm of Charlemagne', 919–45; A. Mundó, 'Sur quelques manuscrits liturgiques languedociens de l'epoque carolingienne (vers 800)', in *Cahiers de Fanjeaux* 17 (1982), 93. For the crucial reform enterprises of Benedict of Aniane: Mundó, 'I "corpora" e i "codices regularum" nei tradizione codicologica delle regole monastiche', in *Atti del 7o congresso internazionale di studi sull'alto medioevo: Norica – Subiaco – Cassino – Montecassino*, (Spoleto, 1982), 2.477–520); K. Zelzer, 'Zum Text zweier Stellungen der Regula Benedicti', *Wiener Studien* 81 (1968): 225–52; Zelzer, 'Zur Stellung des Textus receptus und des interpolierten Textes in der Textgeschichte der Regula S. Benedicti', *Revue benedictine* 88 (1978): 205–46.

[141] Toneatto, 'Manoscrito', 999. Toneatto discovered, through investigation of the physical construction of the codex, that ff. 9–92 were composed together as a unit.

Catalonia relating to expansion into unpopulated areas, a movement begun with the first *aprisiones* farther north, then continued in Catalonia chiefly under the auspices of the counts of Barcelona.

Happily, Lucio Toneatto has studied the codex closely, and has remarked that it contained 'miscellaneous' texts on scientific and religious themes, for his main interest was the *Ars gromatica Gisemundi*, which occupies our attention here.[142] Toneatto's work has revealed the original structure of the now jumbled text, compiled by the monk named Gisemundus who identifies himself at folio 81 r, and which occupies ff. 76 r–89 r of the codex. At folio 76 r, line 30 appears the rubric 'EPISTOLA IULII CAESARIS'. This portion of the *Ars Gisemundi* was excerpted from Pseudo-Boethius and concerns conquering many peoples, wiping out their cities, and planting new *coloniae*. Wifred the Hairy himself supported a settlement drive in his day; indeed Ripoll became central to it. Toneatto's support for dating of the gromatic compilation to the late ninth century reinforces the notion that Gisemundus' text was intended for use in settlement enterprises.[143] Gisemundus could have compiled his *Ars* on a commission from Wifred or Dagui, the abbot of the young monastery, precisely because of the situation faced by settlers of open land. Ripoll possessed wide and varied tracts in deserted areas, so the purchasing, clearing, surveying, and organization of land were of immediate concern.[144] If Gisemundus did indeed include passages on various controversies that could arise, then he had to have had a purpose in doing so. The mountainous features of the area made surveying difficult; surveyors could turn to Gisemundus' tract for guidance, as could parties to disputes where boundaries of estates were hard to determine. Recent study has shown how boundary-setting for property did in fact follow Gisemundus' dictates.[145]

Gisemundus' sources included the body of works now known collectively as the Corpus agrimensorum Romanorum: texts by Julius Frontinus, Hyginus, Pseudo-Hyginus, Siculus Flaccus, Agennius Urbicus, Marcus Junius Nipso, and the anonymous Casae litterarum, Liber regionum I and II, and De sepulchris.[146] The Pseudo-Boethian

---

[142] Toneatto, 'Manoscrito'; L. Toneatto, 'Note sulla tradizione del *Corpus agrimensorum romanorum*', *MEFRM* 94 (1982): 197–8. We shall return to this remark.

[143] Toneatto, 'Manoscrito', 999. See also L. D. Reynolds, *Texts and Transmission: a Survey of the Latin Classics* (Oxford, 1983), 1–6, esp. 5. Zimmermann, *Écrire et lire*, 680.

[144] On the settlement initiative, see Abadal, *Dels visigots als catalans*, 485–96; more recently, Jarrett, *Rulers and Ruled in Frontier Catalonia, 880–1010: Pathways of Power* (London, 2010), 23–72.

[145] A. M. Mundó, *De quan hispans, gots, jueus, àrabs i francs circularen per Catalunya* Seminari de Paleografia, Diplomàtica i Codocologia Monografies (Bellaterra, 2001), 25 note 18.

[146] C. Thulin, ed., *Corpus agrimensorum romanorum* (Stuttgart, 1971 reprint from 1913). See also O. A. W. Dilke, *The Roman Land Surveyors: an Introduction to the Agrimensores* (Newton Abbot, 1971).

'Geometria I' of the eighth century and the works of Julius Honorius and Orosius complement the gromatic corpus.[147] The models for the compilation are not found in the 1047 catalogue of Ripoll's library, but the Pseudo-Boethian work hints at a connection to Corbie.[148] Gisemundus, therefore, probably worked outside the school and scriptorium of Ripoll, perhaps before or just after the house was established or endowed with comital properties in 885. The 'Geometria I' figures more prominently than any single source, with forty-three excerpts, while Frontinus (twenty-one) and Pseudo-Hyginus (twenty) are next; no other source contributes more than eight excerpts to the total of 123. Toneatto calculated that 57 per cent of Gisemundus' *Ars* comes from the collective *Corpus agrimensorum*, 27 per cent from Pseudo-Boethius, and 5 per cent from the others.[149] The remaining 11 per cent of text comes from a combination of the geographical portion of Orosius's *Seven Books of History against the Pagans* and the mind of Gisemundus himself.

Moreover, Gisemundus was responsible for the very concept and structure of the text. The largest single portion that deviates from the *agrimensores* concerns the geography of Spain. This material, taking up f. 81v, line 32 to f. 82 r, line 24 clearly indicates the local interests of the compiler. A drawing of circles labelled with place names of Iberian cities strongly suggests a Catalonian production of the manuscript. Since this section of original material in the *Ars Gisemundi* demonstrates the compiler's local and regional interests, and the compilation itself along with explanatory notes addresses issues relevant to the expansion of settlement and Ripoll's role therein, we can conclude that Gisemundus worked, if not at Ripoll itself, then at another regional centre, perhaps the cathedral of Girona, and produced his *Ars* for the use of the monks at the new monastery of Ripoll as they engaged in the settlement of the valley.[150]

Gisemundus provides a geographical overview of Spain based on that of Orosius but modifies his model considerably. In this short section, known as the *Descriptio Hispaniae*, he informed readers that Spain is a triangle, the corners of which are the region of Narbonne, Cádiz, and the city of Brigantia (modern La Coruña), where a high lighthouse rises.[151] Following Orosius, Gisemundus revealed that the boundaries of Hispania

---

[147] On Pseudo-Boethius, see E. A. Zaitsev, 'The Meaning of Early Medieval Geometry: From Euclid and Surveyors' Manuals to Christian Philosophy', *Isis* 90 (1999): 522–53. Perhaps the most interesting aspect of this section of the *Ars Gisemundi* is its debt to Orosius, *The Seven Books of History against the Pagans*, book 1.

[148] Toneatto, 'Note', 288; M. Viladrich, 'Ripoll: Ara fa un mil.lenni: un escriptori obert al món', in *Catalunya a l'època carolíngia*, 139–43, with English at 489–91.

[149] Toneatto, 'Note', 307–8.

[150] This is also the conclusion of Viladrich, 'Ripoll', 140, reached independently.

[151] Orosius, *Seven Books of History against the Pagans*, trans. A. T. Fear (Liverpool, 2010), 44.

Citerior are enclosed within the district of Carthage (modern Cartagena).[152] Yet in doing so, Gisemundus followed the outlines of ecclesiastical jurisdiction, departing from Orosius's more classical naming of tribes and occasionally cities. But then Gisemundus struck out on his own, inserting a more detailed explanation of Spanish geography in between Orosius's very brief survey of Hispania Citerior and Ulterior. According to Gisemundus, Romans set the boundaries by means of fortifications and rivers that pertained to Hispania Citerior. He gives the measure of the Ebro at 329 miles (today reckoned at 565 mi./ 910 km). Its valley and the rest of north-eastern Spain, although Gisemundus did not mention it, constituted the province of Tarraconensis, the other part of Hispania Citerior. Gisemundus labelled many other regions of Spain by their late Roman as well as contemporary names, departing from Orosius's archaic use, even for his own time, of Citerior and Ulterior. For instance, Gisemundus gives the relative locations of Lusitania and Baetica, the names of Roman provinces, but also adds Gallicia, Asturias, Cantabria, and 'Vasconia'. He shows knowledge of the geography of church provinces, cities, and rivers, but makes some choices of inclusion and exclusion that seem odd at first glance.

The text fails to mention Tarraconensis, hotly contested between barbarians, Roman imperial forces, and Roman usurpers in the fifth century and an ecclesiastical province until the Muslim conquest of the eighth. Its absence from the geographic description of Spain is remarkable, since an ecclesiastical controversy of the 880s–90s involving the metropolitanate was contemporary with Gisemundus. In 885 the would-be Archbishop Sclua sought ordination by Gascon clergy in order to take over the bishopric of Urgell, despite the presence of the incumbent Ingobert.[153] His plot, involving regional bishops and counts, the archbishop of Narbonne, and even kings Charles the Fat and Odo, ultimately failed. What this episode points to is the awareness in the Spanish March of a heritage of ecclesiastical organization. The bishoprics south of the Pyrenees came under the authority of Narbonne in the wake of the Frankish conquest of the eighth and ninth centuries, and bishops seem to have been content with Narbonese authority. Gisemundus's omission could then suggest his compliance with the established hierarchy, that is, Carolingian rule in

---

[152] Orosius, *Seven Books of History against the Pagans*, trans. Fear, 44.

[153] R.-H. Bautier, 'La prétendue dissidence de l'épiscopat catalan et le faux concile de « Portus » de 887–890', *Bulletin philologique et historique (jusqu'à 1610) du Comité des Travaux Historiques et Scientifiques* 1961 (Paris, 1963): 477–98; J. Jarrett, 'Archbishop Ató of Osona: False Metropolitans on the Marca Hispanica', *Archiv für Diplomatik*, 56 (2010), 1–42, esp. at 9–12; and Chapter 3 in this volume.

the church. It seems that Gisemundus made a point of omitting Tarraconensis from his discussion while retaining the Narbonensis as one of the corners of Spain. The parallel passage from Orosius mentions only Brigantia and Carthago Nova (modern Cartagena) as noteworthy cities, while Gisemundus adds his own discussion of others.[154] Gisemundus may have slighted an ecclesiastical province, but the city of Tarragona, the old metropolitan see, is not forgotten in the manuscript.

It is significant that the text, which expands on Orosius, also leaves out other important Visigothic cities. It does not mention Toledo, the metropolitan see of Carthaginensis in the Visigothic period, even though Gisemundus spells out in detail which cities belonged to that province. Orosius emphasized Roman provinces and barbarian tribes, following the ancient republican organization. Gisemundus centuries later followed the imperial administration, centring his description of Spain on Cartagena, even though Toledo was by far the more important city in the early Middle Ages.[155] Gisemundus gives more information on the other Spanish church provinces: Emerita (modern Mérida) as the metropolitan of Lusitania, and Bracara (Braga) of Gallicia, but Seville is not named for Baetica. Moreover, Gisemundus describes the river Baetis (now known as the Guadalquivir) as *ubi Cordoba sita est* 'where Córdoba is sited', before following the river's course to the coast, where it empties into the Atlantic in the vicinity of Cádiz. Seville also lies on the river, but merits no mention. Gisemundus may have neglected Seville because it did not appear in Orosius's work, but Gisemundus had no trouble departing from his source for other purposes. This could reflect the importance of Córdoba in the late ninth century, as the seat of the Umayyad emirs of al-Andalus; Seville, the see of Leander and Isidore, was no longer the most important city in its own province, as seen from the Spanish March. The same holds for Toledo, once the royal city of the Visigoths and home to a series of church councils. Toledo was also home to Archbishop Elipandus, ringleader of the Adoptionists, denounced as heretics a century before Gisemundus wrote. Cities that were important in the seventh century were not the foci of discussion late in the ninth.

---

[154] Orosius, *Seven Books of History against the Pagans*, trans. Fear, 44–5.
[155] See N. Lozovsky, 'Carolingian Geographical Tradition: Was It Geography?', *EME* 5 (1996): 25–43 for the notion that early medieval geography did not always have accuracy as its goal in terms of reflecting contemporary realities.

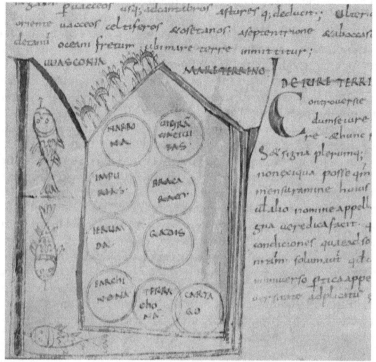

Figure 1. Ministerio de Educación, Cultura y Deporte. Archivo de la Corona de Aragón, Colecciones, Manuscritos, Ripoll 106, fol. 82r, detail of a triptych drawn by hand in the lower left corner

The image resembling a map, on folio 82 (see Figure 1), appears to be a drawing of an open triptych. The identity of the person who copied it into the manuscript remains unknown, but it is certainly contemporary with the text. Perhaps the copyist sketched a triptych belonging to the cathedral of Girona, Gisemundus's putative home. Enclosed in the frame of the triptych are circles labelled with the names of Iberian cities. The drawing betrays a Catalonian bias, listing Empúries, Girona, and Barcelona. It also includes Narbonne, the ecclesiastical and often political capital of the area under Carolingian rule, and Braga, Cádiz, and Cartagena farther west and south. These non-Catalonian cities are the same ones mentioned in the text; here the drawing also mirrors the text in omitting Toledo and Seville. Tarragona, although left out of the textual discussion, does merit an appearance in the drawing. It alone of these former Visigothic metropolitans finds inclusion, in this way, in Gisemundus's brief *Descriptio*.

The drawing also depicts, outside the triptych, Wasconia (Gascony) and Mare Terreno. This is the Tyrrhenian Sea in Orosius and is the western arm of the Mediterranean. Gisemundus included Gascony in his description of a special arch near Salamanca. The arch, with a square base, faces Asturias, and beyond that Gascony on its left side, which would be north, and other parts of Spain from the other sides. Gisemundus uses the term *Asturias*, a territorial designation, rather than Orosius's *Astures*, denoting the people who lived there under Roman rule. Things had changed since the fifth century as far as that part of Spain was concerned, but Gisemundus retained the designations of 'Vaccaeos, Celtiberi, et Oretani' as the tribes surrounding Hispania Ulterior without explanation. This is not without precedent, for Carolingian sources frequently referred to the eighth-century Avars as 'Huns' because they occupied the same space. Gisemundus followed typical Carolingian practice here as elsewhere in his compilation, using precisely what he needed of his sources and building on them where necessary.[156]

Relevant extracts from Isidore's *Etymologiae* follow Gisemundus' text. Isidore's book iii, chapters 7–13 (ff. 86v–89 r) treat numbers, arithmetic, and music, but above all geometry. In sum, Gisemundus' work, along with its Isidorian companions, clearly signals creativity in the compilation of practical quadrivial texts, using available materials to build something new and fitting the needs of the region's people.

The *Ripoll* Contra Iudaeos

One final text in Ripoll 106 casts some light on the social context of the intellectual activity in the Spanish March. This text, given the rubric *Gesta graecorum de passione Domini contra Iudaeos*, suggests the presence of a Jewish population in the Spanish March, and a comprehensive study of Jews in the Carolingian world remains a major desideratum.[157] Yet we do know from surviving evidence that at least some Carolingian-era scholars held and articulated negative attitudes towards Jews.[158] Along with Agobard of Lyon, Claudius of Turin, also an immigrant from Spain, has

---

[156] N. Lozovsky, 'Carolingian Geographical Tradition', 25–43.

[157] J. J. Contreni, 'Charlemagne and the Carolingians: the View from North America', *Cheiron* 37 (2002): 111–54. B. S. Bachrach, *Early Medieval Jewish Policy in Western Europe* (Minneapolis, 1977); and see now the work of Johannes Heil, cited in notes 158–9. For broader medieval context, K. R. Stow, *Alienated Minority: the Jews of Medieval Latin Europe* (Cambridge, MA, 1992); M. R. Cohen, *Under Crescent and Cross: the Jews in the Middle Ages* (Princeton, 1994); and C. Geisel, *Die Juden im Frankenreich: Von den Merovinger bis zum Tode Ludwigs des Frommen* (Frankfurt, 1998).

[158] On this larger question, see J. Heil, *Kompilation oder Konstruktion?: die Juden in den Pauluskommentaren des 9. Jahrhunderts* (Hanover, 1998).

received attention.[159] Work in Catalan has started to address the conditions of the tenth-century March, nearly contemporary with the inclusion of the *Gesta graecorum* in the Ripoll library; any local concern about Jews in the March arose from actual lived experience.[160] As such, Ripoll 106 could provide valuable clues about the religious diversity of the March and what Christian educators thought about it.

Despite this promising context, the *Gesta graecorum* text itself gives no outright indication of anti-Judaic sentiment amongst the clergy or laity of the March. The text is really a very early copy of the *Evangelium Nicodemi* (*Gospel of Nicodemus*), an apocryphal account of Jesus's trial before Pontius Pilate, his Crucifixion and Resurrection, and most intriguingly, his descent into Hell.[161] The themes of this Gospel first appeared in Greek and in the late-antique context of Christian efforts to confront Jews. The descent episode is clearly not based on the canonical Gospels, but rather is an expansion of a reference to such an event in the Apostle's Creed.[162] In the context of the ninth-century Spanish March, the text's appearance in a schoolbook of the Ripoll monastery suggests its appropriateness for young monks as they familiarized themselves with the story of Christ's redeeming power and victory over death, while also perhaps indicating a desire to stabilize local society by strengthening Christians in their own faith and even urging Jews to convert to Christianity. While some texts copied into Ripoll 106 were designed for students learning the liberal arts, several others were clearly meant for religious instruction. This is surely the correct context in which the *Gospel of Nicodemus* is to be understood.

After telling the story of the last days of Jesus on earth, the *Nicodemus* text begins to deviate markedly from the canonical Gospels on folios 129 r–133v of the Ripoll manuscript. Roman soldiers inform the Jewish leaders that

---

[159] J. Heil, 'Agobard, Amolo, das Kirchengut und die Juden von Lyon', *Francia* 25:1 for 1998 (1999): 39–76, as well as his ' Claudius von Turin – Eine Fallstudie zure Geschichte der Karolingerziet', *Zeitschrift für Geschichtswissenschaft* 45 (1997): 389-412 and Heil, 'Nos nescientes de hoc velle manere – "We Wish to Remain Ignorant about This": Timeless End, or Approaches to Reconceptualizing Eschatology after AD 800 (AM 6000)', *Traditio* 55 (2000): 73–103.

[160] D. Romano, 'Notes sobre l'activitat dels jueus a Catalunya l'any mil', in I. Ollich i Castanyer, ed. *Actes del Congrés Internacional Gerbert d'Orlhac i el seu temps: Catalunya i Europa a la fi del Ir mil.leni* (Vic, 1999), 697–700 with bibliography; M. Isabel Miró Montoliu, 'Els jueus i l'ensenyament de les primeres lletres', in ibid., 701–11; A. Mundó, 'Els jueus a Barcelona dels segles IX a l'XI', in *Catalunya romànica* 20 (Barcelona, 1992), 86–8, reprinted in *Obres completes I: Catalunya 1, de la romanitat a la sobirania* (Barcelona, 1998), 583–7.

[161] See the fuller treatment of this text in C. J. Chandler, 'A New View of a Catalonian *Gesta contra Iudaeos*: Ripoll 106 and the Jews of the Spanish March', in C. J. Chandler and S. A. Stofferahn, eds, *Discovery and Distinction in the Early Middle Ages: Studies in Honor of John J. Contreni* (Kalamazoo, 2013), 187–204.

[162] Z. Izydorczyk and J. D. Dubois, 'Introduction', in Z. Izydorczyk, ed., *The Medieval Gospel of Nicodemus: Texts, Intertexts, and Contexts in Western Europe* (Tempe, AZ, 1997), 17. J. Kroll, *Gott und Hölle: Der Mythos vom Descensuskampfe* (Leipzig, 1932), 83.

Jesus's body is not in the tomb, certain Jews bribe them to tell Pilate that the disciples have stolen the body, and the Jewish high priests come to believe in Jesus and proclaim the miracle of Christ's Resurrection. Nicodemus then enters the narrative and gives his witness to the miracle. Joseph of Arimathea also appears and gives his story. The reader learns that others besides Jesus had risen from the dead as well and that a man named Simeon had two sons, Leucius and Charinus, who had actually participated in this great Resurrection. Hastening along, the party finds these two brothers adoring wood fashioned into the sign of the Cross.

Ripoll 106 is one of only seven *Nicodemus* manuscripts that include the representation of the Cross in this particular respect; the others date from the later Middle Ages. The adoration of wood shaped into a cross could, in the early medieval Spanish March, have been understood in relation to the eighth- and ninth-century controversy over religious images. The controversy over religious images, of course, persisted into the ninth century in both the Greek and the Latin Christian worlds. In the West, the most outspoken critic of the Byzantine attitude to images was the hispanus Theodulf of Orléans; Claudius of Turin, another hispanus, went even further in his condemnation of representational images altogether.[163] It could have been that Muslims and Jews in Spain followed more strictly the scriptural prohibition against worshipping images, so Christians under their rule either adopted similarly rigid positions against images, or developed apologetic arguments to the contrary. At any rate there were greater differences in how members of the faiths understood God, yet those posed no significant barriers to cultural assimilation in Spain. Moreover, feasts of the Cross were ninth-century insertions into the liturgy elsewhere in the Carolingian realms.[164] The *Libellus* of the Paris Colloquy of 825 declared that the Cross was not an 'image' in the same sense as other, more controversial images. Despite that, Claudius rejected the cult of the Cross, rousing the ire of both Jonas and Dungal. The Cross was a prominent subject throughout Carolingian literature; writers from Einhard to Hrabanus Maurus, Dungal, and Agobard devoted energy to it.[165] In emphasizing the Cross as a symbol of salvation, the

---

[163] Theodulf's famous work against the adoration of images is the *Opus Caroli regis contra synodum (Libri Carolini)*, MGH *Leges 4 Conc. 2, Supplementum 1*, eds A. Freeman and P. Meyvaert (Hanover, 1998). See also D. Ganz, 'Theology and the Organization of Thought', in R. McKitterick, ed., *The New Cambridge Medieval History*, vol. 2, c.700–c.900 (Cambridge: Cambridge University Press, 1995), 758–85. See now T. F. X. Noble, *Images, Iconoclasm, and the Carolingians* (Philadelphia, 2009) for a full treatment of the controversy over religious images.

[164] Noble, *Images*, 194, 269–76, and 291; C. Chazelle, *The Crucified God in the Carolingian Era: Theology and Art of Christ's Passion* (Cambridge, 2001), 139–42.

[165] Noble, *Images*, 276–7, 309–49.

Gospel of Nicodemus thus served to support the use of a material object in worship.[166]

The *Gospel of Nicodemus* in Ripoll 106 also treats the closely related *Descensus*, narratively ushering the reader down into Hell. Jesus enters the world of the dead, but instead of falling into the enemy's power, saves the dead just as he saved the living with his Cross. The *rex gloriae* then extends his hand and announces that those who follow him can overcome damnation by the wood of the Cross, just as he did. Authors across the Carolingian realms were familiar with these ideas. Audradus of Sens, Notker, John Scottus, Otfrid of Weissenburg, and the anonymous *Heliand* author all wrote on the *Descensus* theme, emphasizing divine victory over death, sin, and Satan.[167] Celia Chazelle, while concentrating on a different overall theme, shows through her own citation of their works that these 'mainstream' Carolingian authors knew the same language as the *Evangelium Nicodemi* used.[168] They knew the text; its appearance in the Spanish March was not unique. Yet it will be observed that the copy of *Nicodemus* in Ripoll 106 did not arrive through Carolingian channels, but rather came from Spain. Amongst the group of *Nicodemus* manuscripts from the peninsula, the copy in Ripoll 106 is one of the oldest and belongs to the C family of manuscripts, which alone from the Spanish branch of transmission mentions the wood of the Cross. Indeed Zbigniew Izydorczyk points out that Spain was important for the transmission of the *Nicodemus* text.[169] Further study can perhaps determine whether at least some elements of the Carolingian 'mainstream' received the text via Spain in the first place.

CONCLUSIONS

Catalonian culture was a dynamic creation of the fusion of tradition received from the Visigothic kingdom, as seen in law and the texts of Isidore, with the imported texts from beyond the Pyrenees. This dynamic need not be seen as tension or in any way antagonistic, for the Carolingian cultural programme itself featured Gregory the Great, Isidore, and Bede, just as the rich cultural heritage of the Visigothic period embraced foreign as well as indigenous authors. Usuard in the ninth century and others in

---

[166] Ibid., 775 on Claudius removing crosses even from churches in Turin; 287–313 on Claudius, his teaching, his activity, and responses to him. Even Theodulf recognized the Cross as a *res sacrata* rather than an 'image': *Opus Caroli regis*, 2.26–20. For Carolingian thoughts on the Crucifixion more generally, see Chazelle, *The Crucified God*, esp. 39–52 for Theodulf and the *Opus Caroli regis* in particular. Noble, *Images*, 158–206 treats the *Opus* in detail.

[167] Chandler, 'A New View', 197–8.   [168] Chazelle, *The Crucified God*, 133–4.

[169] See Z. Izydorczyk, *Manuscripts of the Evangelium Nicodemi: a Census* (Toronto, 1993), 150.

the tenth are examples of the interchange across the Pyrenees. The result of this fusion is embodied in the careers of two figures from the post-Carolingian period. Gerbert of Aurillac is famous for having travelled to the March to take in its superior quadrivial learning in the late tenth century, while the lesser-known but regionally famous Oliba went to some lengths to strengthen cultural ties between Catalonia and Francia in the early eleventh century, even as political bonds are held to have weakened. Many of the texts he gathered during his abbacy (1008–46) to quadruple Ripoll's stock came from the Frankish heartland.[170] Oliba's programme, although not properly understood as part of the Carolingian *renovatio*, certainly built on its foundations and drew heavily from its achievements.[171] Manuscript Ripoll 40, the eleventh-century codex containing Carolingian legal material, is evidence of the Carolingian legacy to Oliba.

It is misguided, therefore, to attribute the entirety of cultural development in the Spanish March to its Visigothic patrimony, just as it would be to label it simply 'Carolingian'. Yet 'Carolingian' enterprises are in large part defined by the interplay between centre and regions. In terms of politics, this manifested itself through kings finding ways to extend patronage to local players, whether monasteries or individuals, or installing 'their' bishops and counts. In the case of culture, the dynamic is evident in local variations on common, court-sponsored themes. When the locals in the March had access to them, they turned to 'Carolingian' models, like Bede, Usuard, or the *Dionysio-Hadriana*. Otherwise, they were free to copy Visigothic-era texts that fit their needs for biblical, patristic, or legal purposes. By the tenth century, the script in Catalonia was Carolingian minuscule, its monastic rule Benedictine, and its ecclesiastical province that of Narbonne. Its schools featured Carolingian as well as Visigothic-era texts, even as they forged relationships with institutions north of the Pyrenees and south of the Ebro. It is reasonable to conclude that, culturally as well as politically, Catalonia was a creation of the dynamism fostered when the Carolingian renaissance reached the Spanish March. During the tenth century, this culture was free to engage the wider world increasingly on its own terms. The chapter that follows will explore what those terms were.

---

[170] P. Riché, *Ecoles et enseignement*, 158–61.
[171] On Oliba's career, R. d'Abadal i de Vinyals, *L'abat Oliba, bisbe de Vic, i la seva època* (Barcelona, 1948). Reprinted in *Dels visigots als catalans*, 141–278.

Chapter 6

THE MARCH TOWARDS SOVEREIGNTY?
(947–988)

In the summer of 987, Borrell II, count of Barcelona, gave to the priest Donadeo two properties in Osona and Manresa.[1] The charter recording the gift is interesting and significant in many respects. First, it shows Borrell's authority outside the county of Barcelona, for indeed he was count of Osona and Manresa as well, and owned land in those areas in addition to exercising political jurisdiction there. He is recorded as giving to Donadeo the same properties the priest's father, Galindo, had earlier held, which indicates a patronage relationship between the two families. The document specifies that the properties were included within the *termini* of castles and thus highlights the basic sociopolitical organization of these areas in the tenth-century Spanish March. And in an unusual scribal practice, Altemirus, the priest (*presbiter*) who drew up the document, used Greek letters to spell his name and title (Αλμθημυροζ πρεσβυτερ), revealing that some Greek was included in the curriculum somewhere in the Spanish March.[2] Evidence considered in the previous chapters hints that there was knowledge of Greek at the monastery of Santa Maria de Ripoll. For understanding the political links between the Spanish March and the Frankish monarchy, however, this charter's dating clause carries even more significance. Altemirus dated the donation to '*IIII idus iulii, Christo regnante regem expectante*', a phrase that refuses to recognize the succession of Hugh Capet after the death of young Louis V, the last Carolingian king. Hugh's accession to the throne has for a long time marked not only the definitive end

---

[1] CC 4, no. 1523.

[2] M. Zimmermann, *Écrire et lire en Catalogne (IX–XII siècle)* (Madrid, 2003), 695–723. See also his earlier 'La connaissance du grec en Catalogne du IXe au XIe siècles', in M. Sot, ed., *Haut Moyen Âge: culture, education et société. Études offertes à Pierre Riché* (La Garenne-Colombes, 1990), 493–516 and A. Mundó, 'La cultura i els llibres [a Catalunya, ss. VIII a XII]', in *Obres completes*, vol. 1 (Barcelona, 1998), 462–83. See also B. M. Kaczynski, *Greek in the Carolingian Age: the St Gall manuscripts* (Cambridge, MA, 1988), 33–42 and W. Berschin, *Greek Letters and the Latin Middle Ages, from Jerome to Nicholas of Cusa* (Washington, DC, 1988), 126–32.

of the Carolingian dynasty, but also of the effective integration of the Spanish March to the kingdom via ties to the monarchy.

For generations of historians, the events of the years 985–8 have represented the ultimate detachment of Catalonia from the Frankish kingdom.[3] It is indeed difficult to conclude otherwise. In these years, the Muslim leader al-Mansur sacked Barcelona, taking prisoners and booty; Borrell, count of Barcelona, Girona, Osona, and Urgell, sought military aid from the king of the Franks, Lothar; Hugh Capet succeeded to the throne of the West Frankish kingdom; Borrell repeated to the new king his request for aid but did not travel to Francia to perform homage to Hugh in order to receive it. The sources for the middle and late 980s are well studied for the evidence they give on the relationships between counts and kings. But is it evidence of a severing of ties? A more nuanced view would hold that the entire course of the tenth century, especially the career of Borrell (947–93), saw the more gradual change in conditions that the crises of 985–8 punctuated. Charters showed deference to kings in their dating clauses, some of which also include rhetoric upholding the legitimacy of the Carolingian line. The preceding pages have served to highlight Catalonia's history as part of the Carolingian empire, pointing out the ways in which relationships with people and ideas north of the Pyrenean region influenced its development into the tenth century. This final chapter follows the same scheme, even as it almost reverses the direction of perspective. That is, during the later tenth century, rather than kings forging links of integration such as appointing counts, encouraging approved religious observances, and the like, it was the counts, bishops, and abbots of the Spanish March who sought to maintain links to the monarchy. This chapter points out ways the received interpretations can be revised in the light of more recent work on early medieval politics, and how our understanding changes when we approach the evidence without a sense of inevitability of Catalonian independence in mind. For the conquering Carolingians building and

---

[3] P. Freedman, 'Symbolic Implications of the Events of 985–988', in *Symposium internacional*, vol. 1, 117–29. See also the work he cites, Abadal, *Els primers comtes catalans*, Biografies Catalanes (Barcelona, 1958). Moreover, as Freedman noted, many works, especially those of Michel Zimmerman, are very important to any discussion of the transition of Catalonia from Carolingian Spanish March to sovereign principality. See a theme running through the work of M. Zimmermann, especially 'Aux origines de la Catalogne. Geographie politique et affirmation nationale', *Le Moyen Âge* 89 (1983): 5–40; the articles collected in his *En els orígens de Catalunya: emancipació política i afirmació cultural*, trans. into Catalan by A. Bentué (Barcelona, 1989); M. Zimmermann, 'La Catalogne de Gerbert', in N. Charbonnel and J.-E. Iung, eds, *Gerbert l'européen: Actes du colloque d'Aurillac 4–7 juin 1996* (Aurillac, 1997), 79–101; 'Hugues Capet et Borell. À propos de l'«independence» de la Catalogne', in X. Barral i Altet, D. Iogna-Prat, A. Manuel Mundó, J. M. Salrach and M. Zimmermann, eds, *Catalunya i França meridional a l'entorn de l'any Mil* (Barcelona, 1991), 59–64 and 'Naissance d'une principauté: Barcelone et les autres comtés catalans aux alentours de l'an Mil', in ibid., 111–35.

holding an empire in the eighth and ninth centuries, it was important for kings to build relationships with local figures in the Spanish March. In the tenth century, rather than seek independence, figures in the March needed ties to the Carolingian kings as a basis to legitimate their positions locally. When approaching this crucial period from the ninth century rather than from the eleventh, continuity becomes more apparent, and we can see how the institutions the Carolingians cultivated formed the basis of Catalonian political structures.

This chapter will first address the historiography of the Catalonian counts from the early modern period to the twentieth century. This effort at once reveals how for centuries nationalist perspectives became entangled with historical interpretations and seeks to correct that trend. Next, I offer a brief study of how surviving texts portray the relationships between Carolingian kings and the counts of the Spanish March. I add an overview of related ecclesiastical affairs during the middle and later parts of the tenth century. The chapter then returns to the business of counts and kings, with special emphasis on Borrell II, count of Barcelona, Girona, Osona, Cerdanya, and Urgell, whose career spanned most of the second half of the tenth century. His actions as count, both within his domains and in terms of his relationships with other powerful figures, have long stood as laying the foundation for an independent Catalonia that opened up to the world and turned away from the Frankish kings. A reconsideration of the evidence, however, will allow for a more nuanced understanding that embraces continuity. In this way, the events of the 980s mark the end of Carolingian Catalonia only because they brought about the end of the Carolingian dynasty, not because they allowed the rulers of the Spanish March to achieve independence.

CHARACTERIZING THE COUNTS

Of all the modern ideologies that can influence interpretations of early medieval politics and society, nationalism is certainly amongst the unwarranted and unwelcome. The practical independence of the counts of the Spanish March has been a contentious issue in historiography since at least the seventeenth century, when the modern study of the history of the Spanish March began in the context of the struggle between France and Spain for control of Catalonia.[4] Catalan independence from either modern state later became a prominent

---

[4] A more detailed discussion of the historiography of the Spanish March can be found in Chandler, 'Carolingian Catalonia: the Spanish March and the Franks, c.750–c.1050', *History Compass* 11 (2013): 739–50.

theme in the writing of history. Pierre de Marca, a magistrate, churchman, and governor of Catalonia in the middle of the seventeenth century, was the first to undertake a serious study of the region. In 1640, Catalonia, along with Portugal, revolted against rule from Madrid, paving the way for a brief period of French control. After the Treaty of the Pyrenees (1660) by which Spain ceded northern Catalonia to France, de Marca was a member of the commission charged with setting the boundary between the two countries.[5] Later, he served as bishop of Toulouse, the city that had functioned as the administrative centre in the early formation of the Spanish March under the Carolingians. Long interested in local histories and diligent in the study of archival sources, de Marca composed a geographical and historical account of Catalonia, the province that for much of his adult life he had been dedicated to administering on behalf of the French crown.[6] His secretary, Etienne Baluze, later Richelieu's librarian and famous as a scholar and editor of medieval source texts, edited, finished, and greatly expanded de Marca's history and augmented it with documentary appendices. Many of the manuscript originals of the documents, some preserved by the earlier work of the Catalan scholar Jeroni Pujades,[7] have since been lost, making these efforts quite valuable to modern historical scholarship. Yet it has been de Marca's characterization of the counts that set the stage for nationalist interpretations of early medieval history. An agent of the French crown, de Marca cast the independently acting counts of the Spanish March as usurpers of royal authority.

The eighteenth and nineteenth centuries also saw strenuous efforts to preserve and study the manuscripts related to the early medieval history of the Spanish March. The nearby French region of Languedoc came under the scrutiny of the Benedictines Dom Joseph Vaissette and Dom Claude Devic, whose endeavours appeared in several volumes beginning in 1730.[8] Almost a full century later, the Dominican friar Jaime Villanueva travelled throughout Spain in order ultimately to publish the historical

---

[5] For these developments and their influence on nationalist thought, see P. Sahlins, *Boundaries: the Making of Spain and France in the Pyrenees* (Berkeley, 1989).

[6] P. de Marca, *Marca Hispanica sive limes hispanicus* (Toulouse, 1688).

[7] J. Pujades, *Coronica Universal del Principat de Cathalunya* (Barcelona, 1609) available online at http://bib.cervantesvirtual.com/servlet/SirveObras/06922741089536262977857/index.htm as of 16 July 2017.

[8] J. Vaisette and C. Devic, *Histoire générale de Languedoc* (Toulouse, re-edited in 1875) available online at http://openlibrary.org/books/OL14011752M/Histoire_g%C3%A9n%C3%A9grale_de_Languedoc_avec_des_notes_et_les_pi%C3%A8ces_justificatives_par_Cl._Devic_J._Vaissete as of 16 July 2017.

and liturgical texts of all that country's churches.[9] Cities, churches, and monasteries located in places where Catalan language and culture throve were included in both works. The division between Spain and France in the Pyrenees held firm, keeping the scholarly efforts confined by the mountains.

Most influential of all efforts in this period to preserve manuscripts was the activity at the Archive of the Crown of Aragon in Barcelona. Prosper de Bofarull became archivist in 1814 and set about reorganizing and augmenting the archive's holdings. Like de Marca, Bofarull made a significant contribution to the study of the Carolingian March. He especially set out to remedy de Marca's bias against the counts who had ruled the Spanish March independently in the late Carolingian period and whom de Marca had painted as traitors. Bofarull defended Catalan national independence by indicating the historical developments, which were neither usurpation nor treason, that resulted in the counts of the Spanish March, and of Barcelona in particular, achieving independence by the end of the tenth century.[10]

Since the 1990s, studies have emphasized the fluidity of ethnic identity and have demonstrated that no modern national identity can be traced in an unbroken line to the post-Roman or even Carolingian periods. In certain European areas, however, nationalist sentiment has persisted in medievalist scholarship right through the twentieth century and into the twenty-first.[11] This is true for Catalonia, now of course a semi-autonomous region within Spain and for long a region with a proud history independent from that of the rest of Spain. In particular, Catalan historiography, based on Bofarull's defence of the counts, has regarded the late Carolingian period (from the 870s to the 980s) as the period of 'national formation' when 'our counts' marched 'our country' to 'sovereignty'.[12] Leading Catalan historians used such language, even as they warned against reading modern, nationalist style state-formation into the events of the tenth-century Spanish March. While no one now would overtly argue that the counts of the tenth century were attempting to create modern Catalonia, subtle nationalism remains embedded in the language historians use even in more recent studies of the period. In part, this is because of a turn in the last decades to social history, which largely accepts as settled the issues of political history addressed in earlier

---

[9] J. Villanueva, *Viage literario a las iglesias de España*, 22 vols. (Madrid, 1802–52) available online at http://archive.org/search.php?query=creator%3A%22Villanueva%2C+Jaime%2C+1766–1824%22 as of 16 July 2017.

[10] P. de Bofarull i Mascaró, *Los condes de Barcelona vindicados* (Barcelona, 1836).

[11] See the related discussion in P. J. Geary, *The Myth of Nations* (Princeton, 2003).

[12] Abadal, *Els primers comtes catalans*, especially 291–341. Salrach, *El procés*, even from the title itself.

generations. This chapter questions and corrects this trend by examining the history of the tenth-century Spanish March, not to pinpoint the constitutional birth of Catalonia, but rather to explain the actions of counts and bishops in the March vis-à-vis the Frankish kings in the terms of early medieval political culture. Simply put, as seen from the March, kings were still the centres of political institutions.

The time has come to correct the use of problematic expressions in the classic – and still in many ways valuable – works on the subject, those by Ramon d'Abadal i de Vinyals and Josep Maria Salrach. Expressions like 'our counts' and its derivatives are peppered throughout Abadal's works. Writing during the dictatorship of Francisco Franco, Abadal focused on the attempt to discern Catalonia's de facto independence during the tenth century, admitting that *de jure* independence did not come until 1258. He realized the nationalism and teleology that factor into historical studies of this sort but in the end could not fully escape them while engaged in constitutional history. For example, he consistently referred to the territory as 'our counties' and the men who governed them as 'our counts'; he characterized a gathering of counts and bishops in 977 'as if they wanted to prefigure . . . the unity of the country that it would later have'.[13] A different reading can construe Abadal's meaning as more like 'the counts/counties we are concerned with in this discussion', but his historical work could not truly break away from his own political career and activism. Nothing much changed between Abadal's account in the 1950s and Salrach's own, obviously nationalistic, celebratory 1978 exposition (published only a few years after Franco's death), which in many respects has remained the best overview of the period. Salrach's major book of 1987, *El procés de feudalització*, still uses the expression 'comtes/comtats catalans' and others, especially 'la terra catalana'. Even in more recent works, he reiterates the same grand narrative.[14] More recently, Michel Zimmermann stated that it is the historian's task to avoid nationalism and anachronism, and that modern historians cannot really even use the term 'Catalonia' except in inverted commas to show that we do not really mean to say that the term or concept behind it existed in the tenth century. Yet in his search for the origins of sovereignty, he falls into the same trap, stating that in 985 'Catalonia is not just a principality with

---

[13] Abadal, *Els primers comtes catalans*, 300–1.

[14] J. M. Salrach, 'La Catalunya comtal', in *Princeses de terres llunyanes: Catalunya i Hongria a la edat mitjana* (Barcelona, 2009), 73–88, in which his overview continues to perpetuate an ethnically charged, 'Goths vs Franks' interpretation of political culture, against which various parts of the present study argue.

neither name nor institution; it is a principality without a prince'.[15] By that he means that the counts of Barcelona possessed superior wealth and position in relation to the other counts in the region, who in turn recognized that superiority but without legal mechanism or title. So even though there was no Catalonia in the modern sense, the term and concept continue to be projected back onto the tenth century.

The impact of the Franco regime on the historiography of early medieval Catalonia was very strong indeed. For much of the twentieth century, the bulk of scholarship on the political structures of the early medieval Spanish March focused on either the development, or formation, of an independent principality.[16] Catalan scholars, especially, tried to determine the constitutional birth of their nation. Yet the end of 'Carolingian' Catalonia, that is, the definitive moment of Catalonia's political separation from the Frankish kingdom, is impossible to pinpoint because it was a process rather than a singular event, similar to its integration into the Carolingian empire during the late eighth and ninth centuries. Furthermore, the local ruling elites in tenth-century Catalonia were not seeking constitutional independence as fervently as twentieth-century Catalan historians. Counts acted autonomously, yet locals used language recognizing the Frankish monarchy in their charters. Bishops remained warm to kings even while they abstained from Frankish church councils. This was a stance rooted in the history of the ninth century. Clearly, the constitutional approach is unhelpful.

Standing in the shadow of these classic interpretations, those interested in the region during its ninth- and tenth-century history have considered the question of political development pretty well settled. They have, for good reason, given their attention to other issues of importance. Yet even Michel Zimmermann's magnum opus and body of work on literate culture highlights the ways that Catalonia was politically, as well as culturally, independent from the Carolingian world.[17] Meanwhile, others have turned to economic history, including Salrach himself, or to social history, in just about all cases focusing intently on the local or regional levels.[18] Archaeologists have been very active and very important

[15] M. Zimmermann, 'La formació d'una sobirania catalana (785–988)', in *Catalunya a l'època carolíngia: art i cultura abans del romànic (segles IX i X)* (Barcelona, 1999), 41–7 at 46, quoted from English translation at 442.

[16] Abadal, *Els primers comtes catalans*, 291–341. Salrach, *El procés*. More recently, M. Zimmermann, 'La formació d'una sobirania'.

[17] Zimmermann, *Écrire et lire*, as Chapter 5 in this volume addresses.

[18] The literature is rich. See, for example, J. Salrach, 'Conquesta de l'espai agrari i conflictes per la terra a la Catalunya carolíngia i comtal', in *Catalunya i França meridional a l'entorn de l'any Mil* (Barcelona, 1991), 203–11; Salrach, 'Entre l'Estat antic i feudal. Mutacions socials i dinàmica

in the last two decades or so, as well.[19] The most recent books on what can be termed political history, by Jonathan Jarrett and Josep Maria Salrach, are not concerned with the relationship between the Spanish March and the Frankish kingdoms, but with 'pathways of power' or 'justice and power' within 'Catalonia' itself.[20] That is to say, they bypass the question of the relationship of the Spanish March to the Carolingian monarchy.

Approached from a perspective that consciously and assiduously avoids teleology, 'Catalonia' in the tenth century emerges as a region whose political and social leaders imagined themselves as subjects within the Frankish kingdom. Likewise, kings involved themselves in the affairs of the Spanish March when necessary. In the end, a paradox emerges. The history of the March in the tenth century, when it supposedly detached from the kingdom, is similar in several ways to that of the ninth, when it was demonstrably integrated into Carolingian empire. Frankish kings issued diplomas for recipients in the March, all of whom sought royal intervention in their affairs, while at the same time it cannot be said that royal authority stood behind the governance or diplomacy the region's counts and bishops conducted. Earlier chapters of this book have addressed important questions about the nature of the Carolingian Empire and the tensions between its centralizing impetus and regional differences. This last reveals how those tensions resulted not in a breaking of links between the March and the monarchy, but rather of their exhaustion.

REPRESENTATIONS OF AND RELATIONS WITH KINGS

Once again, this study will turn to royal diplomas as well as charters produced in the Spanish March. The same advantages and cautions apply for the purposes of this chapter as for others in the book, with a slight

---

político-militar a l'Occident carolingi i als comtats catalans', in *Symposium internacional*, vol. 1, 191–252; J. F. Ruiz Domenech, 'Las Estructuras Familiares Catalanes en la alta Edad Media', *Cuadernos de Arqueología e Historia de la Ciudad* 16 (1975): 69–123; J. Bolòs, 'Onomàstica i poblament a la Catalunya septentrional a l'alta edat mitjana', in P. Sénac, ed., *Histoire et Archéologie des terres catalanes au Moyen Age* (Perpignan, 1995), 49–65.

[19] See, again amongst many others, G. Boto Varela, 'Topografía de los monasteries de la marca de Hispania (ca. 800–ca. 1030)', in *Monjes i monasteries hispanos en la alta edad media* (Aguilar de Campoo, 2006), 149–203; J. A. Adell i Gisbert and J. J. Menchon i Bes, 'Les fortificacions de la frontera meridional dels comtats catalans, o les fortificacions de la Marca Superior del Al-Àndalus', *Lambard: Estudis d'Art Medieval* 17 (2004–5): 65–84.

[20] J. Jarrett, *Rulers and Ruled in Frontier Catalonia, 880–1010: Pathways of Power* (London, 2010) and J. M. Salrach, *Justícia i poder a Catalunya abans de l'any mil* (Vic, 2013). J. Jarrett, 'Caliph, King, or Grandfather: Strategies of Legitimization on the Spanish March in the Reign of Lothar III', *The Mediaeval Journal* 1 (2011): 1–22 does examine the ties between count and king.

change in emphasis for certain issues that are important for questions about the later tenth century. Chief amongst those issues is the use of titles. As was evident for earlier periods, charters and diplomas were not merely tools for conveying information about legal rights. They also communicated ideas about how the powers behind their drafting saw themselves and others in their world. Royal diplomas can, therefore, reveal what kings wished to be communicated when they engaged with parties from the Spanish March. Meanwhile, charters produced in the March can show how counts projected their authority and claimed status. The titles deployed and the phraseology used to date local charters tell us how locals understood the power and authority of both kings and their own counts.[21]

Again, almost all of the locally produced charters that survive to the present day do so because they were preserved in monastery and church archives, and as such all the provisos and cautions apply to their interpretation as we saw in earlier phases of this study. Cartulary copies may contain errors or changes to the texts, but for the most part the use of titles and especially dating clauses can be usefully charted. Those who composed charters in their own time had more reason to demonstrate the authority of the count or king than later copyists. Losses even of royal documents have occurred over the centuries, so at times we are left with reconstructions, both medieval and modern. Sometimes, because of natural disaster or military raid, documents could be destroyed. On those occasions, witnesses would be mustered to reconstruct documents based on memories, a practice established in Visigothic law.[22] A few royal diplomas were lost and now can only be deduced from later material. Because Carolingian kings routinely granted confirmations of rights and properties their predecessors had made, documents refer to earlier grants that may no longer survive.[23] Kings would not only uphold but also extend grants made by their predecessors, sometimes at the behest of intermediary parties, so by reading the grants that claim to be confirmations we can see the maintenance of relationships between the monarchs and their subjects in the Spanish March.[24]

---

[21] On titles, M. Zimmermann, 'Catalogne et Regnum francorum: les enseignements de la titulature comtale', in *Symposium internacional*, vol. 2, 209–63.

[22] See the stimulating treatment in J. A. Bowman, *Shifting Landmarks: Property, Proof and Dispute in Catalonia around the Year 1000* (Ithaca, 2004), 151–64.

[23] Citations to royal diplomas below include the pages containing editorial explanations of reconstruction on a case-by-case basis.

[24] G. Koziol, *The Politics of Memory and Identity in Carolingian Royal Diplomas: the West Frankish Kingdom (840–987)* (Turnhout, 2012), 69–74 on intercessors and 99 for confirmations.

The last Carolingians were not 'do-nothing' kings.[25] On the contrary, evidence shows them to have been quite active, even in regard to the Spanish March, working to maintain the instruments of kingship in the changed circumstances of the tenth century. Charles the Simple's son Louis IV, who returned from exile in England to assume the throne in 936, features in no fewer than ten documents related to parties in the Spanish March.[26] Early in his reign, the king confirmed the properties and immunity of the monastery of Santa Maria de Ripoll.[27] During the 940s, a controversy revolved around the relationship between the monasteries of Banyoles and Sant Pere de Rodes. For a time, Sant Pere was subordinated, but two royal grants ensured its independence, immunity, and right to elect abbots.[28] The existence of the second diploma may serve as evidence that the first act needed strengthening. As the dust was settling on that issue, the king handed over the nearby castle (now Castelló d'Empúries) to the authority of Abbot Hildesindus of Sant Pere.[29] In 952 he granted immunity to the monastery of Cuixà.[30] Two diplomas, one concerning the rights and properties of the convent of Sant Pere de les Puel.les and the other those of Sant Cugat, both lost in the sack of Barcelona in 985, had to be reconstructed.[31] The absence of a later royal confirmation prevented Abadal from piecing together the language for Sant Pere de les Puel.les, but a later document from Lothar III for Sant Cugat provides the basis for understanding what the lost document entailed. For present purposes, the details of which villas were owned by Sant Cugat and what their boundaries were are less important than the royal act itself. A new monastery founded near the middle of the century, Santa Cecília de Montserrat, received confirmation of its immunity thanks to the intervention of Louis's wife Gerberga and Count Odalric.[32] Lest it seem that monasteries were the only concerns that Louis had in the Spanish March, two documents indicate his dealings with other parties. Wifred-Borrell left the right to mints to the bishop of Vic, specifying that they had to obtain royal permission to keep it. The traces of a document no longer extant suggest that Bishop Gotmar did exactly that. Gotmar also intervened to secure immunity for three brothers, one a priest, for their properties in Girona and Besalú.[33] Monasteries, counts, and bishops throughout the Spanish March clearly

---

[25] For a rehabilitation of these kings' reputations after a long period of scorn, R. McKitterick, *The Frankish Kingdoms under the Carolingians, 751–987* (London, 1983), 305–39.

[26] Koziol, *The Politics of Memory*, 85–8, with 89–91 on the tricky issue of the new king's 'accession acts' to recipients in Burgundy; Abadal, *Els primers comtes*, 271–90.

[27] CC 2, 159–65.   [28] CC 2, 226–8 and 229–31.   [29] CC 2, 232.   [30] CC 2, 91–3.

[31] CC 2, 74 and 191–3; see also Bowman, *Shifting Landmarks*, 156–7.   [32] CC 2, 255–7.

[33] CC 2, 300–1 and 387–90.

valued and maintained their relationships with the king, who in turn acted the part of a good ruler.

Although not the last king of the Carolingian dynasty, Louis's son and successor Lothar III was the last king to have a meaningful reign, as his son Louis V held the crown for only a matter of months. For Lothar's reign (954–86) eight diplomas are known to have been issued for recipients in the Spanish March, and seven of those acts were confirmations.[34] This fact has led the king to be viewed as distant and only passively involved in the affairs of the March. But instead he should be understood as maintaining a presence in the region, especially as royal authority was still very much recognized as the source of legal legitimacy there.[35] Important monasteries especially sought royal confirmations. Cuixà won such recognition thanks to the intercession of Queen Gerberga, Lothar's mother, who stepped in on behalf of monasteries in the Spanish March during her husband's reign.[36] The monastery of Santa Maria de Ripoll, already a prestigious and powerful institution in the Spanish March and supported by the comital dynasty of Barcelona, Osona, Urgell, and Girona, and their relatives in Cerdanya and Besalú, still sought royal confirmation for its rights, which Lothar was apparently happy to grant.[37] Abbot Sunyer came to the king in Laon from the *partibus Gothici*, no short journey, in 968 to receive a grant to rule two monasteries, to both of which the king confirmed properties and privileges.[38] Decades after his father had been called to intervene in the affairs of Sant Pere de Rodes, Lothar confirmed the monastery's immunity in 982.[39] Lothar's last grant for a party in the Spanish March was aimed at remedying the destruction of documents resulting from the sack of Barcelona in 985.[40] This document was issued for the monastery of Sant Cugat, and in typical Carolingian fashion the monastery was confirmed in its rights to property, immunity, and election of the abbot. Again, we see that kings did intervene, not least because their commands were thought necessary by their subjects in the Spanish March, even if the royal

---

[34] This compares to a full dozen acts involving Count Arnulf of Flanders and monasteries related to him, four more than for all of the Spanish March and the most of all recipients of Lothar's diplomas: Koziol, *The Politics of Memory*, 259–61. Flanders was an area crucial to Lothar's power.

[35] J. Jarrett, 'Caliph, King, or Grandfather: Strategies of Legitimization on the Spanish March in the Reign of Lothar III', *The Mediaeval Journal* 1 (2011): 1–22, provides a good analysis of the role of the monarchy in the mindset of counts in the Spanish March.

[36] CC 2, 94–8.

[37] CC 2, 166–74. See Abadal's discussion of the circumstances of this diploma's production, including the considerable expansion of Ripoll's holdings.

[38] CC 2, 202–4.   [39] CC 2, 235–44.   [40] CC 2, 194–200.

presence was not constant.[41] It is also striking that large and wealthy monasteries were the ones that received most of the royal confirmations of rights. In many respects, the royal patronage of such houses here mirrors the situation in other areas of the Carolingian realms. Indeed, royal backing was an important factor determining why some monasteries became rich and important. On the one hand, it might seem that those powerful institutions would need such support least, but on the other, they remained the kings' primary connections to the region, the last bonds between monarch and March.

Michel Zimmermann notes, as an important reminder about the context of the tenth century, that distancing from royal authority was common to the entire West Frankish kingdom.[42] Yet the counts, bishops, abbots, and others in the Spanish March continued to rely on royal authority throughout the tenth century. Owing in large degree to the Visigothic legacy, locals continued to hold kings to be the foundation of legitimate, legal order.[43] Working from the proposition that the dating of documents is not simply a way to organize records but also an opportunity to show political alignments, historians have tried to mine the dating clauses of charters to understand more about the relationships between regional magnates and kings.[44] Nowhere is this truer than the Spanish March. Zimmermann goes so far as to claim that during the reign of Radulf (923–36), the counts of the Spanish March 'were in a state of insurrection', based on the circumlocutions employed in dating clauses.[45] This has been an important issue in modern historiography for a long time, as the review of scholarship at the beginning of this chapter shows. It continued to capture the attention of historians right through the twentieth century, and in a volume observing the one-thousandth anniversary of the accession of Hugh Capet, further studies on West Frankish and Catalonian political activity used the dating clauses in documents to

---

[41] For additional diplomas of Lothar: CC 2, 395; the existence of the document is known only in a reference in a later papal bull. See below, in the context of comital authority or 'sovereignty', for two other diplomas Lothar issued: CC 2, 210–14; CC 2, 393–4.

[42] M. Zimmermann, 'La formació d'una sobirania', 41–7 (English at 440).

[43] Visigothic law stated that royal grants were inviolable and fully alienable: *Liber iudiciorum sive Lex Visigothorum*, 5.2 in *Leges Visigothorum*, ed. K. Zeumer, *MGH LL nat. Germ.* 1 (Hanover, 1901, repr. 2005), 33–456, at 21–211. Jarrett, 'Caliph, King, or Grandfather?', 14; P. Bonnassie, 'From the Rhône to Galicia: Origins and Modalities of the Feudal Order', in J. Birrell, trans., *From Slavery to Feudalism in South-Western Europe* (Cambridge, 1991), 104–31, at 107.

[44] H. Fichtenau, '"Politische Datierung" des frühen Mittelalters', in *Intitulatio II*, ed. H. Wolfram (Vienna, 1973), 453–540.

[45] Zimmermann, 'La formació d'una sobirania', 41–7 (English at 440); see note 2 in this chapter and further discussion later on. He points out that a little later, the royal genealogies registered that Catalonia (*ipsa terra*) remained without a king for seven years (*sine rege annos septem*).

chart loyalty to the Carolingian kings.[46] Charters reflect that affairs were conducted 'while awaiting a king' (*rege expectante*), or are dated from the reign of Christ (*Christo regnante*) or from the years following the death of the latest Carolingian. I return to this issue further on in this chapter.

Modern scholarship has also paid careful attention to the titles bestowed upon the region's counts in surviving documents. The most illustrious, *princeps*, was used to honour Wifred the Hairy's memory, as first seen in 906. Wifred-Borrell and Sunyer also used it for themselves to reinforce their own authority by connecting it to their father's. In a later generation, *princeps* became almost standard when used by the leading member of a comital family in the Spanish March, whether based in Barcelona or Empúries.[47] The titles associated with counts in documents may signal an upgrading of comital power, as kings could no longer intervene in local affairs. They used regular titles like *comes*, enhanced with hyperbolic terms like *inclitus, gloriosissimus, illustrissimus, reverentissimus*.[48] During the tenth century, the counts of Barcelona even imitated kings by the use of *gratia Dei*,[49] while, as noted above, across the region counts asserted their status relative to one another by using the title *marchio*.[50] Yet as the examples of Louis IV and Lothar III show, kings did occasionally play a role in local business, lending royal support to claims of property and rights. Meanwhile, no count in the Spanish March ever took the title of king.

On the contrary, counts continued to travel to kings, albeit sporadically, during the tenth century on behalf of churches in the March. Wifred, count of Besalú (d. 957) was the last count in the Spanish March to pay homage to a Frankish king, and did so in the context of a revolt against his own, comital authority.[51] Clearly this was a case of the count relying on royal authority to strengthen his own position in the March. Nevertheless, scribes throughout the region used Frankish regnal years in document dating clauses. Monastic libraries and scriptoria kept royal genealogies up to date, and scribes remembered that royal grant was the foundation of legal order and comital power over deserted fiscal

---

[46] See the contributions of J. Dufour, 'Obédience respective des Carolingiens et des Capétiens (fin Xe siècle-début XIe siècle)', in X. Barral i Altet, D. Iogna-Prat et al., eds, *Catalunya i França meridional a l'entorn de l'any Mil* (Barcelona, 1991), 21–44 and M. Zimmermann, 'Hugues Capet et Borell', in ibid., 59–64.

[47] Zimmermann, 'La formació d'una sobirania', 41–7 (English at 441) overplays the significance of the title.

[48] Zimmermann, 'La formació d'una sobirania', 41–7 (English at 440).

[49] Sant Cugat, no. 2 and 4 for Wifred-Borrell, no. 65 and 66 (dated 963) for Miro, Borrell's son associated in rule.

[50] For the eastern, 'German' kingdom in the tenth century, Stieldorf, *Marken und Markgrafen* makes important observations about the gradually shifting meaning of the title *marchio*.

[51] CC 2, 391–2.

lands.[52] The dating practices used for documents produced in the Spanish March have been a source of some controversy. Some have argued that they show continued dependence on the monarchy, others that this is inconceivable and that the practice simply marks adherence to traditional ways of marking time. Abadal admits that the tradition was strong but also observes that it would not have existed in the first place without the Frankish conquest.[53] During the tenth century, supposedly a time of distant and cool relations with the kings, the role of the king had not disappeared from the minds of those who drew up the documents.

THE CHURCH IN THE TENTH-CENTURY SPANISH MARCH

As was the case in the late ninth century, the ecclesiastical politics of the tenth century Spanish March are significant for what they can reveal about independence-mindedness on the part of regional actors. Historians for decades have taken an interest in the ecclesiastical administration of Catalonia, recalling its history as part of the Visigothic province of Tarraconensis and incorporation into the province of Narbonensis as a consequence of the Carolingian conquest. As previous chapters of this study have shown, the notion that ninth- and tenth-century people in the March also recalled that history and yearned for separation from Carolingian administrative patterns has long generated scholarly interest in the subject.[54] Perhaps by the mid-tenth century, ecclesiastical neglect by their archbishop and provincial synods did indeed spark a desire to form a Catalonian province, for the episode of Cesari, founding abbot of Santa Cecília of Montserrat and would-be archbishop of Tarraconensis has long been taken as a signal of Catalonian striving for ecclesiastical separatism.[55] More probably, however, it was simple, more localized ambition just as in the case of Sclua discussed in Chapter 4. In the 940s, Cesari established his new monastery in what was then very much a frontier area, with what seems to have been a good degree of support from the comital family. Count and *marchio* Sunyer, his wife Countess Riquilda, and the bishop of Vic, located within Sunyer's

---

[52] Zimmermann, 'La formació d'una sobirania', 41–7 (English at 440).

[53] Abadal, *Els primers comtes*, 339–40 explains this phenomenon in terms of a persistent legalistic thought – it would have been illegal for counts to take royal titles, so they did not, preferring to remain subordinate to Frankish kings.

[54] See studies as recent as A. Pladevall, 'L'organització de l'Església a la Catalunya carolíngia', in *Catalunya a l'època carolíngia* (Barcelona, 1999), 53–8 (English trans. 444–8, at 445).

[55] The entry points into Cesari's story are Abadal, *Els primers comtes*, 271–90; also his *Dels visigots als catalans*, ed. J. Sobrequés i Callicó, 2nd ed., 2 vols (Barcelona, 1974), vol. 2, 25–55. More recently, and critical of received interpretations, J. Jarrett, 'Archbishop Ató of Osona: False Metropolitans on the Marca Hispanica', *Archiv für Diplomatik*, 56 (2010), 1–42, esp. at 13–16.

territory in Osona, all played important roles in the organization and endowment of the new abbey.[56] Later on, he apparently travelled to a church council at Compostela, where he was named archbishop of Tarragona. Upon his return to the Spanish March, however, he found that none of the bishops would recognize his authority. A letter he wrote to Pope John XIII secured him no support.[57] As a result of Sunyer's successful campaign in 940–1, the Christian lords did control Tarragona for a time, so perhaps it could have seemed reasonable to reconstitute the province.[58] In the end, Cesari failed at his scheme, perhaps losing support from the ruling family during the career of Borrell II, who supported better-established centres at Ripoll and Vic, and who lost control of Tarragona at any rate.[59]

Decades later Ato, bishop of Vic, also had a brief spell as putative archbishop of Tarraconensis, based in his own see.[60] It seems that Borrell engineered the elevation in 970 when he, Ato, and Gerbert of Aurillac travelled to Rome. Apparently, they asked Pope John XIII to effect the translation, and the pope assented. Ato, however, was murdered soon after, and the whole enterprise came to nothing.[61] The Spanish March had been attached to the province of Narbonne in the aftermath of the Carolingian conquests in the area in the late eighth and early ninth centuries. Consequently, re-establishing the province of Tarragona would have removed the bishops south of the Pyrenees from the jurisdiction of their northern neighbour. It might be tempting to detect a nascent nationalism, or at least a desire for a collective independence from Narbonne, driving the move to resurrect the old Tarraconensis. Yet Cesari had practically no support within the Spanish March for his designs, and the curious murder

---

[56] CC 4, no. 543.

[57] CC 4, no. 1080 gives the text of Cesari's letter to Pope John XIII requesting recognition as archbishop. It has attracted the interest of scholars for its physical characteristics as well: Jarrett, 'Archbishop Ató', 13–14 and works cited therein.

[58] D. Bramon, ed., *De quan erem o no musulmans: textos del 713 al 1000. Continuació de l'obra de J. M. Millàs i Vallicrosa* (Vic, 2000), nos. 411–12. P. Sénac, 'Note sur les relations diplomatiques entre les comtes de Barcelone et le califat de Cordoue au Xe siècle', in P. Sénac, *Histoire et Archéologie des Terres Catalanes au Moyen Âge* (Perpignan, 1995), 87–101; A. Benet i Clarà, 'Castells, guàrdies i torres de defensa', in Udina, *Symposium internacional*, vol. 1, 393–407, at 386–8.

[59] R. Martí, 'Concreció territorial del comtat de Barcelona', *III Congrés d'Història de Barcelona. La ciutat i el seu territori, dos mil anys d'història* (Barcelona, 1993), 247–53; Jarrett, 'Archbishop Ató', 16–18. Charters documenting Borrell's support of Ripoll and Vic are found in CC 4, nos. 783 and 791, for Ripoll, and for Vic CC 4, no. 744 and *Archivo Condal*, no. 204.

[60] R. Martí, 'Delà, Cesari i Ató, primers arquebisbes dels comptes-príceps de Barcelona (951–953/ 981', *Analecta Sacra Tarraconensia* 67 (1994): 369–86; R. Ordeig, 'Ató de Vic, mestre de Gerbert d'Orlhac', in I. Ollich i Castanyer, ed., *Actes del Congrés Internacional Gerbert d'Orlhac i el seu temps: Catalunya i Europa a la fi del Ir Mil.leni* (Vich, 1999), 593–620; R. Ordeig, 'Ató, bisbe i arquebisbe de Vic (957–971)', *Studia vicensia* 1 (1989): 61–97.

[61] Jarrett, 'Archbishop Ató', 18–21.

of Ato leads to the conclusion that he was not a universally respected figure in his own right. Both he and Borrell stood to gain in status, if not in material benefit, by the bishop's elevation, were it to have taken place. There is no separatism evident, but manoeuvring for greater authority and prestige within the ecclesiastical organization of the Spanish March itself suffices to explain the motivations of the figures involved. It is clear from the rest of the documentary record addressed above that representatives of churches and monasteries in the Spanish March sought and received royal diplomas confirming their rights and privileges, so the notion that these same individuals and their peers also struggled against trans-Pyrenean ecclesiastical dominion is misguided.[62]

At the local level, bishops exercised power in their localities, almost as if unconcerned by the higher ecclesiastical politics of the age.[63] Vivas, bishop of Barcelona, was in a position to grant rights and privileges, just as his predecessors and contemporaries received them from Frankish monarchs. Two surviving documents are blanket grants to the inhabitants in different castle jurisdictions. The first, dated to 974, concerned the settlement of Montmell. In it Vivas guaranteed the people immunity from other powers, exemption from personal and pecuniary dues, and his own protection of their rights.[64] A similar grant followed in 990, given to the settlers of Bello Loco, also known as Ribas. They were to enjoy free possession of lands and buildings and exemptions from burdens except work on the castle. Castle labour remained an imposition apparently because the castle required it; Vivas based his demand, rhetorically at least, on local custom.[65] Groups of settlers were not the only people Bishop Vivas favoured. In an act of 978, he granted a castle to an individual, Witard of Mura. While making a significant gift that enhanced Witard's position, Vivas reserved the lands and rights of the churches in the area as well as other properties, and his lordship over Witard for the castle.[66] All three gifts had the consent of the Barcelona clergy and Count Borrell. Because Vivas was alienating the property of the bishopric, the chapter had an interest, and so their consent was needed according to

---

[62] As noted above, see, Pladevall, 'L'organització de l'Església a la Catalunya carolíngia', esp. at 54 and 55 (English trans. 444–8, at 445).

[63] For an overview, P. Freedman, 'Le pouvoir épiscopal en Catalogne au Xe siècle', in *Catalunya i França meridional a l'entorn de l'any mil (Barcelona, 2–5 juliol 1987)* (Barcelona, 1991), 174–80, where Freedman concludes by supporting the notion of rivalries within the Spanish March, rather than separatist notions, fuelling the controversies.

[64] J. M. Font Rius, ed., *Cartas de población y franquicia de Cataluña* (Madrid-Barcelona, 1969), no. 7.

[65] Rius, ed., *Cartas de población y franquicia de Cataluña*, no. 10.

[66] Rius, ed., *Cartas de población y franquicia de Cataluña*, no. 8.

Visigothic law.[67] As this property included a castle and was entrusted to Borrell's man Witard, the count had a voice in the matter as well.[68]

Although the surviving documentation of Vivas's activity is not the most likely place to find evidence of his opinion on the matter, his case gives no indication that would-be archbishops like Cesari and Ato were leaders of a wide-ranging movement throughout the Spanish March to establish a province independent from Narbonne. The simpler, and preferable, interpretation, once the examination of events is shorn of anticipation of Catalonia's political independence, is that most bishops were more concerned with administering their dioceses and protecting or augmenting their churches' patrimonies. Cesari and Ato were outliers, not leaders, whose actions can be explained in terms of personal ambition, not national separatism.

COUNTS AND KINGS IN THE TENTH CENTURY

Counts in the Spanish March continued to jockey amongst themselves for position and face various challenges under the reigns of Charles the Simple's successors. From about 940, Empúries and Roussillon were ruled by Gausfred, the only son of his predecessor Gausbert and grandson of the infamous Sunyer II. Gausfred's uncles were in turn bishops of Elna from 916 to 947, after the incumbency of a cousin of Sunyer II. They were succeeded in turn by Gausfred's son Sunyer.[69] In 976 Gausfred and Sunyer donated to the monastery of Sant Pere de Rodes a stretch of shoreline and some inland properties they claimed to have redeveloped after depopulation.[70] By that point in the tenth century, it is unlikely that the location was still underpopulated, for the wars of the Muslim conquest and Christian 'liberation' were two centuries in the past. For his part, Gausfred seems to have cultivated the closest ties to the Frankish king of any contemporary count in the March; Lothar called him 'dux' and 'friend'.[71] Such a relationship would be coveted in the competition for status in the Spanish March. Clearly Borrell II was more powerful than Gausfred in terms of the land controlled, so Gausfred curried favour with the king in order to affirm his own status vis-à-vis his peers. The old count

---

[67] *Lex Visigothorum*, V.1.3 in *MGH LL nat. Germ.*, 209.

[68] Jarrett, *Rulers and Ruled*, 162 points out that Witard was a *nobilis palatii*.

[69] Abadal, *Els primers comtes*, 292. The family relationships are spelled out clearly in Aurell, 'Jalons pour une enquête sure les strategies matrimonials des comtes catalanes (ix^e–xi^e s.)', 301 (Table III).

[70] CC 5, no. 434.

[71] CC 2, 393–4; Jarrett, 'Caliph, King, or Grandfather', 11–16 provides a fuller study with which I do not disagree.

died in 991, and the counties he had governed were divided between his other two sons: Wilabert acquired Roussillon and Hugh, Empúries.

To the west of the coastal counties, Miro of Cerdanya died in 927. His widow Ava became the chief administrator of Cerdanya while their sons were minors. In 941 Ava is documented as sharing power with her sons, Sunifred, Wifred, Oliba Cabreta, and Miro *levita*.[72] The next year, Sunifred seems to have come of age.[73] Sunifred ruled Cerdanya with the *pagi* of Berguedà and Conflent; Oliba Cabreta was associated in rule in a fashion similar to the arrangement between Wifred-Borrell and Sunyer in Barcelona earlier in the century. Wifred, Miro's second son, took Besalú. Wifred fell in 957 to a revolt within his own county, so his brother Sunifred took his place.[74] Sunifred thus ruled Cerdanya and Besalú until his own death in 968, which brought about a new partition. His younger brother Oliba Cabreta took Cerdanya and its associated *pagi*, while Besalú went to a fourth brother Miro III (Miro *levita*), later bishop of Girona. Miro died in 984, and Oliba Cabreta reunited all that branch of the family's counties under his rule. Oliba retired to the monastery of Monte Cassino in 988, leaving his sons to succeed him.[75] Wifred, the oldest, became count in Cerdanya, the younger Bernard Tallaferro in Besalú, while other brothers became bishops.[76] These men governed areas in the Spanish March after the end of the Carolingian dynasty, under the reign of the new king, Hugh Capet. As their cases show, dividing inheritances amongst surviving sons was commonplace in the Spanish March to the end of the Carolingian period. The webs of relationships can become somewhat complicated for students of the period to trace, and in each generation counties could be conjoined or separated, bringing fluctuations in the amount of wealth and power accruing to individuals.

This period saw continued direct interactions between the counts and the Frankish kings. Wifred of Besalú is the last count documented to have come in person to the royal court, in 952 in the context of the revolt he faced. Here is clear evidence of a count trying to translate a relationship with the king into power back home.[77] The next thirty years passed with three royal diplomas being issued for beneficiaries in the Spanish March,

---

[72] Abadal, *Els primers comtes*, 292–3.

[73] CC 5, no. 258 shows Sunifred as count making a donation to Sant Pere de Rodes in 942.

[74] CC 5, no. 342 shows Sunifred, Ava, and Oliba executing Wifred's will. See also A. Benet i Clarà, 'Una revolta Berguedana contra el comte Oliba Cabreta', *L'Erol: revista cultural del Berguedà* (1983): 29–34.

[75] On this generation, Abadal, 'L'abat Oliba i la seva època', in *Dels visigots als catalans*, 2, 141–273 is still important.

[76] Aurell, 'Jalons pour une enquête sur les strategies matrimonials des Comtes Catalanes (ixe-xie s.)', 300–4 (Table IV).

[77] CC 2, 77–9. He gained for Sant Pere de Camprodon a grant of immunity.

all for monasteries.[78] Gausfred of Empúries is the next count known to
have petitioned a king for a diploma, when he received two in 981.
The language employed by the royal scribe indicates that Gausfred, called
dux in both documents, was not present in person but rather sent word to
the king.[79] In one grant, we have evidence of the *dux* seeking royal
affirmation for exercising his own prerogative in what is termed deserted
land; although it is unlikely to have been truly depopulated, wasteland
was held to belong to the fisc, so locals had to claim royal legitimation for
their actions. Similar circumstances prevailed for Santa Maria de Ripoll
and Sant Pere de Rodes, although these monastic communities had
recourse to previous royal confirmations of ownership. The Ripoll
archives were lost in the nineteenth century, so no original manuscripts
from the Carolingian period of the abbey's history survive. But from
copies preserved in Rome and Paris, it has been possible to reconstruct
Lothar's diploma.[80] There was an interval of nearly forty years between
Lothar's grant and the previous one by his predecessor Louis IV, and in
that time the monastery had come to acquire a good deal of property,
much of it from grants by Count Sunyer. These new estates had to be
covered in the royal confirmation. It seems that a royal grant was still
understood in the Spanish March as the basis for legal action, even if the
king's authority needed only to be recognized. As for Rodes, Abbot
Ildesindus, who was also bishop of Elna, sought royal confirmation of
the properties granted to his community by Count Gausfred.[81] The cases
of these two grants to monasteries show that, while comital acts were
important, and indeed foundational for the landed endowments of the
houses, royal confirmations were also sought and received. Kings were
still seen as accessible higher powers.

Borrell II, son and successor of Sunyer to the counties of Barcelona,
Girona, and Osona, accrued land, wealth, and titles beyond his contemporaries in the Spanish March.[82] Having inherited the co-rule of three
counties from his father in 947, he added the county of Urgell in 948 at
the death of his uncle Sunifred II and in 966 came into sole rule at the
death of his brother Miro. These developments left Borrell the most

---

[78] All discussed above: CC 2, 91–3, dated 952 for Cuixà, granted by Louis IV; CC 2, 94–8, dated 958
for Cuixà, granted by Lothar; CC 2, 202–3, dated 968 for Abbot Sunyer to control two
monasteries, granted by Lothar.

[79] CC 2, 210–4 for the monastery of Sant Genis les Fonts; CC 2, 393–4 for a grant of fiscal rights.
Abadal, *Els primers comtes*, 298 argues that the title *dux* is something akin to courtesy, not
a recognition of Gausfred's superiority over other counts in the region. Jarrett, 'Caliph, King,
or Grandfather', 11–16 offers a sound reading of Gausfred's relationship with the king.

[80] CC 2, 166–174. Abadal, *Els primers comtes*, 298–9.   [81] CC 2, 235–44.

[82] Jarrett, *Rulers and Ruled*, 129–66 is a thorough study of the connections and acts of Borrell as ruler
within his territory, especially in Osona and Manresa.

powerful count in the March and also the subject of the lion's share of scholarly attention. Because so much historiography on the independence of Catalonia from the Frankish kingdom has focused on events involving Borrell, so too will this examination. Like his father, he was often called *princeps*. He is given that title in a church consecration in the diocese of Girona in 947, the year he succeeded his father.[83] King Lothar in a grant of immunity for Sant Pol de Mar and Sant Feliu de Guixols commanded that *nullum principem* interfere with the abbeys, though he named no one in particular.[84] Richer called him *dux citerioris Hispaniae Borrellus*; later Borrell claimed the title *Hibereo duci atque marchiso* in a document emanating from his own court.[85] Gerbert, who knew Borrell personally, referred to him amongst 'the princes of Spain' in a letter of early 985.[86] The use of such a title was not new in this generation, so contrary to what many might hope to detect, there was no more separation from the monarchy up to 985 than before.

Borrell *the* Princeps

Charter evidence gives us a better picture of the power Borrell II wielded as count.[87] Like his grandfather Wifred I, Borrell exercised a degree of power by selecting his aunt Adelaide as abbess of Sant Joan.[88] Adelaide was his uncle Sunifred of Urgell's widow, and so the dynasty kept the governance of the convent under family control, at least for a time.[89] Borrell attained a stature that his predecessors as counts of Barcelona had in the eyes of observers when he was called *princeps* in 977.[90] Contemporaries noted Borrell's status as the autonomous ruler of most of the Spanish March, distributing land and rights like a king of an earlier generation. One obvious way the counts of Barcelona acted like kings was their use of *aprisio* grants. Previously a royal grant, because the land came from the royal fisc, the counts appropriated this prerogative in the tenth century as organized settlement pushed the frontier south. Tenth-

---

[83] CC 5, no. 274.   [84] CC 2, 202–4.

[85] Sant Cugat, no. 217; Richer, *Histories* 3.43 and 3.44, ed. and trans. J. Lake (Cambridge, MA, 2011), 62–7.

[86] The English is that of *The Letters of Gerbert, with His Papal Privileges as Sylvester II*, trans. H. Platt (New York, 1961), no. 51.

[87] Most recently and thoroughly Jarrett, *Rulers and Ruled*, 129–66. The discussion in this chapter does not seek to duplicate the depth or detail Jarrett offers, but rather maintains the study's overall focus on ties between those on the Spanish March and the kings. See also Abadal, *Dels visigots als catalans*, vol. 1, 146–52; Abadal, *Els primers comtes*, 249–90, which emphasizes the locals' relationships with Frankish kings, and 293–7.

[88] *Archivo Condal*, no. 128.

[89] See Udina's discussion of the problematic identification of Adelaide in *Archivo Condal*, xxii–xxiv.

[90] *Archivo Condal*, no. 181.

century *aprisiones* served the same function as earlier grants: settlement and economic production in new areas along with obligations for military service. *Aprisiones* provided their possessors with nearly invincible claims to the land they held.[91] In the tenth-century context, *aprisiones* balanced not the power of the counts vis-à-vis the kings, but helped counts maintain a strong presence and ties to individuals in localities increasingly controlled by viscounts and castellans, while also claiming that their authority to do so devolved from the kings.[92] In other ways, too, Borrell exceeded the efforts of his predecessors, especially in terms of diplomacy with his Muslim neighbours and the papacy. For decades, these activities have been seen as marking the detachment of Catalonia from the Frankish kingdom. But they should more plausibly be understood as Borrell's manipulation of circumstances to maintain and enhance his own position in his own milieu, without regard to staking claim to independence.

Diplomacy with Rome and Córdoba

A long tradition of interpretation holds that the counts of the Spanish March could not withstand the power of the caliphs of Córdoba, so they sought out protection from other sources.[93] Papal bulls began to replace royal diplomas.[94] Secular magnates took trips to Rome beginning in 951. Even group trips of counts, bishops, and abbots became a regular practice. According to this line of thinking, the popes filled the vacancy created by royal 'withdrawal', and a document from 956 hails both the pope and the king as sovereign powers.[95] It is true that in Rome, the counts of the March could make contact with the new powers of Europe, as Borrell met Emperor Otto I there in 970. But under more scrutiny, it remains to be seen what true assistance the pope could render against the very real military power of the caliph. This arrangement could perhaps provide for legal stability, but not real protection as we usually understand the term. At the same time, the same modern body of research asserts that the counts sought military security through submitting themselves to the caliphs of Córdoba. Yet, counts in the Spanish March ever since Wifred

---

[91] Bowman, *Shifting Landmarks*, 47–51.

[92] Jarrett, 'Caliph, King, or Grandfather', 9–10, as well as J. Jarrett, 'Settling the Kings' Lands: *Aprisio* in Catalonia in Perspective', *EME* 18 (2010): 320–42. An older articulation of the issue is in Lewis, *The Development of Society*, 281–2.

[93] This is the underlying message behind Abadal, *Els primers comtes*, 291–325. More recently it has been reinforced by M. Zimmermann, 'La formació d'una sobirania', 41–7 (English at 440–441).

[94] Abadal, *Els primers comtes*, 302–12. This phenomenon is well studied. See also A. R. Lewis, *The Development of Southern French and Catalan Society, 718–1050* (Austin, 1965), 191–2; Salrach, *El procés*, 2, 105–6.

[95] Zimmermann, 'La formació d'una sobirania'.

the Hairy had hostile relations with the Muslim commanders at their doorstep, and the sources provide evidence of armed conflict as well as negotiations for peace. While it may be true that Arabic sources portray the peace agreements as complete submission of the Christians to the caliphs, there is nothing to indicate that the counts saw such submission. Even if the relationship can truly be characterized as such it did not override the counts' relationships to the Frankish kings.

As the direct presence of the Frankish kings supposedly faded, the counts in the March did not presume to act completely as their own lords. For one alternative, Borrell is taken to have strengthened his relationship with the papacy.[96] In 950 the monk Sunyer of Cuixà travelled by himself to Rome; at Christmas 951, a group including Count Sunifred of Cerdanya, Bishop Wisadus of Barcelona, the nobles Tassi and Sala, and other unknowns sought papal privileges for monasteries in the Spanish March. The relationship with Rome both reinforced and was strengthened by the influence of Cluny.[97] These links to institutions beyond the Spanish March are firmly based on evidence, such as that considered here, and constitute what some Catalans call the region's 'opening up to the world'. Part of this 'opening up' featured Borrell cultivating his own relationships with aristocratic families and monastic houses based north of the Pyrenees as well.[98] All this points to intensifying contact with Aquitaine, Burgundy, and Italy at the very time the Spanish March has traditionally been held to be detaching itself from the Carolingian world. It is true that Sunyer, Tassi, and Sala undertook their journeys to confirm rights and privileges from the pope, rather than from kings in Francia as in previous generations. Yet even given all that, papal bulls could buttress one's legal claim to property or rights of immunity, but could not shield one from a Muslim raid. Furthermore, when modern studies are quick to point to missions to Rome, they seem to forget the diplomas of Louis IV and Lothar III addressed earlier in this chapter. Journeying at Christmastime 968, Oliba Cabreta secured a privilege for Arles in Vallespir from the pope, and gained more for Cuixà.[99] Earlier that same year, however, Abbot Sunyer did travel to visit the king in person for the same reason, as noted above. If we are to correct the modern misplaced emphasis on

---

[96] Abadal, *Els primers comtes*, 302–12. This phenomenon is well studied. See also Lewis, *The Development of Society*, 191–2; P. Kehr, *Das Papsttum und der katalanische Prinzipat bis zur Vereinigung mit Aragon* (Berlin, 1926).

[97] A. Mundó, 'Monastic Movements in the East Pyrenees', in N. Hunt, ed., *Cluniac Monasticism in the Central Middle Ages* (Hamden, CT, 1971), 98–122.

[98] M. Zimmermann, 'La formació d'una sobirania' (English at 441). See also Aurell, 'Jalons pour une enquête sur les strategies matrimonials des Comtes Catalanes (ix^e–xi^e s.)', 290–2.

[99] Abadal, *Els primers comtes*, 305–6.

separation from the Carolingian world, the contemporary evidence of royal acts of the 950s and 960s cannot be forgotten.

As another supposed alternative to Frankish royal sovereignty, Borrell turned to a nearer power as overlord. The prevailing body of modern research following Abadal asserts that the counts sought military security through submitting themselves as 'vassals' to the caliphs. In total, the count sent four embassies to Córdoba, in 953, 966, 971, and 974. On the first occasion, Miro, son of Sunyer the 'king of Barcelona and Tarragona' served as envoy to Córdoba.[100] The embassy of 953 also featured envoys from Otto I and Hugh of Arles. One of the conditions of peace seems to have been returning Tarragona to Muslim hands and re-establishing the old frontier as it had been in the early tenth century.[101] The great Caliph Abd al-Rahman III died in 961, succeeded by his son al-Hakam II, already forty years old and experienced in government. Al-Hakam was a man of peace and culture, a lover of arts and letters. His reign is recognized as a cultural golden age in al-Andalus.[102] Yet peace was no longer constant. A Christian attack, presumably led by or representing Borrell and perhaps his cousin Oliba Cabreta, on Tortosa in 964 alarmed Caliph al-Hakam II to the extent that he set off for Almería, ostensibly to launch a counter-attack by sea. News reached him of ultimate Muslim victory, so he settled for merely an inspection of the fleet.[103] The following year saw a Muslim attack on the Barcelona region, probably in retaliation for the Christian expedition.[104] Subsequent to these two most recent setbacks, the Christians once again sought peace. Messengers to al-Hakam II in c.966 brought gifts in the form of slaves, hides, tin, and Frankish armour and swords in order to secure peace. The conditions of peace were that the rulers of Barcelona and Tarragona dismantle fortifications close to the frontier and agree to cease cooperation with other Christians, and to warn the caliph of potentially harmful acts by other

---

[100] Ibn Khaldun, in Bramon, *De quan erem o no musulmans*, nos. 418–19. Abadal identified 'Mughira' as Borrell, but Bramon translates the name as Miro, Sunyer's son who died in 966. Abadal also asserted that the negotiations marked a shift in direction of Borrell's political orientation away from Franks. See note 165.

[101] Abadal, *Els primers comtes*, 315–16, citing E. Levi-Provençal, *Histoire de l'Espagne musulmane* (Le Caire, 1944), vol. 1, 329.

[102] See such works as the essays collected in V. B. Mann, J. D. Dodds, and T. F. Glick, eds, *Convivencia: Jews, Muslims, and Christians in Medieval Spain* (New York, 1992); and M. R. Menocal, *The Ornament of the World: How Muslims, Jews, and Christians Created a Culture of Tolerance in Medieval Spain* (Boston, 2002).

[103] Ibn al-Hatib, in Bramon, *De quan erem o no musulmans*, no. 421.

[104] Bramon, *De quan erem o no musulmans* no. 423; Martínez, 'Catalunya i al-Àndalus (segles viii-x)', 29–35 (English at 431–5).

Christians.[105] It is quite striking when one reflects on the three generations of poor results from campaigning against Muslims on the part of Wifred the Hairy, Wifred-Borrell, Sunyer, and Borrell II. Only Sunyer had any successes, but Borrell negotiated away the gains made at Tarragona and Tortosa.

From 966 onwards, many Christian embassies from all over Spain went to Córdoba, some repeatedly. Even the Byzantine emperor John (in 972) and the German king and Emperor Otto II (in 974) sent envoys as well, though no one has described these acts as political submission.[106] In 971, a mission from Borrell brought a letter promising, according to the eleventh-century Arab historian Ibn Hayyan, 'total obedience and vassallage' to the caliph.[107] Some historians have taken these terms as evidence of the counts of the Spanish March growing yet more distant from the kings of the Franks. Ibn Hayyan's report also provides an aside, alluding to the representative of the viscount, which serves as evidence that Borrell governed so much territory that he had to assign responsibilities in the city of Barcelona itself to a subordinate. Ibn Hayyan noted that three years later the 'vicar of Borrell . . . the tyrant of Barcelona, that is to say, Witard, lord of the city' personally delivered a letter from Borrell in 974 to express the *marchio*'s 'love and submission' to the caliph.[108] Specifically, Witard's mission concerned renewing Borrell's relationship with al-Hakam II. According to Abadal, Borrell agreed to remain in '*obedencia*' towards the caliph and that this was nothing other than equivalent to *fidelitas* in the Frankish world.[109] Abadal argued that the first two embassies (in 953 and 966) probably represent only peace and friendship, but that the last two (those of 971 and 974) had a more precise scope, showing that Borrell established vassalage towards al-Hakam, a vassalage 'incompatible and opposed to fidelity towards the Frankish king'.[110] Thus he concluded that the new power and splendour of Córdoba contributed in a major way to the disappearance of Frankish authority in Catalonia. More recent work concurs with Abadal's interpretation.[111] Mikel de Epalza goes so far as to claim that the diplomacy with al-Hakam II constituted a submission to Muslim rule, in

---

[105] Ibn Khaldun and al-Maqqari, in Bramon, *De quan erem o no musulmans* no. 424.

[106] Abadal, *Els primers comtes*, 318 citing Levi-Provençal, *Histoire de l'Espagne musulmane*, vol. 1, 400–1.

[107] Ibn Hayyan, in Bramon, *De quan erem o no musulmans* nos. 425–6. We do not have the letter, but rather Ibn Hayyan's report of it.

[108] Ibn Hayyan, in Bramon, *De quan erem o no musulmans* nos. 430–1.

[109] Abadal, *Els primers comtes*, 318–20.   [110] Abadal, *Els primers comtes*, 315–21, quote at 320.

[111] Sánchez Martínez, 'Catalunya i al-Àndalus (segles viii–x)', in *Catalunya a l'època carolíngia: art i cultura abans del romànic (segles IX i X)* (Barcelona, 1999) 29–35 (English at 434); Zimmermann, 'La formació d'una sobirania', 41–7 (English at 441).

exchange for regional autonomy, akin to the Treaty of Tudmir (or 'of Orihuela') agreed in the early eighth century.[112]

Yet the nature of the source merits consideration, as well as the meaning of vassalage. The most prominent modern historians concerned with this subject seem to be taking a non-contemporary Arab account at face value. Ibn Hayyan wrote in the eleventh century, long after the events in question took place. He did live and work in Córdoba, where he studied and preserved earlier texts, and may have had access to official records, but that still reveals nothing about Borrell's approach to the treaties. The *fidelitas* Borrell owed to the Frankish king had no bearing on how he behaved as a ruler in his own territory, and his documents discussed above base his authority to a degree on recognition of Frankish kingship. Abadal showed no evidence that the count's relationship with the caliph had any more practical impact. Borrell recognized the kings' supremacy in allowing documents to be dated by their reigns and also conducted his own diplomacy with caliphs – as had *marchiones* in the ninth century. He secured peace in 966 by promising to break off alliances, yet the documents are still dated according to the regnal years of the Franks. One wonders whether notarial practice would have changed had he really placed himself under complete obedience to al-Hakam, unlikely as the notion may seem. It is more likely that Borrell used the embassies of 'submission' in the 970s to assuage tensions between himself and the caliph, who had attacked him earlier, rather than to find a new sovereign. Just as the dating clauses of charters, in Abadal's representation, merely paid lip service to Frankish kings while the counts themselves acted autonomously,[113] so did the agreements with caliphs articulate a position legally inferior but with no actual repercussions. Borrell, and possibly Sunyer before him, therefore, recognized the theoretical hegemony of the Frankish king and the military superiority of the caliph in order to establish legitimacy for their own authority and to secure peace.

There is some support from two sources for the notion, long held, that the tenth-century diplomatic missions 'unmistakably express the evident hegemony of the Caliphate over the Christian kingdoms of the period and the obvious submission of their leaders to Córdoba' and their moral, if not legal, separation from the Frankish kingdom.[114] Firstly, there are indications that people at that time believed the counts were isolated. Ibn

---

[112] M. de Epalza, 'Descabdellament politic i miliatr dels musulmans a terres catalanes (segles viii–xi)', in *Symposium internacional*, 49–80, at 55–9 for the treaties, 57 for al-Hakam II and the counts of Barcelona. See also P. Chalmeta, *Invasión e islamización: La sumisión de Hispania y la formació de al-Andalus* (Jaén, 2003), 206–13 on the early 'pactos' of the conquest of Spain.

[113] Abadal, *Els primers comtes*, 339–40.

[114] Sánchez Martínez, 'Catalunya i al-Àndalus (segles viii–x)', 29–35 (English at 431–5).

Khaldun reports that to the general and vizier al-Mansur 'it became clear that the people of Barcelona had severed ties with the king of *Ifrang* [i.e., Francia]'.[115] Yet Ibn Khaldun's analysis of political thinking centuries before his own time is not exactly trustworthy. During his reign, al-Mansur attacked all the Christian realms of Spain, notably Barcelona in the 980s. Secondly, in observing the state of affairs, the king of the Franks himself urged Borrell not to submit to the Muslims. Ibn Khaldun, not only much later but also from the perspective of one observing as an outsider, may have misrepresented the relationship between count and king. King Hugh's own words, admittedly from late in the 980s, lend credibility to the notion that Borrell had pledged obedience to the caliph, as we shall see. Through Borrell's former associate Gerbert of Aurillac, the count was informed that if he would obey the king rather than the 'Ishmaelites', he was to send messengers to the king.[116] The king's message followed in the wake of a devastating attack, when Borrell was at his weakest. This need not reflect any standing diplomatic arrangements, but rather the possibility of submission to superior Muslim force. Borrell was navigating the perilous waters of late tenth-century diplomacy, finding his course as he could.

The climactic events of 985–8 proved very important to the nationhood of Catalonia, in its mythic historiography if not in lived experience.[117] Therefore, just as in the case of the diplomatic missions, these crucial events need to be situated properly in their context. Submitting to the caliph, whatever Borrell's true intentions, did not in fact bring security. Al-Mansur was the real power in Córdoba after the succession of al-Hisham II and began a long series of campaigns against the Christians of the north. The name al-Mansur means 'the Victorious', and this man was co-regent for the young Hisham, son of al-Hakam II, together with the boy's mother from 976. He was made inspector of the troops of the capital, which gave him great power. He also secured the offices of vizier and prefect of Córdoba. In 979 he married the daughter of Ghalib, general of the frontiers and the only man powerful enough to rival al-Mansur. Al-Mansur thus elevated himself to the status of a non-hereditary 'dictator' by 981, defeating his father-in-law and only rival with the help of Castilian and Navarrese troops.[118] By then he had already begun waging brutal war against the Christians of Iberia. Famous, or perhaps

[115] Bramon, *De quan erem o no musulmans*, no. 439.   [116] CC 2, 441.

[117] Zimmermann, 'La prise de Barcelone par al-Mansûr', *passim*; Freedman, 'Symbolic Implications', 122–9.

[118] Abadal, *Els primers comtes*, 327. See also the brief treatment of the caliphate in R. Puig, 'El concepte musulmà d'estat', in *Symposium internacional*, vol. 2, 103–13.

infamous, amongst historians for his nearly annual summer raiding campaigns, al-Mansur brought in Berber and slave warriors to take the field in his campaigns and is known to have sacked León, Pamplona, and Santiago de Compostela.[119] Frequent campaigns were probably intended to keep the Christians of the north and north-east in line. Not only this, but they also would have helped the power in Córdoba to enforce its authority over the Muslim governors of frontier areas, such as the Banu Qasi, who from time to time acted quite independently of emirs and caliphs. Al-Mansur's career as something of a military dictator can arguably be seen as contributing to the enfeebling of the Umayyad caliphate of Córdoba and its dissolution into the *taifas* of the early eleventh century.[120]

According to Arabic sources, al-Mansur carried out four attacks against the Spanish March during Borrell's rule: in 978 he defeated Borrell for the first time; in 982, Girona and other places felt his reach; he campaigned to the plains near Barcelona in 984; and in 985 he sacked and burned Barcelona. The sources say very little about al-Mansur's first forays into Barcelona territory, other than that they were part of a series of short campaigns beginning in 978.[121] Given the nature of these later sources, it is possible, however, that a composite picture of repeated raids before the major campaign to sack Barcelona is impossible and even ill-advised. Chronology can be confused by different authors, so the story that has been transmitted may just be jumbled reporting of the single campaign of 985. From what material does survive from the Muslim perspective, some comes from the early eleventh century. Whether in 982 as a separate effort or later as part of the campaign to Barcelona, al-Mansur targeted Girona.[122] The plain near Barcelona saw an attack, with al-Mansur's forces 'taking booty and captives ... killing and destroying everything', in the dramatic language of al-Udri, who was born in al-Andalus within a generation of the events.[123] The best explanation for these expeditions is economic expediency, as opposed to religious zeal or political policy. Al-Mansur needed booty and prisoners to give to his troops in order to keep their support; after all, he was not the

[119] De Epalza, 'Descabdellament politic i miliatr', 67–75; R. Collins, *Early Medieval Spain Unity in Diversity, 400–1000*, 2nd ed. (New York, 1995), 195–7.

[120] As does, e.g., Collins, *Early Medieval Spain*, 263–4.

[121] Al-Udri, in Bramon, *De quan erem o no musulmans*, no. 440; *Dikr bilad al-Andalus*, in Bramon, *De quan erem o no musulmans*, nos. 441 and 442.

[122] *Dikr bilad al-Andalus*, in Bramon, *De quan erem o no musulmans*, no. 444.

[123] Al-Udri, in Bramon, *De quan erem o no musulmans* no. 445; *Dikr bilad al-Andalus*, in Bramon, *De quan erem o no musulmans*, no. 445.

caliph despite the power he wielded as vizier.[124] That also explains why the army returned to al-Andalus and did not stay to occupy the Spanish March. Indeed, throughout the tenth century, including al-Mansur's own numerous campaigns, conquest was not at issue. Instead, Muslim rulers sought to take tribute, including slaves, or else to punish Christians for not sufficiently observing Muslim political and military superiority.[125] Al-Mansur was not a party, apparently, to the peace agreement with Borrell conducted by the previous regime, and so had no need to feel bound by it, yet neither did he set out for conquest.

Finally, in the spring of 985, Barcelona fell. Al-Udri heightens the drama by recounting how al-Mansur took a bath in rose water before departing.[126] Another source erroneously reports that Borrell died in the battle.[127] Some sources specify that the Spanish March marked the limits of the territories of the Franks and of Rome, or that Borrell was 'king of *Firanga* [i.e., Francia]', or else give brutal details of the sack of the city.[128] Al-Mansur's successes against Borrell show that, whatever the level of authority Borrell had within the Spanish March, he had no real power beyond it. The military weakness of marcher counts for fully a century is astounding. These attacks prompted Borrell to seek help from King Lothar, as all who have investigated the period recognize. One wonders, then, how much separation he had achieved or even sought from the king of the Franks. At any rate, a royal precept for San Cugat in 986 confirmed rights and possessions the monastery held before the 985 debacle.[129] On the accession of young Louis V in 986, the abbot of Aurillac, long a friend of Borrell's, wrote to Gerbert, who had studied in the Spanish March for a few years in the late 960s, asking if the Frankish army could help Borrell.[130] Gerbert did not have a favourable answer.[131]

---

[124] Amongst other general accounts of the Muslim rulers of al-Andalus in the tenth century, see Richard Fletcher, *Moorish Spain* (Berkeley, 1992), 53, 72–8.

[125] De Epalza, 'Descabdellament politic i militar', esp. 67–75.

[126] Bramon, *De quan erem o no musulmans*, no. 447.

[127] Ibn al-Kardabus, in Bramon, *De quan erem o no musulmans*, no. 449.

[128] Ibn al-Hatib, in Bramon, *De quan erem o no musulmans*, nos. 453 and 452; Ibn al-Abbar, in Bramon, no. 450; Ibn al-Hatib, in Bramon, *De quan erem o no musulmans* nos. 453–4.

[129] CC 2, 194–200.

[130] See the essays collected in I. Ollich i Castanyer, ed. *Actes del Congrés Internacional Gerbert d'Orlhac i el seu temps: Catalnuya i Europa a la fi del Ir mil.lenni* (Vic, 1999), especially R. Ordeig i Mata, 'Ató de Vic, mestre de Gerbert d'Orlhac', 593–620, and A. M. Mundó, 'Entorn de l'astrolabi de Gerbert', 665–77.

[131] Abadal, *Els primers comtes*, 332–3. See also the studies in O. Guyotjeannin and E. Puoulle, eds, *Autour de Gerbert d'Aurillac. Le pape de l'an mil. Album de documents commenteés* (Paris, 1996), including M. Zimmermann, 'Le pélerinage romain d'un Catalan: Testamen de Borrell, Vic 19 octobre 970', 20–5 and Zimmermann, 'Abbatiale de Ripoll: Formule de consécration d'église (960–980)', 26–35.

Nevertheless, when Borrell saw his friend Gerbert attain high position upon the succession of Hugh Capet, he may have seen in it an opportunity finally to obtain aid. According to Richer, Hugh and Borrell exchanged letters (Hugh's emanating from the pen of his secretary, Gerbert), and Hugh and his advisors knew about developments in Spain and intended to help Borrell.[132] Hugh, in his letter written in early 988, however, insisted that Borrell travel to Aquitaine to promise fidelity and help lead the army, like other *fideles* of the king; if the count would obey the king rather than the 'Ishmaelites', he was to send messengers to the king by Easter.[133] For his part, nearly three years after the fall of his city, Borrell knew through the return of ransomed captives that al-Mansur was turning his attention elsewhere, interested as he was only in the money of the captives he took from the Spanish March, which was by no means rich enough to sack time and time again. Ultimately, nothing came of Hugh's proposal. This series of events has been held to have ended de facto Frankish dominion over the Catalan counties.[134] The same years saw what proved to be the definitive end of the Carolingian dynasty, especially once the revolt in 988–91 of Charles of Lotharingia, the uncle of the recently deceased King Louis V and last Carolingian claimant for kingship, failed.[135] Hugh Capet was very concerned with Charles and so would not have been able to help Borrell even if he had had the desire. Relations between the counts of the Spanish March and kings were for all intents and purposes over, Lothar's 986 precept for Sant Cugat the last in a line of grants that spanned two centuries.[136] That, at least, is how generations have understood the end of de facto Frankish dominion over the Catalan counties, along with the contemporary, definitive end of the Carolingian dynasty. Yet all stress de facto, not *de jure*, local sovereignty, and are right to do so. Even the concept of sovereignty in this context is difficult to understand and articulate.

Borrell and 'Sovereignty'

Creators of documents in the Spanish March were quite reluctant to recognize Hugh, just as they had shown unwillingness to recognize his

---

[132] Richer, 4.12, ed. Lake, 222–5; Abadal, *Els primers comtes*, 331–8.   [133] CC 2, 441.

[134] Sánchez Martínez, 'Catalunya i al-Àndalus (segles viii–x)', 29–35 (English at 431–5) at 434, with overstated claims.

[135] See now on these issues Dufour, 'Obédience', 21–44. Note especially the point that controversies regarding regnal years indicate that the king was an important figure in political thought in the Spanish March.

[136] CC 2, 194–200, as above.

non-Carolingian predecessors.[137] Their refusal to recognize a non-Carolingian king is evident in dating clauses for documents produced in Spanish March. One charter from Borrell's county of Girona dates to October 987, or 'the first year in which King Louis, son of Lothar, died'.[138] Another, from Besalú is dated to the second year of Louis's death. Some note that Hugh was just a duke: *Ugone rege, qui fuit dux.* Borrell himself appears in documents with the same title, *dux Gothiae*, perhaps to show himself Hugh's equal.[139] Such sentiment was far from unanimous, however, as even in Girona, documents by the end of 987 are given dates in the simpler format of Hugh's regnal year.[140] A series of charters can help show Borrell's own state of mind in 987–8. First is the one cited at the beginning of this chapter for its use of the phrase *Christo regnante regem expectante.*[141] Another follows closely in the spring of the same year and shares the '*Christo regnante rege expectante*' formula, adding that the year was the one in which King Louis died.[142] Borrell was involved in the transactions both of these charters record, so they perhaps reveal his own position. These were mundane matters, one a gift and one a sale (albeit for the sum of ten *mancusos*), not grand affairs of the elite, but Borrell and his scribes made a statement of wider political significance nonetheless. Next is a charter from November 987, also a routine sale of land dated to the first year of Hugh's reign, revealing Borrell's ultimate recognition of Hugh's right to the crown, for Borrell himself was party to the document.[143] That is followed by three charters from December 987, also all giving the year as the first of King Hugh's reign.[144] The last charter issued in 987 uses a different dating formula: *anno I regnantem Karlo rege*, in recognition of the Carolingian scion Charles of Lotharingia, who fought for his claim to kingship.[145] Charters from early 988 exhibit the same inconsistency, some recognizing Hugh's kingship, while one other dates according to the reign of Charles.[146] The Spanish March was not the only area of controversy, to judge by the dating clauses of charters. Throughout the West Frankish kingdom, from north to south, scribes can be seen to be favouring the Carolingian dynasty, hostile to them, or

---

[137] M. Zimmermann, 'La formació d'una sobirania', 41–7 (English at 442). See also the discussion on dating clauses above, p. 306.

[138] CC 5, 511.

[139] CC 5, no. 524; Sant Cugat, nos. 234, 237, 242, 244, 245, 247, 248, and others composed by the scribe Bonushomo.

[140] Zimmermann, 'La formació d'una sobirania', 41–7 (English at 442) asserts that scribes engaged in an effort to 'erase' the 'royal memory', but I must admit that I cannot draw the same conclusion.

[141] CC 4, no. 1523. Note also that the Spanish March was not the only area where people grappled with Hugh's succession: Dufour, 'Obédience', 26–7.

[142] CC 4, no. 1524.   [143] CC 4, no. 1525.   [144] CC 4, nos. 1526, 1527, and 1528.

[145] CC 4, no. 1529.   [146] CC 4, nos. 1531, 1533, and 1534 date by Hugh, no. 1535 by Charles.

indifferent. Those in the March seem to have placed a greater emphasis on the legitimacy of that line of kings.[147] By the end of 988, dating by Hugh's reign takes over in the surviving charters from Osona and Manresa. The change in this aspect of documentary practice in the territories Borrell ruled serves to mark the end of 'Carolingian Catalonia'.

De jure independence for Catalonia was not achieved until the Treaty of Corbeil in 1258, agreed to by kings Jaume I of Aragon-Catalonia and Louis IX of France. In the tenth century, as noted, the counts exercised powers previously recognized as those of the king, even if they sought royal confirmation for doing so. The counts of Barcelona were the most powerful in the region.[148] These counts acquired land, at first by claiming deserted and resettled areas, and after 950 by outright purchase, and used those resources to build networks of loyal followers. The counts of Barcelona, by also ruling in Osona, had far more opportunity to acquire, organize, and militarize land on the frontier.[149] Although this chapter has emphasized continuing connections to kings throughout the tenth century, it has become clear that royal authority did not penetrate as deeply into the society of the Spanish March as it once did. Comital power was more important than royal, and there would be no further cases of individual lay land-holders receiving confirmation of their rights from Carolingian kings. Yet it is equally clear that the same institutions and practices that the Carolingians manipulated to secure their authority in the March, that is, the office of the count, the network of bishops, recognizing claims to land cleared by *aprisio*, and even the patronage of monasteries, were all those that functioned as the exercise of power in the face of an altered royal presence. While it has never been the aim of this study to engage in the debate over the 'Feudal Revolution', seeking instead to highlight the continuity in the relations between people in the Spanish March and the kings, the observations in this chapter complement very nicely the argument that Charles West makes in his recent book, *Reframing the Feudal Revolution*.[150] West argues that, for the region of the Marne and Moselle rivers in eastern France and western Germany, there was much continuity from the Carolingian period to the post-Carolingian period that followed. In Catalan scholarship, the labels

---

[147] Dufour, 'Obédience', 30–3.

[148] Or in Zimmermann's words, 'La formació d'una sobirania', 41–47 (English at 441), they 'enjoyed an unquestionable supremacy'.

[149] This observation is obvious and is a constant in the scholarly literature. See, e.g., Jarrett, *Rulers and Ruled*, 141–3, 154–5, 165–6; A. Benet i Clarà, 'Castells, guàrdies i torres de defensa', in *Symposium internacional*, vol. 1, 393–407; Zimmermann, 'La formació d'una sobirania', 41–7 (English at 441).

[150] C. West, *Reframing the Feudal Revolution: Political and Social Transformation between the Marne and the Moselle, c.800–c.1100* (Cambridge, 2013), esp. Part II: 'The Long Tenth Century, c.880–c.1030', 107–69.

'feudal' and 'comital' are widely used to describe the period. West shows that 'declining' kingship can stand ironically as the result of the success of the Carolingian political project, and that the disappearance of royal authority was the cause rather than the consequence of the rising power of regional and local aristocrats. The evidence from the Spanish March, as presented here, supports these conclusions and extends their geographical scope.

IDENTITY IN THE SPANISH MARCH AT THE END OF THE CAROLINGIAN PERIOD

The notion of Gothic identity in the tenth-century Spanish March remains an issue in some corners of modern scholarship.[151] Concerning how individuals who lived in the Spanish March may have identified themselves, there certainly is no evidence that they called themselves 'Goths'. Yet there is equally no proof of the opposite. Such is the nature of the surviving source material. Recent work can point to a series of narrative texts by which the Franks or, at least, the political elites of the Frankish kingdom, came to build an identity.[152] No such text or series of texts exists for the locals of the Spanish March, but other royal documents such as diplomas contributed to the identity-building enterprise. As the previous chapters have demonstrated, it was in most cases from this royal perspective that individuals were called 'Goths'. Right through twentieth-century historical scholarship, the claim to Gothic identity was important.[153] Jesús Lalinde Abadía has demonstrated that there is no direct link between the use in Septimania and the Spanish March of the term 'Goths' in the early Middle Ages and the modern usage of the label 'Visigoths' to denote those who entered Gaul and then Spain in late antiquity.[154] Instead, he favours attributing Gothic identity to a military class on the basis of an old pattern of land-holding that involved military service.[155] Although there may have been a tradition of identifying certain members of society as 'Goths' because of their specific land-holding or military service, there was no

[151] See in particular J. Lalinde Abadía, 'Godos, hispanos y hostolenses en la órbita del rey de los fancos', in *Symposium internacional*, vol. 2, 35–74 and F. Udina i Martorell, 'El llegat i la consciència romano-gòtica. El nom d'Hispània', in ibid., 171–200.

[152] Most recently, Reimitz, *History, Frankish Identity and the Framing of Western Ethnicity, 550–850* (Cambridge, 2015).

[153] Even near the end of the century, Udina i Martorell, 'El llegat i la consciència romano-gòtica' as cited in note 151 and L. Suárez Fernández, 'León y Catalunya: paralelismos y divergencias', in *Symposium internacional*, vol. 2, 141–57.

[154] Lalinde Abadía, 'Godos, hispanos y hostolenses', 37–41.

[155] Ibid., esp. 45–51 and for our period 56–60. P. Amory, *People and Identity in Ostrogothic Italy* (Cambridge, 1995) mounts a similar argument.

biological continuity with the Goths of late antiquity in the way that modern notions of ethnicity presume.

One of the major themes of this study is that during the early Middle Ages, most people were far less concerned with ethnic identity than modern investigators. Surely, kings and writers, whether of narrative or documentary texts, cared about articulating a sense of identity and maintaining the cohesion of their political communities. The use of the vocabulary of *gentes* and their laws was one of the hallmarks of Carolingian royal political and legal culture and, as we saw in earlier chapters, various kings emphasized their relationships with hispani and Goths as a way to emphasize their imperial status. One strategy the kings and their courts employed to articulate these notions was in issuing diplomas to recipients in the Spanish March. Royal diplomas as seen elsewhere in this chapter provide few clues indeed. Lothar III in 968 granted confirmation of rights and properties to two small monasteries under one abbot, named Sunyer. The abbot is said in the text to have come to the king *a partibus Gothici regni*.[156] That contrasts with the language apparent twenty years earlier, in a grant from his father to the monastery of Sant Pere of Rodes in Peralada, referring to the recipients coming *a regione Yspaniae* to an audience with the King Louis IV.[157] Louis also issued a diploma to Abbot Cesari of Montserrat using similar language, indicating that the abbot had travelled from Hispania.[158] The most we can conclude from this paltry evidence is that the geographical concepts of Gothia and Hispania continued to hold meaning for the royal court, especially when the recipients of grants travelled to court in order to receive them. If the requests for grants came in other ways, such as in writing or perhaps while in conjunction with a council or assembly, the scribal practice made no note of the geography. All were faithful to the king, regardless of their homes and bases of operation.

A final observation concerning the legacy of the Carolingians and its connections to culture and identity in 'Gothia' remains. The *Chronicon Moissiacense Maius*, the text that begins as a universal chronicle and then incorporates a history of the Franks under the Carolingians, stands as testament to the integration of the 'Gothic' south into the Carolingian empire. A manuscript now in Paris, BnF lat. 5941, contains narrative history similar to and relating to the *Chronicon*, amongst other texts, fragments of Einhard's *Vita Karoli* and references to Benedict of Aniane. This twelfth-century manuscript is heavily interpolated and less reliable as a witness to eighth-century history than its eleventh-century counterpart. But the manuscript's trustworthiness as an 'accurate' source for

---

[156] CC 2, 203. [157] CC 2, 230. [158] CC 2, 256.

history is not the real issue here. Instead, the current state of the codex shows that the early medieval material at some point was bound with a later copy of the *Gesta comitum Barcinonensium*, the legendary account of the counts of Barcelona that traces their mythical descent from Charlemagne. Scholars of the manuscript take this as evidence that the earlier chronicle and associated material were written or copied at Aniane, the monastery of Benedict, and then later made their way to Ripoll, where they were found in the modern era.[159] The codex thus stands as evidence that the Carolingian heritage was still important in the Spanish March well after the end of the dynasty, and that Carolingian history was still central to the identity of the rulers of Catalonia well into the Middle Ages.

CONCLUSIONS

In the late tenth century, Catalonia was part of the Frankish kingdom, even though its own political organization owed very little to direct Frankish royal influence. Certainly the counties themselves were no longer exactly the same as they had been in the early days of the conquest. The counts exercised royal prerogatives, like counts elsewhere in the kingdom.[160] But independent counts were not a new development in the tenth century. One need only to look at the examples of Bernard of Septimania and Bernard of Gothia to find *marchiones* who were more concerned with their own aggrandizement and roles in the politics of the wider kingdom than with administering the March as a loyal agent of the king. The main difference between them and the heirs of Wifred the Hairy is that the latter counts did not raise armies in open rebellion.[161] The tenth-century counts were more or less forced to turn to self-government out of isolation from a meaningful royal presence,

---

[159] R. Kramer, 'Great Expectations: Imperial Ideologies and Ecclesiastical Reforms from Charlemagne to Louis the Pious (813–822)', PhD diss. (Freie Universität Berlin, 2014), 342–4. I thank Dr Kramer for showing me his dissertation and the references to this fascinating manuscript history.

[160] I appreciate the parallel argument of Zimmermann, 'La formació d'una sobirania', 41–7 (English at 442), giving as example power of the counts of Flanders in their territory. Yet, in noting the degree to which counts maintained ties to kings, Zimmermann defers to the concept of feudalism, even while observing that the relationship with the king was 'the keystone of the feudal system which had still to be constructed'. But see West, *Reframing the Feudal Revolution* as cited in note 150, whose articulation is far more persuasive.

[161] See, for deeper exploration of the long-term development of the descendants of Wifred the Hairy, N. L. Taylor, 'Inheritance of Power in the House of Guifred the Hairy: Contemporary Perspectives on the Formation of a Dynasty', in R. F. Berkhofer III, A. Cooper, and A. J. Kosto, eds, *The Experience of Power in Medieval Europe, 950–1350: Essays in Honor of Thomas N. Bisson* (Aldershot, 2005), 126–51.

while those of the ninth century sought their fortunes within a much better integrated empire. What is unique in the late Carolingian era about the Spanish March in the context of a diminished West Frankish monarchy is its simultaneous diplomacy with the caliphate. No other former province of the West Frankish kingdom linked itself to a 'foreign' power as Borrell's embassies to Córdoba suggest he did. No other former province, however, was as near a foreign power as were the counties of the March. Counts in Aquitaine and Burgundy could assert their own power with little fear of retribution from the crown, but Borrell could see the example of his contemporaries in León and Navarre who called themselves kings. Perhaps his peaceful, even theoretically submissive, relationship with the caliphs spared him their military wrath. It was only when al-Mansur, a usurper in his own right, needed a quick infusion of wealth that Muslim forces sacked Barcelona. Thus, the counts in the March, adhering to legal traditions, kept their comital titles in deference to the Frankish monarchy, but also protected themselves in making only modest claims to power within the peninsula.

At the same time, characterizing the entire tenth century as the period of Catalonia's 'march towards sovereignty' misses the mark. Certainly, the counts of the Spanish March in the tenth century did what they could to enhance their own status, to build their authority, and to secure their territories. Nobles throughout the Carolingian period did the same. The fact that the monarchs were neither willing nor able to arrange the affairs of the Spanish March simply meant that the counts there had to make their own way in the tumultuous world of the tenth and eleventh centuries.

CONCLUSION

Carolingian Catalonia, 778–987

Catalonia was a Carolingian creation. Searching for the constitutional birth of Catalonia, earlier scholars, perhaps inadvertently, gave the region undue attention as the principality that it later became, distorting our understanding of its Carolingian and post-Carolingian development. Even though most historians of the region's early medieval history have been aware of anachronism and tried to account for it in their investigations, eschewing the words 'Catalan' and 'Catalunya', still, in emphasizing the 'march towards sovereignty', Catalonia's place in the wider tenth-century world of political decentralization can easily become lost. What is more, viewing stronger ties to other political centres such as the caliph in Córdoba or the papacy as a substitute for connections to the monarchy may be a mistake, again deriving from the desire to find the point at which Catalonia became constitutionally separate from the Frankish kingdom. Indeed, the symbols of sovereignty and submission in the documents of the years 985–8 are widely seen as marking the ultimate detachment of Catalonia from the Frankish kingdom. Although the events of those years do indeed provide an end point to the region's Carolingian period, this study has emphasized that the constitutional origins of modern Catalonia are impossible to pin down. As for the relationships between Catalonian secular and ecclesiastical governors and Roman popes, by the middle of the tenth century the major monasteries and bishoprics in the Spanish March were held by members of the comital families, and counts sought papal protection for these churches. It is important to remember that the institutions of the papacy could be understood as having developed during the same period as did the Spanish March itself.[1] By forging and strengthening direct relationships with popes, the counts, bishops,

---

[1] See T. F. X. Noble, *The Republic of St. Peter: the Birth of the Papal State, 680–825* (Philadelphia, 1984).

and abbots of the March were continuing to participate in the legacy of the Carolingian world.

Paul Freedman has observed that Catalonia never really was Frankish.[2] It is worth considering what that might mean. Ninth-century evidence shows that while the region cannot be called 'Frankish' in terms of its demographics, it certainly was 'Carolingian' in that it functioned like other provinces in the politics of the monarchy, church, and secular aristocracy. As the region of the Carolingian realm most endangered by the Adoptionist heresy, Gothia (the Spanish March and Septimania) had to be brought more in line with mainstream, court-sponsored religious culture. Concerning these developments, Catalonia was very much like other areas Charlemagne conquered, despite its own peculiar situations. The well-known *aprisio* charters of Charlemagne and his descendants shed light on the effort kings made to enforce their authority in the March by linking themselves to local figures without the mediation of counts. This was a common development, highlighting the royal strategy of establishing ties with parties who participated in politics on the ground, while illustrating one of the varied ways the centre incorporated far-off peoples and places. The foundational works on Carolingian politics emphasize the role of monasteries, which were less prominent in the Spanish March under Charlemagne, although kings did grant privileges to abbeys, such as Santa Maria de Arles and Sant Esteve de Banyoles.[3] That the two efforts of religious reform and sociopolitical patronage were simultaneous under Charlemagne makes the Spanish March an optimal demonstration for the dual orientation of Carolingian vitality: expansion and renaissance.

This study began with a review of developments in the area that would become Catalonia in the late Visigothic period and eighth century. While the Visigothic province of Gallia had been the site of rebellions, individuals based there did not seek to overthrow royal authority and establish independent rule. Yet self-rule did fall to the north-east, that is, the province of Gallia along with Tarraconensis, in the wake of the Muslim conquest of Spain. Later, unlike Asturias and other mountainous areas of northern Iberia, which had not been completely subjected to Muslim rule, the north-east was incorporated into the Arab-Berber administration. Those conditions prevailed for a few generations at most, however, as the Frankish conquest of Septimania in 759 and the Carolingian

---

[2] P. Freedman, 'Symbolic Implications of the Events of 985–988', in *Symposium internacional*, vol. 1, 117–29.

[3] Chief amongst them M. Innes, *State and Society in the Early Middle Ages: the Middle Rhine Valley, 400–1100* (Cambridge, 2000) and H. Hummer, *Politics and Power in Early Medieval Europe: Alsace and the Frankish Realm, 600–1000* (Cambridge, 2005).

occupation of Girona, Urgell, and Barcelona in the period 785–801 pushed out the Muslim powers, often with the assistance of local Christians. Thus it is only in the second half of the eighth century, and from a Frankish perspective, that sources identify individuals and groups as Goths. The sources do not explicitly explain what their labels meant, which has allowed modern readers to attribute to them ethnicity, but the labels just as easily could have indicated membership in a political class. In a relatively straightforward way, Pippin, Charlemagne, and young Louis the Pious integrated members of the local and regional political class into Carolingian sociopolitical networks. Referring to their allies as Goths highlighted the kings' prowess and extension of Christian rule into new territories.

In the last decades of the eighth century and the first half of the ninth, Carolingian kings gradually incorporated Septimania and the Spanish March more fully into the Frankish kingdom. Politically, rulers assigned individuals responsibility for the defence and administration of law and order in the region. Their armies made attempts to expand the reach of their authority while immigrants from elsewhere in Spain arrived in Frankish-held territory seeking economic opportunity. Kings appropriated the policy of *aprisio* in order to provide that opportunity and work the newcomers, called hispani because of their origins in Hispania beyond royal control, into royally sponsored political networks. Meanwhile, the religious observance of the former Visigothic regions was reformed along the lines of the Carolingian programme. Charlemagne and his advisors were troubled by the doctrine of Spanish Adoptionism and took steps to see the introduction of proper Christian teaching. The leading preacher in this effort, Benedict of Aniane, later played a crucial role in the establishment of an updated Rule of St Benedict in monasteries throughout the Carolingian realm. Royal patronage of monasteries in the Spanish March encouraged locals to adopt the Rule as well. The success of royal efforts to integrate the March into the kingdom is shown by the case of Count Bera of Barcelona. With family roots in Septimania and having governed parts of the Spanish March for nearly twenty years, Bera was accused of disloyalty and removed from office. The fact that his accuser was called a Goth by Frankish writers indicates that locals held Carolingian authority in high esteem; the way to remove Bera was to involve the emperor, Louis the Pious. Likewise, the *aprisio* settlers had recourse to Charlemagne to uphold their claims against the actions of their neighbours and counts. An uprising in the 820s led by Aizo has puzzled historians for generations. Given the nature of the evidence, little is known about Aizo's background, leading to a great deal of speculation about his motives and objectives. Despite what Catalan scholars of the twentieth century argued, none of the evidence for any of these cases indicates tensions between locals in the Spanish March and their Frankish rulers brought about by conflicts rooted in ethnicity or identity politics.

Aizo's uprising paved the way for the rise of Bernard of Septimania, the first of a series of Frankish magnates holding office in the Spanish March to cause trouble for Carolingian kings. Yet neither Bernard nor any of his successors, including his son William, the great nobles Humfrid and Odalric, and the recalcitrant Bernard of Gothia, however powerful and ambitious, sought to throw off Carolingian authority over the region. Rather, they negotiated the competition amongst the Carolingian rival kings, alternatively backing Charles the Bald, Pippin II of Aquitaine, or Louis the German. At the same time, documentary and historiographic texts from the ninth century paint the Carolingian emperors and kings as ruling over Goths and hispani, accentuating the dynasty's claims to enhanced, imperial authority. This practice dates as far back in time as Charlemagne's use of Lombard as well as Frankish royal titles following his conquest of Italy. In the context of Charles the Bald's struggle against Pippin II of Aquitaine and disagreements with high nobles, the use of such terminology demonstrates two truths. The first is that Charles positioned himself as the legitimate ruler over the people of Septimania and the Spanish March, while the second is that the labels for different identities were more significant for royal claims and aggrandizement than they were for the quotidian functioning of politics on the ground.

In the 820s, Aizo rose against Carolingian rule and carved out a space of his own, but rather than indicate that the whole of the Spanish March failed to be integrated, this in fact shows the opposite. Indeed, no other political contestant in the area could act outside the orbit of the monarchy. Bernard of Septimania's son William wrested control of Barcelona in the late 840s. He did so not to foster a separatist movement but rather to move against Charles the Bald to the benefit of Pippin II of Aquitaine as well as himself. The authority of the monarchy endured, as the testimony of diplomas sought by monasteries, churches, and individuals in the March confirms. By 870, Charles was secure in his rule of the West Frankish Kingdom and returned to the pattern of appointing lesser nobles with local power bases to *honores* in the March. Amongst this group was Wifred 'the Hairy', famous in Catalonia as a founding father who in his own time remained steadfast in his recognition of the Carolingian dynasty. In all of these stories, no trace of what modern observers might call ethnic identity serves to explain political action. Indeed, from the perspective of the court sources, which are the only ones to employ such terminology, identity labels serve only to highlight the power of the rulers. They were not merely kings of the Franks, but held sway over a distant land they called Gothia. It may be more accurate to say that the labels these sources used were more important as markers of geography than of identity. The geographic frontier had been firmly incorporated into the political networks of the kingdom.

Wifred the Hairy took charge of several counties in the 870s, thanks to royal appointments. He also took the initiative to sponsor what must have been a spontaneous wave of migration into the plain of Vic, the area lost in Aizo's uprising. By the time of Wifred's death, he had cultivated his own power in the Spanish March but was not strong enough to take on nearby Muslim powers successfully. Nor did he seek to rule independently of the monarchy that had appointed him. His sons succeeded him during the reign of Odo, a king who was not Carolingian, without securing royal recognition first. For generations, their succession has been seen as a nascent Catalan nationalism. But this presses the evidence too far. Monasteries and churches continued to seek royal confirmation of rights and possessions, and even the counts themselves called upon royal authority to help settle disputes at the high levels of secular and ecclesiastical politics. Notably through the tenth century, the counts, bishops, and abbots sought out members of the Carolingian family when they needed royal intervention more frequently than they called upon Odo's descendants. Even in the context of shifting Carolingian royal power, that family still served as the legitimate authority in the Spanish March. Identity labels such as Goth, Frank, or hispanus seem to have been less important, even from the royal perspective, than they had been in the ninth century.

The questions of Carolingian influence and cultural identity extend beyond political activities and into the world of learned culture. The Carolingian period is known for its 'renaissance' as well as its empire, after all, and surviving evidence from the Spanish March shows that schools and teachers in the region followed the programme as far as they could. The foremost concern of the intellectual reform effort was to have authoritative texts used in correct ways, and at least some of those texts found their way to the March. Examination of those and other texts indicates that elements of the Carolingian renaissance reached into the region, marking it as a typical part of the empire, which overall saw the court-sponsored reform take on different forms according to regional variations. Given the rich literate culture of the Visigothic era, which in its own right made an imprint on Carolingian thought, the regional tradition in the Spanish March had strong foundations.

It is inaccurate to conclude that cultural development in the Spanish March during the ninth and tenth centuries emanated solely from its

Visigothic patrimony, just as it would be to take it as merely a regional derivative of a Carolingian standard. The study above reveals that, when people in the Spanish March had access to texts considered to be authoritative, they copied and used them. Local libraries owned works by Bede or Usuard, who travelled through the Spanish March; a copy of the *Dionysio-Hadriana* survives from the March as well. When such books were unavailable, there were others, products of the leading church figures of the Visigothic age. By the middle and late tenth century, when Carolingian royal power was changing, the learning of the Spanish March was so renowned that Gerbert of Aurillac journeyed there to study astronomy and mathematics. The Latin in the books he read was written in the script fostered by the Carolingian reform. The Rule of the monasteries he visited was that of St Benedict, another product of the reform. In terms of intellectual culture, as in political structures, Catalonia was a creation of the connections forged across the Pyrenees in the wake of the Carolingian conquest.

The history of Catalonia in the tenth century is treated in the classic modern historiography as a march towards nationhood. Certainly a principality centred on Barcelona did develop, as did the Catalan language and various other customs, during the course of the Middle Ages. Political autonomy, for its part, did emerge in the second half of the tenth century, as local political figures in the Spanish March, especially Borrell II of Barcelona, took over many of the duties of kings in this period. They did so out of necessity, continuing to use the title of count, and in a few cases *marchio*, but never styling themselves kings. Loyal autonomy like this is puzzling for those who know that the counts of Barcelona eventually also became kings of Aragon as a result of marriage between the neighbouring comital and royal families. Why the 'Catalans' should continue to cast themselves in a subordinate position while their neighbours to the west claimed regal dignity has been the chief question considered by modern scholars. The answer has been sought in an almost mystical, 'Visigothic' penchant for legalism, but the history of integration into Carolingian political networks is a better explanation. In the earlier period of the eighth and ninth centuries, kings sought to build relationships with political brokers in the Spanish March. Those efforts succeeded to such a degree that, even by the late tenth century, the reverse was true. Leaders in the March relied on ties to the Carolingian kings as the means to legitimate their positions locally. Seen in these terms, the political divorce between Borrell and Hugh Capet in the late 980s marks the end of Catalonia's Carolingian history because it ended the Carolingian dynasty's rule, not because it allowed the rulers of the Spanish March to achieve independence. Nobles and churches in the March had preferred

Carolingian to Robertian kings for generations at any rate; Hugh's reign definitively ended any chance for a renewal of the relationship between the old dynasty and the March. The diminution of Carolingian overlordship during the tenth century presented the counts of the March with both challenges and opportunities. Borrell had already engaged in diplomacy with the caliphs of Córdoba in an effort to protect his lands from military aggression. He could not rely on a Frankish king and so had to take further initiative himself. Yet none of this constitutes the formation of a new nation. Certainly, the counts of the Spanish March in the tenth century did what they could to enhance their own positions and defend their lands and interests. They simply had to make their own way in a thorny, late and post-Carolingian world.

All told, the Carolingian rulers largely succeeded in their efforts to integrate the region, and the Spanish March retained elements of its Visigothic heritage. The two developments are not mutually exclusive. It was, of course, never the Carolingians' goal to eradicate local culture, so much as to bring the region and its people into the Christian fold led by God's chosen kings. For example, the personal names recorded in the region's rich charter evidence carried Gothic linguistic elements deep into the ninth and tenth centuries. These ranged from Visigothic royal names, such as Athanagild and Alaric, to other Gothic names such as Ricimir and Ansemundus.[4] Meanwhile, no evidence has ever suggested significant Frankish migration over the Pyrenees in the wake of the conquest, though the charters do feature names that perhaps indicated other identities, including Franco and Longovardus along with the toponyms Villa Franchone, Pugna Francorum, and Insula Longobardi.[5] Trans-Pyrenean names like these are vastly outnumbered by indigenous Gothic nomenclature. Fifty charters from the ninth and tenth centuries show 'got' or 'god', even 'gud' as a linguistic element in names of both men and women. The most frequently occurring name with this element is Gotmar, carried by two bishops of Girona and the first bishop of Vic. Although it is far from certain that this and other names like Godo, Gudila, Godvira, and Eldregota indicate Gothic ethnicity, much less any attempt to distinguish individual locals from their Frankish neighbours, names are a part of a collective cultural practice, so the

---

[4] Athanagild: *Archivo Condal*, nos. 10 and 14. Alaric: *Archivo Condal*, nos. 90 and 173. Ricimir: *Archivo Condal*, no.2; Marquès, ed., *Cartoral*, no. 19. Ansemundus CC 2, 58; Marquès, ed., *Cartoral*, no. 4.

[5] Franco: *Archivo Condal*, no. 16. Longovardo: *Archivo Condal*, no. 15. Villa Francone: *Archivo Condal*, nos. 19 and 53. Pugna Francorum: CC 2, 78. Insula Longobardi: *Archivo Condal*, no. 38. See also A. M. Mundó, *De quan hispans, gots, jueus, àrabs i francs circulaven per Catalunya*, Seminari de Paleografia, Diplomàtica i Codocologia Monografies (Bellaterra, 2001).

evidence shows that naming patterns continued to adhere to tradition.[6]

Personal and place names point to survivals of social and cultural practices that date to the period before Carolingian overlordship. Appropriately, a great deal of scholarly attention has highlighted the survival of Visigothic law. This code survived to the end of the tenth century, when it was redacted by a *iudex* and close associate of Count Borrell named Bonushomo. Subsequently, elements of the ancient law became the basis for the famed *Usatges* of Barcelona, the fundamental law of the county during its height in the high Middle Ages.[7] Thus, law was an important element of the survival of Visigothic culture during the Carolingian period and beyond. All the same, the Carolingians were famous for allowing local legal practices to survive, rather than extending Salic law to all inhabitants of the empire. Modern historians have shown the subtlety of the Frankish impact on law and society in various regions.[8] Law is one example of something supposedly distinctive about the Spanish March that ironically serves to underscore how much it had in common with other regions under Carolingian rule. The persistence of Visigothic law was a component of a strong Visigothic cultural survival, but it did little to prevent counts and bishops in the ninth and tenth centuries from recognizing military and political Carolingian overlordship. Being 'Goths' had no bearing on membership of the Frankish kingdom. Indeed, well into the tenth century, the ecclesiastical and secular elite of the Spanish March continued to imagine themselves as part of that kingdom.[9]

Several aspects of Catalonian culture can be attributed to Carolingian influence. For example, Smaragdus of St-Mihiel's *Explanatio in Regulam Sancti Benedicti*, a commentary on the Rule, became an important vector of the Rule's transmission to other parts of Spain.[10] The Carolingian triumph over Spanish Adoptionism did not sever the church of the March from the old Visigothic hierarchy so much as solidify its association with the Carolingian reform movement. After all, the province of Narbonne, to which the churches of the Carolingian Spanish March belonged, had

---

[6] Godo: *Archivo Condal*, no. 30. Gudila: CC 3, no. 71. Godvira and Eldregota: CC 4, no. 6.

[7] See the discussion in, for example, Bowman, *Shifting Landmarks: Property, Proof, and Dispute in Catalonia around the Year 1000* (Ithaca, 2004), 81–99 and 132–3.

[8] For example, W. Brown, *Unjust Seizure: Conflict, Interest, and Authority in Early Medieval Society* (Ithaca, 2001).

[9] The vocabulary in this sentence intentionally evokes the concepts in Benedict Anderson, *Imagined Communities: Reflections on the Origin and Spread of Nationalism* (London, 1991).

[10] A. Linage Conde, 'El monacato mózarabe hacia la benedictinización', in *Cristianità d'occidente e cristianità d'oriente (secolo VI–XI)* Settimane di Studio della Fondazione Centro Italiano de Studi sull'Alto Medioevo LI (Spoleto, 2004), 445.

itself been part of the Visigothic kingdom. The controversies surrounding Sclua, Ermemir, and Servus Dei in the late ninth century arose not from separatist sentiment, but rather from simple ambition. There was no sense of a Gothic community standing in opposition to their Frankish rulers, and in fact the ecclesiastical controversies depended on the kings for their resolutions.

The political and social development typical of medieval Catalonia originated in the late ninth- and tenth-century expansion of settlement along the frontier. Holders of castles became increasingly powerful people on local scenes, but the counts remained authoritative. The preceding discussion has not emphasized the frontier aspect of Catalonian society both in order to draw attention to the region in its own right, albeit a part of the wider Carolingian world, and to avoid imposing 'frontier' as a theoretical model that could distort conclusions drawn. The political and social developments just mentioned certainly owe much to their frontier context, but castles also sprang up everywhere in post-Carolingian Europe as localism and decentralization of power began to become the hallmarks of social and political organization. One important factor for Catalonia's eventual political detachment from Francia, namely, the migration into and settlement of formerly Muslim land, resembles the histories of other parts of Christian Spain.[11] In this aspect of its history, the March's frontier setting and its interaction with Muslim Spain are important, but the governing institutions that moved with those people owed a great deal to its incorporation into the Frankish kingdom.

The contribution of al-Andalus to the political development of Catalonia mirrors the intellectual impact of Islamic learning. In their interactions across the frontier and borrowings from Arabic texts, Catalonian schoolmasters cultivated arts and sciences to the point that they had something to give the Franks. Indeed, their accomplishments drew Gerbert of Aurillac to the March so that he could study mathematics and astronomy. This aspect of the study of a 'frontier' is greatly valuable for understanding the nature of the empire itself. But the Carolingian world had frontiers elsewhere, and various regional practices within them existed alongside a mainstream culture emanating from the court and engaged by lay and ecclesiastical elites throughout the realms. Thus, culture, like political and social organization, in the Spanish March during the ninth century and into the tenth fits the 'model' (even though the term may be too strong) of a region within the Carolingian empire that has arisen in recent historical studies.

[11] Lewis, 'Cataluña como frontera military (870–1050)', *Anuario de Estudios Medievales* 5 (1968): 15–29.

Looking back from the end of the Carolingian dynasty in the late tenth century, Catalonia may appear as having been only superficially integrated into the kingdom now ruled by Hugh Capet. As we have seen, the counts in Catalonia exercised their power locally and engaged in diplomacy with only a few nods towards the authority of the king. Over the course of the tenth century, the royal presence waned in terms of the issuance of diplomas just as counts succeeded by inheritance rather than royal appointment. Bishops and abbots came from comital families rather than royal circles. Such conditions were facts of life throughout the late Carolingian period. In the ninth century, counts used the resources of the March in their political machinations involving Frankish kings. Catalonia functioned for them as did properties and *honores* in Burgundy, Neustria, or elsewhere. These men were members of an aristocracy with a wide reach. Meanwhile, local nobles actually administered the March. Such was the situation in all corners of the Frankish realms where great magnates held high offices. Thus the 'Carolingian-ness' of Neustria, Champagne, or Lotharingia has not been questioned.[12] Given multiple *honores*, powerful aristocrats had to leave the daily governance of their regions in the hands of others. In this way, the distance of Catalonia from real Frankish control or royal centralization was no different than it was for any other part of the ninth-century empire. Only in the tenth century, when royal power was re-configured, did local autonomy eventually become a foundation for a new polity. It is important to remember that the royal presence diminished throughout the West Frankish kingdom during the tenth century; Catalonia was not unique. It is distinct as a former Carolingian province not because of its survival as a principality during the tenth and eleventh centuries, but rather because of its twelfth-century conjunction with the kingdom of Aragon. The resulting 'statehood' grew from its rulers also being kings in their own right, while other southern French principalities were eventually re-absorbed by the crown. In the Capetian kingdom and Ottonian empire, rulers buttressed their legitimacy with links to the Carolingian past, including marriage to women of the Carolingian family.[13] Even in Italy, a conquered region where the Frankish impact was important but subtle, as it was in Catalonia, rulers after the end of the Carolingian line in 875 still drew

---

[12] C. West, *Reframing the Feudal Revolution: Political and Social Transformation between the Marne and Moselle, c.800–c.1100* (Cambridge, 2013), esp. chapters 4 and 5.

[13] See for example G. M. Spiegel, 'The *Reditus regni ad stirpem Karoli Magni*: a New Look', *French Historical Studies* 7 (1971): 145–74.

legitimacy from their closeness to the former imperial family.[14] The counts of Catalonia likewise built on certain Carolingian legacies, even as they drew upon older traditions, and looked to chart their own course. Indeed, until the end of the tenth century these counts relied heavily upon the legitimacy of the Carolingian monarchy to substantiate their own rule. They did not need to claim marriage or kinship links to the Carolingian dynasty because, unlike their contemporaries in Germany and Italy, they did not aspire to royal title. The budding principality was, in the end, a creation of Carolingian political prowess; incorporation into the Frankish empire had a formative influence in the society of Catalonia. New families wore royal crowns, and the power of local figures was perhaps more important than ever before. The beginning of the eleventh century was a time when Catalonia, like the rest of Europe, was no longer Carolingian, but used the Carolingian heritage to build a new society.

---

[14] For orientation, see P. Delogu, 'Lombard and Carolingian Italy', in R. McKitterick, ed., *The New Cambridge Medieval History*, vol. 2, c.700–c.900 (Cambridge, 1995), 290–319, esp. 310–19.

BIBLIOGRAPHY

MANUSCRIPTS CONSULTED

Arxiu Capitular de Barcelona

Codex 28
Codex 64
Codex 69
Codex 79
Codex 131
Codex 137
Codex 178–1, aka Fragmenta Codicum 1
Codex 187-B, aka Fragmenta Codicum 10, B 14

Archivo de la Corona de Aragón, Colecciones Manuscritos

Ripoll 40
Ripoll 42
Ripoll 46
Ripoll 49
Ripoll 52
Ripoll 59
Ripoll 74
Ripoll 83
Ripoll 106
Ripoll 116
Ripoll 151
Ripoll 168
Ripoll 225
Ripoll 229

Bibliography

Archivo de la Corona de Aragón, Fragmentos Manuscritos

Frag. 22
Frag. 33
Frag. 157
Frag. 395
Frag. 396

Biblioteca de Catalunya

MS 569
MS 945
MS 2363
MS 2541
MS 3724

EDITED PRIMARY SOURCES

d'Abadal i de Vinyals, R., ed. *Catalunya Carolíngia 2: Els diplomes carolingis a Catalunya.* 2 vols. Barcelona, 1926–52.

Catalunya Carolíngia 3: Els comtats de Pallars i Ribagorça. 2 vols. Barcelona, 1955.

Admonitio generalis. MGH Fontes iuris germanici antique in usum scholarum 16. Eds. H. Mordek, K. Zechiel-Eckes, and M. Glatthaar. Hanover, 2012.

Agobard. Opera omnia. CCCM, 52. Ed. L. Van Acker. Turnhout, 1981.

Aimoin. *De Translatione ss. martyrum Georgii monachi, Aurelii et Nathaliae. PL,* 115. Ed. J.-P. Migne. 1852, 939–60.

Translatio sancti Vincentii. PL, 126. Ed. J.-P. Migne. Paris, 1852, 1013–28.

Alcuin. *Adversus Elipandum Libri IV. PL,* 101. Ed. J.-P. Migne. Paris, 1844, 243–300.

Contra Felicem Urgellitanum libri VII. PL, 101. Ed. J.-P. Migne, Paris 1844, 119–230.

Epistola 7. *MGH Epistolae karolini aevi,* 2. Ed. E. Dümmler. Berlin, 1895, 32.

Versus de laude metricae artis. MGH Poet. lat. carolini aevi 1. Ed. E. Dümmler. Berlin, 1881, 347–8.

Ancienne Chronique d'Uzès. HGL 2. Toulouse, 1875, col. 13–29.

Ancienne chronique d'Uzès. In *Histoire Générale de Languedoc,* 2. Eds C. Devic and J. Vaisette. Toulouse, 1875, cols. 239.

Annales Alamannici. In *MGH SS,* 1. Ed. G. H. Pertz. Hanover, 1826, 40–60.

Annales d'Aniane. In *Histoire Générale de Languedoc,* 2. Eds C. Devic and J. Vaisette. Toulouse, 1875, cols. 1–12.

Annales de Saint-Bertin. Eds. F. Grat, J. Vielliard, and S. Clémencet. Paris, 1964.

Annales Fuldenses. In *MGH SS,* 1. Ed. G. H. Pertz. Hanover, 1826, 337–415.

Annales Laureshamenses. In *MGH SS,* 1. Ed. G. H. Pertz. Hanover, 1826, 22–39.

Annales Regni Francorum 741–829 qui dicuntur Annales Laurissenses maiores et Einhardi. In *MGH SSrG,* 6. Ed. G. Kurze. Hanover, 1895.

Annales Xantenses et Annales Vedastini. In *MGH SRG,* 12. Ed. B. von Simson. Hanover, 1909.

The Annals of Fulda. Trans. T. Reuter. Ninth-Century Histories 2. Manchester, 1992.

Bibliography

The Annals of St-Bertin. Trans. J. L. Nelson. Ninth-Century Histories 1. Manchester, 1991.

Ansegisus. *Karoli Magni, Hludowici et Hlotharii imperatorum capitularia. MGH Leges 1.* Ed. G. H. Pertz. Hanover, 1835, 256–325. Also *MGH Capit. 1.* Ed. A. Boretius. Hanover, 1883, 382–450.

Ardo. *Vita Benedicti Anianensis.* In *MGH SS,* 15. Ed. G. Waitz. Hanover, 1887, 198–220.

Astronomer. *Vita Hludowici imperatoris.* In *MGH SS,* 2. Hanover, 1829, 604–48. English trans. T. F. X. Noble, trans. *Charlemagne and Louis the Pious: Lives by Einhard, Notker, Ermoldus, Thegan, and the Astronomer.* University Park, PA: The Pennsylvania State University Press, 2009, 219–302.

Baraut, C. 'Els documents, dels segles IX i X, conservats a l'Arixiu Capitular de la Seu d'Urgell.' *Urgellia,* 2 (1979): 7–145.

'Les acta de consagracions d'esglésies del bisbat d'Urgell.' *Urgellia* 1 (1978): 11–182.

Barrau-Dihigo, L., ed. *El 'Gesta comitum Barcinonensium'.* Barcelona, 1925. New ed. L. Barrau-Dihigo and J. M. Torrents. Croniques Catalanes 2. Barcelona, 2007.

Bede. *Opera Didascalica. CCSL 123 A.* Ed. C. W. Jones. Turnhout, 1975.

The Reckoning of Time. Trans. F. Wallis. Liverpool, 1999.

Benedict of Aniane. *Disputatio Benedicti levitae adversus Felicianem impietatem.* In *PL,* 103. Ed. J.-P. Migne. Paris, 1844, 1399–1411.

Testimoniorum nubecula de incarnatione Domini, sancta et indiuidua Trinitate et iteratione baptismatis deuitanda pernicie. In *PL,* 103. Ed. J.-P. Migne. Paris, 1844, 1381–99.

Blumenshine, G., ed. *Liber Alcuini contra haeresim Felicis: Edition with an Introduction.* Vatican City, 1980.

Boethius. *Institution arithmétique.* ed. and French trans., J. -Y. Guillaumin. Paris, 1995, 2nd ed. 2002.

Bramon, D., ed. *De quan erem o no musulmans: textos del 713 al 1000. Continuació de l'Obra de J. M. Millàs i Vallicrosa.* Barcelona and Vic, 2000.

Capitulare Septimanicum. MGH Capit. 2. Ed. A. Boretius and V. Krause. Hanover, 1897, 256–8.

Capitulare monasticum. MGH Capit. 1. Ed. A. Boretius. Hanover, 1883, 343–9.

Casas Homs, J. M. 'Una gramàtica inèdita d'Usuard.' *Analecta Montserratensia* 10 (1964): 77–129.

Chronicon Moissiacense. MGH SS, 1. Ed. G. H. Pertz. Hanover, 1826, 280–313.

Codex Carolinus. MGH Epistolae Merowingici et Karoli aevi 1. Berlin, 1892, no. 61.

Concilium Aquisganense (800). MGH Conc. 2.1. Hanover 1906, 220–225.

Concilium Aquisganense (816). MGH Conc. 2.1. Hanover 1906, 307–464.

Concilium Francofurtense (794). MGH Conc. 2.1. Hanover 1906, 110–171.

Constable, O. R., ed. *Medieval Iberia: Readings from Christian, Muslim, and Jewish Sources.* Philadelphia, 1997.

Constans i Serrats, L. G., ed. *Diplomatari de Banyoles 1 (De l'any 822 al 1050).* Banyoles, 1985.

Constitutio de Hispanis. MGH Capit. 1. Ed. A. Boretius. Hanover, 1883, 261.

277

Bibliography

Council of Attigny (874). MGH Conc. 4. Ed. W. Hartmann. Hanover, 1998, 597–600.

Council of Tusey. MGH Conc. 4. Ed. W. Hartmann. Hanover, 1998, 12–42.

Devic, C., and J. Vaissette, eds. *Histoire générale de Languedoc.* Toulouse, 1879–92.

Dhuoda. *Handbook for Her Warrior Son: Liber Manualis.* Ed. and trans. M. Thiébaux. Cambridge, 1998.

  Manuel pour mon fils. Ed. P. Riché. Sources Chrétiennes 225. Paris, 1975.

  Handbook for William: a Carolingian Woman's Counsel for Her Son. Trans. C. Neel. Washington, DC, 1999.

Divisio imperii. MGH Leges 1. G. H. Pertz. Hanover, 1835, 140–1.

Dubois, J., ed. *Le martyrologe d'Usuard: Texte et commentaire* Bruxelles, 1965.

Dutton, P. E., ed. and trans. *Charlemagne's Courtier: the Complete Einhard.* Peterborough, ON, 1998.

Einhard. *Vita Karoli, MGH SS rer. Germ. 25.* Hanover and Leipzig, 1911. English trans. T. F. X. Noble. *Charlemagne and Louis the Pious: Lives by Einhard, Notker, Ermoldus, Thegan, and the Astronomer.* University Park, PA: The Pennsylvania State University Press, 2009, 7–50.

Epistola de litteris colendis, MGH Capit. 1. Ed. A. Boretius. Hanover, 1883, 78–9.

Ermoldus Nigellus, *In honorem Hludowici. MGH Poetae latini aevi Carolini, 2.* Ed. E. Dümmler. Berlin, 1884, 1–91. English trans. T. F. X. Noble. *Charlemagne and Louis the Pious: Lives by Einhard, Notker, Ermoldus, Thegan, and the Astronomer.* University Park, PA: The Pennsylvania State University Press, 2009, 119–86.

Fàbrega Grau, Á. *Santa Eulalia de Barcelona: revisión de un problema histórico.* Rome, 1958.

Font Rius, J. M., ed. *Cartas de poblacion y franquicia de Cataluña 1.* Madrid-Barcelona, 1969.

Gerbert of Aurillac. *The Letters of Gerbert, with His Papal Privileges as Sylvester II.* Trans. H. Platt. New York: Columbia University Press, 1961.

Gil, J., ed. *Corpus Scriptorum Muzarabicorum.* 2 vols. Madrid: Consejo Superior de Investigaciones Cientificas, 1973.

Hincmar of Rheims. *De ordine palatii. MGH Fontes iuris Germanici antique 3.* Hanover, 1980.

Julian. *Sancti Iuliani Toletanae sedis episcopi opera. CCSL 115.* Ed. J. N. Hillgarth. Turnhout: Brepols, 1976.

Junyent i Subirà, E., ed. *Diplomatari de la catedral de Vic, segles IX–X.* 2 vols Vic: Patronat d'Estudis Ausonencs, 1980.

Kats, J. M. J. G. *Chronicon Moissiacense Maius: a Carolingian World Chronicle from Creation to the First Years of Louis the Pious.* Prepared and revised by D. Claszen, 2 vols. (MPhil thesis, Leiden, 2012) available online at https:// openaccess.leidenuniv.nl/handle/1887/20005.

Les premiéres annales de Fontanelle (Chronicon Fontanellense). In *Mélanges de la Société de l'Histoire de Normandie.* Ed. J. Laporte. Rouen, 1951, 63–91.

Liber iudiciorum sive Lex Visigothorum, 5.2. In *Leges Visigothorum. MGH LL nat. Germ. 1.* Ed. K. Zeumer. Hanover, 1901, repr. 2005, 33–456.

Lupus. *Servati Lupi Epistolae.* Ed. P. K. Marshall. Leipzig, 1984.

Lex Visigothorum 10.2.4, MGH LL nat. Germ. 1. Ed. K. Zeumer. Hanover, 1902.

Bibliography

Mansi, J. D., ed. *Sacrorum conciliorum nova et amplissima collection.* Florence, 1767. Paris, 1902.

Marca, P. de, ed. *Marca hispanica sive limes hispanicus.* Paris, 1688.

Marquès, J. M., ed. *Cartoral, dit de Carlemany, del bisbe de Girona (s. IX–XIV)* 1. Barcelona, 1993.

Millàs i Vallicrosa, J. M. *Textos dels historiadors àrabs referents a la Catalunya. Carolíngia.* Barcelona, 1987.

Miro, A. 'Les comtes de Toulouse en Pallars et Ribagorce au IXe siècle: princes souverains ou agents du prince?', *Territorio, Sociedad, y Poder* 6 (2011): 23–52.

Nithard. *Histoire des fils de Louis le Pieux.* Ed. and trans. P. Lauer. Paris, 1964. *Historiarum Libri IIII.* In *MGH SS*, 2. Hanover 1829, 649–72.

Oosthout, H. and J. Schilling, *Anicii Manlii Severini Boethii De arithmetica. CCSL 94 A.* Turnhout, 1999.

Opera omnia in PL 125: 1035C–1070C and 126: 94D–99A. Ed. J.-P. Migne. Paris , 1851.

Ordeig i Mata, R. 'La consagracio i la dotacio d'esglesies a Catalunya en els segles IX–XI.' In *Symposium internacional sobre els orígens de Catalunya (segles VIII–XI).* 2 vols. Barcelona, 1991. Vol. 2, 85–102.

Ordeig i Mata, R., ed. *Catalunya Carolíngia 4: Els comtats de Osona i Manresa.* Barcelona, 1999.

Les dotalies de les esglésies de Catalunya (segles IX–XII) 1. Vic, 1993.

Pardo i Sabartés, M., ed. *Mensa episcopal de Barcelona.* Barcelona, 1994.

Paschasius Radbertus. *Epitaphium Arsenii. Abhandlungen der königlichen Akademie der Wissenschaften zu Berlin, Philologische und historische Klasse.* Ed. E. Dümmler. 2 (1900): 1–98.

Paulus Orosius. *The Seven Books of History against the Pagans.* Trans. R. J. Deferrari. Washington, DC, 1964.

Ponsich, P., and Ordeig i Mata, R., ed. *Catalunya Carolíngia 6: Els comtats de Rosselló, Conflent, Vallespir i Fenollet.* Barcelona, 2006.

Pope John VIII. *Epistola Mironi et Sunefrido germane suo. MGH Epistolae karolini aevi 5.* Berlin, 1928.

Puig y Puig, S. *Episcopologio de la Sede Barcinonense.* Barcelona, 1929.

Regino. *Chronicon.* In *MGH SS 1.* Ed. G. H. Pertz. Hanover, 1826, 537–612. *Reginonis Prumiensis Chronicon.* In *MGH SSRG 50.* Ed. F. Kurze. Hanover, 1890.

Richer. *Histoire de France (888–995).* Ed. R. Latouche. Paris, 1930–7.

Richer of Saint-Rémi. *Histories.* Ed. and trans. J. Lake. 2 vols. Cambridge, MA, 2011.

Rius Serra, J., ed. *Cartulario de Sant Cugat del Vallés* 1. Barcelona, 1945.

Sobrequés Vidal, S., Riera i Viader, S., Rovira i Sola, M., Ordeig i Mata, R., ed. *Catalunya Carolíngia 5: Els Comtats de Girona, Besalú, Empúries i Peralada.* Barcelona, 2003.

Scholz, B. W. with B. Rogers (trans.) *Carolingian Chronicles: Royal Frankish Annals, Nithard's Histories.* Ann Arbor, 1972.

Tessier, G. *Recueil des actes de Charles II le Chauve.* 3 vols, Paris, 1943–55.

Thegan. *Vita Hludowici imperatoris.* In *MGH SS*, 2. Hanover 1829, 585–604.

Theodulf of Orléans. *Capitula ad presbyteros.* PL 105. ed. Migne. Paris, 1851, 191D–224A.

Bibliography

Opus Caroli regis contra synodum (Libri Carolini). MGH Leges 4 Conc. 2, Supplementum 1. Ed. A. Freeman and P. Meyvaert. Hanover, 1998.

Thulin, C., ed. *Corpus agrimensorum Romanorum.* Stuttgart, 1971 reprint from 1913.

Udina Martorell, F., ed. *El Archivo Condal de Barcelona en los siglos IX–X. Estudio crítico de sus fondos.* Barcelona, 1951.

Villanueva, J. *Viage literario a las iglesias de España,* 22 vols. Madrid, 1803–51.

Vives, J., ed. *Concilios Visigóticos e Hispano-Romanos.* Barcelona, 1963.

Wallace-Hadrill, J. M., ed. *The Fourth Book of the Chronicle of Fredegar with Its Continuations.* London, 1960.

SECONDARY SOURCES

d'Abadal i de Vinyals, R. *Catalunya Carolíngia 1: El domini carolingi a Catalunya.* Barcelona, 1986.

Dels visigots als catalans. Ed. J. Sobrequés i Callicó. 2nd ed. 2 vols. Barcelona, 1974.

'El paso de Septimania del dominio godo al franco a través de la invasión sarracena (720–768).' *Cuadernos de Historia de España* 19 (1953): 5–54.

Els primers comtes catalans. Biografies Catalanes. Barcelona, 1958.

Els temps i el regiment del comte Guifré el Pilós. Ed. J. Sobrequés i Callicó. Sabadell, 1989.

Historia dels catalans, vol. 2: *Alta Edat Mitjana.* Barcelona, 1963.

La batalla del Adopcionismo en la desintegración de la Iglesia visigoda. Barcelona, 1949.

'La Catalogne sous l'Empire de Louis le Pieux.' *Études Roussillonnaises: Revue d'histoire et d'archéologie méditerranéennes* 4 (1954–5): 239–72; 5 (1956): 31–50, 147–77; 6 (1957): 267–95.

'La expedición de Carlomagno a Zaragoza: el hecho histórico, su carácter y su significación.' Paper presented at the Coloquios de Roncevalles, agosto 1955. Zaragoza, 1956.

'La família del primer comte barceloní, Berà.' *Cuadernos de Arqueología e Histoira de la Cuidad* 10 (1967): 187–93.

'La instutició comtal carolingia en la pre-Catalunya del segle IX.' *Anuario de Estudios Medievales* 1 (1964): 29–75.

La plana de Vich. Vich, 1954.

L'abat Oliba, bisbe de Vic, i la seva època. Barcelona, 1948.

'La reconquesta d'una regió interior de Catalunya: la Plana de Vic (717–886).' In *Dels visigots als catalans.* Ed. J. Sobrequés i Callicó. 2nd ed. 2 vols. Barcelona, 1974. Vol. 1, 309–22.

'L'Entrada des sarraïns a la peninsula i l'enfonsada del regne de Toledo. La reacció dels francs i llur occupació de Septimània.' In *Catlunya carolíngia 1: El domini carolingi a Catalunya.* Ed. J. Sobrequés i Callicó. Barcelona, 1986, 1–37.

'Un diplôme pour le comte Oliba.' *Annales du Midi* 61 (1949): 346–52.

'Un gran comte de Barcelona preterit: Guifré-Borrell (897–911).' *Cuadernos de Arqueología e Historia de la Ciudad de Barcelona* 5 (1964): 83–130.

Adell i Gisbert, J. A. and J. J. Menchon i Bes. 'Les fortificacions de la Frontera Meridional dels comtats catalans, o les fortificacions de la Marca Superior del Al-Àndalus.' *Lambard: Estudis d'Art Medieval* 17 (2004–5): 65–84.

Bibliography

Airlie, S. 'The Aristocracy.' In *The New Cambridge Medieval History*, vol. 2, c. 700–c.900. Ed. R. McKitterick. Cambridge, 1995, 431–50.

'Bonds of Power and Bonds of Association in the Cout Circle of Louis the Pious.' In *Charlemagne's Heir: New Perspectives on the Reign of Louis the Pious (814–840)*. Ed. P. Godman and R. Collins. Oxford, 1990, 191–204.

'The Palace of Memory: the Carolingian Court as Political Centre.' In *Courts and Regions in Medieval Europe*. Ed. S. R. Jones, R. Marks, and A. J. Minnis. York, 2000, 1–20.

Power and Its Problems in Carolingian Europe. Farnham, 2012.

'Semper Fidelis? Loyauté envers les Carolingiens comme constituant de l'identité aristocratique.' In *La royauté et les élites dans l'Europe carolingienne*, R. Le Jan, ed. (début IXe siècle aux environs de 920). Villeneuve d'Ascq, 1998, 129–43.

'True Teachers and Pious Kings: Salzburg, Louis the German, and Christian Order.' In *Belief and Culture in the Middle Ages: Studies Presented to Henry Mayr-Harting*. Eds. R. Gameson and H. Leyser. Oxford, 2001, 89–105.

Albertoni, G. *L'Italia carolingia*. Rome, 1997.

Allen, M. I. 'The *Chronicle* of Claudius of Turin.' In *After Rome's Fall: Narrators and Sources of Early Medieval History. Essays presented to Walter Goffart*. Ed. A. C. Murray. Toronto, 1998, 288–319.

Althoff, G. *Amicitia und Pacta: Bündnis, Einung, Politik und Gebetsgedenken im beginnenden 10. Jahrhundert*. Hanover, 1992.

Alturo, J. 'El conocimiento del latín en las Cataluña del siglo IX: un capítulo de su historia cultural.' *Euphrosyne* 21 (1993): 301–18.

'El glossari contigut en el manuscrit París, Bibl. Nat. Lat. 2306.' *Espacio, Tiempo, y Forma* 3 (1990): 11–19.

'El Glossari *in Regulam Sancti Benedicti* de l'arxiu de la catedral de Barcelona.' *Studia monastica* 37 (1995): 271–9.

'El sistema educativo en la Cataluña altomedieval.' *Memoria Ecclesiae XII: Instituciones de enseñanza y archivos de la iglesia hispano-mozarabe en las dioceses de España*. Ed. A. H. Ballina. Oviedo: Actas del XII Congreso de la Asociación celebrado de León, 1998, 31–61.

'Escritura visigotica y escritura carolina en el contexto cultural de la Catluña del siglo IX.' In *Memoria Ecclesiae II: Las raices visigoticas de la Iglesia en España: en torno al Concilio III de Toledo. Actas de Congreso celebrado en Toledo (21 y 22 de Septiembre de 1989)*. Ed. A. H. Ballina. Oviedo: Asociación de Archiveros de la Iglesia en España, 1991, 33–44.

'La cultura llatina medieval a Catalunya. Estat de la qüestion.' In *Symposium Internacional sobre els orígens de Catalunya*. Barcelona, 1991, 21–48.

'La Glossa VI del ms 74 de Ripoll: un epítom isidorià incorporat al Liber glossarum.' *Faventia* 18 (1996): 67–91.

'Los folios de guarda del manuscrit Paris, Bibl. Nat. Lat. 6113: un *Commentarium in Lucam* de Beda del siglo IX.' *Historia. Instituciones. Documentos* 19 (1992): 1–6.

'Manuscrits i documents llatins d'origen català del segle IX.' In *Symposium Internacional sobre els Orígens de Catalunya*. Barcelona, 1991, 273–80.

281

Bibliography

Studia in codicum fragmenta. Bellaterra, 1999.

'Un manuscrito del *Liber de dono perseuerantiae* de san Agustín copiado en Gerona an torno al decenio 870–880.' *Revue des Études Augustiniennes* 43 (1997): 105–10.

'Un Seduli amb glosses de Remi d'Auxerre copiat a començos de segle X (a Barcelona?).' *Analecta sacra Tarraconensia* 69 (1996): 5–28.

Alturo, J. and A. H. Ballina. 'El sistema educativo en la Cataluña altomedieval.' *Memoria ecclesiae* 12 (1998): 31–61.

Amann, E. *L'Epoque Carolingienne*. Ed. A. Fliche and V. Martin. Histoire de l'Eglise 6. Paris, 1947.

Amory, P. 'The Meaning and Purpose of Ethnic Terminology in the Burgundian Laws.' *Early Medieval Europe* 2 (1993): 1–28.

People and Identity in Ostrogothic Italy. Cambridge, 1995.

Anderson, B. *Imagined Communities: Reflections on the Origin and Spread of Nationalism*. London, 1991.

Anderson T., Jr. 'Roman Military Colonies in Gaul, Salian Ethnogenesis and the Forgotten meaning of *Pactus Legis Salicae* 59.5.' *Early Medieval Europe* 4 (1995): 129–44.

Angenendt, A. *Das Frühmittelalter: die abendländische Christenheit von 400 bis 900*. Stuttgart, 1990.

Kaiserherrschaft und Königstaufe: Kaiser, Könige und Päpste als geistliche Patrone in der abendländischen Missionsgeschichte. Arbeiten zur Frühmittelalterforschung. Berlin, 1984.

'Taufe und Politik in frühen Mittelalter.' *Frühmittelalterliche Studien* 7 (1973): 143–68.

Angenendt, A. *Kaiserherrschaft und Königstaufe: Kaiser, Könige und Päpste als geistliche Patrone in der abendländischen Missionsgeschichte*. Berlin, 1984.

'Taufe und Politik in frühen Mittelalter.' *Frühmittelalterliche Studien* 7 (1973): 143–68.

Archibald, L. 'Dhuoda.' *German Writers and Works of the Early Middle Ages: 800–1170*, 148. Eds. W. Hasty and J. Hardin. New York, 1995, 14–16.

Aurell, M. 'Jalons pour une enquête sure les strategies matrimoniales des comtes catalans (IXe-XIe s.).' In *Symposium internacional sobre els orígens de Catalunya (segles VIII-XI)*. Barcelona, 1991, 281–364.

'Pouvoir et parenté des comtes de la Marche Hispanique (801–911).' In *La royauté et les élites dans l'Europe carolingienne (début IXe siècle aux environs de 920)*. Ed. R. Le Jan. Villeneuve d'Ascq, 1998, 467–81.

Auzias, L. *L'Aquitaine carolingienne*. Toulouse, 1937.

Bachrach, B. S. *Armies and Politics in the Early Medieval West*. Aldershot, 1993.

Charlemagne's Early Campaigns (768–777). Leiden, 2013.

Early Carolingian Warfare: Prelude to Empire. Philadelphia, 2001.

Early Medieval Jewish Policy in Western Europe. Minneapolis, 1977.

'On the Role of the Jews in the Establishment of the Spanish March (768–814).' In *Hispanica Judaica: Studies in the History, Language and Literature of the Jews in the Hispanic World*. Ed. J. M. Sola-Solé. Barcelona, 1980, 11–19.

Bibliography

'Pirenne and Charlemagne.' In *After Rome's Fall: Narrators and Sources of Early Medieval History. Essays Presented to Walter Goffart.* Ed. A. C. Murray. Toronto, 1998, 224–5.

'A Reassessment of Visigothic Jewish Policy.' *American Historical Review* 78 (1973): 11–34.

Balañà i Abadia, P. 'Els musulmans i el pirineu català.' In *Mil.lenari de Catalunya i la Cerdanya.* Barcelona, 1989, 37–50.

L'Islam a Catalunya (segles VIII–XII). Col.lecció Nissaga 13. Barcelona, 1997.

Banniard, M. 'Language and Communication in Carolingian Europe.' In *The New Cambridge Medieval History*, vol. 2:, c.700-c.900. Ed. R. McKitterick. Cambridge, 695–706.

Viva Voce: communication orale et communication écrite en occident latin (IVe–IXe siècle). Paris, 1992.

Baraut, C. 'La intervenció carolíngia antifeliciana al bisbat d'Urgell i les seves conseqüències religioses i culturals (segles viii-ix).' In *Jornades internacionals d'estudi sobre el bisbe Feliu d'Urgell.* Ed. J. Perarnau. Barcelona, 2000, 155–93.

Barbero, A. 'La integración social de los "hispani" del Pirineo oriental al reino carolingio.' In *Mélanges offerts à René Crozet.* Eds. P. Gallais and Y.-J. Riou. Poitiers, 1966, 67–75.

Barceló, M. 'Wisigoths et Arabes en Catalogne.' In *Histoire de la Catalogne.* Eds. J. Nadal Farreras and P. Wolff. Barcelona, 1982, 217–36.

Barnwell, P. S. *Kings, Courtiers and Imperium: the Barbarian West, 565–725.* London, 1997.

Barral i Altet, X. et al., eds. *Catalunya i França meridional a l'entorn de l'any mil / La Catalogne et la France méridionale autour de l'an mil.* Colloque international DNRS, Hugues Capet 987–1987, La France a l'an mil. Barcelona, 1991.

Barrow, J. 'Ideas and Applications of Reform.' In *The Cambridge History of Christianity*, vol. 3: *Early Medieval Christianities c.600–c.1100.* Ed. T. F. X. Noble and J. M. H. Smith. Cambridge, 2008, 345–62.

Bautier, R.-H. 'La campagne de Charlemagne en Espagne (778): la réalité historique.' In *Roncevaux dans l'histoire, la légende et le myth: Actes du colloque organisé à l'occasion du 12e centenaire de Roncevaux, Saint-Jean-Pied-de-Port, 1978*, nouv. série, 135. Bayonne, 1979, 1–47.

'La prétendue dissidence de l'épiscopat catalan et le faux concile de « Portus » de 887–890.' *Bulletin philologique et historique (jusqu'à 1610) du Comité des Travaux Historiques et Scientifiques* 1961 (Paris, 1963): 477–98.

Beer, R. 'Die Handschriften des Klosters Santa Maria de Ripoll.' *Sitzungsberichte der philosophisch-historischen Klasse der Kaiserlichen Akademie der Wissenschaften* 155, 158 (1908).

Benet i Clarà, A. 'Castells i línies de reconquesta.' In *Symposium internacional sobre els orígens de Catalunya (segles VIII-XI).* Barcelona, 1991, 365–91.

El procés d'independència de Catalunya. Sallent, 1988.

'Una revolta Berguedana contra el comte Oliba Cabreta.' *L'Erol: revista cultural del Berguedà* (1983): 29–34.

Bensch, S. P. *Barcelona and Its Rulers, 1096–1291.* Cambridge, 1995.

Bibliography

Berschin, W. *Greek Letters and the Latin Middle Ages, from Jerome to Nicholas of Cusa.* Washington, DC, 1988.

Bischoff, B. 'Aus Alkuins Erdentage.' *Mittelalterliche Studien: Ausgewählte Aufsätze zur Schriftkunde und Literaturgeschichte,* 1 (1967), 12–19.

'Benedictine Monasteries and the Survival of Classical Literature.' In *Manuscripts and Libraries in the Age of Charlemagne.* Trans. M. Gorman. Cambridge, 1994, 134–160.

Die Abtei Lorsch in Spiegel ihrer Handschriften, 2nd edn. Lorsch, 1989.

'Libraries and Schools in the Carolingian Revival of Learning.' In *Manuscripts and Libraries in the Age of Charlemagne.* Trans. M. Gorman. Cambridge, 1994, 93–114.

Lorsch im Spiegel seiner Handschriften. Munich, 1974.

Bishko, C. J. 'The Pactual Tradition in Hispanic Monasticism.' Reprinted in *Spanish and Portuguese Monastic History, 600–1300.* Aldershot, 1984, 1–16.

Bisson, T. N. *The Medieval Crown of Aragón: a Short History.* Oxford, 1986.

Björkvall, G. and H. Andreas. 'Verslehre und Ververtonung im lateinischen Mittelalter.' In *Artes im Mittelalter.* Ed. U. Schaefer. Berlin, 1999, 309–23.

Blackburn, M. 'Money and Coinage.' In *The New Cambridge Medieval History,* vol. 2, c.700-c.900. Ed. R. McKitterick. Cambridge, 1995, 538–59.

Blumenshine, G. B. 'Alcuin's Liber Contra Haeresim Felicis and the Frankish Kingdom.' *Frühmittelalterliche Studien* 17 (1983): 222–33.

Bofarull y Mascaró, P. *Los condes de Barcelona vindicados, y cronología y genealogía de los reyes de España considerados como soberanos independientes de su marca.* Barcelona 1836, repr. 1990.

Bolòs, J. 'Onomàstica i poblament a la Catalunya septentrional a l'alta edat mitjana.' In *Histoire et Archéologie des terres catalanes au Moyen Age.* Ed. P. Sénac. Perpignan, 1995, 49–65.

Bolòs, J., and V. Hurtado. *Atles del comtat de Besalú (785–988).* Atles dels comtats de la Catalunya carolíngia. Barcelona, 1998.

Atles del comtat de Girona (785–993). Atles dels comtats de la Catalunya carolíngia. Barcelona, 2000.

Atles del comtat de Manresa. Barcelona, 2001.

Atles del comtat d'Osona. Barcelona, 2001.

Atles dels comtats de Pallars i Ribagorça. Barcelona, 2012.

Atles dels comtats d'Empúries i Peralada (780–991). Atles dels comtats de la Catalunya carolíngia. Barcelona, 1999.

Atles del comtat d'Urgell. Barcelona, 2006.

Bolòs, J., V. Hurtado, and R. Català. *Atles dels comtats de Rosselló, Conflent, Vallespir i Fenollet.* Barcelona, 2009.

Bonnassie, P. *From Slavery to Feudalism in Southwestern Europe.* Trans J. Birrell. Cambridge, 1991.

'From the Rhône to Galicia: Origins and Modalities of the Feudal Order.' In *From Slavery to Feudalism in South-Western Europe.* Trans J. Birrell. Cambridge, 1991, 104–31.

La Catalogne du milieu du Xe siecle à la fin du XIe siècle: croissance et mutations d'une societe. Toulouse, 1975.

'Sur les "origines" de la Catalogne: quelques remarques et orientations de recherche.' In *Symposium Internacional sobre els orígens de Catalunya*. Barcelona, 1991, 437–45.

Bonnery, A. 'A propos de Concile de Francfort (794). L'action de moines de Septimanie dans la lutte contre l'Adoptianisme.' In *Das frankfurter Konzil von 794: Kristallisationspunkt karolingischer Kultur*, vol. 2. Ed. Rainer Berndt. Mainz, 1997, 767–86.

Booker, C. *Past Convictions: the Penance of Louis the Pious and the Decline of the Carolingians*. Philadelphia, 2009.

Boshof, E. *Ludwig der Fromme*. Darmstadt, 1996.

Bowlus, C. R. *Franks, Moravians, and Magyars: the Struggle for the Middle Danube, 788–907*. Philadelphia, 1995.

Bowman, J. A. 'Councils, Memory and Mills: the Early Development of the Peace of God in Catalonia.' *Early Medieval Europe* 8 (1999): 99–130.

'Countesses in Court: Elite Women, Creativity, and Power in Northern Iberia, 900–1200.' *Journal of Medieval Iberian Studies* 6 (2014): 54–70.

Shifting Landmarks: Property, Proof, and Dispute in Catalonia around the Year 1000 Ithaca, 2004.

Brown, G. 'Introduction: the Carolingian Renaissance.' In *Carolingian Culture: Emulation and Innovation*. Ed. R. McKitterick. Cambridge, 1994, 1–51.

Brown, W. *Unjust Seizure: Conflict, Interest, and Authority in Early Medieval Society*. Ithaca, 2001.

Brown, W., M. Costanbeys, M. Innes, and A. J. Kosto, eds. *Documentary Culture and the Laity in the Early Middle Ages*. Cambridge, 2013.

Brunhölzl, F. 'Die Bildungsauftrag der Hofschule.' In *Karl der Grosse: Lebenswerk und Nachleben* vol. 2: *Das geistige Leben*. Ed. B. Bischoff. Dusseldorf, 1965, 28–41.

Bruyning, L. F. 'Lawcourt Proceedings in the Lombard Kingdom before and after the Frankish Conquest.' *Journal of Medieval History* 11 (1985): 193–214.

Buc, P. 'Ritual and Interpretation: the Early Medieval Case.' *Early Medieval Europe* 9 (2000): 183–210.

Buckler, F. W. *Harunu'l-Rashid and Charles the Great*. Monographs of the Medieval Academy of America 2. Cambridge, MA, 1931.

Bührer-Thierry, G. 'La reine adultère.' *Cahiers de civilisation medieval, Xe–XIIe siecles* 35 (1992), 299–312.

Bulliet, R. *Conversion to Islam in the Medieval Period*. Cambridge, MA, 1979.

Bullough, D. A. *Alcuin: Achievement and Reputation*. Leiden, 2004.

'Alcuin and the Kingdom of Heaven: Liturgy, Theology, and the Carolingian Age.' In *Carolingian Essays: Andrew W. Mellon Lectures in Early Christian Studies*. Ed. U.-R. Blumenthal. Washington, DC, 1983, 1–70.

'*Europae Pater*: Charlemagne and His Achievement in the Light of Recent Scholarship.' *English Historical Review* 85 (1970): 59–105.

'Roman Books and Carolingian Renovatio.' In *Carolingian Renewal: Sources and Heritage*. Manchester, 1991, 1–37.

Burns, R. I. 'The Significance of the Frontier in the Middle Ages.' In *Medieval Frontier Societies*. Eds. R. Bartlett and A. MacKay. Oxford, 1989, 307–30.

Cabaniss, A. 'The Heresiarch Felix.' *The Catholic Historical Review* 39 (1953): 129–41.

Bibliography

Cabestany Fort, J.-F. 'El culte de Santa Eulàlia a la catedral de Barcelona (s. ix–x).' *Lambard* 9 (1997): 159–65.

Calmette, J. 'Les origines de la premiére maison comtale de Barcelone.' *Mélanges d'archeologie et d'histoire* 20 (1900): 299–306.

Carlo, A. M. *Tratado de paleografía española*, 3 vols. 3rd ed. Madrid, 1983.

Carroll, C. 'The Bishoprics of Saxony in the First Century after Christianization.' *Early Medieval Europe* 8 (1999): 219–46.

Castrillo Llamas, M. C. 'El *Liber manualis* de Dhuoda: una fuente para el estudio de la educación en la edad media.' *La voz del silencio* 1 (1992): 33–51.

Castro Correa, A. 'Visigothic vs. Carolingian script. Context (I).' *Littera Visigothica* (March 2014). http://litteravisigothica.com/visigothic-vs-carolingian-script-context1 (ISSN 2386–6330).

Catlos, B. A. *The Victors and the Vanquished: Christians and Muslims of Catalonia and Aragon, 1050–1300.* Cambridge, 2004.

Cavadini, J. C. 'Elipandus and His Critics at the Council of Frankfort.' In *Das Frankfurter Konzil von 794: Kristallisationspunkt karolingischer Kultur*, 2: Kultur und Theologie. Ed. R. Berndt. Mainz, 1997, 787–807.

The Last Christology of the West. Philadelphia, 1993.

'The Sources and Theology of Alcuin's *De fide sanctae et individuae trinitatis*.' *Traditio* 46 (1991): 123–46.

Chalmeta, P. 'El sugar de una formación: Al-Andalus.' In *El Islam y Cataluña.* Barcelona, 1999, 39–49.

Invasión e islamización: La sumisión de Hispania y la formación de al-Andalus. Jaén, 2003.

Chandler, C. J. 'Agobard and Adoptionism: a Controversy Continues.' In proceedings of *Colloque international: Lyon dans l'Europe carolingienne – Autour d'Agobard (816–2016).* Lyons, forthcoming.

'Barcelona, BC 569, Dhuoda's *Liber manualis*, and Lay Culture in the Carolingian Spanish March.' *Early Medieval Europe* 18 (2010): 265–91.

'Between Court and Counts: Carolingian Catalonia and the *aprisio* Grant, 778–897,' *Early Medieval Europe* 11 (2002): 19–44.

'Carolingian Catalonia: the Spanish March and the Franks, c.750–c.1050.' *History Compass* 11 (2013): 739–56.

'Heresy and Empire: the Role of the Adoptionist Controversy in Charlemagne's Conquest of the Spanish March.' *International History Review* 24 (2002): 505–527.

'Land and Social Networks in the Carolingian Spanish March.' *Studies in Medieval and Renaissance History*, third series, 6 (2009): 1–33.

'A New View of a Catalonian *Gesta contra Iudaeos*: Ripoll 106 and the Jews of the Spanish March.' In *Discovery and Distinction in the Early Middle Ages: Studies in Honor of John J. Contreni.* Eds. C.J. Chandler and S. A. Stofferahn. Kalamazoo, MI, 2013, 187–204.

Chaume, M. 'Onfroi, marquis de Gothie: ses origines et ses attaches familiales.' *Annales du Midi* 52 (1940): 113–36.

Chaytor, H. J. *A History of Aragón and Catalonia.* London, 1933.

Bibliography

Chazelle, C. *The Crucified God in the Carolingian Era: Theology and Art of Christ's Passion*. Cambridge, 2001.

Cherewatuk, K. '*Speculum matris*: Dhuoda's Manual.' *Florilegium* 10 (1991): 49–63.

Christys, A. 'Christian-Muslim Frontiers in Early Medieval Spain.' *Bulletin of International Medieval Research* 5 (1999): 1–19.

'St-Germain-des-Près, St Vincent, and the Martyrs of Cordoba.' *Early Medieval Europe* 7 (1998): 199–216.

'The Transformation of Hispania after 711.' In Regna *and* Gentes: *the Relationship between Late Antique and Early Medieval Peoples and Kingdoms in the Transformation of the Roman World*. Eds. H.-W. Goetz, J. Jarnut, and W. Pohl. Leiden, 2002, 219–41.

Cingolani, S. M. 'The Family of Wilfred I, the Hairy: Marriage and the Consolidation of Power, 800–1000.' *Imago Temporis: Medium Aevum* 4 (2010): 119–40.

Les Gesta Comitum Barchinonensium (versió primitiva), la Brevis Historia i altres textos de Ripoll. Valencia, 2012.

Claussen, M. A. 'Fathers of Power and Mothers of Authority: Dhuoda and the *Liber manualis*.' *French Historical Studies* 19 (1996): 785–809.

'God and Man in Dhuoda's *Liber manualis*.' *Studies in Church History* 27 (1990): 43–52.

The Reform of the Frankish Church: Chrodegang of Metz and the Regula canonicorum in the Eighth Century. Cambridge, 2008.

Codero y Zaidín, F. 'El Godo o moro Aizón.' In *Estudios críticos de historia árabe española* vii. Madrid, 1917.

Cohen, M. R. *Under Crescent and Cross: the Jews in the Middle Ages*. Princeton, 1994.

Collins, R. *The Arab Conquest of Spain, 710–797*. Oxford and Malden, MA, 1994.

The Basques. The Peoples of Europe. Oxford and New York, 1986.

'The Basques in Aquitaine and Navarre: Problems of Frontier Government.' In *War and Government in the Middle Ages: Essays in Honor of J. O. Prestwich*. Eds. J. Gillingham and J. C. Holt. Cambridge, 1984, 3–17.

Charlemagne. Toronto and Buffalo, 1998.

'Charlemagne and His Critics, 814–829.' In *La royauté et les élites dans l'Europe carolingienne (début IXe siècle aux environs de 920)*. Ed. R. Le Jan. Villeneuve d'Ascq, 1998, 193–211.

'Charles the Bald and Wifred the Hairy.' In *Charles the Bald, Court and Kingdom*. Eds. M. T. Gibson and J. L. Nelson. *Aldershot*, 1990, 169–88.

Early Medieval Spain: Unity in Diversity, 400–1000. 2nd ed. New York, 1995.

'Julian of Toledo and the Education of Kings in Late Seventh-Century Spain.' In *Law, Culture and Regionalism in Early Medieval Spain* [originally published as 'Julian of Toledo and the Royal Succession in Late Seventh-Century Spain']. Aldershot, 1992, 1–22.

Law, Culture, and Regionalism in Early Medieval Spain. Aldershot, 1992.

'Law and Ethnic Identity in the Western Kingdoms in the Fifth and Sixth Centuries.' In *Medieval Europeans*. Ed. A. P. Smyth, 1–23. London, 1998.

'Literacy and the Laity in Early Medieval Spain.' In *The Uses of Literacy in Early Mediaeval Europe*. Ed. R. McKitterick. Cambridge, 1990, 109–33.

Bibliography

'Pippin I and the Kingdom of Aquitaine.' In *Charlemagne's Heir: New Perspectives on the Reign of Louis the Pious (814–840)*. Eds. P. Godman and R. Collins. Oxford, 1990, 363–89.

'The "Reviser" Revisited: Another Look at the Alternative Version of the *Annales Regni Francorum*.' In *After Rome's Fall: Narrators and Sources of Early Medieval History: Essays Presented to Walter Goffart*. Ed. A. C. Murray. Toronto, 2000, 191–213.

'Sicut lex Gothorum continent: Law and Charters in Ninth- and Tenth-Century León and Catalonia.' *English Historical Review* 100 (1985): 489–512.

'Spain: the Northern Kingdoms and the Basques, 711–910.' In *The New Cambridge Medieval History*,vol. 2, c.700-c.900. Ed. R. McKitterick. Cambridge, 1995, 272–89.

'Visigothic Law and Regional Custom in Disputes in Early Medieval Spain.' In *The Settlement of Disputes in Early Medieval Europe*. Eds. W. Davies and P. Fouracre. Cambridge, 1986, 85–104.

Visigothic Spain, 409–711. Oxford, 2004.

Constable, G. '*Nona et Decima*: an Aspect of Carolingian Economy.' *Speculum* 35 (1960): 224–30.

Contreni, J. J. 'By Lions, Bishops Are Meant; By Wolves, Priests': History, Exegesis, and the Carolingian Church in Haimo of Auxerre's *Commentary on Ezechiel*.' *Francia: Forschungen zur westeuropäischen Geschichte* 29 (2003): 1–28.

Carolingian Learning, Masters and Manuscripts. Variorum Collected Studies Series. Aldershot, 1992.

'Counting, Calendars, and Cosmology: Numeracy in the Early Middle Ages.' In *Word, Image, Number: Communication in the Middle Ages*. Eds. J. J. Contreni and S. Casciani. Rome, 2002, 43–83.

'The Carolingian Renaissance: Education and Literary Culture.' In *The New Cambridge Medieval History*, vol. 2, c.700–c.900. Ed. R. McKitterick. Cambridge, 1995, 709–57.

'The Carolingian School: Letters from the Classroom.' In *Giovanni Scoto nel suo tempo: L'organizzazione del sapere in età carolingia*. Settimane di Studio della Fondazione Centro Italiano de Studi sull'Alto Medioevo. Spoleto, 1989, 81–111.

The Cathedral School of Laon from 850 to 930: Its Manuscripts and Masters. Münchener Beiträge zur Mediävistik und Renaissance-Forschung. Munich, 1978.

'Charlemagne and the Carolingians: the View from North America.' *Cheiron* 37 (2002): 111–54.

'The Pursuit of Knowledge in Carolingian Europe.' In *'The Gentle Voices of Teachers:' Aspects of Learning in the Carolingian Age*. Ed. R. E. Sullivan. Columbus, 1995, 106–141.

Linage Conde, A. 'El monacato mózarabe hacia la benedictinización.' In *Cristianità d'occidente e cristianità d'oriente (secolo VI–XI)* Settimane di Studio della Fondazione Centro Italiano de Studi sull'Alto Medioevo. Spoleto, 2004, 337–461, at 382–3 and 415–20.

Coope, J. A. *The Martyrs of Córdoba: Community and Family Conflict in an Age of Mass Conversion*. Lincoln, NE, 1995.

Bibliography

Cordoliani, A. 'Los manuscritos de cómputo eclesiástico en las bibliotecas de Barcelona.' *Analecta sacra Tarraconensia* 23 (1950): 103–29.

Corradini, R., M. Diesenberger, and H. Reimitz, eds. *The Construction of Communities in the Early Middle Ages: Texts, Resources and Artefacts.* The Transformation of the Roman World 12. Leiden, 2003.

Costa, M.-M. 'Les genealogies comtals catalanes.' In *Symposium internacional sobre els orígens de Catalunya (segles VIII–XI).* Barcelona, 1991, 447–62.

Coupland, S. 'The Coinages of Pippin I and II of Aquitaine. ' *Revue numismatique* 6 (1989): 194–222.

Curta, F. *The Making of the Slavs: History and Archaeology of the Lower Danube.* Cambridge, 2001.

Davies, W. 'Sale, Price and Valuation in Galicia and Castile-León in the Tenth Century.' *Early Medieval Europe* 11 (2002): 149–74.

Small Worlds: the Village Community in Early Medieval Brittany. Berkeley and Los Angeles: University of California Press, 1988.

Davies, W., and P. Fouracre, eds. *Property and Power in the Early Middle Ages* Cambridge, 1995.

The Settlement of Disputes in Early Medieval Europe Cambridge, 1986.

Davis, J. R. *Charlemagne's Practice of Empire.* Cambridge, 2015.

'A Pattern for Power: Charlemagne's Delegation of Judicial Responsibilities.' In *The Long Morning of Medieval Europe: New Directions in Early Medieval Studies.* Eds. J. R. Davis and M. McCormick. Aldershot, 2008, 235–46.

Declercq, G. *Anno Domini: the Origins of the Christian Era.* Turnhout, 2000.

de Bruyne, D. 'Un document de la controverse adoptianiste en Espagne vers l'an 800.' *Revue d'Histoire Ecclésiastique* 27 (1931): 307–12.

de Epalza, M. 'Mozarabs: an Emblematic Christian Minority in Islamic al-Andalus.' In *The Legacy of Muslim Spain.* Ed. S. K. Jayyusi. Leiden, 1992, 149–70.

'Descabdellament politic i miliatr dels muslumans a terres catalanes (segles viii-xi).' In *Symposium internacional sobre els orígens de Catalunya.* Barcelona, 1991, 49–80.

de Fluvià, A. *Els primitius comtats i vescomtes de Catalunya.* Barcelona, 1989, 125–232.

de Hartmann, C. C. 'The Textual Transmission of the Mozarabic Chronicle of 754.' *Early Medieval Europe* 8 (1999): 13–29.

de Jong, M. 'Carolingian Monasticism: the Power of Prayer.' In *The New Cambridge Medieval History*, vol. 2, c.700–c.900. Ed. R. McKitterick. Cambridge, 1995, 622–53.

'The Empire That Was always Decaying: the Carolingians (800–888).' *Medieval Worlds: Comparative & Interdisciplinary Studies* 1 (2015): 6–25.

The Penitential State: Authority and Atonement in the Age of Louis the Pious, 814–840. Cambridge, 2009.

de la Granja, F. 'A marca superior en la obra de Al-Udri.' *Estudios de la Edad Media de la Corona de Aragón*, VIII (1967): 457–61.

de Marca, P. *Marca hispanica sive limes hispanicus*, 2 vols. Paris, 1688.

de Molins, A. E. *Catálogo del Museo Provincial de Antigüedades de Barcelona.* Barcelona, 1888.

Bibliography

Deér, J. 'Karl der Große und der Untergang des Awarenreiches.' In. *Karl der Große: Lebenswerk und Nachleben*, vol. 1 *Persönlichkeit und Geschichte*. Ed. H. Beumann. Düsseldorf, 1965, 719–91.

Deliyannis, D. 'Year-Dates in the Early Middle Ages.' In *Time in the Medieval World*. Eds C. Humphrey and W. M. Ormrod. Rochester, NY, 2001, 5–22.

Delogu, P. 'Lombard and Carolingian Italy.' In *The New Cambridge Medieval History*, vol. 2, c.700–c.900. Ed. R. McKitterick. Cambridge, 1995, 290–319.

Delort, R., ed. *La France a l'an mil* Paris, 1990.

Dhondt, J. *Etudes sur la naissance des principautés territoriales en France, IXe au Xe siècle*. Bruges, 1948.

'Le titre du marquis à l'époque carolingienne.' *Archivum Latinitatis Medii Aevi* 19 (1948): 407–17.

Diaz y Diaz, M. C. *Index scriptorum Latinorum medii aevi Hispanorum*. Salamanca, 1959.

'Las reglas monásticas españolas allende los Pirineos.' In *L'Europe héritière de l'Espagne wisigothique*. Eds. J. Fontaine and C. Pellistrandi. Madrid, 1992, 159–75.

Diem, A. 'The Carolingians and the *Regula Benedicti*.' In *Religious Franks: Religion and power in the Frankish Kingdoms: Studies in honour of Mayke de Jong*. Eds. R. Meens, D. van Espelo, B. van den Hoven van Genderen, J. Raaijmakers, I. van Renswoude, and C. van Rhijn. Manchester, 2016, 243–61.

Dilke, O. A. W. *The Roman Land Surveyors: an introduction to the agrimensores*. Newton Abbot, 1971.

Dodds, J. D. 'Islam, Christianity, and the Problem of Religious Art.' In *The Art of Medieval Spain, AD 500–1200*. New York, 1993, 27–37.

Dronke, P. *Women Writers of the Middle Ages: a Critical Study of Texts from Perpetua (+ 203) to Marguerite Porete (+ 1310)*. Cambridge, 1984.

Duckett, E. S. *Alcuin, Friend of Charlemagne: His World and Work*. New York, 1951. *Medieval Portraits East and West*. Ann Arbor, 1972.

Dufour, J. 'Obédience respective des Carolingiens et des Capétiens (fin Xe siècle-début XIe siècle).' In *Catalunya i França meridional a l'entorn de l'any Mil*. Eds. X. Barral i Altet, D. Iogna-Prat, et al. Barcelona, 1991, 21–44.

Duhamel-Amado, C., and A. Catafau. 'Fidéles et aprisionnaires en réseaux dans la Gothie des IXe et Xe siècles.' In *La royauté et les élites dans l'Europe carolingienne (début IXe siècle aux environs de 920)*. Ed. R. Le Jan. Villeneuve d'Ascq, 1998, 437–65.

Dupont, A. 'Considerations sur la colonisation et la vie rurale dans la Roussillon et la Marche d'Espagne.' *Annales du Midi* 57 (1955): 223–45.

'L'aprision et le régime aprisionaire dans le Midi de la France.' *Le Moyen Age* 71 (1965, 1966): 177–213, 375–99.

Dutton, P. E. *The Politics of Dreaming in the Carolingian Empire*. Lincoln, NE, 1994.

Dutton, P. E. and A. Luhtala. 'Eriugena in Priscianum.' *Mediaeval Studies* 56 (1994): 153–63.

Duval, P. M. 'Les plus anciennes routes de France: les voies gallo-romaines.' In *Les routes de France. Depuis les origines jusqu'à nos jours*. Ed. G. Michaud. Paris, 1959, 9–24.

Bibliography

Effros, B. '*De Partibus Saxoniae* and the Regulation of Mortuary Custom: a Carolingian Campaign of Christianization or the Suppression of Saxon Identity?' *Revue Belge de Philologie et d'Histoire* 75 (1997), 267–86.

Engels, O. 'Der Weltklerus und das Pfarrnetz.' In *Symposium internacional sobre els orígens de Catalunya (segles VIII–XI)*. Barcelona, 1991, 477–90.

Schutzgedanke und Landherrschaft im östlichen Pyrenäenraum (9.-13. Jahrhundert). Münster in Westfalen, 1970.

Escalona, J., ed. *Building Legitimacy: Political Discoures and Forms of Legitimacy in Medieval Socities*. Leiden, 2004, 223–262.

'Family Memories: Inventing Alfonso I of Asturias.' In *Building Legitimacy: Political Discoures and Forms of Legitimacy in Medieval Societies*. Eds. I. Alfonso, H. Kennedy, and J. Escalona. Leiden, 2004, 223–62.

Estey, F. N. 'The *Scabini* and the Local Courts.' *Speculum* 26 (1951): 119–29.

Everett, N. *Literacy in Lombard Italy, c.568–774*. Cambridge, 2003.

Faulkner, T. *Law and Authority in the Early Middle Ages: the Frankish* Leges *in the Carolingian Period*. Cambridge, 2016.

Fedalto, G. 'Il significato politico de Paolino, Patriarca de Aquileia, e la sua posizione nella controversia Adozionista.' In *Das frankfurter Konzil von 794: Kristallisationspunkt karolingischer Kultur*. Ed. R. Berndt, vol. 1, Mainz, 1997, 103–23.

Feliu i Montfort, G. 'Els inicis del domini territorial de la Seu de Barcelona.' *Cuadernos de historia económica de Cataluña* 14 (1976): 45–61.

'La pagesia catalana abans de la feudalització.' *Anuario de Estudios Medievales* 26 (1996): 19–41.

La presa de Barcelona per Almansor: història i mitificació; discurs de recepció. Barcelona, 2007.

'Societat i economia.' In *Symposium internacional sobre els orígens de Catalunya (segles VIII–XI)*. Barcelona, 1991, 81–116.

Ferreiro, A., ed. *Visigoths: Studies in Culture and Society*. The Medieval Mediterranean Peoples, Economies, and Cultures, 400–1453. Leiden, 1999.

Fichtenau, H. *The Carolingian Empire*. Trans. P. Munz. Oxford, 1957.

Das Urkundenwesen in Österreich vom 8. bis zum frühen 13. Jahrhundert. Vienna, Cologne, Graz, 1971, 56–72.

'"Politische" Datierungen des frühen Mittelalters.' In *Intitulatio*, Vol. II: *Lateinische Herrscher- und Fürstentitel im neunten und zehnten Jahrhundert*. Vienna, 1973, 453–522.

Firey, A. 'Carolingian Ecclesiology and Heresy: a Southern Gallic Juridical Tract against Adoptionism.' *Sacris erudiri* 39 (2000): 253–316.

Fletcher, R. *The Barbarian Conversion from Paganism to Christianity*. New York, 1998.

Moorish Spain. Berkeley, 1992.

Fluvià, de. *Els primitius comtats i vescomtes de Catalunya*. Barcelona, 1989.

Font i Rius, J. M., A. M. Mundó, M. Riu i Riu, F. Udina i Martorell, and J. Vernet i Ginés. *Procés d'independéncia de Catalunya (ss. VIII–XI): La fita del 988*. Trans. M. Strubell and T. Strubell. Barcelona, 1989.

Fontaine, J. 'La figure d'Isidore de Séville à l'époque carolingienne.' In *L'Europe héritière de l'Espagne wisigothique*. Eds. J. Fontaine and C. Pellistrandi. Madrid, 1992, 195–212.

Bibliography

'Mozarabie hispanique et monde carolingien: les échanges culturels entre la France et l'Espagne du VIIe au Xe siècle.' *Anuario de Estudios Medievales* 13 (1983): 17–46.

Fontaine, J. and C. Pellistrandi, eds. *L'Europe héritière de l'Espagne wisigothique.* Madrid, 1992.

Fouracre, P. *The Age of Charles Martel.* London, 2000.

'Cultural Conformity and Social Conservatism in Early Medieval Europe.' *History Workshop Journal* 33 (1992): 152–61.—

'Frankish Gaul to 814.' In *The New Cambridge Medieval History*, vol. 2, c.700–c.900. Ed. R. McKitterick. Cambridge, 1995, 85–109.

'"Placita" and the Settlement of Disputes in Later Merovingian Francia.' In *The Settlement of Disputes in Early Medieval Europe.* Eds. W. Davies and P. Fouracre. Cambridge, 1986, 23–44.

Franklin, C. V. 'The Date of Composition of Bede's *De schematibus et tropis* and *De arte metrica*.' *Revue bénédictine* 110 (2000): 199–203.

Freed, J. B. 'Nobles, Ministerials, and Knights in the Archbishopric of Salzburg.' *Speculum* 62 (1987): 575–611.

'Reflections on the Medieval German Nobility.' *American Historical Review* 91 (1986): 553–75.

Freedman, P. H. *Church, Law, and Society in Catalonia, 900–1500.* Variorum Collected Studies Series. Aldershot, 1995.

'Cowardice, Heroism and the Legendary Origins of Catalonia.' *Past and Present* 121 (1988): 3–28.

The Diocese of Vic: Tradition and Regeneration in Medieval Catalonia. New Brunswick, 1983.

'Le pouvoir episcopal en Catalogne au Xe siècle.' In *Catalunya i França meridional a l'entorn de l'any Mil.* Eds. X. Barral i Altet, D. Iogna-Prat et al. Barcelona, 1991, 174–80.

The Origins of Peasant Servitude in Medieval Catalonia. Cambridge, 1991.

'Symbolic Implications of the Events of 985–988.' In *Symposium Internacional sobre els orígens de Catalunya.* Vol. 1. Barcelona, 1991, 117–29.

Freeman, A. 'Theodulf of Orléans: a Visigoth at Charlemagne's Court.' In *L'Europe héritière de l'Espagne wisigothique.* Eds. J. Fontaine and C. Pellistrandi. Madrid, 1992, 185–94.

Frez, A. 'El adopcionismo i la evoluciones religiosas i politicas en el reino astur.' *Hispania: Revista Española de Historia* 58 (1998): 971–93.

'El adopcionismo: disidencia religiosa en la Penínusla Ibérica (fines del siglo VIII–principios del siglo IX).' *Clio i Crimen: Revisto del Centro de Historia de Crimen de Durango* 1 (2004): 115–34.

Fried, J. 'Karl der Große, die Artes liberales, und die karolingishe Renaissance.' In *Karl der Große und sein Nachwirken: 1200 Jahre Kultur und Wissenschaft in Europa*, 1 Wissen und Weltbild. Eds. P. Butzer, M. Kerner, and W. Oberschelp. Turnhout, 1997, 25–43.

Ganshof, F. L. *The Carolingians and the Frankish Monarchy: Studies in Carolingian History.* Trans. J. Sondheimer. Ithaca, 1971.

Bibliography

Frankish Institutions under Charlemagne. Trans. B. Lyon and M. Lyon. Providence, 1968.

'L'Église et le Pouvoir Royale dans le Monarchie Franque sous Pépin III et Charlemagne.' In *Le Chiese nei Regni dell'Europa Occidentale e i loro Rapporti con Roma sino all'800*, 7. Settimane di Studio della Fondazione Centro Italiano de Studi sull'Alto Medioevo. Spoleto, 1960, 95–141.

Ganz, D. *Corbie and the Carolingian Renaissance.* Sigmaringen, 1990.

'The *Epitaphium Arsenii* and Opposition to Louis the Pious.' In *Charlemagne's Heir: New Perspectives on the Reign of Louis the Pious (814–840).* Eds. P. Godman and R. Collins. Oxford, 1990, 527–50.

'Theology and the Organization of Thought.' In *The New Cambridge Medieval History*, vol. 2, c.700–c.900. Ed. R. McKitterick. Cambridge, 1995, 758–85.

García Moreno, Luis A. 'Spanish Gothic Consciousness among the Mozarabs in al-Andalus (VIIIth–Xth Centuries).' In *The Visigoths: Studies in Culture and Society.* Ed. A. Ferreiro. Leiden, 1999, 303–23.

García Villada, Z. *Bibliotheca Patrum Latinorum Hispaniensis.* Vienna, 1915.

Garipzanov, I. *Symbolic Language of Authority in the Carolingian World (c.751–877).* Leiden, 2008.

Garrison, M. 'The Franks as the New Israel? Education for an Identity from Pippin to Charlemagne.' In *The Uses of the Past in the Early Middle Ages.* Eds. Y. Hen and M. Inne. Cambridge, 2000, 114–61.

Gaskoin, C. J. B. *Alcuin: His Life and Work.* New York, 1966.

Gázquez, J. M., and G. Puigvert i Planagumà. 'Los "Excerpta" de Beda (*De Temporum Ratione* 18 y 23) en Ripoll (ACA. Ripoll 59 y Vat. Reg. Lat. 123).' *Emerita* 64 (1996): 296–305.

Geary, P. J. *The Myth of Nations: the Medieval Origins of Europe.* Princeton, 2002.

Phantoms of Remembrance: Remembering and Forgetting in the Tenth and Eleventh Centuries. Princeton, 1985.

'Un fragment récemment découvert du *Chronicon Moissiacense*.' *Bibliothèque de l'École des Chartes* 136 (1978): 69–73.

Geisel, C. *Die Juden im Frankenreich: Von den Merovinger bis zum Tode Ludwigs des Frommen.* Frankfurt, 1998.

Gibson, M. T., and J. L. Nelson, eds. *Charles the Bald: Court and Kingdom.* 2nd rev ed Aldershot, 1990.

Glick, T. F. *From Muslim Fortress to Christian Castle: Social and Cultural Change in Medieval Spain.* Manchester, 1995.

Islamic and Christian Spain in the Early Middle Ages. Princeton, 1979.

Gillett, A. 'Introduction: Ethnicity, History, and Methodology.' In *On Barbarian Identity: Critical Approaches to Ethnicity in the Early Middle Ages.* Ed. A. Gillett. Turnhout, 2002, 1–18.

Gillett, A., ed., *On Barbarian Identity: Critical Approaches to Ethnicity in the Early Middle Ages* Turnhout, 2002.

Godman, P. *Poets and Emperors: Frankish Politics and Carolingian Poetry.* Oxford, 1987.

Goetz, H.-W. 'Concepts of Realm and Frontiers from Late Antiquity to the Early Middle Ages: Some Preliminary Remarks.' In *The Transformation of Frontiers from Late Antiquity to the Carolingians.* Eds. W. Pohl, I. Wood, and H. Reimitz. Leiden, 2001, 73–82.

Bibliography

'*Gens*, Kings and Kingdoms: the Franks.' In *Regna and* Gentes: *the Relationship between Late Antique and Early Medieval Peoples and Kingdoms in the Transformation of the Roman World.* Eds. H.-W. Goetz, J. Jarnut, and W. Pohl; with collaboration of S. Kaschke. Leiden, 2002, 307–44.

'Social and Military Institutions.' In *The New Cambridge Medieval History*, vol. 2, c.700–c.900. Ed. R. McKitterick. Cambridge, 1995, 451–80.

Goetz, H.-W., J. Jarnut, W. Pohl., eds. Regna and Gentes: *the Relationship between Late Antique and Early Medieval Peoples and Kingdoms in the Transformation of the Roman World.* Transformation of the Roman World 13. Leiden, 2003.

Goffart, W. 'Does the Distant Past Impinge on the Invasion Age Germans?' In *On Barbarian Identity: Critical Approaches to Ethnicity in the Early Middle Ages.* Ed. A. Gillett. Turnhout, 2002, 21–38.

The Narrators of Barbarian History. Princeton, 1988.

Goldberg, E. J. 'More Devoted to the Equipment of Battle than the Splendor of Banquets: Frontier Kingship, Martial Ritual, and Early Knighthood at the Court of Louis the German.' *Viator* 30 (1999): 41–78.

'Popular Revolt, Dynastic Politics, and Aristocratic Factionalism in the Early Middle Ages: the Saxon *Stellinga* Reconsidered.' *Speculum* 70 (1995): 467–501.

Struggle for Empire: Kingship and Conflict under Louis the German, 817–876. Ithaca, 2006.

Gómez Pallarés, J. 'Textos latinos de cómputo en manuscritos visigóticos de los siglos X–XI.' In *Lateinische Kultur im X. Jahrhundert. Akten des I. Internationalen Mittellateinerkongresses, Heidelberg, 12.-15. IX. 1988.* Ed. W. Berschin. Stuttgart, 1991, 133–42.

González Rolán, T. 'La tradición de los Dicta Catonis y el Ripollensis 106.' *Habis* 5 (1974): 93–106.

Goody, J. *Development of the Family and Marriage in Europe.* Cambridge, 1983.

Grierson, P., and M. Blackburn. *Medieval European Coinage: With a Catalogue of the Coins in the Fitzwilliam Museum, Cambridge 1: the Early Middle Ages.* Cambridge, 1986.

Griffe, É. *Histoire religieuse des anciens pays de l'Aude. Tome I: des origines chrétiennes à la fin de l'époque carolingienne.* Paris, 1933.

Guerreiro, R. 'La rayonnement de l'hagiographie hispanique en Gaule pendant le haut Moyen Âge: circulation et diffusion des *Passions* hispaniques.' In *L'Europe héritière de l'Espagne wisigothique.* Eds. J. Fontaine and C. Pellistrandi. Madrid, 1992, 137–57.

Guichard, P. *Al-Andalus: estructura antropológica de una sociedad islámica en Occidente.* Barcelona, 1976.

Guyotjeannin, O. and E. Puoulle, eds. *Autour de Gerbert d'Aurillac. Le pape de l'an mil. Album de documents commentés.* Paris, 1996.

Hainthaler, T. 'Von Toledo nach Frankfurt: dogmengeschichtliche Untersuchungen zur adoptianistischen Kontroverse.' In *Das frankfurter Konzil von 794: Kristallisationspunkt karolingischer Kultur.* Ed. R. Berndt, vol. 2, Mainz, 1997, 809–60.

Halphen, L. *Charlemagne and the Carolingian Empire.* Trans. G. de Nie. New York, 1977.

Bibliography

Halsall, G. *Warfare and Society in the Barbarian West, 450–900*. London, 2003.

Harmand, L. *L'Occident romain: Gaule, Espagne, Bretagne, Afrique du Nord (31 av. J. C. à 235 ap. J. C.)* Bibliothéque Historique. Paris, 1960.

Harnack, A. von. *History of Dogma*. Trans. J. Millar. 3rd German ed. 5. New York, 1958.

Harrison, D. 'Structures and Resources of Power in Early Medieval Europe.' In *The Construction of Communities in the Early Middle Ages*. Eds. R. Corradini, M. Diesenberger and H. Reimitz. Leiden, 2003, 17–38.

Hartmann, W. *Die Synoden der Karolingerzeit im Frankenreich und in Italien*. Konziliengeschichte Reihe A. Paderborn, 1989.

Häse, A. *Mittelalterliche Bücherverzeichnisse aus Kloster Lorsch. Einleitung, Edition und Kommentar*. Wiesbaden, 2002.

Haywood, J. *Dark Age Naval Power: a Reassessment of Frankish and Anglo-Saxon Seafaring Activity*. London, 1991.

Heather, P. 'Disappearing and Reappearing Tribes.' In *Strategies of Distinction: the Construction of Ethnic Communities, 300–800*. Eds. W. Pohl *with* H. Reimitz. Leiden, 1998, 95–111.

Heene, K. *The Legacy of Paradise: Marriage, Motherhood, and Women in Carolingian Edifying Literature*. Frankfurt am Main, 1997.

Helmut H. 'Beda Venerabilis in Spain.' *MLN* 70 (1985): 120–37.

Heil, J. 'Agobard, Amolo, das Kirchengut und die Juden von Lyon.' *Francia* 25:1 for 1998 (1999): 39–76.

'Claudius von Turin – Eine Fallstudie zure Geschichte der Karolingerziet.' *Zeitschrift für Geschichtswissenschaft* 45 (1997): 389–412.

Kompilation oder Konstruktion?: die Juden in den Pauluskommentaren des 9. Jahrhunderts. Hanover, 1998.

'Nos nescientes de hoc velle manere – "We wish to remain ignorant about this": Timeless End, or Approaches to Reconceptualizing Eschatology after AD 800 (AM 6000).' *Traditio* 55 (2000): 73–103.

Heil, W. *Alkuinstudien 1: Zur Chronologie und Bedeutung des Adoptianismusstreites*. Düsseldorf, 1970.

'Der Adoptianismus, Alkuin, und Spanien.' In *Karl der Große: Lebenswerk und Nachleben* vol. 2 *Das geistige Leben*. Ed. B. Bischoff. Düsseldorf, 1965, 95–155.

Helvétius, A.-M. 'L'Abbatiat laïque comme relais du pouvoir aux frontières du royaume: le cas du nord de la Neustrie au IXe siècle.' In *La royauté et les élites dans l'Europe carolingienne (début IXe siècle aux environs de 920)*. Ed. R. Le Jan. Villeneuve d'Ascq, 1998, 285–99.

Hen, Y. *The Royal Patronage of Liturgy in Frankish Gaul to the Death of Charles the Bald (877)*. London, 2001.

Herlihy, D. 'Church Property on the European Continent, 701–1200.' *Speculum* 36 (1961): 81–105.

Herrin, J. *The Formation of Christendom*. Princeton, 1987.

Hildebrandt, M. M. *The External School in Carolingian Society*. Leiden, 1992.

Hillgarth, J. N. 'Spanish Historiography and Iberian Reality.' *History Theory* 24 (1984): 23–43.

Bibliography

Hitchcock, R. *Mozarabs in Medieval and Early Modern Spain: Identities and Influences.* Aldershot, 2008.

Hlawitschka, E. *Franken, Alemannen, Bayern und Burgunder in Oberitalien, 774–962: Zum Verständnis de fränkischen Königsherrschaft in Italien.* Freiburg im Breisgau, 1960.

Hoffmann, H. H. 'Fossa Carolina. Versuch einer Zusammenschau.' In *Karl der Grosse, Lebenswerk und Nachleben.* Ed. W. Braunfels. Düsseldorf, 1965, vol. 1, 437–53.

Holder, A. '(Un)dating Bede's *De arte metrica.*' In *Northumbria's Golden Age.* Ed. J. Hawkes and S. Mills. Stroud, 1999, 390–5.

Holtz, L. 'Alcuin et la renaissance des arts libéraux.' *In Karl der Große und sein Nachwirken: 1200 Jahre Kultur und Wissenschaft in Europa, vol. 1: Wissen und Weltbild.* Eds. P. Butzer, M. Kerner, and W. Oberschelp. Turnhout, 1997, 45–60.

Donat et la tradition de l'enseignement grammatical: étude sur l'Ars Donati et sa diffusion (IVe–IXe siècle) et édition critique. Paris, 1981.

Hubert, J. 'Les routes du Moyen Age.' In Les routes de France. Depuis les origines jusqu'à nos jours. Ed. G. Michaud. Paris, 1959, 25–56.

Hummer, H. *Politics and Power in Early Medieval Europe: Alsace and the Frankish Realm, 600–1000.* Cambridge, 2005.

'The Production and Preservation of Documents in Francia: the Evidence of Cartularies.' In *Documentary Culture and the Laity in the Early Middle Ages.* Eds. W. C. Brown, M. Costambeys, M. Innes, and A. J. Kosto. Cambridge, 2013, 189–230.

Hurtado, V., J. Mestre, and T. Miserachs. *Atles d'història de Catalunya.* Barcelona, 1992.

Innes, M. 'Archives, Documents and Landowners in Carolingian Francia.' In *Documentary Culture and the Laity in the Early Middle Ages.* Eds. W. C. Brown, M. Costambeys, M. Innes, and A. J. Kosto. Cambridge, 2013, 152–88.

'Charlemagne's Government.' In *Charlemagne: Empire and Society.* Ed. J. Story. Manchester, 2005, 71–8.

'"Immune from Heresy": Defining the Boundaries of Carolingian Christianity.' In *Frankland: the Franks and the World of the Early Middle Ages. Studies in Honour of Dame Jinty Nelson.* Eds. P. Fouracre and D. Ganz. Manchester, 2008, 101–25.

'Kings, Monks, and Patrons: Political Identities and the Abbey of Lorsch.' In *La royauté et les élites dans l'Europe carolingienne (début IXe siècle aux environs de 920).* Ed. R. Le Jan. Villeneuve d'Ascq, 1998, 301–24.

'Memory, Orality, and Literacy in an Early Medieval Society.' *Past and Present* 158 (1998): 3–36.

State and Society in the Early Middle Ages: the Middle Rhine Valley, 400–1100. Cambridge, 2000.

'Teutons or Trojans? The Carolingians and the Germanic Past.' In *The Uses of the Past in the Early Middle Ages.* Eds. Y. Hen and M. Innes. Cambridge, 2000, 227–49.

Innes, M., and R. McKitterick. 'The Writing of History.' In *Carolingian Culture: Emulation and Innovation.* Ed. R. McKitterick. Cambridge, 1994, 193–220.

Bibliography

Izydorczyk, Z. *Manuscripts of the Evangelium Nicodemi: a Census.* Toronto, 1993.

Izydorczyk, Z. and J.-D. Dubois. 'Introduction.' In *The Medieval Gospel of Nicodemus: Texts, Intertexts, and Contexts in Western Europe.* Ed. Z. Izydorczyk. Tempe, AZ, 1997, 17.

James, E. 'Septimania and Its Frontier: an Archaeological Approach.' In *Visigothic Spain: New Approaches.* Ed. E. James. Oxford, 1980, 223–41.

James, E., ed. *Visigothic Spain: New Approaches* Oxford, 1980.

Jarnut, J. 'Nomen et gens: Political and Linguistic Aspects of Personal Names between the Third and the Eighth century.' In *Strategies of Distinction: the Construction of Ethnic Communities, 300–800.* Eds. W. Pohl *with* H. Reimitz. Leiden, 1998, 113–16.

Jarrett, J. 'Archbishop Ató of Osona: False Metropolitans on the *Marca Hispanica.*' *Archiv für Diplomatik* 56 (2010): 1–42.

'Caliph, King, or Grandfather: Strategies of Legitimization on the Spanish March in the Reign of Lothar III.' *The Mediaeval Journal* 1 (2011): 1–22.

'Centurions, Alcalas, and *Christiani Perversi*: Organisation of Society in the Pre-Catalan "Terra de Ningú."' In *Early Medieval Spain: a Symposium.* Eds. A. Deyermond and M. J. Ryan. London, 2010, 97–128.

'Power over Past and Future: Abbess Emma and the Nunnery of Sant Joan de les Abadesses.' *Early Medieval Europe* 12 (2003): 229–58.

Rulers and Ruled in Frontier Catalonia, 880–1010: Pathways of Power. London, 2010.

'Settling the Kings' Lands: Aprisio in Catalonia in Perspective.' *Early Medieval Europe* 18 (2010): 320–42.

Jeudy, C. 'Donat et commentateurs de Donat à l'abbaye de Ripoll au Xe siècle (ms. Barcelone, Archivo de la Corona de Aragón, Ripoll 46).' In *Lettres latine du Moyen Age et de la Renaissance.* Eds. G. Cambrier, C. Derous, and J. Préaux. Brussels, 1978.

Johnston, H. *Tales of Nationalism: Catalonia, 1939–1979.* New Brunswick, NJ, 1991.

Johrendt, J. *Papsttum und Landeskirchen im Spiegel der päpstlichen Urkunden (896–1046).* Hanover, 2004.

Kaczynski, B. M. *Greek in the Carolingian Age: the St Gall Manuscripts.* Cambridge, 1988.

Kats, J. M. J. G. 'Chronicon Moissiacense Maius: a Carolingian World Chronicle from Creation to the First Years of Louis the Pious.' Prepared and revised by D. Claszen, 2 vols. MPhil thesis, Leiden, 2012. Available online at https://openaccess.leidenuniv.nl/handle/1887/20005.

Keefe, S. A. *A Catalogue of Works Pertaining to the Explanation of the Creed in Carolingian Manuscripts.* Turnhout, 2012.

Kehr, P. *Das Papsttum und der katalanische Prinzipat bis zur Vereinigung mit Aragon.* Berlin, 1926.

Kelleher, M. A. 'Boundaries of Law: Code and Custom in Early Medieval Catalonia.' *Comitatus* 30 (1999): 1–10.

Keller, W. E. *Der Karlsgraben-Fossa Carolina.* Treuchtlingen, 1993.

Kennedy, H. 'The Muslims of Europe.' In *The New Cambridge Medieval History*, vol. 2, c.700–c.900. Ed. R. McKitterick. Cambridge, 1995, 249–71.

Kienast, W. *Die fränkische Vassalität von dem Hausmeiern bis zu Ludwig dem Kind und Karl dem Einfältigen.* Frankfurt am Main, 1990.

'La pervivencia del derecho godo en el sur de Francia y Cataluña.' *Boletín de la Real Academia de Buenas Letras de Barcelona* 35 (1973–4): 265–95.

King, P. D. *Law and Society in the Visigothic Kingdom.* Cambridge, 1972.

Kloft, M. T. 'Der spanische Adoptianismus.' In *794 – Karl der Große in Frankfurt am Main: ein König bei der Arbeit.* Eds. J. Fried, R. Koch, L. E. Saurma-Jeltsch, and A. Thiel. Sigmaringen, 1994, 55–62.

Koch, A. *Kaiserin Judith: Eine politische Biographie.* Husum, 2005.

Kosto, A. 'Hostages in the Carolingian World (714–840).' *Early Medieval Europe* 11 (2002): 123–47.

Making Agreements in Medieval Catalonia: Power, Order, and the Written Word, 1000–1200. Cambridge, 2001.

Koziol, G. *The Politics of Memory and Identity in Carolingian Royal Diplomas: the West Frankish Kingdom (840–987).* Turnhout, 2012.

Kramer, R. 'Adopt, Adapt and Improve: Eealing with the Adoptionist Controversy at the Court of Charlemagne.' In *Religious Franks: Religion and Power in the Frankish Kingdoms: Studies in Honour of Mayke de Jong.* Eds. R. Meens, D. van Espelo, B. van den Hoven van Genderen, J. Raaijmakers, I. van Renswoude, and C. van Rhijn. Manchester, 2016, 32–50.

'Great Expectations: Imperial Ideologies and Ecclesiastical Reforms from Charlemagne to Louis the Pious (813–822).' PhD diss., Freie Universität Berlin, 2014.

Kroll, J. *Gott und Hölle: Der Mythos vom Descensuskampfe.* Leipzig: B. G. Teubner, 1932.

Kunitzsch, P. 'Les relations scientifiques entre l'Occident et le monde arabe à l'époque de Gerbert.' In *Gerbert l'européen: Actes du colloque d'Aurillac 4–7 juin 1996.* Eds. N. Charbonnel and J.-E. Iung. Aurillac: Société des lettres, sciences et artes 'La Haute-Auvergne', 1997, 193–203.

Laistner, M. L. W. *A Hand-List of Bede Manuscripts.* Ithaca, 1943.

Lattin, H. P. 'Lupitus Barchinonensis.' *Speculum* 7 (1932): 58–64.

Lauranson-Rosaz, C. 'Le Roi et les grandes dans l'Aquitaine carolingienne.' In *La royauté et les élites dans l'Europe carolingienne (début IXe siècle aux environs de 920).* Ed. Regine Le Jan. Villeneuve d'Ascq, 1998, 409–36.

L'Auvergne et ses marges (Velay, Gévaudan) du VIIIe au XIe siècle: Le fin du monde antique?. Le-Puy-en-Velay, 1987.

Law, V. 'The Study of Grammar.' In *Carolingian Culture: Emulation and Innovation.* Ed. R. McKitterick. Cambridge, 1994, 88–110.

Le Jan, R. *Famille et pouvoir dans le monde franc (VIIe–Xe siècle): essai d'anthropologie sociale.* Paris, 1995.

'Introduction.' In *La royauté et les élites dans l'Europe carolingienne (début IXe siècle aux environs de 920).* Ed. R. Le Jan. Villeneuve d'Ascq, 1998, 7–16.

Le Jan, R., ed. *La royauté et les élites dans l'Europe carolingienne.* Villeneuve d'Ascq, 1998.

Lalinde Abadía, J. 'Godos, hispanos y hostolenses en la órbita del rey de los francos.' In *Symposium internacional sobre els orígens de Catalunya (segles VIII-XI).* Barcelona, 1991, vol. 2, 35–74.

Bibliography

Levi-Provençal, É. 'España musulmana hasta la caída del califato de Córdoba (711–1031).' In *Historia de España dirigida por R. Menéndez Pidal* vol. 4 (Madrid, 1950), 142.

Histoire de l'Espagne musulmane. 3 vols. Leiden, 1950 and 1967.

Levison, W. *England and the Continent in the Eighth Century.* Oxford, 1946, repr. 1966.

Lewis, A. R. 'Cataluña como frontera militar (870–1050).' In *Anuario de Estudios Medievales*, 5. Barcelona, 1968, 15–29.

The Development of Southern French and Catalan Society, 718–1050. Austin, 1965.

'Land and Social Mobility in Catalonia, 778–1213.' In *Geschichte in der Gesellschaft: Festschrift für Karl Bosl zum 65. Geburtstag.* Eds. F. Prinz, F.-J. Schmale, and F. Seibt. Stuttgart, 1974, 312–23.

Liebeschutz, H. 'Wesen und Grenzen des karolingischen Rationalismus.' *Archiv für Kulturgeschichte* 33 (1950): 17–44.

Lifshitz, F. *The Name of the Saint: the Martyrology of Jerome and Access to the Sacred in Francia, 627–827.* Notre Dame, IN, 2006.

The Norman Conquest of Pious Neustria: Historiographic Discourse and Saintly Relics, 684–1090. Toronto, 1995.

Limerick, P. N. *The Legacy of Conquest: the Unbroken Past of the American West.* New York and London, 1987.

Limerick, P. N., C. A. Milner II, and C. E. Rankin, eds. Trails: Toward a New Western History. Lawrence, KS, 1991.

Linehan, P. *History and the Historians of Spain.* Oxford, 1993.

López, G. R. 'The Arrival of the Visigoths in Hispania: Population Problems and the Process of Acculturation.' In *Strategies of Distinction: the Construction of Ethnic Communities, 300–800.* Eds. W. Pohl with H. Reimitz. Leiden, 1998, 153–87.

'Las relaciones entre la Península Ibérica y la Septimania entre los siglos V y VIII, según los hallazgos arqueológicos.' In *L'europe héritière de l'Espagne wisigothique.* Eds. J. Fontaine and C. Pellistrandi. Madrid, 1992, 285–301.

'On the Supposed Frontier between the Regnum Visigothorum and Byzantine Hispania.' In *The Transformation of Frontiers from Late Antiquity to the Carolingians.* Eds. W. Pohl, I. Wood, and H. Reimitz. Leiden, 2001, 95–115.

López Perreira, J. E. *Crónica muzárabe de 754.* Zaragoza, 1980.

Estudio crítico sobre la Crónica Mozárabe de 754. Zaragoza, 1980.

Lowe, E. A. 'An Unedited Fragment of Irish Exegesis in Visigothic Script.' *Celtica* 5 (1960): 1–7.

Lozovsky, N. 'Carolingian Geographical Tradition: Was It Geography?' *Early Medieval Europe* 5 (1996): 25–43.

Lynch, J. H. *Godparents and Kinship in Early Medieval Europe.* Princeton, 1986.

'Spiritale Vinculum: the Vocabulary of Spiritual Kinship in Early Medieval Europe.' In, *Religion, Culture, and Society in the Early Middle Ages: Studies in Honor of Richard E. Sullivan.* Eds. T. F. X. Noble and J. J. Contreni. Kalamazoo, MI: 1987, 181–204.

MacLean, S. *Kingship and Politics in the Late Ninth Century: Charles the Fat and the End of the Carolingian Empire.* Cambridge, 2003.

Madoz, J. 'Los "Excerpta Vincentii Lirinensis" en la controversia adopcianista.' *Revista Española de Teología* 3 (1943): 475–83.

Bibliography

Magnou-Nortier, E. *La société laïque et l'église dans la province ecclééesiastique de Narbonne (zone cispyrénéenne) de la fin du VIIIe a la fin du XIe siècle.* Toulouse, 1974.

'L'Admonitio Generalis: Étude critique.' In *Jornades internacionals d'estudi sobre el Bisbe Feliu d'Urgel. Crònica i estudis.* Barcelona, 2000, 195–242.

Malbos, L. 'La capture de Bernard de Septimanie.' *Le Moyen Age* 76 (1970): 7–13.

Mann, V. B., J. D. Dodds, and T. F. Glick, eds. *Convivencia: Jews, Muslims, and Christians in Medieval Spain.* New York, 1992.

Manzano Moreno, Eduardo. 'The Creation of Medieval Frontier: Islam and Christianity in the Iberian Peninsula, Eighth to Eleventh Centuries.' In *Frontiers in Question: Eurasian Borderlands, 700–1700.* Eds. D. Power and N. Standen. New York, 1999, 32–54.

Marenbon, J. 'Alcuin, the Council of Frankfort and the Beginnings of Medieval Philosophy.' In *Das frankfurter Konzil von 794: Kristallisationspunkt karolingischer Kultur.*vol. 2: *Kultur und Theologie.* Ed. R. Berndt. Mainz, 1997, 603–15.

Martí, R. 'Concreció territorial del comtat de Barcelona.' In *III Congrés d'Història de Barcelona. La ciutat i el seu territori, dos mil anys d'història.* Barcelona, 1993, 247–53.

'Delà, Cesari i Ató, primers arquebisbes dels comptes-prínceps de Barcelona (951–953/981).' *Analecta Sacra Tarraconensia* 67 (1994): 369–86.

Martinell, M. 'Una mujer del s. IX, Duoda.' *Laurentianum* 31 (1990): 27–38.

Martínez Gázquez, J, and G. Puigvert i Planagumà. 'Los *excerpta* de Beda (De temporum ratione 19 y 23) en Ripoll (ACA, Ripoll 59 y Vat. reg. lat. 123).' *Estudios Medievales* 64 (1996): 295–305.

Mateu y Llopis, F. '*De la Hispania Tarraconense visigoda a la Marca Hispánica carolina.*' *Analecta Sacra Tarraconensia* 19 (1947): 1–122.

Mayeski, M. A. *Dhuoda: Ninth Century Mother and Theologian.* Scranton, PA, 1995.

Mayr-Harting, H. 'The West: the Age of Conversion (700–1050).' In *The Oxford Illustrated History of Christianity.* Ed. J. McManners. Oxford, 1990, 92–121.

McCarthy, M. J. 'Hincmar's Influence during Louis the Stammerer's Reign.' In *Hincmar of Rheims: Life and Work.* Eds. R. Stone and C. West. Manchester, 2015, 110–29.

'Power and Kingship under Louis II the Stammerer, 877–879.' PhD diss., University of Cambridge, 2012.

McCarthy, D. P. 'The Emergence of *Anno Domini.*' In *Time and Eternity: the Medieval Discourse.* Eds. G. Jaritz and G. Moreno-Riaño. Turnhout, 2003, 31–54.

McCormick, M. *Charlemagne's Survey of the Holy Land: Wealth, Personnel, and Buildings of a Mediterranean Church between Antiquity and the Middle Ages.* Washington, DC, 2011.

Eternal Victory: Triumphal Rulership in Late Antiquity, Byzantium and the Early Medieval West. Cambridge, 1990.

Origins of the European Economy. Cambridge, 2001.

McCullough, J. M. 'Historical Martyrologies in the Benedictine Cultural Tradition.' In *Benedictine Culture 750–1050.* Eds. W. Lourdaux and D. Verhelst. Leuven, 1983, 114–31.

McGuire, A. C. 'Liturgy and the Laity in the Ninth Century.' *Ecclesia Orans* 13 (1996): 463–94.

Bibliography

McKeon, P. R. 'The Carolingian Councils of Savonnières (859) and Tusey (860) and their Background.' *Revue Bénédictine* 84 (1974): 74–110.

McKitterick, R. *Charlemagne: the Formation of a European Identity.* Cambridge, 2008.

The Carolingians and the Written Word. Cambridge, 1989.

The Frankish Church and the Carolingian Reforms, 789–895. London, 1977.

The Frankish Kingdoms under the Carolingians 751–987. New York, 1983.

The Frankish Kings and Culture in the Early Middle Ages. Aldershot, 1990.

History and Memory in the Carolingian World. Cambridge, 2004.

'The Legacy of the Carolingians.' In *Carolingian Culture: Emulation and Innovation.* Ed. R. McKitterick. Cambridge, 1994, 317–23.

'Unity and Diversity in the Carolingian Church.' *Studies in Church History* 32 (1996): 59–82.

McKitterick, R., ed. *The New Cambridge Medieval History,* vol. 2, c.700–c.900. Cambridge, 1995.

The Uses of Literacy in Early Medieval Europe. Cambridge, 1990.

McWilliam, J. 'The Context of Spanish Adoptionism: a Review.' In Conversion and Continuity: Indigenous Christian Communities in Islamic *Lands,* Eighth to Eighteenth Centuries. Eds. M. Gervers and R. Jibran Bikhazi. Papers in Mediaeval Studies 9. Toronto, 1990, 75–88.

Menocal, M. R. *The Ornament of the World: How Muslims, Jews, and Christians Created a Culture of Tolerance in Medieval Spain.* Boston, 2002.

Mercier, J. 'Les problèmes politico-religieux en Catalogne (IXe-XIe siècles).' In *Actes del Congrés Internacional Gerbert d'Orlhac i el seu temps: Catalunya i Europa a la fi del Ir Mil.leni.* Ed. I. Ollich i Castanyer. Vic, 1999, 115–34.

Meyer, H. B. 'Zur Stellung Alkuins auf dem Frankfurter Konzil.' *Zeitschrift für katolische Theologie* 81 (1959): 455–60.

Miles, C. *The Coinage of the Visigoths of Spain: Leovigild to Achila II.* New York, 1952.

Millàs i Vallicrosa, J. M. *Textos dels historiadors àrabs referents a la Catalunya carolíngia.* Barcelona, 1987.

Mínguez, J. M. 'Ruptura social e implantación del feudlismo en el noroeste peninsular (siglos VII-X).' *Studia Historica. Historia Medieval* 3 (1985): 7–32.

Miró Montoliu, M. I. 'Els jueus i l'ensenyament de les primeres lletres.' In *Actes del Congrés Internacional Gerbert d'Orlhac i el seu temps: Catalunya i Europa a la fi del Ir mil.leni.* Ed. I. Ollich i Castanyer. Vic, 1999, 701–11.

Mohr, W. 'Die kirchliche Einheitspartei und die Durchführung der Reichsordnung von 817.' *Zetschrift für Kirchengeschichte* 72 (1961): 1–45.

Mordek, H. 'Karolingische Kapitularien.' In *Überlieferung und Geltung der Normativer Texte des frühen und hohen Mittelalters.* Ed. Hubert Mordek. Sigmaringen, 1986, 25–50.

Mordek, H. and G. Schmitz, Papst Johannes VIII. und das Konzil von Troyes (878) *in* Geschichtsschreibeung und geistiges Leben im Mittelalter, Festschift für H. Löwe. Cologne and Vienna, 1978, 179–225.

Morera Sabater, J. M. 'Un conato de secesión eclesiástica en la Marca Hispánica en el siglo IX.' *Anales del Instituto de Estudios Gerundenses* 15 (1962): 293–315.

Morris, R. 'Dispute Settlement in the Byzantine Provinces in the Tenth Century.' In *The Settlement of Disputes in Early Medieval Europe.* Eds. W. Davies and P. Fouracre. Cambridge, 1986, 125–48.

Bibliography

Morrison, K. F. *The Two Kingdoms: Ecclesiology in Carolingian Political Thought*. Princeton, 1964.

Müller-Mertens, E. *Karl der Grosse, Ludwig der Fromme und die Freien: wer waren die liberi homines der karolingischen Kapitularien (742/743–832)? Ein Beitrag zur Sozialgeschichte und Sozialpolitik des Frankenreiches*. Berlin, 1963.

Mundó, A. M. 'Aspectes de la cultura i de la ideologia catalana en el primer període comtal.' In *Mil.lenari de Catalunya i la Cerdanya*. Barcelona, 1989, 51–71.

De quan hispans, gots, jueus, àrabs i francs circulaven per Catalunya. Seminari de Paleografia, Diplomàtica i Codocologia Monografies. Bellaterra, 2001.

'El commicus palimpsest Paris B.N. Lat. 2.269. Amb notes sobre la litúrgia i manuscrits visigòtics a Septimania i Catalunya.' In *Liturgica I. I.A. Schuster in memoriam*. Montserrat, 1956, 151–276.

'Els jueus a Barcelona dels segles IX a l'XI.' In Catalunya romànica 20. Barcelona, 1992, 86–8. Reprinted in *Obres completes I: Catalunya 1, de la romanitat a la sobirania*. Barcelona, 1998, 583–87.

'Els manuscrits del "Liber iudiciorum" de les comarques gironines.' In *La formació i expansió del feudalisme català: Actes de col.loqui organizat pel Col.legi Universiari de Girona (8–11 de gener de 1985)*. Ed. J. Portella i Comas. Girona, 1985, 77–86.

'Entorn de l'astrolabi de Gerbert.' In *Actes del Congrés Internacional Gerbert d'Orlhac i el seu temps: Catalunya i Europa a la fi del Ir Mil.leni*. Ed. I. Ollich i Castanyer. Vich, 1999, 665–77.

'I "corpora" e i "codices regularum" nei tradizione codicologica delle regole monastiche.' In *Atti del 7o congresso internazionale di studi sull'alto medioevo: Norica – Subiaco – Cassino – Montecassino*. Settimane di Studio della Fondazione Centro Italiano de Studi sull'Alto Medioevo. Spoleto, 1982, vol. 2, 477–520.

'Importación, exportación y expoliaciones de codices en Cataluña (siglos VIII al XIII).' In *Coloquio sobre Circulación de codices y escritos entre Europa y la Peninsula en los siglos VIII–XIII*. Compostela, 1988, 87–134.

'La cultura i els llibres [a Catalunya, ss. VIII a XII].' In *Obres completes*, 1. Barcelona, 1998, 462–83.

'La cultura artística escrita.' In *Catalunya romànica*, 1. Barcelona, 1994, 133–62.

'La cultura escrita dels segles IX al XII a Catalunya.' In *Obres completes*. Barcelona, 1998, 547.

'Les changements liturgiques en Septimnie et en Catalogne pendant le période prémomaine.' *Les cahiers de Saint-Michel de Cuxa* 2 (1972): 29–42.

'Monastic Movements in the East Pyrenees.' In *Cluniac Monasticism in the Central Middle Ages*. Ed. N. Hunt. Hamden, CT, 1971, 98–122.

Obres completes. Barcelona, 1998.

'Producció i conservació del material escrit a Catalunya: escriptors i biblioteques pels volts l'any Mil.' In *Catalunya i França meridional a l'entorn de l'any Mil*. Eds. X. Barral i Altet, D. Iogna-Prat, A. M. Mundó, J. M. Salrach, and M. Zimmermann. Barcelona, 1991, 378–81.

'Sur quelques manuscrits liturgiques languedociens de l'epoque carolingienne (vers 800).' *Cahiers de Fanjeaux* 17 (1982): 81–95.

Bibliography

Mundó, A. M., and A. Gudayol. 'Manuscrits altmedievals amb caplletres i altres il. lustracions.' In *Catalunya romànica*, 26. Barcelona, 1997, 447–51.

Murray, A. C. 'Immunity, Nobility, and the Edict of Paris.' *Speculum* 69 (1994): 18–39.

Nagel, H. *Karl der Große und die theologischen Herausforderungen seiner Zeit: Zur Wechselwirkung zwischen Theologie und Politik im Zeitalter des großen Frankenherrschers*. Freiburger Beiträge zur mittelalterlichen Geschichte 12. Frankfurt am Main, 1998.

Nees, L. *A Tainted Mantle: Hercules and the Classical Tradition at the Carolingian Court*. Philadelphia, 1991.

Nehlsen, H. 'Zur Aktualität und Effektivität germanischer Rechtsaufzeichnungen.' In *Recht und Schrift im Mittelalter*. Ed. P. Classen. Sigmaringen, 1977, 449–502.

Nelson, J. L. *Charles the Bald*. New York, 1992.

'Charlemagne and Empire.' In *The Long Morning of Medieval Europe: New Directions in Early Medieval Studies*. Eds. J. R. Davis and M. McCormick. Aldershot, 2008, 223–34.

'Dispute Settlement in Carolingian West Francia.' In *The Settlement of Disputes in Early Medieval Europe*. Eds. W. Davies and P. Fouracre. Cambridge, 1986, 45–64.

'Frankish Identity in Charlemagne's Empire.' In *Franks, Northmen, and Slavs: Identities and State Formation in Early Medieval Europe*. Eds. I. H. Garipzanov, P. J. Geary, and Przemyslaw Urbanczyk. Turnhout, 2008, 71–83.

The Frankish World, 750–900. London, 1996.

'The Franks, the Martyrology of Usuard, and the Martyrs of Cordoba.' *Studies in Church History* 30 (1993): 67–80.

'Kingship and Empire in the Carolingian World.' In *Carolingian Culture: Emulation and Innovation*. Ed. R. McKitterick. Cambridge, 1994, 52–87.

'Kingship and Royal Government.' *The New Cambridge Medieval History*, vol. 2, c.700–c.900. Ed. R. McKitterick. Cambridge, 1995, 383–430.

'La cour impériale de Charlemagne.' In *La royauté et les élites dans l'Europe carolingienne (début IXe siècle aux environs de 920)*. Ed. R. Le Jan. Villeneuve d'Ascq, 1998, 177–91.

'Literacy in Carolingian Government.' In *The Uses of Literacy in Early Mediaeval Europe*. Ed. R. McKitterick. Cambridge, 1990, 258–96.

'The Siting of the Council at Frankfort: Some Reflections on Family and Politics.' In *Das frankfurter Konzil von 794: Kristallisationspunkt karolingischer Kultur*. Ed. R. Berndt, vol. 1: Politik und Kirche. Mainz, 1997, 149–65.

Nicolau d'Olwer, L. 'L'Escola poètica de Ripoll en els segles X–XIII.' *Anuari d'Institut d'Estudis Catalans* 6 (1920): 3–84.

'Le cadre historique et social.' In *La Catalogne à l'epoque romane*. Paris, 1932.

Noble, T. F. X. *Images, Iconoclasm, and the Carolingians*. Philadelphia, 2009.

'Louis the Pious and the Frontiers of the Frankish Realm.' In *Charlemagne's Heir: New Perspectives on the Reign of Louis the Pious (814–840)*. Eds. P. Godman and R. Collins. Oxford, 1990, 333–47.

'The Papacy in the Eighth and Ninth Centuries.' *The New Cambridge Medieval History*, vol. 2, c.700–c.900. Ed. R. McKitterick. Cambridge, 1995, 563–86.

Bibliography

The Republic of St. Peter: the Birth of the Papal State, 680–825. Philadelphia, 1984.

'The Revolt of King Bernard of Italy in 817: Its Causes and Consequences.' *Studi Medievali* 45 (1974): 315–26.

'Tradition and Learning in Search of Ideology: the *Libri Carolini*.' In *'The Gentle Voices of Teachers': Aspects of Learning in the Carolingian Age.* Ed. R. E. Sullivan. Columbus, 1995, 227–60.

Noble, T. F. X., trans. *Charlemagne and Louis the Pious: Lives by Einhard, Notker, Ermoldus, Thegan, and the Astronomer.* University Park, PA, 2009.

Odegaard, C. E. *Vassi and Fideles in the Carolingian Empire.* New York, 1972, originally published 1949.

Oexle, O. G. 'Bischof Ebroin von Poitiers und seine Verwandten.' *Frühmittelalterlichen Studien* 3 (1969): 138–210.

Ollich i Castanyer, I. 'Roda: l'Esquerda. La ciutat carolíngia.' In *Catalunya a l'època carolíngia: art i cultura abans del romànic (segles IX i X).* Ed. J. Camps. Barcelona, 84–8, trans. as 'Roda: l'Esquerda. The Carolingian Town', ibid., 461–3.

'Vic: la ciutat a l'època carolíngia.' In *Catalunya a l'època carolíngia: art i cultura abans del romànic (segles IX i X).* Ed. J. Camps. Barcelona, 1999, 89–94, trans. as 'Vic: the Town in the Carolingian Age', ibid., 464–6.

Ollich i Castanyer, I., ed. *Actes del Congrés Internacional Gerbert d'Orlhac i el seu temps: Catalunya i Europa a la fi del Ir mil.leni.* Vic, 1999.

Olsen, G. W. 'One Heart and One Soul (Acts 4:32 and 34) in Dhuoda's "Manual."' *Church History* 61 (1992): 23–33.

Ordeig, R. 'Ató, bisbe i arquebisbe de Vic (957–971).' *Studia vicensia* 1 (1989): 61–97.

'Ató de Vic, mestre de Gerbert d'Orlhac.' In *Actes del Congrés Internacional Gerbert d'Orlhac i el seu temps: Catalunya i Europa a la fi del Ir Mil.leni.* Ed. I. Ollich i Castanyer. Vich, 1999, 593–620.

Orlandis, J. 'Le royaume wisigothique et son unité religieuse.' In *L'Europe Héritière de l'Espagne wisigothique.* Eds. J. Fontaine and C. Pellistrandi. Madrid, 1992, 9–16.

Palmer, J. 'Defining Paganism in the Carolingian World.' *Early Medieval Europe* 15 (2007): 402–25.

Parés i Saltor, X. 'Rituals impresos a Catalunya.' *Revista catalana de teologia* 21 (1996): 377–86.

Patzold, S. *Episcopus. Wissen über Bischöfe im Frankenreich des späten 8. bis frühen 10. Jahrhunderts.* Ostfildern, 2008.

Pearson, K. L. R. *Conflicting Loyalties in Early Medieval Bavaria: a View of Socio-Political Interaction, c.680–900.* Aldershot, 1999.

Pecher, W. D. *Der Karlsgraben – wer grub ihn wirklich?* Treuchtlingen, 1993.

Penelas, M. 'Some Remarks on Conversion to Islam in al-Andalus.' *Al-Qantara* 23 (2002): 193–200.

Peranau i Espelt, J. 'Feliu d'Urgell: Fonts per al seu estudi i bibliografia dels darrers seixanta anys.' *Arxiu de textos catalans antics* 16 (1997): 435–82.

Pizarro, J. M., ed., *The Story of Wamba: Julian of Toledo's Historia Wambae Regis.* Washington, DC, 2005.

Bibliography

Pladevall, A. 'L'organització de l'Església a la Catalunya carolíngia.' In *Catalunya a l'època carolíngia: art i cultura abans del romànic (segles IX i X)* Barcelona, 53–8.

Pohl, W. 'Conceptions of Ethnicity in Early Medieval Studies.' *Archaeologia Polona* 29 (1991): 39–49. Reprinted in *Debating the Middle Ages: Issues and Readings*. Eds. L. K. Little and B. H. Rosenwein. Oxford, 1998, 15–24.

'The Construction of Communities and the Persistence of Paradox: an Introduction.' In *The Construction of Communities in the Early Middle Ages*. Eds. R. Corradini, M. Diesenberger, and H. Reimitz. Leiden, 2003, 1–16.

Die Awaren: Ein Steppenvolk in Mitteleuropa, 567–822 n. Chr. Munich, 1988.

'Telling the Difference: Signs of Ethnic Identity.' In *Strategies of Distinction: the Construction of Ethnic Communities, 300–800*. The Transformation of the Roman World, 2. Eds. W. Pohl with H. Reimitz. Leiden, 1998, 17–69.

Pohl, W., I. Wood, and H. Reimitz, eds. *The Transformation of Frontiers: From Late Antiquity to the Carolingians*. Leiden, 2001.

Ponsich, P. 'El problema de l'ascendència de Guifré el Pelós.' *Revista de Catalunya* 23 (1988): 35–44.

'El problema de la partició del comtat de Rosselló entre els casals de Cerdanya i d'Empúries a la mort del comte Miró I, el Vell (896).' *Estudis universitaris catalans* 30 (1994): 9–24.

Pössel, C. 'Authors and Recipients of Carolingian Capitularies.' In *Texts and Identities in the Early Middle Ages*. Eds. R. Corradini, R. Meens, C Pössel, and P. Shaw. Vienna, 2006, 253–74.

Power, D. and N. Standen. 'Introduction.' In *Frontiers in Question: Eurasian Borderlands, 700–1700*. Eds. D. Power and N. Standen. New York, 1999, 1–31.

Power, D. and N. Standen, ed., *Frontiers in Question: Eurasian Borderlands, 700–1700*. New York, 1999.

Pujades, J. *Coronica Universal del Principat de Cathalunya*. Barcelona, 1609. Available online at http://bib.cervantesvirtual.com/servlet/SirveObras/069227410-8953626297857/index.htm as of 16 July 2017.

Radding, C. and A. Ciaralli. *The Corpus Iuris Civilis in the Middle Ages: Manuscripts and Transmission from the Sixth Century to the Juristic Revival*. Leiden, 2007.

Read, J. *The Catalans*. London and Boston, 1978.

Reilly, B. F. *The Medieval Spains*. Cambridge, 1993.

Reimitz, H. *History, Frankish Identity and the Framing of Western Ethnicity, 550–850*. Cambridge, 2015.

'Social Networks and Identities in Frankish Historiography: New Aspects of the Textual History of Gregory of Tours' Historiae.' In *The Construction of Communities in the Early Middle Ages*. Eds. R. Corradini, M. Diesenberger, and H. Reimitz. Leiden, 2003, 229–68.

Remensnyder, A. *Remembering Kings Past: Monastic Foundation Legends in Medieval Southern France*. Ithaca, 2005.

Reuter, T. 'The End of Carolingian Military Expansion.' In *Charlemagne's Heir: New Perspectives on the Reign of Louis the Pious (814–840)*. Eds. P. Godman and R. Collins. Oxford, 1990, 391–405.

'Plunder and Tribute in the Carolingian Empire.' *Transactions of the Royal Historical Society 5th series* 35 (1985): 75–94.

Reuter, T., ed. *Medieval Nobility: Studies on the Ruling Classes of France and Germany from the Sixth to the Twelfth Century.* Amsterdam, New York, and Oxford, 1979.

Reynolds, L. D. *Texts and Transmission: a Survey of the Latin Classics.* Oxford, 1983.

Reynolds, R. E. 'The Organisation, Law, and Liturgy of the Western Church, 700–900.' In R. McKitterick, ed. *The New Cambridge Medieval History* , vol. 2, c.700–c.900. Cambridge, 1995, 587–621.

'A Visigothic-Script Folio of a Carolingian Collection of Canon Law.' *Mediaeval Studies* 58 (1996): 321–25.

'The Visigothic Liturgy in the Realm of Charlemagne.' In *Das frankfurter Konzil von 794: Kristallisationspunkt karolingischer Kultur.* vol. 2, ed. R. Berndt, Mainz, 1997, 919–945.

Reynolds, S. *Fiefs and Vassals: the Medieval Evidence Reinterpreted.* Oxford, 1994.

Riché, P. *The Carolingians: a Family Who Forged Europe.* Trans. M. I. Allen. Philadelphia, 1993.

Daily Life in the World of Charlemagne. Trans. J. A. McNamara. Philadelphia, 1978.

Ecoles et enseignement dans la Haut Moyen Age, Fin du Ve si cle – milieu de Xie siècle. Paris, 1989.

Education and Culture in the Barbarian West: Sixth through Eighth Centuries. Trans. J. J. Contreni. Columbia, SC, 1976.

'Gerbert d'Aurillac en Catalogne.' In *Catalunya i França meridional a l'entorn de l'any Mil.* Eds X. Barral i Altet, D. Iogna-Prat, A. M. Mundó, J. M. Salrach, and M. Zimmermann. Barcelona, 1991, 374–7.

'Les moines bénédictins, maîtres d'école VIIIe-XIe siècles.' In *Benedictine Culture, 750–1050.* Eds. W. Lourdaux and D. Verhelst. Leuven, 1983, 96–113.

'Les réfugiés wisigoths dans le monde carolingien.' In *L'Europe héritière de l'Espagne wisigothique.* Eds. J. Fontaine and C. Pellistrandi. Madrid, 1992, 177–183.

Riess, F. 'From Aachen to Al-Andalus: the Journey of Deacon Bodo (823–76).' *Early Medieval Europe* 13 (2005): 131–57.

Narbonne and Its Territory in Late Antiquity: from the Visigoths to the Arabs. Farnham, 2013.

Riu, M. 'L'Església catalana al segle X.' In *Symposium internacional sobre els orígens de Catalunya (segles VIII-XI).* Barcelona, 1991, 161–90.

Rivera Recio, J. F. *El Adopcionismo en España siglo VIII: Historia y Doctrina.* Toledo, 1980.

Romano, D. 'Les juifs de Catalogne aux alentours de l'an Mil.' In *Catalunya i França meridional a l'entorn de l'any Mil.* Eds X. Barral i Altet, D. Iogna-Prat, A. M. Mundó, J. M. Salrach, and M. Zimmermann. Barcelona, 1991, 317–31.

'Notes sobre l'activitat dels jueus a Catalunya l'any mil.' In *Actes del Congrés Internacional Gerbert d'Orlhac i el seu temps: Catalunya i Europa a la fi del Ir mil. leni.* Ed. I. Ollich i Castanyer. Vic, 1999, 697–700.

Rosenwein, B. H. *Negotiating Space: Power, Restraint, and Privileges of Immunity in Early Medieval Europe.* Ithaca, 1999.

Rhinoceros Bound: Cluny in the Tenth Century. Philadelphia, 1982.

Bibliography

To Be the Neighbor of Saint Peter: the Social Meaning of Cluny's Property, 909–1049. Ithaca, 1989.

Ross, J. B. 'Two Neglected Paladins of Charlemagne: Erich of Friuli and Gerold of Bavaria.' *Speculum* 20 (1945): 212–235.

Rouche, M. *L'Aquitaine des Wisigoths aux Arabes, 418–781.* Editions de l'Ecole des hautes études en sciences sociales. Paris, 1979.

Roura, G. *Girona carolíngia: comtes, vescomtes i bisbes (del 785 a l'any 1000).* Girona, 1988.

Ruiz Domenec, J. F. 'Las Estructuras Familiares Catalanes en la alta Edad Media.' *Cuadernos de Arqueología e Historia de la Ciudad* 16 (1975): 69–123.

Safran, J. M. 'Identity and Differentiation in Ninth-Century al-Andalus.' *Speculum* 76 (2001): 573–598.

Sahlins, P. *Boundaries: the Making of France and Spain in the Pyrenees.* Berkeley and Los Angeles, 1989.

Salrach, J. M. 'Conquesta de l'epsai agrari i conflictes per la terra a la Catalunya carolíngia i comtal.' In *Catalunya i França meridional a l'entorn de l'any Mil.* Eds. X. Barral i Altet, D. Iogna-Prat, A. M. Mundó, J. M. Salrach, and M. Zimmermann. Barcelona, 1991, 203–11.

El procés de feudalització (segles III-XII). Ed. P. Vilar. 2nd ed. Història de Catalunya 2. Barcelona, 1998.

El procés de formació nacional de Catalunya (segles VIII–IX). 2 vols. Barcelona, 1978.

'Entre l'Estat antic i feudal. Mutacions socials i dinàmica polítíco-militar a l'Occident carolingi i als comtats catalans.' In *Symposium internacional sobre els orígens de Catalunya (segles VIII-XI).* Barcelona, 1991, 191–252.

Justícia i poder a Catalunya abans de l'any mil. Vic, 2013.

'La Catalunya comtal.' In *Princeses de terres llunyanes: Catalunya i Hongria a la edat mitjana.* Barcelona, 2009, 73–88.

'La Catalunya de Gerbert entre dues èpoques: estructura del territori i dinàmica polítíco-econòmica.' In *Actes del Congrés Internacional Gerbert d'Orlhac i el seu temps: Catalunya i Europa a la fi del Ir Mil.leni.* Ed. I. Ollich i Castanyer. Vic, 1999, 45–67.

'Memoria, poder i devoció: donacions catalanes a La Grassa (segles xi-xii).' In *Histoire et Archéologie des terres catalanes au Moyen Age.* Ed. P. Sénac. Perpignan, 1995, 103–17.

'Prácticas judiciales, transformación social y acción política en Cataluña (siglos IX–XIII).' *Hispania* 47 (1997): 1009–48.

'Societat i poder als comtats pirinencs als segles IX i X.' In *Mil.lenari de Catalunya i la Cerdanya* Barcelona, 1989, 23–36.

Sánchez Martínez, M. 'Catalunya i al-Àndalus (segles viii-x).' In *Catalunya a l'època carolíngia: art i cultura abans del romànic (segles IX i X)* Barcelona, 1999, 29–35.

Saunders, J. J. *A History of Medieval Islam.* London and New York 1965; reprinted 1996.

Schäferdiek, K. 'Der adoptianische Streit im Rahmen der spanischen Kirchengeschichte.' *Zeitschrift für Kirchengeschichte* 80–1 (1969–70): 291–311, 1–16.

Schmauder, M. 'The Relationship between Frankish *Gens* and *Regnum*: a Proposal Based on the Archaeological Evidence.' In Regna *and* Gentes:

the Relationship between Late Antique and Early Medieval Peoples and Kingdoms in the Transformation of the Roman World. Eds. H.-W. Goetz, J. Jarnut, and W. Pohl, with the collaboration of S. Kaschke. Leiden, 2003, 271–306.

Schmitz, G. 'The Capitulary Legislation of Louis the Pious.' In *Charlemagne's Heir: New Perspectives on the Reign of Louis the Pious.* Eds. P. Godman and R. Collins. Oxford, 1990, 425–36.

Schröder, I. *Die westfränkischen Synoden von 888 bis 987 und ihre Überlieferung.* Monumenta Germaniae Historica Hilfsmittel 3. Munich, 1980.

Screen, E. 'The Importance of the Emperor: Lothar I and the Frankish Civil War, 840–843.' *Early Medieval Europe* 12 (2003), 25–51.

Semmler, J. 'Benedictus II: una regula – una consuetuda.' In *Benedictine Culture 750–1050.* Eds. W. Lourdaux and D. Verhelst. Leuven, 1983.

'Benediktinische Reform und kaiserliches Privileg. Die Kloster im Umkreis Benedikts von Aniane.' In *Società, istituzioni, spiritualità. Studi in onore di Cinzio Violante,* 2 vols. Eds. G. Arnaldi, A. Bausola, O. Capitani, C. Cesa, E. Cristiani, C. D. Fonseca, F. Gabrieli, and P. Zerbi. Spoleto, 1994. Vol. 2, 787–823.

Sénac, P. 'Charlemagne et l'Espagne musulmane.' *Cheiron* 37 (2002): 55–80.

'Las incursions musulmanes más allá de los Pirineos (siglos VIII–XI).' In *El Islam y Cataluña.* Barcelona, 1999, 51–5.

'Note sur les relations diplomatiques entre les comtes de Barcelone et le califat de Cordoue au Xe siècle.' In *Histoire et Archéologie des Terres Catalanes au Moyen Âge.* Ed. P. Sénac. Perpignan, 1995, 87–101.

Simonet, F. J. *Historia de los Mozarabes de España.* Madrid, 1903.

Smith, J. M. H. 'Fines imperii: the Marches.' In *The New Cambridge Medieval History.* Vol. 2. Ed. R. McKitterick. Cambridge, 1995, 169–89.

'Gender and Ideology in the Early Middle Ages.' In *Gender and Christian Religion.* Ed. R. N. Swanson. Woodbridge, 1998, 51–74.

Province and Empire: Brittany and the Carolingians. Cambridge, 1992.

Southern, R. W. *The Making of the Middle Ages.* New Haven, 1953.

Spiegel, G. M. 'The reditus regni ad stirpem Karoli Magni: a New Look.' *French Historical Studies* 7 (1971): 145–74.

Stalls, C. *Possessing the Land: Aragon's Expansion into Islam's Ebro Frontier under Alfonso the Battler 1104–1134.* The Medieval Mediterranean: Peoples, Economies, and Cultures, 400–1453. Leiden, 1995.

Stevens, W. M. 'Fields and Streams: Language Practice of Arithmetic and Geometry in Early Medieval Schools.' In *Word, Image, Number: Communication in the Middle Ages.* Eds. J. Contreni and S. Casciani. Rome, 2002, 113–204.

Stieldorf, A. *Marken und Markgrafen: Studien zur Grenzsicherung durch die fränkisch-deutschen Herrscher Monumenta Germaniae Historica Schriften,* 6. Hanover, 2012.

Stocking, R. L. *Bishops, Councils, and Consensus in the Visigothic Kingdom, 589–633.* Ann Arbor, 2000.

Stofferahn, S. A. 'Changing Views of Carolingian Women's Literary Culture: the Evidence from Essen.' *Early Medieval Europe* 8 (1999): 69–97.

Stow, K. R. *Alienated Minority: the Jews of Medieval Latin Europe.* Cambridge, MA, 1992.

Bibliography

Suárez Fernández, L. 'León y Catalunya: paralelismos y divergencias.' In *Symposium internacional sobre els orígens de Catalunya*, vol. 2. Barcelona, 1991, 141–57.

Sullivan, R. E. 'The Carolingian Age: Reflections on Its Place in the History of the Middle Ages.' *Speculum* 64 (1989): 267–306.

'The Carolingian Missionary and the Pagan.' *Speculum* 28 (1953): 705–40.

'Carolingian Missionary Theories.' *The Catholic Historical Review* 42 (1956): 273–295.

'The Context of Cultural Activity in the Carolingian Age.' In *'The Gentle Voices of Teachers': Aspects of Learning in the Carolingian Age*. Ed. R. E. Sullivan. Columbus, 1995, 51–105.

'The Medieval Monk as Frontiersman.' In W. W. Savage, Jr., ed. *The Frontier: Comparative Studies*. Norman, OK, 1979, 25–49.

Symposium internacional sobre els orígens de Catalunya (segles VIII–XI). 2 vols. Barcelona, 1991.

Tabacco, G. *The Struggle for Power in Medieval Italy: Structures of Political Rule*. Cambridge, 1989.

Taylor, N. L. 'An Early Catalonian Charter in the Houghton Library from the Joan Gili Collection of Medieval Catalonian Manuscripts.' *Harvard Library Bulletin* 7 (1996): 37–44.

'Inheritance of Power in the House of Guifred the Hairy: Contemporary Perspectives on the Formation of a Dynasty.' In *The Experience of Power in Medieval Europe, 950–1350: Essays in Honor of Thomas N. Bisson*. Eds. R. F. Berkhofer III, A. Cooper, and A. J. Kosto. Aldershot, 2005, 126–51.

Tenberken, W. *Die Vita Hludowici Pii auctore Astronomo*. Rottweil, 1982.

Thompson, E. A. *The Goths in Spain*. Oxford, 1969.

Toneatto, L. 'Manoscrito dell'Ars gromatica Gisemundi.' In *Codices artis mensoriae i manoscriti degli antichi opusculi latini d'agrimensura (V–XIX sec.)*. vol. 3. Settimane di Studio della Fondazione Centro Italiano de Studi sull'Alto Medioevo. Spoleto, 1995, 997–1012.

'Note sulla tradizione del *Corpus agrimensorum romanorum*.' *MEFRM* 94 (1982): 191–313.

Toubert, P. 'Conclusion.' In *La royauté et les élites dans l'Europe carolingienne (début IXe siècle aux environs de 920)*. Ed. R. Le Jan. Villeneuve d'Ascq, 1998, 519–26.

Tremp, E. *Die Überlieferung der Vita Hludowici imperatoris des Astronomus*. MGH Studien und Texte I. Hanover, 1991.

Turner, F. J. *The Frontier in American History*. New York, 1920.

Udina i Abelló, A. M. 'Els comtats catalans en el context de l'Europa carolíngia: aspectes polítics i jurídics.' In *Actes del Congrés Internacional Gerbert d'Orlhac i el seu temps: Catalunya i Europa a la fi del 1 r Mil.leni*. Ed. I. Ollich i Castanyer. Vich, 1999, 69–88.

'L'aprisió i el problem del repoblament.' In *Symposium internacional sobre els orígens de Catalunya (segles VIII–XI)* Barcelona, 1991, 159–70.

La successió testada a la Catalunya altomedieval. Barcelona, 1984.

Udina i Martorell, F. 'El llegat i la consciència romano-gòtica. El nom d'Hispània.' In *Symposium internacional sobre els orígens de Catalunya*, vol. 2. Barcelona, 1991, 171–200.

Bibliography

'Llegat, sediment i consciència visigòtica a la Catalunya dels segles VIII–XI.' In *Catalunya i França meridional a l'entorn de l'any Mil.* Eds. X. Barral i Altet, D. Iogna-Prat, A. M. Mundó, J. M. Salrach, and M. Zimmermann. Barcelona, 1991, 368–73.

Ullmann, W. *The Carolingian Renaissance and the Idea of Kingship.* London, 1969.

Vaisette, J. and C. Devic. *Histoire générale de Languedoc.* Toulouse, re-edited in 1875. Available online at http://openlibrary.org/books/OL14011752 M/Histoire_g %C3%A9 n%C3%A9rale_de_Languedoc_avec_des_notes_et_les_pi%C3% A8ces_justificatives_par_Cl._Devic_J._Vaissete as of 16 July 2017.

Vallvé, J. *La division territorial de la España musulmana.* Madrid, 1986.

Vanderputten, S. 'Faith and Politics in Early Medieval Society: Charlemagne and the Frustrating Failure of an Ecclesiological Project.' *Revue d'histoire ecclésiastique* 96 (2001): 311–32.

VanLandingham, M. *Transforming the State: King, Court, and Political Culture in the Realms of Aragon (1213–1387).* The Medieval Mediterranean: Peoples, Economies, and Cultures, 400–1453. Leiden, 2002.

Varela, G. B. 'Topografía de los monasteries de la marca de Hispania (ca 800-ca. 1030).' In *Monjes i monasteries hispanos en la alta edad media.* Aguilar de Campoo, 2006, 149–203.

Velázquez, I. '*Pro patriae gentisque Gothorum statu* (4th Council of Toledo, Canon 75, A. 633).' In *Regna* and *Gentes: the Relationship between Late Antique and Early Medieval Peoples and Kingdoms in the Transformation of the Roman World.* Eds. H.-W. Goetz, J. Jarnut, and W. Pohl; with collaboration of S. Kaschke. Leiden, 2003, 161–217.

Verhulst, A. 'Economic Organization.' In *The New Cambridge Medieval History*, vol. 2, c.700-c.900. Ed. R. McKitterick. Cambridge, 1995, 481–509.

Veyrard-Cosme, C. 'Littérature latine du haut Moyen Âge et ideologie politique: l'example d'Alcuin.' *Revue des Études Latines* 72 (1994): 192–207.

Vezin, J. 'Le commentaire sur la Genése de Claude de Turin, un cas singulier de transmission des textes wisigothiques dans la Gaule carolingienne.' In *L'Europe héritière de l'Espagne wisigothique.* Eds. J. Fontaine and C. Pellistrandi. Madrid, 1992, 223–9.

'Manuscrits presentant des traces de l'activité en Gaule de Theodulphe d'Orléans, Claude de Turin, Agobard de Lyon et Prudence de Troyes.' In *Coloquio sobre Circulación de codices y escritos entre Europa y la Peninsula en los siglos VIII-XIII.* Compostela, 1988, 157–71.

Vicens Vives, J. *Approaches to the History of Spain* Trans. J. C. Ullman. Berkeley and Los Angeles, 1967.

Viladrich, M. 'Ripoll: Ara fa un mil.lenni: un escriptori obert al món.' In *Catalunya a l'època carolíngia: art i cultura abans del romànic (segles IX i X).* Barcelona, 139–43.

Villanueva, J. *Viage literario a las iglesias de España*, 22 vols. Madrid, 1802–52. Available online at http://archive.org/search.php?query=creator%3A%22Villanueva%2 C+Jaime%2 C+1766–1824%22 as of 16 July 2017.

Vones-Liebenstein, U. 'Katalonien zwischen Maurenherrschaft und Frankenreich. Probleme um die Ablösung westgotich-mozarabischer Kirchenstrukturen.'

Bibliography

In *Das Frankfurter Konzil von 794: Kristallisationspunkt karolingischer Kultur*. Vol. 1: Politik und Kirche. Ed. R. Berndt, Mainz, 1997, 453–505.

Wallace-Hadrill, J. M. *Early Germanic Kingship in England and on the Continent*. Oxford, 1971.

The Frankish Church. Oxford, 1983.

Wallach, L. *Alcuin and Charlemagne: Studies in Carolingian History and Literature*. Cornell Studies in Classical Philology. Ithaca, 1959, emended and reprinted 1968.

Ward, E. 'Agobard of Lyons and Paschasius Radbertus as Critics of the Empress Judith.' *Studies in Church History* 27 (1990), 15–25.

'Caesar's Wife: the Career of the Empress Judith, 819–829.' In *Charlemagne's Heir: New Perspectives on the Reign of Louis the Pious (814–840)*. Eds. P. Godman and R. Collins. Oxford, 1990, 205–27.

Wemple, S. F. *Women in Frankish Society: Marriage and the Cloister 500 to 900*. Philadelphia, 1981.

Werner, K. F. 'Important Noble Families in the Kingdom of Charlemagne – a Prosopographical Study of the Relationship between King and Nobility in the Early Middle Ages.' In *The Medieval Nobility: Studies on the Ruling Classes of France and Germany from the Sixth through the Twelfth Century*. Ed. T. Reuter. Amsterdam, New York, and Oxford, 1979, 137–202.

'Missus-Marchio-Comes: entre l'administration centrale et l'administration locale de l'empire carolingien.' In *Histoire comparée de l'administration (IVe-XVIIIe siècle)*. Beihefte der Francia, 9. Eds. W. Paravicini and K. F. Werner. Munich, 1980, 191–239.

West, C. *Reframing the Feudal Revolution: Political and Social Transformation between the Marne and Moselle, c.800–c.1100*. Cambridge, 2013.

Whittaker, C. R. *Frontiers of the Roman Empire: a Social and Economic Study*. Baltimore, 1994.

Wickham, C. *Early Medieval Italy: Central Power and Local Society 400–1000*. Ann Arbor, 1989.

'European Forests in the Early Middle Ages: Landscape and Land Clearance.' In *Land and Power: Studies in Italian and European Social History, 900–1200*. London, 1994, 155–99.

Framing the Early Middle Ages: Europe and the Mediterranean, 400–800. Oxford, 2007.

'Land Disputes and their Social Framework in Lombard-Carolingian Italy, 700–900.' In *The Settlement of Disputes in Early Medieval Europe*. Eds. W. Davies and P. Fouracre. Cambridge, 1986, 105–24.

The Mountains and the City: the Tuscan Apennines in the Early Middle Ages. Oxford, 1988.

'Pastoralism and Underdevelopment in the Early Middle Ages.' In *Settimane di Studio del Centro Italiano di Studi sull'Alto Medioevo*. Spoleto, 1985, 401–51.

'Problems of Comparing Rural Societies in Western Europe.' In *Land and Power: Studies in Italian and European Social History, 900–1200*. London, 1994, 201–27.

'Rural Society in Carolingian Europe.' In *The New Cambridge Medieval History*, vol. 2, c.700-c.900. Ed. R. McKitterick. Cambridge, 1995, 510–37.

Bibliography

Wilmart, A. 'L'Ordre des parties dans la traité de Paulin d'Aquilée contre Félix d'Urgel.' *Journal of Theological Studies* 39 (1938): 22–37.

Wolf, K. B. *Christian Martyrs in Muslim Spain.* Cambridge, 1988.

'The Earliest Spanish Christian Views of Islam.' *Church History* 55 (1986): 281–93.

Wolff, P. 'Aquitaine et ses marges.' In *Karl der Große: Lebenswerk und Nachleben* vol. 1: *Persönlichkeit und Geschichte.* Ed. W. Braunfels. Düsseldorf, 1965, 269–306.

Wolfram, H. 'The Creation of the Carolingian Frontier-System c.800.' In *The Transformation of Frontiers: From Late Antiquity to the Carolingians.* Eds. W. Pohl, I. Wood, and H. Reimitz. Leiden, 2001, 231–45.

Wood, I. 'The Code in Merovingian Gaul.' In *The Theodosian Code.* Eds. J. Harries and I. Wood. London, 1993, 161–77.

'Disputes in Late Fifth- and Sixth-Century Gaul: Some Problems.' In *The Settlement of Disputes in Early Medieval Europe.* Eds. W. Davies and P. Fouracre. Cambridge, 1986, 7–22.

The Merovingian Kingdoms, 450–751. London, 1994.

Wormald, P. 'Charters, Law and the Settlement of Disputes in Anglo-Saxon England.' In *The Settlement of Disputes in Early Medieval Europe.* Eds. W. Davies and P. Fouracre. Cambridge, 1986, 149–68.

'The *Leges Barbarorum*: Law and Ethnicity in the Post-Roman West.' In *Regna and Gentes: the Relationship between Late Antique and Early Medieval Peoples and kingdoms in the Transformation of the Roman World.* Eds. H.-W. Goetz, J. Jarnut and W. Pohl. Leiden, 2003, 21–53.

'Lex Scripta and Verbum Regis: Legislation and Germanic Kingship from Euric to Cnut.' In *Early Medieval Kingship.* Eds. P. Sawyer and I. Wood. Leeds, 1977, 105–38.

'Review of *A Jewish Princedom in Feudal France, 768–900.*' *English Historical Review* 89 (1974): 415–16.

Wormald P., and J. L. Nelson, eds. *Lay Intellectuals in the Carolingian World.* Cambridge, 2007.

Wright, N. 'The Metrical Art(s) of Bede.' In *Latin Learning and English Lore,* vol. 1. Eds. K. O'Brien O'Keeffe and A. Orchard. Toronto, 2005, 150–70.

Wright, R. 'Early Medieval Pan-Romance Comprehension.' In *Word, Image, Number: Communication in the Middle Ages.* Eds. J. J. Contreni and S. Casciani. Florence, 2002, 25–42.

Late Latin and Early Romance in Spain and Carolingian France. Liverpool, 1982.

Zaitsev, E. A. 'The Meaning of Early Medieval Geometry: From Euclid and Surveyors' Manuals to Christian Philosophy.' *Isis* 90 (1999): 522–53.

Zapke, S. 'Notation Systems in the Iberian Peninsula: From Spanish Notations to Aquitanian Notation (9th–12th Centuries).' In *Hispania Vetus: Musical-Liturgical Manuscripts from Visigothic Origins to the Franco-Roman Transition (9th–12th Centuries).* Ed. S. Zapke. Bilbao, 2007, 189–243.

Zelzer, K. 'Zum Text zweier Stellungen der Regula Benedicti.' *Wiener Studien* 81 (1968): 225–52.

'Zur Stellung der Textus receptus und des interpolierten Textes in der Textgeschichte der Regula S. Benedicti.' *Revue bénédictine* 88 (1978): 205–46.

Bibliography

Zimmermann, M. 'Abbatiale de Ripoll: Formule de consécration d'église (960–980).' *Autour de Gerbert d'Aurillac. Le pape de l'an mil. Album de documents commenteés* Eds. O. Guyotjeannin and E. Puoulle. Paris, 1996, 26–35.

'Aux origines de la Catalogne. Geographie politique et affirmation nationale.' *Le Moyen Age* 89 (1983): 5–40.

'Catalogne et Regnum francorum: les enseignements de la titulature comtale.' In *Symposium internacional sobre els orígens de Catalunya (segles VIII-XI)* vol. 2. Barcelona, 209–63.

'Conscience gothique et affirmation nationale dans la genèse de la Catalogne (IXe-XIe-siècles).' In *L'Europe héritière de l'Espagne wisigothique*. Eds. J. Fontaine and C. Pellistrandi. Madrid, 1992, 51–68.

'De pays catalans à la Catalogne: genese d'une représentation.' In Histoire et archéologie des terres catalanes au Moyen Age. Ed. P. Sénac. Perpignan, 1995, 71–85.

Écrire et lire en Catalogne (IX–XII siècle). Madrid, 2003.

En els orígens de Catalunya: emancipació política i afirmació cultural. Trans. into Catalan A. Bentué. Barcelona, 1989.

'Entre royaume franc et califat, soudain la Catalogne.' In *La France de l'an mil*. Ed. R. Delort. Paris, 1990, 75–100.

'Hugues Capet et Borell. À propos de l'«independence» de la Catalogne.' In *Catalunya i França meridional a l'entorn de l'any Mil*. Eds. X. Barral i Altet, D. Iogna-Prat, A. M. Mundó, J. M. Salrach, and M. Zimmermann. Barcelona, 1991, 59–64.

'La Catalogne de Gerbert.' In *Gerbert l'européen: Actes du colloque d'Aurillac 4–7 juin 1996* Eds. N. Charbonnel and J.-E. Iung. Aurillac, 1997, 79–101.

'La Connaissance du grec en Catalogne du IXe au XIe siècle.' *Haut Moyen-Age: Culture, Éducation et Société. Études offertes à Pierre Riché*. Ed. M. Sot, 494–515. Centre de Recherche sur l'Antiquité Tardive et le Haut Moyen-Age de l'Université Paris-X-Nanterre. La Garenne-Colombes, 1990.

'La formació d'una sobirania catalana (785–988).' In *Catalunya a l'època carolíngia: art i cultura abans del romànic (segles IX i X)*. Barcelona, 1999, 41–7.

'La prise de Barcelone par Al-Mansûr et la naissance de l'historiographie catalane.' *Annales de Bretagne et des pays de l'Ouest* 87 (1980): 191–218.

'Le monde d'un catalan au Xe siècle: analyse d'une compilation isidorienne.' In *Le métier d'historien au Moyen Age*. Ed. B. Guené. Paris, 1977, 45–78.

'Le pélerinage romain d'um Catalan: Testamen de Borrell, Vic 19 octobre 970.' In *Autour de Gerbert d'Aurillac. Le pape de l'an mil. Album de documents commenteés* Eds. O. Guyotjeannin and E. Puoulle. Paris, 1996, 20–5.

'Le vocabulaire latin du malédiction du IXe au XIIe siècles.' *Atalaya* 5 (1994): 37–55.

'Les goths et l'influence gothique dans l'empire.' *Les Cahiers de Saint-Michel de Cuxa* 23 (1992): 31–46.

'L'Usage du droit wisigothique en Catalogne du IXe au XIIe siècle.' *Mélanges de la Casa de Velázquez* 9 (1973): 233–81.

'Naissance d'une principauté: Barcelone et les autres comtés catalans aux alentours de l'an Mil.' In *Catalunya i França meridional a l'entorn de l'any Mil*. Eds. X. Barral

Bibliography

i Altet, D. Iogna-Prat, A. M. Mundó, J. M. Salrach, and M. Zimmermann. Barcelona, 1991, 111–35.

'Origines et formation d'un etat Catalan (801–1137).' In *Histoire de la Catalogne*. Eds. J. N. Farreras and P. Wolff. Barcelona, 1982, 237–71.

'Un formulaire du Xème siècle conservé à Ripoll.' *Faventia* 4 (1982): 25–86.

'Western Francia: the Southern Principalities.' In *The New Cambridge Medieval History*, vol. 3, c.900–c.1024. Ed. T. Reuter. Cambridge, 1999, 420–55.

Zuckerman, A. J. *A Jewish Princedom in Feudal France, 768–900*. New York, 1972.

INDEX

Index

Index